Offering a broad perspective of the philosophy, theory, and aesthetics of early Indian music and musical ideology, this study makes a unique contribution to our knowledge of the ancient foundations of India's musical culture. Lewis Rowell reconstructs the tunings, scales, modes, rhythms, gestures, formal patterns, and genres of Indian music from Vedic times to the thirteenth century, presenting not so much a history as a thematic analysis and interpretation of India's magnificent musical heritage.

In Indian culture, music forms an integral part of a broad framework of ideas that includes philosophy, cosmology, religion, literature, and science. Rowell works with the known theoretical treatises and the oral tradition in an effort to place the technical details of musical practice in their full cultural context. Many quotations from the original Sanskrit appear here in English translation for the first time, and the necessary technical information is presented in terms accessible to the nonspecialist. These features, combined with Rowell's glossary of Sanskrit terms and extensive bibliography, make *Music and Musical Thought in Early India* an excellent introduction for the general reader and an indispensable reference for ethnomusicologists, historical musicologists, music theorists, and Indologists.

Lewis Rowell, professor of music theory at Indiana University, has written extensively on Indian music and on the philosophy of music.

# MUSIC
AND
# MUSICAL THOUGHT
IN
# EARLY INDIA

# MUSIC

AND

# MUSICAL THOUGHT

IN

# EARLY INDIA

*Lewis Rowell*

Munshiram Manoharlal
Publishers Pvt. Ltd.

ISBN 81-215-0867-3
First Indian edition 1998




Printed and published by
Munshiram Manoharlal Publishers Pvt. Ltd.,
Post Box 5715, 54 Rani Jhansi Road,
New Delhi 110 055.

# CONTENTS

PREFACE ix
ACKNOWLEDGMENTS xiii
THE SOUNDS OF SANSKRIT xv
ABBREVIATIONS xvii
ABOUT THE FRONTISPIECE 3

1 INTRODUCTION 5

1.1 Music and Musical Thought in Early India 5
1.2 The Divisions of Music 9
1.3 Microcosm and Macrocosm 16
1.4 Chronology and Sources 18

2 THOUGHT 23

2.1 Introduction 23
2.2 Continuities of Indian Thought 24
2.3 Systematic Thinking 27
2.4 Symbolic Thinking 32

3 SOUND 35

3.1 Introduction 35
3.2 The Divisions of Sound 35
3.3 The Theory of Sound 38
3.4 Sound: A Lexicon 41
3.5 Causal Sound: *Nāda* 43
3.6 *Ākāśa,* the Medium of Sound 47
3.7 Sound and the External World 50
3.8 Three Ancient Conceptions of Musical Sound 51

4 CHANT 56

4.1 Introduction 56
4.2 Sāmavedic Chant 57

4.2.1 The Role of Memory 64
4.2.2 Chironomy 65
4.2.3 Duration and Tempo 67
4.2.4 Dynamics 68
4.3 The Phonetic Treatises 68
4.4 Some Distinctive Features of Sanskrit and Their Musical Consequences 70
4.5 Nārada's *Śikṣā* and the Organization of Musical Pitch 75
4.6 Milieu 85

5 THEATER 91
5.1 Introduction 91
5.2 The *Nāṭyaśāstra* 96
5.3 The Preliminary Rituals 101
5.4 The Incidental Music 108
5.5 Instruments 112
5.6 Epilogue 117

6 *ŚĀSTRA* 119
6.1 Introduction 119
6.2 Musical Scholarship 124
6.3 Musical Discourse 130
6.4 The Language of Musical Speculation 134
6.5 Notations 140

7 PITCH 144
7.1 Introduction 144
7.2 The Gamut and Its Tuning 145
7.3 Philosophical Arguments on *Śruti* and *Svara* 149
7.4 The Gamut and Its Variables 152
7.5 Sonance 157
7.6 The *Tāna*s 160
7.7 Melodic Choices 162
7.8 The Concept of *Rāga* 166

8 TIME 180
8.1 Introduction 180
8.2 The Idea of Time in Ancient India 182

8.3 *Tāla* 188
8.4 Chironomy 193
8.5 Rhythmic Patterns 196
8.6 The Concept of State 199
8.7 Timing 202
8.8 The *Deśī Tāla*s 207
8.9 The Influence of Metrics 215
8.10 The Rhythms of Indian Music 222

9 FORM 225
9.1 Introduction 225
9.2 Formal Archetypes 230
9.2.1 The Human Body 232
9.2.2 Organic Growth 233
9.2.3 Ritual 236
9.2.4 Creation 237
9.3 Formal Components 243
9.4 Formal Tactics 247
9.4.1 *Upohana* 248
9.4.2 *Upavartana* 250
9.4.3 *Prastāra* 251
9.5 Ritual Forms 252
9.6 Minor Forms 265

10 SONG 269
10.1 Introduction 269
10.2 The *Prabandha*s 274
10.3 Song Forms 276
10.4 A Garland of Songs 280
10.5 Expansion of the Genre 281
10.6 Cultural Mapping 284
10.7 The Theory and Practice of Song 290

11 STYLE 295
11.1 Introduction 295
11.2 Gender 298
11.3 Qualifications 301
11.4 *Guṇa*s and *Doṣa*s 304

11.5 The Qualities of Musical Sound 308
11.6 Style as a Composite 312
11.7 Levels of Ornamentation 319
11.8 *Rasa* 327
11.9 The Values of Indian Music 334

12 AFTERTHOUGHTS 338

NOTES 345
GLOSSARY OF SANSKRIT TERMS 381
BIBLIOGRAPHY 387
INDEX 397

## TABLES

1 The Six Orthodox Systems of Indian Philosophy 28
2 The Forms of the *Ātman* according to the *Maitri Upaniṣad* 37
3 Two Perspectives on Sound Production, according to the Krama System of Kashmir Shaivism 47
4 The Twenty-Five Mute Consonants of Sanskrit 47
5 Three Ancient Conceptions of Musical Sound 52
6 The Sanskrit Morphophonemes 73
7 The Seven *Svaras* 78
8 Correspondences to the Seven *Svaras* 89
9 The *gaṇa* Elās as a Cultural Map of Medieval Indian Song 288
10 Coordinates of Style from Mataṅga's *Bṛhaddeśī* 314
11 Coordinates of Musical Style in the *Saṅgītaratnākara* 319

# PREFACE

What was music like in early India? What were its sounds, rhythms, tunes, and forms? How did it differ from today's music, or from music in the ancient and medieval West? What was it about? What did it mean to those who sang and played it, and to their hearers?

I have undertaken this book as an exercise in musical archaeology, with the hope of giving provisional answers to these questions. The aim was not only to pursue a technical investigation of the materials and struetures of music but also to increase our awareness and understanding of the intellectual foundations of India's ancient musical culture. I shall reserve further explanations for chapter 1, but one guiding assumption of this project must be clearly stated here. My study has been motivated by the unshakable conviction that the organization of music (by which I mean not only sounds, but also behaviors and concepts) has been continuously informed and molded by the prevailing framework of ideas. Accordingly my purpose has been not only to determine as precisely as possible what we may call the "facts" of music (the tunings, scales, modes, rhythms, gestures, patterns, and formal structures) and the conceptual basis for these facts but also to place these facts and concepts within their proper cultural context and examine their many connections with the fabric of ideas in early Indian philosophy, cosmology, religion, literature, science, and other relevant bodies of thought.

I am particularly gratified that this book appears as a part of the Chicago Series in Ethnomusicology, because I have always thought of it as a study in historical ethnomusicology. Readers will find few references to ethnomusicological theory and method in these pages, but I shall return to make the connections explicit in my final chapter.

Any book could have been several different books, and this one is no exception. Specialists in ancient Indian music and music theory would welcome, and perhaps expect, a comprehensive study that proceeds step by step through each of the surviving texts, attempting to resolve every philological question, proposing and defending each of the necessary reconstructions of the many textual gaps and passages mangled in the scribal tradition, explaining each musical concept and tracing its development throughout the corpus of literature, reconciling the many contradictions, and exploring the wider realm of these concepts with far-reaching etymological analyses. Such a book would indeed be welcome. It would also be massive, ponderous, largely in Sanskrit, quite beyond the reach of most of those who are curious about the early history of Indian music, and, alas, by another author. In short, this is not that book, and I mention all of this to defuse unrealistic expectations.

Some of my fellow specialists may also feel uncomfortable with the level of generalization that I permit myself in this study, but I am convinced that much of what we do know about the music of ancient and medieval India remains all but inaccessible as the result of scholarly hesitation to venture any statement whatsoever to which a qualification can be attached. Valid general statements can and should be made, and I count on the intelligence of the reader to recognize that there may be qualifications and exceptions to all such statements.

I have proceeded under the assumption that, despite the intractability of the sources, it is nevertheless possible to assemble an intelligible synthesis of early musical doctrines and the supporting fabric of ideas—a synthesis that will be not only informative but also accessible to various segments of a broad readership: to Western musicians with a lively curiosity but no expertise in either Indian music or intellectual history; to ethnomusicologists with expertise in other world cultures as well as a professional interest in the music of India; to specialists in other fields of Indic studies who may wish to learn how Indian music and musical teachings have been influenced by their own body of literature; and most of all, to general readers whose curiosity has been whetted by their own experience with Indian music today and who wish to learn more about its background. I hope this study will also be of some value to the handful of Western students of ancient Indian music, not for the general synthesis I present, but for the individual translations, analyses, and points of interpretation along the way.

This study has been preceded by a series of technical articles published in various journals during the last fifteen years; for these see the bibliography. This volume differs from the earlier publications in two ways: first, readers will find additional technical material and supporting evidence in the separate articles, and I have provided citations to point the way. In this volume I have confined the technical material to concise illustrations of the principal point(s) under discussion, and I have been highly selective in choosing passages for translation and musical issues for illustration. In no case has any unrevised material been transferred to this study. And second, I have ventured much farther here in matters of interpretation and analysis of the cultural background than was possible in a series of articles on individual topics. Above all, I have attempted here to present the subject as a whole, not in compartments.

The book is organized thematically, not chronologically, and is based on a set of keywords; I think of it as a thematic analysis, not a historical account per se, and my views on the problems of Indian music history will emerge clearly in chapters 1 and 12. Once the reader is past chapters 1 and 2 there is no reason to read in any particular sequence. The development of concepts for the organization of pitch is presented in two installments: first, an account of their early evolution based on the evidence of one of the ancient phonetic manuals (§ 4.5); and second, a step-by-step exposition of the entire system of musical pitch in chapter 7. Chapters 7–9 constitute what I see as the technical core of the study; they will be of special interest to musicians. I hope, however, that other readers will persevere when technical issues arise; in each case the accompanying commentary will offer explanations and interpretations from various branches of Indian learning that can be read profitably without reference to the figures or musical notations. (Western staff notation appears only in chapters 4 and 7, and rhythmic notation only in chapter 8; I have devised my own system of notation for reconstructing musical forms, one based on the traditional gesture language of *tāla,* but no musical expertise is required to decipher it.)

Readers should expect to encounter many Sanskrit words, but in virtually every case they appear in the form of single terms, in transliteration, and have been provided with either a translation or an explanation. A glossary of Sanskrit terms has also been provided for quick reference. The book includes a large number of English translations from the major Sanskrit treatises on music, and I have selected a wide range of translation styles—from the painstakingly literal to the happily periphrastic. My own translations, of which there are many, fall somewhere in between. It has seemed better to me to give some indication of the breadth and diversity of Indian musical scholarship than to take advantage of the translator's prerogative to channel his subject into his own lexicon and style.

Scholarship does not stand still when we are working on a project, and I should like to have seen the fruits of several current works in progress, including D. R. Widdess's study of the *rāga*s of early Indian music, the second edition of Mukund Lath's *Study of Dattilam,* R. Satyanarayana's translation of Pārśvadeva's *Saṅgītasamayasāra,* and Prem Lata Sharma's translation and critical study of Mataṅga's *Bṛhaddeśī.* Tentative publication information has been included in the notes and bibliography.

I have found this project a musical and intellectual adventure, and I invite readers to share it with me.

# THE SOUNDS OF SANSKRIT

A complete display of the forty-eight Sanskrit morphophonemes appears in table 6, and readers with more than a passing interest in phonetics will find relevant material in § 4.4. My purpose here is to guide English-speaking readers toward a rough approximation of Sanskrit pronunciation. In general consonants are more problematic than vowels, and some of the distinctions are difficult for English speakers.

In this book all Sanskrit words are transliterated according to international conventions. Heavy syllables may be accented, that is, syllables containing a long simple vowel, a diphthong, or a short vowel followed by more than one consonant. For this purpose aspirated consonants are regarded as single consonants.

Vowels are pronounced as follows:

| | | |
|---|---|---|
| *a* | as *u* in *but* | (as in *rasa*) |
| *ā* | as in *father* | (as in *rāga*) |
| *i* | as in *bit* | |
| *ī* | as in *ravine* | |
| *u* | as in *put* | |
| *ū* | as in *rule* | |
| *ṛ* | similar to *ri* in *rick* | |
| *e* | as *ay* in *hay* | |
| *ai* | as in *aisle* | |
| *o* | as in *go* | |
| *au* | as *ow* in *cow* | |

Consonants are generally similar to those of English, with exceptions as noted below. The distinction between aspirated and unaspirated stops is essential, and aspirated consonants should be pronounced with the same heavy aspiration they would normally receive at a syllabic juncture in English, e.g., *kh* as in *bunkhouse, dh* as in *mudhen,* and *th* as in *coathook* (N. B.: not a spirant as in the English word *thin*). A second distinctive feature is the important opposition between the dental (tongue in contact with the teeth) and retroflex (tongue flexed back under the hard palate) consonants, i.e., *t, th, d, dh, n* in contrast to *ṭ, ṭh, ḍ, ḍh, ṇ.*

Note also the following:

| | |
|---|---|
| *c* | as *ch* in *church* but lightly aspirated |
| *ch* | the same, but aspirated more heavily |
| *g* | as in *game* |
| *ñ* | as in the Spanish word *señor* |
| *ś* | as *sh* in *share* |
| *ṣ* | similar to the above |
| *ḥ* | a rough breathing at the end of a syllable or word (*visarga*) |
| *ṁ* | nasalizes the preceding vowel |

Unless in context, Sanskrit verbs appear in their root form and nouns in their uninflected stem form, to which plurals are formed by the addition of *s*. In the case of modern names, diacritics appear only when employed by the author or editor. A number of familiar Sanskrit words that have made their way into the English language are treated as English words.

# ABBREVIATIONS

| | |
|---|---|
| *AB* | Abhinavagupta, *Abhinavabhāratī* |
| *BN* | Bharata, *Nāṭyaśāstra* |
| *IC* | ILankoo, *Cilappatikaaram* |
| *D* | Dattila, *Dattilam* |
| *K* | Kuḍumiyāmalai rock inscription |
| *MB* | Mataṅga, *Bṛhaddeśī* |
| *NB* | Nānyadeva, *Bharatabhāṣya* |
| *NS* | Nārada, *Nāradīyaśikṣā* |
| *PS* | Pārśvadeva, *Saṅgītasamayasāra* |
| *SM* | Someśvara, *Mānasollāsa* |
| *SS* | Śārṅgadeva, *Saṅgītaratnākara* |

# MUSIC

AND

# MUSICAL THOUGHT

IN

# EARLY INDIA

The water that was first created,
the sacrifice-bearing fire, the priest,
the time-setting sun and moon,
audible space that fills the universe,
what men call nature, the source of all seeds,
the air that living creatures breathe—
through his eight embodied forms,
may Lord Śiva come to bless you!

Kālidāsa, *Śākuntala*
Trans. Barbara Stoler Miller

## About the Frontispiece

If any of the numerous gods in the Indian pantheon merits recognition as the tutelary deity of music, dance, and the theater, it is Śiva, shown here in his celebrated pose as *Naṭarāja* (Lord of the Dance).[1] This elegant South Indian bronze embodies a series of apparent contradictions, reconciling the oppositions between perpetual motion and eternal stasis, creation and destruction, reality and illusion. Śiva's dance has been arrested at a point of perfect equilibrium, and he is surrounded by symbols of universal continuity—fire, water, space, and time. All five of Śiva's traditional activities are represented in the symbolic design of this icon: creation, destruction, preservation, veiling (that is, drawing the curtain of illusion before our eyes), and liberation.

The god's multiple limbs manifest ancient Indian doctrines of form and substance: any form is a temporary condition and is to be understood as one among many aspects of reality; matter is flexible and tends to mutate through series of playful transformations; and we obtain knowledge only after scanning an object from multiple perspectives (§§ 2.2, 9.1). The small hourglass drum in Śiva's uplifted right hand represents the *ākāśa* (atmosphere)—the "audible space that fills the universe"—which according to the *Taittirīya Upaniṣad* is the first evolute from the universal soul, the atman (§ 3:6), which causes sound to issue forth at the first moment of creation.

The tongue of flame on Śiva's left palm symbolizes the world of created forms, a world that will one day dissolve into its former state of undifferentiated matter under his trampling feet. He is thus the master of both creation and destruction and of all that lies in between (§ 8.3). With his lower right hand the god reassures his devotees of his benevolence toward them. The lower left arm, curving like the trunk of an elephant (in a reference to his jovial elephant-headed son Ganeṣa, also a patron of the performing arts), points to his uplifted foot, a symbol of release (*mokṣa*): release from gravity, from the phenomenal world, from attachment, and from the blindness of ignorance, symbolized by the demon on which the god stands.

The benedictory verse from *Śākuntala,* one of the most beloved of the surviving plays of the classical Indian theater, invokes Śiva's blessing on the performance by praising his octoform nature and suggesting that the per-

1. For additional analysis see Heinrich Zimmer, *Myths and Symbols in Indian Art and Civilization* (New York: Harper and Row, 1962), 151–75; see also C. Sivaramamurti, *Naṭarāja in Art, Thought, and Literature* (New Delhi: National Museum, 1974).

forming arts of India should be viewed as instruments of sacrifice, a sacrifice bringing unseen benefit to all who participate and all who bear witness. Śiva's eight forms—water, fire, "audible space," earth, air, the sun, the moon, and the person of the sacrificer—encompass the whole realm of nature (§ 5.1). This elemental concept of musical sound invites us to confront the most profound metaphysical questions: the source of music, its goal, its ontological status, its role in universal process, and how it can be known. We shall consider the answers provided by Indian teachings.

This book is for all who take delight in the audible space that fills the universe.

# ONE
# INTRODUCTION

## 1.1 Music and Musical Thought in Early India

Let us begin with the five keywords of my title. By India I mean the entire subcontinent of South Asia, including Pakistan and Bangladesh, before partition. By "early" I mean as early as possible, including the historical eras often identified as "ancient" and "medieval," with the middle of the thirteenth century as a convenient terminus ad quem. I shall have frequent occasion to refer to an important musical document from that century—the *Saṅgītaratnākara* (The mine of musical jewels) of Śārṅgadeva, a monumental synthesis of the many musical doctrines expounded by the authors of the previous millennium. My account thus ends before the successive waves of Persian culture made their full impact on the music of northern India and thereby encouraged the development of separate musical traditions in the North and South. I shall suggest some early evidence for this separation, but it is not among my main themes. Similarly, I shall point out many of the roots of modern Indian musical concepts and practices, but the main emphasis must remain on what Indian music *was* (insofar as that can be determined), not what it now *is*.

By "music" and "musical" I mean not only the phenomena that we ordinarily regard as music in the West but also the entire structure of ideas surrounding and informing the practice of music. When we recall that the ancient Greek concept of *mousike* was held to encompass all of the domains of the nine Muses—from poetry, song, and dance, to history and even astronomy—we should be prepared to encounter a complex structure of ideas with multiple dimensions and many interconnections. The standard Sanskrit word for music is *saṅgīta*—the exact equivalent of the Latin *concentus*. The most precise, if not the most elegant, translation is "concerted song." Our investigation, however, must extend to genres that would not ordinarily be considered to be a part of the realm of *gīta* (song). These include not only the various traditions and styles of sacred chant but also composite genres, especially the theater, in which what we call "music" is an integral part of a composite artform, and within which it is not always possible to separate what is music from what is not. But the word *gīta* provides the semantic core of the idea of music and conveys the quintessential humanism of the ancient Indian concept: musical sound is, first of all, vocal sound. The most powerful and generally accepted ontological conception of music is rooted in a profound cultural metaphor, in which the emanation of vocal sound from deep within the human body has been linked with the process of creation as a "bringing forth" of the divine substance that lies at the heart of our innermost being.

By musical thought I mean the complete ideology of music—including, but not limited to, those technical compartments within which music has been organized into notes, scales, rhythms, forms, and the like, and extending to larger philosophical questions of being, knowledge, and value. I shall outline traditional Indian answers to such questions as, What is musical sound? What does it mean? How is music transmitted? and What cultural values does music represent? The separate chapters will help to channel these questions into a systematic organization, but at the same time they conceal the essential relatedness of all Indian musical thought.

A few preliminary observations on the distinctive patterns of Indian thought will set the stage for the more detailed discussions in chapter 2. Readers familiar with the surgical dichotomies of ancient Western thinking, in which the search for truth proceeds by separating everything that a thing *is* from everything that it *is not,* and eventually penetrating to the core of a concept when no further divisions are possible, will encounter different habits of thought. Inquiry is open-ended in the Indian tradition, and the process of making categories is infinite—at least in theory. Every statement that can be made blurs a finer distinction, and ultimate truth or reality lies beyond the reach of human experience or inference—except perhaps in those moments of suprasensible illumination vouchsafed to the yogin. Indian musical thought has thus been channeled into elaborate taxonomic structures within which subcategories unfold in profusion, subcategories that often are not mutually exclusive and which thereby encourage a certain amount of ambiguity

Truth is revealed, not achieved. It is manifested by authoritative teachings and carried forward by a tradition of literary scholarship. Knowledge of it is always imperfect. Within such a framework of belief, the literature of music has taken on a prescriptive tone, and musical doctrines require no other justification than their prior existence in an authoritative treatise. If apparent contradictions appear, they are the result of our limited knowledge or of accidents of the transmission process. They are to be understood, not discarded and replaced by new teachings. Such is the reasoning behind the

Indian commentarial tradition and the continuous probing for meaning in imperfectly preserved texts.

Musical writings have taken on a life of their own as a result of the many scribal copyings and recopyings over the centuries. It is not fanciful to regard these texts as living organisms—organisms manifesting the typically Indian play of images and plurality of forms that mask the underlying unity. Indian musical scholarship has also been likened to the course of a mighty river (one of the cherished analogies of Indian thought), accepting tributary streams, turning away from dry channels, and mingling separate waters in a central confluence of ideas—disciplining and accepting certain contributions while rejecting others outright. The analogy has no doubt been overworked, and this centrist imagery can cause us to overlook or undervalue the revitalizing force of new musical contributions, as in the movement referred to as *deśī*—an infusion of various provincial musical traditions between ca. A.D. 500 and 1000, an infusion which greatly expanded the boundaries of the ancient musical system and altered the future course of Indian music in far-reaching ways.

Whatever the imperfections of the concept, I shall present the outlines of such a central tradition as documented in Indian literature from late Vedic times to the thirteenth century, a tradition that proved flexible enough to accommodate the mystical doctrines of Tantra (as in Mataṅga's *Bṛhaddeśī*) and the elaborate transcendental philosophy of Kashmir Shaivism (as expounded by the commentator Abhinavagupta).[1] Most of the evidence is from literature, oral as well as written: unlike European music, for which systems of musical notation have existed for more than three thousand years, the music of India has never been recorded in more than a skeletal script. Music, like other branches of learning, is not something to be acquired by reading books or studying scores; it is learned from a master teacher, a guru. The sole purpose of a notation is to remind us of what we have already learned. Paradoxically, this reliance upon a tradition of oral instruction has narrowed the boundaries within which innovation is acceptable. While there is still much to be learned from reconstructing the notations in early musical texts, it must be accepted that knowledge of what the music of early India was like must rest on two sources—the textual evidence and Indian music as it is heard today.

From Vedic times to the thirteenth century is indeed a long time, and certain historical problems must be acknowledged: with the aid of hostile nature and historical accident, Indian scholarship has managed to cover its tracks so successfully that the step-by-step development of music and musical ideas can be perceived only as recorded in the few scattered monuments of musical literature that have survived. And each such document as it has come down to us is itself a tangle of various historical layers and a mixture of quotations, glosses, and commentary in which the precise sequence of contributions is often impossible to determine. As Prem Lata Sharma has observed, "'history' in the context of Indian culture has to be viewed as a complex phenomenon comprised of concurrences and overlappings rather than a simple linear phenomenon."[2]

Students of early Indian intellectual history have learned to accept the price that has to be paid for this inescapable lack of "simple linearity." What it means for the present study is that the advance of musical ideology must often be presented in an admittedly discontinuous format, in the form of successive snapshots instead of the more accurate form of a series of motion picture frames in extremely slow motion. Or to change the metaphor, I shall have to argue across the gaps in the fossil record and run the risk that the resulting narrative may appear more discontinuous than it in fact was. I shall, for example, attempt to trace the evolution of the Indian idea of musical sound—from early metaphoric concepts and primitive acoustical speculations to the refined arguments and subtle distinctions of the later philosophical schools—but the approach must be to present the various manifestations and clarifications of a single, complex idea, as assembled from the available evidence (sketchy as it at times may be).

The general plan of the book is first, to establish the appropriate contexts for music and musical thought—intellectual, cultural, and social—and second, to focus in turn on each of the main technical compartments of music. The chapters will therefore be thematic rather than chronological; each chapter will be a substantial strand in the fabric of musical ideas: thought, sound, chant, theater, pitch, time, form, song, and style. Each of the main strands of ideas will be unraveled into as many component strands as possible, and I shall try to show their relatedness. Although treatises are the main source of evidence, I shall not emphasize the many philological problems that continue to block our full understanding of this corpus of ancient literature. I shall present summaries and interpretations of the major musical texts and also translations of many representative passages so that the special flavor of the literature will be conveyed along with its substance. Where appropriate, I shall draw comparisons to the musical systems and thinking of the ancient West, so that the distinctive character of Indian musical thought will shine the more vividly.

The central premise of this study is that music and musical thought depend upon their cultural context and can be fully understood only with reference to that context. This is true with respect to other world musics, but it carries special meaning in the case of India, where a unique cultural tradition of great antiquity and literacy has given birth to a remarkable musical language. The aim of my study, then, is to explore in a systematic way the philosophy, theory, and aesthetics of early Indian music, with constant reference to the cultural contexts within which the idea of music arose and by which it was given distinctive form and flavor.

## 1.2 The Divisions of Music

In a typical Sanskrit treatise or a chapter thereof, this would be the appropriate location for an *uddeśa*—a list of the principal topics to be expounded. My *uddeśa* is displayed in the form of a schematic diagram (1). The intent is to give some preliminary idea of the range of the ancient Indian concept of music and its many traditional connections with the other performing arts. I will introduce a number of important terms to be encountered in subsequent chapters, although sharper definitions and fuller explanations will follow in due course.

The diagram (1) should be read with the understanding that it constitutes a unified semantic field within which the connecting lines do not represent exclusive pathways between the separate components. "Music," the hypothetical center of the field, is at the same time only a limb of certain larger artistic composites such as drama and dance. So it is helpful to regard the diagram as a flexible and multidimensional array with reversible pathways and numerous unshown interconnections. No particular priorities should be inferred from the arrangement of the diagram; I shall simply take up each of the divisions in turn. The diagram will also serve as a typical model of Indian classificatory schemes, which are more like networks than pyramids because of the many interconnections. In the various technical compartments (especially pitch and rhythm), it should be understood that each of the basic divisions opens out into an array of subtopics.

*Saṅgīta* is the closest equivalent to the Western concept of music, although the inclusion of dance as one of the three main compartments suggests that in early Indian thought *saṅgīta* was regarded as a composite art consisting of melos (*gīta*), syllabic accompaniment (*vādya*), and limb movement (*nṛtta,* or the more general term *nartana*). In later Indian thought and practice, the sense of *saṅgīta* has narrowed to the point where it can more accurately serve as the equivalent of "music." One of the oldest and most cherished explanations of the word is an example of the etymological method known as *nirukta,* codified by Yāska around 500 B.C. Additional examples will follow in subsequent chapters. Yāska's method, which

1. The divisions of music

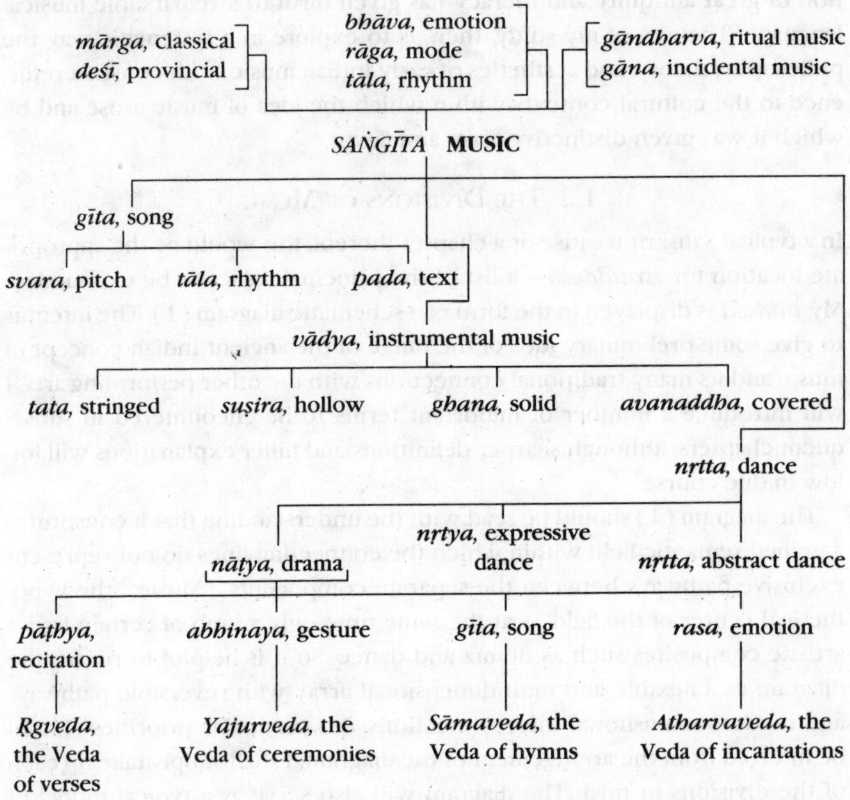


often yields results as fanciful and far from the truth as many of Varro's Latin etymologies, derives the meaning of a word—or as in this case, a symbolic substitute word—from its *bīja* (seed) syllables. Hence, *saṅgīta* is explained as a compound of the implied meanings of the three syllables of the substitute word *bharata: bha* from *bhāva* (emotion), *ra* from *rāga* (the modal-scalar framework for melody), and *ta* from *tāla* (the system of hand gestures by which the rhythmic and metric structure of music is controlled and made manifest).[3] Indian musicians have found this explanation deeply satisfying, despite the convenient blurring of the distinction between short and long vowels (*a* and *ā*) and the equally convenient assumption that all syllabic components of a word have a separate identity as verbal roots or nominal stems. It is obviously invalid as a historical explanation, but failure to pass the test of linguistic credibility is scarcely an adequate reason to dismiss such a long-held belief.

The literal meaning of the word *bharata* is "he who is to be maintained."[4] The reference is to Agni, the god of fire by whose agency the sacrificial offerings are conveyed to the other gods. From this context the word came to refer to the priests who maintained the sacred fire, and thence to anyone responsible for preserving the world order. Many ancient Indian rulers took the name Bharata, but the specific Bharata invoked in the definition of *saṅgīta* is the legendary sage who is said to be the author of the *Nāṭya-śāstra,* unquestionably the most important of the early treatises on music and the theater. It is in this sense that the word *bharata* also means an actor or a dancer. In a derivative form, with the first syllable lengthened, *bhārata* signifies the descendants of the Bharatas and the land they inhabit—India. Because of the close association of drama, music, and dance in the classical theater, *bharata* symbolizes the essential contribution from each of the three performing arts: from drama, emotion; from music, melody; and from dance, rhythm.[5] The subconscious message embedded in this semantic cluster is that India's music is one of its national treasures. It suggests further that music and the associated arts are traditions to be preserved, not replaced in waves of new styles or with technological innovations. And from a more technical point of view, it is hard to find fault with a definition of music as a blend of melody, rhythm, and emotion.

The remaining classifications at the top of (1) are loosely related, although each has a different purpose. *Gāndharva* and *gāna* were the two major musical genres of the ancient theater; their opposition signifies the important distinction between strict or composed music (*gāndharva*) and (relatively) free or improvised music (*gāna*). Like many other terms, *gāndharva* was applied in both a general and a special sense: in a special sense, it signified the ceremonial music of the preliminary theatrical rituals; in a general sense, it came to represent what we might call "formal" music—thereby implying the existence of more relaxed, less strictly prescribed musical styles.[6] The word *gāndharva* is another reference to divine patronage, in this case the host of celestial musicians (the *gandharva*s) who were the Indian equivalents of the angel musicians of the European Middle Ages.[7] *Gāna* is derived more prosaically from the noun "singing"; when opposed to the *gāndharva* genre, it denotes the relatively free style of incidental music performed during the play proper.

What is important here is a very early distinction between composition and improvisation, and (not quite the same thing) between strictly and loosely regulated music—distinctions that have provided a useful explanatory paradigm in later Indian musical thinking. There is no evidence that the incidental plot songs or the instrumental pieces were created spontaneously by the performers of the early theater, but—in their relative freedom, in contrast to the ritual music—it is from this line of music that later improvisational practice appears to have arisen. One of the important themes in this book will be the successive stages by which the theory and practice of early Indian music moved gradually in the direction of increasing freedom and spontaneity, providing ever-increasing performance options while at the same time maintaining certain controls.

The distinction between the *mārga* (path or way, hence the "proper way") and *deśī* (regional, provincial) traditions may be summarized as follows:

| *mārga* | *deśī* |
|---|---|
| The classical phase of the ancient Indian musical theater | The vernacular phase, beginning ca. A.D. 500 |
| A central "Great Tradition" | Many regional "Little Traditions" |
| Primarily Sanskrit texts | Song texts in both Sanskrit and various provincial languages |
| A strict practice of composition | A relatively free practice, moving toward improvisation |
| Employed in the ritual theater music | Music for entertainment, modeled upon the incidental music of the early theater |
| Melody based on the *jāti*s and *grāmarāga*s[8] | Melodic basis expanded to include later types of *rāga*s |

Despite the obvious parallels to the distinction drawn between *gāndharva* and *gāna,* it would be a mistake to overlook the differences. The distinction between *mārga* and *deśī* is essentially historical—undoubtedly the only important distinction of this type in the evolution of Indian musical style. It is similar to the relationship between the ecclesiastical and scholastic traditions of Medieval Latin and the rise of vernacular languages and literature in the later European Middle Ages: if *mārga* is compared to the Latin of Augustine and Aquinas, the *deśī* movement corresponds to the Italian of Dante. The corpus of early musical treatises demonstrates a growing focus upon the *deśī* repertoire during the second half of the first millennium A.D. as the *mārga* tradition declined and was eventually lost as a living practice. It is clear that by the thirteenth century the doctrines of *mārga* were perpetuated solely on the basis of textual information, most of it recorded by scholars who were not themselves practical musicians and who were not interested in attempting to recover details of musical practice other than those set down in the treatises.

Musical options kept pace with the increasing number of provincial traditions: the system of *rāga*s grew from a relatively small number of basic scales (the eighteen *jātis* and the seven original *grāmarāgas*) to the 253 *rāgas* mentioned in the *Saṅgītaratnākara,* and an expansion of similar proportions took place in the number of *tālas*. In the course of this expansion significant changes were introduced, especially in the rhythmic system. This process of gradual evolution from the "prescribed few" to the "optional many" encapsulates India's musical self-image along a popular metaphoric pathway: a highly venerated and ancient tradition flowering outward until it encompassed all the richness and diversity of Indian musical culture. It has become a model for historical explanation. Little is known about the status of secular or entertainment music before the rise of the many *deśī* musics, except for some tantalizing bits of information in the ancient Tamil classics which make it abundantly clear that a cultivated musical tradition existed in the South as early as the last few pre-Christian centuries.[9] The full contribution of early Dravidian culture to the great central stream of Sanskrit musical thought has yet to be determined, but there can be no doubt that the impact of ancient Tamil music upon the *mārga* tradition was felt at a very early time. This realization helps to undermine the notion of a single, unifying nuclear musical tradition. Any such tradition is not born; it must be made. And it can be recognized as such only at a relatively advanced stage of musical development, after theorists have made considerable progress in collecting, codifying, and "leveling" a richly diverse storehouse of raw musical data. The gradual transformation of music and musical ideas from raw data to systematic organization will be among my main themes.

Proceeding down the diagram, we enter the technical domains of *saṅgīta,* divided first into the three performing components: song (*gīta*), instrumental music (*vādya*), and dance (*nṛtta*).[10] The division of *gīta* into the three aspects of tune, time, and text is a natural division and was paralleled in ancient Greece by a similar division of the technical realm of music into the three domains of harmonics, rhythmics, and metrics.[11] It will be useful to explain what is meant by the important terms *svara, tāla,* and *pada*—three terms that will appear again and again in subsequent chapters, and which I shall retain in transliteration. *Svara* refers to (1) the entire dimension of musical pitch, and in a more restricted sense (2) to pitch as objectified in the successive steps of the musical scale.[12] *Tāla* embraces the entire temporal dimension of music, conceived in terms of the system of chironomy by which musical rhythm and form were manifested and brought under control. *Pada* (in the sense of "word") refers to text (and especially to meaningful text, as opposed to meaningless phonetic syllables) and all of the possible units into which a text can be divided.

The classification of musical instruments into four types, based on their acoustic principle, anticipates the system of classification devised by Curt Sachs and E. M. von Hornbostel by some two thousand years: stringed (chordophones), hollow (aerophones), solid (idiophones), and covered instruments (membranophones).[13] Little is known about the intellectual background of this ingenious and sensible scheme; it had become the standard method for classifying instruments by the time of the *Nāṭyaśāstra,* in which a separate chapter is devoted to each of the four categories.[14] A point of considerable interest emerges when the Indian classificatory scheme is compared to the ancient Chinese *pa yin* (the "eight [sources of] sound"), in which musical instruments were grouped according to their most prominent material component—metal, stone, earth (that is, clay), skin, silk, wood, gourd, and bamboo.[15] It seems fitting that a culture with such a notably nonmaterialistic philosophical orientation would have devised a classification based on the principle by which things work, while a more practical and materialistic society would have been more inclined to develop a taxonomy based on the different types of material substance from which their instruments were constructed.

*Vīṇā,* in the ancient literature, was the generic term for a number of different families of stringed instruments, including both lutes and arched harps, with and without frets, and plucked either with the fingers or a plectrum. The archetypal "hollow" instrument was a transverse flute, and the "solid" category is represented only by the pair of small bronze cymbals used to mark the structure of the *tāla.* The "covered" instruments are, of course, drums of various sizes and shapes. Although a chapter on instruments (*vādya,* "to be sounded") was a standard part of a music treatise, the authors frequently took the opportunity to expound appropriate details of the musical system, in preference to purely organological matters. This was particularly true in the case of the solid instruments, about which there was relatively little to say. Consequently Bharata's chapter on the solid instruments is actually an elaborate theoretical exposition of the system of *tāla.* It will become evident that instruments play a relatively limited role in Indian musical thought and that most of the authors were not particularly tool conscious. It should also be noted that the rhythmic-metric system and the instructions for drumming were kept in separate compartments, consistent with the general view that timekeeping and percussion were separate musical functions. While a proper knowledge of *tāla* was essential, a drummer was assigned no more responsibility for coordinating the temporal aspects of performance than any of the other performers. Further interpretation of the role of instruments in early Indian musical thought will follow in chapter 5.

The third component of *saṅgīta,* limb movement, is itself subdivided into three genres. Of these, two involve representation—*nāṭya* (acting, with reference to its physical aspects) and *nṛtya* (expressive dance, mime)—as opposed to the "pure," abstract style of dancing known as *nṛtta*. The complexity of the Indian classification of the arts begins to become apparent here when we note that *nāṭya* is both a subdivision of "limb movement" and, at the same time, a composite art form (drama) that encompasses all the performing arts. The arts of physical representation and bodily movement are also linked by subliminal verbal clues. Readers will have noted the presence of the common root *nṛt* (to dance, represent, act), but it may not be as obvious that the word *nāṭya* (drama, dancing, mimic representation) is a not-too-distant relative. This semantic overlap makes it clear that there is no easy way to determine where dancing ends and acting begins. Their common territory, which is considerable, may be viewed as a gradual progression from nonrepresentational dance to representational dance, miming, and acting proper. The key ingredient in this sequence is the elaborate gesture language of *abhinaya* (literally, "to bring near," that is, to represent before the eyes), which is more a matter of pose, gesture, and facial expression than of footwork. While the expressive techniques of actors and dancers branched off into their own individual domains of recitation and footwork, both actors and dancers were required to be expert in the intermediate style of *abhinaya.*[16]

To complete our survey of (1), we find that drama is divided into an additional set of four components; these are the major modes of expressive communication: recitation, gesture, song (in the general sense of "music"), and emotion. Because of the authority of the Vedas in ancient Indian culture, it is easy to understand why authors were unable to resist drawing the obvious correlations: the *Ṛgveda* for its text, the *Yajurveda* for its descriptions of the ritual actions, the *Sāmaveda* for the musical style in which its verses were intoned, and the *Atharvaveda* for what Basham has described as its atmosphere of "simple animism and sympathetic magic on a lower cultural level than that of the *Ṛg Veda,* deriving from the plebian religion of the Āryans and containing many non-Āryan elements."[17] The meanings are clear: the spoken word is a vehicle of elemental power, physical gesture is equated with ritual action, song is rooted in the traditions of sacred chant, and emotion is communicated from person to person by suprasensible means. I shall return to each of these themes in later chapters. In particular, the idea of *rasa* (sap, juice, essence)—which has acquired a much more specialized meaning than *bhāva*—has become the single most important concept in Indian aesthetics. I shall outline the dimensions of this idea in chapter 11, but for now *rasa* may be defined simply as the pervading emotional tone or mood in any performance.

## 1.3 Microcosm and Macrocosm

What were the social and intellectual contexts within which the idea of music developed in early India? To make the discussion more concrete, imagine the world as seen from two contrasting perspectives—that of the Vedic priest, serene in his life of ritual service; and that of the theatrical producer-director, surrounded by the chaos of rehearsals and the noisy milieu of the ancient Sanskrit drama. What role did music play in their daily routines, and how did they see themselves and the world around them?

In traditional Indian cosmology, the individual is situated at the precise center of a concentric universe, analogous to the location of Mount Meru as the *axis mundi.*[18] Various authors have elaborated the idea of a set of concentric sheaths radiating outward from the still center, beginning with the inner sheaths of the individual and continuing to the outer sheaths of the universe. Although there was never a consensus on the exact number of layers and their contents, the following set of sheaths from the *Taittirīya Upaniṣad* is a typical construction:[19]

| *Inner* ← | | | | → *Outer* |
|---|---|---|---|---|
| earth | atmosphere | intermediate quarters | quarters of heaven | heaven |
| fire | wind | sun | moon | stars |
| one's body | space | trees | plants | water |
| touch | speech | mind | hearing | sight |
| marrow | bone | muscle | flesh | skin |

The scale of the surrounding universe was a matter of no consequence, because all was relative: the macrocosm could be shrunk to our size, or to look at it from the opposite point of view, the microcosm was capable of infinite expansion. The entire universe could be compressed into a drop of water, a grain of sand, or a single spoken word; and hence the potential power of sound. And similarly the innermost center of human existence, which is the source of all sound, has the potential to encompass all worlds that can be imagined. The *Chāndogya Upaniṣad* presents an eloquent exposition of this doctrine:

> He who consists of mind, whose body is life (*prāṇa,* literally "breath"), whose form is light, whose conception is truth, whose soul (*ātman*) is space, containing all works, containing all desires, containing all odors, containing all tastes, encompassing this whole world, the unspeaking, the unconcerned—this Soul

> of mine within the heart is smaller than a grain of rice, or a barley-corn, or a mustard-seed, or a grain of millet, or the kernel of a grain of millet; this Soul of mine within the heart is greater than the earth, greater than the atmosphere, greater than the sky, greater than these worlds. . . . this is the Soul of mine within the heart, this is Brahma. Into him I shall enter on departing hence.[20]

Remember this vision of an infinitely contracting and expanding universe and its subtle connections of breath, soul, and space, for it provides the essential background for the concept of musical sound. All human action occurs at the center of a theater of cosmic dimensions, and human life is a continuous pageant of images, works, and days passing before one's eyes—a timeless existence within which human life is played out in the certain knowledge that it is no more than one among an infinite number of similar worlds of illusion.

The priest saw this world from within, bringing his sensory organs and bodily functions under control, building his fire altar in the form of a symbolic representation of the universe (which was itself conceived in anthropomorphic form), and maintaining the order of things—the *rta*—by his sacrifices and his chanting of the sacred formulas. When he began his recitation by intoning the sacred syllable *om,* he symbolically inhaled the whole world of phenomena, and with the mantras that he uttered, he exhaled vital substance that became one with the universal continuum of spiritual energy. With this as background, it is easy to understand the reverence with which thinkers pondered the physical and metaphysical sources of sound; and similarly, it is easy to see why the melodic and accentual structure of Vedic chant was investigated with the same meticulous attention to detail that we find in the phonetic and grammatical analyses of the sacred texts.

The theatrical producer saw this world from without. His title of *sūtradhāra,* "he who holds the strings," describes his role as that of a master puppeteer, directing and controlling the thoughts, emotions, and actions of the colorful world of Indian society—a world that was fully indexed in terms of social class, gender, hereditary occupations, appropriate feelings, right actions, and all the deepest instincts of human nature. He had to know the entire world of Indian culture, what it meant, and how it was to be represented. Music for him was an essential component of the total spectacle and a means of timing and coordinating all aspects of the performance so that the dominant emotion (the *rasa*) would arise unmistakably in the hearts of the spectators. It is for these reasons that musical doctrines were expounded in such elaborate detail in the early literature of dramatic criticism.

Both priest and producer were concerned with the pursuit of reality in the midst of the illusions of the *theatrum mundi,* but they approached their tasks from opposite directions and with contrasting values: the contrast between a sacred and a secular worldview, between asceticism and hedonism, between sensory control and sensory surrender, between the pursuit of *mokṣa* (liberation) and *kāma* (pleasure). The result has been a constant tension in Indian musical ideology, in that music is valued not only for the delight that it brings through sensory experience but also because it provides a glimpse of the reality that is to be sought beyond the reach of the senses. Hold the images of the priest and the producer in mind as the role of music in sacred chant and the classical theater is explored in chapters 4 and 5.

## 1.4 Chronology and Sources

Indian cultural history begins for us with the high civilization of the Indus River valley in modern Pakistan, the so-called first urbanization including the settlements at Harappa and Mohenjo-Daro and generally dated from around 2500 B.C. This was a civilization of impressive accomplishments in such diverse matters as urban planning, community sanitation, brick construction, agriculture, and the visual arts; but its script remains undeciphered and its culture remains largely a mystery.[21] This flourishing civilization came to an abrupt end about 1750 B.C., for reasons that may include devastating climatic changes, flooding, plague, or even massacre. Archaeological investigations have turned up few traces of the Harappan musical culture apart from some instrument fragments and a small number of replicas of musicians and instruments on their engraved stone seals. The most striking artifact is a haunting statuette of a nude dancing girl.[22]

Vedic civilization was brought to the Indian subcontinent by the invading Indo-Aryans, beginning sometime during the second millennium B.C. Their route took them from the plains of Central Asia through the northwest mountain passes in modern Afghanistan, and then they spread out to the east and south along the plains of northern India as they conquered and intermarried with the indigenous Dravidian population, many of whom were pushed farther and farther south. This cultural encounter has often been described as a classic example of a familiar scenario: invading barbarians meet cultivated plains dwellers and absorb many of the higher values of the local population.

The Aryans brought an impressive culture with them, along with their own traditional kinship and class systems, and were particularly expert in horsemanship, military technology, metal working, musical culture, and the oral literature created and preserved by their priestly class. Their feelings of awe and dependence on the forces of nature were expressed in the powerful hymns of the *Rgveda*. The Aryans gradually traded in their seminomadic ways for village life and farming. This led to the massive deforestation that eventually transformed India's once favorable climate. Although illiterate, the Aryans brought with them the language that was to become the basis for classical Sanskrit, the polished tongue that flourished for more than a thousand years and still serves as the lingua franca of Indian scholarship. The Aryan settlers ultimately spread out westward to the Arabian Sea and eastward to the Bay of Bengal, and had reached as far south as the Vindhya mountain range by about 550 B.C.—a probable date for some of the earliest layers in our corpus of musicological literature.

With this brief background, the following chronology will provide a historical frame of reference for the major musical documents that have survived. These will be presented in the form of short descriptive sketches, along with their probable date and the symbol by which each of them will be identified in subsequent chapters. In the absence of any standard set of abbreviations, the following symbols represent a composite of the name of the author and the title of the treatise (if both are known, and differ). Some comments about dating this corpus of literature will follow the chronology.[23]

| | | |
|---|---|---|
| to 2500 B.C. | PREHISTORIC PERIOD | |
| 2500–1750 B.C. | INDUS VALLEY CIVILIZATIONS | |
| 1500–500 B.C. | ARYAN INVASIONS AND GRADUAL CONQUEST; the age of Vedic civilization | |
| | 1300–1000 B.C. | Composition of the *Rgveda* |
| | ca. 1000 B.C. | The *Mahābhārata* War |
| | 1000–500 B.C. | The later Vedas, *Brāhmaṇas*, and Upanishads |
| 500–300 B.C. | THE RISE OF BUDDHISM AND JAINISM | |
| | ca. 350 B.C. | The grammarian Pāṇini's *Aṣṭādhyayī* |
| | 326 B.C. | Alexander the Great abandons his conquest in the Punjab |
| 322–185 B.C. | THE MAURYAN DYNASTY | |
| | 272–237 B.C. | The emperor Aśoka |
| 100 B.C.–A.D. 300 | THE AGE OF INVASIONS, HINDUISM, AND TANTRISM; rise of the theater tradition; the great age of epic poetry | |
| | 500 B.C.–A.D. 500 | The golden age of classical Sanskrit as defined by Pāṇini; the period of the sutras |
| | 400 B.C.–A.D. 400 | Composition of the *Mahābhārata* |
| | 200 B.C.–A.D. 200 | Composition of the *Rāmāyaṇa* |
| | A.D. 200 | The *Nāṭyaśāstra* (*BN*), attributed to the sage Bharata, a compendious treatise of six thousand verses on the classical theater, of which the six (or in some editions, seven) chapters on music provide the earliest and most detailed information on all aspects of the ancient musical system, as well as elaborate descriptions of the music and musical style employed in the preliminary rituals and the incidental music.[24] |

A.D. 200 The *Dattilam* (*D*), a concise manual of ritual music by the otherwise unknown author Dattila, limited to brief expositions of *svara* and *tāla* in its 244 verses but valuable for its independent confirmation of the doctrines in *BN*.[25]

A.D. 200 The *Cilappatikaaram* (*IC*), "The Anklet," an early Tamil classic including many references to music and dance, a unique system of tuning, the musical scale, the modal system in relation to the zodiac, and much useful material on instruments, genres, forms, and rhythm.[26]

A.D. 320–540 *The classical Gupta period;* the zenith of the theater tradition; the age of ornate lyric poetry

A.D. 500 The *Nāradīyaśikṣā* (*NS*), a short phonetic manual attributed to the early sage Nārada, pertaining largely to the chanting of the *Sāmaveda*. About half of its 239 verses provide instruction in chanting and interesting, although cryptic, information on the early system of musical pitch, its derivation from the Vedic scale, and the mythology of music. The remaining verses are a set of instructions for correct enunciation, accentuation, and separation of the text, and a large number of homely maxims for the daily life and training of the young priest.[27]

A.D. 600–1200 *Medieval dynasties of North and South India;* the age of the six orthodox systems of philosophy

A.D. 650 The Kuḍumiyāmalai rock inscription (*K*), carved into the wall of a cave temple on a hill near Puḍukottai in the state of Tamil Nadu in South India. The inscription has been deciphered as a didactic musical notation demonstrating the tonal properties of the seven original *grāmarāgas* and must be reckoned among the important world monuments of early musical notation.[28]

A.D. 800 The *Bṛhaddeśī* (*MB*), the substantial remains (ca. five hundred verses) of a large and comprehensive treatise attributed to the sage Mataṅga, showing the growing influence of the Tantra and Yoga philosophies and documenting the transition from the *mārga* system to the evolving *deśī* musical practice. *MB* is also the earliest of the extant treatises to include musical notations and is an important early source for the tradition of secular song.[29]

A.D. 1000 *Abhinavabhāratī* (*AB*), a massive and brilliant commentary on *BN* by the Kashmiri Shaivite philosopher Abhinavagupta. Although scholars are still attempting to solve the numerous textual problems and determine more precisely what Abhinavagupta had in mind, his interpretations of the ancient treatises are regarded as authoritative and represent the commentarial tradition at its highest level of virtuosity.[30]

A.D. 1100 *Bharatabhāṣya,* or more accurately, *Sarasvatīhṛdayālaṅkāra* (*NB*) by King Nānyadeva of

| | | |
|---|---|---|
| | | Mithilā. This major work has been incorrectly presumed to be another commentary on *BN,* but some of the ten chapters on music deal with matters beyond the original scope of *BN,* including phonetics, *rāga,* and the new *deśī* songs.[31] |
| | A.D. 1131 | *Mānasollāsa,* or *Abhilaṣitārthacintāmaṇi* (*SM*), compiled by order of the Chālukya king Somésvara III, an encyclopedic treatise on everything a king ought to know, including three substantial chapters on the "enjoyments" of music—song, instrumental music, and dance.[32] |
| A.D. 1018 | *MAHMUD OF GHAZNI INVADES INDIA FROM AFGHANISTAN;* subsequent spread of Islam throughout North India | |
| | A.D. 1240 | The *Saṅgītaratnākara* (*SS*), a comprehensive synthesis of all previous musical learning, written by Śārṅgadeva, the scholarly royal accountant and Āyurvedic physician at the court of the Yādava king Siṅghaṇa at Devagiri. Its seven chapters, amounting to a total of more than five thousand verses, are as follows: *svara, rāga,* "miscellaneous topics," song, *tāla,* instrumental music, and dance. Of the three surviving commentaries, two are especially important—those of Siṁhabhūpāla (fourteenth century) and of Kallinātha (fifteenth century).[33] |
| | A.D. 1250 | The *Saṅgītasamayasāra* (*PS*), a work of 1168 verses by the Jain author Pārśvadeva emphasizing *rāgas* and their performance, the nature of sound, song, *tāla,* dance, and instrumental music.[34] |

In introducing this corpus of literature, a few caveats are necessary. It should be understood that each of the dates assigned above to one of the treatises should be preceded by *ca.,* and that *ca.* may indicate a leeway of several centuries in either direction in the case of the early texts: *BN, D, IC, NS,* and *MB.* There is a tendency in the critical literature for editors and translators to argue in favor of as early a date as possible, and a complementary tendency for other scholars to resist early attributions, often without strong evidence on either side of the controversy. In general I have chosen the earliest date by which the treatise cited *could* have achieved its "final form" (a concept that requires further explanation below), in the certain knowledge that no literary work from this period can be dated with any precision, and also recognizing that each of these texts is almost surely a composite of many earlier historical layers.

Quotations and glosses upon previous material are extremely common, and the possibility cannot be excluded that many of the citations may have been inserted at later stages of copying, so that even the sequence of names mentioned is open to question. It was considered a mark of erudition to quote from previous authorities and to attribute unidentified material to eminent authors; consequently the final form of a treatise as it has come down to us is sometimes more like a selection from an expandable data file than a unified dissertation—or to borrow an analogy from J. A. B. van Buitenen, more like a small library than a book.[35]

Many authors and works are now known only by name or on the evidence of citations in other treatises. The second half of the first millennium A.D. is a particularly dark age in Indian musicological literature, and names such as Kohala, Kaśyapa, Nārada, Śārdūla, and Yāṣṭika remain no more than shadowy figures. These preliminary cautions will be amplified in chapter 6, and the present remarks are intended merely as a reminder that certain reservations are necessary in interpreting a manuscript tradition in which no documents exist in "original" form—whatever that may have been—and in which even the concept of an original form may be misleading. What is important in the end is the text as it survives, whatever its imperfections, and the level of musical development therein recorded. Philological investigations should and will continue, but in the case of most of the above texts the point of diminishing returns has long since passed.

I should also point out that references to the music of early India are by no means confined to formal treatises, and that much useful information is to be found in a wide range of literature: the great epics, plays, poems, and the many genres of technical literature. Much of this material is peripheral to the central concerns of musical authors, but it helps to fill in the picture. And finally, one must acknowledge the depth of the tradition set down in this corpus of music literature. While a particular text may have reached a point after which no further substantive additions were made, it is likely that much of its material may have been drawn verbatim from much earlier texts which no longer exist—or which perhaps never did exist in written form. For these reasons a corpus of musical thought spanning roughly a thousand years between A.D. 250 and 1250 has preserved in fossilized form large quantities of material that may reasonably be attributed to authors as early as the fifth century B.C. and which may, like many other important documents of ancient Indian civilization, have first been formulated in an oral tradition and have been transmitted from teacher to student in the same way before finally becoming fixed in the form of a written text.

# TWO
# THOUGHT

Know thou the soul (*ātman*) as riding in a chariot,
The body as the chariot.
Know thou the intellect (*buddhi*) as the chariot-driver,
And the mind (*manas*) as the reins.
The senses (*indriya*), they say, are the horses;
The objects of sense, what they range over.
The self combined with senses and mind
Wise men call "the enjoyer."

*Kaṭha Upaniṣad* 3.3–4[1]

## 2.1 Introduction

Many of the characteristic features of traditional Indian thinking are evident in this passage from the *Kaṭha Upaniṣad,* one of the great works of metaphysical speculation intended to amplify the teachings of the Vedas and assemble them into a unified, systematic philosophy. Among these features are the highly introspective focus, the detailed analysis of the self, the multiple categories, and the colorful analogy that reaches back into the historical memory of the Indo-Aryan invaders as they swept down onto the plains of northern India with their horse chariots. Also, and importantly, the theme of mental discipline and control of the organs of sense as the means by which a final goal is attained.

To say something meaningful about thought is an ambitious undertaking and should restrain our expectations. By "thought" I mean the entire complex of mental activity, ingrained habits of thinking, instinctive reactions, traditional topics, cultural strategies of explanation, assumptions, values, preferences, connections, linguistic possibilities, and of course the inevitable blind spots and mental quirks that impede our understanding. We shall consider informal as well as formal thinking. Indian scholars, despite their formidable reasoning skills, recognized the limitations of linguistic technique and the dangers of overabstraction and attempted to make their arguments as concrete and colorful as possible. I shall try to follow their example, but a certain amount of abstraction will be unavoidable.

In this chapter I shall indicate the main lines of thought within which musical speculation arose, lines that were rooted in the Vedic tradition, were developed and amplified in the ancillary literature, and were eventually brought into firmer organization during the period of the orthodox philosophical systems—the period during which many of the later musical treatises cited were produced. All of this will provide the intellectual background for the analyses of the musical *śāstra*s in chapter 6. Here I shall point out a number of important continuities of Indian thought and proceed from there with some analysis of the systematic and symbolic dimensions of the philosophical tradition. Having thus established the necessary intellectual foundations, we will be ready to take up in turn each of the main issues in Indian musical speculation.

## 2.2 Continuities of Indian Thought

Truth has always existed. It was first revealed to the ancient sages through their sense of hearing, and it is thus known as *śruti,* "that which has been heard."[2] It must be kept alive by memory (the Sanskrit word for "tradition" is *smṛti,* "that which has been remembered") and amplified by the methods of scholastic inquiry. And finally it is to be uttered, because only then can its full power become manifest. The search is open-ended, since truth can never be known in full. To employ a typical analogy, truth exists in the form of a seed or a kernel—a nuclear idea of enormous potential but in need of analysis and elaboration before its full range of meaning can begin to become apparent. In the effort to understand why Indian musical thought is the way it is, it will be necessary to keep this image constantly before us.

The object of inquiry is that which already exists, in the form of aphorisms, pithy sayings, vivid expressions and images, and terse definitions. Essential information is prepackaged into individual modules corresponding roughly to the length of the mental present, formulated in the laconic sutra (thread) style of literary expression or in metrical couplets (*śloka*s) of standard length and structure, and written upon individual palm leaves trimmed to uniform size. The method of inquiry is to recite, recopy, and ponder this testimony and the accumulation of analysis and interpretation with which it is eventually surrounded, perhaps adding some new insight or point of interpretation. Little wonder that the commentary became the basic form of literary analysis in early Indian civilization.

Indian thought is relentlessly taxonomic. A profusion of categories unfold, each giving way to new subcategories and each lending itself to analysis from multiple perspectives. It is difficult for a Westerner to accept this concept of open-ended inquiry, of a method whose goal—like the goal of

Zeno's racecourse—is unattainable. Every statement turns out to be false in that it is inescapably an oversimplification that blurs finer distinctions. And because Indian thought tends to be inclusive rather than exclusive, contradictions abound, and the resulting categories are never as neatly organized or as mutually exclusive as we would like them to be. Faced with these contradictions and ambiguities, the commentator had his work cut out for him. It has often been pointed out that formal systems of Indian logic have never accepted the law of the excluded middle (which holds that in the case of an apparent contradiction, a proposition either is or is not true), and hence Indian taxonomies seldom are arrayed in sharp dichotomies and exclusive categories.

Indian thought relies upon authority. As Richard Lannoy put it, "oldest is best!"[3] and in most systems of Indian philosophy the testimony of reliable persons and scriptures has been regarded as a source of valid knowledge and therefore among the major *pramāṇa*s (standards) on which correct inference can be based.[4] The important *pramāṇa* identified as *śabda* (sound) *pramāṇa* refers specifically to uttered testimony. The message here is that truth is to be proclaimed, and its utterance carries vital power; hence the emphasis upon the efficacy of mantras (formulas), the importance of memory, and the divine power of Vāc, the speech principle as deified in the *Ṛgveda*.[5]

Mediation has always been seen as an obstacle to full understanding. It is paradoxical that Indian thought has had as its goal the search for ultimate meaning and truth unmediated by language and logical thinking, under the influence of the traditional concept of essential reality masked by the phenomenal illusion known as maya. The search has led thinkers in the direction of metaphysics and nonmaterialist ontologies. But the paradox lies in this: despite the inherently inadequate tools of language and logical thinking, authors have resorted to the most rigorous analysis of their language, alongside their attempts to capture elusive meaning in the form of the many atmospheric, vegetative, and animal analogies that are such a colorful feature of the literature of music and the other compartments of the technical literature.

Indian thought is dynamic, not static, and emphasizes processes and transformations rather than permanent certainties. It identifies with the processive world of Heraclitus and Empedocles in preference to the static worldview of Parmenides: becoming is valued above being. This attitude reveals the influence of the traditional Hindu worldview of a continuous process of creation and dissolution under the successive patronage of Brahmā,

Viṣṇu, and Śiva. It is a worldview, as Heimann points out, that encourages a biological and long-term view of life, history, and time—in which nothing is isolated from its antecedents and its consequences (according to the doctrine of karma), the present is to be held in proper perspective and viewed with some objective detachment, the potential is to be valued above the actual, and a continuous, interpenetrating life force provides subtle connections among all creatures and things.[6] It is not surprising that nineteenth-century German thinkers, and especially Goethe and Schopenhauer, were attracted to Indian philosophy, nor is it surprising that the pervading values of nineteenth-century romanticism were so close to the values that have informed Indian music and thought for millennia. Despite the differences in musical language and style, this was the era in which the intellectual orbits of East and West made their closest approach. But despite their common assumptions, each remained unable to comprehend the phenomenal basis of the other's music.

Indian thought is also, as Lannoy has indicated, "hylozoistic," which he defines as a "tendency to draw no clear distinction between matter, life, and mind."[7] The major schools of systematic philosophy differed on the question of whether reality was monistic or pluralistic, but running throughout their counterarguments is a clear sense of the interconnectedness of all things. Accordingly, authors sought constantly to identify universals and set them above the limitations of the individual and the particular. The influence of this line of thinking is evident in the traditional concepts of form and substance: form is merely a temporary condition of flexible substance.

Whether substance is, as some have argued, nothing more than a persuasive illusion, or as others have claimed, actual matter that is subject to series of transformations, few Indian thinkers would deny the underlying unity of the animate and inanimate worlds and the mind—the instrument by which all things are known. If substance always exists in mutable form, as an essential core that persists during all its manifestations to the senses, then we can more readily understand the traditional preferences for a plurality of forms, for the appearance of deities in their various incarnations,[8] and for some of the most characteristic processes in the arts—processes in which visual and audible constructions of all sorts appear in series of playful transformations and are savored in their successive aspects. That part of reality which can be known is always multidimensional and can be known only after exploration from multiple perspectives, as when we circumambulate a temple or (as the six blind men discovered in a familiar parable) an elephant. The aim of art was not perfection of form but a profusion of forms, and the object was more to explore possibilities than to achieve closure or demonstrate ideal forms and proportions.

## 2.3 Systematic Thinking

Indian philosophy is known for its elaborate "systems"—schools of thought (about the universe, the self, and the search for true knowledge) that were worked out by generations of thinkers over many centuries. The limited scope of this study must rule out even a sketchy exposition of the main systems, but some discussion is necessary if only to lay out some of the main lines of thought as essential background for the musical doctrines to be investigated. The various schools of formal thought can be divided in a number of ways: philosophies as opposed to religions (neither an easy nor an obvious distinction), speculative as opposed to practical systems, Aryan and non-Aryan, orthodox (schools that accept the authority of the Vedas) as opposed to heterodox schools (those that do not), and numerous finer distinctions.[9]

Although as usual precise dating is not possible, a traditional division into four main phases has been widely accepted. The Vedic period (to about 500 B.C.) is the period of the scriptures—the four Vedas and their auxiliary texts. From 500 B.C. to about A.D. 200 has been designated as the period of the epics (the *Mahābhārata* and the *Rāmāyaṇa,* of which the former includes the *Bhagavadgītā*); this same period witnessed the rise of three of the main heterodox schools—Buddhism, Jainism, and the Cārvāka school of materialism, which is known largely by the efforts of subsequent schools to refute its doctrines. From A.D. 200 until 700 was the age of the sutras, the collections of laconic sayings and cryptic verses upon which later scholars built their comprehensive systems. This is also a crucial formative period for systematic musical thought; the earliest of the major musical treatises were written in a similar style, a style that encouraged and rewarded the attention of later commentators. The fourth and final period (A.D. 700 to 1700, or perhaps the present) is the age of the scholiasts, an age in which the teachings of the ancient authors were elaborated and amplified into formal philosophical systems.

I shall not dwell on the important religious traditions of Buddhism and Jainism, since the distinctive features of their teachings were largely irrelevant to musical thought, or perhaps it is more accurate to say that the influence of their differences from traditional Hinduism is not apparent in the musicological literature—with the one possible and interesting exception of the Jain author Pārśvadeva, whose thirteenth-century treatise entitled

*Saṅgītasamayasāra* (*PS*) has yet to be studied in the detail it deserves. I shall also defer discussion of the mystical movement known as Tantra (beginning in the seventh and eighth centuries A.D.) and the religiophilosophic school of Kashmir Shaivism (after the ninth century A.D.) which came later to have an enormous influence upon musical thought, as reflected in the writings of Abhinavagupta. The remainder of this section, then, will be devoted to some introductory comments on the six orthodox *darśanas* (literally, points of view), their common assumptions, and a few of the more important variations (see table 1).[10]

The six systems differ in several aspects, among them (1) emphasis, in that some systems incline more to metaphysics, others to practical conduct; (2) whether they are monistic or pluralistic, a vital distinction in Indian thought; (3) the nature of the theistic outlook and the theory of creation; (4) the purpose of the system; (5) the specific set of categories; and (6) the epistemological method advocated. Although all six are regarded today as "completed" systems, their general doctrines and specific arguments (especially those of Advaita Vedanta) are still very much alive and flourishing in India today.

On the other hand, certain important lines of thought run through all the great systems, although to recognize them is to run the risk of glossing over the many equally important differences in application, interpretation, and

Table 1 The Six Orthodox Systems

| System | Founder | Emphasis |
| --- | --- | --- |
| Nyāya: "analysis" | Akṣapāda Gautama | Logical realism |
| Vaiśeṣika: "the school of individual characteristics" | Ulūka Kaṇāda | Realistic pluralism |
| Sāṅkhya: "the enumeration" | The sage Kapila | Evolutionary dualism |
| Yoga: "harnessing [the mind and senses]" | Patañjali[a] | Disciplined meditation |
| Mīmāṃsā: "investigation" | Jaimini | Interpretation of the Vedic teachings on ritual |
| Vedānta: "the end of the Vedas" | Bādarāyaṇa | Interpretation of the natural philosophy of the Vedas |

[a]The author of the *Yōga Sūtras* is almost certainly not the great grammarian and author of the *Mahābhāṣya* (2d century B.C.).

context. First, philosophy is not restricted to the proverbial ivory tower but is accompanied and supported by a practical, sensible way of life, featuring such things as meditation, devotional rituals, self-control, sensory deprivation, breathing exercises, and the like. It is for this reason that the six major systems are paired (as shown in table 1), each pair consisting of a speculative and a practical member. Second, despite individual variations, each of the six systems rests on metaphysical presuppositions (as opposed to the Cārvāka school) and asserts that ultimate reality is situated beyond the illusory world of phenomena, obscured by the "veil" of maya. Third, each of the systems has accepted the crucial doctrine of karma, which acknowledges a continuous chain of cause and effect in which our actions are followed by inevitable consequences that determine our state in subsequent reincarnations. This influential doctrine rests on the assumption that the soul is immortal, with *mokṣa* (liberation) or nirvana (extinction) as the goal—annihilation through escape from the cycle of birth and rebirth.

Fourth, all share in the highly introspective focus on the analysis of the self or soul (*ātman*): ultimate philosophy is a lens trained inward, and the concept of the self has been subjected to a penetrating analysis without a parallel in world philosophy. It is defined in many stages, phases, layers, or *tattva*s: pure transcendent being, consciousness, ego, intellect, mind—all represented by important technical terms and arranged in complex hierarchies. And fifth, all six systems stress that which is latent—pure potential, dormant energy, an infinite well of subtle life force—whether conceived as the primal waters, the reservoir of vital air situated at the center of the human body, or the continuous vibration of all creation. This is the source of the sage's power and the force that connects all things; it cannot be perceived directly, but its presence may be inferred.

As brief illustrations of the range of these doctrines, especially that of the *ātman,* I present the relevant views of two of the major systems. In the monistic and relatively uncomplicated structure of the Vaiśeṣika system, the basic substances (*dravya*s) are nine in number: earth, water, fire, air, ether (*ākāśa,* the medium for sound), time, space, self, and mind (*manas*). In the more elaborate set of categories of the dualistic Sāṅkhya system, we find a fuller development which takes the form of an evolution of the manifested universe, as the result of an interaction between ultimate substance (*prakṛti*) and one of an infinite number of *puruṣa*s (a concept that may be defined as "pure consciousness of the individual self"). The evolution proceeds by means of the cooperative interplay of twenty-four *tattva*s, as arranged on the following diagram:

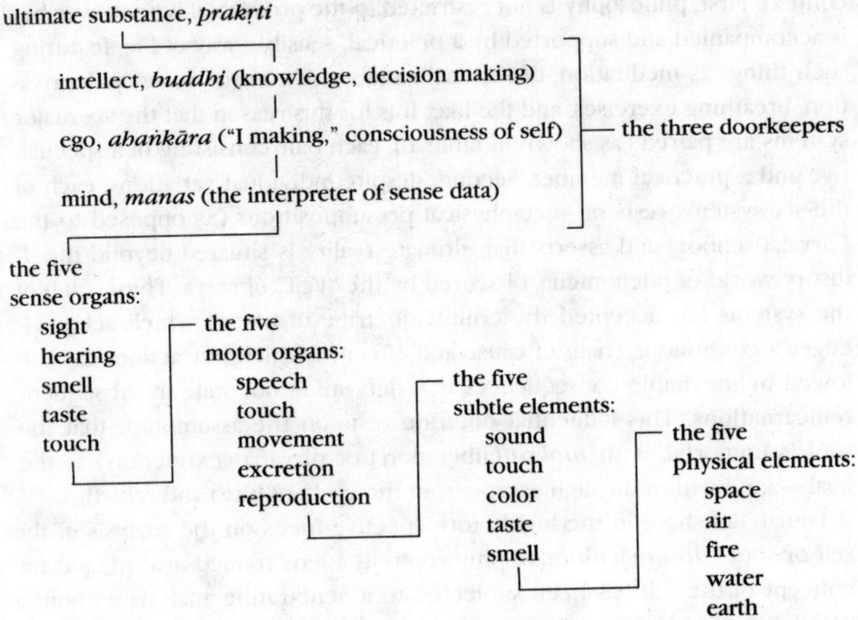


There are several conclusions to be drawn from this display. The elaborate structure of the Sāṅkhya system and its counterparts in the other orthodox systems have encouraged the development of a profound philosophy of mind and a complex psychology that emphasizes the theory of perception. Within these lines of thinking, epistemology plays a more important role than ontology. The underlying assumptions that (1) matter is permanent and (2) force is persistent imply that nothing can ever "come into being" or "pass away" in the Aristotelian sense. Substance can undergo transformation, but it retains its essential nature. Process is all-important and all-pervasive, and that process, although it may not have a specific ultimate goal, always has a direction along the continuum from subtle to gross matter.

Above these twenty-four *tattva*s the exponents of the later school of Kashmir Shaivism add eleven transpersonal and transcendental categories: beginning with five manifestations of the universal self (as pure being, consciousness or energy, will, knowledge, and action), followed by *māyā* (the first manifestation of the "impure creation" and the power that obscures), then *kalā* (the limited power of action) and its four effects: discrimination, choice, time, and limitation. No mere enumeration of topics can give more than a hint of the lofty abstractions and fierce complexities of these systems, but the tendency to infer subtle, unmanifested, transcendental principles stands out as one of the hallmarks of systematic Indian thinking and could not have failed to influence the idea of music as it developed. It is also easy to understand how deeply the notion of an independent, immaterial, transpersonal, universal self or will would have appealed to a thinker such as Arthur Schopenhauer. European philosophers of the nineteenth century may not have been acquainted with the full details of the traditional Indian philosophies, but they found something profoundly sympathetic in the attitudes outlined above and the characteristic Indian weltanschauung.

Another significant concept of the Sāṅkhya system will provide further insight into Indian ways of thinking: universal substance (*prakṛti*) is further conceived in the form of a rope fashioned from three intertwined strands or *guṇas*: *sattva* (often translated as "goodness"), the principle of illumination, intelligence, pleasure, whiteness, and pure light; *rajas* (passion), the principle of activity, stimulation, pain, redness, and fire; and *tamas* (darkness), the principle of inertia, obstruction, heaviness, indifference, darkness, and earth. All reality arises from the continuous interaction of the three principles, with one or another always dominating. In a familiar analogy, the three *guṇa*s have been likened to the wick, oil, and flame that combine to produce light from a lamp.

The classical exposition of this doctrine appears in the fourteenth chapter of the *Bhagavadgītā,* as Kṛṣṇa instructs Arjuna in the "Discipline of Distinction of the Three Strands":

> Goodness, passion, and darkness,
> The Strands that spring from material nature,
> Bind, O great-armed one,
> In the body the immortal embodied (soul). . . .
>
> Goodness causes attachment to bliss,
> Passion to action, son of Bharata,
> But darkness, obscuring knowledge,
> Causes attachment to heedlessness likewise. . . .
>
> Of action well done, they say
> The fruit is spotless and of the nature of goodness;
> But the fruit of passion is pain;
> The fruit of darkness is ignorance.[11]

It is important to note that the *guṇa*s were conceived as essential components of substance, not as qualities or attributes, but in a typical Indian twist, the resulting substance was held to be one, not a composite. The notion that something may be both composite and incomposite at one and the same time sets the Indian tradition apart from one of the cardinal ontological principles of the ancient West, under which one of the most basic distinctions that can be made is to separate otherwise similar things into those which are composite and those which are not. On the other hand, the Western doctrine of the four humors (with the conventional correspondences to the four temperaments, the four physical elements, and the four properties of nature) is an obvious parallel to the theory of the three *guṇa*s, and there are also some broad parallels between early Indian and Western medical practice and pharmacology, in that disease was regarded as an imbalance, and health as a balance, of the bodily elements. And in both traditions what may perhaps have begun as a practical method of diagnosis and therapy has developed into an influential theory of personality. To mention one example, *rajas* was considered to be the dominant characteristic of a king (*rāja*) and his warlike *kṣatriya* class; it has subsequently become the basis for a personality stereotype that runs through Indian history and literature and has also become one of the essential components in the definition of poetic and/or musical style.[12] And as a final observation, the concept that any object or process can best be defined by enumerating its qualities, or *guṇa*s, has evolved into one of the standard strategies of musical explanation.

## 2.4 Symbolic Thinking

We have been examining the conscious, rational level of thinking—a mode of inquiry that was honed to a razor edge of precision by the great Indian philosophers, but within which the inherent limitations of language and logical reasoning would inevitably set obstacles in the seeker's path. Symbolic thinking—in the form of vivid metaphors, similes, and analogies—became a popular means for getting at the essence of things that are either too subtle or too complicated to grasp by ordinary observation or reasoning. This type of thinking, which the Belgian musicologist Jan L. Broeckx has labeled "analogical thinking" (as opposed to his three other categories—the generative, actualized, and syntactical modes of musical thinking),[13] has become one of the most powerful tools of Indian musical speculation.

Authors took their analogies from the familiar creatures, objects, and surroundings of the everyday world: a clay pot, as a universal symbol for any type of container; digging a well, as an illustration of the way in which a student should obtain knowledge from a teacher; the string running through a necklace of gemstones, as a symbol of the rhythmic continuity by which a musical performance should be integrated; a tigress carrying her cubs in her teeth, as an analogy for the precise, delicate enunciation of a sacred text; insects building an anthill, as a symbol of industry and patience; the spices used in cooking, as an analogy for the way in which the various actions and emotions during the course of a play fuse into one dominant emotional tone; a woman's jewelry, as a symbol for ornamentation in music; and the relative viscosity of fluids such as water, milk, oil, and honey, as symbols of melodic continuity—all delivered in a tone that was both moralistic and affectionate, and often seasoned with no small amount of humor.

Specific examples of these and other analogies will appear frequently in subsequent chapters, and the present discussion is intended primarily as an introduction to this characteristic mode of thinking. I wish, however, to highlight one particular metaphor with important implications for music—the description of musical sound as an emanation along an outward spiral pathway. The metaphor works in both directions: the way of action (the *karmamārga*) radiates outward from the center, whereas the way of perception and of knowledge (the *jñānamārga*) proceeds in the opposite direction.

The metaphor of outward passage is a standard topic of Indian culture, as expressed in explanations for the emission of breath or musical sound from the central cavities of the human body, or the pattern of natural growth that can be observed in the leaves of a lotus, or the concentric ripples produced by a stone dropped into a pool of water. Emanation is a continuous process, gradually losing some of its force and concentration as the vital breath or life force proceeds along its spiral or radiating course and emerges in gross, manifested form—as articulate speech sounds, meaningful words, or musical sounds and rhythms.

The metaphor is supported by a wealth of cultural imagery, particularly in the Tantric philosophy of *kuṇḍalini yoga,* in which the bodily channels are visualized in the form of a coiled serpent extending upward and passing through various bodily regions, the *cakras.*[14] An earlier and more abstract version of the same pathway is the Upanishadic conception of the body in terms of five superimposed layers,[15] interpreted in the Advaita Vedantic teachings of Śaṅkara as five "sheaths" that surround the pure self: from inner to outer, these are (1) the sheath of "bliss," likened to the plane of deep sleep; (2) the sheath of understanding; (3) the sheath of mind; (4) the sheath of vital breath; and (5) the gross physical body, the sheath of "food."[16] And, in a related analogy, the *Aitareya Āraṇyaka* refers to the human body as the divine vina and outlines a set of point-by-point correspondences between the sound-producing features of the vina and the body.[17] This line of anthropomorphic imagery is also reversible, allowing one to endow a musical instrument with human properties or to view the human body as a cosmic instrument.

Other implications of the metaphor of outward passage include a progression from the lower to the higher, from subtle to gross (matter), from continuous to discontinuous, and from the nonmanifest to the manifest: lower in this context refers to the so-called knot of Brahmā (the *brahmagranthi*), conceived as the life source of the human body and situated near the root of the navel;[18] and upper, in the sense that human thought, breath, speech, and song are conceived as upward processes. The consequences of this line of imagery for the traditional system of values are as follows:

| *Greater value* | *Lesser value* |
| --- | --- |
| inner | outer |
| lower | higher |
| subtle | gross |
| continuous | discontinuous |
| nonmanifest | manifest |

In contrast, the inward pathway—the way of perception and of knowledge, affect as opposed to effect—signifies a process of increasing focus, distillation, and concentration of energies, leading to greater purity, understanding, and eventual detachment from the phenomenal world. According to the teachings of Yoga, by means of fixation and intense concentration on the object of perception, followed by a stage-by-stage withdrawal of perception from the phenomenal illusion toward which those perceptions were directed, the yogin may be able to achieve *samādhi* (absorption)—the trancelike state in which the distinction between subject and object disappears.

The special relevance of this line of thinking for the theory of musical sound will become apparent in chapter 3.

# THREE
# SOUND

> The Word is measured in four quarters. The wise
> who possess insight know these four divisions.
> Three quarters, concealed in secret, cause no movement.
> The fourth is the quarter that is spoken by Men.
>
> *Ṛgveda* 1.164.45[1]

> Sound is not what one should desire to understand. One should know the hearer.
>
> *Kauṣītaki Upaniṣad* 3.8[2]

## 3.1 Introduction

Sound is everywhere, within and around us—a continuum of vital force and latent energy. Only a part of it can be heard: the world of manifest, audible sounds with their individual phonetic, morphological, and semantic distinctions occupies no more than a small fraction of the total field of sound; the greater part is within, unmanifest and beyond the grasp of conscious experience. The sounds that are uttered, according to the *Kauṣītaki Upaniṣad,* are subject to all the illusions of the phenomenal world; what these sounds mean, or suggest, is all-important. Consequently the source and the goal of sound are of greater intrinsic interest than the phenomenon itself.

This chapter is concerned with both audible and inaudible sound. I shall draw upon the Upanishadic literature to establish the traditional cultural background for the idea of sound before proceeding to some of the refinements and hairsplittings of the later philosophical systems. My contention, here and elsewhere in this study, is that musical thought has been molded more by the gradual diffusion of deeper layers of cultural ideas in relatively unsophisticated form than by the systematic arguments of professional philosophers.

## 3.2 The Divisions of Sound

The four divisions mentioned in the passage from the *Ṛgveda,* three inaudible and one audible, form the basis for much of the later speculation about the metaphysical nature of sound, and especially for the influential concept of *śabdabrahman* as formulated by the grammarian Bhartṛhari (ca.

A.D. 450–500) and described in his *Vākyapadīya* as "that beginningless and endless one, the imperishable Brahman of which the essential nature is the Word, which manifests itself into objects and from which is the creation of the Universe."[3] Only a cumbersome translation such as "the speech-sound principle as ultimate reality" can come close to the meaning of Bhartṛhari's expression. In a later section we shall encounter a similar concept with particular reference to musical sound: *nādabrahman,* a concept implying that the successive gradations of musical sound, both manifest and unmanifest, are identified with the creative vital force by which the entire universe is animated.[4] The cultural ideology of sound is obviously not confined to the domain of physics, nor can questions of musical sound be easily separated from their larger context of the sounds of human speech and the general theory of sound.

An analysis of the sacred syllable *om* and its many symbolic associations will provide some useful cultural background for the ancient theory of sound. The brief *Māṇḍūkya Upaniṣad* is devoted entirely to an interpretation of the four quarters of the word as manifested by the successive phonetic elements of *om,*[5] but in this case the proportions have been reversed: three of the components are audible and the fourth, inaudible. The syllable *om,* which is intoned at the beginning and end of every Vedic lesson and recitation, is analyzed into three elements: *a* + *u* (that is, the diphthong *o*) + *m;* it is often written as *aum. Om* has been interpreted as the eternal syllable that contains in itself the entire phenomenal universe, and as the nucleus from which all audible sounds proceed and to which all such sounds must ultimately return. In fact the word for "syllable," *akṣara,* is usually analyzed as *a* + *kṣara* (imperishable).[6] Sound is permanent.

The final phase of *om* is not represented by any phonetic component, because it transcends the limitations of human utterance, and hence the following schema: first *a* (the "primal sound" as well as the first letter of the Sanskrit alphabet), followed in turn by *u* and *m,* and finally by the silence "that follows and surrounds the syllable."[7] These four phases also represent, according to the same text, threefold time (past, present, and future) and that which transcends threefold time. They are also likened to the three stages of consciousness (the waking state, dreaming, and deep sleep) plus a fourth, noncognitive state—the unthinkable and ungraspable. *Om* has in fact been said to represent all forms of the world soul (*Ātman*) (see table 2).[8]

Table 2 provides a wealth of material for analysis and helps to explain why the utterance of audible sound has become invested with such a heavy load of symbolic associations. I can only touch upon a few of these. It is more than coincidence that three of the forms of "vital breath" (*prāṇa*) ap-

Table 2 The Forms of the *Ātman* according to the *Maitri Upaniṣad*

| Form | First Stage | Second Stage | Third Stage |
|---|---|---|---|
| Sound | *a* | *u* | *m* |
| Sex | Feminine | Masculine | Neuter |
| Light | Fire | Wind | Sun |
| Deity | Brahmā | Rudra (Śiva) | Viṣṇu |
| Sacrificial fire | Domestic fire | Southern, expiatory fire | Primary, eastern fire |
| Understanding | *Ṛgveda* | *Yajurveda* | *Sāmaveda* |
| World | Earth, *bhūr* | Atmosphere, *bhuvas* | Sky, *svar* |
| Time | Past | Present | Future |
| Heat | Breath | Fire | Sun |
| "Swelling"[a] | Food | Water | Moon |
| Intelligence | Intellect, *buddhi* | Mind, *manas* | Egoism, *ahaṅkāra* |
| Vital breath | Forward breath | Downward breath | Diffused breath |

[a] In the sense of "increase," i.e., nourishment, the enlargement of a river by its tributary waters, and the waxing of the moon.

pear among these correspondences, emphasizing the important point that the ancient Indian conception of sound is essentially human, vocal sound. The liturgical role of sound is likewise emphasized by the inclusion of the so-called Great Vyāhṛtis (utterances)—*bhūr* (earth), *bhuvas* (atmosphere), and *svar* (heaven)—the ceremonial salutation of the "three worlds" which is uttered immediately after *om* in daily prayers.[9] When Prajāpati, the creator god of the later Vedic period, created language, he first meditated upon the three worlds, and from his meditation arose the threefold knowledge (the first three of the Vedas); as he meditated upon these, the three words of invocation issued forth: *bhūr, bhuvas, svar;* and from these arose the syllable *om* which encompasses and integrates all human speech, just as "leaves are held together by a spike."[10] Because of these symbolic associations, *om* has been held to be a valuable object of meditation, especially in the philosophy of Yoga, and an instrument that leads toward liberation. Elsewhere in the *Maitri Upaniṣad* the process of meditation is compared to a spider mounting by means of his thread to obtain free space; by intoning *om* the meditator similarly ascends toward freedom.[11]

The utterance of the sacred syllable is, then, at once an invocation to the gods, a salutation to the structure of the created universe, an aid to meditation, a protection against error, a hymn of praise to life in all its forms and manifestations, and a symbol of integration and completeness—completeness, that is, in the sense that the whole is not only greater than the sum of its parts: the three phases and their individual distinctions are absorbed into a whole within which all these distinctions and attributes are dissolved. Sound is clearly something to be taken seriously.

The passages examined in this section illustrate a deeply engrained cultural habit of thinking in which sound is conceived as a series of gradations—three, four, or (in some cases) many more—proceeding from the inaudible to the audible, each stage fusing imperceptibly into the next, and following the metaphoric pathway of the outward spiral.[12] The most common set of divisions is 3 + 1, but it may appear in either positive or negative form (that is, with three quarters "concealed in secret" and one audible, or the reverse, as in the case of *om*). In either of these versions, one of the divisions represents an ultimate stage that transcends action and consciousness—the stage of nondistinction and ultimate silence. I shall have frequent occasion in later chapters to emphasize the special role of silence in Indian thought, in which nothingness is often valued more highly than somethingness.[13]

How is silence heard? Perhaps in the way that we "hear" the light that shines within a person, according to the *Chāndogya Upaniṣad*—by closing our ears and listening to the sound of a fire blazing within.[14] Or, in the words of the *Maitri Upaniṣad,* "by closing the ears with the thumbs they hear the sound of the space within the heart. Of it there is this sevenfold comparison: like [the sound of] rivers, a bell, a brazen vessel, a wheel, the croaking of frogs,[15] rain, [or] as when one speaks in a sheltered place."[16]

In India, as elsewhere in the ancient world, the concept of musical sound arose and developed in the midst of an aura of cultural symbolism. Because of its many associations with the sounds of human speech, it was expounded within the context of articulatory phonetics and was pursued with the same intellectual rigor and keenness of observation. Audible sound has become a means of knowledge because of its ability to reveal the inaudible. In the testimony of the *Maitri Upaniṣad,* "The body is a bow. The arrow is *Om.* The mind is its point. Darkness is the mark."[17]

## 3.3 The Theory of Sound

So that we may approach the theory of sound from a cross-cultural perspective, I present representative passages from two early authors, one Indian and one Western:

We worship that divine sound, the life of consciousness in all beings and the supreme bliss, manifested in the form of the universe. By the adoration of sound, the gods Brahmā, Viṣṇu, and Śiva are truly worshipped, for they are the embodiment of sound. The Soul,

Take sound, to start with. Noise is audible because its body penetrates the ears, impinging on the sense; voices and sounds are bodily in nature, since they strike with impact on the senses. . . . Words and tones, since they can hurt, are, beyond any doubt, made of material stuff. . . . The ear having a desire to speak, stirs the mind. The mind strikes the fire abiding in the body, and that fire strikes the wind. Then that wind abiding in the region of Brahmā, rising along the upward paths, manifests the sound successively in the navel, the heart, the throat, the head, and the mouth. (Śārṅgadeva, *Saṅgītaratnākara* 1.3.1–4)[18]

is struck by different sorts of atoms when a horn is muted, crooning low, or blares away full blast, or when the swans in plaintive cry raise their clear dirges over Helicon. (Lucretius, *De rerum natura* 4)[19]

Let us begin with the West. Although Lucretius's brand of atomistic materialism was not endorsed in full by all ancient Greek and Latin authors, he still represents the main line of thought clearly enough. The realm of physics provides straightforward explanations of the production and transmission of sound: it is a material substance, born of impact and transmitted by the successive impacts of an assortment of atoms upon the organ of hearing, whence it moves elsewhere in the body. That is about all there is to it. Since the time of Archytas of Tarentum (fourth century B.C.) Greek authors have defined sound as a "blow" or a "striking," *plaga* and the later Attic *plege*. The nature of the impact (fast or slow, powerful or feeble) determined the nature of the sound (high or low, loud or soft), and that portion of the sound sustained after the initial impact was held to be nothing more than the automatic residue of the impact.[20] Aristotle refined this line of thinking in his *De Anima,* and it continued to be the standard explanation for sound as late as Boethius. Even Plato, whom we would hardly expect to have favored such a physical explanation, evidently subscribed to the same hypothesis: "We may in general assume sound to be a blow which passes through the ears, and is transmitted by means of the air, the brain, and the blood, to the soul, and that hearing is the vibration of this blow which begins in the head and ends in the region of the liver. The sound which moves swiftly is acute, and the sound which moves slowly is grave. . . . A great body of sound is loud, and a small body of sound the reverse" (*Timaeus* 67b–c).[21]

Śārṅgadeva's view is radically different: Sound is vital substance and an extension of the all-pervading continuum of universal sound, born of mind, activated by heat energy, and discharged along the spiraling channels of the human body in the form of a continuous stream of breath, acquiring resonance as the flow of sound passes through the various chambers, and finally emerging in the form of individual syllables, pitches, and time durations. It is not clear whether the use of *ātman* in this passage refers to the world soul or merely to the individual consciousness, nor is there any need to draw such a distinction: the two are one. Whatever the efficient cause, the interaction of differing forms of elemental substance deep within the body impels the sound upward and outward in much the same way that fire and wind combine to produce smoke, a popular analogy in Indian philosophy. There is still "contact" in Śārṅgadeva's description of sound, but the emphasis is more upon friction and continuous process than upon a precisely timed impact.

I have emphasized the quintessentially human nature of the Indian concept of sound, and that vocal sound has become the primary model for all musical sound. Musical instruments (especially the vina, conch shell, and drum) appear frequently in analogies in the ancient literature, but their status is that of little more than a tool; the primary connection between the universal substratum of sound and the individual musical sounds is by way of human vital breath (*prāṇa*). Sound, according to the testimony of Śārṅgadeva, is manifested, not caused, and the sounds that are uttered represent only one category among its many manifestations. By sound the gods exist, with sound they are worshiped, and the entire world process of continuous creation and dissolution subsists by means of sound.

It will be useful to indicate the principal variations among the views of the later philosophical systems.[22] Is sound a substance or merely a quality inherent in a substance? The Mīmāṁsā thinkers preferred the former explanation, but they appear to have been in the minority. The Nyāya, Vaiśeṣika, and Tantric schools maintained that sound is a quality inherent in one of the elemental substances—air, ether, earth, and the like. Is sound one or many? In this case a loose consensus was reached, namely, that sound is essentially one. Is sound eternal or transitory? Eternal, according to the Mīmāṁsās and several of the other schools; transitory, according to the Nyāyas.

What is the proper medium of sound? A later section will be devoted to this question, but a brief introduction will be helpful. Most of the philosophical schools have held that sound is primarily associated with the *ākāśa,* translated sometimes as "space" but more often as "ether," the first of the elements evolved from the universal consciousness (once again the *Ātman*).[23] A minority view was held by the Sāṅkhya and Vedānta thinkers, who maintained that sound inheres in earth, water, fire, and air—in much the same manner that colors and odors inhere—but not in the *ākāśa. Dik* is another common word for "space," but it signifies ordinary, directional, inert, objective space, not the type of space that is saturated with subtle, vital energy (*ākāśa*). Sound has something of the nature of each of the physical elements: the solidity of earth (when manifested in bodies or instruments), the vaporousness and viscosity of water, the stimulating power and purifying force of fire, and the mobility and pervasiveness of wind. But its primary element is the *ākāśa*.

Another debate arose over the issue of causation: Is sound caused, as the Nyāyas claimed, or is it manifested? If sound is subject to causation, it cannot be eternal, because eternal substance cannot have a cause; and if the Vedas are truly self-sufficient (as they must be), then the word must be eternal and without a cause. On the strength of these assumptions, most of the orthodox schools (including the Mīmāṁsā, Sāṅkhya, and Vedāntic philosophers) have defined sound not as an effect but as a manifestation—of inner consciousness, vital breath, and/or the primordial cause of the evolved universe. Buddhist thought has dissented sharply from this line of reasoning, holding instead that sound is the result of disturbances in the elemental substances; sound therefore subsists in nothing and is subject to generation and destruction. Materialist explanations of the nature of sound have also been advanced, not differing greatly from the atomistic concept expounded by Lucretius, but they have not been widely endorsed—probably because this line of argument goes against the grain of so many crucial assumptions in traditional Indian thought.

If there is a central core to the idea of sound as developed in the systematic Indian philosophies, it is that sound is a quality, inhering in the substratum of *ākāśa* which pervades both the outer spaces of the world and the inner spaces of the body. It is one, universal, eternal, causal (but not caused), permeating both personal and transpersonal consciousness, and manifested along the human pathway from inner to outer space. Its discharge in the form of vital breath is both an act of worship and an affirmation of universal process.

## 3.4 Sound: A Lexicon

The Sanskrit language is particularly rich in words for "sound," and some preliminary analysis will help to distinguish the various shades of meaning. It is also useful to recognize the common tendency to use words in both a general and a special sense, and for this reason it is not unusual to find the same word used with reference to sound in general, to the sounds of speech, and to musical sound, often within the same passage. I shall distinguish between the following terms: *śabda, dhvani, sphoṭa, vāc, svara, śruti,* and *nāda*.

*Śabda* is the least specialized word for sound. While it can be conceived as a series of gradations, like several of the other terms, *śabda* more often refers to ordinary, everyday sound—as in the sounds of human speech and the cries of animals. *Śabda* has no specific meaning with reference to music. *Dhvani,* a word with a wide semantic range in connection with both speech and music, is somewhat more specialized: the root meaning is "to resound or reverberate." I like to think of it as implicative or consequential sound. In poetic theory *dhvani* has become an important technical term for an implied meaning, an allusion, or poetic suggestion, a doctrine expounded by the critic Ānandavardhana (ca. A.D. 850).[24] So *dhvani* in literary contexts signifies sound with a meaning, sound that refers to something other than its own phonetic nature. But nothing of this specialized usage appears to color *dhvani* when it is applied to music, as in Mataṅga's *Bṛhaddeśī,* where the reference is to musical sounds in general.[25]

*Sphoṭa* is another literary term with an extremely specialized meaning: deriving from a verbal root meaning "to burst," *sphoṭa* signifies the eternal and imperceptible aspect of sound as the vehicle of meaning, flooding the mind with a burst of pure meaning in response to the uttered sounds. It is an instantaneous and indivisible perception, fusing in a single stroke the separate phonetic elements of a word or the words in a sentence. The idea behind *sphoṭa* adds some valuable background to this linguistic survey, but the word has seldom been applied to music.

*Vāc,* personified in the Vedas as the goddess of speech and identified at times with the goddess Sarasvatī (the patroness of both speech and music), may refer to ordinary human speech, sound in general, animal sounds, or to the divine speech principle as a creative power.[26] The word appears mainly in metaphorical or mythological contexts and holds no particular significance for music.

The three remaining terms are of considerable importance for music and musical thought, and additional analysis will follow in this and later chapters; here it will suffice to indicate the basic distinctions. *Svara,* as introduced in chapter 1, means (1) the domain of musical pitch in the most general sense; and more important, (2) a specific manifested musical sound—manifested, that is, in the form of one of the seven steps of the musical scale, as represented by the sol-fa syllables *sà, ri, ga, ma, pa, dha, ni* (which are equivalent, in a loose way, to the Western sol-fa syllables *do, re, mi, fa, sol, la, ti*).[27] The seven *svaras* must be recognized, though, as *generalized* scale steps, unspecified as to their precise pitch or tuning. As an example, *ma* may refer either to the fourth scale degree (*fa*) or to a raised or lowered version of this degree. The word *svara* is usually explained, perhaps not very accurately, as "that which manifests itself," that which shines forth by means of its own nature.[28] There is more to it than this, but we may interpret the basic idea of *svara* as a *graspable* musical sound, a sound that is intelligible in that it corresponds to one of the basic steps of the musical system, not falling into the cracks.

In contrast, *śruti* signifies a limen, a threshold of musical pitch. In formalized musical thought, twenty-two such *śruti*s were conceived within the span of an octave. Despite the literal meaning of the word, "that which has been heard,"[29] the *śruti*s are not heard or performed separately. The role that they play in music is as minute pitch quanta, not discernible in themselves but inferred as the subtle differences between one perceivable musical sound and another. Each of the seven *svara*s was separated from its neighbors by intervals of two, three, or four *śruti*s: 2/22 is the equivalent of the Western semitone, whereas 3/22 and 4/22 may be considered "major" and "minor" whole tones.[30] But I must emphasize that early authors did not regard the *śruti*s as identical in size, nor can it be assumed that they constituted a tuning system of precise calibration. As a verse in an ancient text states,

> Just as there is no definite path for fishes moving in the water,
> nor for birds in the sky,
> So it is in the case of the *śruti*s that control our perception of
> the *svara*s.[31]

*Nāda,* the final term, is an extremely important term for musical sound with a wide range of meanings and associations. In the next section I shall delve into its many meanings with the aid of a passage from *MB*.

### 3.5 Causal Sound: *Nāda*

For a more complete statement on the nature and production of musical sound, I turn to the earliest exposition of the concept of *nāda-brahman* (usually translated as "causal sound") in the *Bṛhaddeśī* of Mataṅga:[32]

> Now I shall expound the highest definition of *nāda:*
> Without *nāda,* song cannot exist; without *nāda,* the scale
> degrees cannot exist;
> Without *nāda,* the dance cannot come into being; for this
> reason the entire world becomes the embodiment of *nāda.*
> In the form of *nāda,* Brahmā is said to exist; in the form of
> *nāda,* Viṣṇu;
> In the form of *nāda,* Pārvatī; in the form of *nāda,* Śiva.
> That [inner region] which is said to be the abode of Brahmā is
> called the *brahmagranthi:*[33]
> Vital air is situated in its center; from [this mass of] vital air fire
> arises;

From the combination of fire and air *nāda* is born.

From *nāda* is produced *bindu,* and from *nāda* everything that has speech (*Vāc*) as its essence.

This is what some people say, [and further:]

Air, moving about hither and thither in the lower and upper regions, having arisen from the bulbous region (the *brahmagranthi*),

[When] agitated produces the entire process of *nāda*.

This is what others say.

People [also] say that the syllable *na* signifies breath and the syllable *da,* fire;

These are the two root-meanings of the word *nāda,* as I have correctly explained.

*Nāda* derives from the root *nad, nadati* and is fivefold:

[Its five phases are] *sūkṣma* (subtle), *atisūkṣma* (very subtle), *vyakta* (manifest), *avyakta* (unmanifest), and *kṛtrima* (artificial).

*Sūkṣma nāda* resides in the interior cave, and *atisūkṣma,* in the heart;

*Vyakta* is situated in the middle of the throat, and *avyakta,* in the palate;

But *kṛtrima* [is] in the region of the mouth. In this manner *nāda* is known by the wise to be fivefold.

Thus I have expounded, in a charming way, the evolution of *nāda*.

This important passage, which has been widely quoted and analyzed by later authors, summarizes many of the themes encountered in the preceding pages. Mataṅga's metaphysical explanation of the origin of sound is grounded in the ancient Āyurvedic concept of universal vibration and reveals also the influence of the mystical doctrines of Tantrism, to which he evidently subscribed. The word *nāda* is correctly identified as a derivative from the verbal root *nad* (to sound, thunder, roar, or bellow),[34] in the sense of a loud sound, a spreading sound with powerful reverberations. The semantic development of the term is of considerable intrinsic interest, in that it demonstrates how phonetic similarities reveal the persistence of common root meanings in words that have become specialized. Mataṅga's exposition depends upon the common phonetic and semantic properties of three words: *nada* (a roarer or bellower), *nadī* (river), and *naḍa* (reed). The sense here is not obscure: the reverberation of a powerful sound and the flow of a river are seen as manifestations of the same process, in which vital energy courses along a channel (the internal channels of the body, the riverbed), and from this arose the idea of a "conduit" for vital substance in any of its forms—sound, speech, breath, water, vegetative growth, semen, and the like. In the Tantric-Yoga philosophy the *nāḍīs* are the subtle channels or "veins" spreading outward from their source at the center of the body, through which the life energies flow to and from the extremities and the organs of sense perception. The meaning of *bindu* (drop) in this passage is "spreading out," in the sense of a drop of liquid falling upon a surface, a common Indian analogy.

Mataṅga's etymological explanation of the word *nāda* draws once again upon the traditional *nirukta* method of analysis.[35] In this case the syllable *na* apparently represents the second syllable of *prāṇa* (breath), but the connection between *da* and fire is obscure—unless it has something to do with the verbal root *dah* (to burn). One of the commentators on the *SS* relates this etymology to the Tantric custom of assigning a presiding deity for each "seed syllable" of a word or formula, and in this case the syllables are under the respective patronage of Prāṇa (breath) and Agni, the god of fire.[36] We are struck more by the ingenuity of this explanation than by its contribution to the meaning of the word, but if true, it represents yet another connection with the occult philosophy of Tantrism.

Like many other technical terms, *nāda* is a word with a broad range of application. It appears to be used in four distinct senses in *MB:* (1) in the special sense of "primordial sound," the pervading causal sound that animates the universe (as in the passage under analysis); (2) as a general word for musical sound, scarcely differentiated from other words for sound such as *śabda* and *dhvani;* (3) as a technical term for the process of emerging vocal sound as it wells up from its inner source and flows outward along the bodily channels; and (4), most specific of all, as a term signifying what eventually became the standard beginning gambit in Indian musical performance—the improvised exposition of a *rāga*.[37] Once again the line of semantic development is reasonably clear: the systematic exploration of the characteristic pathways and tonal landmarks of the chosen *rāga* is seen as an analogy to the manner in which vocal sound follows the bodily pathways, touching in turn each of the centers of resonance and organs of articulation. It is further interesting to observe that many singers begin their improvisation by vocalizing on the syllable *na,* in preference to an open vowel—conceivably a form of phonetic testimony to their inner experience. Mataṅga's exposition of the theory of *nāda* is an attempt to establish an explicit connection between the first and third of these meanings, thereby suggesting that the *musica humana* and the *musica mundana* are one.

The other feature of particular interest in this passage is Mataṅga's description of the five phases or grades of *nāda*, arranged in an outward progression from the "interior cave"[38] to the mouth. He seems to have gotten some of his terms reversed, and later authors took issue with him on this point.[39] The correct order is probably very subtle, subtle, unmanifest, manifest, and artificial. None of this is in any way exceptional in Indian thought; individual details are subject to revision, but the overall conceptual framework remains much the same.

Mataṅga's five grades of *nāda* represent a significant step in the continuing evolution of the theory of sound production, and they closely parallel the grades of articulate speech as formulated by successive authors seeking to identify the "four quarters of the Word."[40] The grammarian Bhartṛhari divided the principle of speech (*vāc*) into three stages: *paśyantī*, the metaphysical source of articulate speech within the individual consciousness; *madhyamā*, an intermediate stage in which speech is conceived by the mind; and *vaikharī*, the actual sounds uttered by the speaker and heard by the listener.[41] Somānanda (ca. A.D. 875–925) accepted Bhartṛhari's three stages but postulated a fourth, "ultimate" stage (*parā*) on the grounds that the association of *paśyantī* with the individual organism was a limiting condition and inappropriate for representing the speech principle in its transcendent form.[42] Later authors of the influential Krama system of Kashmir Shaivism interpolated a fifth, intermediate category (*sūkṣmā*), as shown in table 3, and the number of stages seems to have stabilized thereafter at five—for both speech and musical sound.[43] Table 3 presents two of the many pentadic formulations of the Krama system,[44] including a number of by now familiar terms.[45] The two pentads are not to be correlated with each other, since each represents a different aspect of the process of sound production: speech as it arises within the individual speaker, and sound in the abstract as it acquires its differentiations. The similarities in concept will be readily apparent.

Several characteristic habits of Indian thought are evident in table 3: the tendency to expand the number of categories to the "right" number by adding both ultimate and intermediate categories, the botanical metaphors, and the confusing application of established terms in new contexts or new order. There can be no doubt that this fivefold explanation of sound production has been strongly influenced by the ancient classification of the sounds of Sanskrit, in which the letters are arranged in five ranks (*vargas*), in outward

Table 3 Two Perspectives on Sound Production, according to the Krama System

| From Absolute to Gross Sound | Aspects of the Articulate Sound |
|---|---|
| *parā Vāk:* the ultimate speech principle | *vimarśa:* undifferentiated, universal sound |
| *sūkṣmā:* the first stirrings | *bindu:* the seed or spreading drop |
| *paśyantī:* absolute, undifferentiated sound within the individual | *nāda:* the sprout, still an undifferentiated unity |
| *madhyamā:* sound beginning to acquire phonetic and morphological distinctions | *sphoṭa:* sound as it begins to form into "leaves" |
| *vaikharī:* uttered and heard sounds | *śabda:* fully differentiated sounds |

Table 4 The Twenty-Five Mute Consonants of Sanskrit

| | Stops | | | | |
|---|---|---|---|---|---|
| | Voiceless | | Voiced | | |
| | Unaspirated | Aspirated | Unaspirated | Aspirated | Nasals |
| Velar | k | kh | g | gh | ṅ |
| Palatal | c | ch | j | jh | ñ |
| Retroflex | ṭ | ṭh | ḍ | ḍh | ṇ |
| Dental | t | th | d | dh | n |
| Labial | p | ph | b | bh | m |

sequence according to the place of articulation: the throat (velar), the palate, the "roof of the mouth" or alveolar ridge (retroflex), the teeth (dental), and the lips (labial).[46] As a sample of this arrangement, table 4 is a display of the twenty-five stop consonants. Further exploration of this significant link between musical sound and phonetics will follow in chapter 4.

Mataṅga's description of the generation of musical sound, with its many symbolic associations with the gods, elemental substances, and the structure of the universe, has become one of the most powerful cultural models for the idea of musical sound. Few later authors have deviated from his line of thinking, which reinforces so many of the traditional continuities of Indian thought. As a consequence, the theory of sound as emerging vital substance became established as one of the pillars of Indian musical teachings.

## 3.6 Ākāśa, the Medium of Sound

In this section I shall explain more fully the concept of *ākāśa* in ancient Indian metaphysics, focusing on its special role as the medium for the transmission of sound. This is no simple concept but rather an entire semantic field that includes such things as breath, soul, energy, motion, space, wind, and most important of all, ether. The word *ākāśa* is a derivative of the verbal root *kāś,* "to become visible, shine, be brilliant" (much the same range of meanings as the Greek *phaino* and the German *scheinen*). In formalized Indian thought, *ākāśa* was conceived as a subtle and ethereal fluid that pervades the entire universe as the special vehicle for life (in the form of breath), energy, and sound. Although they inhabit the same territory, *ākāśa* differs from both *dik* (directional space, space in the abstract) and *vāyu* (air, wind). It will also be useful to distinguish the concept of *ākāśa* from the ancient Greek idea of ether (*aither*), while noting the many resemblances.

The idea of *ākāśa* developed in later Vedic times and is especially prominent in the cosmological speculations of the Upanishads. The concept was rejected by the early Buddhist and the materialistic Cārvāka schools but was endorsed enthusiastically, and with some special twists, by the Jains. One passage from the *Taittirīya Upaniṣad* refers to *ākāśa* as the first evolute from the universal soul (*Ātman*): "From this Soul, verily, space (*ākāśa*) arose; from space, wind; from wind, fire; from fire, water; from water, the earth; from the earth, herbs; from herbs, food; from food, semen; from semen, the person."[47] The implications are clear: *ākāśa* takes priority over the other elements because, like breath, it has issued forth from the universal *Ātman*. It is subtle matter, infinite, eternal, without divisions, and does not depend upon anything else for its existence. It is entirely independent of any limitations of time or space. To translate the word as "space" is to gloss over its distinctive nature, and I prefer to translate *ākāśa* as "ether" or, better still, "atmosphere." The Greek word *atmos* is, by the way, a cognate of the Sanskrit *ātman,* consistent with the early Western conception of the atmosphere as the sphere of vapor that surrounds the world—a compound of air, breath, and soul.

In another grand cosmic vision, the *Bṛhad-Āraṇyaka Upaniṣad* describes the *ākāśa* as part of a multidimensional world tapestry: past, present, and future (represented by the upper, middle, and lower levels of the cosmos) are "woven, warp and woof" across the *ākāśa,* while the *ākāśa* is itself "woven, warp and woof" across the Imperishable (*akṣara*)—the "unseen Seer, the unheard Hearer, the unthought Thinker, the ununderstood Understander," that is, Brahman.[48] If sound, then, is identified as the primary quality or attribute of the substance that pervades the cosmic tapestry, we can readily understand the cultural priority assigned to speech, hearing, and the inherent power of sound.

In early Greek cosmological speculation, *aither* was conceived as the shining, fiery layer of upper air situated above the misty lower band of *aer.*

The association with fire goes back at least as far as Heraclitus, who contended that the nature of the soul was fire, and hence that the *aither* was a divine essence and the final resting place of souls.[49] Elsewhere among the pre-Socratic philosophers the soul was held to be a part of the cosmic fire, giving rise to the living warmth of the human body, and the rarified upper air was thought to be alive. Aristotle, however, distinguished ether (the "fifth essence," or quintessence) from both air and fire, holding that the ether was uncorruptible and unchanging—the stratum of the heavenly bodies, the celestial spheres, and the intervening spaces. His formulation remained the basic Western explanation for more than a millennium. It is interesting, though, that the Stoics (first century B.C. to second century A.D.) developed a view of ether that did not differ substantially from the Indian concept of *ākāśa,* investing it with the universal spirit (*pneuma*) that pervades all earthly matter and, as a result of its continuous interaction with matter, serves as a universal medium for the transmission of force. As late as the seventeenth century, René Descartes argued that ether was a kind of pervasive, subtle matter—an intermediate substance between the luminous matter of the heavens and the gross matter of the earth. Other philosophers of the same century contended that ether was the medium for the transmission of light, heat, and magnetism, as well as sound. In fact the concept of ether was never decisively rejected until Einstein's first paper on special relativity in 1905, and many contemporary physicists still regard the issue as far from closed.[50]

How did the early Indian notion of *ākāśa* differ from the views outlined above? First, *ākāśa* is not limited to the upper air, nor does it have an elemental relationship with fire; from the beginning it was considered to have a subtle nature all its own. Like the categories of time and space, *ākāśa* is both universal and eternal: a continuum of undifferentiated life, breath, and energy that fills both external space and the internal spaces of the human body, interpenetrating freely. Nothing can be added to it, nor can anything be taken away. Sound is its primary attribute, just as sight is the special attribute of fire, and touch, of air. The entire universe was conceived as a humming field of continuous, subtle, inaudible sound, pulsating with vital energy and potential. The *ākāśa* provides the essential connections between ultimate reality, humanity, and the elemental components of the physical universe.

I close this section with a brief quotation from one of the early authorities on music, to show that *ākāśa* was not the only elemental substance invoked in discussions of musical sound. The theory of tone quality set forth in this passage closely resembles the ancient Western concept of the four bodily humors (blood, phlegm, yellow bile, black bile) and their corresponding four temperaments (sanguine, phlegmatic, choleric, and melancholic), a concept endorsed by both Galen and Hippocrates. In contrast, early Indian physiology recognized three humors, each of which influenced the nature of musical sound in a particular way. The passage, from *MB,* attributes this testimony to the legendary sage Tumburu.

> Other authorities contend that *śruti*[51] is fourfold, divided into the following varieties: excess of air, excess of bile, excess of phlegm, balance of the humors. And thus Tumburu said: "Dry, higher sound is acknowledged to be *vātaja* (born of air) by the experts. Sound that is deep, solid, and continuous is to be known as *pittaja* (born of bile), while sound that is unctuous, delicate, and sweet should be known as *kaphaja* (born of phlegm). The sound resulting from a harmonious balance of these three qualities conjoined is declared to be *sannipātaja* (born of conjunction)."[52]

I shall return to these cultural stereotypes for tonal quality in chapter 11.

## 3.7 Sound and the External World

As we have seen, early Indian acoustical speculation emphasized inner sound: sound as it is conceived and produced in the individual and, to a lesser extent, sound as it is apprehended by the hearer. Acoustics in this tradition is as much a philosophy of mind as it is a physical science, and once sound emerges from the individual body, it ceases to be the object of intense curiosity. Because of the powerful ideological connections between the universal *Ātman,* the pervading *ākāśa,* and the reservoir of vital breath within the individual, the transmission of sound is taken for granted, and its efficacy is assumed—as, for example, when reciting a mantra or chanting the sacred texts—almost in the form of a contractual obligation with the forces of nature. The ultimate effectiveness of sound and the perpetuation of its chain of cause and effect is assured by the doctrine of karma. I have no doubt overstated the case, but it is nonetheless surprising that Indian thinkers have shown no great interest in the propagation of sound from place to place or from person to person, with the exception of the two general theories to be presented below. The contrasting views of ancient Greek and Chinese thinkers will help to put the matter into perspective.

In their studies of Indian acoustical speculation, Umesha Mishra and Brajendranath Seal have analyzed two competing theories of the propagation of sound: (1) circular transmission, in which the sound travels outward in concentric circles, in analogy to the motion of waves generated in standing water;[53] and (2) spherical transmission, in which the molecules of sound reproduce themselves by impacting on other molecules, spreading outward toward the ten directions (the four cardinal points of the compass, the four intermediate points, up, and down).[54] The latter is known as the *kadamba*-bud theory, with reference to the way in which the bud of the *kadamba* tree (*Nauclea cadamba*) sends forth series of filaments in all directions. Each of these conceptions has interesting implications for the cultural ontology of musical sound, implications which have somehow failed to generate intense debate: whether, for example, sound is one or many, continuous or atomistic, by what agency it is propagated, and whether its wave motion is transverse or longitudinal. If these issues have not been explored as fully as one might have expected, it must mean that satisfactory answers were already provided in the traditional explanations.

## 3.8 Three Ancient Conceptions of Musical Sound

This chapter has focused on the *being* of music and its essential substance, an important and at times disturbing issue in musical thought.[55] Early philosophies of music in both East and West attempted to answer certain basic questions about the nature of musical sound: Sound must have a source; whence does it arise? Sound is invisible and intangible; how can it become objectified and thereby grasped by the mind? Sound is transient, constantly slipping away from us; how can its repeatability be assured? Sound appears to make things happen; by what means? And sound is apparently transmitted across distance; how is this possible?

In the musical ontologies of three ancient high cultures—India, Greece, and China—we can detect similar strategies of explanation, even though the answers to the individual questions are strikingly, profoundly different. This is the scenario: Musical sound is first explained as a manifestation of some type of elemental substance—air, ether, breath, vapor, fluid, energy, or even spirit—taking full advantage of whatever ideas are conveniently associated in the language of the culture (such as the pairing of "breath" and "spirit" in the Greek *pneuma,* the Latin *anima,* the Hebrew *rua,* and the Sanskrit *ātman*). In a second stage a metaphysical principle is identified as the agency by which the effects of sound are produced: for example, the principle of harmony in the ancient and medieval West, the vital energy emanating from the all-pervasive *Ātman* in early Indian thought, and the principle of *chhi* in traditional Chinese cosmological speculation. In the third and final stage, this line of explanation is encapsulated in a colorful image, a vivid metaphor that draws on a number of long-established cultural preferences and values—almost a form of cultural advertising. The results are displayed in table 5, which will serve as a summary of this discussion.

Table 5 Three Ancient Conceptions of Musical Sound

| | India | Greece and Medieval Europe | China |
|---|---|---|---|
| Principle | *Ātman* | harmony | *chhi* |
| Metaphor | emerging vital breath | a tensed string | friction of yin and yang[a] |
| Value | continuity | articulation | correlation with other elements of nature |
| Concept of sound | emergence (flow) | impact (point) | resonance |
| State | outpouring | equilibrium of opposing tensions | pulsating waves |
| Nature | immaterial | material substance | intermediate (vaporous energy) |
| Agent | Word | number | natural forces |
| Mode | dynamic | static | dynamic |
| Action | direct reception of vital substance | sympathetic response to form | mutual influence of related objects and forces |

[a] Or perhaps the winds of the directions blowing through the bamboo "humming tubes."

Over time these conceptions of the power of sound tend first to be elaborated with subtle arguments and fine distinctions and then to be trivialized as they gradually work their way down into general cultural awareness, often in greatly simplified form—sayings, maxims, or clichés. Culture seems to have a way of blurring the arguments of the great intellects and of selecting those proposals which are the most consistent with traditional preferences. This is not to claim that philosophy is ineffective, but merely to recognize that its more powerful propositions have generally been understood only in adulterated form. Musical thought is no exception.

The early Indian conception of musical sound as emerging vital substance is a remarkable synthesis of a number of ideas, some of which have already been mentioned: (1) the divine origin of sound; (2) the notion of a transpersonal world soul; (3) the breath as living substance and agent of universal process; (4) the special nature of the medium of *ākāśa*; (5) the efficacy of ritual action; (6) utterance as an act of worship and means of knowledge; (7) the stimulating power of heat energy; (8) the metaphoric identification of thought, breath, sound, and semen as means by which we act upon the world; (9) the mythical association of sound and speech (*vāc*); (10) the metaphor of a creative spiral (visualized in the form of the bodily channels for the discharge of sound); (11) a preference for unimpacted sounds; and (12) the potential valued above the actual.

The evolution of Indian music has since early times been responsive to this cluster of cultural values. The consequences have included the following: (1) the establishment of vocal sound as the primary paradigm for music; (2) the continuous drone as a symbolic representation of the continuum of unmanifest sound; (3) song traditions that emphasize the precise articulation of the text; (4) the atavistic roles of gesture (as in the system of *tāla*) and respiration as symbolic reenactment of ancient ritual; (5) a unique concept of vocal timbre featuring a certain characteristic nasality (which seems to have arisen in part from directing the singer's awareness to the resonance available in the various facial cavities); (6) an emphasis upon circular and spiral melodic and rhythmic formations; and (7) a decisive preference for organic and incremental forms (in preference to hierarchical and syntactical structures)—emphasizing such things as linearity, continuity, and progressive growth. The evolution of the drone, evidently a product of the fifteenth to seventeenth centuries,[56] appears to be a case of art imitating nature—a subconscious attempt to externalize the universal continuum of unmanifest sound—and to imply thereby that each individual performance arises from, and returns to, the substratum of undifferentiated vital sound: to paraphrase an old Talmudic saying, if you wish to understand the inaudible, listen closely to the audible.

I have already referred to the ancient Western concept of sound as *impact*—the impact, apparently, of a plucked string, with the consequence that the sounds of music were conceived as a nexus of points, not a smooth continuum.[57] The dominant metaphor in this interpretation is the tensed string of the primitive hunting bow, the *bios,* as Heraclitus said in one of his cryptic aphorisms, whose name was life but whose work was death.[58] His equation of the hunting bow and the lyre becomes explicit in another of his sayings: "The hidden harmony is better than the obvious. . . . People do not understand how that which is at variance with itself agrees with itself. There is a harmony in the bending back, as in the cases of the bow and the lyre."[59] In a few pithy sentences Heraclitus has introduced us to the principle of harmony, conjuring up an image of a world in a state of equilibrium, bound together by opposing tensions and regulated by unseen connections among all its components—inanimate, animate, and divine.

Harmony is the metaphysical principle which has dominated early Western musical thought, defined by the Pythagoreans as "the harmonization of opposites, the unification of disparate things, and the conciliation of warring elements."[60] The principle was manifest not only in the proportioned sounds of music but also in a healthy human life, social intercourse, political deliberations, and the structure of the universe. The entire world was seen as a delicate balance of the four elements and their characteristic properties, an idea that was slowly worked out by the pre-Socratics. In their worldview musical substance was not a special category; any raw material would do—the pitched sounds of music, the unpitched sounds of speech, even the movements of the body—so long as they were receptive to the harmonic number proportions.[61] The harmonic principle was illustrated in three types of music: the music of the cosmic spheres (the *musica mundana*), the equilibrium of mind and body in the individual (the *musica humana*), and the ordinary sounds of music (the *musica instrumentalis*).[62] But it was not until considerably later, in the writings of the Neoplatonists, that there was thought to be any direct transmission or sharing of substance across a distance. The cosmic instrument, the human instrument, and the musical instrument were governed by the same principle, the same number proportions, and the same need for balance amidst the pull-and-tug of opposing forces. But in the influential worldview of Aristotle and his followers, things act upon one another by means of their form, not their substance: according to this line of thinking, substances respond sympathetically by receiving the imprint of form and thus taking on likenesses. To be even more explicit, we respond, therefore, to the sounds and structures we call "music" because of what was thought to be our natural affinity for certain specified shapes, numbers, and ratios—not, as in the Indian worldview, by receiving the direct flow of sound and emotion in the form of immaterial, vital substance.

Ancient Chinese thinkers conceived of sound as "a manifestation of Nature in equilibrium and disequilibrium,"[63] a concept eloquently explained in this passage from the *Yo Chi* (Record of ritual music and dance), a remarkable document from the late Chou period: "The *chhi* of earth ascends above; the *chhi* of heaven descends from the height. The *yang* and the *yin* come into contact; heaven and earth shake together. Their drumming is in the shock and rumble of thunder; their excited beating of wings is in wind and rain; their shifting round is in the four seasons; their warming is in the sun and moon. Thus the hundred species procreate and flourish. Thus it is that music is a bringing together of heaven and earth."[64]

Musical sound is thus held to be caused by friction, the friction between heaven and earth, and between the yin (the passive, negative, female principle) and the yang (the active, positive, masculine principle).[65] The medium for sound was the *chhi* (often translated as "vital force"), a concept I shall explain presently. The universe was seen as a slowly pulsating mass held together by opposed but mutually necessary forces. In such an organic worldview all things have their proper stations and individual rhythms and are able to exert influence across distance. Sound itself was not considered to be fundamentally different from such things as flavors and colors, and for this reason Chinese acoustics has taken on an unusually qualitative tone, emphasizing the correlations between musical sounds and other objects of perception. Chinese acoustical thought is also "pneumatic"—like their medicine, meteorology, and even geology—once again invoking the familiar semantic cluster of wind, breath, and spirit.[66]

The essential concept here is the idea of *chhi,* a subtle blend of vapor, air in motion, nutritive energy, mental qualities, and spiritual force.[67] Sound in this theory is not one but many: it is born of the natural friction of the universe and transmitted in the form of pulsating waves of *chhi*. Action is produced as the result of resonance between homologous things—not because of any similarity in form (as in Greek thought) or substance, but because of their similar *position* within a universe in which all phenomena and all qualities were indexed and aligned in columnar format under the appropriate member of the Five Agents (*wu hsing*): wood, fire, earth, metal, and water.[68] The vaporous nature of the *chhi,* as its character reveals, is the steam arising from a pot of cooking rice, and indeed ancient texts speak of the collective *chhi* hovering above the heads of an approaching army like a great cloud of steam, from which the morale of the enemy army could be discerned by diviners.

Human breath plays no important role in early Chinese musical speculation; the image of moving air is provided by the winds of nature, blowing through bamboo tubes of varying lengths (the so-called "humming tubes") aligned toward the various directions.[69] The world of ancient China, like that of the Greeks, was held together by a harmonic principle (*ho*), although with interesting and subtle differences. Both cultures shared a passion for numbers and precise standards of measurement for sound (among other things), a passion that is notably absent from the Indian literature of musical acoustics (see table 5).

# FOUR
# CHANT

*Om!* We will expound pronunciation (*śikṣā*):
the sound (*varṇa*);
the accent (*svara*);
the quantity (*mātrā*);
the force (*bala*);
the articulation (*sāma*);
the combination (*santāna*).
—Thus has been declared the lesson on Pronunciation.

*Taittirīya Upaniṣad* 1.2[1]

Whenever a sacred formula is recited in a distorted manner, lacking in correctness of tone or vowel, it injures the sacrificer's person, his offspring, and his beasts.

*Nāradīyaśikṣā* 1.1.6[2]

## 4.1 Introduction

Sacred chant is the subject of this chapter. Subtopics will include (1) the majestic hymns of the *Sāmaveda* and their performance traditions, (2) the instruction manuals, (3) the important relationship between early phonetic theory and the evolving idea of music, (4) the development of concepts for the organization of musical pitch, and (5) the intellectual environment and routines of the Vedic priest. Chant traditions in other parts of the world have often provided valuable evidence for the early development of music, its pitches, scales, rhythms, accents, formal structures, and performance practice; in all of these respects the chant traditions of ancient India are particularly informative. I shall focus on one text with more to say about the subject of music than any of the other phonetic treatises—the *Nāradīya-śikṣā* (*NS*), that is, the *śikṣā,* or phonetic manual attributed to the legendary sage Nārada.[3] The six principal topics of phonetic theory are outlined in the above passage from the *Taittirīya Upaniṣad* and amplified slightly in (2). It will be clear that these are issues of vital importance in the regulation of any form of vocal utterance—ordinary speech, elevated speech, recitation, chant, or singing. As a result, the ancient theory of speech became a fertile breeding ground for the theory of music.

2. The six topics of *śikṣā*

| | |
|---|---|
| *varṇa* | the elements: individual sounds and letters |
| *svara* | distinctions of quality: accents, timbre, pitches, vowel grade |
| *mātrā* | distinctions of quantity: durations, syllable quantity, meter |
| *bala* | dynamics, articulatory force, resonance, the organs of utterance |
| *sāma*[4] | correct delivery, continuity, performance as a whole |
| *santāna* | the euphonic laws, the proper connection of syllables |

The *NS,* like the other phonetic manuals, emphasizes the severe penalties incurred by the chanter who fails to perform his task accurately, whether by mispronouncing the text, accenting it incorrectly, erring in either the length or the tonal quality of a syllable, failing to render the text with sufficient clarity, or simply suffering a mental lapse. Some minor errors could be expiated, but others entailed drastic and unavoidable consequences; and as will soon be evident, the Sanskrit language provided a variety of traps into which a careless chanter could readily fall. Many of the *śikṣā*s include the following warning: "If a mantra is defective either in accent or quality of sound, or is employed in performing the wrong rite, it does not convey the proper meaning. It then becomes a thunderbolt in the form of speech and kills the sacrificer, as when [the demon] accented incorrectly the compound *Indraśatruḥ.*"[5] The reference here is to a sacrifice performed by the serpent-demon Vṛtra, who was then slain by Indra's thunderbolt as a direct consequence of the distortion in meaning that resulted from his misaccentuation.[6] The authors of the phonetic treatises did not hesitate to draw the moral: if the efficacy of a ritual utterance is assured, it can also backfire on the incompetent performer.

## 4.2 Sāmavedic Chant

The four primary Vedas are the oldest and greatest of India's literary treasures, as well as scriptural sources for later religious traditions. They were written in the Vedic language, ancestral to the Sanskrit language as formalized by Pāṇini around 500 B.C. One of the hymns from the tenth book of the *Ṛgveda,* addressed to Vāc as the divine Word, sets forth the purpose of each of the four collections:

> One man with utmost care creates the verses (*ṛcs*);[7]
> another sings a song in chanted meters.
> A third, the Brahmin, tells forth the wisdom of being,
> while yet a fourth prescribes the rules of sacrifice.[8]

I shall mention each of these in turn. By far the most important is the *Ṛgveda,* a collection of 1028 hymns (in more than ten thousand verses) addressed to the principal Indo-Aryan deities personifying the various forces of nature.[9] The *Sāmaveda* is a much smaller collection of hymns, mostly from the *Ṛgveda,* set to melodies (*sāman*s) and rearranged for liturgical use. The third line of the above verse refers to the *Atharvaveda,* a more popular assortment of magical spells, incantations, and prayers. The *Yajurveda,* which has come down to us in two recensions (the so-called Black and White *Yajurveda*s), contains sacrificial formulas and directions for the Vedic ceremonies.

In a penetrating interpretation of the above verse, Raimundo Panikkar describes the different roles "assigned to those who concelebrate [the Vedic sacrifices]": "the creation of poetry (corresponding to the Ṛg Veda with the *hotṛ* or offerer as priest), the melodious recitation of it bringing out all its inherent sound vibrations (the Sāma Veda with the *udgātṛ* as the singer or celebrant), the exposition of its meaning and of the wisdom contained in it (the Atharva Veda with the *brahman*-priest), and its application in the sacrificial action (the Yajur Veda with the *adhvaryu* as the minister)."[10] Or to put it another way, the Word itself, the Word as sound, the Word as meaning, and the Word translated into action. The "inherent sound vibrations" will be among the main concerns in this study, along with the means devised to capture the exact nature and structure of these vibrations, both in thought and in practice.

Only the members of the three highest classes in traditional Hindu society, the *dvija* (twice-born), may learn and recite the Vedas, and their teaching is reserved for members of the priestly class (Brahmans). According to Wayne Howard, every Brahman "belongs by birth to one Veda, one *śākhā* (school) of this Veda, one *gotra* (ancestral family), and one *sūtra* (manual of aphoristic rules)."[11] Chant styles will thus vary from place to place and from one *śākhā* to another. But within each local tradition the system has succeeded in preserving both the text and the individual performance style with remarkable fidelity. For our purposes it will be sufficient to distinguish between the melodic styles of the *Ṛgveda* and the *Sāmaveda.*

It is open to question whether the style in which the *Ṛgveda* is intoned is better described as "recitation" or "chant." It is delivered in a restricted pitch compass and conceived in terms of three tonal accents (*svara*s)—the *udātta* (acute), *anudātta* (grave), and *svarita* (circumflex), of which the last is a compound accent and the source of considerable controversy.[12] In contrast, the hymns of the *Sāmaveda* are conceived and rendered in specifically musical terms, in a pitch compass that extends at times to a full diatonic heptad. It follows then that the instruction manuals pertaining to the

*Sāmaveda* would contain some of the most informative material on the early musical system, both in theory and in practice.

But a word of caution is appropriate here: it is tempting to overinterpret this material and read more into it than the authors intended. The instruction books were designed as jogs to the memory, not as full performance scripts. And despite the valuable equation between the Sāmavedic scale and the secular musical scale as set forth in the *NS*,[13] we cannot fix the exact pitch intervals between the scale degrees with any certainty; nor can the matter be resolved on the evidence of surviving chant traditions, which differ considerably in their choice of pitches. But there is a still more important problem to be addressed in a later section of this chapter. The "tones" (*svaras*) are described in three distinct aspects: as accents (with particular reference to the *Ṛgveda*), of which there are three primary accents (those mentioned in the previous paragraph) and a number of secondary ones; as scale degrees, of which there are seven; and as "shadings" (*śruti*), of which there are five.[14] These distinctions go far beyond any simple classification of musical pitches as high or low. We see instead a sophisticated and multidimensional concept of musical sound, a concept designed for an oral tradition in which pitch, timbre, and dynamic intensity have not yet become clearly distinguished from one another.

A few words of explanation about the Sāmavedic repertoire and its traditions of performance may be useful.[15] The corpus of the *Sāmaveda* (the *saṁhitā*) is approximately 15 percent of the length of the *Ṛgveda*, consisting both of 1,549 verses of text and a large number of melodies assembled from a much smaller number of melodic fragments. This technique of melodic composition, known in the West as *centonization*, is a common practice in other bodies of sacred chant and appears to be an instinctive and effective strategy for organizing a large liturgical repertoire without overloading the chanter's mental circuits with too much information.[16] At no time is there an exclusive one-to-one correspondence between text and music, and the same text verse may appear in different contexts and be set to different melodies. The three surviving schools of the *Sāmaveda* differ not only in their text selection and ceremonial requirements but also in their notation, performance style, and in their method of distorting the text by means of phonetic alterations.[17]

These alterations, which are perhaps the most distinctive feature of the *Sāmaveda* tradition, reveal a number of typical Indian preferences for musical form, among them the techniques of infixing, formal inflation, and simultaneous variation.[18] The phonetic changes include the following: changes of vowel grade (that is, lengthening or shortening the vowel in question), letter substitutions, inserted nonsense syllables (*stobha*), pauses, repetitions, syllabic infixes, and other similar devices. The sacred text becomes expanded through a kind of phonetic play, which functions as a simultaneous response to the text and may originally have been devised to conceal its meaning from hostile demons and those unworthy to hear it. It may also have been a means for adapting preexistent melodies to the chosen texts.[19] I should emphasize that this practice is in no way a matter of improvisation; the various alterations, additions, and deletions are strictly prescribed within each individual school or regional tradition and must be committed to memory with as much fidelity and performed as accurately as the text itself.

In this unusual performance practice we may find a clue to the early history of Indian melody. If the phonetic interpolations serve as a simultaneous commentary on a source text, then it is possible to think of the more elaborate melodic style of the *Sāmaveda* as a gloss on a simpler pattern of tonal accents. If there is anything to this interpretation, the idea of melody may have been first conceived as a garland of simultaneous variations on an underlying set of tonal distinctions (the three main Vedic accents mentioned above)—distinctions which were easy to demonstrate and recognize in practice but which resisted easy definition and, perhaps for that reason, were valued more highly than a fully actualized melody.

The *saṁhitā* of the *Sāmaveda* is arranged in two different formats: one according to meter and the particular deity addressed, and the other according to the requirements of the various rituals.[20] A sample verse will serve as a demonstration of the typical phonetic alterations and will also give something of the flavor of this body of literature. The verse appears below in three parallel versions: first, an English translation; second, the original Vedic text in transliteration; and third, the same text as expanded by the phonetic alterations and interpolations.[21] The verb *anvāra-bhāmahe* ("we place our confidence") occurs at the end of the first line of the couplet, and the names of the various gods will be easily recognizable, each in the accusative case, as indicated by the terminal *m*.

> We place our confidence in Soma, the king, in Varuṇa, in Agni, in
> Āditya, in Viṣṇu, in Sūrya, and in Bṛhaspati, the priest.
>
> Somam rājānam varuṇam agnimanvāra bhāmahe
> Ādityam viṣṇum sūryam brahmaṇañca bṛhaspatim.
> Somam rājānam varuṇām . agnimanvāra bhāmahe— hovā— hā i .

Ādityam viṣṇu ṁ sūryam . hovā— hā i . Brahmāṇā—ñcā— .
hovā—hā i .
Bṛhā—uvā— . pā—tīm .

I must emphasize that this verse was transcribed from a modern notation and that it cannot be assumed that this particular version of the phonetic alterations is of any great antiquity; only that it is consistent with ancient tradition and the verse may indeed have been performed in precisely this way or a very similar way. Because the main point of the example is to show what happens to the text, all pitch indications have been removed. (The original notation is that of the Kauthuma school, in which the *svara*s are shown in the form of numerals both above and within the line of text.)[22] Periods mark the division of the verse into *parvan*s (knot, joint, or member), units to be sung with a single breath and concluding with a brief pause. The meter of the verse is a variant of the Vedic Anuṣṭubh, which normally appears as four half lines of eight syllables each with caesura after each quarter, but here it lacks a syllable in the third quarter (that is, $\frac{8+8}{7+8}$).[23]

The first half line is distorted only by the lengthening of the final syllable of *varuṇām,* but the phonetic changes and additions mount up to the end of the verse. The dashes, beginning with the end of the verb *anvārabhāmahe,* indicate syllables that are prolonged with ornamental clusters of *svara*s. The three statements of the meaningless vocalise *ho vā—hāi* should be thought of as laudatory interjections; it should also be noted that *hāi* is a diphthong distributed over two syllables. In the third quarter observe the separation of the final *ṁ* in *viṣṇuṁ,* which thereby regularizes the meter of the verse by restoring the missing eighth syllable. The last three words of the original text (*brahmaṇañca bṛhaspatim*) are greatly elongated, separated, increased in vowel grade, and contain substitutions. The final word is broken into two *parvan*s.

I turn next to the musical aspects of the Sāmaveda tradition, of which three are particularly informative: form, rhythmic and metric organization, and melodic content. There is quite a bit to say about the last of these, so I shall reserve discussion of melody and pitch organization for a separate section. With respect to form, some preferences can be deduced from the typical patterns of liturgy, and as is often the case, from the frequent appearance of certain numbers. The relevant numbers here are three, five, and seven—numbers of considerable cultural significance in Indian and many other world cultures. The structural levels on which these numbers are manifested do not always arise in recitation for purposes of study or personal devotions, but they come to the fore in the more formal recitations that accompany the Vedic sacrifices. The hymns, as they are performed in the various ceremonies, appear as successive clusters of verses (typically in multiples of three, *tṛcas*) set to the same or different melodies. Making due allowance for the many cultural differences, the overall effect is not unlike the psalm sequences heard in a typical Anglican evensong service, and indeed the liturgical purposes are much the same: invocation, praise, petition, oblation, and the like.

The individual chant complex (*stotra,* "laud") is assembled from a number of repetitions of the cluster of three source verses (*tṛcas*)—usually, but not invariably, in multiples of three, depending on the requirements of the ceremony and other traditional practices. The text that results is thus not a complete and coherent hymn but an expanded musical setting of a detail from a hymn. A day of performance may require as few as twelve or as many as thirty-three *stotras*, and the sacrifice being performed may be complete within a single day or may have a duration of more than twelve days. What seems important here is that the larger rhythms of daily life and sacrificial practice are replicated in miniature on several structural levels of the chant rituals, resulting in a hierarchical concept of musical structure that reflects the cosmic order (the *ṛta*).

One extremely significant model for the clusters of threes may be the celebrated Gāyatrī meter, which is employed for nearly one-fourth of the *Ṛgveda.* The standard Gāyatrī stanza consists of three identical lines of eight syllables, each (if normal) unregulated at the beginning of the line but concluding with two iambs (◡–◡⏓).[24] Of all the texts composed in this popular meter, the most famous is the mantra that is also known as the Gāyatrī, a short prayer addressed to the sun god Savitṛ as the "stimulator":

> We meditate upon the glorious splendor
> of the Vivifier divine.
> May he himself illumine our minds![25]

The Gāyatrī is recited daily at sunrise and sunset and is surrounded by an elaborate body of symbolic associations.[26] In its most typical form, the structural hierarchy I have been outlining may be summarized as follows:

| | | |
|---|---|---|
| several trisyllabic *gaṇas*[27] | = | one line of text |
| three such lines (as above) | = | one Gāyatrī stanza |
| three such stanzas | = | one *stotriyā* |
| *stotriyās*, (often) in multiples of threes | = | one *stotra* |
| twelve to thirty-three such *stotras*, | | |

| | | |
|---|---|---|
| divided among three services (morning, noon, evening) | = | one day |
| one or many days | = | one soma pressing, a complete sacrifice[28] |

No hierarchy can ever be this perfect, and the summary obviously fails to take into consideration the different poetic meters available and the many modifications, exceptions, and performance variables (liturgical, textual, and musical). But none of these can completely conceal the deeply embedded ternary rhythm that pervades both the materials and the structure of this body of chant.

A rhythm of fives is similarly embedded within this structure as demonstrated in the liturgical interaction of the trio of priests: the precentor or chief singer (*udgātṛ*), the eulogizer (*prastotṛ*), and the respondent (*pratihartṛ*), whose ceremonial roles are loosely parallel to those of the celebrant, deacon, and subdeacon of the Roman Catholic mass. The performance of each individual *stotriyā* is generally divided into the following sequence of five components (*bhaktis*):

| Name | Liturgical function | Performed by |
|---|---|---|
| *prastāva* | invocation and eulogizing address | eulogizer |
| *udgītha* | the primary section | precentor |
| *pratihāra* | a response | respondent |
| *upadrava* | an optional interlude or prefinal | precentor |
| *nidhana* | a conclusion | all three chanters |

Two purely phonetic components (*praṇava* and *hiṅkāra*) augment the basic structure of the liturgy. *Praṇava* refers to the sacred syllable *om,* with which the precentor introduces the *udgītha; hiṅkāra* consists of the syllable *hum,* intoned by various chanters as an introduction to the *prastāva* and the *pratihāra*. Of the required components, only the final chorus is not preceded by one of these symbolic vocalises. These two purely phonetic components of the *Sāmaveda* repertoire provide early evidence for the practice of beginning a musical performance or a section thereof with a vocalise on meaningless syllables, a practice that has since become a virtual cliché in the music of India. It survives in the form of *upohana,* the typical beginning gambit in the ritual music of the ancient theater, and in the improvisatory *ālāpana* of later Indian song.[29] The essence of the idea seems to be that uttered sounds are invested with an elemental meaning and power of their own, quite apart from whatever denotative meaning they may convey at other times; they evoke resonances and associations with particular deities and elemental substances and thereby help to bring the chanter into alignment with the structure of the world he is charged with celebrating and preserving. They serve at the same time as affirmations and marks of emphasis within the texts they introduce and divide.

In the sequence of five *bhakti*s we see a structure whose influence has spread considerably beyond its original liturgical setting. I regard this pattern as one of India's major formal archetypes, as I shall argue in chapter 9.[30] We find similar sequences in the early theater music and one important derivative in the structure of the *prabandha,* the main song genre of the medieval period.[31] It comes as no surprise to discover a formal pattern with a beginning, a middle, and an end, or (in more specific terms) an introduction, main section, and conclusion. The characteristic feature in this pattern is the presence of affixes: responses, interjections, and prefinals—brief changes of pace and focus that reflect upon the previous section, provide a ceremonial buffer between two sections, or anticipate what is to follow. These are typical components of liturgy as performed by an ensemble of priests with specialized roles. It is easy to supply the liturgics: invocations, acclamations, affirmations, expressions of awe, moments of reflection, place markers, expressions of religious community, marks of emphasis that serve to highlight important points, and genial collegial dialogue. In later Indian music the typical patterns of sacred ceremony have become transformed into patterns of abstract musical form, just as liturgical formulas of the West (for example, the Kyrie eleison and Agnus Dei of the Roman Catholic mass) have become transformed into ternary and binary designs that can be realized by purely musical means. In this interpretation the rhythms of ceremony (as well as the rhythms of movement, speech, and formal poetry) provide important models for the rhythms of music.

The liturgical functions of these formal components were held in great awe by early authors and were described with a number of colorful analogies. The *Chāndogya Upaniṣad,* which is a treasury of symbolic material pertaining to the Sāmavedic tradition, includes the following passage:

> One rubs the fire-sticks together—that is a Hiṅkāra.
> Smoke is produced—that is a Prastāva.
> It blazes—that is an Udgītha.
> Coals are formed—that is a Pratihāra.
> It becomes extinct—that is a Nidhana.[32]

### 4.2.1 The role of memory

It is necessary to emphasize the vital role of mnemonics. For many centuries the Vedas were transmitted orally, with many controls to insure precise rendering of the text. As a consequence, the texts have survived with greater accuracy than the musical system with which they were performed. Young trainees were put through memory-building routines that boggle the mind: recitation of the text both with and without consciousness of its meaning, recitation both forward and backward, recitation both with phonetic junctures (sandhi) between words and with separations between words, metrical recitation and recitation in a continuous flow (except for the obligatory caesuras), and recitation of pairs of syllables in distorted (*vikṛti*) sequences and complex designs, with and without sandhi, accents, and pauses.[33] The aim was to instill an automatic and total command of the text that would rule out even the slightest possibility of error. A chanter was expected to respond immediately with the correct opening letter when chapter and verse were cited by his teacher.

These routines proved to be powerful techniques for learning a text and preserving its accuracy by periodic refreshment, but the ancient Vedins were not content to stop here. Convinced that memory was too important a thing to be left to the mind, they built in redundancy by developing additional reinforcing techniques. Perhaps the most valuable of these were the *mudrā*s, the finger positions and motions which were used to represent the more musical aspects of the chant and which are as essential in performance as they are in learning and remembering.[34]

### 4.2.2 Chironomy

Contemporary Sāmavedic schools differ in several respects, but all three depend upon similar systems of chironomy. There can be no doubt of the antiquity of this practice, and the early phonetic manuals provide ample evidence that the same repertoire of gestures was employed to signify the same categories of musical information.[35] The *mudrā*s were designed to convey a wealth of information with just a few simple and convenient motions of the hand. The individual *svara*s are marked off on the right hand by touching the finger joints with the tip of the thumb. The same hand is also used to indicate certain melodic sequences, tonal prolongations, and tones that are to be shaken—by gliding the thumb across several finger joints or rubbing the side of one of the fingers. The special function of the right hand is thus to display single pitches, pitch clusters, ornamental pitches, and pitches that are to be highlighted in some way. Because this hand was, and is, the "good" hand in Indian tradition,[36] the indication of tonal distinctions was obviously the priority task. The left hand is assigned quite a different role and information content: it is used to show certain long syllables, to represent (on appropriate occasions) the three original Vedic accents, and particularly to mark the correct number of repeated words or syllables. The result of this interesting specialization is that the function of the right hand is primarily tonal, and the function of the left hand, temporal, in that the left hand is used more for counting and indicating special durations.

Western musicians will inevitably see a parallel to the Guidonian "Hand," a popular diagram and system of mnemonics that was developed during the European Middle Ages, on which a much larger gamut of pitches was displayed on the finger joints of one hand and touched by the index finger of the other hand.[37] But in this case the only function of the hand was to specify pitch, with no apparent use of finger positions or motions to represent ornaments, durations, accents, or formal repetitions. Herein lies a distinct contrast between the Indian and European attitudes toward melody and its measurement: the musical scholars of medieval Europe were gradually developing a concept of melody as a series of discrete units, each roughly equivalent and represented by a single visual symbol and syllable. Despite the complexity they obviously heard in their music and represented with neumes of different shapes (in their early notations), their preoccupation with synchronization led them to formulate a simpler concept of melody in which the various units could be easily measured and aligned with the accompanying parts. Indian chanters had quite different concerns. They preferred to think of melody as a more complex series of clusters and events, and therefore they found it more useful to indicate a variety of information with the simple means available to them. In general the Indian system of chironomy seems to have been designed to show the mobile dimensions of the chant, to represent the dynamic as well as the static aspects of melody.

Because the various *svara*s were associated by convention with particular regions of the body and stages of the articulatory process, it seems inevitable that the *mudrā*s became something more than mere aids to the memory. They became a part of the ritual and functioned in a number of different ways: as sacramental signs of inner process, as an external scale for inner space, and as symbolic links between the uttered sounds and their guardian deities. I have emphasized the act of counting, surely an essential technique in an oral tradition with many repetitions on different structural levels. In this respect it is possible to trace a clear connection between the *Sāmaveda mudrā*s and the finger counts (the *jāti*s) of later *tāla* systems, which mark off and count the small units between the major divisions of a rhythmic cycle. And finally, as additional insurance against error, the chanters keep their place among the many repeated verses by laying down sticks in traditional patterns, one stick for each verse.

### 4.2.3 Duration and Tempo

The temporal aspects of the chant were regulated, as one would expect, by the syllabic quantities of the text—as measured in *mātrā*s (a unit equal to one short syllable) and their multiples. Three basic durations were recognized: short, long, and protracted (*pluta*), in an invariant ratio of 1:2:3 *mātrā*s. The same durations form the basis for the system of *tāla.*[38] *Pluta* is in many respects the most interesting of the three and played a special role in the delineation of musical rhythms, but its role is minuscule in Vedic recitation. As W. Sidney Allen points out, *pluta* "occurs but three times in the *RV* and it is in all cases related to the special type of speech function."[39] Certain combinations or distortions of syllables have the effect of prolonging or reducing these *mātrā* values by halves or quarters, resulting in a complex but precise representation of the durations of the original text.

Finding absolute measures for the various durations was a problem for early authors, as it was in other bodies of ancient metrical theory, and the solutions were often naive. The *Pāṇinīyaśikṣā,* perhaps the oldest and most authoritative of the phonetic manuals, prescribes the following values: "One *mātrā* is equivalent to the cry of the blue jay, two *mātrā*s to that of the crow, three *mātrā*s to that of the peacock, and one-half *mātrā* to that of the mongoose."[40]

The question of tempo proved equally resistant to quantification, although authors were more successful in specifying the relationships between the three conventional speeds. The *Nāradīyaśikṣā* includes the following verse, borrowed from many of the other phonetic manuals: "One should perform in the fast style (*vṛtti*) when studying, but in the moderate style when reciting, and in the slow style when instructing a pupil."[41]

I suspect that the three tempos were taught and found more by tradition and instinct than by any precise calculations, but the *Mātrālakṣaṇam* (a treatise of uncertain date) provides a specific ratio for the three: 3:4:5, in which each of the *mātrā*s is divided into three, four, or five *kalā*s (apparently in the sense of absolute time units).[42] In this treatise the moderate and slow speeds are referred to as "augmented" (*vṛddha*), and each of the three is associated with a color and a deity: fast with red, for the red horses of the wind god Vāyu; moderate with dark blue, for the blue back of Bṛhaspati, the "Lord of Prayer"; and slow with white, for the white horses of Sūrya, the sun god.[43] The 3:4:5 ratio sounds practical for recitation and chanting (in which we would hardly expect to find tempo variations in geometric proportions), but it is difficult to see any connection between this set of ratios and the prevailing ratio of 1:2:4 by which the ancient system of *tāla* was governed.[44] I leave the matter with the obvious comment that music tolerates, and perhaps demands, a much wider and more readily calculated range of tempos than any style of verbal recitation.

#### 4.2.4 Dynamics

In addition to the performance variables already mentioned, we read of different dynamic grades or styles of utterance. The authoritative *Taittirīya Prātiśākhya* outlines a set of seven dynamic levels: inaudible, murmur, whisper, mumbling, soft, moderate, and loud.[45] And the *Chāndogya Upaniṣad* dedicates a number of performance styles to various of the Vedic deities: "'I choose the roaring, animal-like form of the Sāman'—such is the Udgītha belonging to Agni. The indistinct form belongs to Prajāpati; the distinct, to Soma; the soft and smooth, to Vāyu; the smooth and strong, to Indra; the heron-like to Bṛhaspati; the ill-sounding, to Varuṇa. One may practise all these, but one should avoid that belonging to Varuṇa."[46]

The tradition of Sāmavedic chant, as will soon be apparent, is a treasury of information with respect to the early evolution of pitch concepts, but it tells us little about the history of Indian musical rhythm. For this type of information we must look instead to the music of the early theater. In the musical settings of the *Sāmaveda* hymns, the original durations of the text were expanded in a process similar to the phonetic expansion of the text itself, but in the process no new principles of rhythmic organization were introduced, nor is there any evidence of an independent means of temporal control other than the system of metrics by which the original texts were regulated.

### 4.3 The Phonetic Treatises

The mind stirs up the body's fire;
The fire then sets in motion wind;
The wind then, moving through the chest,
Produces pleasurable sound.

As stirred in heart by means of fire of friction,
Less is it than the least; in throat, it is doubled;
And know that on the tongue-tip it is trebled;
Come forth, it is the alphabet!—They say thus.

*Maitri Upaniṣad* 7.11.4–5[47]

Before we proceed to investigate the many links between music and articulatory phonetics in the cryptic teachings of the *Nāradīyaśikṣā,* it will be useful to place the phonetic treatises within their larger context and distinguish the two main genres from one another. The keyword for this section is *śikṣā:* in a general sense the word signifies the entire field of articulatory phonetics; in a narrower sense it denotes what I shall refer to as the phonetic "manuals."

The subject of phonetics was a privileged discipline in early Indian scholarship because of the authority accorded to the Vedas and the consequent demand for scrupulously accurate performance of the sacred texts. *Śikṣā* was the first of a set of six ancillary disciplines that were known collectively as "Limbs of the Vedas" (Vedāṅgas): phonetics, ritual, grammar, etymology, metrics, and astronomy. Their joint task was to insure correct performance—through the study of articulation, ritual procedures, grammatical and semantic analysis, the metrical basis of the texts, and the proper scheduling and timing of ceremonies. Important as the Vedāṅgas may have been in preserving various aspects of the Vedic tradition, they were held in lesser esteem than the Vedas themselves and were classified as "traditional knowledge" (*smṛti*) rather than "revealed knowledge" (*śruti*).[48]

Two genres of phonetic treatises must be distinguished. The *śikṣā*s are relatively brief and consist of short theoretical expositions and practical advice for the trainee. While certain *śikṣā*s were addressed to a particular Veda (as, for example, the teachings of the *Nāradīyaśikṣā* to the *Sāmaveda*), their precepts were intended to apply to all the recensions or schools of that Veda, and their practical wisdom could be taken to heart by all student-priests. The *prātiśākhya*s provide reference tools for the specialist, examining in comprehensive detail the special problems of word order, word separation, accent, articulation, and similar matters pertaining to one particular śākhā (school) of the appropriate Veda. While there may at one time have been as many *prātiśākhya*s as there were individual schools of the Vedas (1,130, according to Vidhata Mishra), only six have survived.[49] In contrast, about sixty-five *śikṣā*s still exist, thirty-one of them assembled in the Banaras edition of the *Śikṣāsaṁgraha*.[50] The relative status of the two genres is clear from the following oft-quoted remark: "If *Śikṣā* and *Prātiśākhya* are found at variance, the *Śikṣā* is said to be the less authoritative, as the deer is weaker than the lion."[51] Nevertheless, for musical purposes one deer has proved to be more informative than the entire pride of surviving lions.

The phonetic literature can be dated with no more certainty than any other body of ancient Indian literature. Siddheshwar Varma has proposed 500–150 B.C. as the period of the *prātiśākhya*s.[52] The original *śikṣā*s are probably even older, but most of the extant manuals appear to have been compiled at a much later date than the few surviving *prātiśākhya*s. The most comprehensive and authoritative of these, the *Pāṇinīyaśikṣā* (from which many of the other *śikṣā*s borrow extensively), has been attributed to the great fifth-century B.C. grammarian and has consequently been hailed as the original *śikṣā,* but both claims seem dubious. The phonetic manuals, like most other early Indian writings, consist of successive accretions of material from the hands of multiple authors, so the best solution is to suggest a range, rather than a specific date. In the case of Nārada's *śikṣā,* there can be little doubt that some of the material—perhaps most of it—is from pre-Christian centuries, but the later layers and final compilation cannot have been much earlier than the sixth or seventh centuries A.D. It would be particularly useful to be able to date the musical material it contains, but I can see no reliable basis for doing this. It may be the earliest literary work to examine questions of musical pitch in such detail.

It would take us too far afield to discuss in detail the early contributions to phonetic theory, other than to endorse Allen's pertinent observation: "The authors of our treatises were clearly phoneticians rather than priests, and a scientific curiosity, coupled with keen audition and an effective methodology, led to descriptions which must surely have transcended their original terms of reference."[53] I will indicate, however, a number of ways in which the distinctive features of the Sanskrit language and its parent tongue have left their marks upon the musical language of India and influenced the evolution of musical doctrines.

## 4.4 Some Distinctive Features of Sanskrit and Their Musical Consequences

Perhaps the single most striking feature of Sanskrit is *sandhi* (junction), a process in which the words of a sentence or poetic line are written and pronounced as a continuous string of syllables, within which certain letter substitutions and changes of vowel grade mark the coalescence of separate words and members of compounds. These alterations are governed by a complex set of rules, but the two main principles were, as Macdonell observes, assimilation and the avoidance of hiatus.[54] The purpose of the latter was to insure the continuity and flow of the utterance as a whole, without sacrificing the necessary distinctions that would permit its meaning to be communicated—reconciling, as it were, the conflicting demands of melody and meaning. The process of assimilation is particularly significant and works in two directions: regressive assimilation, in which the influence of an initial sound causes the preceding final sound to mutate to a similar position within the mouth (as in American English, where the expression "What do you want?" is often pronounced "Whaddo you want?"); and the rarer progressive assimilation, in which an initial sound assimilates to the position of the preceding final.

What have been the consequences for music and musical thought? It will be evident that in the case of this and the other distinctive features, any significant aspect of a language must be preserved in one form or another when performing texts in that language. Our interests must go deeper than this. I can see a number of implications for both performance and analysis of the musical utterance, whether that utterance is conceived as elevated speech, chant, or song. With respect to performance, the influence of sandhi has helped to develop the concept of a melodic line with minimal interruptions and a strong sense of progression, reinforced by many gliding transitions between the individual *svara*s and melodic clusters (the *gamaka*s).[55] In analysis, the task was to help the chanter to retrace this process, to undo the continuous stream of sound and thus come to understand both the meaning and the morphological structure of a text; as a consequence, word and syllable separation became one of the major concerns of the *śikṣā* literature. The ideal musical performance was one in which the singer would attempt to sustain the illusion of continuous melodic flow, with precise yet noninterruptive enunciation of the necessary articulations. Articulatory requirements were clearly more stringent in recitation and chanting than in song, and the phonetic junctions were reflected in both the accentuation and the timing of the Vedic texts. It therefore became imperative for the ancient phoneticians to make a thorough exploration of the dimensions of pitch and rhythm and to develop concepts for their representation. Here is one possible explanation for the rise of a theory of music.

Aspiration is a second characteristic feature of Sanskrit and its Vedic ancestor, providing the basis for numerous essential phonetic distinctions. Aspiration—and here I use the term in its broadest sense—is heard, for example, in the distinctions between the three sibilants (*ś, ṣ,* and the ordinary dental *s*), in the special type of final aspiration known as *visarga* (in which *s* is converted into *ḥ* and pronounced in voiced form as *ha*), and also to a lesser extent in the roles of the four glides or semivowels (*y, r, l,* and *v*), in addition to the initial *h*.[56] Pulmonic processes were the subject of intense debate among the ancient phoneticians and have left their mark upon musical concepts, not least of all because of their focus on the role of the breath in the production of musical sound. In the Sāmavedic chant, interjected *stobha* syllables such as *hāu, ho vā, hāi,* and *hum* color the timbre of the chant line with the frequent aspirations and cause the chanter's respiration to mingle with the smoke that carries the sacrificial fire offerings up to the gods.

But most important of all for musical purposes is the vital distinction between aspirated and unaspirated consonants (*kh, ch, th, ph, gh, jh, dh,* and *bh,* as opposed to *k, c, t, p, g, j, d,* and *b*)—a distinction that lies at the heart of the language and its preferred means of discriminating between otherwise similar sounds. The process of aspiration furnishes one of the most crucial distinctions in the sets of syllables that are recited or sung to represent the various drum strokes and dance steps (*dhā* and *dhin,* for example, as opposed to *dā* and *din*). While the particular selection of syllables has varied from time to time, from North to South, from one type of drum to another, and from one regional practice to another, and despite the lack of any permanent one-to-one correspondence between individual strokes and syllables, the distinction between aspirated and unaspirated makes it possible to articulate certain significant oppositions: left and right (hand or foot), drumheads of higher and lower pitch, stress and nonstress, damped and undamped strokes, two-hand strokes as opposed to single-hand strokes. The only other prominent phonetic opposition in the traditional drum languages is that between voiced and voiceless consonants, especially *d* as opposed to *t.*[57] The syllables chosen for recitation were obviously designed to fit "trippingly on the tongue" but also to mimic the sonic distinctions in an appropriate way.

Ancient Western authors were not unaware of the role of the breath in the production of vocal sound, and aspiration—in the form of the so-called rough and smooth breathing—was a distinctive feature in Attic Greek. Zeno defined speech in terms that most Indian phoneticians would have endorsed enthusiastically: "a stream of air extending from the principal part of the soul to the throat and the tongue and the appropriate organs."[58] But the phonetic specialists of ancient India appear to have been unique in their recognition of the vital role of pulmonic processes in the production of sound, and their consequent emphasis on musical sound as process.

Nasality (*anunāsika*) is the third feature to be examined, with particular reference to the role of nasal closure. In this category I include (1) the regular assimilation of final nasals to the class of the subsequent initial (for example, *an jo* becomes *añjo*), and (2) the special type of nasal closure known as *anusvāra,* transliterated as *ṁ* or *ṃ.*[59] Like the other forms of assimilation mentioned above, the role of (1) is to encourage continuity; but *anusvāra* is performed with a nasalized lengthening of the previous vowel, and in external combination it is followed by a slight hiatus in the stream of written or enunciated words. So from the point of view of phonetics, nasality is associated with both continuity and separation.

Early musical authors must have been aware of the potential for an unpleasant amount of nasality in vocal sound, for it is commonly listed among the defects (*doṣa*s) of singing.[60] Nevertheless, despite their warnings and the protests of those who have become accustomed to it, a certain degree of nasality is typical in Indian vocal production today, and it cannot be dismissed as a recent development. Even the art of instrument building has sought to imitate nature: I refer here to the many types of string instruments in which a nasal quality is simulated by various means. Perhaps the best conclusion to draw with respect to nasality is that the variety of final nasals[61] and their tendency to be assimilated to the position of the following sound have led reciters and chanters to enunciate them with particular clarity and emphasis, and this in turn has encouraged the spread of the nasal influence to the neighboring vowel sounds. And finally, such an emphasis upon final nasal closure—as in the syllable *om*—invites the chanter to hum on this final sound.

The fourth phonetic issue to be examined here is the distinctive arrangement of the letters of the Sanskrit alphabet according to place of articulation, a feat of sound classification unmatched by any of the other phonetic traditions in the ancient world. Table 6 is a complete display of the forty-eight morphophonemes and a useful reference for the other phonetic features I have discussed. A full appreciation of this remarkable system would be beyond the scope of this study, but the table will bear witness both to the complexity and subtlety of the required phonetic distinctions and to the pro-

Table 6 The Sanskrit Morphophonemes

| | Velar | Palatal | Retroflex | Dental | Labial |
|---|---|---|---|---|---|
| Vowels | | | | | |
| Simple | | | | | |
| Short | a | i | ṛ | ḷ | u |
| Long | ā | ī | ṝ | | ū |
| Diphthongs | | | | | |
| Short | | e | | | o |
| Long | | āi | | | āu |
| Consonants | | | | | |
| Visarga | ḥ | | | | |
| Anusvāra | ṁ | | | | |
| Stops | | | | | |
| voiceless unaspirated | k | c | ṭ | t | p |
| voiceless aspirated | kh | ch | ṭh | th | ph |
| voiced unaspirated | g | j | ḍ | d | b |
| voiced aspirated | gh | jh | ḍh | dh | bh |
| Nasals | ṅ | ñ | ṇ | n | m |
| Semivowels | | y | r | l | v |
| Sibilants | | ś | ṣ | s | |
| Aspirate | h | | | | |

found way in which the metaphor of the outward pathway mirrors the structure of the sounds of the language.[62]

It will be clear that the traditional explanation of the production of musical sound is modeled upon the paradigm for the articulation of speech sounds; this passage from the *Pāṇinīyaśikṣā* is a typical version:

> The soul, apprehending things with the intellect, inspires the mind with a desire to speak; the mind then excites the bodily fire, which in its turn impels the breath. The breath, circulating in the lungs, is forced upwards and, impinging upon the head, reaches the speech-organs and gives rise to speech-sounds. These are classified in five ways—by tone (*svara*), by length (*kāla,* "time"), by place of articulation (*sthāna,* "register"), by process of articulation (*prayatna,* "effort"), and by secondary features (*anupradāna*).[63] Thus the phoneticians have spoken: take careful heed.[64]

At least three of the five features mentioned in the passage from the *Pāṇinīyaśikṣā* have become formal topics in the theory of ancient Indian music: *svara,* in the sense of pitch; *kāla,* in the sense of duration; and *sthāna,* register.[65] When the scientific observations of the ancient speech scholars became mingled (late in the first millennium A.D.) with the mystical physiological teachings of Tantra and Yoga, the merger between articulatory phonetics and the art of singing became a permanent feature of Indian musical explanation.[66]

As the final topic, I shall briefly consider the role of the syllable in Indian music and musical thinking—another important legacy from early linguistic science. This is a large issue, which we will return to later. In one form or another the concept of syllable dominates all descriptions of Indian language and music, and virtually all melodic and rhythmic concepts are syllabic in nature: musical ideas are conceived in terms of syllables and syllable complexes, learned and remembered by an indigenous system of sol-fa syllables, and (beginning in the later medieval period) notated in a syllabic script. There is also a common tendency to generate musical ideas in a number of parallel syllabic tracks—recited syllables, sung syllables representing the scale degrees (the *svàra*s), syllables that are onomatopoeic of drum strokes, syllables representing specific dance steps—all of these encoded in the form of units of like size that permit ready transposition between one such track and another. Why is it that such an apparently atomistic concept as the syllable has proved so valuable in a musical culture where continuity and process have been prized more highly than static values?

To find a partial answer to this question, it is necessary to discard the simplistic notion of a syllable as a single unit of sound. Linguists by and large have abandoned the syllable in analyzing the sound features of world languages and have concentrated instead on the identification of even smaller phonetic units. But the sophisticated Indian concept of the syllable as the core of a complex cluster of sound phenomena became a permanently viable means of representing the many sounds of speech and music. The syllable served as the basic unit of cognition, to which any number of transitions, ornaments, and other secondary features could readily adhere and become assimilated by the ear and the mind. The task for music theory was to describe the musical materials and their structure in terms of this syllabic core, but it remained for oral instruction to demonstrate and teach the many additional sound distinctions too subtle to be captured in the filter of syllabic description.

From a broader perspective, Indian culture has designated the syllable as the abiding part of any vocal utterance; recall from the discussion of the syllable *om* in chapter 3 that the idea of syllable has been invested with a large number of symbolic associations. The conventional analysis of the word *akṣara* (syllable) as "the imperishable" and "that which flows not away" is a clear indication that ancient scholars believed, or wished to believe, in the permanence of the syllable. *Akṣara* has often been identified with the syllable *om,* sometimes with the essence of speech itself, sometimes with the patron goddess of speech, and occasionally with the unchanging, transcendental world principle.[67] As a result, the musical meaning of a syllable will include not only its outward form (as uttered or conceived in the mind) and specific reference of the moment (as the name of a scale step or drum stroke) but also the many microfeatures that will always escape the grasp of the mind and the senses.[68]

## 4.5 Nārada's *Śikṣā* and the Organization of Musical Pitch

The short phonetic manual ascribed to the ancient sage Nārada is one of three extant *śikṣā*s of the *Sāmaveda* and unquestionably the most important and comprehensive of the three.[69] It consists of a total of 239 metrical couplets (*śloka*s), divided into two cantos (*prapāṭhaka*s) of eight chapters (*kaṇḍikā*s) each. The first canto contains most of the material pertaining to music; the second canto is largely devoted to phonetics and correct enunciation and concludes with some practical advice for the daily life and conduct of the young student-priest. The dominant meter is the standard Anuṣṭubh of epic Sanskrit, but the metrical inconsistencies in several sections of the treatise suggest the presence of borrowed material.[70]

The *NS* is particularly rich in its exposition of the topics of *svara* and in the many mythological references, but less rich in instructions for recitation and textual analysis. In this section I shall take up the concepts that form the basis for the theory of musical pitch. I shall then focus on the milieu of the Sāmavedin, his life, his training, and the mythology that informed his worldview.

How does one musical sound differ from another? Some are shorter or longer than others, but this distinction is not problematic: the scale of durations is a quantitative scale that facilitates counting, measurements, and comparisons. The tonal aspects of musical sound must at first have seemed more qualitative than quantitative to those who listened: how then does one musical sound differ from another with respect to tone? The very generality of the word is a sign of the problems that lie ahead. It is easy for us to jump to the conclusion that by "tone" we mean primarily "pitch."[71] And from the perspective of recent music in the West, pitch is neither a complex nor a controversial issue: one sound is higher or lower than another, depending mainly on the nature of the sound source and the frequency with which it vibrates. The timbre—the quality or "color" of the sound—is for the most part a separate issue. But from the perspective of early civilizations, the analysis and description of the tonal dimensions of musical sound was no obvious matter.

What do the terms "high" and "low" mean? Loud and soft, up and down, tense and lax? And, if "up and down," does "up" mean up with respect to the height of a pipe, the position of a particular string as the instrument is held, the stance of a singer's body, or does it mean up, as we have come to assume, as measured along the abstract continuum of musical space that is the domain of musical pitch? We take certain associations for granted: to a pianist, up and down are inseparable from right and left. An Indian chanter or singer may have used the terms "up and down" to represent where he believed the sound was produced within his body.

There is a natural relationship between the descriptors high, loud, bright, tense, as opposed to low, soft, dull, lax. My main argument here is that it took early Indian authors some time to disentangle these oppositions. Loud-soft is perhaps the most obvious opposition between one sound and another, and in this respect it is interesting to note that many of the Sanskrit words for sound mean not merely "sound" but a "loud sound," as if a reference to a quality (a sound or a color) is to emphasize not only the presence but the intensity of that quality.

It takes time for a culture to turn a set of descriptors borrowed from everyday experience into an abstract scale for the measurement of musical sounds. The ancient Chinese, with their bureaucratic passion for national standards of weight and measurement, went the farthest in proclaiming absolute pitch standards on the basis of precisely scaled bamboo tubes and stone chimes, but they continued to associate musical pitches with the timbres and special materials from which their instruments were constructed. The early Greeks achieved a virtuoso control of relative pitch measurement in the form of interval ratios, but their system remained on a certain level of abstraction in the absence of any fixed standards. Ancient Indian observers—lacking technology, relatively uninterested in numbers, distrusting material substance, and without any frame of reference for musical sounds other than their own bodies—began by describing what they heard. Their success was spectacular, especially in describing the sounds of speech, but how did they describe the sounds that we call "music"? To sharpen the question, how did they manage to separate the multiple perspectives from which sound can be described and arrive at a set of objective descriptors so that their observations could be translated into a system? The story is an interesting one, and much of its confused early history is recorded in the successive layers of Nārada's *śikṣā.*

I shall briefly examine concepts of register, scale degree, scale, mode, timbre, and accent, leaving a fuller account of the pitch system for chapter 7. The idea of register (*sthāna*) seems to have come easily: "There are three registers of speech—the chest, the throat, and the head—and these are called *savana*s;[72] in performing the *sāman*s, [a similar division is made with respect to] the high and low notes. There are seven *svara*s in the chest, and likewise [seven] in the throat and the head, but not all seven are manifested in the chest."[73]

So by the time when these particular verses were composed, the three vocal registers had already developed into a continuous heptatonic scale extending to nearly three octaves, in theory if not in practice. Why three? Apart from the general cultural significance of the number three, the idea may have arisen in the attempt to associate various tripartitions of musical space (such as the three places in which vocal resonance is felt and the three accents used for chanting the hymns of the *Ṛgveda*) with the three daily soma oblations. With the expanded pitch gamut of the *Sāmaveda,* the tripartition which had become familiar at the local level (in the accentual system of the *Ṛgveda*) was transferred to the three separate vocal registers, each of which was now filled in with a full set of scale degrees. From this process it is possible to infer three instinctive "laws" for the systematic exploration of musical space: (1) expand the system to a set of boundaries that seem natural, (2) fill in the gaps, and (3) apply structural divisions and principles developed at the local level to the system as a whole. Not much has been made of the concept of the octave in Indian musical speculation. This is a consequence not only of their relative lack of interest in musical intervals (an issue to which I shall return)[74] but also because octave doublings were accepted as conventions of melodic style.

The concept of *svara,* in the sense of scale degree, is crucial.[75] Nārada's exposition of this important topic begins with the following *uddeśa,* or table of contents: "Seven the *svara*s, three the *grāma*s, twenty-one the *mūrcchanā*s, forty-nine the *tāna*s—thus the circle of *svara*s (the *svaramaṇḍala*) is formed."[76] This group of scalar concepts forms a "circle" not only (1) because it is a complete exposition that includes all possibilities but also (2) because each of the items mentioned can be represented by a circular motion of the thumb across the finger joints, touching each of the *svara*s in turn. The seven *svara*s, which I described in chapter 3 as "generalized" degrees of the diatonic scale, are displayed in table 7 with their traditional syllabic abbreviations and etymologies.[77] The *grāma*s are the three basic scales, beginning on the first, third, and fourth *svara*s. The *mūr-*

Table 7 The Seven *Svaras*

| Degree | Name | Abbreviation | Derivation | Meaning |
|---|---|---|---|---|
| 1 | *ṣaḍja* | *sa* | *ṣaḍ* (six) + *ja* (born) | Born of the six organs of utterance |
| 2 | *ṛṣabha* | *ri* | *ṛṣabha* (bull) | Bellowing like a bull[a] |
| 3 | *gāndhāra* | *ga* | *gandha* (fragrance) | The fragrant note |
| 4 | *madhyama* | *ma* | *madhya* (middle) + the superlative suffix *ma* | "Middlemost" |
| 5 | *pañcama* | *pa* | *pañca* (five) | The fifth note |
| 6 | *dhaivata* | *dha* | perhaps from *dhī* (perceive, think) | Unclear |
| 7 | *niṣāda* | *ni* | *ni* (down) + *sad* (sit) | The final note |

[a]The etymology of this word is interesting: the root *ṛṣ* means "to flow," and thus the sense of the word *ṛṣabha* (bull) is "he whose flowing semen impregnates the herd"; from this the meaning attenuates to the best or most excellent of anything, and its application to the second degree of the musical scale is an indication of some priority attached to that degree.

*cchanā*s are the complete set of systematic rotations of each of the three *grāma*s (3 × 7 = 21): that is, 1 up to 1, 2 up to 2, and so forth. The forty-nine *tāna*s comprise an incomplete collection of pentatonic and hexatonic versions of the *mūrcchanā*s, lacking one or two of the scale degrees, and their numbers do not add up as neatly because of certain duplications and restrictions. I shall amplify these preliminary discussions and provide illustrations in chapter 6.

Nārada's exposition of the seven *svara*s begins as follows: "Because *ṣaḍja* arises from the combination of nose, throat, chest, palate, tongue, and teeth, it is known as "six-born." When air, rising from the navel and united with the throat and head, bellows like a bull, the sound is called *ṛṣabha*. When air, rising from the navel and united with the throat and head, carries fragrance to the nose, the sound is rightly known as *gāndhāra*."[78]

It will be apparent from table 7 that the seven sol-fa syllables (*sa, ri, ga, ma, pa, dha, ni*) derive in an obvious way from the initial syllables of the *svara* names. This system is among the world's most significant oral notations and is still in use today. We see in the system a notable parallel to the set of solmization syllables devised by the Italian monk Guido of Arezzo in the eleventh century (*ut, re, mi, fa, sol, la*), except that Guido's set—derived from the opening syllables of the first six lines of the Latin hymn "Ut queant laxis," each of which begins one degree higher than the preceding line—represents *specific* pitch relationships.[79] While the Guidonian set is semantically neutral and tells us nothing about the earlier history of the scale, the *svara* names are a colorful mixture of qualities and quantities and permit some historical interpretation (see below).

The next topic for consideration is *grāma* (scale).[80] There is not much to say about the concept of scale, other than to point out that there were three, each of them a collection of the seven *svara*s: two in common practice (those beginning on *sa* and *ma*, degrees one and four) and one (beginning on *ga*, the third degree) that is practiced, as Nārada informs us, "nowhere else than in heaven!"[81]

The three topics we have examined—*sthāna, svara* (with its set of subtopics), and *grāma*—provide the framework for the early system of musical pitch: one diatonic system with a theoretical range of three octaves, with seven nonspecific degrees in each octave and authorized scales beginning on three of these degrees; each of the three scales is available in a complete set of rotations and may drop one or two of its degrees.[82]

Nārada's exposition of these scalar concepts includes one vital piece of information found in no other source. In the fifth chapter of the opening canto, the *svaras* of the Sāmavedic scale are equated with those of the "worldly" (*laukika*) scale. The results of this equation are displayed in (3).[83]

3. The equation of the Sāmavedic and secular scales according to the *NS*

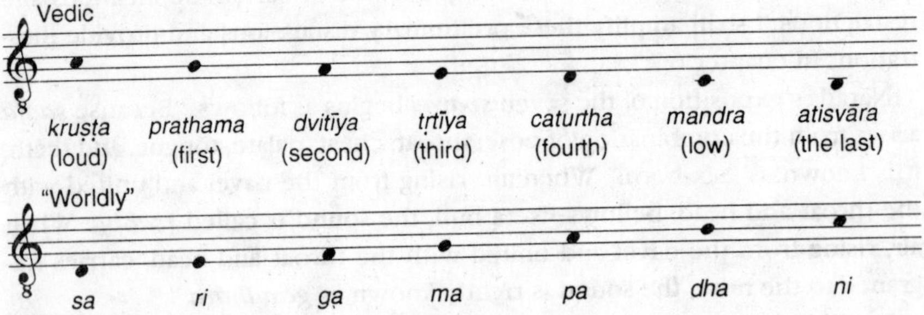


It is quite impossible to determine the exact pitch relationships in either of the two scales, but the sequence of intervals in the secular scale (in which the successive steps, according to later authors, occur at intervals of two, three, or four *śrutis*)[84] is generally accepted as a reasonable approximation of ancient practice. It will be recognized as the equivalent of the Dorian mode (*protus authenticus*), the first of the set of eight modes by which the tonal structure of Gregorian chant has been defined since the early Middle Ages. This formation turns up again and again in melodic repertoires and modal systems from many different parts of the ancient world, and it must be one of the oldest—and perhaps also one of the most instinctive and deeply satisfying—scalar constructions.[85]

The Vedic scale was evidently generated from a nucleus at the upper end of the scale, as the names for its degrees suggest, spreading downward in response to the greater melodic demands of the *Sāmaveda* tradition: *prathama, dvitīya,* and *tṛtīya* are the likely members of the original nucleus, as well as the counterparts of the three Ṛgvedic accents. The secular scale, on the other hand, was clearly generated in an upward direction—if *pa* is the fifth degree. None of this is in any way exceptional in the early development of scale systems.

We know nothing else about the early history of the secular scale, but passages elsewhere in Nārada's manual imply certain priorities (in the form of correspondences between the *svaras*, deities, and the four social classes):[86] the highest ranking is assigned to *svaras* 1, 4, and 5 (*sa, ma,* and *pa*), followed by 2 and 6 (*ri* and *dha*), and finally 3 and 7 (*ga* and *ni*). These priorities appear to validate Curt Sachs's contention that musical systems tend to seek out and crystallize around the basic consonant intervals—the octave, perfect fifth, and perfect fourth.[87] The result has often been a ranking of scale degrees in three tiers: (1) strong/stable, (2) neutral/intermediate, and (3) weak/unstable; and the priorities outlined above are not inconsistent with those of other, unrelated scale systems (particularly in the common tendency to treat the third and seventh degrees as variable or unstable members). None of these properties, however, should be read into the Sāmavedic scale, nor may it be inferred that its intervals were identical to those of the worldly scale, especially since no consensus exists in contemporary *Sāmaveda* practice.[88]

Nārada has expounded the concept of mode (melody type) in connection with the secular scale, not (as in the West) with the tonal basis of the chant. The generic term is *rāga.*[89] Two verses will serve as an introduction: "Madhyamagrāma is recognized by a dominance of *gāndhāra,* by comings and goings of *niṣāda,* and by the weakness of *dhaivata.* When *niṣāda* is lightly touched, with an abundance of *gāndhāra,* and when *dhaivata* is shaken, that is declared to be Ṣaḍjagrāma."[90] These verses and their neighbors provide skeletal descriptions of the seven original *grāmarāga*s and must be among the later accretions in Nārada's little phonetic manual.[91] It is not clear whether this passage was composed at an earlier or a later date than the descriptions of the *jāti*s (mode classes) in the *Nāṭyaśāstra,* but the *grāmarāga*s and the *jāti*s represent the two oldest surviving levels of the later *rāga* system.[92] The idea of *rāga* has not changed in any substantial way since its initial formulation during the second half of the first millennium A.D., although its development may be analyzed in a series of distinct stages, and the number of recognized *rāga*s has expanded from the original limited set to perhaps as many as several thousand.

Although the names of the two *grāmarāga*s in the above passage are identical to the names of the two basic scales (the *grāma*s on *sa* and *ma*), the terms of reference have become much more specific. Instead of a relatively neutral set of scale degrees from which any melodic functions can only be inferred, we now find explicit references to strong notes, weak notes, transient notes, shaken notes, and (in the accompanying verses) to altered notes and notes to be performed "in association" with certain others. The descriptions presented here are still too sketchy to permit reconstruction without recourse to the detailed descriptions in later texts, but the concept of *rāga* can be clearly discerned.

A *rāga,* then, is a mode, a melodic construction that may take the form of a "particularized scale" or a "generalized tune":[93] a scalar collection of *svara*s with distinct functions (such as initial, final, pivotal, weak, profuse, high boundary, low boundary, unstable, and the like). As a consequence the original neutral structure of the collection is transformed into a dynamic model in which many or all of the *svara*s have individual missions. This model is in effect a script for improvisation and/or composition—strict enough to distinguish it from all other such scripts (by means of its unique set of rules) but loose enough to provide for many options and contingencies and thereby generate an infinite number of compositions and performances. It is no exaggeration to say that there has been no more important concept in the long history of Indian music. The essence of the idea of *rāga* lies in the concept of an array of individual scales, each of which has become particularized by certain intonations, tendencies, strong and weak members, typical ornaments, and characteristic melodic pathways: in the process becoming much more than a scale, but at the same time much less than a fixed melody.

In contrast, the *grāma*s are not modes but simply collections of the available *svara*s with no special functions attached to the various degrees of the scale. Neither are the *mūrcchanā*s modes. They are, rather, purely mechanical rotations of and through the basic scales and are precisely equivalent to the seven octave species of ancient Greek music in their systematic display of each of the seven possible arrangements of the intervals within a diatonic octave.[94]

In 1.7.9 Nārada adds to the cluster of pitch concepts: "*Dīptā* (brilliant), *āyatā* (extended), *karuṇā* (mournful), *mṛdu* (soft), and *madhyama* (moderate)—these are the five [*śruti*s]; he who lacks knowledge of these *śruti*s is no master teacher."

This is an enigmatic passage, but there is a valuable understanding to be gained from it. The five *śruti*s enumerated—or *śruti-jāti*s (species of *śruti*), as they were later called—are presented as modifiers of the *svara*s of the Sāmavedic scale, and they should not be confused with the set of twenty-two *śruti*s with which the secular octave was divided.[95] It is accurate to describe both sets of *śruti*s as tonal inflections or shadings, but of what? Of pitch, loudness, timbre, or a mixture of some or all of these? The twenty-two *śruti*s are unquestionably microtonal pitch distinctions, but it is not at all clear whether the five *śruti*s mentioned by Nārada are measures of pitch, in terms of high and low, or of something else. I am arguing in favor of "something else."

The following five verses lay down the conditions under which each of the *śruti*s is to be performed on one or another of the *Sāma svara*s: whether, for example, a particular *svara* is followed by a pause, another given *svara,* or is involved in a particular type of junction between words. The rules are complex, and the conditions are ambiguous in Nārada's text, which is after all more a set of general guidelines than an exhaustive set of rules. The *śruti*s were obviously intended as "qualifiers" that served to adapt the note-for-note structure of the chant to its changing contexts (tonal, temporal, and phonetic). Most later authors have simply assumed that the five *śruti*s were equivalent to "sharps" and "flats" and were employed in a manner similar to the medieval Western practice of *musica ficta,* but N. Ramanathan was right on the mark when he maintained that Nārada's *śruti*s were proposed as measures of tonal quality or timbre rather than as measures of pitch.[96]

The result is an entirely different kind of music as particular syllables or scale degrees are brightened, dulled, or altered in dynamic level, for the sake of emphasis, deemphasis, or to adjust the "melody" of the line in some other appropriate way. These distinctions are always present, in chant or in song, but the greater our consciousness of pitch, the lower our awareness of the many qualitative distinctions which are often learned more by imitation than by verbal instruction. Nārada's testimony is a reminder that while the domain of song had begun to rely almost exclusively upon pitch for its tonal distinctions, the tradition of recitation and chant continued to be regulated by a subtle mixture of pitch, dynamic, and timbral distinctions.

Of the five *śruti*s, *dīptā* occurs in the greatest variety of tonal contexts and is mentioned more frequently than the others. I take it to mean simply "intensity," perhaps in the sense both of a louder and a more strident tone. In contrast, *karuṇā* and *mṛdu* appear to be more relaxed, subdued intonations, and *madhyama* seems to be present for the sole purpose of describing a *svara* performed without any special inflection. The role of *āyatā* is not obvious, and it is mentioned only once; it may represent a slight lengthening of the note. Nārada further connects the two most important *śruti*s with the three Ṛgvedic accents in an equation that seems entirely natural and reinforces these tentative conclusions: the bright *śruti, dīptā,* is to be performed on both *udātta* (acute) and *svarita* (circumflex), while the soft *śruti, mṛdu,* is to be rendered on *anudātta* (grave).[97]

Accent is the last concept to be examined. Confusingly, the three accents used for the chanting of the *Ṛgveda* are also known as *svara*s, the third such set of *svara*s we have encountered in Nārada's phonetic manual.[98] Here we can draw upon the entire phonetic literature, including no less an authority than the grammarian Pāṇini, who referred to *udātta* as "high," *anudātta* as "low," and *svarita* as "a compound tone."[99] The authoritative *Ṛk-Prātiśākhya* describes the three accents in somewhat different terms:

*udātta* is "extended," *anudātta* is "relaxed," and *svarita* is "cast down" or "shaken."[100] *Udātta* and *anudātta* are precisely what their names suggest—an "elevated" and an "unelevated" tone; the problem arises with *svarita,* which is generally recited today at a higher level of pitch than the *udātta*.

J. F. Staal speculates that "an attempt might be made to explain this development by assuming that the original Vedic accent was not a musical accent but a stress accent."[101] This is a question that has still not been settled. J. E. B. Gray's interpretation provides some useful perspective on this and the related issues we have been considering: "[Pāṇini's] terms do not ensure any correct interpretation, however, since 'upwards' and 'downwards' have no settled meaning. . . . In such cases, then, one must resort to definition by saying that tension, hardness, and narrowness of the intrabuccal space are the factors which make a sound 'upwards.' . . . Relaxation, softness, and wideness of the intrabuccal space are the factors which make a sound 'downwards.'"[102]

This is a complex matter, and the proper interpretation of the three accents depends also upon such things as vowel length, sandhi, hiatus, closed or open syllables, nasality, aspiration, style of recitation, and the nature of the preceding and following accents. I do not see this as a "musical" issue, except in the very largest sense, but the influence of this habit of thinking in terms of three "tones," whether they were differentiated primarily in terms of pitch or stress, was pervasive in early Indian musical thought. The *Nāradīyaśikṣā* does little to resolve these questions, although several chapters are devoted to Ṛgvedic accentuation.[103] Its main contribution is yet another set of provocative equations: "*Niṣāda* and *gāndhāra* [arise from the] *udātta, ṛṣabha* and *dhaivata* from the *anudātta,* but the following have their origin in the *svarita: ṣadja, madhyama,* and *pañcama.*"[104] The resulting priorities are as follows; they may be compared to the general set of priorities inferred from the secular scale.[105]

| Vedic accents | *Svaras* of the secular scale |
|---|---|
| *udātta:* elevated | *ga* and *ni:* 3 and 7 |
| *svarita:* compound | *sa, ma,* and *pa:* 1, 4, and 5 |
| *anudātta:* unelevated | *ri* and *dha:* 2 and 6 |

What do these equations mean? The pitch compass and style of recitation heard today, even that of the "lute-throated" Nambudiri tradition of Kerala described in such meticulous detail by Gray and Staal, provide no firm grounds for fixing either the intervals between the three accents or their range, which varies from a minor third to a perfect fifth.[106] In no way, therefore, is it safe to draw any conclusions about their possible influence upon the structure of the secular scale, apart from the following: within the limited pitch compass associated with Ṛgvedic recitation, it is not difficult to conceive of three generalized "tones" in the sense of "region of voice"—clear enough in practice, but not completely differentiated in terms of pitch, intensity, timbre, and expenditure of breath. Such distinctions were both unnecessary and irrelevant within an oral tradition. It is only when using these tones as a model for a more "musical," pitched style that ears more attuned to this parameter would attempt to pick out finer gradations and distinctions and seek out concepts with which to represent these distinctions. In short, the concept of pitch is something that emerged from a multidimensional model of vocal sound, and it took some time to sort out.

The author of the *Nāradīyaśikṣā* was neither a towering intellect nor a brilliant innovator, but he too was trying to sort out what he heard. His passion for cataloging the many sounds of music took him farther than the descriptive techniques of his time permitted. He drew on a wide range of descriptors and formulated them as best he could in what must have seemed a natural arrangement:

| | | |
|---|---|---|
| *udātta* (elevated)/*dīptā* (bright)/*kruṣṭa* (aloud) | = | high/loud/bright/tense |
| *svarita* (compound)/*madhyama* (moderate) | = | intermediate |
| *anudātta* (unelevated)/*mṛdu* (soft)/*karuṇā* (mournful)/*mandra* (low) | = | low/soft/dull/lax |

The final step was to match these three "levels" with the relative strength and weakness, the stability and instability, that had become associated with the various degrees of the early modal system. But his equations sowed massive confusion for subsequent authors, whose general reaction was to endorse Nārada's statements without fully understanding the original terms of reference, and some of this confusion is still evident in Indian scholarship today. It is not often that we are accorded a glimpse of musical thought in such a formative stage. Nārada's manual records only a few of the first steps toward the systematic organization of pitch, perhaps long after these steps had been taken. But first steps are always the hardest.

## 4.6 Milieu

> We have drunk the Soma. We have become immortal. We have gone to the light. We have found the gods. . . . That drop, O Fathers, which, when drunk in our hearts, enters us mortals, itself immortal, to that Soma we would offer worship with an oblation.[107]

With these words a young trainee may have begun his working day. The life of a *sāmavedin* revolved around the *savana*s—the sacrificial pressings of the intoxicating liquid obtained from the soma plant. This plant is addressed as a deity in the Vedas and is the subject of 120 hymns in the *Ṛgveda,* including the entire ninth book.[108] The source of the juice, which was strained through a woolen filter into a wooden trough where it was mixed with water and milk, has not been convincingly identified, and its effects have been described as ranging from mildly intoxicating to hallucinogenic. The soma juice was regarded as the elixir of immortality when consumed by either gods or humans, and the soma oblations were viewed as solemn sacrifices by which the cosmic order (the *ṛta*) was maintained. In *RV* 9.74 the stalk of the plant is addressed as "pillar of the sky," "well-extended prop of the earth," and "navel of the *Ṛta*"—the *stambha* or *axis mundi* around which the entire cosmos revolves.[109] These epithets and the plant's intoxicating properties suggest some type of mushroom, but the evidence is inconclusive.[110]

Most of the phonetic manuals focused upon instructions for the *sāmavedin*'s official duties, but Nārada's *śikṣā* concludes with a set of homely verses offering practical advice on a variety of matters. From them we get a vivid picture of daily life punctuated by the sacrifices. The young student-priest is admonished to get up early, eat a healthy diet, keep his sinuses clear by inhaling the fumes of medicinal plants, clean his teeth with twigs of various plants, spend some time in daily meditation, attend to his studies, cultivate the right mental attitude, not linger over his meals, and avoid the company of women.[111] A misogynistic tone pervades these instructions, a tone not unknown in priestly circles: "Gambling, reading books, keeping company with actors and dancers, fondness for women, laziness, and sleep—these are the six obstacles to knowledge."[112]

Another recurrent theme in this section is the process of teaching and learning by which the sacred knowledge was transmitted orally. Knowledge obtained not from a teacher but from a book is as worthless as a woman illegitimately pregnant and as barren as an infertile woman, and knowledge obtained from an incompetent teacher brings evil consequences as surely as the bite of a serpent.[113] Five things are learned from one's teacher: how to begin the ceremonies, proper orientation by fixing the position of the scale syllables on the finger joints, the science of pronunciation, knowledge of the sacred texts, and skill in recitation.[114] The student-priest should not accept knowledge passively from a teacher but should dig it out of him, just as we obtain water from the earth.[115] And just as ants build up huge anthills with fine particles of dust, so should the pupil industriously build up knowledge.[116]

The sixth and seventh chapters of book 1 contain practical instructions for recitation. Chapter 1.6.1–2 refers to the practice of accompanying the Sāmavedic chant on an instrument known as the *gātravīṇā* (bodily vina). Some scholars have interpreted this as an actual instrument, but it seems more plausible that the verses draw an elaborate analogy between the vina and the human body, in which the body is symbolically fingered like a stringed instrument, as the chanter marks off the notes and syllable durations with various finger *mudrās*:

> The *gātraviṇā,* to which the *Sāma*-chanters sing, is equipped for the manifestation of the musical notes, indicated by the thumb and fingers. The two hands should [first] be held with fingers together and resting on the knees; the student should imitate his *guru,* his mind intent on knowledge. Having first uttered the syllable *Om* and then the threefold Great Utterances,[117] followed by the *Gāyatrī* stanza,[118] one should then begin the recitation. After having spread out all the fingers, one should establish the circle of *svaras* on them, and one should keep the thumb and fingers separated.[119]

The recitation would then proceed as described in §4.2.2, with the right thumb marking each of the *svaras* on the appropriate finger joint and the left hand reserved for the indication of prolonged, repeated, or connected syllables.

A later pair of verses presents a set of associations between the notes of the Sāmavedic scale and various regions of the body: "The region of *kruṣṭa* is the head, and that of *prathama,* the forehead; *dvitīya* is situated between the eyebrows, and *tṛtīya,* in the ears. The region of *caturtha* is declared to be the throat, while *mandra* is located in the chest; the region of the heart is ordained for the low *atisvāra.*"[120] This passage, however, seems not to refer to any scaling of bodily space by means of gestures but rather to the metaphoric locations for the resonance of the individual *svaras*.

Throughout these instructions for proper performance, the chanter is advised to cultivate self-control ("like a tortoise who has drawn his limbs together"), even pronunciation, and synchronization of the syllables and their accompanying gestures, and to avoid any distortion of the text or the notes. The transitions between syllables are to be rendered smoothly and precisely, yet without too obvious a connection, just as there is no visible line of division between shade and sunlight. The *sāmans* should be sung as smoothly as the path of a hawk circling in the sky. One should not attack the syllables with excessive force, nor with pressure of the tongue, nor too loudly, nor with a quivering voice. The syllables should be recited in the same manner that a tigress carries her cubs with her teeth, neither biting them nor holding them so loosely that they might fall. A chanter whose breath becomes faint at the end of a line is just as defective in recitation as is a beautiful woman reciting poetry to a deaf husband. All of these instructions refer specifically to the Sāmavedic chant, but one important chapter (1.3, which appears to be a later interpolation) sets forth the ten merits and fourteen defects of song, to which I shall return in chapter 11.[121]

Mythological and cosmological references occupy nearly one-third of the opening canto.[122] These verses include a ceremonial affirmation of Nārada's authority, a brief account of the evolution of chant, and an awesome reminder of the power of music and the fearful consequences of incorrect recitation. The three basic scales are related to the three worlds: earth, atmosphere, and heaven. But by far the most important topic is the complex set of relationships established between the seven *svara*s and the various colors, social classes, animal cries, bodily regions, sages, and deities (see table 8). A few sample verses will suggest the tone and style: "*Ṣaḍja* screams the peacock, but the bull roars *ṛṣabha;* goats bleat *gāndhāra,* and the crane shrieks *madhyama.* In the springtime the cuckoo whistles *pañcama,* but the horse utters *dhaivata,* and the elephant, *niṣāda.*"[123]

The cluster of ideas in these verses (musical notes, colors, social classes, and animal cries) is not random, and it demonstrates that mythology can pun. The keyword here is *varṇa* (cover, appearance), the first of the six standard topics of phonetic theory, used here in the special sense of individual sounds, vowels, letters, syllables, musical notes, and phonetic units of any kind. But the word *varṇa* covers an unusually wide semantic range, including color (as the "cover" or outward appearance of anything), social class (perhaps deriving originally from the contrasting skin tones of different ethnic groups), and the characteristic sounds of animals and birds.

What can be learned from the array of correspondences in table 8? I have already mentioned the equation which permits reconstruction of the degrees of the *Sāmaveda* scale (column 5) in relation to those of the secular scale (column 1).[124] We can also draw certain conclusions about the priority or relative strength of the various scale steps from the comparisons to social classes and deities, for which the ranking system was well established. We can also deduce something about preferences for the color spectrum, which in this case gravitate toward yellow,[125] and observe the common tendency in myth making to resort to repetitions or to a "mixed" category when it becomes necessary to fill out a group to a culturally significant number

Table 8 Correspondences to the Seven *Svaras*

| Svara | Dynasty 1.2.15–16 | Color 1.4.1–2 | Class[a] 1.4.3–4 | *Sāmasvara* 1.5.1–2 | Animal or Bird Sounds 1.5.3–4 | Bodily origin 1.5.5–6 | *Ṛṣi*[b] 1.5.12–14 | Deity 1.5.14–18 |
|---|---|---|---|---|---|---|---|---|
| Sa | gods | Lotus leaf | *brāhmaṇa* | *caturtha* | Peacock | Throat | Agni-fire | Brahmā |
| Ri | *ṛṣis* | Parrot yellow | *kṣatriya* | *tṛtīya* | Bull | Head | Brahmā-creator | Agni |
| Ga | *pitṛ*s (forefathers) | Gold | *vaiśya* or *śūdra* | *dvitīya* | Goat | Nose | Soma-moon | Divine Cow |
| Ma | *gandharva*s (celestial musicians) | Jasmine | *brāhmaṇa* | *prathama* | Crane | Chest | Viṣṇu-preserver | Brahmā |
| Pa | gods, *pitṛ*s, and *ṛṣis* | Dark | *brāhmaṇa* | *kruṣṭa* | Cuckoo | Chest, head, and throat | Nārada | Soma |
| Dha | the whole host of beings | Saffron | *kṣatriya* | *mandra* | Horse | Forehead | Tumburu | Soma |
| Ni | *yakṣa*s (attendant demigods) | Multicolored | *vaiśya* or *śūdra* | *atisvāra* | Elephant | All registers combined | Tumburu | Āditya (sun) |

[a] The ranking of the four classes (*varṇa*s) is *brāhmaṇa* (priestly class), *kṣatriya* (warrior class), *vaiśya* (merchant class), and *śūdra* (menial class).

[b] See Margaret Stutley and James Stutley, *A Dictionary of Hinduism: Its Mythology, Folklore and Development 1500 B.C.–A.D. 1500* (London: Routledge and Kegan Paul, 1977), 251–52.

(such as seven): *niṣāda,* in particular, seems to have no independent identity in several of the columns. The details of this elaborate system varied from treatise to treatise, but the overall scheme has become a fixture in Indian musical lore.

Just as the monastics of the European Middle Ages went about their daily routines surrounded by the images and rhythms of the Scriptures and the liturgical year, so did the Vedin live and work in the midst of a fully developed mythology and worldview. He saw the world as a network of mythical threads that connected the sounds he uttered to the structure of the universe, the gods, his ancestors, a host of other creatures, the colors he saw, the natural sounds that he heard, and the social structure in which he lived—a world of symbolic resonance.

# FIVE
# THEATER

For ancient sages consider drama
the visible and pacific sacrifice of the gods;
its two modes are shown by Śiva himself
in the body he divides with Umā;
actions of men, born of nature's three strands,
are there displayed in many moods—
and though men have many different tastes,
the play is the one delight of all.

Kālidāsa, *Mālavikā and Agnimitra*[1]

## 5.1 Introduction

In the opening act of *Mālavikā and Agnimitra,* the earliest of Kālidāsa's three surviving plays, the dancing master Gaṇadāsa reflects with satisfaction on the auspicious nature of his profession: his lines provide an appropriate entry into the colorful world of the early Indian musical theater. The poet has managed to work several themes into this brief passage—the divine origin of drama and its roots in religious ritual, the opposition of stereotypical masculine and feminine performance styles as symbolized by Śiva's androgynous nature,[2] the Sāṅkhya concept of the "three strands" (that is, the three *guṇa*s: illumination, passion, and inertia) from which all material substance is woven,[3] and the final reference to the theory of *rasa,* the cornerstone of later Indian aesthetics.[4] I shall reserve a full examination of the idea of *rasa* for chapter 11, but its influence will be evident throughout the following pages. In brief, *rasa* is the dominant emotional tone that arises during the performance of a play. The reference to Śiva is a conventional tribute to the divine dancer in recognition of his role as special patron of the theater—not merely because of his identification with the performing arts (as Naṭarāja, Lord of the Dance)[5] but, more importantly, because Śiva's eight forms encompass all the elemental components of nature.[6] The significance of the drama therefore lies in its ability to represent the entire phenomenal world.

To enter the world of the classical Indian theater is to enter a completely different milieu than the world of the Vedic priest, although he too was one of the stock characters of the Sanskrit drama (and often treated with no great reverence). A play was offered to the cultivated and pleasure-loving members of the Gupta court as a royal gift and a feast for the senses, depicting worldly life in all its richness and intensity and in a range of moods that ran from despair to farce. Although the Indian drama, like many other world theater traditions, is thought to derive from ancient religious ceremonies and flourished originally in open fields and temple corridors,[7] its grand climax and locus classicus came at the brilliant court of Chandragupta II (ca. A.D. 375–415) in Pāṭaliputra, at the confluence of rivers in the Ganges basin. The tradition was well established by the time of the Buddhist author Aśvaghoṣa (first century B.C.–second century A.D.) and continued to prosper throughout the rest of the first millennium, during which time it seems to have been the only thriving genre of dramatic literature in the civilized world. Approximately forty plays have survived, including such works as *The Vision of Vāsavadattā* (Bhāsa, ca. A.D. 350), *The Little Clay Cart* (Śūdraka, third to sixth century A.D.?), and especially *Śākuntala* (Kālidāsa, fl. A.D. 400?), a play that Goethe admired and took as a partial model for his *Faust.* Many of the extant plays are readily available in excellent translations, accompanied by an abundance of critical studies, but live performances are rare today.[8]

And not without reason: few theater traditions demand as much from their audiences. Spectators were expected to know in detail the repertoire of stylized gestures and literary allusions with which subtle meanings could be communicated and to respond with appropriate emotional empathy. This is not to suggest that ordinary people would not attend and enjoy a performance, but their satisfaction would be of a different kind. This was not theater for the masses but theater on an intimate scale in which all the participants would under ideal conditions be "at heart" with one another.[9] To set the stage, I quote from J. A. B. van Buitenen's description:

> The theater itself would be a simple affair: a pavilion or a raised platform with four pillars at the corners supporting a marquee, with a curtain in the rear that was split in the middle. On this simple stage all kinds of variations could be made, but the bare floor provided all that a play essentially needed. The color of the back curtain was important: it would indicate to the audience what mood might be expected. . . . Props were not really needed, though on occasion they might be provided. The pride of the actor was to *show* what he was doing, through elegant gesticulation. . . . Generally, the occasion would be a grand one, worthy of being celebrated by a dramatic pageant, and likely to attract a

> sufficient number of the learned and cultured for an audience to be formed. . . . the Indian drama would often be performed early in the morning, when cultural and religious events are apt to start. . . . The audience before whom all this unfolded was highly critical . . . and all educated men would have, securely lodged in their prodigious memories, hundreds and thousands of stanzas against which a playwright's poetry could be weighed. . . . All of them were able to retain in their minds an adjective that came at the beginning of a stanza, until it was finally wedded to its noun at the end of it. In other words, the pleasure felt by a member of the audience at a play was as much in his own erudition that made him capable of following it as it was in the play itself.[10]

This is no doubt an overstatement. Cynics can rightly point out the inherent contradictions between a highly refined dramatic tradition, where the first aim was to please the connoisseur, and the demands of a living theater. Private theater, whatever its merits, loses much of its vital force when it overstays the social conditions it was created to reflect, to call upon Abhinavagupta's favorite image of a "spotless mirror."[11] But the staying power of the Indian theater may in part be attributed to the fact that it depicted, albeit in ideal terms, a society with roots sunk much deeper than the floating pleasures of court life. It cannot be denied, however, that if the drama was to survive in such a cultural setting, its priority task was to meet the requirements laid down by a learned elite—requirements for refined poetic diction, polished delivery, highly stylized gesture, expression of lofty cultural ideals, meticulous attention to innumerable production details, and (not least of all) the highest standards in musical composition and performance.

We know little about the formative stages of the Indian theater, although A. B. Keith points out a number of contributory influences: passages in dialogue format in some of the Vedic hymns, dramatic adaptations of the great epics, and the possible influence of the New Attic Comedy (*ca.* 340–260 B.C.) after Alexander's expedition to the subcontinent.[12] The genre had stabilized by the time of the earliest surviving plays and had already acquired a substantial body of dramatic criticism as compiled and codified in the *Nāṭyaśāstra,* the work that will be the focus of this chapter. To the general remarks in chapter 1 on the problems of dating I can add only that much of the material contained in this treatise must have been formulated during the final pre-Christian centuries, but that its present literary form cannot have been achieved earlier than the first or second century A.D. What *can* be said is that there is a remarkable harmony between the precepts of *BN* and the texts of the extant plays, and I shall have cause to refer to this work often in later chapters.

Remnants of the classical theater survive in a large number of regional and popular theater traditions throughout the subcontinent, but nowhere with greater persistence than in many of the dramatic and dance genres of Kerala, on the Malabar coast of southwest India.[13] It may not be without significance that the most accurate and complete manuscript of *BN* is written in the Malayalam script of Kerala. Revivals of the classical plays are still presented today, but while their emotional content and plots still strike resonances when presented to a contemporary audience, their complex literary style and mixture of archaic languages render access difficult for all but the literati. The Sanskrit drama can no longer be said to represent a living tradition in the sense of the complete and uninhibited surrender that was expected of its original audience.

James Brandon provides some perspective on the waning years of the Indian theater:

> The performing tradition for Sanskrit plays maintained itself from perhaps several centuries before Christ until around the twelfth century—that is, for a period of twelve hundred to fifteen hundred years. In the fragile and ever-changing world of theater this is a very long time indeed: Javanese shadow theater goes back a thousand years or more; the Nō theater of Japan is entering its seventh century of continuous performance; the classical tradition of performing Greek tragedies lasted perhaps five hundred years; and the Elizabethan theatrical tradition, within which Shakespeare wrote, ended after a mere seventy-five years. Certainly the fact that the performing conventions of the Sanskrit stage were highly codified and were committed to writing at an early date helped to stabilize and preserve the tradition. But even this long life eventually came to an end. The story is not an unusual one: a culture in decay, and a performing art, uprooted from its social context, gradually vanishing. . . . Support for theater performances declined because courts were pillaged and burned during wars of conquest that began in the tenth century and continued for hundreds of years. New Islamic rulers shunned the classic plays, for they were steeped in Hindu philosophy and mythology. Also, according to orthodox Islamic belief, it is blasphemous to portray the human figure, as the actor does in the theater. Sanskrit ceased to be a living language. . . . In time, the troupes of players who embodied the performing tradition dispersed into the countryside or disbanded. The time came

> when no troupe existed to pass on to the next generation the full, living tradition of Sanskrit theater.[14]

Music and the theater are natural partners and close associates in many world cultures; music was an essential component of the theater of Attic Greece, well before the rise of the Indian drama. But few traces of this association are recorded in the writings of the Greek philosophers, the historians, or the theorists of music. The details of the musical system, its rhythmic patterns, its scales, and its formal structures were set down independently and described in abstract terms that tell us next to nothing about the role of music in actual theatrical situations. It is clear that the theater was only one milieu among many within which music flourished, and that music was not assigned the privileged position it held in the world of Indian theater.

In addition to this natural partnership between music, dance, and the stage, there are a number of reasons why the Sanskrit theater exerted a special influence upon musical thought and practice. First and of overriding importance, the body of dramatic theory and criticism provides more detailed information on the musical system and its application in performance than is available for any other ancient culture. Second, the demand for incidental music, much of which had to be produced spontaneously or on short notice, led eventually to a tradition featuring improvisation. And third, because the many components of dramatic theory (in terms of plot, action, and formal structure) have developed into independent models for musical structure, it is possible to identify certain archetypal formal patterns which pervade the performing arts.[15] Fourth, the special relationship that has always existed between Indian music and dance may be traced to their ritual pairing in the preliminary dramatic ceremonies, if not to the popular rituals that preceded the rise of the theater tradition. And fifth, the standard repertoire of emotional states and expressive styles (and especially the heroic masculine and delicately erotic feminine stereotypes) set the emotional tone for the expressive range of later Indian music and laid the foundation for the entire system of musical values.[16] In the last three of these aspects, Indian music may well have developed apart from the theater, with deeper roots than the literary tradition I have been describing, but it was within the context of the Sanskrit drama and dramatic theory that musical doctrines received their definitive form and were molded into conceptual patterns that still resist all pressures for substantive change. Westerners often find it difficult to understand the relationship of dependency that mutually informs and binds together the arts of India, but that dependency is one of the hallmarks of traditional Indian culture—within which anything other than the evolution of the performing arts along close, parallel tracks is inconceivable.

The aim of the classical drama was not only propitiation of the gods but also cultural instruction—instruction in duties, behavior, myth, and feeling. Quite apart from its intrinsic excellence as a body of literature and a source of colorful entertainment, the Indian theater was at once a conveyor of social values, a reinforcement of cultural tradition, and a genre of ritual that provided continuing testimony to the numerous intellectual strands that connected the spectacle on stage with the entire fabric of belief. In the opening chapter of *BN,* Bharata himself addresses the assembly of demons who have threatened to disrupt the performance:

> In drama there is no exclusive representation of you demons or of the gods. Drama is a representation of the emotional states of the threefold universe. It includes concerns of duty, play, material gain, peace, mirth, war, desire, and death. It teaches duty to those who violate duty, desire to those addicted to love; it reprimands those who behave rudely, promotes restraint in those who are disciplined; it gives courage to cowards, energy to heroes; it enlightens fools and gives learning to learned men.[17]

But lest we conclude that the sole purpose of the drama was to correct improper behavior and to reinforce meritorious character traits, Bharata closes his massive treatise with the following reminder: "Among all kingly duties, the presentation of a play has been deemed the most fruitful; the gift of a dramatic spectacle is esteemed highly among all gifts. For the gods are never as pleased when worshipped with garlands and fragrances as they are pleased with the auspicious performance of a play. He who properly cherishes both *gāndharva*[18] and the drama attains [at last] the happy and meritorious state of the blessed lords."[19]

## 5.2 The *Nāṭyaśāstra*

The remainder of this chapter will be devoted to a survey of the *Nāṭyaśāstra,* with particular attention to the sections on music; these amount to approximately fifteen hundred verses, about one-fourth of the treatise. I shall examine the role of music and dance in both the preliminary rituals and the play proper and proceed with an analysis of the sections dealing with musical instruments (*vādya*). Two topics of overriding importance will be reserved for fuller discussion and analysis in later chapters: the organization of pitch (*svara*) and rhythm (*tāla*).[20]

It is no exaggeration to claim, as V. Raghavan has claimed, that the *Nāṭya-*

*śāstra* "is the most elaborate treatise on drama and its production ever written."[21] In its thirty-seven chapters and ca. six thousand verses this work covers in minute detail the widest possible range of topics pertaining to the composition and production of a play and the appropriate audience response. Bharata's concept of drama can be accurately described as a *Gesamtkunstwerk*—a composite art form that transmits the playwright's message by means of a rich blend of poetry, prose, declamation, song, acting, mime, dancing, instrumental music, costume, and makeup. Only the art of scenic design was neglected, leaving the physical surroundings to the imagination of the audience and the descriptive passages in the poetic text.

It is clear from Bharata's account of the origin of drama in the opening chapter that the art of the theater is no trivial entertainment: he describes the knowledge of the theater as a fifth Veda—an audible and visible object of diversion for gods and humans alike and a summary of all learning.[22] Its components are derived from the original four Vedas: from the *Ṛgveda,* recitation; from the *Yajurveda,* acting, gesture, and narrative dance; from the *Sāmaveda,* song; and from the *Atharvaveda,* emotion.[23] Even the author's name has become a symbolic statement: as Raghavan explains, "the word *bharata* also means actor, and is taken as signifying in its three constituent syllables, the three arts of drama, music, and dance based [respectively] on emotion [*bhāva*], melody [*rāga*], and rhythm [*tāla*]. . . . [in sum] a total theater."[24]

A brief summary of the treatise will provide the context for the sections on music. The mythical, physical, and ceremonial foundations of the theater are described in the first five chapters. After Bharata's explanation of the origin of drama, instructions are given for constructing, purifying, and dedicating a theater. This line of thought leads naturally to the ritual preliminaries with which each performance is to be introduced and the style of nonrepresentational dance employed in these ceremonies. Within the chapter on nonrepresentational dance (chap. 4) we find some valuable information on the role of song, drumming, and instrumental music in the opening ceremonies.

Bharata's themes in this opening sequence of chapters are sacrifice, purification, and initiation: the theater is a sacred place, the stage is an altar, the actor is a celebrant, and the performance is an offering. Kapila Vatsyayan elaborates:

> Each single phase, whether it is the consecration of the earth, or the adoption of a particular ground plan for the theater, or the symbolic placing of the different deities, or the oblations . . . is designed to correspond to an altar of the vedic sacrifice. . . . Only he who has purified his body and kept his senses under

> control is capable of consecrating the playhouse. Many regional dance forms which are still performed today in India . . . rigorously observe these preliminary rites before a performance. These include fasting, the consecration of the ground, the installation of a pole, and lastly, the consecration of a pitcher of water. The human being who performs these becomes an "initiate," a special person for the duration of the event, and the physical space . . . acquires a new meaning. . . . it is clear that the rites of the stage are indeed a continuation of the rites and rituals of the different sacrifices described in the *Vedas* and the *Śatapatha Brāhmaṇa.*[25]

With chapter 6 the author begins an important new line of thought—emotion (*rasa*) and the various means by which it is communicated: facial expressions, gestures, poses, footwork, patterns of group movement, and ways of walking across the stage (imitating, for example, the gait of an animal, a child, a drunk, a cripple, or a eunuch). In chapter 13 (on the different gaits) there are some brief but informative remarks on rhythm, tempo, and drumming. But the nucleus of this section is the exposition of *rasa* in chapters 6 and 7, the earliest and most authoritative statement of this central topic in Indian aesthetic theory.[26]

Chapter 14 is a brief interlude (seventy-eight verses) describing some generalities of theatrical performance: the division of the stage into specific zones, each with symbolic meaning, the proper procedure for entrances and exits, regional mannerisms and preferences, the various performance styles and their implementation in different types of plays. Chapter 15 begins a set of six chapters on the composition of poetic texts, including such subjects as grammar, recitation, prose and verse, metrics, figures of speech, diction, the *guṇa*s and *doṣa*s (merits and demerits) of poetry, the use of language (Sanskrit and the various vernaculars, or Prakrits), and a detailed description of the ten major types of plays. Of these, chapter 19 (on modes of address, enunciation, and intonation) contains some interesting material pertaining to music which has not been sufficiently studied.

Dramatic presentation and expression is the subject of chapters 21–27, and this sequence of chapters is of particular importance for dramatic theory. The author returns here to the line of thought introduced in the *rasa* chapter, but his concern now is for practical application: the emotional content of a play, how to construct a proper dramatic plot, development of the central emotion by means of various situations and the interaction of different types of characters, and how meaning is conveyed through the appropriate style of recitation, costume, makeup, dramatic characterization, and the coordination of speech, posture, and gesture. The final chapter in this sequence deals with success (*siddhi*) in dramatic production and how it is to be achieved and measured: criteria for evaluating a play, the qualifications required of the sensitive audience and the competent critic, the appropriate time of day for producing various plays, and how a performance can fail.[27]

With chapters 28–33, Bharata introduces the subject of music. His chapters are arranged in an interesting way: according to the different types of instruments in the theater ensemble. After brief chapters on character types, casting, and the duties of each member of a theater company, the final chapter returns to the subject with which Bharata began his compendious work: the mythical origin of drama, how the members of the theatrical profession fell under a divine curse, and how the drama has been redeemed through the efforts of Bharata. The moral is clear: a performance that observes the precepts laid down in the *Nāṭyaśāstra* will not only please—it will be auspicious.

The chapters on music are as follows: chapter 28 (151 verses) introduces the subject of instrumental music and includes a comprehensive exposition of the system of pitch.[28] Each of the four classes of musical instruments—stringed, hollow, solid, and covered—becomes the subject of one of the subsequent chapters, with two additional chapters on songs and singing. To elaborate, chapter 29 (156 verses) contains material of particular relevance to the vina player, although—as in later chapters—there is greater emphasis on the musical system than on instrumental technique per se. Thus Bharata takes the opportunity to outline the melodic modes (the *jāti*s) appropriate for various emotional states and situations, the four melodic contours (*varṇa*s), the thirty-three ornaments (*alaṅkāra*s), various types and combinations of vina strokes (the *dhātu*s), some remarks on the performance styles, and even the rhythmic outlines of certain musical structures.[29] Chapter 30 (on the hollow instrument, that is, the transverse flute) is a brief chapter of thirteen verses with instructions for modulating the pitch of the flute through shaken, half-holed, and fully open notes.

In contrast, chapter 31 (on the solid instruments, that is, the small bronze cymbals used to signal and control the rhythmic cycle or *tāla*) is a massive chapter of 502 verses which provides the author with the opportunity to lay out the entire system of musical rhythm and to outline the various ritual forms as delineated by the prescribed sequences of hand motions.[30] It is impossible to overstate the importance of this chapter for early rhythmic theory, and it is safe to say that nowhere else in the ancient or medieval world is there to be found such a comprehensive and detailed exposition of the theory and practice of musical rhythm.

The plot songs (the *dhruvās*) are described in the 525 verses of chapter 32. Three aspects of the songs are emphasized: their conventional subject matter, their appropriateness to various dramatic situations, and their metrical structure. The chapter is swollen by the inclusion of many samples of text, from single lines to complete stanzas of considerable length.[31] It concludes with some brief remarks on how the songs are to be accompanied and the desirable qualities a singer should demonstrate.[32] Chapter 33 (on the covered instruments, that is, the drums, a total of 301 verses) concludes the sequence of chapters on music. It is more self-contained than any of the previous chapters and includes virtually everything pertaining to the drummer's profession—from selecting the hide and making the drum to the strokes and rhythmic patterns.

Before we explore the uses of music before and during a play and the roles of the different instruments, it will be useful to consider briefly the textual tradition of the *Nāṭyaśāstra* and the obstacles that hinder our full understanding of this work. Despite its impressive length and the multitude of details it contains, the *Nāṭyaśāstra* is less than crystal clear in its exposition of many aspects of the ancient musical system. This is partly because of the condition of the manuscripts and the different recensions of the text. A second reason for the frequent obscurity of meaning lies in the habits of Indian scholarship and the conventions of exposition which dictated that the maximum amount of information should be set forth in as concise a format as possible, on the premise that a written exposition needs to do no more than call to mind material which will already have been committed to memory in far greater detail; it is an index, as it were, to the contents of one's mind.[33] As one consequence, the treatise, like the many which were to follow, is full of lists; and in these long lists of technical terms and categories, many of the items appear only by name or accompanied by the briefest and most cryptic of definitions. Other fields of study fared no better, and it was understood that what was left unclarified in the early literature remained for later scholars to explicate, often many centuries later. By that time the original tradition may have undergone considerable change or may even have died out. And despite their virtuoso command of the tools of linguistic reconstruction and comparative textual analysis, many—perhaps most—of the commentators lacked expertise in the technical subject under investigation and were therefore unable to provide insight gleaned from practical experience. For all the wealth of information in *BN,* there remains much that cannot be interpreted with any certainty, and therefore any supplementary material represents a source of potential clarification.

Two such sources are particularly important for this work: a short contemporary treatise entitled *Dattilam* (*D*) and the commentary *Abhinavabhāratī* (*AB*) by the eleventh-century Kashmir author Abhinavagupta.[34] The former covers only two of the topics set forth in *BN* (pitch and rhythm, arguably the two most important topics from a musician's viewpoint), but it does so in great detail and with considerable clarity. The value of *D,* which cannot have been written or compiled at a much later date, is that while differing in many details of presentation and wording, it still substantiates the doctrines of *BN* to such a degree that it is possible to reconstruct the main outlines of the early musical tradition with considerable confidence and to make critical comparisons of various topics by examining parallel passages.

Both Bharata and Dattila have been well represented by quotations in subsequent treatises on music and the theater, but the single most important source of further elucidation is Abhinavagupta's great commentary. It is difficult to estimate the relative proportions of Bharata's original text and the text of *AB.* The manuscript sources for *AB* are if anything more corrupt and in greater disarray than those of *BN,* but *AB* is much longer—perhaps two or three times as long. Abhinavagupta wrote at a time when the musical theater tradition was in decline, but he evidently based his commentary on his own experience with a living tradition, and his razor-sharp analyses and explanations have illuminated many obscure passages. Some of his explanations must surely be incorrect or applicable to a later stage in dramatic praxis, but more importantly, his searching discussions have opened up new lines of interpretation and provided analytic tools with which to pry out some of the meanings of the original text.

In his commentary to chapter 32 of *BN,* Abhinavagupta expounds the many distinctions between the two main musical genres—*gāndharva* and *gāna.*[35] As he understood it, the term *gāndharva* was applied in two distinct senses. In a general sense, it signifies the whole art of music (that is, the art that is pleasing to the celestial musicians, the *gandharvas*).[36] In a more technical sense, it signifies the special genre of ritual music prescribed for the preliminary ceremonies of the ancient theater. The genre known as *gāna* includes the incidental music performed during the play.[37] I will now focus on the dramatic setting within which these two genres were practiced; the melodic, rhythmic, and formal constraints of the *gāndharva* repertoire will provide the subject matter for chapters 7–9.

## 5.3 The Preliminary Rituals

When we think of the masterpieces of world drama—*Prometheus Bound, Hamlet, Sotoba Komachi,* or *Śākuntala*—what first comes to mind is the text. And rightly so, for the text remains our most tangible piece of evidence. When we are lucky enough to witness a classical play in modern performance, we can begin to appreciate the myriad details of staging, movement, and timing that are required to animate the text, and the words themselves shrink to somewhat less than 100 percent of our concept of the play. In all likelihood we will still remain unaware of many of the other technical details that contribute to the total spectacle if the director, designer, and lighting director have done their job.

If we regard the early Indian drama primarily as a text, we will get no more than a faint impression of the elaborate preliminary rituals. The formal text of a play will generally begin with the opening benediction and continue with the director's address to the spectators. This excerpt from Śūdraka's *Little Clay Cart* is typical:

> BENEDICTION
>
> May Śiva's Meditation favor thee . . .
> And may the throat of the Blue-Throated God,
> Dark as a thundercloud upon which flashes
> The lightning streak of Gaurī's arm, protect thee!
>
> *After the Benediction enter the Director.*
>
> DIRECTOR: No more of this tiresome waste of time that'll only wear thin our audience's curiosity! I prostrate myself before you gentlemen and beg to announce to you that we have decided to stage a Phantasy for you, which is entitled *The Little Clay Cart.* The poet, of course, was a King whose steps had the poise of an elephant, whose eyes the light of a cakora bird's, whose face the beauty of the full moon, King Śūdraka, stalwart leader of the twiceborn, celebrated poet, profound man of character![38]

But the benediction and director's address are only two among nineteen separate components prescribed for the ritual prologue (the *pūrvaraṅga*), specifically, the thirteenth and nineteenth items. No doubt these preliminaries varied with each new production, or (to a lesser degree) with different performances of the same production, but the evidence indicates that they were planned and executed with meticulous attention to detail—much more so in fact than the actual performance these ceremonies were designed to introduce. The same is true of the music. Most of the available information on the structure and style of the early theater music pertains to the ceremonial music of the *pūrvaraṅga.* The reasons are given by Abhinavagupta in his explanation of the special features of *gāndharva:* the genre of ritual music, unlike the incidental music, was fixed in all aspects of its structure—melodic, rhythmic, and formal. The musical elements dominated the text, and the aim of the genre was *adrṣṭa phala* ("unseen benefit"), not the immediate pleasure of the spectators.[39] The *pūrvaraṅga* was, in a word, a sacrifice: a religious ceremony designed to propitiate the presiding deities, to purify both the performers and the stage, and to lead the audience step by step from the sacred plane of the opening ceremonies into the mundane world depicted in the play.

In the literature of music it is typical to find genres of sacred or ceremonial music recorded more faithfully than secular, everyday music. The monastic authors of the European Middle Ages set down with fidelity the regulations for the music of the church, but relatively little is known about the secular music of their age. It follows then that the special import of the preliminary ceremonies lent an urgency to Indian authors' efforts to spell out the full and precise details. We know that the ritual was sometimes both elaborate and prolonged, from remarks such as the director's reference to "this tiresome waste of time"—a remark that carries intentional irony and an indication that we are now in the mundane world of the play. It is clear that the preliminaries, if designed and executed with zeal, could easily overshadow the following play.

I shall briefly describe the ritual. The participants may be divided into three groups: the director (*sūtradhāra*) and his two assistants, each of whom is also assigned a role in the play; a musical ensemble consisting of singers, drummers, and instrumentalists; and a small group of female dancers, usually four. The musicians, whose numbers could be augmented for special occasions, sat in a niche at the rear of the stage, flanked by the two doors through which all entrances and exits were made, in the following general formation:

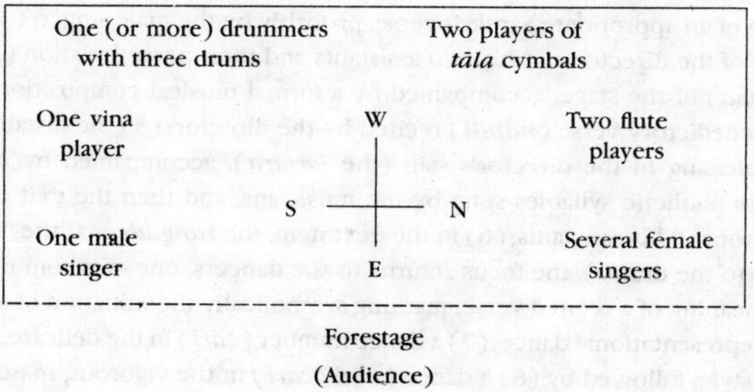

The first nine items of the *pūrvaraṅga* are assigned to the members of the musical ensemble and are performed behind a curtain drawn across the front of the musicians' enclosure. In simpler surroundings, we can assume that the curtain was held by two stage assistants, as is the practice in many genres of Indian theater today. The ceremonies begin with drumbeats summoning the audience into the theater; a carpet is spread out for the musicians, and the instruments are carried in and set in place by assistants. The musicians then enter and take their places; they perform a short vocalise, and then the various instruments are tuned. The instrumentalists then practice a set of strokes and run through the musical gamut on their instruments. Next the entire ensemble rehearses a rhythmic exercise, and finally a formal composition is performed. The central principle is that each stage of the proceedings—from the relative informalities of stage preparation, entrance, and tuning to the formalities of notes, scales, rhythms, and finally an entire composition—is regarded as auspicious, and thus each of the prescribed items is introduced as a separate link in a chain of ritual actions that concludes with the emergence of formalized music.[40] After this, the entire sequence is repeated, this time *as* music. Once this has been accomplished, the curtain is drawn, the musicians are revealed, and the focus of attention shifts to the forestage. The action progresses from the unseen to the seen.

This sequence of musical numbers obviously may have been performed with some dispatch or in a more leisurely manner (ranging perhaps between five and twenty minutes), but the greater part of the prologue was still to come. Ten additional components bring the ritual to a conclusion: (1) a song of praise to the gods (the *gītavidhi*) performed by the musical ensemble, accompanying an elaborate dance routine in which one after another of the female dancers enters, performs a solo dance, and then joins a group dance with those who entered previously; (2) the *utthāpana,* a recitation of an appropriate Sanskrit verse, probably by the male singer; (3) the entry of the director and his two assistants and their perambulation (*parivartana*) of the stage, accompanied by a formal musical composition; (4) the benedictory verse (*nāndī*) recited by the director; (5) the installation and blessing of the director's staff (the *jarjara*), accompanied by meaningless phonetic syllables sung by the musicians, and then the exit of the director and his assistants; (6) in the next item, the *raṅgadvāra* (the "doorway" to the drama), the focus returns to the dancers, one of whom mimes the meaning of a recited verse, marking symbolically the initiation of acting and representational dance; (7) a dance number (*cārī*) in the delicate, feminine style; followed by (8) a dance (*mahācārī*) in the vigorous, masculine style, with longer extensions of arms and legs; (9) a second entry (*trigata,* "threesome") of the director and his assistants (one of whom is the jester in the play), no longer symbolic figures but now in their dual roles as members of the theatrical troupe (each with individual responsibilities and well-defined qualifications)[41] and as characters in the play, moving about the stage informally while carrying on a witty conversation about the play, unaccompanied by any music; and finally (10) the director's address to the spectators. Only the benediction and the director's address were considered to be a part of the dramatic poem; the remaining items were the responsibility of the producer, and while some musical numbers were composed for a specific occasion, others could be drawn from a standard stock of melodies, drum patterns, poetic texts, and dance movements. Much would depend on the demands of the patron, his financial backing, and the performance circumstances. Certain nonmusical numbers, especially the entertaining *trigata,* were often improvised to suit the occasion and sprinkled with local references and topical humor, but the musical numbers, especially the ensembles, must have been rehearsed to the teeth.

Each musical number in the sequence was a formal composition, chosen from among the many types of pieces whose rhythmic and formal schemes are outlined in the *tāla* chapter of *BN.*[42] I emphasize the word "outlined," because these valuable descriptions stop short of a complete performance score. The treatise provides an enormous amount of information on the underlying rhythmic patterns and structures, the hand gestures with which the rhythmic structure was made manifest and kept under control, the tempo and timing of all aspects of the performance, the general performance style, conventions of accompaniment, the subject matter of the verses that were sung or recited, the metrical structure of the text, and whether a song includes vocables or consists entirely of meaningful text; but these descriptions do not go far enough to permit reconstruction of the tunes or melodic rhythms. And similarly, while *BN* provides detailed descriptions of the inventory of poses, gestures, foot movements, and the general dance styles from which a particular performance would draw, the individual choreographic decisions remained to be made. Each specific emotional state could be recognized by its own appropriate music—melodic phrases, rhythmic patterns, and characteristic ornaments—as well as by an array of appropriate poses, movements, gestures, facial expressions, styles of makeup, and costume colors. It is debatable to what extent even the most informed modern reconstruction can recreate the ancient tradition of performance, but happily this is not deterring Indian scholars today. The extent to which a competent and historically accurate modern performance might fail to match the original is probably less than the variation between one ancient production and another.

The *parivartana* of the director and his assistants merits some special attention. Entrances and exits are often among the most spectacular effects in the theater, but their entrance is particularly impressive: one assistant carries white flowers, the other a golden jar of water, and the director himself carries the *jarjara*—the symbolic staff with which Indra scattered the demons. All three are clothed in white and have already performed a purificatory ritual backstage. They proceed to establish the center of the stage with an oblation to Brahmā, and the staff is raised as a symbol of the primeval sacrificial pillar and world axis. In close triangular formation the three proceed to each of the four corners of the stage, saluting and propitiating the guardian deities of the four directions. These ceremonies are a rich treasury of material for the anthropologist, invoking ancient rites of fertility, initiation, purification, sacrifice, and orientation in cosmic space. They also begin a series of transitions: from mythical to secular time, from the abstract to the particular, from inchoate to organized musical sound, and from cosmic space to the terrestrial plane of activity.[43] The perambulation of the three is accompanied by a composition in which the number of beats, the hand gestures, the number of rhythmic cycles, and the progressively increasing tempo are clearly specified, and to which the movements of the trio must be precisely synchronized. The formal designs of the accompanying music were intended to provide a counterpoint to the geometric salutation of the zones of the stage and to underscore the increasing tension and speed of the music.

Two additional features of the *pūrvaraṅga* require some explanation. First, meaningless syllables (*śuṣkākṣara*s) play several vital roles in the ceremonies: as introductions to songs and dance numbers, as interludes during the director's perambulation, and especially at the symbolic moment of the blessing of the *jarjara.* There is an important parallel here to the ceremonies of the Roman Catholic mass and other ritual traditions: just as music (and indeed time itself) is suspended during the elevation of the host, so in the theater ritual is meaningful text replaced by pure sound, untinged by any secular associations and unencumbered by any limitations of meaning. And second, the conventional feminine and masculine stereotypes are set before the audience in the two successive dances *cārī* and *mahācārī,* making it clear that the following drama is a form of social instruction and a celebration of human behavior as it ought to be; it is a drama that seeks to reinforce the established social order and reaffirm its harmony. In this respect the classical Indian theater is a drama not of conflict but of reconciliation.

The preliminary ritual I have been describing is of course a general plan. It surely must have varied depending upon the occasion, the patron, the audience, the location and size of the theater, and the type of play that followed. The usual presiding deity was Śiva, and the style of dancing employed in the opening numbers of the *pūrvaraṅga* was the vigorous style of dance known as *tāṇḍava* (from Taṇḍu, the first human to receive the doctrines of Śiva from the Rudras),[44] a fertility dance symbolizing the cosmic dance of Śiva with its alternating periods of creation and destruction. Thus, each of the dancers might mime one of Śiva's conventional aspects, perhaps in his pose as Lord of the Dance (Naṭarāja), poised on one leg in the midst of a circle of flame and holding various symbols in his several arms. This masculine style of expression was entirely appropriate for the heroic romance, but an alternate style of ritual (known as the Lāsya) was prescribed for the many plays featuring the delicately erotic feminine sentiment.

The Lāsya style of *pūrvaraṅga* is best described as an integrated sequence of ten solo numbers for a female dancer, unified by a poetic content that runs a gamut of conventional literary topics pertaining to a woman's emotional life. Most of the numbers were accompanied by the musical ensemble, and the solo dancer was also required to recite appropriate Sanskrit verses and to mime with expressive gestures the content of various songs sung by one of the female singers. In all probability the Lāsya sequence was taken into the theater from an earlier, independent dramatic genre. It is often compared to the popular *Bhāṇa* monodrama, in which a single actor represents a number of different characters by means of stock dramatic conventions: different speaking voices, imaginary conversations, repetition of unheard lines, and offstage voices. The Lāsya genre may also be an ancestor of the conventional sequence of danced and mimed numbers in a modern Bharata Nāṭyam recital. Because of its gentler, playful, and more amorous style, the Lāsya type of *pūrvaraṅga* was presented as an offering to Śiva's consort, Pārvatī, and thus the dedicatory ceremonies would take place within a more delicate and intimate atmosphere than the standard type of *pūrvaraṅga* as outlined above.

The *pūrvaraṅga,* like many other genres of ritual, is an elaborate and many-leveled structure that invites inspection from multiple perspectives. It is at once a descent (from the divine to the terrestrial plane), an emerging creation (in which names, forms, and distinctions arise out of inchoate matter—particularly with reference to the opening musical numbers), an orientation in cosmic space, a propitiary sacrifice, and an initiation (for both actors and spectators). And on a more mundane level, the *pūrvaraṅga* is also a rehearsal, a preview (in the sense of a potpourri of literary, dramatic, and musical allusions: an overture, in effect, in which the main tunes are introduced), a dramatic proposition, a stimulus to the spectator's imagination, and a step-by-step organic development of sound, movement, and meaning that builds steadily into the opening scene of the play, with an increasing focus and magnification that serves to purify and concentrate the separate thoughts and feelings of the members of the audience and direct them toward the central theme of the performance.

The ceremonies were further designed to introduce the performers in their multiple roles and transformations along a continuum running from abstraction to literal representation: first unseen, then as geometric blocks in a sacred mandala design (as in the intricate pattern for the perambulation of the stage), as abstract celebrants in a sacrifice of cosmic import, as symbols of conventional emotional states, as idealized character types, as members of the troupe (the director, the jester), as individuals in a specific role in the play or as mentioned in a particular song text, and finally, as themselves.

With each phase of the ceremony the audience is encouraged to accept the many conventions that make the illusions of drama possible: that the singer seated at the rear of the stage is the voice of the dancer and the poet; that the meaning of the play will be communicated by both the poetic text and the language of gesture; and most important of all, that each component of the dramatic spectacle is a clue that points to one pervading emotional state, the *rasa,* into which the audience should expect to be drawn as the play unfolds. The final aim would be achieved, wrote Abhinavagupta, when the heart of each spectator, like a "spotless mirror," would become a perfect reflection of the central emotion brought forth in the performance.[45]

## 5.4 The Incidental Music

> *Dhruvā*s (songs) depending on the context and made to express Sentiments suited to the situation, embellish the drama just as the stars illumine the sky. . . . One should first of all bestow care upon songs. For songs have been called the resting place (lit. bed) of the drama. The song and the playing of musical instruments being well-executed, the performance of the drama does not encounter any risk.
>
> Bharata, *Nāṭyaśāstra* 32.487, 493[46]

The category of incidental music includes the many types of functional music performed during the play: interpolated songs and dances, signal music (similar to Shakespeare's alarums and flourishes), instrumental interludes, music for entrances and exits, music to evoke a particular mood or milieu, music to underscore dialogue or dramatic action, and the like. There is ample evidence in the surviving play texts that all of these devices were part of the standard practice of the early Indian theater, in addition to the specific instructions in the *Nāṭyaśāstra* and later works on dramatic theory. Bharata's directions for the appropriate style and structure of instrumental music are scattered throughout *BN,* with a particular concentration in the chapter on drumming,[47] but the most important source of evidence is chapter 32, on the interpolated plot songs (*dhruvās*). As we might expect, it was easier to provide samples of song texts than to describe the instrumental music. The author was content to leave the instrumental music with a few general precepts pertaining to such things as expressive style, rhythmic patterns, conventions of accompaniment, and its synchronization with the stage action, but the instructions for the *dhruvā* songs are much more specific. The chapter on the *dhruvās* is a rich collection of typical song texts on various standard poetic topics, in a wide assortment of Sanskrit and Prakrit meters, and it also includes a detailed classification of songs according to their proper use in the play.

The *dhruvās* fall into two broad categories: those included in the formal text of a play and the larger number that were to be interpolated by the producer. The sample texts in the *Nāṭyaśāstra* are consistent in meter, tone, style, and imagery with the songs in the extant plays, and they give a clear picture of the literary genre, if not of the music. The *dhruvās* were sung by the singer(s) at the rear of the stage, not the actors, and their primary purpose was description. Bharata's guiding principle was that the entrance of any major character must be preceded by a verbal description in another's words, with special reference to the subject's appearance and emotional state. Thus, in the third act of Kālidāsa's *Mālavikā and Agnimitra,* King Agnimitra describes the entrance of Mālavikā with these evocative words:

> Broad hipped,
> slender-waisted,
> bosom full and bold;
> my life itself advances,
> casting sidelong glances. . . .
> Her cheeks are pale as stalks of cane;
> her ornaments are few—
> an early jasmine vine whose buds are rare
> and leaves still new.[48]

The topics were standard, and an array of conventional similes, metaphors, and other figures of speech provided the poet with a large repertoire of descriptive terms that would be readily understood by his audience. Two sample texts from Bharata's *dhruvā* chapter will serve as illustrations. To portray the thoughts and emotions of a queen whose consort is absent, the following:

> O fair lady, now has come the joyous evening of the spring which is full of sweet-smelling flowers, and which causes emaciation of one who is separated from her lover.[49]

And to represent a storm interlude:

> The sky covered with rain-clouds, fringes of which are illumined by the flash of lightning, is maddening the herd of elephants which being lashed by storm, are shivering [with cold].[50]

The songs are classified in a variety of ways. An individual song has five "causes"—its name, the occasion for its use, the number of syllables in the metric line, whether the meter is an even or an odd number,[51] and its *tāla.*[52] There are also five occasions: entrance songs, exit songs, songs used as interludes, songs for the purpose of clarifying or developing a particular mood, and songs that signal a subtle shift in the underlying emotion.[53] The six "aspects" of a song are its tempo, the nature of the instrumental accompaniment, and its prescribed pauses, words, letters, and syllables.[54] In this list of a song's essential components we have a valuable clue both to the meaning of the term *dhruvā* (fixed, firm, constant) and to the performance practice of the early theater: a *dhruvā* is so called because it is a song with a *specified* poetic and musical content, with the obvious implication that the contemporary tradition of song had already begun to move toward an improvisatory style in which many of the textual and musical features were not prescribed.

In verse 400 we are told that the composer-poet of a song should first consider the theme of the play, the specific performance occasion, the characters around whom the play revolves, the dominant and subsidiary emotions appropriate to the situation, the season of the year, the time of day, the age and mental condition of the character represented, and the locale. And finally, the songs were further divided into six main types and assigned to appropriate roles (male or female, high, middle, or lowly): a song to be sung in an elevated style, a vehement song, a song dependent upon the dramatic action of the moment, a slow song sung in a free style, a richly emotional song in the erotic sentiment, and a subdued song in the pathetic sentiment.[55] To these were added two additional song types for inferior characters, expressing the comic, pathetic, and fearful *rasas*—the only emotional states authorized for the lower social classes.[56] The *dhruvā* chapter also contains a wealth of information on the metrical and formal structure of the plot songs. Perhaps the most valuable piece of information is the list of eighteen "limbs" (*aṅga*s) or formal components from which the various songs were assembled, demonstrating that the individual song could vary from a brief couplet to a complex structure with several contrasting musical sections.[57]

Because clear projection of the text was regarded as essential, a song would usually be sung first without accompaniment or with extremely light accompaniment, and then, if desired, repeated with heavier instrumentation and drumming. It is clear that much repetition was often necessary, and that a song could be stretched or trimmed to suit the stage requirements. Bharata permits certain exceptions to his general rule that an entrance song must precede the appearance of any of the major characters: when a character enters singing or weeping, or makes a sudden entrance, or enters with an important announcement, or when any wondrous event or calamity occurs.[58] Most of the songs were to be sung in Prakrit, the language of most of the female characters, implying that the song would be assigned to the female singer(s) in the ensemble, but Sanskrit was the appropriate language for all references to superior male characters. In this case the male singer or *pāṭhya*—whose name suggests that his style of performance was closer to declamation than to singing—would undoubtedly be the featured performer. The intermediary songs, those prescribed to fill a hiatus in the performance, are sung when the principal characters are "gloomy, absent-minded, angry, asleep, intoxicated, or . . . enjoying other's company, being under heavy weight, or being in a swoon, or . . . fainting due to poisoning, or being in error, or . . . adjusting or fixing up clothes and ornaments, and in covering any of their faults."[59] One such opportunity would occur during the lyrical dream sequence in act 5 of Bhāsa's *Vision of Vāsavadattā,* a sequence that consists mainly of mime.[60] The passage also suggests an amusing but practical solution when, as must have happened on occasion, an actor forgot his lines.

The instrumental music appears to have been associated mostly with movement on stage, especially in underscoring the typical walking styles of different characters: royalty, superior women in love, inferior women in fear, jesters, dwarfs, and lame, wounded, or confused persons. The rhythmic styles appropriate to the various gaits are outlined (in terms of their tempo, hand strokes, and recited drum syllables) in chapter 33 of *BN,* which thus provides a valuable supplement to the rhythmic patterns set forth in the earlier chapter on *tāla*.[61] Drama critics clearly believed that the language of rhythm could communicate as fully and as precisely as the language of stylized gesture.

Three styles of instrumental music are mentioned in chapters 29 and 33: *tattva* ("thisness," that is, the true or essential state), a style used for slow movements and songs, in which the instrumental music is a precise duplication of the stage movement or the vocal line; *anugata* (following), a moderate style in which the musicians provided a coordinated rhythmic accompaniment but without duplicating the exact rhythms of the actor or singer; and *ogha* (flood), a torrent of strokes that was completely independent of the physical actions or the melody. There is also evidence that different scales, modes, or *rāgas* were not only matched to the various moods, emotions, and dramatic situations but were also linked with particular times of day and with the standard five phases or "junctures" (sandhi) of the plot.[62] The conventional assignment of modern *rāgas* to specific times of day is probably a survival of this practice.

V. Raghavan's summary of the function of the instrumental music provides a fitting conclusion for this section:

> Twice Bharata says that what has not been said in the words of the play is to be embellished through music. What he seems to mean is that actions—such as gathering flowers, or watering plants, or drawing a picture—which are only mentioned in the text, should have musical accompaniment throughout. There is to be no gap; song, instrument, word, action should flow in one unbroken sequence, says Bharata (28.7). There is a saying in Sanskrit: Anything strange is like "a drama without a drum." The drum is the very spirit of the drama. Music, says Bharata, forms the bed, that is, the bedrock of drama (32.436). "The songs based on *rasa* and context make the drama dazzle as the heaven with the stars. As without color, a drawing is not beautiful, so is drama not attractive without music" (32.425). "What is production?" asks Bharata. He answers, "It is the union of song, instrument and action" (32.378, G.O.S. ed.).[63]

## 5.5 Instruments

In India, as elsewhere among the high cultures of antiquity, musical instruments are objects of special attention in the fabric of cultural ideas and a rich source of symbolic, mythical, and literary allusions. This material is of considerable intrinsic interest, but it can also provide valuable and unique information on music in the abstract and its organization into a formal system. Let us see what we can make of it.

We may separate this material into four main strands of ideas. First, the purely organological material which for obvious reasons is of the highest importance not only to performers but also to those who study man's tools and what he does with them: the different categories of instruments and their subcategories, how to choose the proper material and make an instrument, how to give it shape and due proportion, how to hold it, its various accessories (plectra, drumsticks, and the like), and how to maintain it. A second strand of ideas pertains to playing techniques (drum strokes, fingering, and similar matters), and here we begin to encounter material that is also useful for more "musical" purposes.

Third, the surrounding web of cultural ideas: how an instrument was "discovered" by humans or "presented" by gods, instruments as a source of metaphor and myth, the occasions for their use, the ceremonies for installing or dedicating an instrument, and the special qualifications required of the performer.[64] Fourth, and most important for this study, the technical details of the music played on a particular instrument, its characteristic musical style, and its coordination with other instruments, singers, dancers, and the action on stage. I shall pass lightly over the first two of these idea strands, and I will emphasize more heavily the symbolism of musical instruments and what can be learned about the musical system and its application in instrumental performance.

Instruments, as culture objects, play somewhat less of a role in Indian musical thinking than in the West. This is partly because of the typically anthropocentric orientation of traditional Indian thought; implements and other extensions of the human body have not been viewed with as intense interest as the body itself and what the body means. It is also a direct consequence of the cultural importance attached to human speech and vocal sound since ancient times, as detailed in chapters 3 and 4. And indeed the most popular and successful of Indian instruments have been those capable of replicating the characteristic pitch slides, quivers, and ornamental clusters of the vocal style. Drums are the exception, and I shall take them up presently.

Early Indian literature is sprinkled with references to various instruments—flutes, conch shells, drums, and lutes (as generic types)—and their special properties, but the instrumental chapters of *BN* provide the oldest and most comprehensive description of the theater orchestra and the roles of its members. I have mentioned that the traditional classification of instruments into the stretched, hollow, solid, and covered families forms the excuse for the chapter divisions in the musical portion of the *BN. Vādya,* in the general sense of instruments and their characteristic music, became one of the standard topics in later Sanskrit musical treatises, and it is instructive to note the proportionate amount of material devoted to the instruments of each class. For example, the number of verses pertaining to each of the four classes in *BN* and *SS* (the earliest and latest of the musical documents with which this study is concerned) is as follows:

| | Stretched | Hollow | Solid | Covered |
|---|---|---|---|---|
| *BN* | 156 | 13 | 502 | 301 |
| *SS* | 419 | 380 | 49 | 364 |

The discrepancies are enormous, and the conclusions to be drawn from the proportions are not self-evident. In *BN* the chapter on the solid instruments is actually a chapter on the system of *tāla*—its purpose, gestures, patterns, forms, tactics, and other abstract properties of the rhythmic system. There is no mention whatsoever of the construction or playing techniques of the cymbals, which are, to be sure, minimal. And similarly, the 156 verses of the chapter on stringed instruments include no more than 35 verses on the vina and its playing techniques; the rest of the material pertains to the melodic system and is of general interest. The drum chapter, on the other hand, is relatively self-sufficient.[65]

In *SS* the proportions for the first three classes are radically different and signal a change in the general attitude toward instruments. Because the author has removed his exposition of *tāla* to a separate chapter,[66] the number of verses allotted to the solid category has been greatly reduced; what remains is a description of the cymbals and instructions for playing them. Śārṅgadeva has also expanded the organological material in the stretched and hollow categories, although these sections still include many of the traditional topics that are not the unique concern of any instrumental family. Clearly the interest in musical organology increased during the millennium that separates the two treatises, but at the same time the fact remains that early musical scholars were more interested in what could be played upon their instruments than in their physical properties.

Drone instruments are conspicuously absent from Bharata's theater ensemble (in contrast to the continuous drone heard in today's music). Despite claims for the antiquity of the practice, there is no convincing evidence for the drone until the sixteenth or seventeenth centuries,[67] unless we are prepared to accept the argument that such an essential musical component was considered self-evident by all the major authors. I am not. But this is not to say that droning was never a part of the early theater music: the early vina may have had drone strings, and the reiteration of a low-pitched string is a natural technique on plucked instruments; so it is entirely possible that certain passages or compositions introduced this device. But if they did, it seems strange that none of the surviving accounts of the pitch system would have recorded the scale degree appropriate for such a drone figure, especially since the concept of a general "final" or tonic for the entire scale system had not yet developed.[68]

The vina (as a general type) was the principal melodic instrument, and early iconographic evidence shows numerous types of ovoid lutes and arched harps, with and without frets and played with either the fingers or a plectrum. Both instruments are descended from the ancient hunting bow and are the ancestors of many different types that are still in use today. The vina was seen as the alter ego of the human body, in a metaphor that works both ways: the vocal tract as the human vina, or the vina as the physical equivalent of the human voice. In this connection an important passage from the *Aitareya Āraṇyaka* (3.2.5) outlines a set of correspondences between the divine vina (the body) and the ordinary wooden vina: the head is equated with the upper gourd resonator or the end of the vina's neck, the belly with the sounding board or hollow body of the vina, the tongue with the plectrum, the fingers (in the sense of the notes produced) with the strings, the scale degrees produced "by human effort" with those produced by plucking the instrument, the vocal consonants with the contact between finger and string, and the "tightly stitched" body (that is, with reference to the network of veins) with the set of tensed strings; and both vinas are described as covered with a "hairy hide."[69]

This is no trivial set of correspondences, and it demonstrates how deeply rooted in Indian tradition is the analogy between the vina (as the protomelodic instrument) and its human counterpart. To point out but one particularly appropriate aspect of this comparison, the grid of parallel strings and crosswise frets is an unmistakable analogue to the grid of speech sounds and articulatory organs as outlined in the early phonetic literature, each considered as a model for the production of sound. Each of the two grids also provides for the scaling of musical space—the internal space of the human body and external space as marked off along the body and strings of the instrument.

In contrast to this treasury of musical imagery, and despite its considerable symbolic importance in many world cultures, the role of the flute and other wind instruments is surprisingly limited in the early literature. Once human breath has emerged from the body, it apparently ceases to be regarded as vital breath (*prāṇa*) and functions as ordinary instrumental sound. A possible reason for this lack of interest may lie in the fact that the sounds of the flute are modulated by actions on an external device rather than being the sole result of the internal actions and emissions of the human body.

If the generic vina is the alter ego of the human voice, or its protagonist, the drum is its counterego or antagonist. The polarity of melody and drumming is one of the deepest layers in the Indian musical tradition, manifest not only in such things as caste distinctions, taboos, and gender stereotypes[70] but also in the basic conception of music as a counterpoint between the two opposing dimensions—each with its own pitch structure and distinctive syllabic language, both controlled and integrated by the system of *tāla.* The intrinsic complexity and equally complex interaction of these two dimensions partly explains why Indian musicians have never developed a system of harmony, a question that seems to intrigue Westerners. To have developed a system of harmony would have first required an unacceptable simplification of both the pitch and temporal dimensions. More to the point, it would also have required a foreign imagination and an urge to meet a need that was not felt.

The common equation (drumming = rhythm) is a serious misrepresentation of the Indian concept and experience of music: the rhythm of drumming is one thing, and the controlling, structural rhythm of *tāla* is another. *Tāla*—in the broadest sense of timekeeping, from the shortest durations to the longest spans of the musical structure—is the abstract essence of the rhythmic system, has total integration of the performance as its chief aim, and is the mutual responsibility of the solid instruments and the gestures of many or all of the performers. Percussion—in the form of the drum strokes, their patterns, and their syllabic representations—has accompaniment and opposition as its aims; this is the reason why drumming has been treated as a separate compartment in Indian musical thought and practice. Instead of considering pitch and rhythm as the two major musical domains, each conceived as abstract scales (for musical space and time), it is more accurate to think of the melodic and drum sounds of Indian music as coordinate dimensions of pitch, held in check within the regulating framework of rhythm.

The drumming chapter of *BN* is organized around sixteen major topics: the sixteen syllabic sounds (each of which represents a single stroke by one or both hands), four ways of combining strokes on the various drumheads, the procedure for applying paste to the heads, six stroke patterns, three ways of regulating the intervals between strokes (*yati*), the three tempos (*laya*), three degrees of synchronization (*gati*) with the melodic line, three relationships of the right or left hand to the right or left drumheads, three styles of combining light and heavy syllables (when recited), three modes of beginning or *pāṇi* (that is, either anticipating, synchronized with, or following after the singer), an additional set of five hand strokes, three ways of muting the stroke by dampening the vibration of the head, three tunings of drumheads by the application of black clay, the eight "conformities" between drumming and song, eighteen *jāti*s (different playing styles and "gaits"), and twenty additional playing styles and special effects produced by combinations of the preceding. The point to be extracted from this long list of topics, apart from its practical value as an index to the art of Indian drumming, is that the drummer seems to have inhabited a self-sufficient musical world, as a counterdimension to all other musical activity.[71]

The remaining topics in the chapter are the mythical origin of the drum in the sound of rain upon lotus leaves; the function of drumming in the theater; the seating plan for the theater ensemble; the role of drums in the rituals of the *pūrvaraṅga;* how to accompany stage action and dancing; preparing for a performance; the faults of a bad drummer and the merits of a good one; the construction and dimensions of many types of drums; the ceremonies for dedicating a new drum;[72] and even how to select a good hide—one that is not "old, torn, pecked by crows, covered with . . . fat, [or] soiled by smoke or fire."[73]

In his book *Rhythm and Tempo,* Curt Sachs contended that "no other civilization is India's equal in drum playing."[74] And among the high musical cultures of later antiquity, it is only in India that we find such a wealth of evidence testifying to a highly developed system of drumming, accompanied by a distinctive body of musical ideology. While drums played a prominent role in the solemn ceremonies of ancient China, rhythm itself appears to have been taken much for granted, apart from the predictable requirement that all the rituals must be precisely synchronized. And in Attic Greece the idea of rhythm evolved as an abstract doctrine for which the primary models were the accents, durations, patterns, and inflections of formal poetry.[75] Part of my story in subsequent chapters will be an account of the early development of rhythmic concepts and structures in relative independence from the metrical influence of Sanskrit verse. In the temporal dimension, the crowning achievement of the ancient Indian musical system was the creation and integration of two concepts of rhythm: the surface rhythms of drumming and the structural rhythms of *tāla.*

## 5.6 Epilogue

In the drama that flourished during the middle centuries of the first millennium A.D., we see a highly refined—perhaps, some may say, even an "overbred"—synthesis of a long tradition of folk drama and sacred ritual with roots so deep as to be indiscernible. Of all the performing arts, it is drama that reaches out the farthest to its audience, seeking maximum impact and emotional involvement and response. It is noteworthy that early Indian playwrights and producers sought to achieve this impact—in the form of a state of total empathy, drenched with emotion—not by such obvious means as conflict, disequilibrium, and the flash of raw passion, but by a much more difficult and roundabout process: the cumulative evocation of a world in harmony with itself, striking resonance from every sight and sound, and following an emotional script which Indian culture has crafted with as much precision as the poet has crafted the individual play. The essence of the classical Indian theater is comedy—not farce, satire, or burlesque, but the same vein of gentle romantic comedy that echoes throughout *A Midsummer Night's Dream.*[76]

Indian music and dance grew to maturity within the context of the theater. They have remained steadfastly under the guidance of the aesthetic principles that informed the classical Sanskrit drama, and it is thanks to the literature of dramatic criticism that their early stages have been so fully and faithfully recorded.

# S I X
# ŚĀSTRA

> [The prospective poet] must apply himself in the first instance to *śāstra*, for it is that upon which [the composition of] poems depends. Without making use of a lamp one cannot survey in the dark the caravan of things as they really are.
>
> Rājaśekhara, *Kāvyamīmāṁsā* 11.16–18[1]

> He who throws away the precepts of *śāstra* and lives to indulge his desires does not attain to success, nor to happiness or the ultimate goal. Let therefore *śāstra* be your yardstick in establishing what is your task and what is not, and, with the knowledge of what the dictates of *śāstra* prescribe, pray do your acts in this world.
>
> *Bhagavadgītā* 16.23–24[2]

## 6.1 Introduction

This chapter is an introduction to the early Indian musicological literature, the literature of *saṅgītaśāstra.* The word *śāstra* signifies first a set of rules for right action (doing, making, or performing), then the teaching of those rules, and finally the instruments by which those rules are transmitted: dictum, doctrine, and document. As the second element in the compound *saṅgītaśāstra, śāstra* refers both to the general notion of a field of study (*ology*) and to a particular treatise or group of treatises on a given subject—in this case music.

It is often difficult for outsiders to grasp the reasons for the authority of *śāstra* in Indian thought, described in one Sanskrit proverb as "the all-seeing eye, without which one is truly blind,"[3] and which the ninth-century critic Rājaśekhara hailed as a lamp piercing the darkness of illusion and revealing "things as they really are." The assumption that a preexistent body of learning constrains, or ought to constrain, a poet's efforts to discern and describe things "as they really are" is apt to strike an unsympathetic Western critic as self-fulfilling, as well as an outright rejection of the principles of objective observation and scientific method. And in a sense it is. Two complex and thorny issues are involved here: the relationship between theory and practice and the deeper question of the proper relationship between human action (karma) and its consequences.

There have been times in Western history when theory has been praised more extravagantly than practice, notably in the Middle Ages. Perhaps the most quoted testimony is the remark of Boethius (A.D. 480–524) that "it is far greater and nobler to know what someone does than to accomplish oneself what someone else knows, for physical skill obeys like a handmaid while reason rules like a mistress. . . . How much more admirable, then, is the science of music in apprehending by reason than in accomplishing by work and deed!"[4] But this view has not prevailed in more recent centuries and has indeed been flatly contradicted by the popular notion that a theorist (of the arts, or of anything) is simply an accurate observer, skillful analyst, or wise codifier of the principles displayed in what artists make, or do, by instinct. Nothing could be more foreign to the Indian point of view.

The Sanskrit language provides two sets of oppositions for the distinction between theory and practice. One of these is less useful for the present discussion: the opposition between the words *lakṣya* (to be marked) and *lakṣaṇa* (a characteristic mark, token, or sign); this opposition embodies the objective viewpoint with regard to an artistic creation or performance, that is, those characteristics it ought to exhibit (*lakṣya*) and those that it does in fact exhibit (*lakṣaṇa*).[5] More important for our purposes is the opposition between *śāstra* (the body of traditional learning) and *prayoga* (the practical application of these doctrines). This opposition represents the subjective point of view—that is, what we ought to do and what we actually do. One may risk the generalization that the subjective position is always a privileged one in Indian thought, and that the self-awareness and motivations of the subject have generally been regarded with deeper interest than the objects of action or perception.

A second reason for the failure of outsiders to comprehend the full implications of the shastric tradition lies in our relative neglect of the question of *action,* a topic that has dominated Indian philosophy since ancient times. As J. A. B. van Buitenen puts it, "The attention and deliberation devoted by Indian, especially Hindu, thinkers to the nature of actions, their components, their conditions, and their consequences are to the non-Indian student staggering."[6] One has to search for anything comparable in Western thought. The problem of action in Western philosophy has been generally confined to the domain of ethics and is largely a matter of getting our goals straight, with little discussion of the abstract value of action per se. Accordingly, many Western thinkers have seen action as a straightforward matter of achieving our objective—whether that be happiness, health, social welfare, material gain, or salvation—and have been inclined to rate an action as successful based on the question Did it accomplish its end? not Was it performed in accordance with the received wisdom of our culture?

But in Indian philosophy, codes of ethics have tended more toward the juridical than the teleological. The idea of right action and the formulation of codes of conduct have developed into a general cultural assumption—that is, that action is to be performed for its own sake, not as a means of attaining a particular objective. To attempt to summarize the message of the *Bhagavadgītā* in a few words goes beyond presumption, but the essence of what Kṛṣṇa said to Arjuna in chapter 16 is that action performed for the sake of satisfying our desires leads to bondage (because our judgment is always clouded by what we want), but "disinterested" action, action as enjoined by the *śāstra*s, leads to liberation.[7] Aristotle assumed that the good was what is desired by all men, but the early Indian sages took what they thought was a more realistic point of view.

The noun *śāstra* is a derivative of the verbal root *śās* (to correct, punish, and hence to teach), and the standard word for pupil (*śiṣya,* a gerundive form from the same root) means "he who is to be punished." The phonetic similarity between *śāstra* and *śastra* (sword) provided Indian scholars with an irresistible opportunity for one of their beloved puns, suggesting both that the chastening rod of instruction often held a sharp edge and that the systematic study of a particular field required intellectual dissection. The English language retains traces of the same pun, by means of a devious semantic route via Latin, in the words "castigate" (correct) and "castrate" (cut). The essential point behind this subconscious line of argument is that the technical literature of any subject is above all a means for intellectual discipline. From this comes the authority of *śāstra.*

The development of the scientific or shastric literature in ancient India was a consequence of increasing specialization, dating back perhaps to later Vedic times. A need developed for expertise which could not be met within the traditional Vedic specialties, requiring the creation of methods and areas of inquiry that cut across the older intellectual divisions. Grammar, for example, may have been the first of these studies; it is clearly a subject which could be usefully generalized and applied to the study, interpretation, and preservation of the Vedas. Medicine, law, and astronomy followed, and within a few centuries the shastric literature encompassed such exotic and diverse subjects as agriculture, architecture, armaments, burglary, elephant keeping, falconry, painting, politics, prostitution, and music.[8] The traditional Hindu classification of the four ends of life—that is, righteousness (*dharma*), material gain (*artha*), pleasure (*kāma*), and liberation (*mokṣa,* the ultimate goal)—furnished another conceptual framework for organizing the technical literature.[9] It is the latter two toward which the study of music aims.

One wildly comical scene from Śūdraka's *Little Clay Cart* will serve both to give a vivid (although exaggerated) sense of the role of shastric teachings in everyday life and also to refute the popular notion that Indian literature lacks a sense of humor.[10] In act 3, Śarvilaka, described as "a Brahmin turned burglar," mounts what seems like an interminable assault on the house of the sleeping Cārudatta, searching his memory at each step of the way for the precepts of the burglary *śāstra*s, praying to the burglar's guardian deities, quoting appropriate Sanskrit verses, and shaping his entrance hole so that "the neighbors would congregate in the morning to discuss my craftsmanship." And the householder Cārudatta, not to be outdone, after waking and discovering the theft, remarks with manic detachment, "What an elegant hole!" and after quoting another Sanskrit *śloka,* complete with outrageous metaphor:

> The bricks are neatly stacked and put aside—
> The hole, wide-waisted, to the head grows thinner. . . .
> It is as though from fear to touch a sinner
> This noble mansion broke its heart and died!

he affirms with sententious moral fervor, "Indeed, even in crime there can be artistry."[11]

The musicological literature has much in common with the literature of other intellectual disciplines, and we shall presently consider in some detail its style, scholarly traditions, habits of thought, expository strategies, and modes of discourse. By way of introduction, and with appropriate reservations, I quote from A. B. Keith's useful, although unsympathetic, analysis of the shastric tradition:

> A characteristic which in greater or less degree pervades the whole of the scientific literature is the love of subdivision and of inventing distinctions. Everything has to be schematized without regard to the nature of the subject-matter. Thus in the *Kāmasūtra* even the meticulous specification of detail of this kind is carried out with perfect solemnity. . . . In the subdivisions of which India is so fond there is often much ingenuity in finding legitimate grounds of distinction, but there is always present the tendency to lose sight of the broad and important lines of demarcation while concentrating on minutiae. Moreover the practice of accepting as given what has been traditionally handed down has a serious effect. It often results in ingenious efforts to reinterpret the old, in lieu of frankly abandoning it, thus causing

> waste of energy in subtleties. . . . There was, of course, constant progress . . . but it was hampered by the necessity of making out that change was not really taking place.[12]

Readers will have the opportunity to test these conclusions in what follows, and may find as I do that while we may concede each of Keith's contentions, the picture that emerges is not as one-sided as it may at first appear. And in rebuttal, it should be pointed out that the scientific methods of the ancient West did not always lead to equally productive results, and that certain fields of study have fared better than others in traditional Indian thinking. Grammar, botany, pharmacology, and law were brilliantly successful in their early formulations, eclipsing comparable achievements in the West, while sciences such as anatomy, physiology, chemistry, and mechanics were clearly hampered in their development. The status of music lies somewhere in between.

I would like to suggest several ways in which Indian musical scholarship has reflected the shaping influences of the shastric tradition. As a first consequence, the musical thought of early India is not directed at the proverbial "cutting edge" of what is new; on the contrary, its objects lie at the heart of all that has been established by ancient authority. If the metaphor of a cutting edge is at all appropriate in this context, it must refer not to the explorer, hacking out new pathways through uncharted territory, but to the gardener who seeks to trim away the overgrown brush from existing pathways, thereby removing the limitations and gradually extending the perimeters of the present core of knowledge. The primary method is therefore prescriptive rather than descriptive, and the object of study—organized sound—can hardly be imagined apart from its attendant aura of elemental world process, the vital principles by which process is manifested, and the vestigial memories of ancient ritual by which process was controlled. Against this background, musical thought is profoundly commentarial; its purpose is to contribute new detail, perspectives, analyses, and interpretations. It seeks to correct when necessary (but not to contradict), to reconcile, and to bring into systematic order. The documents with which we shall be concerned are to be regarded as dilations of, and commentaries upon, the bare kernel of truth as revealed to the ancient sages.

As a second major consequence, musical thought has taken delight in elaborate taxonomic systems with a profusion of categories. Simplicity and parsimony are not valued for their own sake, apart from the obvious need to preserve an oral tradition by compressing as much meaning as possible into as few words as possible. So musical thought is pluralistic with regard to concepts, groupings, and structures, including multiple perspectives and points of view. The musical systems it has produced are likewise inclusive rather than exclusive, and in no way have the many successive systems of *rāgas* and *tālas* been considered to exhaust the available options. The musical systems of India remain open-ended and retain the power to generate new formations, so long as these do not violate the traditional guidelines.

Third, the objects of musical thought have not been regarded as isolated acoustical phenomena; they represent merely one aspect of the world process which is made manifest in each of the artistic domains. Horace's celebrated dictum *Ut pictura poesis* is particularly appropriate in the integrated worldview of India:[13] the idea of music is by no means confined to a unique set of principles, materials, and structures. Its essential features are shared with the other arts, and readers should expect to encounter similar terms and organizing principles in arts as seemingly diverse as music and architecture, poetry and sculpture.

And finally, *śāstra* is barren without *prayoga.* The practice of Indian music, as prescribed in the literature of *saṅgītaśāstra,* is a daily affirmation of the teachings of the great philosophical traditions and their practical recommendations for such things as concentration, memory, mental attitude, self-discipline, perception, testimony, and the attainment of knowledge. The way of the thinker may differ in degree, but not in essence, from the way of the music studio, and the transaction between teacher and student, guru and *śiṣya,* is symbolic of the authority vested in the traditional methods of learning. There is much in common between the practice of music, the disciplines of yogic meditation, religious ritual, and the repetitive routines of everyday village life. The Indian focus on the self and on self-awareness has encouraged the development of theories of performance, as opposed to theories of composition, and the emphasis has fallen more heavily upon the musical process and improvisation than upon the reification of musical objects. Action and cognition rank higher than the production of sound artifacts. In all these aspects *śāstra* is the bow, *prayoga* the arrow.[14]

## 6.2 Musical Scholarship

In the rest of this chapter I shall take up in turn various aspects of early Indian musical scholarship: its assumptions, the physical circumstances that have influenced the forms in which musical learning has been recorded, its transmission and reception, characteristic modes of discourse, strategies of explanation, codes and notations, grammatical and metrical style, and conventions of literary expression. It will be clear from the preceding discussion that a number of deep-seated cultural assumptions underscore the scholarly frame of mind: among these, that old is best, oral is true—that is, learning from a teacher is more reliable than book learning—and knowledge in written form is to a certain extent to be regarded as suspect and to be used as an index to the contents of one's own mind. An understanding of the reasons behind these attitudes is vital if we are to put this literature into proper perspective.

Why is it that the Vedic texts have been better preserved by oral transmission than texts from later periods which have been transmitted in writing? Certainly as the result of special mnemonic techniques[15] and the authority accorded to the scriptures, but also because of the general belief in the validity of testimony. To this day it is easy to detect traces of this profound respect for spoken testimony in scholarly circles: in the elevated style of intonation with which a quotation is "performed," heavily endowed with pitch inflections and rendered with an obvious relish of the metric structure, and in the sense of finality with which a citation from an earlier authority is used to clinch an argument and drive the point home. In sharp contrast to attitudes in the West, ancient learning is held to be infallibly true, like a body of constitutional law: it needs to be amplified, studied deeply to discern the author's intent, applied to different situations and contexts, and supplemented by means of finer distinctions; and the form in which it has been received demands painstaking reconstruction and skillful interpretation. Such is the task of musical scholarship.

All early books were copied by hand, as in the European Middle Ages, and technology has not yet put all the copyists out of work; every surviving text has passed through the hands of many generations of scribes. Palm leaves and strips of birchbark trimmed to a uniform size were dried and pressed between endboards, and the whole package was tied around with cord. All of these materials proved to be highly perishable in India's hot and dusty conditions and vulnerable to invasions of worms and physical deterioration. In the West scholars have been able to reach farther back into the manuscript tradition because of the longer life of the physical materials—the parchment scrolls or papyruses—but Indian scholars have been compelled to place their trust in the integrity of the text under study and the grammatical-literary form in which it has been recorded. It is unlikely that there is a single manuscript in India today which is more than a few hundred years old, and in the case of popular texts surviving in many copies, too much evidence can present as great an obstacle as too little evidence.

What then might happen to a book? First, in its unbound state it would be subject to loss (when the cord broke, or as leaves were added) and could easily acquire additional material. It is easy to imagine scribes picking their way through an inherited library in a state of disarray, reassembling and tying whole sheaves of material without being fully aware of their contents. And indeed many treatises survive in an obviously scrambled state. Books were regarded as personal property because the owner had paid for the copying, and hence if a manuscript was copied by a learned person, he might not hesitate to "correct" it—often to the point of leveling out all case endings across an entire verse, thereby eliminating the original grammatical distinctions—embellish it with his own comments, develop its line of argument with further illustrations, propose and refute counterarguments, or insert a verse that struck him as having some metaphoric application to the topic under discussion. Even if he was careful to restrict his additions to the margins (which were not large), a later scribe might easily recopy all of the material in the standard format, thus effectively removing all traces of the glossing. If, as was often the case, the scribe was ignorant, he could easily drop words and entire lines, confuse one letter with another, and commit many other obvious errors which scholars have learned to expect and correct automatically.

These problems have been compounded by the special characteristics of the Indian scripts, particularly in the case of the Devanagari script in which classical Sanskrit was set down: first, because of the large number of characters required (generally accepted as fourteen vowels and thirty-five consonants, in contrast to the twenty-four letters of Attic Greek or the twenty-six of modern English); and second, because of the unusually high potential for confusing one letter with another (as, for example, *b* and *v*, *d* and *ḍh*, *gh* and *dh*, *bh* and *m*).[16] The distinguishing mark was often an added hook, stroke, or superscript dot, and a hungry worm could in a single meal generate enough confusion to confound a panel of editors and alter forever the meaning of a passage.

J. A. B. van Buitenen's summary is appropriate:

> The pages between two boards, then, could become the beginning of a modest library. It was like an expanding folder: nothing was easier than to insert at the appropriate leaf a number of other leaves cut to the same size and covered with texts that expanded on the original, made exceptions, and added further illustrations. . . . For a book, a dating over eight centuries makes [no sense]. For a library, it does: one may date a library between its founding and the time when no new acquisitions were made.[17]

The present text of Mataṅga's *Bṛhaddeśī* (*MB*) is a case in point.[18] Only two manuscript sources have been discovered, both fairly recent and one much shorter than the other, so substantial portions of the text as we know it rest on a single manuscript. But it has long been known that such a treatise existed, and Mataṅga has been quoted—sometimes at length—by virtually every musical authority since Abhinavagupta. These citations provide a useful basis for comparison with the text of the 1926 Trivandrum edition, and some of the discrepancies and uncertainties may be resolved as the work proceeds. But the two manuscripts available to Śāstrī are themselves typical products of a long chain of copying and recopying, as well as a baffling hodgepodge of inconsistent material—metrical verses, prose passages, passages in dialogue format, inserted quotations, and material so garbled that it defies understanding. It is impossible to say just what has been lost, but the internal evidence indicates that the text may at one time have included a canto on instruments; and quotations attributed elsewhere to Mataṅga (if we assume the attribution to be correct, which is a big if) suggest that additional cantos on *tāla* and dancing may also have been part of the original, larger work. And there are other obvious gaps in the material. What more can be done to improve the state of the present text? Continue to compare it with citations in other texts, attempt to clarify the meaning of the text as it stands, resolve the internal and external contradictions on a provisional basis, and wait for more manuscripts to turn up. The problem is no less serious in the case of other musical texts, for a variety of reasons: the present text of *D* depends on a single manuscript,[19] and so many copies of *BN* are floating around that it is unlikely that scholars can ever agree on one canonical version.

To an outsider this sounds appalling, but Indian scholars have lived with it for millennia and have developed techniques appropriate to the nature of the problem. If a tradition has been broken and an "original" text cannot be recovered, all that remains is to attack the existing text with all the tools of textual scholarship, including grammatical, semantic, metrical, and etymological analysis. One of the oldest traditions of Indian scholarship has been for a ruler to commission a team of pandits to compile a private library for him, examining all the available texts, correcting where appropriate, and producing a synthesis of their learning. The team would always have included experts on grammar, but not necessarily experts in the various fields under study, and they were more than likely to miss the meaning of a word used in a special, technical sense.

The extreme brevity of many of the early texts is a problem in itself, particularly in the texts formulated in the aphoristic sutra style (prose) or the rhymed couplets of the *śloka* meter, the dominant meter in the ancient musicological literature.[20] The intent was clearly to produce an oral literature, by encoding maximum information in the fewest words and also in the most rhythmic and predictable literary style, taking full advantage of every shortcut and mnemonic aid. As a result the texts are often little more than strings of keywords, designed to jog the memory and recall what was already deposited during face-to-face instruction. This procedure is highly effective for a living tradition, and surely no one should be expected to remember what months have how many days when the answer can be readily found in a short mnemonic verse. But when a tradition is no longer practiced, an index of this type can often seem as barren of meaning as a telephone directory. What this led to in Indian scholarship was the development of a commentarial style (*bhāṣya*) that met the special needs of the literature. The virtue of the commentary was that it allowed full explication while at the same time preserving the authoritative form of the text being explained. Special codes were devised to condense the question-and-answer format into few words. M. Winternitz describes the *bhāṣya* style as

> a highly developed form of learned prose . . . [that] originated in the form of a disputation, naturally from a type of scientific pursuit. In particular, in *sabhā*s, the assemblies of learned men held in courts of princes or at houses of rich and prominent people, this played an important part. Every new theory had to be defended here in these learned discussions, in case it was meant to be established. Hence it follows that scientific literature in India is almost wholly scholastic and dialectical. The dull style of scientific discussion is very often agreeably interrupted by insertion of obviously intelligible similes or by references to events of daily life. . . . The language is simple and clear and the sentences are short, as they have the tendency to be in actual conversation.[21]

So from an early date, the commentary was established as a favorite form of textual scholarship, and it was accepted that a commentator's job required him not only to explain what the text meant but also to comment upon the grammatical and metrical structure of the text and justify the emendations he was expected to make. In this connection, something must be said on behalf of the process of emendation: It is not the text itself which remains beyond criticism, but the essential thought and utterance embodied in the text. Texts are corrupt by nature, generally in predictable ways, and they are to be corrected at every opportunity, even at the risk of *suppressio veri.* The ideal scholar, to be sure, is one who is able to combine grammatical expertise with knowledge in a special subject, but even a trained grammarian who lacks this special expertise can accomplish much in improving a corrupt text. At best a skillful commentator could penetrate deeply into the meaning of a cryptic text, make vital editorial improvements where needed, and supply priceless supplementary information from his own experience. At worst a commentator would merely paraphrase the text, define its terms with cognate words, supply misleading etymologies, explain the obvious, and ignore the crucial matters that demanded explanation.

But apart from the *bhāsya*s and other related styles of commentaries, in a sense all the Indian musicological literature is a massive, running commentary on itself—a tradition of testimony in the form of borrowed material of various kinds, interpolated quotations and memorial verses (*kārikā*s), conventional illustrations and metaphors, and standardized modes of explanation that serve to constrain the growth of new doctrines. In such a tradition authorship must be viewed as multiple, and the most appropriate metaphor for the Indian scholarly tradition is once again a botanical one: in music, as in other fields of study, the body of traditional learning has often been likened to the main stalk of a plant which is subject to numerous new grafts and prunings, but in which the organic "program" of the original stock—its kernel of essential truth—will control and limit the accumulation of new material by means of its inherent impulses and constraints. The trunk of knowledge will ultimately accept only those accretions and amplifications which are consistent with its internal programming and will reject those which are not compatible. But in the meantime, false knowledge is to be feared above all, more so than ignorance, and because of its inherent defects, knowledge in written form is to be distrusted and valued below true knowledge obtained, as the *Nāradīyaśikṣā* advises, from a living teacher.[22]

There are obvious morals for the interpretation of written evidence, and these have not been lost upon Indian scholars: obtain as early and as grammatical a text as possible, be guided by predictability in literary style, expect and correct the obvious errors, respect the pandit's expertise, be on the lookout for successive layers of material and value them accordingly, and above all, compare. But there is one method of interpretation that has developed as a natural consequence of a homogeneous body of knowledge that has gradually acquired definition as a result of explanatory accretions. It can be best described as a tendency toward "reflexive explanation," that is, applying the clarifications and illustrations found in later texts to the cryptic statements found in earlier texts. While this sort of interpretation is often justified and of great value, it can at times distort the meaning of the original by introducing material reflecting a later stage in musical practice.[23] The consumer of Indian scholarship has a difficult choice to make: whether to treat each text in relative isolation, like a snapshot, or run the risk of viewing it as a partly obscure frame in a cinematographic film sequence that becomes progressively clearer as a result of later photographic enhancement.

## 6.3 Musical Discourse

> *Gāna* has been declared by the sages to be twofold, namely, *nibaddha* (composed) and *anibaddha* (improvised). That which is composed of *dhātu*s (sections) and *aṅga*s (limbs) is called *nibaddha. Ālapti,* which is free from such structural limitations, is known as *anibaddha* and has already been dealt with by us. *Nibaddha* is now being expounded. *Nibaddha* has three names—*prabandha, vastu,* and *rūpaka. Dhātu* is the structural element of *prabandha* and is shown to be fourfold: the first is *udgrāha,* then *melāpaka, dhruva,* and *ābhoga.* These will now be defined seriatim. (Śārṅgadeva, *Saṅgītaratnākara* 4.4c–8b)[24]

Many of the traditional strategies of Indian musical explanation are evident in this passage: the emphasis on name and number, the categorical manner in which the exposition unfolds, and the didactic tone resulting from the many process comments. To separate content and the tactics of exposition from the style of literary expression is always an artificial division, and particularly so in the case of a literature in which authors have preferred to set forth their technical expositions in the form of verse. Nevertheless, I shall reserve comments on poetic style and literary expression for the following section.

Our corpus of musicological literature spans at least one thousand years, and common sense alone suggests that we should expect considerable diversity. So it comes as something of a surprise to discover how relatively homogeneous the literature is. And the homogeneity does not lie on the surface: despite superficial variations in the style of exposition, it is possible to identify a number of common features—certain expository tactics, ways of thinking, and modes of musical discourse—that are characteristic of this body of literature and have helped to insure that musical doctrines have developed along authorized pathways.

Indian musical explanation, like Indian explanation in general, is profoundly categorical, and the essential formula for musical discourse is threefold: name, number, and definition. A typical way of presenting a subject is first to assert that Subject *X* is fourfold and then proceed to name and define the four aspects. The same procedure is then applied to each of the four divisions and continues until the limits of knowledge have been reached. Accordingly, expositions of the subject of music tend to be lists of technical terms, which accounts for the prevalence of nouns and the almost complete suppression of verbs.

Definition typically takes the form of a list of *lakṣana*s—the characteristic properties, attributes, or distinguishing marks of whatever one is seeking to define. As an example, Dattila's exposition of the *jāti*s (mode classes) lists ten characteristics by which an individual *jāti* can be recognized: initial note, predominant note, high note, low note, a hexatonic form of the scale, a pentatonic form, weak note, frequent note, final note, and internal cadence note.[25] Such lists tend to occur in numbers of some cultural significance, and once an authoritative treatise has established a precedent for defining a given topic in a certain number of *lakṣaṇa*s, this precedent is generally respected by later authors.

Such an inclusive approach to the mental act of definition avoids the surgical distinctions drawn by ancient Greek authors, in whose expositions a technical subject is systematically dissected into mutually exclusive domains. Intervals, for example, differ from one another in that one is larger than another, one is rational and another irrational, one composite and another incomposite, one is consonant and another dissonant, and so on.[26] This type of either-or mentality is utterly foreign to Indian thought, in which the categories are fluid and often overlapping. A concept or object is identified by the preponderance of its characteristic marks—not, as in Greek thought, by distinguishing it in every possible way from all others of its class. This reluctance to think in exclusive categories can be a source of frustration to those who prefer a tidier world, but it is one of the hallmarks of Indian scientific discourse.

A standard format provided additional insurance against confusion or loss of part of a manuscript. Just as a typical Peripatetic treatise was divided into a *proemion* (preamble), *archai* (statement of first principles), and *stoicheia* ("elements," an exposition of the individual topics), so were early Indian treatises organized along predictable lines. A treatise, and often each of its component chapters or poetic cantos, would usually begin with a benedictory verse (*maṅgalācaraṇa*) in honor of an appropriate deity, densely packed with metaphors and symbolic associations, and written in an elevated style that set it apart from the rest of the text. Through clever allusions, etymologies, and even puns, an ingenious author was able to suggest some allegorical relationship between the surface content of his verse and the subject matter he was about to expound.

The *maṅgalācaraṇa* with which Śārṅgadeva introduces the dance canto of the *Saṅgītaratnākara* is a typical and attractive example of this strategy:

> We bow to the energetic (*sāttvika*) Śiva, whose body movement (*āṅgika*) is the phenomenal world,
> whose articulate expression (*vācika*) constitutes all verbal expression, and whose ornaments (*āhārya*) are the moon, stars, etc.[27]

Śiva is once again invoked as Lord of the Dance,[28] and the four attributes mentioned in the verse are the same set of terms introduced in the *Nāṭyaśāstra* as the four components of expressive dance (*abhinaya*): *sāttvika,* internal emotion; *āṅgika,* bodily movement; *vācika,* speech; and *āhārya,* costumes and makeup—or to put it another way, essence, appearance, expression, and adornment.[29] The implicit moral of the verse is that Śiva's attributes constitute the prototypical forms of artistic presentation, and the student of dance will do well to justify his continued patronage.

The next item was usually an *uddeśa,* a table of contents, in the form of a bare list of the principal topics to be expounded. In addition to the master *uddeśa,* individual chapters and major sections would often begin in a similar manner. These were obviously useful not only as jogs to the memory but also as insurance that the material would survive scribal incompetence or the dismemberment of the manuscript. After the *uddeśa* the author would proceed with a seriatim exposition of the various topics, in a highly compartmentalized style that left little opportunity for integrating the subject as a whole—a task that remained the responsibility of a living teacher. There was no consensus on the proper number or order of musical topics, but the topics of Śārṅgadeva's seven cantos provided one of the most typical and influential models: *svara,* the organization of pitch; *rāga,* melody; *prakīrṇa,* "miscellany"; *prabandha,* song; *tāla,* rhythm, meter, and form; *vādya,* instruments (chiefly drumming); and *nartana,* dance.[30] We can also observe an interesting tactic of closure: nearing the end of a particular chapter or section, an author would frequently summarize the topic he had just presented by enumerating the various possibilities and subtopics, adding them up to a grand total.

Another distinctive feature of the literature is the inclusion of colophons. The regular sequence of poetic lines or prose paragraphs is interrupted by partial lines announcing the end of a particular topic, the beginning of a new topic, the end of a quotation, the introduction of a different point of view, or a different speaker (in dialogue formats). An author would often begin or end a treatise or chapter with a salutory or valedictory phrase such as Mataṅga's "Let auspicious knowledge flourish!" (at the conclusion of his *prabandha* canto).[31] The colophons have helped to preserve the material in proper format, but it goes without saying that they have on occasion been omitted, misplaced, mangled, or miscopied into the main text. Nevertheless, because of their information content and their multiple roles (as punctuation, attribution, running index, and sometimes even as ceremonial affirmation), the colophons must be regarded as one of the most characteristic and valuable features of the scholarly tradition.

Two extremely useful code words belong in the same category as the colophons: *iti* (thus, in the sense of "thus spake"), which invariably marks the end of a quotation, and *ādi* (beginning with), which has the force of *et cetera* when suffixed to a noun or nominal compound.[32] The merits of such shortcuts are beyond dispute, but they also have their drawbacks. While *iti* is unequivocal in indicating where a quotation comes to an end, it is not always clear just where a quotation begins. The resulting ambiguity can easily be remedied in oral instruction by a change in tone of voice, but this is a serious matter in a literature that depends so heavily upon quotations. And with respect to the convention of *ādi,* if an author wanted to refer to the four aspects of *abhinaya* alluded to in Śārṅgadeva's benedictory verse, he might use the expression *sāttvikādi*—an elided version of *sāttvika-ādi,* "that standard list of things which begins with *sāttvika.*" Here again there is a potential for ambiguity unless the listener or reader understands the context, knows this particular list of terms, and can supply the rest of the list from his memory bank.

From a broader perspective, it is notable that so many of these information markers occur at the end of a semantic unit and thus signal a momentary resolution of the accumulated tension, in much the same way that full comprehension of a sentence in German comes only with the arrival of the final verb. We can only speculate why it has proved more useful to erect verbal signposts at the end of material instead of at the beginning, but it may be related to the general tendency toward end accent that I will argue for in subsequent chapters.[33]

The conventional lists of *guṇa*s (merits) and *doṣa*s (defects), which usually appear in sets of ten, are another characteristic mode of musical discourse. This tradition is very ancient, and it contributes heavily to the prescriptive, even moralistic, tone. As a result, the early musicological literature is value laden, and the various clusters of values that occur again and again in the *śāstra*s furnish valuable clues to the intangible and qualitative aspects of musical style that are so conspicuously absent in other bodies of ancient music theory. It is no exaggeration to say that in no other body of early musical thought has there been such an emphasis on the aesthetic domain and such precise information on musical values, qualities, and cultural preferences. It is also self-reinforcing, in that respect for authority has encouraged later authors to perpetuate the conventional lists.[34]

It will be useful to sort out the differences between four standard topics of dramatic, poetic, and musical criticism: *guṇa*s, *doṣa*s, *lakṣaṇa*s, and *alaṅkāra*s (ornaments). The word *alaṅkāra* means "to make sufficient," and its etymology is a powerful testimony to the role of ornament in Indian culture. The message is that an ornament is not mere decoration, icing on the cake, but is an essential component of any artistic presentation. Just as a woman is undressed without her ornaments, so is poetry or music barren without *alaṅkāra*s.[35] To return to the four topics: the *lakṣaṇa*s of a particular *rāga,* song, or poetic text are its inherent properties, its essential features and distinguishing marks; its *alaṅkāra*s are added properties, and their purpose is to provide beauty in certain conventional ways. Both are necessary. Its *guṇa*s are meritorious qualities, and its *doṣa*s are blemishes. The task of the poet or composer was to make a judicious selection from among the appropriate *lakṣaṇa*s and *guṇa*s, with the addition of a tasteful selection of *alaṅkāra*s, while avoiding *doṣa*s at all costs. The implication is that art, like nature, becomes beautiful only when ornamented in certain conventional ways, just as food becomes flavorful not as the result of the basic ingredients but through the judicious addition of spices.[36]

The moralizing tone is further implemented by the concluding verses offering rewards for observing, as well as blame for ignoring, the precepts of the *śāstra*s. These are the so-called *phalasūtra*s, aphorisms stating what will be the "fruit" (*phala*) of the proper action or true knowledge: "He who observes these precepts obtains merit, both in this world and in the next!" but also, "He who does not know the matters herein expounded—he is no proper teacher!" And similarly, the homely maxims and colorful animal fables contribute to the didactic tone of much of the literature: for example, a rare event is compared, with typical and charming hyperbole, to a sea tortoise who reportedly rises to the surface once every hundred years and who, upon reaching the ocean surface, puts his head through the noose of a rope conveniently floating by.

## 6.4 The Language of Musical Speculation

To Westerners it may seem paradoxical that early Indian writers chose to expound most of their technical literature in the form of metrical verse. In fields of learning where precision and unambiguous expression were demanded, why would an author prefer poetry to prose and subject his expositions to the constraints of metrical regulation?

We have already touched upon some of the reasons: the physical materials that have left their mark on the length of the line and the number of lines on a standard manuscript leaf, a long-standing tradition of poetic exposition, a handy system of codes, and above all, the special requirements of an oral literature—conciseness, memorability, predictability, rhythm, formulaic construction, suitability for oral delivery, and appropriateness for teaching and learning. Because the Vedas were themselves cast in the form of verse, it seemed an obvious choice for their ancillary literature, and from there the tendency spread into various fields of knowledge.

One meter dominates the early musicological literature—the *śloka,* which may be simply described as an unorganized series of unrhymed couplets containing four half-lines or *pāda*s (the four "paws" of a quadruped) of eight syllables each: that is, $\frac{8}{8}+\frac{8}{8}$ syllables, with caesura at the end of each *pāda. Śloka*s are often referred to as "epic couplets" in recognition of their role as the standard meter of India's two great epics, the *Mahābhārata* and the *Rāmāyaṇa;* they subsequently became the most common meter for Sanskrit narrative and didactic verse. The ancestor of the *śloka* was the popular Anuṣṭubh meter of the later Vedic literature, and to a great extent, its special properties have been influential in shaping the course of Indian musical thought and its characteristic modes of explanation. We shall need to examine its metrical structure in some detail in an attempt to see how it affected literary content.

The *śloka* is considered to be quantitative verse, but the sequence of short and long syllables is only partly determined: with a few minor and technical exclusions, the first four syllables of each *pāda* are undetermined, but the last four fall into predictable patterns—in accordance with the general tendency in world poetry for lines to display relative freedom at their beginnings and a fairly rigid cadence structure. With reference to the rhythm of the *śloka* as a whole, we can say that it is basically iambic but with at least one prominent disruption of the iambic sequence at the end of the first and third *pāda*s. The most common form of the couplet, then, may be displayed as follows:

| | *pāda a* / *pāda c* | *pāda b* / *pāda d* | |
|---|---|---|---|
| Line 1 | + + + + \| ⏑ – – ⏓ \| | + + + + \| ⏑ – ⏑ ⏓ ‖ | } *śloka* |
| Line 2 | + + + + \| ⏑ – – ⏓ \| | + + + + \| ⏑ – ⏑ ⏓ ‖ | |

There is quite a bit to say about this pattern. First, the parallel construction of the two lines tended to encourage semantic parallelism, and similarly the regular caesuras concluding each of the *pāda*s provided additional opportunity for semantic division. As a result, the material was set forth in balanced, rhythmic form and neatly "chunked." Topics were often confined to a single couplet, although there were of course many exceptions, and we expect a full stop at the conclusion of every other line. In written texts a single vertical stroke marks the end of line 1, and a double stroke the end of line 2, followed by the number of the *śloka.* In technical expositions the final element of each couplet is often the main verb of the sentence, and just as often all of the remaining words are either nouns or nominal compounds interspersed with connectives.

The general rhythmic shape of the couplet is cleverly designed to take advantage of the subtle contrast in cadence structure between *pāda*s a/c and b/d. The resulting pattern of verse was easy to learn and easy to remember, and its characteristic durational patterns made it easy for scholars to spot errors and correct them—if not with the author's original words (which was often possible), then at least with an appropriate semantic, grammatical, and metrical replacement. The caesuras did not necessarily imply a full stop when the verse was recited, but they usually required either the end of a word or one of the elements in a compound. This metrical pattern proved ideal for the exposition of musical material, particularly when the reciter was enumerating sets of technical terms or defining a topic by means of its *lakṣaṇa*s, *guṇa*s, and *doṣa*s.

The *śloka* was by no means the only meter found in the musicological literature: *āryā* was a popular substitute,[37] and others appear from time to time, especially when earlier authors were being quoted; and prose passages are not rare. But even in the midst of a prose exposition, *śloka*s will return again and again to lend rhythmic punctuation to the discourse and give the ring of authority. We can analyze, explain, and argue in prose, but when we wish to proclaim or affirm doctrine, it feels right to revert to verse. Part of the special appeal of the *śloka* couplets lies in the relative brevity of the eight-syllable *pāda*s. Most of the elegant meters featured in the later tradition of ornate court poetry were organized in *pāda*s of eleven, twelve, or even more syllables, which provided ample scope for virtuoso poetic diction, but which lacked the regular, homely rhythm that seems to have been preferred by most authors writing in technical fields. There were some exceptions: the literature of certain disciplines, notably mathematics and astrology, is marked by a decided tendency toward more elaborate verse structures.

A typical verse from *SS* will serve as a sample of the literary style. *Ālapti,* the subject of the sentence and the term being defined, is the name for the improvised prelude to a formal song, a prelude in which the singer must create a spontaneous exposition of the characteristic features of the chosen *rāga.* Three versions of the verse are displayed in (4): (1) the transliterated Sanskrit text in continuous format, (2) the same text in separated form, divided into *pāda*s and accompanied by a literal English translation of each of the elements, and (3) a restructured English translation.[38]

The main sentence is confined to *pāda c:* "*Ālapti* is defined by the experts ("this-knowers") [as]." The foursquare construction of Śārṅgadeva's definition falls neatly into the internal structure of the couplet: a main sentence plus three eight-syllable compounds, each modifying the subject of the sentence (*ālaptir*), as shown by the agreement of case endings.[39] Only the final element in each compound is inflected. Each of the three compounds consists of three elements run together: either noun + noun + adjective/participle (*pāda*s *a* and *b*) or adjective + noun + adjective/participle (*pāda d*), in which the syntactical relationships among the various elements must be deduced by a mixture of traditional analytic conventions and common sense, and they require the translator to supply the necessary connectives.

Lexical interchangeability was an essential strategy in this style of exposition, so that any desired meaning could be expressed in any given number and pattern of syllables. If, for example, the main sentence of the above verse had to be moved to *pāda d* and the final five syllables had to be replaced for metrical considerations, *ālaptir parikīrtitā* would be an acceptable substitution.[40] While this technique may have inhibited an author's poetic fancy, it more than compensated in its ability to survive the accidents of time and be restored by any competent scholar. Similarly, an assortment of particles, conjunctions, and other types of verse fillers proved useful in rounding out the texts to the requisite number and pattern of syllables. And finally, authors drew upon an array of expressions asserting the authority of the "experts." The literature is full of expressions such as "as is known by learned men," typically in the instrumental case (as in *tajjñair,* "by those who know these things") and again available in enough varieties to suit any metrical location. To quote an earlier authority was to corroborate an assertion, and most Indian schools of logic have held that testimony is a valid basis for inference. It is for this reason that special stylistic means were devised for rendering testimony, whether formal or informal, attributed or, as in this case, unattributed.

The tone is highly prescriptive: a verb is apt to appear in the optative

4. Analysis of a typical *śloka*

(1) *varṇālaṅkārasaṁpannā gamakasthāyacitritā*
*ālaptirucyate tajjñairbhūribhaṅgimanoharā*

(2)

| [with] melodic contours | [and] ornaments | endowed, | [by] melodic transitions | [and] composed phrases | colored, |
|---|---|---|---|---|---|
| *varṇa* | *alaṅkāra* | *sampannā* | *gamaka* | *sthāya* | *citritā* |
| *pāda a* | | | *pāda b* | | |

| *Ālapti* is said | by the experts | [to be], [because of its] many curves | charming. |
|---|---|---|---|
| *ālaptir ucyate* | *tajjñair* | *bhūri bhaṅgi* | *manoharā* |
| *pāda c* | | *pāda d* | |

*Ālapti* is defined by experts [as that which is] profuse with melodic contours and ornaments, colored by melodic transitions and composed phrases, [and] charming because of its many curves.

mood (*ought, should*) or as a gerundive (a future passive participle with the force of "must," as in Latin). The passive voice was preferred to the active, and two particular constructions are common: (1) the *yat . . . tad* construction, which places the relative clause *before* the clause it relates to; and (2) the rhetorical figure known as anacoluthon, a break in the construction of the sentence following an initial noun phrase. Sentences often begin with a gerund (a past active participle), for example, "having performed X, one should then proceed to . . ." And the frequent deployment of a past passive participle at the end of a sentence—as in *parikīrtitā* ("as has been proclaimed") or *smṛtā* ("as tradition has maintained")—is still another means of placing the stamp of authority on the doctrine presented.

I have referred to the relative sparsity of verbs in this expository style. To some extent this is the result of recasting the verbal elements into participial form and placing them in grammatical agreement with the noun that they modify, and hence the verb "to be" is generally suppressed. Word order is very free, and the meaning is controlled by an extremely precise syntax. Common case relations include the partitive genitive ("of all the foregoing"), the standard accusative as direct object, the instrumental of means, the ablative of cause ("from this reason"), and the locative of respect ("in the case of"). Frequently a sentence will consist solely of nouns and adjectives in the nominative case, as in a typical definition format: "Topic *X* [is] fourfold, [viz.] *A, B, C, D.*" Brevity was the object, and the result was a highly aphoristic and scholastic style of discourse.

A person does not need to know Sanskrit to realize that any language contains the means to express all of these relations in a simpler manner through direct discourse. The material is presented in coded form, not only to meet the demands for economy, memorability, survivability, and metric structure, but also, as has sometimes been suggested, to preserve a certain secrecy and to vest intellectual property rights in those qualified to know by means of study and initiation. Our authors had no concern for a wide readership, copyright did not apply, and knowledge *was* property, because a person had paid for the copying of a book with either his money or his labor.

But in addition to the general encoding of musical teachings within the technical conventions of poetic exposition, there are more specific codes which present absolute barriers to those who lack the key to unlock their secrets. I will mention only a few. Because of the metrical format, authors were disinclined to include numerals in a text; and as alternatives to the standard words for the cardinal and ordinal numbers, they would frequently resort to a code of words with specific numerical or cultural associations: for example, *indu* (the moon) = 1; *netra* (the eyes) = 2; *agni* (with reference to the three sacrificial fires) = 3; *veda* (for obvious reasons) = 4; *bāṇa* (arrow) = 5, because of the five arrows in the love god's quiver, and so forth.

Discussions of metrics are especially cryptic in their reliance upon a shorthand in which syllable sequences (of two, three, four, or more syllables) can be represented by a single syllable taken from a standard formula.[41] Rhythmic durations could also be represented by single syllables, numerals by another code of single syllables based on alphabetical order, and numerous other details were presented in cryptic form—obviously a complicating habit in a subject where precise measurements and accurate ritual performance are required. Even the divisions between one statement and the next were subject to certain conventions and are not always clear in the texts: verses are numbered, and two symbols for punctuation are used—a vertical line at the end of *pāda b* and two vertical lines to mark the end of a couplet—but these did not automatically signal the completion of a statement or topic. In the end these conventions and obstacles must be seen in a moral perspective: as the *Nāradīyaśikṣā* maintains, it is only with effort that we are able to tap water from the earth, churn butter out of curds, or strike fire from wood; and so it is when we wish to obtain knowledge, whether from a teacher or a book.[42] No pain, no gain.

## 6.5 Notations

The physical evidence for early Indian music has been the theme of this chapter, and it will be obvious that the "best" evidence has not yet been mentioned—musical notation. Here is the problem: while there is an abundant supply of musical notations in the corpus of musicological literature, they are simply not as specific as we would like them to be. Ancient Greek musicians had developed adequate notations for pitch and rhythm well before the beginning of the Christian era;[43] were Indian musicians less observant, less inventive, or less concerned with the preservation and transmission of their art? The status of musical notation in early documents has yet to be fully studied, but some progress is being made.[44] We will not become bogged down in technicalities, but it will be useful to understand the role of notation in the transmission of music and musical learning.

There are many types of notations in the early musical treatises. What can be said about them is that they are verbal, mnemonic, and minimal, and that they were devised to meet the special needs of an oral tradition. Above all they are syllabic. Indian authors were realists, and in no way did they expect an example of notation to be a graphic display of the musical utterance in all its details. Judging from the example set by the ancient grammarians and phoneticians, the observation of vocal sound had already passed far beyond the stage of being content with a simple one-to-one correspondence between sound and symbol. There were too many sounds for the available symbols, and the role of contextual features was clearly recognized. The same disregard for a precise one-to-one correspondence persists in modern Indian notations.

Not only must early musicians have been keenly aware of the influence of context upon the performance and perception of musical sounds, but they must have also realized the inherent limitations of any notation devised to render the intricacies of a musical system with such a profusion of microtonal shadings, melodic transitions, ornamental clusters, and complex rhythms.[45] Their solution, which was entirely consistent with traditions of teaching and learning and which still obtains today, was to place musical notation in a more realistic perspective: preserve the music in skeletal form as a spur to the memory, but impart its full details in face-to-face instruction, by demonstration and imitation, teacher seated across from student.

We would scarcely have expected ancient Indian scholars to have hit upon staff notation, the brilliant solution found by medieval European monastics.[46] Staff notation, for all its merits, is not an obvious solution, but letters and numerals must have been possible alternatives. There is actually one numeral notation still practiced in India, the notation used in the Kauthuma school of Sāmavedic chanting, in which the intralinear and supralinear numerals represent both melodic configurations and syllabic durations of the text.[47] But it is impossible to say how ancient this tradition is, and there are no explicit references to this style of notation in the musicological literature. The single-letter alternative, which served the Greeks well, seems to have been ruled out by the syllabic nature of the Sanskrit language and the scripts devised for its rendering—which are, without exception, syllabaries in which the basic consonant symbols are modified by various secondary symbols (hooks, affixed strokes, and the like) to represent the vowels and their grades. For this and many other reasons, the syllable became the primary model for the notation of music.

What syllables were used? Most important of all, the set of sol-fa syllables representing the seven degrees of the scale: *sa, ri, ga, ma, pa, dha,* and *ni,* the so-called *sargam* notation.[48] These syllables have no direct relationship to the sounds, but they derive in an obvious way from the *svara* names and are easy to articulate. A second notational solution was the set of onomatopoeic syllables for the various drum strokes. In this system the essential sonic distinctions—such as the oppositions between high and low pitch (of the heads) free and damped strokes, finger and palm strokes, single- and two-hand strokes—are represented by typical phonetic oppositions: voiced-voiceless (*dā* vs. *tā*), open-closed (*dā* vs. *din*), and unaspirated/aspirated (*dā* vs. *dhā*).[49] The drum notations are organized in syllabic chains in which (1) the same stroke may be represented by a number of different syllables, depending upon the context; and (2) the same syllable may be chosen to represent different, although sonically appropriate, sounds. As D. R. Widdess has observed, the notation is presented in the form of "words" (*bol*s) rather than individual syllables.[50] It is striking that the pitch and drum syllables inhabit two distinct planes: the former with no natural relationship to the actual pitches, and the latter with a marked iconic resemblance to the drum sounds. This contrast may be either a cause or an effect of the fundamental conception of the streams of melodic and percussive sounds as separate, though coordinate, musical dimensions—a conception more relevant to the Indian experience of music than the abstract opposition between the spatial and temporal dimensions.

The hand motions of *tāla* were also notated, both by the full name of each gesture and by the first syllable of that name, and entire compositions were set down in that format.[51] Durations proved more resistant than pitches and were notated according to several conventions: by spacing on the page (which was unreliable), by groupings of syllables, or by the vowel quantities of the accompanying text. In their temporal aspects the early notations give no more than a faint indication of the rhythmic vitality and complexity of the performance tradition.

The earliest-known example of specific pitch notation is the seventh-century Kuḍumiyāmalai rock inscription, consisting of seven short compositions demonstrating the properties of the seven original *grāmarāgas*.[52] The notation is based upon the seven solmization syllables, but with each syllable "inflected" by changes of vowel (that is, with *sa,* the first degree of the scale, appearing in four forms: *sa, se, su,* and *si*) and occasionally by superscript dots. These inflections, which have puzzled generations of scholars and which have been assumed to represent microtones, now appear to indicate the direction of each successive melodic interval, with reference to the articulatory position of each of the vowels within the mouth. The result is a subtlety which has not been preserved in subsequent pitch notations, and which I interpret as further evidence for the deep-seated tendency in Indian notational practice to forgo precise symbol-to-sound equivalence in favor of contextual relationships.

In later musical treatises, beginning with Mataṅga's *Bṛhaddeśī,* it became the custom to include short musical examples demonstrating the typical properties and contours of the various *rāgas*. The aim here was to specify not the individual notes of a composition but the general features of a melody type. These examples appear in the form of regular sequences of the standard *sargam* syllables, sometimes run together in unbroken strings and sometimes spaced out in a grid of poetic lines that includes both the *svaras* and an accompanying text. These valuable examples demonstrate that the idea of *rāga* consists of much more than an abstract collection of scale degrees; it is, in fact, a melody—not in the sense of a tune in which one prescribed note follows another, but in the sense of a melodic pathway that can be rendered in a plain or an ornate style, departing from and returning to the melodic framework, but deeply individualized in its patterns, contours, and overall structure.

What these examples do *not* fix, at least with the precision many would like, is the microstructure of melody: the tuning of the scale, the exact intervals between one degree and its neighbors, and the characteristic transitions and ornaments that we know were and are associated with individual *rāgas*.[53] Western notations are similarly imprecise in specifying the ornamental and transitive elements of musical sound, all those expressive elements that we value so highly in an effective performance. In this respect we can hardly criticize Indian notation for failing to achieve what others have not managed to achieve. But a larger question remains: what is the status of a pitch notation that overlooks not only exact tuning but even the approximate size of melodic intervals? Indian scholars have pondered this question, and many have proposed solutions for fixing the tunings of the early scales; but in no way have these provided a convincing basis for interpreting the earliest notated examples in more than skeletal form.

The problem of notation is a problem of expectations. There is no problem in transcribing the early notations, so long as it is realized that only the bare bones of the music can be uncovered. But students of ancient music, like archaeologists, have learned to be grateful for all the bones that come their way. What we can conclude in the end is that Indian notation does precisely what it was intended to do—record the musical utterance in minimal form, enough to distinguish it from anything else and to call its details back to mind. That is what early musicians expected, and that is what they got.

# SEVEN
# PITCH

Immediately consequent upon *śruti,* creamy and resonating, the sound that delights the listeners' minds by itself is called *svara.*

Śārṅgadeva, *Saṅgītaratnākara* 1.3.24c–25b[1]

## 7.1 Introduction

The goal in this and the two subsequent chapters is to understand how the Indian mind has cataloged and organized the sounds of music. The two keywords for this chapter are *śruti* and *svara,* especially the latter, in both (1) its general meaning as the conceptual-perceptual structure of the entire dimension of pitch, and (2) its specialized meaning as an individual musical note. According to Śārṅgadeva, the chief attributes of a single musical sound were its distinctness, viscosity, resonance, and capacity to bring pleasure. Its qualities were at least as important to him as its quantities. The point is worth remembering.

We can observe three distinct levels of accomplishment in the efforts of ancient musicians to gain control over the domain of pitch, and the same three stages will provide the format for my discussion. They follow a pathway which the Peripatetic philosophers found useful for their investigations—from potential to progressively more actualized forms of musical organization. Analysis in these terms is by no means intended as a historical account: in the evolution of a musical tradition—ancient or modern, literate or nonliterate—the actuality of music must precede the more abstract notion of a musical "potential," the system of possibilities from which individual choices are made. And similarly, no set of separate stages will yield a true picture of the way in which a music develops, because music simply does not develop in a systematic, organized manner.

There are two naive interpretations of the process by which a systematic theory of music arises: first, that a body of theory is invented, prescribed, and then implemented in musical practice; and a second and somewhat more credible interpretation, that keen observers pay close heed to musical practice and faithfully record its details, which eventually become established as musical laws. A more realistic interpretation must recognize the simultaneous development of, and mutual feedback between, an established musical practice and the mental gymnastics by which that practice can be taught, learned, remembered, and recorded.

For convenience, then, my exposition will focus on the efforts of Indian musical scholars as they (1) constructed a gamut of possibilities and organized it into a scale of fairly precise increments; (2) proposed an array of melodic choices, in several different categories; and (3) actualized these concepts in the form of melodic models and individual compositions. The first of these stages is clearly precomposition; the latter two represent types of musical activity that we may describe as either composition or performance. I shall identify the third stage by its later name, *rāga*. In (5) I will index the various pitch concepts under their traditional Sanskrit names:

5. The domain of *svara*

(1) The gamut and its tuning
*svara:* note, scale degree
*śruti:* intonation, microtone
*grāma:* scale
*mūrcchanā:* scale rotations
*tāna:* pentatonic and hexatonic versions of the *mūrcchanās*
*sthāna:* register
*sādhāraṇa:* altered notes
*vādi:* sonance

(2) Melodic choices
*varṇa:* contour
*alaṅkāra:* ornament
*gamaka:* transition

(3) *Rāga*
The *jāti*s: the mode classes
The *grāmarāgas*
*Rāga* in later Indian music

## 7.2 The Gamut and its Tuning

We return to the twin concepts of *svara* and *śruti* for a final consideration of their roles in the early system of pitch organization. Indian scholars have pondered their relationship since ancient times, with the goal either of expressing their tuning in precise mathematical terms or of explaining their various manifestations with lines of argument drawn from the traditional philosophies. I shall attempt to give the gist of these arguments and draw some conclusions.

To rephrase the definitions put forward in earlier chapters, *svara* (in its limited sense as "scale degree") represents a graspable musical sound—one of the degrees of the heptatonic scale and the basic unit of musical meaning. The *śruti*s represent the potential divisions of the pitch continuum, an unheard musical substratum of background sound scaling the octave into twenty-two unspecified microunits.[2] To make the discussion more concrete, the following diagram sets forth the conventional tunings of the two basic scales. The intervals between the seven *svara*s in each of the two scales are expressed in terms of the number of *śrutis*:

| | *sa* | | *ri* | | *ga* | | *ma* | | *pa* | | *dha* | | *ni* | | (*sa*) |
|---|---|---|---|---|---|---|---|---|---|---|---|---|---|---|---|
| *sa-grāma* | | 3 | | 2 | | 4 | | 4 | ⤧ | 3 | | 2 | | 4 | |
| *ma-grāma* | | 3 | | 2 | | 4 | | 3 | | 4 | | 2 | | 4 | |

The equivalent in modern staff notation is:

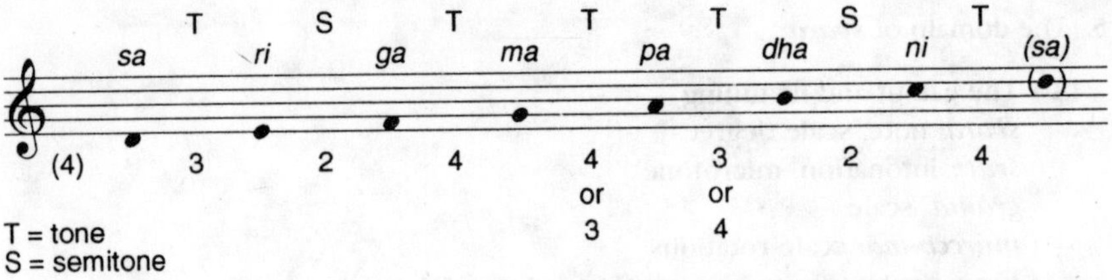


Although we do not know the exact size of these units, there can be no doubt that both scales—which differ only in their interchange of the intervals between degrees 4/5 and 5/6 (*ma*/*pa* and *pa*/*dha*)[3]—are versions of the familiar type of scale that ancient Greek authors referred to as *diatonic*, in recognition that the whole tone (*tonos*) was the regular size of step. Within the scale the pattern of tones and semitones in any given octave segment would display some rotation of the interval sequence *TSTTTST*: that is, a selection of seven degrees, separated by five tones and two semitones in a fixed sequence, with a total of twelve semitones to the octave. The particular rotation shown here (in which the semitones occur as the second and sixth intervals) produces the pattern that the medieval Roman Catholic church knew as *autentus protus, primus tonus*, or Dorian; the Greeks named it Phrygian.[4] It is important to point out that we have no other reliable evidence in ancient Indian sources for the tuning of this scale, particularly with respect to the exact size of the *śrutis*.

Much depends on this last point. There can be three possibilities: either (1) an equal division of the octave into twenty-two identical or roughly equal *śruti*s; or (2) the *śruti*s were of unequal but unspecified size, allowing the intervals to gravitate toward what have been regarded as "natural" intervals, generally those expressible in simple integral ratios such as 3:2, 4:3,

9:8, 10:9, and the like, approximating the system of just intonation;[5] or (3) a consensus on the exact sizes of the intervals was never achieved—they were determined on the basis of oral instruction and were never more than rough approximations of the intervals mentioned, except perhaps within a particular teacher-student line. The first two possibilities are still being argued today, with no consensus emerging.[6] I incline toward (3) in the absence of any definitive evidence in the early literature.

The first possibility, twenty-two-tone equal temperament, or some approximation thereof, seems unlikely on natural grounds because of the huge and pervasive deviations from the interval sizes preferred by early Western and most other musical traditions. The system of 1200 centitones per octave devised by A. J. Ellis for the measurement of intervals in twelve-tone equal temperament provides a basis for comparison.[7] If one *śruti* was equivalent to 55 centitones (1200 ÷ 22 ≅ 54.545454), the interval of two *śruti*s is indeed a remarkable approximation of one of the four semitones of just intonation: 16:15 = 112 cents.[8] The problem, however, lies in the two "whole tones," whose difference exceeds by far the range of deviation permitted in any of the principal historical tunings, as the following comparison will indicate:

| 22-tone equal temperament | just intonation | 12-tone equal temperament |
|---|---|---|
| 4 *śruti*s = 218 | 9:8 = 204, the "major" tone | 200 |
| 3 *śruti*s = 164 | 10:9 = 182, the "minor" tone | 200 |

If this ancient tuning is similar to any of the early known tunings in the West, it is closer, at least in concept, to just intonation than to the celebrated Pythagorean tuning, in which all the whole tones are of equal size: 9:8 = 204 cents. The range of deviation is simply greater—so much greater, in fact, that it strains credibility to think of both the 3-*śruti* and 4-*śruti* intervals as whole tones or equivalent "steps" of the scale. This difficulty has led later authors to postulate a set of *śruti*s of variable magnitude, thus allowing them to manipulate the tuning of the scale into rough conformity with the simple and elegant low-order integral ratios of just intonation.

In support of the proposition that the intervals of the system did conform to those of just intonation, proponents have interpreted Bharata's experiment with two vinas (*BN* 28.24)—in which he demonstrated the existence of the twenty-two *śruti*s—in such a way that the so-called *pramāṇa-śruti,* the standard measure (*pramāṇa*) of tuning, turns out to be the well-known syntonic comma (81:80 = 22 cents), the difference between the two whole tones of just intonation.[9] But even if this claim is correct, the discovery of a single significant interval can scarcely stand as the proof of an entire system, and it seems more than unlikely that a consensus on such an exact system of tuning could have been achieved without some of its details turning up in the early literature.

So far I have focused on the smaller intervals, the steps of the basic scale; but there is one interesting question involving the tuning of a crucial pair of the larger intervals. Examination of this issue will not help to resolve the question of which tuning was prevalent, but it will serve to introduce the concept of *sonance*—the agreement (consonance), disagreement (dissonance), or neutrality that exists between one note and another. The *śāstra*s agree that the intervals of 9 and 13 *śruti*s are particularly significant and provide the standard for consonant agreement between one *svara* and another—as, for instance, between *sa*/*ma* and *sa*/*pa* in the *sa-grāma* (degrees 1/4 and 1/5). Whether these intervals are reckoned on the basis of equal temperament or natural ratios, they are close approximations of the perfect fourth and perfect fifth—the intervals that are usually held to be second only to the octave in the ranking of consonances.

| 22-tone equal temperament | just intonation | 12-tone equal temperament |
|---|---|---|
| 9 *śruti*s = 491 | 4:3 = 498 | 500 |
| 13 *śruti*s = 709 | 3:2 = 702 | 700 |

The intervals of 2 and 20 *śruti*s were regarded as dissonant, once again approximating the minor second and major seventh intervals by any means of derivation and forbidden under certain conditions. The interval of 1 *śruti* exists only as a standard of measure for the larger intervals, and its complement (the interval of 21 *śruti*s) had no status at all. The remaining intervals were considered to be neutral and are largely ignored in the literature. I shall reserve a fuller discussion of sonance for a later section, but it is worth remarking here that the ancient musicians were not particularly interval-minded and did not develop any independent concepts of interval function or behavior per se, that is, when considered apart from the relationship between two specific *svara*s. I consider this remarkable in view of the traditional value attached to the "in-between" in Indian thought.

If the *śruti*s really were of variable size and were found more by instinct and by demonstration than by calculation, we can understand this hesitation to become more specific. For scholars of Western music, the relative indifference with which early Indian musicians viewed the abstract relationships between the *svara*s will stand in sharp contrast to the passion with which ancient Greek authors developed their elaborate doctrines of pitch intervals and analyzed their many differences.[10] Some of the reasons for this neglect will soon become apparent.

To put the entire question of tuning into perspective, it is useful to recall that musical experience in ancient India—music as heard, as taught in face-to-face instruction, as learned, and as remembered—had accustomed practitioners to live in a world of subtle microtonal shadings which to them were more familiar, more tangible, and more real than anything they could hope to set down in the form of written knowledge. Modern Indian practice has evolved into a close approximation of twelve-tone equal temperament, from which seven *svara*s (or in certain cases, more or fewer) are ordained for each *rāga,* but in which individual notes may be shaded up or down from this standard. Once learned and "locked into place" at the beginning of a performance, each set of *svara*s becomes a collection of unique possibilities, and the difference between one scale step and another is understood, not as a calculated interval with an identity of its own, but as a matter of jumping or sliding from one fixed location to another.

## 7.3 Philosophical Arguments on *Śruti* and *Svara*

Although the mathematical basis of the *śruti*s remains obscure, their ontological status has captured the interest of Indian authors since ancient times, and a number of subtle arguments have been put forward to explain their special role vis-à-vis the *svara*s. In the *Bṛhaddeśī,* Mataṅga cites and analyzes five traditional views on *śruti* and *svara.*[11] This passage will provide some useful insights into the language, doctrines, and intellectual habits of the major philosophical systems. The sage introduces his subject with the following brief preamble: "Now will be explained the various views on the nature of the *śruti*s, such as 'identity' and the like: it is generally said of the *śruti*s [that the relationship between them and the *svara*s is one of] identity, reflection, causation, transformation, or manifestation."

The five arguments cited by Mataṅga are: (1) *śruti* and *svara* are identical, in the same sense that a class and the members of that class are identical, since no differences are perceived by the organ of hearing; (2) the *svara*s are heard as the reflections of the *śruti*s, just as the appearance of a human face in a mirror is a reflection of reality; (3) the *śruti*s are the material cause of the *svara*s, just as a ball of clay is the material cause of an earthenware pot; (4) the *śruti*s become transformed into the *svara*s, as milk is transformed into curds; and (5) the *svara*s are manifested by the *śruti*s,[12] just as a pot and other objects standing in darkness become manifested when a lamp is lit. These homely analogies—the clay pot, the lamp, a reflection in a mirror—are all staples of Indian epistemology and are argued in exquisite detail (and often to different conclusions) by exponents of the various systems. What is interesting here is the application of these analogies to the perception of musical sounds.

Mataṅga proceeds to reject the first three arguments: (1) the identity argument, because the distinction between *svara* and *śruti* is perceived differently by different minds, but more importantly, because the two concepts are related to one another as the "supported" to the "supporter," and hence they cannot be said to be identical; (2) the reflection argument, because if the *svara*s are nothing more than reflections of the *śruti*s, they are unreal and are therefore false knowledge; and (3) the causation argument, on the grounds that the reality of the *śruti*s can be established only by inference and circumstantial evidence; and further, the analogy to a ball of clay is a false analogy in that the ball of clay is no longer available once it has been fashioned into a pot, whereas the *śruti*s remain available. Mataṅga then accepts both the transformation and the manifestation arguments, but the subsequent discussion makes clear his position (which was endorsed by many later authors) that the seven *svara*s are manifested by the *śruti*s. Let us try to understand this line of argument by an extension of Mataṅga's analogy of the lamp: the scale degrees are made manifest by the movement of sound along the background continuum of pitch quanta, in much the same way that flashes of light appear when a lamp is carried past the panes of a leaded window, or perhaps past the windows of a darkened house. We can perceive the bursts of light as the lamp passes predetermined positions, but we can only infer the movement of the lamp. Mataṅga summarizes: "This is what I reply [to the previous claims]: the *śruti*s are perceived through circumstantial evidence, inference, and/or direct perception, and then become the means for the manifestation of the *svara*s."[13]

We see here a sample of reasoning that gives a profound glimpse into the heart of ancient Indian musical speculation and demonstrates how deeply concepts of musical sound are rooted in traditional thinking. The ancient Greek position was that the proper sounds of music—as they are collected in melodic and harmonic intervals and patterns of duration and stress—take on form and become perceptible because they manifest that special class of simple ratios by which the world is organized, thus coming into harmony with one another and striking a sense of recognition in our organs of perception, which have a natural affinity for the same ratios. The Indian position cannot be put quite as simply, but it too is grounded in a basic metaphysical assumption: that a substratum of continuous, imperceptible reality persists as the essential background for all human actions and cognitions, and that the mental forms in which we think, perform, and perceive music arise as spontaneous manifestations along this underlying scale of possibilities. The continuity of the real world can be grasped only by inference from our encounters with the discontinuities and limitations of ordinary experience. The *svaras* exist by the authority of culture and tradition, and the unique contribution of Indian thinkers to the ontology of musical sound lies in the subtle distinction they drew between a scale of latent possibilities for conceiving and perceiving musical sounds (the *śrutis*) and the actualized sounds (the *svaras*) with their special attributes—resonance, perceptibility, melodic function, and their capacity to give pleasure.

The process by which the *svaras* become manifest is similarly indebted to traditional Indian thinking. The basic idea is that a specific scale degree is manifested at the upper limit of its "range," that is, each of the *svaras* is separated from its neighbors by a band of two, three, or four *śrutis*, but each is manifested only at the upper edge of this band, when the accumulation of *śrutis* is complete.[14] This is in striking contrast to early Western musical thought, in which pitches were traditionally conceived as points,[15] not bands. It is possible to relate the Indian concept of *svara* to at least three cultural streams of thought: (1) the notion of sound manifested by means of upward progression reflects the metaphoric pathway along which sound arises within the human body; (2) the idea of the spontaneous manifestation of a graspable musical sound is reminiscent of the *sphoṭa* ("disclosure") theory argued by the early grammarians, in which the meaning of a word floods the listener's mind in an act of spontaneous perception at the end of a series of individual sounds and syllables; (3) R. Sathyanarayana has pointed out the influence of the concept of *saṁskāra* as proposed in the philosophical systems: by *saṁskāra* the thinkers meant the residue of qualities or attributes of experience (as, for example, from a prior existence) that are acquired in a progressive and cumulative manner. In other words, the spontaneous perception of a musical sound occurs as the outcome and experiential residue of an accumulation of *śrutis*, in which each transfers its essential properties to the next. To extract the central proposition from Sathyanarayana's extraordinary analysis: "Thus the *śrutis* are not regarded as discrete, self-contained and independent entities but as the locus traced by the *śruti* moving vertically in a tonal continuum. The *svaras* are regarded as those regions of the continuum where there is manifestation, illumination, or expression."[16]

The thinkers of early India gradually fashioned a dynamic concept of musical sound to represent the vitality and mobility they heard in their music. After some acquaintance with Indian music we cannot fail to be struck by the appropriateness of this line of thinking, in which subtle motion along a continuum of pitch becomes manifest in the form of individual sound events, each a microworld of sound variations, oscillations, and transitions. One of the main tasks of musical thought is to construct appropriate imagery with which to explain the paradox of music conceived as both atomistic and continuous—projecting the illusion of a sensuously moving stream of sound while traversing a network of fixed points. In early musical and grammatical explanation the sound sequences were often likened to a string of gemstones, unified by a current of continuous energy but revealed as a series of discrete, perceptible, meaningful sound events.

## 7.4 The Gamut and its Variables

We return to our agenda (5) for further consideration of the gamut of pitches. In (6) is a display of the basic *sa-grāma* transcribed from Mataṅga's *Bṛhaddeśī.*[17] The aim here was to show the position of each of the *svara*s against the background of their component *śruti*s; the procedure was to construct a nexus of eleven intersecting lines and then imagine them circumscribed by a circle.

6. The *sa-grāma* according to *MB*

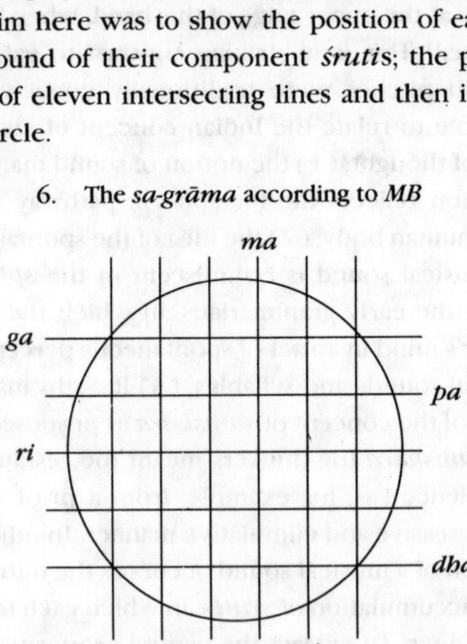


This type of diagram and the numerous references to the "circle of *svara*s" (*svaramaṇḍala*) make it clear that the pitch system was regarded as a continuum that repeated at the interval of an octave, and we must wonder why the concept of the octave (qua interval) played such an insignificant role in Indian musical speculation. As usual terminology provides some useful evidence: the Greek word *diapason* ("through all [the notes]") identifies the eighth sound (Latin: *octava*) as the replica of the first and the completion of the set, thus stressing the vital role of this interval as the most perfect and consonant of all. In contrast, the Sanskrit equivalent—*saptaka* ("the [set of] seven")—emphasizes the contents of the octave instead of its boundary interval. The three registers (*sthānas*) are simply labeled as lower, middle, and upper, and it is taken for granted that their contents are identical, in theory if not in practice. It is *not* taken for granted that the ascending and descending forms of the scale amount to the same thing, as demonstrated by the numerous *rāgas* whose structure differs in ascent and descent

Three of the remaining pitch concepts, which combine to suggest options for traversing the musical gamut, depend upon this view of the scale as a repeating continuum from which segments may be selected and subjected to permutations: *grāma,* as I have pointed out, signifies the basic collection of *svaras* displayed in consecutive order; the *mūrcchanās* comprise a set of systematic rotations of a given octave segment, or perhaps we should say *saptaka,* with a total of seven *mūrcchanās* for each of the two basic scales; and the *tānas* are collections of five or six of the available *svaras* within any given set of seven.

7. The gamut

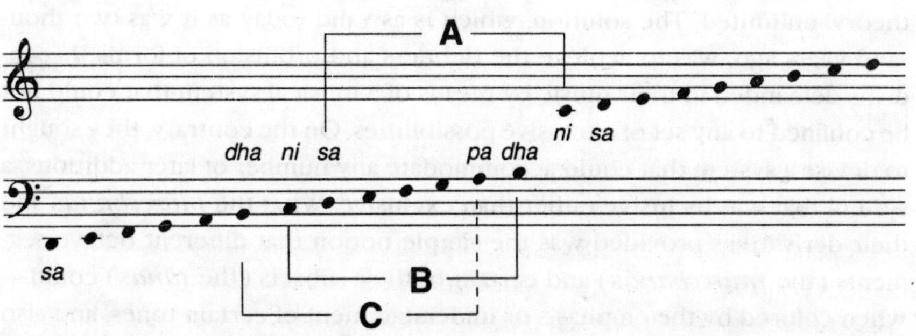


In (7) is a display of the entire gamut in Western staff notation, running through the three full octaves of the *sa-grāma,* with square brackets indicating the successive *mūrcchanās*: bracket *A* encloses the seven scale degrees from lower *sa* to higher *ni,* and this *saptaka* is conceived as the first of the seven possible *mūrcchanās* for this scale. Bracket *B* encloses its first rotation downward, from *ni* to *dha,* and bracket *C* continues the process of systematic rotation. The *mūrcchanās*, then, represent what the ancient Greek musicians knew as "octave species"—the seven possible permutations of the interval sequence within a diatonic octave.[18] The word *mūrcchanā* is used here in the sense of "spreading" or "expanding," and we find the same word applied to a category of multiple vina strokes or a cluster of vocal ornaments.[19] We see here one manifestation of a powerful concept in the history of Indian music: that melodic development proceeds by systematic permutations of the available forms. But the *mūrcchanās* appear to have played a relatively limited role in the ancient system of pitch, and the various rotations of the underlying scale were regarded more as theoretical possibilities than as practical options for performance.

What does this tell us about the relationship between theory and practice? A hallmark of the early Indian way of thinking about music was to identify and name all possible permutations of the basic elements, but with the realization that only certain authorized (and far more specific) melodic constructions can become the basis for actualized music, as, for example, in the form of an individual *rāga.* It was the job of theory to provide the widest selection of possibilities, but it remained for practice to select the most pleasing of these arrangements. There is a reason for this: any purely mechanical set of permutations of a given system (of which the diatonic scale is an excellent example) will sooner or later exhaust the available possibilities and will admit no others. Such an outcome would violate a basic assumption of Indian culture, namely, that the number of available forms is, at least in theory, unlimited. The solution, which is as valid today as it was two thousand years ago, was to achieve the richness and profusion of forms that Indians demanded in their music by means of a musical system that could not be confined to any set of exclusive possibilities. On the contrary, they sought to devise a system that could accommodate any number of later additions, a system that was inclusive rather than exclusive. What the *mūrcchanās* and their derivatives provided was the simple notion that different octave segments (the *mūrcchanās*) and certain of their subsets (the *tānas*) could—when colored by the emphasis or understatement of certain tones, and also by distinctive ornaments and melodic pathways—form the structural basis for a unique melodic construction: a *jāti,* a *grāmarāga,* or a *rāga.* The *tānas* present a special problem, to which I shall return.

The concept of *sādhāraṇa* ([the note or notes] "occupying a mean position") introduces a second major variable of the system. As alternatives to the seven basic *svaras* of the scale, the musical gamut provided for two "altered" or auxiliary degrees: *antara-svara* (the intermediate *svara*) and *kākalī* (a low or sweet sound), raised two *śrutis* from *ga* and *ni,* respectively, and often referred to as *antara-ga* and *kākalī-ni.* In (8) we see their locations along the scale of the *sa-grāma* and the changes thereby produced in the intervals between each pair of scale degrees.[20]

8.

These two altered notes were conceived and explained in an interesting way: because they fell within the interval between two of the standard scale degrees and thus produced a redistribution of the number of *śruti*s within that interval, they were thought to share something of the nature of each of the two surrounding *svara*s. Bharata describes this overlapping of tonal territory with one of his vivid analogies: "There is a time of year when one feels cold in the shade but sweats in the sun; this is the period when spring cannot be said to have not arrived but winter is not fully over."[21] The consequent distinction between the original seven *śuddha* (pure) scale degrees and the two *vikṛta* (altered, distorted) degrees reflects an important antithesis between "pure" and "impure" constructions that spread eventually throughout the entire musical system.[22] There is no reason to suppose this is anything other than a natural habit of thought, but Indian authors implemented it with a passion, drawing instinctively on the philosophical distinction between *prakṛti* (primary, natural substance) and *vikṛti* (transformed substance).

Several questions arise: Why two altered scale degrees? Why only two? Why *these* two? What do they tell us about the ancient Indian musical system, or about scale systems in general? We know that the two altered *svara*s were rare, limited to certain melodic contexts, and that they were regarded as "extra" notes. They were considered to be unstable; and at no time could they serve as the *aṁśa,* the predominant note in any *jāti* or *grāmarāga.* They are obviously upward inflections of the two basic degrees that they replace (that is, "sharps" rather than "flats")—in modern Western terminology, "leading tones." Students of medieval European music will not fail to notice the similarity to the concept of *musica ficta,* and I would not deny that some instinctive musical impulses may be inferred from this evidence, in the form of the near-universal tendency to approach strong, stable scale degrees by the smallest authorized interval. Nowhere in the early Indian system of pitch organization do we find anything analogous to the Western concept of "flat," the downward inflection of a scale degree.

In the original form of the *sa-grāma* and when both the altered notes were present (as was often the case), there is some evidence of a tendency to think of the scale as a pair of identical trichords flanking the central and stable *ma.*[23] Both forms of the scale are displayed in (9):

9.

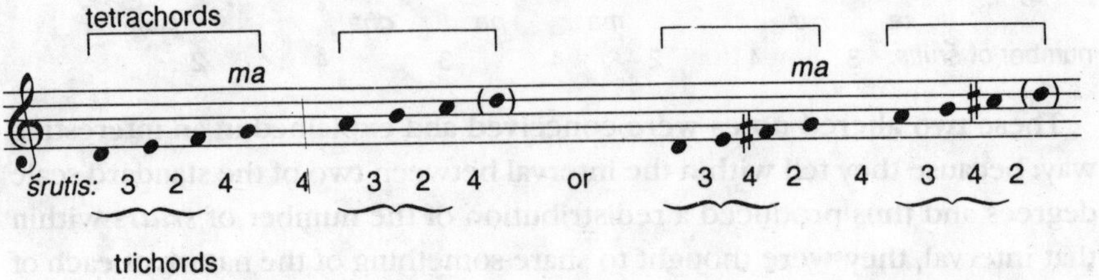


This point did not escape later authors, and the partitioning of the scale into two identically tuned segments comes as a logical consequence of the demand for consonant agreement (the thirteen-*śruti* interval that Westerners know as the *diapente,* or perfect fifth) between *sa/pa, ri/dha,* and *ga/ni*—that is, scale degrees 1/5, 2/6, and 3/7. The result is a symmetry that cannot arise in the basic form of the *ma-grāma,* which may explain the apparent preference for the scale from *sa.* We could also interpret this as evidence for tetrachordal thinking, as marked by square brackets in (9). But while tetrachordal scale construction was the guiding principle in ancient Greece, there are no indications that early Indian musicians relied upon this principle of "chunking" in the construction of either their scales or their melody types.

But, to return to (9), in either of these scale forms the lower and upper segments of the scale are identical, and the effect of each of the elevated degrees is to effect a closer proximation to the next-higher stable degree, *ma* or *sa.* The demand for symmetry may explain why there were two and only two altered notes, and perhaps also why these two (and not, for example, *ma*). We are approaching an important question: What behavioral characteristics and tendencies were assigned to the various *svara*s? How were these bare bones transformed into living melodic tissue?

The priority degrees of the scale, as I observed earlier, were *sa, ma,* and *pa*—degrees 1, 4, and 5. In the modern *rāga* system of South India, *sa* and *pa* are the only unalterable degrees, and the individual *rāga*s have been divided into two large categories: those with *ma* and those with raised *ma.*[24] But in the ancient musical system we have been examining, *ma* was the indispensable degree in any scale and was not subject to any alteration. It is probably incorrect to infer from this that *ma* functioned as a tonal center, or that it was the equivalent of *mese* in the ancient Greek system, but its persistence and stability within the scale suggests that the basic Indian scale at that time manifested the type of tonal equilibrium that we now describe as plagal—by which we mean simply that the relation between degrees 1 and 4 was stronger than that between degrees 1 and 5, and the natural division of the octave was thereby 1–4–8, rather than 1–5–8.[25]

The special role of *ma* may also tell us something about what Bence Szabolcsi has identified as a tendency for early pitch systems either to crystallize around a central "pivotal tone" or to gravitate toward a "ground tone."[26] In the case of the Indian system, as with the Greeks, the idea of a pivotal tone seems to have preceded the concept of a ground tone toward which all melodic activity would sooner or later subside. In the absence of any fixed standard other than the relative positions of the notes, *sa* had not yet begun to assume its later role as the tonic and ground tone, not only of each individual *rāga* but of the entire musical system; it must be regarded as little more than a convenient point of reference, stability, and as we have seen, some priority in the ranking of the scale degrees.

## 7.5 Sonance

I have touched on the vital issue of tonal function: how a tone *behaves*, as opposed to what it *is*. Most musical thinking is a happily unconscious mixture of functional and neutral concepts, and there is no better source of information than a culture's lexicon of musical terms. For example, the eighteenth-century composer and theorist Jean-Philippe Rameau referred to the seventh degree of his scale as the *notte sensible* and the fifth degree as the *dominante.*[27] Before leaving the early Indian musical gamut, we must inquire what (if any) functional tendencies have been built into the system, as opposed to the greater number of tonal tendencies that become evident when we make specific melodic choices in composition or in performance. What evidence can be detected for such things as tonal focus (that is, tonality in the broadest sense), tension and resolution, agreement and disagreement, stability and instability, the priorities of certain notes, and tonal relationships in general? This is a large question, which can be only partially considered.

The most explicit of Indian functional concepts is called (in English) *sonance:* the presence or degree of affinity or "valence" between one note and another. Or to put it in even simpler terms, the extent to which tones agree or disagree with one another. The subject of consonance and dissonance has been one of the great issues in the history of musical thought in the West, and an account of the development of this concept would fill a large book. The notion is far from a simple one, involving, for example, whether the two terms signify smooth blending as opposed to harsh discord, or stable sounds as opposed to unstable ones. The potential valence, the "bonding" properties, of musical tones is a crucial, if imperfectly understood, issue, and the Indian solution (although the question has not been carried as far as it has been in the West) is of considerable intrinsic interest.

The concept of sonance produces a fourfold division of the musical possibilities: notes are either sonant (*vādi*), consonant (*saṁvādi*), dissonant (*vivādi*), or "assonant" (*anuvādi,* that is, neutral or subordinate). The *vādi,* as its name implies, is the note that "speaks" or "resounds," and the remaining terms, by virtue of their different prefixes, mean, respectively, "to speak in concert with," "to speak in opposition to," and "to speak in a subordinate manner."

Śārṅgadeva, in the *Saṅgītaratnākara,* draws upon an old analogy comparing these four possibilities to the roles, relationships, and mutual obligations of the members of a feudal society: "The sonant . . . is considered to be the ruler, while the consonant, being in concert with it, is called the minister; the dissonant being antagonistic is likened by the sages to an enemy; the assonant, however, since it follows the king as well as the ministers, is like a servant."[28] And Mataṅga, in a passage from the *Bṛhaddeśī,* explains these relationships in musical terms: "That from which the essential nature of a *rāga* (*rāgasya rāgatvaṁ,* literally the '*rāga*-ness of a *rāga*') arises is the *vādi;* that which assists in establishing this nature is the *saṁvādi;* that which promotes it is the *anuvādi;* and that which destroys it is known as *vivādi.*"[29]

The sonant note, then, is the single fixed point of reference from which all other tonal affinities are reckoned. When actualized in a particular scale formation or melodic construction, it becomes the *aṁśa,* the "denominator" (as in a fraction), and by extension, the note that determines the individual roles and limitations of the remaining notes, in much the same way that the executor of an estate might be charged with dividing the inheritance and distributing the various shares in the estate. The *aṁśa,* for practical purposes, serves as the tonal center and predominant note in a given *jāti* or *rāga.*

Consonant and dissonant relationships, in contrast to the more elaborate and comprehensive scheme developed by ancient and medieval Western musicians, were each limited to two possibilities. And each category, as we have seen, approximates one of the six distinct interval classes (*ic*) of Western equal temperament: that is, consonance is associated with the intervals of nine or thirteen *śruti*s (*ic* 5: the perfect fourth and its octave complement, the perfect fifth), and dissonance with the intervals of two or twenty *śruti*s (*ic* 1: the minor second and major seventh).[30] Within the Indian system of twenty-two *śruti*s per octave these interval pairs *do* constitute equivalence classes, but this is as far as the system goes.

There is a lot to say about this arrangement, and what has been left unsaid is almost as interesting as what has been said. Nowhere in the literature is there any attempt to identify the remaining intervals or their classes, nor do these intervals have any identity of their own—apart from specific note pairs. The quality of consonance or dissonance is situated in the note, not in an abstract interval. Western musicians will not be surprised to find these intervals designated as consonant or dissonant; but they may fail to remember that consonance and dissonance, which we now tend to associate with simultaneous sounds (intervals or chords), were originally devised as measures for the successive sounds of a melody. In this respect the parallel to the ancient Western experience of music is more exact than it may appear. There are, however, two surprises: the relative neutrality of all other pitch relationships and the sparing way in which sonant relationships are applied in an individual melodic construction.

In the *jāti*s, which I shall soon examine, any of several different *svara*s could be designated as the *aṁśa,* thus affecting the reckoning of all the other tonal relationships, as well as the range within which the melody would be allowed to develop. Several note pairs might be in consonant agreement, but only one note was installed as the official *saṁvādi* (by virtue of its relationship to the *aṁśa*), and consequently it could not be dropped from the scale under any circumstances. With these two strong and closely related *svara*s thus identified as an axis of tonal stability, we see clear indications of a rudimentary principle of structural consonance; but there is no evidence of any tendency toward vertical thinking or the possibility of simultaneous consonance. All we can say is that the consonant pairing of the sonant/*aṁśa* and its *saṁvādi* appears to be an obvious ancestor of the later drone interval, which did not become a fixture of Indian musical practice until as late as the fifteenth or sixteenth century.[31]

The concept of sonance has mutated over the course of time, as subsequent musicians sought to reconcile the puzzling rules of the ancient literature with the musical experience of their day. The notion of *vivādi* reflects this shift in thinking: in modern Hindustani music, for example, the term *vivādi* now signifies a note foreign to the *rāga.* But in the ancient system, *vivādi svara*s were those situated two *śruti*s above or below the *aṁśa.* As a consequence, *vivādi* relationships would not necessarily arise in a given melody type: the intervals of two and twenty *śruti*s will appear twice in any diatonic scale, but "dissonance" as such will not occur except with reference to the *aṁśa.*

From the melodic point of view, there is no obvious reason why an interval of two *śruti*s (= the Western semitone) should be regarded as dissonant. Semitones after all are the lifeblood of melody, and the ear relishes these close connections among notes. What the early concept of *vivādi* probably signifies is that a close neighbor to the focal tone should be treated as a sensitive and unstable tone, perhaps shaken, deemphasized, or passed over in some ornamental figure, and above all should not be allowed to overshadow the center of tonal focus in any way. I shall have more to say later about the role of the *aṁśa* in the various *jāti*s and *grāmarāgas*.

The designation of all other notes as functionally subordinate or neutral also has some interesting implications. What it means is that beyond these few valences—all of which follow from the choice of *aṁśa*—all other functional properties of the notes will be assigned within the context of each different melody type. Tonal behavior is not something that arises from deep-seated tendencies in the system; it is the result of deliberate choice and can be donned like a favorite sari and set of accessories. And Śārṅgadeva's political analogy is by no means a superficial one: in the early Indian world of feudal princely states, the distinctive quality of life was a direct consequence of the character and personality of the ruler, his choice of advisors, the relationships he maintained with his subjects, and even the enemies he made. And in a similar way, the individuality of each melody type depended upon the choice of *aṁśa,* the immediate consequences of that choice (limitations of range and the roles assigned to certain scale degrees), and the remaining choices, which were subject to considerable freedom so long as they did not violate the existing rules for tonal conduct.

## 7.6 The *Tānas*

Each of the seven *mūrcchanā*s of the two basic scales could be converted into a hexatonic or pentatonic version by omitting one or two of the *svaras*. I have deferred consideration of this final variable of the system until now, because the criteria for inclusion and exclusion depend to a certain extent upon the sonant categories and the ranking of the scale degrees. It was clearly more convenient to identify the missing note(s) than to list the larger number that would be present, but the result was once again to emphasize the negative.

If there is a specific algorithm for converting the fourteen *mūrcchanā* octave rotations into the eighty-four *tānas* mentioned by Bharata and Dattila, it resists easy formalization.[32] The specifications are as follows:

For the hexatonic *tānas*,
  in the *sa-grāma:* drop *sa, ri, pa,* or *ni;*
  in the *ma-grāma:* drop *sa, ri,* or *ga.*
For the pentatonic *tānas*,
  in the *sa-grāma:* drop one of the pairs *sa/pa, ga/ni,* or *pa/ri;*
  in the *ma-grāma:* drop one of the pairs *dha/ri* or *ga/ni.*

We have accounted for the numbers: 12 options × 7 possible rotations = 84, but why these and not others? Is there an internal logic that has eluded us? The considerable differences between the two scales cannot be explained solely by the one-*śruti* discrepancy in their tuning. First the problem of the hexatonic versions: in (10) is a display of the two *grāmas* with their tuning in *śrutis*, their indispensable *svaras* (blackened note heads), and the *svaras* that were subject to omission (empty note heads):

10.

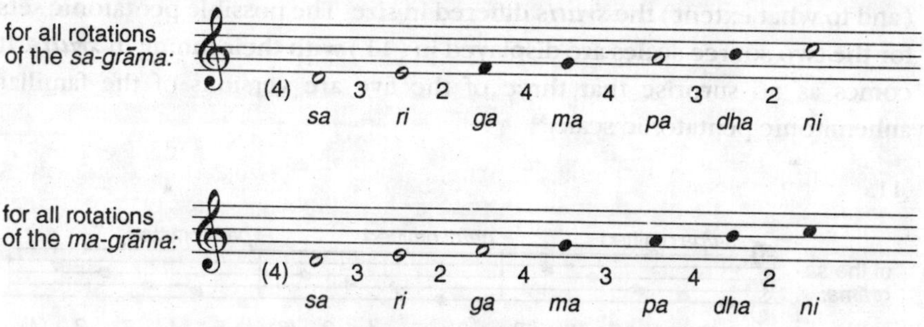


The set of background priorities for the scale degrees must be among the criteria for inclusion or exclusion. *Ma,* for example, could never be dropped from either scale, situated as it was nine *śrutis* above and thirteen below *sa.* But *sa* could be dropped from either scale. And *pa* could not be dropped from the *ma-grāma,* on the strength of a curious but not atypical piece of reasoning: now located twelve (instead of thirteen) *śrutis* above *sa* and therefore no longer in consonant agreement, *pa* was held to be indispensable because it had moved into a nine-*śruti* relationship with *ri.* If the logic behind this line of explanation is elusive, it does demonstrate the importance attached to the fifth degree of the scale, which in modern practice may be omitted but cannot be altered in pitch.

The algorithm for the pentatonic versions is somewhat clearer, although not totally consistent: the note pairs identified for possible omission exclude the indispensable *ma,* and, more important, they are in consonant agreement—with the one exception of the pair *pa/ri* in the *sa-grāma* (ten *śruti*s). These specifications entail two significant consequences: First, the requirement that only note pairs separated by intervals of nine, ten, or thirteen *śruti*s may be dropped has the effect of balancing the resulting scale forms, that is, by insuring that the scale contains two nonconsecutive gaps of minimal size, instead of two consecutive gaps or a single larger interval. And second, the pentatonic sets thus produced would, because of their derivation as subsets of a larger referential set, be more likely to be conceived and perceived as "gapped" scales—unlike other world versions of the same pentatonic scales, in which the larger intervals are *not* thought of as gaps or "skips" but as "steps" equivalent to the smaller intervals of the scale.

But the suspicion grows that these decisions, whatever they may have meant in actual musical practice, were reached originally on aesthetic and essentially irrational grounds, and that their formalization in these terms gives no more than the appearance of rigor. And to complicate an already complicated matter, it must surely have made a difference whether or not (and to what extent) the *śruti*s differed in size. The possible pentatonic sets for the two source scales are displayed in (11) with their tuning in *śruti*s. It comes as no surprise that three of the five are versions of the familiar anhemitonic pentatonic scale.[33]

11.

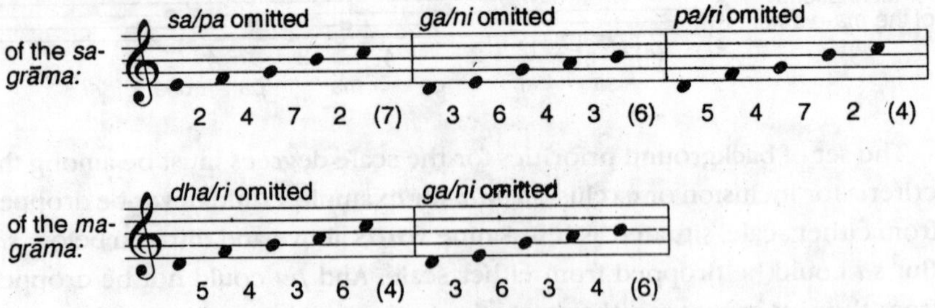


## 7.7 Melodic Choices

> A song without any *alaṅkāra* would be like a night without a moon, a river devoid of water, a vine without any flower, and a woman without any ornament.
>
> Bharata, *Nāṭyaśāstra* 29.75[34]

In the many studies of the melodic dimension in Indian music, few authors have been able to resist citing Bharata's famous dictum. Indian melody, consistent with the other traditional arts of the subcontinent, is inherently and profoundly decorative, and the small cluster of concepts with which the decorative aspects of melody are grasped amounts to a general theory of melodic contour, one which is relatively independent of both the underlying structure of the musical gamut and the detailed restrictions of the individual *jātis*, *grāmarāgas*, and *rāgas*. This section is organized around three topics: *varṇa* (melodic shape), *alaṅkāra* (ornament), and *gamaka* (transition).[35] Of the three, the idea of *gamaka* was the latest to develop. Mataṅga was apparently the first author to use the word in this special sense, and descriptions of the individual *gamakas* begin to appear only in the thirteenth century. *Varṇa* and *alaṅkāra* are among the standard topics of the earliest treatises.

The musicians of ancient India seem to have reached an easy consensus on the concept of *varṇa*, and all the authors of our corpus of literature accept the standard set of four: the *sthāyī* (stable), *sañcārī* (meandering), *ārohī* (ascending), and *avarohī* (descending) contours. A melodic unit, then, might dwell upon or prolong a single tone, it might proceed in a steady upward or downward direction, or it might exhibit a pattern with frequent changes of direction. This is reminiscent of the slightly different set of four melodic figures expounded by the Hellenistic author Cleonides under the general topic of *melopoeia* (melodic composition): succession, plexus or network, repetition, and prolongation.[36] The intent behind these conventional sets of obvious melodic shapes was not to specify the overall contour of a melody (which would be impossible) but to fix the shape of a given melodic unit, which in the case of the four *varṇas* was a single word of the poetic text.[37] The concept was highly appropriate for a florid style of singing in which the individual words were frequently prolonged, and it subsequently proved equally useful in instrumental music where the *varṇas* were defined as clusters of vina strokes.

But although both *varṇa* and *alaṅkāra* may have arisen within the context of *gīta,* Bharata's exposition is located in his chapter on stringed instruments; it is entirely separate from his presentation of the elements of the musical gamut and directly precedes his explanation of the different finger strokes (the *dhātus*).[38] In the later history of musical ornamentation, both *varṇa* and *alaṅkāra* have developed into abstract melodic concepts, freely translatable between vocal and instrumental performance; and the size of the unit determining the *varṇa* is often a matter of instinct and convention. It is, we may say, a melodic "gesture" or "event."

The term *alaṅkāra* refers to the pattern of surface decoration within an individual *varṇa,* and here the possibilities could in no way be restricted to any obvious set of exclusive choices. As was the case with so many other topics of the musical system, *alaṅkāra* developed in an explosion of possibilities—from Dattila's thirteen, to Bharata's thirty-three, and subsequently to the sixty-three enumerated by Śārṅgadeva and the still-larger numbers mentioned in later treatises.[39] Unsurprisingly, the scope of the concept narrowed during the course of this explosion: while the earliest lists of the *alaṅkāras* were intended to exhaust all the conventional categories of ornaments (including oscillations on a single tone and slides from one tone to another), the later lists were confined to progressions that could be described in terms of specific patterns of *svaras*. In the later medieval period the more irrational melodic ornaments—irrational, that is, in that they could not be described as patterns of fixed scale degrees—were grouped under the heading of *gamaka*.

Of Dattila's short list of *alaṅkāras*, some are shakes or quivers on a sustained tone, some are back-and-forth "swings" between two adjacent or nonadjacent tones, some are rapid touchings of a single higher or lower tone (to be struck "like lightning"), and others are patterns with specific contours (with, for example, the lowest tone situated at the beginning, middle, or end of the progression).[40] Certain *alaṅkāras* were restricted to an appropriate *varṇa*—an *alaṅkāra* that must end on a low tone is obviously out of place in an ascending melodic contour—but others were unrestricted as to context. Many of the same *alaṅkāras* are still practiced today in the melodic exercises with which the Indian student expands his technique and learns the characteristic patterns of the individual *rāgas*. Śārṅgadeva hinted at the pedagogical applications of the concept: "The aim of demonstrating the *alaṅkāras* is to create delight, knowledge of the *svaras*, and the variety of melodic shapes."[41]

To put the three terms into their proper perspective, it is useful to imagine the decorative dimension in Indian music as a hierarchy: if *varna* represents the generalized shape of a given unit of melody, *alaṅkāra* signifies the specific pattern of decoration within this general shape, and *gamaka* refers to the transitive elements around and between the individual *svaras*—the microlevel of melodic structure. And in addition to this progression from contour to pattern to microstructure, we can also infer another progression: from ornaments as conceived to ornaments as performed; once again from the potential to the actual. The idea of *varṇa* is readily grasped by the mind and described in words, but the microscopic subtleties of the *gamakas* resist description and are best learned by demonstration and imitation. The first descriptions of the *gamakas* appear in *PS;* Pārśvadeva's list of seven has been expanded to fifteen in *SS,* and the number has grown in subsequent treatises.[42] Pārśvadeva's list includes such familiar ornaments as a tremor on a single tone, one tone sliding gradually into another, a second tone begun without a new stroke or articulation, two degrees of oscillation between two tones (one rapid and one slow), and other staples of the Indian melodic tradition.

No useful purpose would be served by an exhaustive enumeration of the many ornaments listed in the early treatises, but we may note that many of the individual *alaṅkāra*s have become models for the types of melodic permutations which Indian musicians and their audiences take such delight in: progressions in which the musician gradually adds or subtracts notes, arabesques, palindromes, progressions in which the same ornamental figure is applied systematically to each successive step of the scale, and other patterned ways of traversing the gamut. What seems important here is the depth of the decorative impulse and its meaning in the musical aesthetics of India.

The etymology of the word *alaṅkāra* provides a powerful clue: I pointed out in chapter 6 that the literal meaning of the word is "to make sufficient," and the obvious implication is that decoration is an essential aspect of structure and a necessary condition if music is to give pleasure. Traditional Indian aesthetics has not emphasized the concept of natural beauty; this is entirely consistent in a culture where material substance has been assigned relatively low value and where the differences between one manifestation and another have not been regarded as lasting or essential. Less is not more: if matter in its primal state (*prakṛti*) will always lie beyond the grasp of sense perception, there is no reason to consider any appearance as natural or to attach any particular value to it; and if cultural ideology has not taught us to relish the display of matter in what we assume to be its natural state, the logical consequence is to add and take delight in the touches that give beauty. We can adduce evidence for this line of argument from the citation from Bharata, the role of spices in cuisine, feminine fashions and makeup, the barrenness and limited color spectrum of much of the Indian landscape, the important role of ornamental figures in poetic and dramatic theory, and the many decorative styles and conventions in the visual arts.

In the tradition of pervading ornamentation we see one of the sharpest contrasts between the musical experience of India and that of the West. Just as Western students of Indian music find it next to impossible to hear and reproduce the minute embellishments and transitions with which the musical surface is etched, so do Indian students labor when required to produce straight tones as a pedagogical exercise, thus avoiding the impulse to fall into the familiar decorative patterns with which their entire musical experience has been saturated. The achievement of ancient Indian authors was to recognize the profundity of the decorative impulse in their music and to provide, at a very early date, the conceptual means for its realization. Without the example of the great phoneticians before them, they might have been tempted to gloss over the microstructural domain of music. And although the abundance of decoration in the musical tradition has encouraged authors to emphasize the organization of the musical surface at the expense of long-range or syntactical thinking, their decisions were in accord with one of the most fundamental aims of Asian art, namely, to achieve the maximum refinement of a limited spectrum: "from less, more."

## 7.8 The Concept of *Rāga*

> The profoundly learned in *rāga,* even Mataṅga and his followers, have not crossed the ocean of *Rāga;* how then may one of little understanding swim across?
>
> Nānyadeva, *Sarasvatīhrdayālaṅkāra* 7.13[43]

We would do well to heed Nānyadeva's warning. The subject of *rāga* is indeed an endless ocean, and my exposition will not venture beyond the coastal waters charted by authors of the first millennium. My aim here is to identify the principles by which the earliest sets of melody types were generated, as set forth in the first few layers of the textual evidence, and in this way to suggest how the idea of *rāga* evolved. I will examine two classes of scalar modes, the *jāti*s and the *grāmarāga*s, the earliest-known ancestors of the later *rāga*s.

Nānyadeva's words of caution echo one of the aphorisms in Nārada's phonetic manual, which asserts that even legendary master musicians such as Nārada and Tumburu were unable to specify the exact melodic path of the Sāmans because the *svara*s were so subtle and so elusive.[44] Indian authors have traditionally left some room in their expositions for a je ne sais quoi, recognizing that the full details of musical practice can only be communicated in face-to-face instruction; this tendency is clearly evident in their presentations of *rāga* and its ancestral melody types. From the earliest times it has been apparent that a *rāga* is much more than a scale or configuration of notes with pivotal, strong, and weak degrees and other melodic functions; it is also apparent that its affective properties, intangible as they may be, are at least as important as the technical specifications.

The word *rāga* derives from the verbal root *rañj:* "to be colored [especially red], to be affected or moved, to take delight in."[45] Hence the term occupies a rich semantic field that includes such things as color, feeling, intensity, passion, love, and beauty. The primary aim of *rāga,* then, is to bring delight by stimulating an emotional response in the hearer. The affective content of a given *rāga* rests on a cultural consensus, is embedded in the many technical specifications, and should be communicated automatically if the performance is competent. It is evident that we are dealing with an important theory of musical meaning, as well as a cluster of theoretical constructs, and that we need to examine the connections that authors have drawn between the technical and expressive domains of *rāga.*

As far as can be determined, extramusical associations have guided the evolution of the idea of *rāga* from the beginning, and the early development of the concept is recorded in the critical literature on the Indian theater. Although the word *rāga* appears in the *Nāṭyaśāstra,* it is not used in its later and fully developed sense. What is crucial in this work is the association of particular melodic constructs—the *jāti*s—with specific emotional states, dramatic situations, and types of characters. Music has the power to evoke a repertoire of conventional emotions depending on a rich network of cultural associations (including colors, fragrances, facial expressions, times of day, figures of speech, and modes of diction), which are triggered by the musical clues implanted in the structure of a given melody. The link between melodic structure and the emotional response generated by that structure was the sonant note, or *aṁśa,* the note emphasized in the melody and from which the remaining melodic functions were reckoned. According to Bharata, the *aṁśa* determined not only the "*rāga*" (by which he meant the ethos of the melody) but also the framing notes (initial, final, high, low) and the entire network of tonal relationships.[46]

What exactly is a *rāga?* Is it like anything in Western music? I have been struck by Harold Powers's definition of *rāga* as "a continuum with scale and tune as its extremes,"[47] that is, something more specific than an array of pitches, but more variable than a composed melody. *Rāga*s and their ancestral melody types are generally described in terms of a particular selection of scale degrees, their tuning, and the functions of the various notes, but there is usually more to it than this. Examples of notated *rāga*s in treatises beginning with *MB* provide convincing evidence that individual *rāga*s can also be identified by their characteristic melodic progressions and overall design. In the later stages of the evolution of the *rāga* system, a particular *rāga* may incline toward the scalar or tunelike end of the continuum. Its constituent tones may be relatively neutral and ready to accommodate a wide range of melodic figures, or they may be charged with tensions and energies that shape individual performances into a similar melodic profile. I think of a *rāga* as a tonal matrix or framework, complete not only with nodal points and the functions assigned to the individual *svara*s but also furnished with characteristic ornaments, shapes, and pathways. The result is a set of deeply etched tonal grooves that guide a performer's spontaneous decisions into the proper channels.

How did this all come about? The earliest ancestral phase of the *rāga* concept for which we have reliable written evidence is the system of eighteen *jāti*s (classes) outlined in *D* and *BN:* seven generic or pure *jāti*s (the *svarajāti*s) and eleven "mingled" (*saṅkara*) *jāti*s.[48] From the pure *jāti*s an indefinite number of "distorted" (*vikṛta*) varieties could be derived. The mingled *jāti*s arise from combinations of the various generic and distorted *jāti*s. Note once again the familiar antithesis between *śuddha* (pure) and *vikṛta* constructions; also note that the seven "pure" degrees of the diatonic scale have given birth to the seven pure *jāti*s, as shown in (12). Still other *jāti*s were theoretical possibilities, but the repertoire of *gāndharva* was confined to the eighteen. The *jāti*s are situated closer to the scalar end of Powers's continuum than to the end represented by "tune," and the functions of the individual *svara*s are not fixed as precisely as they are in most later *rāgas*. In some of the *jāti*s, for example, as many as five, six, or even all seven of the scale degrees are available as potential *aṁśa*s, thereby influencing the emotional coloring and tonal relationships of the melodic structure they are able to generate.

A conspectus of the seven generic *jāti*s appears in (12), each displayed in scalar form in the octave above its designated final. In connection with this figure and later displays of the structure of the various *jāti*s, it is essential to point out that (1) the particular octave in which the notes are deployed is in no way to be regarded as an authorized melodic range or *ambitus;* and (2) nothing should be inferred about tendencies for tonal gravitation within this selection of notes (as we do, for example, when displaying the scales of Western tonal music with *do* as the common ground tone), apart from the obvious fact that the final, *nyāsa,* will linger in the mind.

I remarked earlier that the octave as an interval is insignificant in Indian musical thinking. As W. Sidney Allen has observed, "it should be mentioned here that in the musical treatises each octave is referred to as the '*dviguṇa*' or 'double' of its predecessor, and it would be tempting to conclude from this that the authors were further acquainted with the theory of vibrational frequency-ratios; this interpretation is invalidated, however, by the commentator's statement that 'double' means simply 'double in effort.'"[49] What is all-important is the *saptaka,* the collection of seven *svara*s available in each register.

12. The seven generic *jātis*

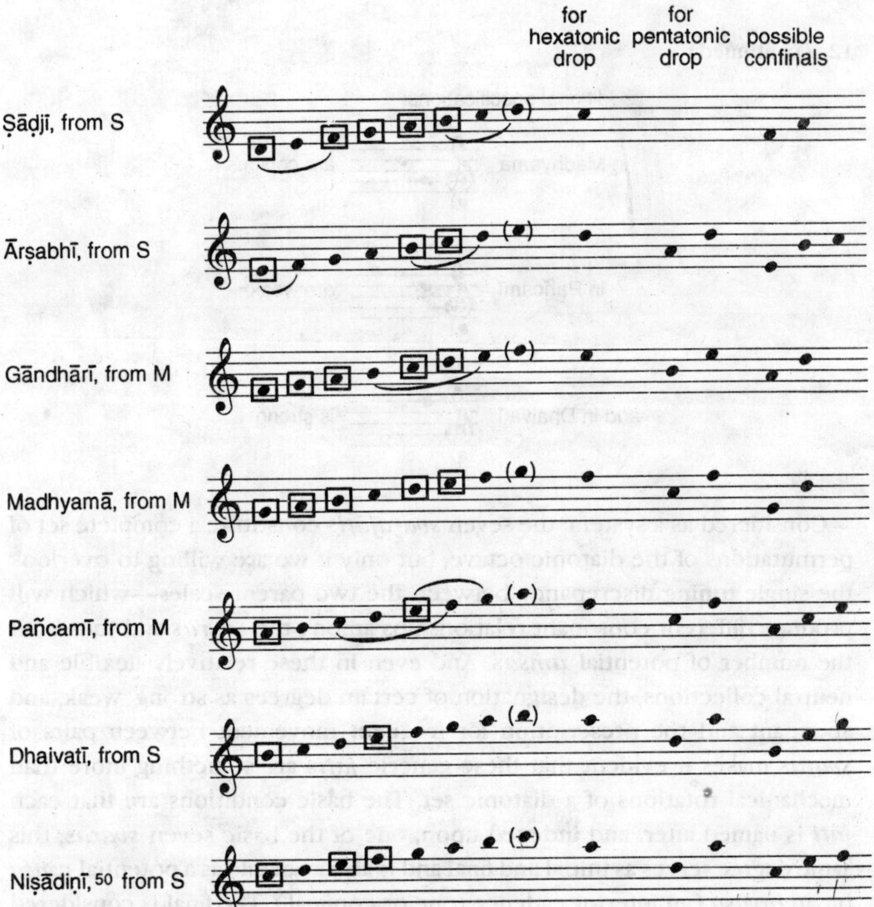


**From** ***S:*** **derived from the** ***sa-grāma***[51]
**From** ***M:*** **derived from the** ***ma-grāma***
**Emboxed notes: possible** ***aṁśas***
**First** ***svara*** **in each of the above: initial, final, possible** ***aṁśa,*** **or confinal**
**Final is in low octave**
**⁀: *saṅgati* (association) or *sañcāri,* back-and-forth movement between two *svaras***

12. (continued)

additional specifications:

in Madhyamā  are copious

in Pañcamī  are weak

and in Dhaivatī  is strong

Considered as a system, the seven *svarajātis* constitute a complete set of permutations of the diatonic octave, but only if we are willing to overlook the single tuning discrepancy between the two parent scales—which will produce different consonant relationships among the *svaras* and thus limit the number of potential *aṁśas*. And even in these relatively flexible and neutral collections, the designation of certain degrees as strong, weak, and abundant and the prescription for frequent movement between pairs of *svaras* makes it evident that these generic *jātis* are something more than mechanical rotations of a diatonic set. The basic conditions are that each *jāti* is named after, and indexed upon, one of the basic seven *svaras*; this same degree serves as initial and final and is also available as a potential *aṁśa* or *apanyāsa* (an interior cadence tone or confinal). The final is considered to be in the lower octave. Hexatonic and pentatonic versions of these *jātis* are produced by dropping the note or note pair indicated in (12).[52]

Each of the *jātis* would be actualized in performance and recognized by means of its ten characteristics—its *lakṣaṇas*:[53]

1. *graha:* the initial
2. *aṁśa:* the sonant
3. *tāra:* the highest note permitted—generally the *svara* located a fifth above the *aṁśa,* but with *ni* in the upper octave as the absolute limit[54]
4. *mandra:* the lowest note permitted—often the final, the *aṁśa* in the lower octave, or even the note below the final[55]
5. *ṣāḍava:* a hexatonic variant produced by omitting a designated *svara*
6. *auḍuvita* (or *auḍuva*): a pentatonic variant produced by omitting a designated pair of *svaras*[56]

7. *alpatva* ("scarceness"): a note that is weak, infrequent, or omitted altogether

8. *bahutva* ("muchness"): a note used copiously or as a nodal point in the melody, often the sonant or consonant

9. *nyāsa:* the final

10. *apanyāsa:* a confinal—a *svara* appropriate for an internal cadence

To this standard list of ten *lakṣaṇa*s, certain authors add the intriguing concept of *antaramārga* (internal pathway), realized in performance by *saṅgati* or *sañcāri*—frequent movement between two associated *svara*s, as shown by the curving lines in (12). In this respect the *jāti*s begin to approach the idea of tune. One can infer a great deal about the structure of the *jāti*s from the list of their characteristics, but the single most important variable was the flexibility allowed in the choice of *aṁśa.* If we bear in mind that both the ambitus and the entire network of tonal relationships would be determined by this choice, it is evident that as many as twenty-five individual melodic structures could be generated from the set of seven pure *jāti*s.[57]

Of these, only eleven are set forth in the ancient musicological literature, and the reasons for their selection are obscure. The eleven mingled *jāti*s are explained as derivatives from as few as two, or as many as five, of the parent *jāti*s. Their options include as few as one, or as many as seven, of the potential *aṁśa*s. The set does not exhaust all of the possible initial and final notes, and as a system it reveals no pattern whatsoever. The fact that several of the names coincide with names of major geographical regions of ancient India suggests that this classification was an early attempt to incorporate certain distinctive regional traditions within the established framework of the *jāti* system.[58] Even at this early date the theorists have been at work.

Rather than display the entire set of eleven with their various properties, I shall make two comparisons to illustrate the range of differences between otherwise similar *jāti*s. Ṣāḍjī, the first of the *svara-jāti*s, is displayed in (13) along with its derivative, Ṣaḍjamadhyamā; the latter, as its name implies, is explained as a composite of the two generic *jāti*s Ṣāḍjī and Madhyamā. Ṣaḍjamadhyamā has all the earmarks of a purely theoretical concoction, with so many options that it has no identity of its own: all its scale degrees are potential *aṁśa*s, and its other variables include the initial and final degrees of both its parents. In addition, Ṣaḍjamadhyamā permits the use of the two altered *svara*s (but only in ascent) when certain degrees were designated as the *aṁśa.* If such a *jāti* ever existed as a recognizable and individual melody type, its identity must have been communicated by distinctive melodic properties other than those recorded in the literature.

13. Ṣāḍjī compared to Ṣaḍjamadhyamā

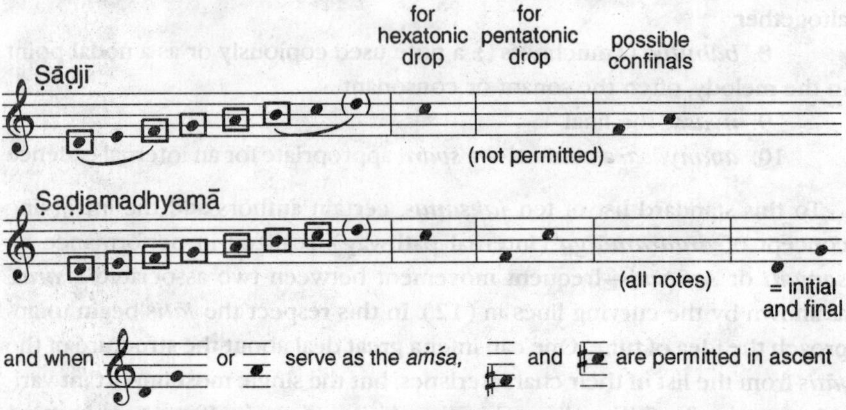


In the five mingled *jāti*s shown in (14), on the other hand, we find grounds for a more productive comparison: all five share the same final (*ga*) but differ in initial, strong, and weak notes, the number and selection of possible *aṁśa*s, and in the restrictions for hexatonic and pentatonic performance. Each of the five retains some individuality, despite the number of options that remain open. In particular, Nandayantī ("gladdening"), with its single initial, final, and sonant, resembles the Hypolydian mode of the medieval European modal system.[59]

14. Comparison of five mingled *jātis*

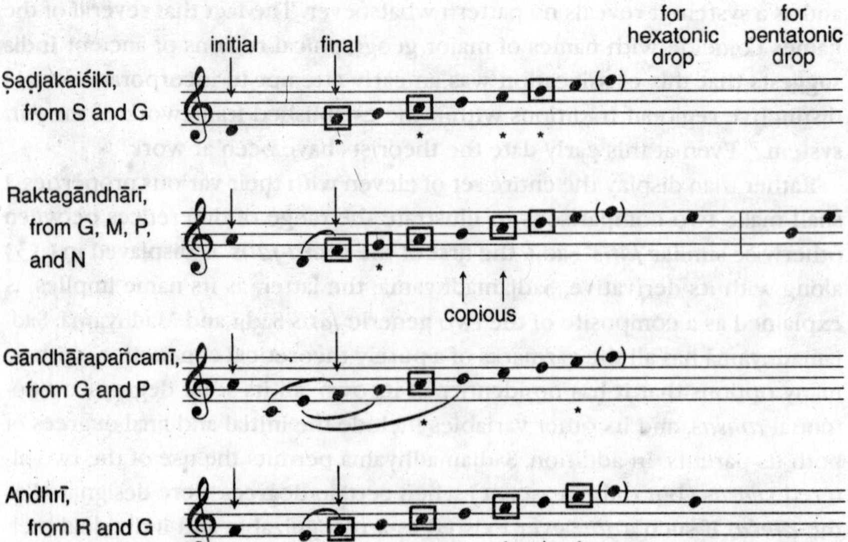

Nandayantī, from R, G, and P

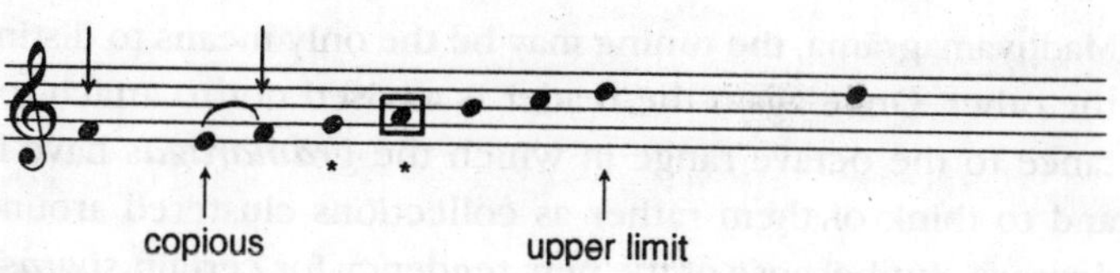


* possible confinals
Emboxed notes: possible *aṁśas*
Hexatonic and pentatonic versions permitted only where notes are shown
From *S, R, G, M, P, D,* and/or *N:* derivation from *śuddha jātis*[60]

A second and quite different stage in the evolution of the *rāga* concept is recorded in sources dating from the middle of the first millennium[61] in the form of the so-called *grāmarāga*s ("scalar" *rāga*s). The *jāti*s are not mentioned in these sources, so it is entirely possible that the two systems represent separate but contemporaneous traditions rather than successive historical layers. The *jāti*s and *grāmarāga*s first appear side by side in *MB,* although the *grāmarāga*s have already begun to multiply (to a total of thirty).[62] By this time the *jāti*s were a closed tradition, and all later developments occurred within the framework of the idea of *rāga.* On the evidence of these sources, D. R. Widdess has concluded that the original seven *grāmarāga*s were the predominant modes in musical practice during the middle years of the first millennium A.D.[63] There is also evidence that they were known in China during the Northern Zhou Dynasty (ca. A.D. 570) under Chinese transliterations of their original Sanskrit names.[64]

The original *grāmarāga*s are once again a set of seven, but the frame of reference has altered in interesting ways. Instead of an array of scales with finals on each step of the basic scale, as in the generic *jāti*s, the finals are now restricted to the fourth and fifth degrees (*ma* and *pa*). And instead of a large number of potential sonant notes, there is now one and only one for each *grāmarāga.* In five of the seven, the initial and *aṁśa* have been assigned to the same *svara* (*sa* in the upper octave), thus separating their function from that of the final. Like the system of pure *jāti*s, the system of *grāmarāga*s was devised to meet the demands for regularity and completeness, but with different tactics: instead of a systematic rotation through all the possible permutations of a diatonic octave, the objectives now seem to be two: to limit the number of possible interval sequences and to establish three of the *svara*s (*sa, ma,* and *pa,* degrees 1, 4, and 5) in specialized roles and as nodal degrees.

The seven primary *grāmarāga*s are displayed in (15), with their initial, final, and sonant notes, their derivation, and their tuning in *śruti*s.[65] It will be particularly instructive to compare this display to (12). In the case of scales that are otherwise described in identical terms, as in Ṣaḍjagrāma and

Madhyamagrāma, the tuning may be the only means to distinguish one from the other. Once again the reader is advised not to attach too much importance to the octave range in which the *grāmarāga*s have been illustrated and to think of them rather as collections clustered around their priority degrees. But because of the new tendency for certain *svara*s to play specialized roles throughout the system, it makes some sense to display the seven *grāmarāga*s as permutations within a common octave—lower *sa* to upper *sa.*[66]

15. A conspectus of the seven primary *grāmarāgas*

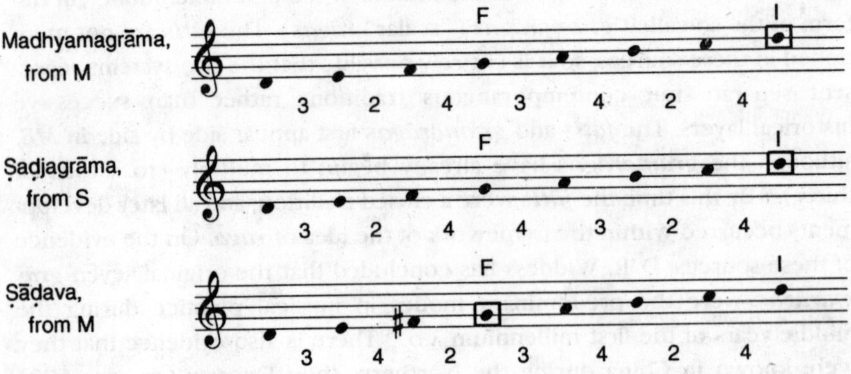

Emboxed notes: *aṁśa*
*F:* final
*I:* initial
From *M:* derived from the *ma-grāma*
From *S:* derived from the *sa-grāma*

The seven *grāmarāgas* displayed in (15) may be further reduced to three familiar arrangements of the diatonic octave, differentiated in terms of their derivation from the *sa-* or the *ma-grāma* (and consequently in their tuning) and also by their functional degrees.[67] Interestingly, one of the seven is hexatonic—Kaiśikamadhyama ("subtle" *madhyama*), an obvious variant of Kaiśika that may have been inserted to fill out the system to the desired number. The *grāmarāgas* may also have been differentiated by strong and weak degrees, *sañcāri,* oscillations, and other unspecified characteristics; the garbled and virtually undecipherable descriptions in the *Nāradīyaśikṣā* suggest strongly that such was indeed the case. And further, the *grāmarāgas* reveal a greater and more systematic application of the altered *svaras* on *ga* and *ni,* which I compared earlier to the *musica ficta* "leading tones" of medieval Western chant; this phenomenon cannot be completely unrelated to the tendency to regard *ma* and *sa* as pivotal functional degrees, not only of the individual *grāmarāgas* but of the system itself.[68] This is a crucial point, and I shall return to it below. In the seven *grāmarāgas* we see once again an attempt to construct a set of exclusive possibilities within the diatonic system, a system that now appears to be moving in the direction of a set of common degree functions with a force that cuts across the entire pitch system.

It is time to step back from this ocean of detail and put the subject of *rāga* into broader perspective. Much of this chapter has been an attempt to demonstrate the distinctive features of the Indian approach to the nature and organization of musical pitch. This approach not only was in harmony with, but continued to be guided by, the prevailing cultural ideology and habits of thinking. In search of a broader perspective on pitch, I am posing two general questions; each will suggest interesting side issues. What natural or even universal tendencies can be detected in the ancient Indian strategies for the organization of pitch? And what has been the later history of the concept of *rāga?*

In the sets of *jātis* and *grāmarāgas* we have seen two early and ingenious attempts to construct a viable musical system from the material at hand. Each of the attempts was characterized by a certain amount of wishful thinking, in that its proponents sought to reconcile three objectives that were and are essentially incompatible: (1) to incorporate as much as possible of the musical practice of the day; (2) to produce a closed, finite system of some rigor; and (3) to leave the system open-ended in some important respects so as to accommodate future possibilities. That they succeeded to the degree they did is a tribute to their keen intellect and their musical sensitivity. The subsequent history of the *rāga* system testifies that Indian musicians set a higher value on the inclusiveness of their system than on its ability to exhaust all of the available possibilities in a systematic manner. Theorists in turn saw the rapid expansion of musical possibilities as a challenge to their imagination and set to work with the typically Indian passion for classification and organization. The demands of theory and practice will inevitably collide under these conditions, and the development of a musical tradition of this antiquity and complexity will just as inevitably be a continuing dialectic between *śāstra* and *prayoga.*

Students of ancient Greek music and medieval European chant will recognize most of the theoretical constructs devised for pitch organization and the classification of melody types. We have seen how Indian authors approached their material with what appear to be instinctive strategies for grasping and then manipulating the pitch structure of music: isolate, name, and number your basic units; collect them into groups; derive from preexistent patterns whenever possible; limit the possibilities and express the limitations in the form of rules; seek to provide for flexibility and variety by introducing procedures for systematic permutation; fit what already exists into the system; if it doesn't fit, make it fit; classify your material according to established cultural patterns; devise a set of oppositions (such as between "pure" and "derivative" material) so that the system can expand in an orderly manner; and provide the means for developing the individuality of melody.

But beyond these I would identify several additional features as natural components in the early Indian organization of the domain of pitch. First of all, the diatonic scale. This scale is so pervasive in the history of music in the ancient world and has such useful technical properties and such evident aesthetic appeal that, as Robert Gauldin has written, we should scarcely be surprised to discover it "alive, well, and living on some distant planet."[69] This scale is remarkable not only in and of itself but also for the way its patterning invites transposition and other forms of systematic permutation. I regard the following as "laws" of diatonicism: (1) tonal focus (and perhaps, even *dual* tonal focus);[70] (2) adjacent but dissimilar whole steps; (3) a tendency to crystallize around nodal degrees separated by intervals of a perfect fourth/fifth, with these "strong" degrees filled in by "weaker," less stable members; and (4) a tendency to develop and expand the system by exploiting the special role of the semitone as a leading tone.

Those who have grown up with twelve-tone equal temperament, as I have, may lift an eyebrow at the second of these claims; but I contend that the diatonic system is inherently a far more complex achievement than it may appear to be, and that its early history demonstrates a clear preference for an octave divided first into a lower and an upper part (tetrachords). Each part is balanced against the other and framed by strong scale degrees, and each part is divided into three steps (two tones and one semitone) of dissimilar size, with the structure of each part clarified by the position of the smallest interval.[71] This falls short of a full description of the earliest stages in the evolution of the *rāga*-system, but it is evidently the guiding principle by which the various known scales were brought into conformity with one another. Indian musicians, like their counterparts elsewhere in the ancient world, must have turned instinctively to this system and manipulated it with some brilliance; but it did not suit enough of their material to survive as the exclusive basis for the system. In the end, as in the West, a more chromatic system was required, and by the thirteenth century a rough system of twelve-tone equal temperament (still allowing for the shading of individual pitches upward or downward) had begun to replace the system of twenty-two *śruti*s.

The exact status of the ancient tuning system cannot be determined. As Powers observes: "whatever links there may be between ancient Indian practice and that of the present day are to be found in a gradually developing aesthetic and classification theory, not in tuning and acoustics. Indeed, whatever acoustic foundation may have existed for the *śruti*-doctrine up until the 7th or 8th centuries, after that time it developed as a purely scholastic tradition."[72] In modern Indian practice, despite the claims of some of the more mathematically minded scholars and the many dilettantes who have traditionally taken up tuning as a cause, there is little or no connection between the twenty-two *śruti*s and the division of the octave into twelve semitones.

Of all the elements which seem to arise automatically in a diatonic system, tonal focus (that is, tonality in the broadest sense) is perhaps the most powerful, and the Indian system provided for it in a variety of ways, but chiefly in the development of specialized roles for the scale degrees. It seems a natural tendency to describe and thus control a repertoire of melodies in terms of five nodal scale degrees: the first, the last, the high, the low, and the central tone. These, together with the underlying scale and the secondary melodic functions, may be said to represent the modality of early Indian music.

Late in the first millennium the system of *rāga*s must have expanded in exponential fashion: scores, even hundreds, of new *rāga*s were churned up from the Ocean of *Rāga* like the treasures brought up from the churning of the cosmic ocean presided over by Viṣṇu in his second incarnation as the giant sea tortoise.[73] The original set of seven *grāmarāgas* had become thirty by the time Mataṅga's *Bṛhaddeśī* had reached its canonical form, and to them had been added a large number of *bhāṣā* (vernacular) and *deśī* (provincial) *rāgas*. By the thirteenth century the number of recognized *rāgas* had reached between two and three hundred, and no one can say precisely just how many *rāgas* are practiced today in the traditions of North and South India. Surely there are several hundred in common use.

What seems important to emphasize is that while the specifications of the many individual *rāgas* have undergone almost constant (if slow) change, some going out of fashion while others become popular, and while new *rāgas* continue to appear under old names, still the idea of *rāga* is not greatly changed. *Rāgas* are now identified by their selection of *svaras* in ascent and descent, by their shaken notes and other *gamakas*, and by whether they follow a straight or a "crooked" (*vakra*) path, but also by the traditional *lakṣaṇas* outlined above.

The *grāmarāgas* and the *jātis* were eventually seen as part of the older classical or *mārga* tradition and as such were set aside, perhaps as early as the thirteenth century; but many of their properties still survive in some of today's most popular *rāgas*. Mataṅga's recognition of the *deśī* tradition, along with the endorsements of subsequent authors, encouraged the assimilation of a wide range of regional tastes and preferences, and a large number of new melodic formations began to find their way into the system of authorized *rāgas*. India's centrist tradition obligingly accepted these graftings, which must have proved difficult to classify. Also, by the thirteenth century the idea of *rāga* had become independent of the moribund theater tradition, but its affective role was argued as hotly as ever; and eventually the conventional association of a *rāga* with an appropriate time of day or season of the year replaced the older association between the *rāgas* and appropriate dramatic situations.

Two crucial changes in the overall *rāga* system occurred not later than the fifteenth century: the designation of *sa* as the final, and thus the tonic, for the entire system, and the introduction of the continuous drone. These two innovations must be seen as evolutionary, not revolutionary, in that they must have been devised to reinforce existing tendencies or preferences; but they served to stabilize the development of the system, so that all later accretions would be in harmony with the preexistent functions and structure of the system. The recent history of *rāga* is studded with brilliant feats of explanation and virtuoso attempts to construct a theoretical framework that will accommodate the hundreds of existing *rāgas*. Most notable are Veṅkaṭamakhī's proposal for a set of seventy-two *melas* (in his seventeenth-century treatise *Caturdaṇḍī Prakāśikā*)[74] to organize the *rāgas* of Karnatic music and the system of ten *ṭhāṭs* that V. N. Bhātkhaṇḍe devised early in the twentieth century for the classification of modern Hindustani *rāgas*.[75] Each of these had essentially the same purpose: to provide an algorithm for reducing the number of basic scale types and thus a means for classifying both existing and future *rāgas*. To this day new *rāgas* are being created, old ones are neglected, and others are undergoing subtle alterations over time.

But the idea of *rāga* is more than a brilliant technical solution to the problem of classifying a wide range of exotic melodic material, and it is more than a record of evolving style in an ancient musical tradition. It is, as I shall attempt to show in a later chapter, one of the most explicit and unequivocal statements on musical meaning ever devised by a culture. In its underlying and self-fulfilling assumption that a particular melodic structure insures the communication of affect from person to person, the tradition of *rāga* has become one of the primary means by which Indian culture has become sensitized and perhaps even instructed in emotive life. Although it is generally accepted in the West that music can have meaning, the nature of that meaning and the process by which musical meanings can be communicated from person to person have been vigorously debated, with no consensus in sight. It is among the remarkable achievements of Indian culture, and is largely a result of the ideology within which the idea of *rāga* arose and developed, that these questions need not be asked.

# EIGHT

# TIME

The vision of time varies according to whether time is regarded as power, the Self, or a divinity. In a state of ignorance [time] is the first thing to manifest itself, but in the state of wisdom it disappears.

Bhartṛhari, *Vākyapadīya* 3.9.62[1]

Whoever reverences Time as Brahma, from him time withdraws afar.
For thus has it been said:—

From Time flow forth created things.
From Time, too, they advance to growth
In Time, too, they do disappear.
Time is a form and formless too.

There are, assuredly, two forms of Brahma: Time and the Timeless. That which is prior to the sun is the Timeless (*a-kāla*), without parts (*a-kala*). But that which begins with the sun is Time, which has parts.

*Maitri Upaniṣad* 6.14–15[2]

## 8.1 Introduction

Time has been and continues to be one of the central issues and perennial puzzles of natural philosophy. The epigraph from Bhartṛhari's fifth-century treatise on grammar and the philosophy of language does not exhaust the full range of imagery with which the ideas of time and timelessness have been grasped in ancient Indian literature, but it provides an appropriate introduction to the main lines of thinking to be explored in this chapter and chapter 9.[3]

I shall marshal evidence in support of the following propositions: (1) concepts of temporal organization in the music of early India reflect the influence of the prevailing cultural ideology, just as the concept of vocal sound production has been seen to reflect traditional thinking on the nature of space; (2) among the most powerful pressures on the arts of India have been cultural preferences for the circular disposition of space and the cyclical disposition of time, of which the latter developed gradually during the period covered by this study; (3) the temporal structure of Indian music is signaled both visibly and audibly by a gesture language with symbolic and ritual connotations; (4) the musical experience, as traditionally conceived, appears to demonstrate a confluence of two simultaneous streams of time—a physical, divisible, external time and an internal stream of continuous time, devoid of any distinctions: "Time is a form and formless too," in the words of the *Maitri Upaniṣad;* (5) the words chosen or coined to represent the various temporal concepts contain etymological clues suggesting that temporality in music is understood as a manifestation of the cosmic process of continuous creation; and (6) among the keywords for the organization of time in music have been these: control, limitation, and equilibrium—as if to suggest that time's power must be continually held in check lest it run away with us.

Much of the human experience of temporality in music arises as a result of our perception of time as an immense hierarchy, a hierarchy that extends from the smallest rhythmic units (individual tones, durations, accents, and pulsations) to intermediate levels of structure (patterns, phrases, poetic lines) to the larger, deeper structural levels (formal sections, entire compositions and performances). In the case of Indian music it seems particularly important to recognize and emphasize those aspects of the temporal hierarchy that outlast the duration of the individual musical event: musical seasons, creative lifetimes, the understandings that are handed down from teacher to student, the common features of a repertoire, the open-ended musical frameworks (*rāga*s and *tāla*s) that persist beyond the lifetime of a performer, the abiding properties of the musical system (such as the designation of *sa* as a common final for the entire later *rāga* system), and the glacial evolution of musical practice and its theory over many centuries.

I propose to examine early traditions of music and musical thought in terms of this hierarchy; for convenience, I shall adopt terms such as "surface" and "foreground" to describe the shorter units of rhythmic experience.[4] In the musical hierarchy there can be no fixed lines of division between the foreground rhythms of the musical surface and the larger rhythms and spans of structure, so I shall draw my own lines in a manner consistent with the standard Indian categories.

I will first examine temporal imagery in ancient Indian literature, drawing material from one of the two hymns to time in the *Atharvaveda.* Second, I will analyze the system of *tāla* as it is presented in the early musicological literature, with special attention to its inventory of temporal concepts and constructs. Next I will discuss the topics by which the rhythmic surface was organized and understood (hand motions, durations, proportions, silence, tempo, and the various *tāla* patterns). Finally I will consider the possible influence of text rhythms and the interaction between *tāla* and poetic meters. I will discuss the remaining levels of the temporal hierarchy in chapter 9, under the heading of form.

## 8.2 The Idea of Time in Ancient India

Time draws [the chariot] like a horse with seven reins, a
thousand-eyed, ageless, rich with seed.
Astride it are the seers who understand inspired songs; its
wheels are everything that exists.

Thus Time draws seven wheels; seven are its hubs; immortality
is its axle.

Hither Time advances, carrying all beings; he, the first god, now
hastens onward.

A brimming vessel has been placed upon Time; we see him
now existing in many forms.

He carries away all these beings; they call him Time in the
highest heaven.

In oneness Time bore these existences; in oneness it
encompassed them.

Time the father became Time their son; no glory is higher
than his.

Time begat heaven above; Time also begat these earths.
That which was and that which shall be—urged forth by
Time—spreads out.

Time created the earth; in Time burns the sun.
In Time are all beings; in Time the eye sees afar off.

In Time is mind; in Time is breath.
In Time names are fixed; as Time unfolds all creatures rejoice
in it.

In Time is fervor; in Time is the highest; in Time is spiritual
exaltation.

Time is the Lord of all things; Time was the father of Prajāpati.

By Time this universe was urged forth; by Time it was born and
in Time it is set firm.

Time, having become the brahman, bears the most exalted one.

Time generated all creatures; and in the beginning Time
created the Lord of creatures.

The self-existing one and the creative fervor were born of
Time.

*Atharvaveda* 19.53[5]

I know of no more colorful image of time than the thousand-eyed horse personified in this hymn as the creator-god and source of primordial power. The horse plunges across the sky (presumably pulling the sun chariot) while balancing a "brimming vessel" on his back. The horse and chariot imagery draws upon one of the most familiar metaphors of the Aryan invaders, but the underlying cluster of ideas may reach even farther back to the magical cults of the Indus Valley civilizations and the indigenous Dravidian inhabitants of ancient India. How do we make sense of such a welter of temporal imagery? The more philosophically minded authors of the Upanishads sought to refine and intellectualize it, while later exponents of the orthodox philosophical systems felt constrained to react against it and explain it away.

Time, the hymn continues, exists in many forms: the fertile semen of the horse (a symbol of pure potentiality), the heat energy of the sun, human respiration, the utterance of sounds, the sacrificial formulas with which the gods are invoked and time maintained, the perception of forms by bestowing names upon them, and the defining power of mental activity. This cluster of ideas draws together many important strands in traditional Indian thought. The result is a complex metaphor of time as a cosmic generating principle born of inner energy. The seers who sit astride the chariot, according to the commentarial tradition, are responsible for the control of time by means of their daily sacrifices and chanting of mantras. I would like to emphasize six of the many themes in the hymn, each of which has had implications for the idea of music.

1. Time as described here is no empty or inert dimension: it is conceived as a causal power and procreative force, begetting all creatures, all gods, and the entire world. (And by procreation I mean creation in the fullest sense of the word, including the continuous cycle of biological growth and decay and the cosmic cycle of generation, destruction, and regeneration.)[6]

2. Time is also presented in the hymn as the *urger,* a ripening force and the principle of intensification—working its effects through the agency of heat energy and creative fervor (*tapas*), bringing spiritual purification (*brahman*), articulation (born of breath, the ultimate source of sound), and continuity. As the result of these urgings, time "spreads out"—an early recognition of the role of permutation (*prastāra*) as time unfolds in a series of metamorphoses.

3. Time is also celebrated as the *definer* and the medium for all articulation and clarity, by means of thought, vocal utterance, and the giving of names.[7]

4. Time is seen as both the origin and the fruit of ritual action. In fact time is regarded as dependent upon the correct performance of ritual: in this Vedic concept of world order, time is made to happen by the recitation of sacred formulas and the performance of sacrificial actions.

5. In addition to all these graspable characteristics of time, the hymn includes a clear reference to a transcendental category of time in the form of a deity—a deity which, though multiform, is in reality one. This must be among the earliest references to what has since developed into a conventional antithesis between manifested, divisible time and unmanifested, indivisible time—"that which begins with the sun" and "that which is prior to the sun."[8]

6. And finally, time is circular. Multiple images of circularity dominate the language of the hymn: the chariot wheels with their spokes, hubs, and axles; the sun, the year, the eye, the cycle of human life and the generations, and the cryptic brimming vessel, which has become the object of much commentary. It has been interpreted as the sun, a symbol for the year, a burial urn, or even as a more abstract reference to time as the container for all human actions and events.

These themes merit some elaboration. Certain of the references are conventional topics of ancient cosmological speculation, especially the notions of time as sevenfold (a culturally significant number in most early civilizations), time as fate, time as the destroyer, time as that which eventually reveals all things, time as past, present, and future, and time as manifested in the recurring seasons of the year. It is not clear to what extent the thinking of ancient Mediterranean civilizations may have made its way into Indian thought, but many of the special intuitions of time embedded in the hymn have no parallel elsewhere in antiquity. It is true that many ancient literatures have referred to time as cyclical, and these references rest on more than an objective description of how nature works: the cycle of time can be interpreted as a symbol of man's quest for continuity, as he seeks reassurance that the sun will continue to rise each day, the earth will continue to bring forth crops, the animals will breed, and the individual human being can be assured of some measure of continuity—both backward in time (to his ancestors, the Pitṛs) and forward (by means of his children).

But in later Indian thought, the idea of a cycle took on a double meaning; it became a symbol not only of continuity but also of limitation. The cyclical rhythms of life, and by extension also those of music, not only carry the creative force necessary for their perpetuation, but they must eventually be overcome, as people assert control over their senses and actions (the way of the yogin) and thus seek to transcend the state of illusion wherein they are subject to the limitations of time as manifested in ordinary human experience. For one who is able to accomplish this, as the author of the *Maitri Upaniṣad* wrote, "time withdraws afar."

I am emphasizing here the profound connections between the concept of time, ritual action, and the structure of music. In India, as in many other ancient cultures, the idea of music arose partly within the context of religious ceremony, and traces of ritualistic behavior still inhere in formal music making. This may also be true with respect to the musical event in more recent Asian and Western practice, but in the case of India it carries particular significance. The control of musical structure by symbolic gestures, the special connotations of the breath in the production of musical sound, the elaborate preperformance rituals, the solemnity in which the profession (and especially the teacher-student relationship) has traditionally been held, and the extraordinary degree of empathy generated during a performance are all suggestive of a deep-seated cultural assumption that music is something more than meets the eye and the ear. The implication is that music is a ceremonial, symbolic representation of cosmic process—a sacrificial offering and an oblation.

The link between time and sacrifice is very ancient. In the well-known *Puruṣa-sūkta,* one of the latest compositions in the *Ṛgveda,* the seasons of the year are the elements of sacrifice in the ritual dismemberment of Puruṣa, the cosmic man, whose parts became everything that exists. The appropriate verse, in Walter Maurer's translation, reads: "When with Puruṣa as oblation the gods offered a sacrifice, the spring was its clarified butter, the summer the fuel, the autumn the oblation."[9] The reasoning is deliberately circular: time becomes the means of sacrifice and makes sacrifice possible; but as the direct result of that sacrifice, time is established and maintained in its proper course. If time appears, confusingly, to be both the agent and the outcome of the sacrificial process, it is worth remembering that even at this early time thinkers were slowly groping their way toward a more sophisticated understanding of time. In this connection Raimundo Panikkar has written eloquently on the evolving relationship between time and sacrifice in later Vedic times:

> Time is born with sacrifice, and it is by sacrifice that it is once again destroyed. . . . The Vedas sought the continuity of time through the sacrificial act, but the Upanishads began to question the permanence of this act and this continuity. . . . Continuity was no longer to be found externally, in the ritual or the cosmos, but internally, within man, or more exactly within the Self, the *ātman.* . . . The transition from the cultic time of the Vedas to

> the interiorized time of the Upanishads occurs evidently at the point where respiration, interpreted as a sacrifice, takes the place of the sacrifice of fire.[10]

The keyword here is *respiration,* and the emphasis on breath (which I noted earlier) suggests that the focus of sacrifice is beginning to shift from external, ritual action to internal action—and also nonaction, that is, self-discipline and control of one's physical and mental processes—and accordingly signals a shift of focus from external time to time as internalized. In this interpretation, sacrifice becomes less a mechanical performance of a contractual obligation and more a means of seeking truth where it abides, within the self. In developing and sharpening the concept of internal time and in capturing its image in the form of vital breath, Indian thinkers managed to reconcile the conflicting cultural intuitions of time they had inherited. Their solution was to conceive of two coexisting streams of time: the external time of daily experience, manifested in the seasonal recurrences, daily routines, and also in the sharp discontinuities of life; and the special category of internal time, devoid of divisions, motions, change, and all other such distinctions.

I am suggesting here, and will give additional evidence to support the suggestion, that musical behavior in the Indian tradition has been deeply influenced by, and continues to manifest, this confluence of two temporal streams. Gesture and breath are the archetypal forms of music making and may be interpreted as both symbols and means of sacrifice: like the ancient vedin, the Indian musician controls audible time by actions—the motions of his hand and the outflow of his breath. With the gestures of *tāla* he regulates the illusion of outer time with its gross divisions and audible forms, while with the controlled emission of vocal sound he manifests the true, continuous, inner time. Of the musical dimensions, *tāla* has been assigned the chief responsibility for maintaining proper control in performance; and in the theatric rituals preceding the performance of a play, the exact rendering of the hand gestures, durations, and proportions of the music was considered a matter of greater importance than the correct delivery of the poetic text. Abhinavagupta made the link between *tāla* and ritual action explicit in his remarks accompanying the *tāla* chapter of the *Nāṭyaśāstra,* explaining that the various hand motions had originated in ancient sacrificial gestures.[11]

Later Indian philosophers sought, as Augustine did in the West, to refine and dematerialize the idea of time, to divest it of its many mythological and cult associations and give it a proper place within their complex systems. They came to differ, as we would expect, on certain important points: whether time was real or empirical, whether it could be perceived or only inferred, and whether it was one or many, continuous or atomistic. The arguments were generally subtle, complex, and largely irrelevant to the more simplistic concept of time embedded in the musical tradition. If there is any consensus, it is that time is one, indivisible, eternal, and free of any limiting attributes or qualities such as change, motion, form, and the like; its apparent properties are inferred by the mind as the result of our perception of such things as speed, slowness, duration, succession, simultaneity, priority, and posteriority. An important contribution of the Buddhist, Jain, and Yoga philosophies was their concept of time as a succession of discrete instants—merging, in a celebrated Buddhist image, in the apparent circle of flame produced by a whirling torch, or in the illusion of a stream of water; both of these images have become popular analogies for the continuity heard in music. Perhaps it was a subconscious compensation for the primitive obsession with isolating, naming, and counting individual units of experience that led thinkers to argue in favor of a dynamic concept of time that enabled them to see continuity penetrating and organizing the individual atoms. Surely this type of wishful thinking is present in the conceptual organization of sound.

The aim of the yogin was to perceive what exists between the successive instants, to reject the apparent continuity of experience, and to seek freedom from illusion in all its forms, by widening his perception of the moment in the attempt to find ultimate reality in what has been called the timeless present. In this cultural emphasis on what lies between, we see one of the vital continuities of Indian thought, not unrelated to certain other enduring concepts or habits of thinking: the idea of zero, the cultural meaning ascribed to silence, and the essentially "passive-negative" qualities of Indian thought. The moral is that nothingness as a cultural value is equal to, or even superior to, somethingness.[12]

I have given illustrations of the three temporal concepts noted by Bhartṛhari—time as power (*śakti*), as a deity (*devatā*), or as constituted within the self (*ātman*); but I have not mentioned Bhartṛhari's own view. Bhartṛhari's penetrating analysis of time, grounded in his philosophy of language and informed by the great tradition of Sanskrit grammar, led him to define time as the *sūtradhāra* ("string holder") of the world, a limiting power that causes the world to operate by means of an alternation between restraint (*pratibandha*) and release (*abhyanujñā*). It is notable that he chose the word that defines the ceremonial role of the stage director in the

Sanskrit drama. In addition to this subliminal allusion to time as the *theatrum mundi,* the grammarian has likened time to the line held by a falconer, which permits free flight until the end of the line is reached and then restrains the falcon's flight. In the same manner time permits and then prevents the appearance of successive phenomena.[13] Many ancient cultures have conceived of time as discontinuous, but it is unusual to find time described as manifesting a binary rhythm. Bhartṛhari's explanation was endorsed by later Kashmir Shaivite authors, who made an important place for time in their elaborate systems, as a limiting power (*kāla śakti*).[14] This brief survey of the development of concepts of time in early India has barely scratched the surface of this many-faceted idea, but it has served to identify several strands of thought which have found expression in the temporal structure of music. In particular, we shall note the pervasiveness of the idea of limitation in discussions of musical rhythm.

## 8.3 *Tāla*

> I offer threefold praise to this octoform body (Śiva), whose essence is illusion, holding a token of enjoyment, in whom there is perfect equilibrium of all worldly activity by means of divisions (*kalā*), time (*kāla*), and rest (*laya*).
>
> Abhinavagupta, *Abhinavabhāratī* 31.1

For the perspective of an influential thinker on the cluster of ideas from which many of the basic temporal concepts of ancient Indian music were borrowed, we turn to the benedictory stanza Abhinavagupta composed to introduce the *tāla* chapter of Bharata's *Nāṭyaśāstra.*[15] The eleventh-century author managed to pack a large number of metaphorical references into a few poetic lines, drawing upon a lexicon of conventional allusions to the god Śiva, who has by this time moved into the foremost place among the patron deities of music, dance, and the theater. Some close analysis will help to clarify Abhinavagupta's line of argument.

Equilibrium (*sāmya*) is the main purpose of *tāla* according to both Abhinavagupta and his earlier colleague Dattila; and from equilibrium comes "fulfillment in both this world and the next."[16] In this connection it is useful to recall that Abhinavagupta's comments are attached to a text outlining the ritual requirements for the drama, and that *tāla,* of all the musical dimensions, has been assigned the major responsibility for coordinating, integrating, and maintaining control over all aspects of the performance. The correct performance of ritual is obviously no small matter, and the benefits of *tāla* were intended to go far beyond the admitted pleasures of musical rhythm. And similarly, the equilibrium that Abhinavagupta praises, visualized in the form of Śiva's celebrated pose as Lord of the Dance (Naṭarāja), is something more than a state of simple physical balance or repose; it is the state of cosmic equilibrium precariously maintained in the midst of the continuous creation, preservation, and destruction of the world, its forms, and its creatures. Śiva has assumed all three functions of the divine patrons of world process, functions shared previously with Brahmā and Viṣṇu.

How is this equilibrium achieved and maintained? As the result of the integrated activity of three temporal elements: *kalā,* the division of musical time into individual units; *kāla,* the ongoing stream of time itself; and *laya,* the interstices between the successive units. Abhinavagupta's interpretation has likened the temporal process in music to the three phases of the cyclical evolution of the cosmos: the differentiation of primal matter and its division into perceptible forms; orderly movement in structured time; and finally, the dissolution of all created forms back into their original state of undifferentiated matter; after this the cycle begins once again. The equation reads: equilibrium (rhythmic or cosmic) = division + time + rest. All three phases are made manifest by actions—the hand motions of *tāla* or Śiva's cosmic dance.

Abhinavagupta has proposed his compound *kalā-kāla-laya* as a substitute reading for Bharata's *kalā-pāta-laya,* which the commentator interprets as technical terms of music. In this context, *kalā* signifies a silent gesture, *pāta* ("beat") an audible gesture, and *laya* the span of time between the successive gestures.[17] With these three components the temporal structure of music is manifested. This in essence is the idea of *tāla.*

I shall pass more lightly over the other references in the stanza. Śiva is invoked with one of his conventional epithets—*aṣṭamūrti* (octoform). Once again the poet has something more in mind than a profusion of arms and legs. Śiva's eight forms, according to the traditional explanation, are the five elements (earth, water, fire, wind, sky), the sun and moon, and he who offers a sacrifice.[18] Here is yet another reference to the world as sustained by sacrificial action, and we begin to see more clearly the outlines of the case Abhinavagupta is building on behalf of *tāla.* The elemental components of the world as we know it are held together by the actions of the sacrificer, just as the structure of music is secured by the actions of *tāla.* If Śiva's essence is illusion, as the commentator contended, that illusion consists of apparent motion and the perception of successive forms; reality abides in the absence of motion and the knowledge that all forms are nothing other than different aspects of the One. Form is mutable, matter is malleable, and both subsist in illusion. The goal of *tāla* is to maintain equilibrium during the parade of manifested forms.

The phrase which I have translated as "holding a token of enjoyment" is cryptic, perhaps deliberately so. Beyond the surface reference to the pleasures of the theater and the *jarjara* carried by the stage director in the opening ceremonies, it may be taken together with the word *tridhā* (threefold) as an allusion to Śiva's trident; this has been interpreted as (1) a sign that he has assumed the three functions of creation; (2) a symbolic representation of the three *guṇa*s of the Sāṅkhya philosophy (illumination, darkness, and passion), the three strands from which the fabric of life is woven; or (3) the three subtle arteries of the body in the Yoga philosophy.[19] Any of these interpretations lends additional depth to Abhinavagupta's offering of praise. Śiva is often represented with three eyes (the sun, the moon, and fire), with which he is able to see the past, present, and future. The point of all this "threeness" is to underscore the importance and mutual dependence of the three primary temporal concepts that first stimulated the commentator's imagination and motivated this flight of poetic fancy.

I turn now to the technical features of the *tāla* system. The word *tāla* has an interesting ancestry which is none too clear. The obvious derivation is from the noun *tala* (a flat surface such as the palm of the hand, a pedestal, a fan, or an elephant's ear) and perhaps also from the verbal root *taḍ* (to strike).[20] Following this semantic route, *tāla* thus signifies an action applied to, or making use of, such a flat surface, with division or measurement as its purpose. It is also an important unit of spatial measure in the visual arts, based upon the length of the hand (as measured from the wrist to the tip of the middle finger) or the length of the face. The basic meaning of *tāla,* then, is "span"—a span of space or of time.[21]

Western musicologists may find their suspicions aroused by the sound of the word *tāla,* but as far as I can determine, the word is unrelated to the Latin *talea,* which means a "cutting" (of a plant) or a "bar" (of metal); in the musical terminology of medieval Europe *talea* is a technical term for a rhythmic pattern that was superimposed upon a preexisting plainsong melody and repeated over and over as the rhythmic framework for a composition.[22] This sounds similar to the cyclical *tāla*s of later Indian musical practice and suggests one of those coincidences which we always ought to suspect; but it seems to be nothing more than coincidence.

In early Sanskrit musical treatises *tāla* is both a general term for the entire system of rhythm and a special term for one of the eight hand gestures, in which the left hand slaps down audibly upon the right palm or the left knee.[23] This ambiguity reminds us of the similar treatment of the word *svara.* As a system, *tāla* has been organized by means of the following set of topics. There seems to be no canonical order of presentation in the literature, so I have rearranged them to permit a more effective exposition.[24] The following topics, briefly defined, will serve as a partial index for this chapter and chapter 9.

1. *kalā:* a division of time, also a silent gesture demarcating such a duration
2. *pāta:* an audible gesture, usually a clap
3. *laya:* the rate of gestural succession, that is, "tempo"
4. *yati:* the principle of regulation and rhythmic control; also, in a more specialized sense, the temporal flow (whether even, accelerating, or decelerating)[25]
5. *pāṇi:* the principle of synchronization by which the entrances of the various performers are regulated
6. *pādabhāga:* one formal unit (measure, phrase) of a group of four, literally "a division into [four] paws" (as of a quadruped)
7. *mātrā:* a phrase or line, typically consisting of four *pādabhāgas*; also a time duration (mora), as in verse
8. *parivarta:* a prescribed repetition of a formal unit
9. *vidāri:* a pause or cadence, also a line or phrase ending with such a pause or cadence
10. *aṅga:* a musical section consisting of several phrases or poetic lines
11. *vastu:* a longer type of formal component; a stanza
12. *prakaraṇa:* a collective term for the seven major forms (the *saptarūpas* or *gītakas*) of the ancient ritual music[26]
13. *avayava:* alternative versions of the *gītakas*, versions that arise from the many performance variables
14. *gīti:* text setting; also style in general
15. *mārga:* the relative density of events within a given span of time

This set of topics is obviously designed to accommodate a complex hierarchical system of rhythm, and falls into four distinct levels. The first five topics control what we may consider the *infrastructure* of musical rhythm—gestures, durations, accents, rests, and their synchronization. Together with the patterns they create, these will occupy our attention for most of this chapter. Topics 6–11 constitute the *structural* level of phrases, lines of text, caesuras, formal sections, and poetic stanzas. Topics

12 and 13 may be regarded as *suprastructure*, the level of entire compositions. Topics 14 and 15 pervade all levels of the rhythmic hierarchy. In general I shall defer analysis of the structural and suprastructural levels, along with the tactics by which events on these levels are delineated, to chapter 9. Note that the concept of cycle is conspicuously absent from this set of topics, unless it is present in embryo in the notion of an obligatory repetition (*parivarta*).[27]

Many of the same terms are still in use today, although some of their meanings have shifted along with the rhythmic basis of the later system. For comparison, I present the "ten vital breaths of *tāla*" (*tāla daśa prāṇa*s) by which the modern system of rhythm is organized in Karnatic music.[28]

1. *kāla:* the twelve divisions of "absolute" time: from *kṣaṇa* ("instant," the time required for a needle to pierce one lotus leaf) to *kākapadam* ("crow's foot," a duration 262, 144 times as long)[29]
2. *mārga:* the density of events within a pattern or rhythmic cycle
3. *kriya:* the collective term for the hand gestures by which the temporal structure of music is manifested, including both silent and audible gestures
4. *aṅga:* the component parts of a particular *tāla* cycle as signaled by the gestures
5. *graha:* the point in a *tāla* cycle where the music begins
6. *jāti:* expanded versions of the basic *tāla* patterns, produced by counting with the fingers
7. *kalā:* a variable unit of time specifying the ratio between melodic activity and the structure of the *tāla*
8. *laya:* the three tempos (slow, moderate, fast)
9. *yati:* the rhythmic design of a cycle as manifested by the pattern and relative length of its components
10. *prastāra:* the process of permutations

The contrast is striking: structural and suprastructural topics have vanished from the list, and in their place we see a number of concepts designed for the synchronization, control, and perpetuation of the cycle (*āvarta*), which has now become an implicit assumption of the system. The formal basis of the entire system has shifted from a set of complex modular formal structures to an integrated system designed to facilitate improvisation over a repeated rhythmic cycle. This is essentially the difference between *mārga* and *deśī*—between the prescribed forms of the ritual tradition and the great variety of regional patterns and procedures which began to be codified during the second half of the first millennium. These patterns and procedures display not only a contrasting method of organization but also a different, richer repertoire of *tāla*s, expanding from the five recognized by Bharata and Dattila to the 120 *deśī tāla*s cataloged by Śārṅgadeva.[30]

The question also arises, why such an abundance of temporal concepts? Part of the answer must lie in the evident delight the Indian mind takes in dissecting existing categories and inventing new ones. But the more important part of the explanation is related to the issue of temporal standards and the relativism which a rhythmic system of any complexity and sophistication must provide if it is to be successful. In early, nontechnological civilizations the measures for time in music were as slippery as the measures devised for the dimension of pitch. Long and short syllables and the conventional tempo of speech were, and are, the obvious candidates, but early Sanskrit grammarians had long recognized their lack of precision. If the *mātrā* (referring here to the basic unit of measure in both poetry and music) could be defined no more precisely than as the time required to utter five consonants or blink one's eyelids five times, the best solution was to provide for a flexible set of equations among the several concepts that governed the durational structure. In this way the profusion of temporal relationships and the various hierarchical levels of the music could be specified with great precision, leaving it for comfort and convention to dictate the basic pace. I shall return to these issues of duration and timing in a moment.

## 8.4 Chironomy

The single most distinctive feature of the Indian rhythmic tradition is the way the temporal structure of music is manifested and controlled by means of hand motions—the claps, finger counts, and silent waves that accompany every performance of Indian music. These gestures are obviously practical signals to other members of the ensemble and help to insure a synchronized performance, but they are at the same time mnemonic aids, external manifestations of the internal structure and energies of the music, markers of the passage of time, and symbolic vestiges of their original ritual function. The gesture language of the modern *tāla* systems has discarded many of the complexities displayed in ancient practice, since its role is now limited to defining the exact location within the rhythmic cycle.

Eight gestures, four silent and four audible, provide the basis for the chironomy of the ancient system of *tāla.* These gestures are listed and described in (16), along with translations of their names and the abbreviations by which the gestures will be represented. To catch the eye more readily, silent gestures will appear in *italic* type and sounding gestures in roman. All gestures are performed with the right hand unless otherwise indicated.

16. The gestures of the ancient *tāla* system

The four *kalās* or *niḥśabda* (silent) gestures

*āvāpa* (sowing, as in seeds): palm up with fingers folded (*ā*)
*niṣkrāma* (exit): palm down with fingers extended (*ni*)
*vikṣepa* (scattering): open hand waves to the right (*vi*)
*praveśa* (entrance): fingers closed with palm downward (*pra*)

The four *pātas* or *saśabda* (audible) gestures

*dhruva* (unchanging): a finger snap preceding a beat[31]
*śamyā* (peg): right hand slaps down on left hand or right knee (śa)
*tāla:* left hand slaps down on right hand or left knee (tā)
*sannipāta* (struck together): hands clap together (S)[32]

Some of the names are cryptic, but most are easily identifiable as simple descriptors of the shape or motion of the gesture. In many performances the gestures were, as they may be today, reinforced by the sound of the small pair of bronze *tāla* cymbals, but the gestures alone are sufficient to regulate the performance. What the gestures mean is a complex question.

What they do *not* mean, first of all, is an accent or pulsation in the music. Nothing could be more misleading than to infer that any of these gestures signifies the special quality of metric weight or potential stress that we attribute to, say, each of the four beats of the standard simple quadruple meter in Western music ($\frac{4}{4}$).[33] The pattern of gesture is a code that carries a great deal of information about the underlying musical structure, but it tells us nothing about the melodic rhythm or the accompanying rhythm played by the drummer—except, of course, that structural and melodic rhythms will often be in phase and synchronized with one another.

One gesture can carry many meanings, and the consequent ambiguity is a characteristic feature of the system and the repertoire. Accent and the structural meaning of a gesture are determined primarily by context, particularly at the beginnings and endings of patterns and at points where superimposed patterns come into phase with one another. In this respect *sannipāta*—which is an obvious ancestor of the beat *sam* in modern *tāla* practice (the gesture marking the point where one cycle terminates and the next begins)—has been invested with special meaning as a structure marker and is reserved for initial or final gestures of patterns and formal components. The remaining gestures are more neutral. *Dhruva* is the most neutral of all and plays an insignificant role in the delineation of form; these finger snaps provided additional control of slow tempos and marked the passage of time during certain sections where the regular sequence of meaningful gestures was suspended.[34]

Let us explore the possible meanings of a gesture sequence in the ancient ritual music. The three principal audible gestures—*śamyā, tāla,* and *sannipāta*—can represent either single events (individual syllables or consecutive durations) or the final unit in a pattern or a subdivision of that pattern. In contrast, the silent gestures were reserved for the beginnings of patterns and were restricted to what I shall refer to as the "expanded states"—patterns inflated to two or four times their original length by the prefixing of the appropriate number of silent gestures.[35] The concept of inflatable form is one of the most distinctive structural features of ancient Indian music, and it will become clearer in the patterns diagrammed in §8.5 and in the forms reconstructed in chapter 9. For the moment it will be sufficient to remember that silent gestures mark the early stages in expanded patterns; in the conclusion to this chapter I will touch on the reinterpretation of this role in modern Indian music.

But this association with the beginnings and ends of patterns by no means exhausts the possible meanings of a gesture or sequence of gestures. *Śamyā* and *tāla,* in keeping with their alternation of right and left hands, serve to maintain a binary rhythm of alternating qualities, but with no implication of arsis-thesis or strong-weak. Sounding gestures are also prescribed with increasing frequency near the end of a large formal unit; they serve here as audible and visible signals of the passage of time and impending closure. In contrast, the four silent gestures maintain the neutral background stratum of rhythm in the expanded states, as in (17):

17. Patterns of silent gestures in the expanded states

| | |
|---|---|
| *ā ni vi pra* | a pattern expanded to four times its basic length, within which no other structural meaning is conveyed except when one or more of the silent gestures are replaced by the audible gestures that define the musical structure |
| *ni pra*[36] | a pattern expanded to twice its basic length, again without any other structural significance except when substitute sounding gestures define a superimposed formal pattern |

It is evident that formal meaning is determined not by gesture but by *pattern of gesture,* and that the role of any individual gesture (with the exception of *sannipāta*) will often be ambiguous. Indeed, one of the prime objectives of Indian art is to provide multiple meanings for the senses to savor and the mind to ponder. To summarize, a gesture may represent any or all of the following: the basic structural pulse of the music, one of the standard *tāla* patterns superimposed upon that pulse,[37] an inflated form of one of these patterns, a certain stage in the progress of a large formal component, or the beginning or end of a pattern on any level of the rhythmic hierarchy. When some or all of these patterns fall into phase, the result is accent—not necessarily a stress accent but an accent of pure structure.

The gesture language is thus a language of allusion that adds a new dimension to the complex question of musical meaning. It is a truism to say that music is an art of relationships, implications, and cross-references; the fascinating element here is the extraordinary degree to which formal relationships embedded in the music are made manifest and communicated in a dimension which most Western listeners would regard as extrinsic to music. This would clearly be a misjudgment, and we must revise our concept of Indian music accordingly.

## 8.5 Rhythmic Patterns

Having thus established the repertoire of hand gestures by which rhythmic structure is manifested, we are now in a position to explore the set of patterns described in the early layers of musical texts and thereby identify the basic durations, sequences, and tactics of grouping. But first a word of caution: I shall be examining structural rhythms, not the surface rhythms of melody or drumming. While it is reasonable to infer that the rhythms of structure may often have been replicated in the patterns of performed, surface rhythm, we still have no evidence that would allow us to reconstruct the musical flesh and skin that covered these bones. After some experience with contemporary performance, noting in particular the typical drum patterns, it is possible to draw certain inferences: (1) strings of even durations and regular patterns of binary alternation must surely have been a part of every performer's repertoire and daily experience; (2) the conventional groupings of text syllables into *gaṇa*s of two, three, and four units (metrical feet) were also available as models for rhythmic patterns;[38] and (3) the practice of permutation (*prastāra*), for which there is clear evidence since ancient times, insured that the authorized patterns, whatever they were, would sooner or later appear in all possible variants and contexts. I shall have more to say later about the composite rhythms and the interaction of the various rhythmic layers in early Indian music, but the first task is to examine the five *mārga tāla*s outlined in *Dattilam* and the *Nāṭyaśāstra* and repeated in the later texts.[39]

In (18) each of the five patterns is displayed in the form of (1) the prescribed gestures; (2) the sequence of durations, that is, short *(laghu)*, long (*guru*), and "protracted" (*pluta*), in an invariable ratio of 1:2:3; (3) the proportions of this sequence, which become important when attempting to recognize the expanded versions of these patterns; (4) the traditional Indian rhythmic notation in which I = *laghu,* S = *guru,* and Ś = *pluta;* and (5) the total time span of the pattern as measured in *kalā*s. In this case the *kalā* unit is equated with one long syllable. Each pattern appears here in what I shall call its *syllabic* state (the Sanskrit term is *yathākṣara,* "according to [the nature of the] syllable"), which means simply that each action represents a single syllabic duration, with the durations signified in each case by the nonsensical mnemonics of the *tāla* names.

18. The five *mārga tālas*

(1) Caccatpuṭaḥ:
*guru* · *guru* · *laghu* · *pluta* (S S I Ś) = 4 *kalā*s
2 : 2 : 1 : 3

(2) Cācapuṭaḥ:
*guru* · *laghu* · *laghu* · *guru* (S I I S) = 3 *kalā*s
2 : 1 : 1 : 2

both sharing the three following gesture patterns: S śa tā śa
or
śa tā śa tā
or
tā śa tā śa

(3) Ṣaṭpitāputrakaḥ:
*pluta* · *laghu* · *guru* · *guru* · *laghu* · *pluta* (Ś I S S I Ś) = 6 *kalā*s
3 : 1 : 2 : 2 : 1 : 3
S tā śa tā śa tā (or vice versa)[40]

(4) Sampakveṣṭākaḥ:
*pluta* · *guru* · *guru* · *guru* · *pluta* (Ś S S S Ś) = 6 *kalā*s
3 : 2 : 2 : 2 : 3
tā śa tā śa tā

(5) Udghaṭṭaḥ:
*guru* · *guru* · *guru* (S S S) = 3 *kalā*s
2 : 2 : 2
*ni* śa śa

The 3 basic durations: *laghu* ("light") = short
*guru* ("heavy") = long
*pluta* ("floating") = protracted
} 1 : 2 : 3

Metrical analysis of the 5 mnemonic *tāla* names (in which the distinction between long and protracted durations is not recognized):

| | |
|---|---|
| Caccatpuṭaḥ | – – ⏑ – |
| Cācapuṭaḥ | – ⏑ ⏑ – |
| Ṣaṭpitāputrakaḥ | – ⏑ – – ⏑ – |
| Sampakveṣṭākaḥ | – – – – – |
| Udghaṭṭaḥ | – – – |

This is a surprising set of patterns, for which the obvious comparison to the array of metrical feet available for Greek or Sanskrit verse is misleading in several respects. The set of *tāla*s is a more selective set, and the patterns (with perhaps the sole exception of the rarely used Udghaṭṭaḥ) are somewhat longer and more complex than the most popular poetic feet of Attic Greek verse. More important, they lack entirely the qualities of arsis and thesis which differentiated otherwise similar Greek meters: while the individual units differ in both quantity (because of the durations) and quality (because of the gestures), they are neutral with respect to accent and metric weight. I can best put the comparison this way: metrical feet are essentially surface patterns, whose influence may sometimes spread into the deeper levels of the rhythmic hierarchy (colon, line, phrase, stanza), but the five *mārga tāla*s are structural patterns. They are conceptual rhythms which may indeed appear in the form of successive syllables and durations on the musical surface, but they are even more valuable because they can organize and control the deep structure of music. When this occurs, the rhythms of *tāla* are manifested in the form of gestures and proportions buried in the musical structure and separated by many intervening pulsations and events, much like the letters of the word CANADA on a map of North America.

There is yet another conceptual dimension to these patterns: whether each is regarded as exemplifying threeness (*tryaśra,* "triangular," or *ayugma,* "odd") or fourness (*caturaśra,* "quadrangular," or *yugma,* "even"). Of the five, only Caccatpuṭaḥ has been assigned to the quadrangular class. This apparent profusion of triangularity is striking in view of the prevalence of duple and quadruple meters and the relative scarcity of simple triple meter in world music. And musicians may also be surprised by the irregularity of some of the patterns. But this results from evaluating the set of rhythms from a foreign perspective and with a different set of expectations. The early *tāla* patterns were designed, not as simple sequences that could be repeated many times and maintained automatically as a foundation for a composed or improvised melody, but as deliberately asymmetrical patterns whose components and proportions could be detected in the midst of a complex musical texture. As such, the *mārga tāla*s must have suited admirably, judging from how long they remained the preferred structures of the theatrical ritual music.

When musical needs changed—as must have happened with the rise of improvisation, the advent of the drone, the turn to cyclical rhythm, and the decline of the theater tradition—the rhythmic system adapted to these new needs. The result was the system of *deśī tāla*s, which we will shortly examine.

It will also be apparent that three of the five patterns are palindromes, and that their palindromic structure is not always reinforced by the gesture language. It is difficult to assess what this meant for early rhythmic practice, and the textual evidence is uninformative. It seems not to have meant the widespread cultivation of retrogradable rhythms or melodies. What it suggests to me is that these patterns, along with their characteristic gesture sequences, created agogic accents (accents of length) at both their beginning and their end, and that the transition from one pattern to the next might thus have been made more obvious. One other thing is clear: these are not cyclical patterns in which the final of one also serves as the initial of the next; each initial and final was unique.

Some additional conclusions can be drawn from the gesture sequences illustrated in (18). The most common sequence is the regular alternation of right-hand and left-hand claps (even in the so-called triangular *tāla*s), and therefore even at this relatively uncomplicated level of rhythmic structure a certain potential for rhythmic counterpoint has been built into the system. Of all the audible gestures, *sannipāta* is the least ambiguous and marks either the initial or the final unit in a pattern. *Tāla* patterns are often described with *sannipāta* (if present) at the beginning, but in expanded versions the pattern was almost invariably reversed so as to end with this gesture of summation. Perhaps this is further evidence for the usefulness of palindromes, in that the underlying sequence of gestures can be reversed without doing violence to the pattern it manifests.

## 8.6 The Concept of State

I referred earlier to the concept of *state*, one of the most important of the rhythmic variables. Patterns and entire compositions were conceived and constructed in three such states: the syllabic (*yathākṣara*, also known as *ekakala*, "onefold"), the "twofold" (*dvikala*), and the "fourfold" (*catuṣkala*) states. In the latter two—which I shall refer to as the expanded, inflated, or manifold states—both the proportions and the total duration of the original pattern were doubled or quadrupled. In the course of this doubling or quadrupling some unexpected things happened, so it is essential to understand how the system works.

The solution required two steps: (1) the various durations (short, long, and protracted) were first resolved into an even series of long (*guru*) durations; and (2) the appropriate number of silent gestures was then prefixed to each of the audible gestures that defined the *tāla* in its original, syllabic state. This is a remarkable solution, and surely not the only one possible. Two interesting results are (1) similar patterns on different levels of the rhythmic hierarchy are recognized by their proportions, not by their sequence of durations; and (2) musical patterns are defined, recognized, and indexed, as it were, not by their beginnings but by their endings. If it is true, as the critic Ernest Decsey once wrote, that we perceive relationships among phrases of Western music by the "rhyme" at their beginning (a melodic rhyme),[41] the ancient Indian solution was to create and recognize relationships among rhythmic and formal units by means of the structural rhyme—in effect, a visible and physical rhyme—at their end.

To make the process of structural inflation more concrete, (19) displays the most popular of all the *mārga tāla* patterns (Ṣaṭpitāputrakaḥ) in the three states.[42] Because a full understanding of this process is crucial in grasping the Indian concept of form in music, I ask the reader's indulgence if I appear to belabor the following three points.

1. It will be apparent that the same proportion (3:1:2:2:1:3) is manifested in each of the three states, with totals of six, twelve, and twenty-four *kalās*, respectively. What may not be as apparent from the diagram is the vital difference between the syllabic and the expanded versions: in the former the proportions are those of the three basic durations, but in the latter the proportions represent groupings of identical, long durations. The result in musical practice is that a change into the syllabic state—which typically occurs at the end of a long section or an entire composition—produces an unexpected series of jaggedly irregular durations which, in my interpretation, signal closure. I interpret this effect as a rhythm of deep structure which, when compressed, works its way up through the various structural levels and is finally made manifest on the rhythmic surface. I regard this as one of the primary tactics of Indian musical form.

2. The sequence of prescribed gestures signals both the state and the particular *tāla* being performed: the shape of the *tāla* emerges gradually from the pattern of audible gestures marking the end of each proportional unit, in this case the sequence tā śa tā śa tā **S.** The state is deduced from the pattern of prefixed silent gestures—*ni pra* for the twofold state, and *ā ni vi pra* for the fourfold state. I like to think of the silent gesture sequences as a relatively neutral substratum upon which the audible gestures are superimposed and thereby clarify the form.

3. Note that the gestures are reversible only in the syllabic state. The only option for the manifold states is the version that concludes with *sannipāta.*

19. Ṣaṭpitāputrakaḥ in the three states

The syllabic state:

| | | | | | |
|---|---|---|---|---|---|
| 1 | 2 | 3 | 4 | 5 | 6 |
| tā | śa | tā | śa | tā | **S** |

or

| | | | | | |
|---|---|---|---|---|---|
| **S** | tā | śa | tā | śa | tā |

[3 : 1 : 2 : 2 : 1 : 3]

The twofold state:

| | | | | | | | | | | | |
|---|---|---|---|---|---|---|---|---|---|---|---|
| 1 | 2 | 3 | 4 | 5 | 6 | 7 | 8 | 9 | 10 | 11 | 12 |
| *ni* | *pra* | tā | śa | *ni* | tā | *ni* | śa | tā | *pra* | *ni* | **S** |

3 : 1 : 2 : 2 : 1 : 3

The fourfold state:

| | | | | | | | | | | | | | | | | | | | | | | | |
|---|---|---|---|---|---|---|---|---|---|---|---|---|---|---|---|---|---|---|---|---|---|---|---|
| 1 | 2 | 3 | 4 | 5 | 6 | 7 | 8 | 9 | 10 | 11 | 12 | 13 | 14 | 15 | 16 | 17 | 18 | 19 | 20 | 21 | 22 | 23 | 24 |
| *ā* | *ni* | *vi* | *pra* | *ā* | tā | *vi* | śa | *ā* | *ni* | *vi* | tā | *ā* | *ni* | *vi* | śa | *ā* | tā | *vi* | *pra* | *ā* | *ni* | *vi* | **S** |

3 : 1 : 2 : 2 : 1 : 3

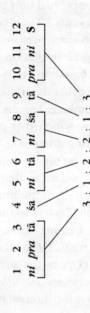

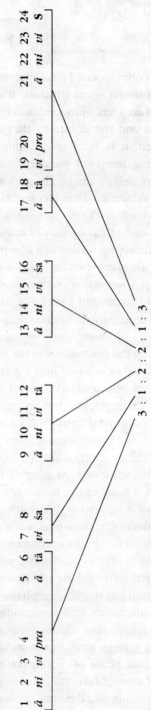

## 8.7 Timing

For convenience I have organized this exposition of *tāla* in a sequence that may at first seem arbitrary. Instead of beginning with abstract principles of rhythm, I have plunged into the most concrete matters—specific hand motions and the durations they represent. Now that these have been established, it is time to examine some of the more fundamental aspects of timing, temporal standards, and—in particular—the shifting proportional relationships among the various components of *tāla.* I shall focus here on five concepts: *laya* (tempo, timing in general), *mātrā* (a measure of duration), *akṣara* (syllable), *kalā* (a conceptual unit of rhythm), and *mārga* (a measure of the density of musical events). Their collective responsibility is to define the timing of a composition or a performance.[43]

I use the word "tempo" with some hesitation, because it tempts us to jump to some obvious conclusions based on the Western experience of musical rhythm and meter. We shall see that the Indian experience of tempo is based on quite a different way of thinking. *Laya* is the primary term for the "pace" of music, and the means by which that pace is evaluated will be among the main issues in the following discussion. In more recent literature *laya* has developed into a general term for rhythm and timing: when a performer is said to have "good *laya,*" we mean that he knows how to "keep time." Tempo, yes, but also good timing in the broadest sense of the word. The old saying "Śrutir mātā, layaḥ pitā" refers to this broad concept of *laya.* Often the first thing a teacher tells a young music student is, "*Śruti* (pitch, good intonation) is the mother [of music], *laya* the father."[44]

The sense of *laya* is more restrictive in the ancient and medieval literature: it signifies the time interval between one *tāla* action and the next. Or to put it somewhat differently, *laya* is the interval between the attack points of successive durations, each initiated by a gesture. It thus represents the phase of rest in the continuous alternation of action and repose which is the essence of the traditional concept of temporality in music, and which Bhartṛhari captured in his analogy of the falconer's line. I have already pointed out that this emphasis on what separates events, on the nothingness that alternates with somethingness, is one of the hallmarks of Indian thinking; I have also adduced other examples of this dynamics of the negative from various branches of Indian scholarship. Etymologically *laya* is linked with the phase of creation in which primal matter exists in an undifferentiated, amorphous state, thus lending emphasis to the role of the *tāla* gestures in creating and defining the world of musical forms.

I am arguing that tempo is essentially a *ratio* between selected layers of the rhythmic hierarchy—in the case of Indian music, a ratio arbitrarily established between the sequence of *tāla* gestures and the standard measures by which all musical durations are reckoned. When we put it this way, the basic idea does not differ greatly from a pattern of conductor's beats controlled by the rate to which a metronome is set (expressed, for example, in the equation between one quarter note and M.M. 60),[45] except for the vital difference between a conductor's gestures and the gestures of *tāla* in the ancient rhythmic system. In the latter, the gestures differ in two important respects: (1) they may occur at a steady or a variable rate, marking equal or unequal durations; and (2) their pattern is not uniform; the variations in pattern delineate both the structure and the progress of the underlying rhythmic form—the "bones" of the music.

When we define tempo in Western music as the speed or rate at which a work is performed, we also assume a ratio between (1) a particular level of pulsation perceived in the music and (2) some internalized standard of temporal measure—perhaps, as some have suggested, the heartbeat. Manifestly this is not the only tempo to be found in music. There is also the tempo of surface rhythm (which is generally much faster than what we conceive as "the beat") and what Wallace Berry has identified as the "tempo of events" (which will be much slower than the beat).[46] All three of these tempos may readily be found in, say, the first movement of Mozart's Symphony in G Minor, K. 550: in the steady surface rhythm of continuous eighth notes, in the conductor's two hand gestures (down, then up) for each measure of $\frac{2}{2}$ time, and in the longer intervals between the beginnings of phrases and themes. But when asked to characterize the tempo, most musicians will unhesitatingly choose the conductor's beat as the rate to define (as fast or slow). It is interesting that unpracticed listeners will often select different rates of pulsation and interpret the tempo (of surface rhythm) as fast, when in reality the structural beats are in a more leisurely tempo.

The solution offered in the ancient system of *mārga tāla*s was to fix, if not all of the ratios between the various levels of rhythmic activity, at least as many as possible—often as many as three or four. This was no simple task, and the system of *deśī tāla*s signals the abandonment of this set of multiple rhythmic equations in favor of a short, repetitive cycle.

I shall attempt to summarize the respective roles of the members of these multiple rhythmic equations: the *tāla* gestures are the structure markers; *laya* is the interval between gestures; the *mātrā* is a conventional standard of time measurement; *akṣara* is a syllable (any sort, any length); *kalā* is a conceptual standard by which rhythmic form is measured; and *mārga* is the relative density of time, as measured by the span of time within which a given sequence of musical events is to be completed. In one way or another, all five of these components must be specified when the temporal structure of a musical composition is defined, and none of them is permanently affixed to any of the others. It becomes obvious that this is no simple set of relationships.

This being the case, it is much too simplistic to describe the temporal hierarchy in terms of a single ratio or set of ratios; nor is it clear on what model or models these equations were constructed. One possible model was the three speeds of recitation, defined variously as 1:2:3 (the short, long, and protracted syllabic durations), 3:4:5, 9:12:16, and 16:20:25.[47] Two ratios in particular permeate the musical system: the arithmetic ratio of 1:2:3, which arises from the three basic durations of the syllabic state; and the geometric ratio of 1:2:4, which pervades all levels of musical activity. Both are natural ratios which take no great amount of intellectual effort to discover, but the ratio 1:2:4 is also widespread in the visual arts and architecture and apparently led to the great engineering advances of the early Indus Valley civilizations when Harappan brick makers discovered the exceptional bonding properties of kiln-fired bricks standardized to these proportions.[48] It may be more than coincidence that the proportions of a great tradition of brick construction were adopted for the regulation of a highly modular system of musical rhythm.

I turn now to the individual standards of measurement. Of the five concepts we have been examining, *mātrā* comes the closest to a fixed unit of measure; the same word denotes the basic unit of measure for Sanskrit verse. Prem Lata Sharma has defined *mātrā* as "a conceptual time-unit that is concretized or manifested in *akṣara* (syllable)," with the useful observation that the relationship is similar to the relationship between *śruti* and *svara.*[49] This traditional line of explanation helps to bring four of our terms into alignment: the syllables (of verse, music, drumming, and dance) and *tāla* gestures are actualized forms, perceptual units that manifest the conceptual units of rhythm (*mātrā* and *kalā*).

By what standard was the duration of the *mātrā* established? In Sanskrit prosody and in the later system of *deśī tāla*s the *mātrā* was equated with one short syllable (*hrasva* or *laghu*), but in the ancient system the *mātrā* was clearly a longer unit, defined none too precisely as the time required to blink the eyelids five times or utter five short syllables of text. According to this equation, the three basic durations of the *mārga tāla*s are as follows: *laghu* = one *mātrā* (five short syllables), *guru* = two *mātrā*s (ten), and *pluta* = three *mātrā*s (fifteen). If we recall that the manifold states were organized in long strings of *guru* durations, it is apparent that the tempo of structural gestures must have been extremely slow, perhaps as slow as M.M. 40. The association of slow pace with ritual music is unsurprising, but no constraints were placed upon either the tempo of surface musical activity or the tempo of musical events.

The term *akṣara* is unproblematic and means nothing more than "syllable" in all possible contexts—a syllable of speech, the letter representing that syllable in any of the traditional scripts, a syllable denoting one of the *tāla* gestures, or any musical unit that can be represented by an uttered syllable: a dance step, a drum stroke, or one of the seven *svara*s. The essential point here is that the syllabic unit, however we define it, has proved such a useful concept for the encoding of musical information: it is unitary, precise, easily remembered and articulated, and firmly rooted in the experience of human language; but at the same time it is flexible in duration and can conveniently represent a complex cluster of musical phenomena. This profusion of syllabic forms is clearly a result of the meticulous phonetic observations of the ancient grammarians. I have argued the role of the syllable in chapter 4 and will not belabor the point here, except to emphasize that the equations among the several types of syllables have often been established in a highly relativistic way: that is, one *tāla* gesture may represent any of the three durations (as in the syllabic state), or a 1 : 1 ratio may be maintained between one gesture and one duration (as in the manifold states), or a single unit of *tāla* may subsume a long string of rapidly articulated drum syllables.

The two remaining terms are problematic, but they lie at the core of the ancient concept of musical rhythm. *Kalā* at first glance is especially confusing because (1) only the placement of the macron distinguishes it from *kāla,* the word for time in general (providing Indian authors with a tempting opportunity for clever wordplay); and (2) the word can denote either a specific duration of time or the gesture by which that duration is separated from its neighbors. Let us clear away some of the confusion. In the sense of gesture, *kalā* signifies one of the four silent gestures;[50] in the sense of duration, *kalā* units (defined in terms of 1, 2, 4, or 8 *mātrā*s) are used to measure the time span of a *tāla,* a formal unit, or an entire composition. The word *kalā* has a wide semantic range, but the core meaning is "a small part of anything," especially a sixteenth part. Two aspects of this semantic field have proved particularly useful for musical purposes: its flexibility (in representing units of variable size) and its association with the geometric series 1, 2, 4, 8, 16, 32, 64. In a hierarchical system of rhythm featuring the inflation of patterns in an invariant ratio of 1 : 2 : 4, it comes as no surprise to uncover references to this numerical series in the etymologies of important terms.

But to grasp the full meaning of the concept of ***kalā,*** it is necessary to explore its relationship to the equally problematic concept of *mārga* (path).

To be precise, *mārga* specifies the duration of the rhythmic path, in effect the time within which a prescribed series of musical actions and events is to be completed. An analogy may help. *Mārga* from a Western point of view is a somewhat eccentric way of expressing the concept of tempo, and indeed that is exactly what is intended—as if to say "Sing the national anthem in eight, or in four, or in two minutes, with all the proportions adjusted accordingly." But *mārga* is experienced not as a prescribed length of time but as the relative density of events within that time span. To return to the national anthem, if we were to sing it, tapping the first beat of each measure and making a mental note at the end of each phrase, and were then to render the same song at twice the speed, and then at four times the speed, with every action proportionate within the contracting span of time, we would have experienced the equivalent of *mārga.* We would have sung all the notes and all the words, tapped all the beats, and marked all the cadences. The events of the song, however defined, would have undergone proportional compression, and this is precisely what is meant by the idea of *mārga.* In (20) is a display of the equations between ***kalā*** and ***mātrā*** in each of the four *mārgas*:

20. Rhythmic equations in the four *mārgas*

| *mārga* | ***kalā*** | ***mātrā*** |
|---|---|---|
| ***dhruva*** (the shortest) | 1 | 1 |
| ***citra*** | 1 | 2 |
| ***vṛtti*** | 1 | 4 |
| ***dakṣiṇa*** | 1 | 8 |

This seems innocent enough, but note what has *not* been specified: the rhythmic equations in (20) fix the ratios between the basic unit of measure (the *mātrā,* which is found by convention) and the structural units (the ***kalā***s), but not the individual time durations of the ***tāla,*** which are also variable. It will be evident that the system depends upon a bewilderingly complex set of rhythmic equivalents, almost as if we were to concoct a recipe with an assortment of measuring spoons and cups that kept expanding or shrinking. Indeed the system was overly complex, and it subsequently underwent drastic alteration in response to new musical needs. What helped to restrain its complexity in ancient ritual practice was the stabilizing 1 : 1 ratio between the ***kalā*** and the ***guru*** duration, which was held invariant in the manifold states. If, then, there existed any general standard of measure, any *pramāṇa,* this was it. Perhaps this is why the major formal structures of the *gāndharva* repertoire appear to have been designed for performance in the expanded versions, a point to which I shall return in chapter 9.

These relationships are summarized in (21). Note in particular the discrepancy between the actual durations of the *tāla* and the underlying framework of conceptual rhythm as expressed in *kalā*s and *mātrā*s.

21. Ṣaṭpitāputrakaḥ *tāla* in the syllabic state and the *citra mārga*[51]

<table>
<tr><td>6 tāla durations</td><td colspan="3">pluta</td><td>laghu</td><td colspan="2">guru</td><td colspan="2">guru</td><td>laghu</td><td colspan="3">pluta</td></tr>
<tr><td>6 tāla gestures</td><td colspan="3">S</td><td>tā</td><td colspan="2">śa</td><td colspan="2">tā</td><td>śa</td><td colspan="3">tā</td></tr>
<tr><td>6 kalās</td><td colspan="2"></td><td colspan="2"></td><td colspan="2"></td><td colspan="2"></td><td colspan="2"></td><td colspan="2"></td></tr>
<tr><td>12 mātrās</td><td></td><td></td><td></td><td></td><td></td><td></td><td></td><td></td><td></td><td></td><td></td><td></td></tr>
</table>

It would take us too far out of our way to trace the later history of these temporal concepts through the Indian musicological literature. What can be said in general is that their domains narrowed, their variations became more limited, their mutual relationships became more fixed, and some were reinterpreted. With the advent of the system of *deśī tāla*s, many of them became irrelevant. In the modern traditions of Karnatic and Hindustani music, the concept of *mārga* survives only as a vestige of its former self. In chapter 9 we shall see concrete illustrations of these rhythmic concepts in the diagrams and reconstructions.

## 8.8 The *Deśī Tālas*

I have referred in previous chapters to the phenomenon of *deśī*—the dynamic expansion of musical resources during the second half of the first millennium; during this time a large number of popular regional traditions were collected, codified, partly homogenized, and set alongside the venerable *mārga* tradition (which in the end they supplanted).[52] In the domain of musical rhythm, this expansion was fully as explosive as it was in the domain of pitch, but the sweeping changes in the system of *tāla* are quite impossible to document from the surviving textual evidence. In fact nothing remains of any of the intermediate stages, and the authors of the medieval period failed to reach a consensus on the number, names, and structure of the many *deśī tāla*s that they recorded. One especially regrettable loss is the sole document which would undoubtedly shed some light on this transition in rhythmic thinking and practice—the lost *tāla* canto of Mataṅga's

*Bṛhaddeśī,* of which no more than a handful of verses survive, in the form of quotations embedded in later treatises.[53] If and when a manuscript containing this canto turns up, scholars will be standing in line to examine it.

I shall deal with the *deśī tāla*s as a "movement" and a set of principles, not an established body of doctrine. As a movement, however, they are of vital importance, for it is from them that the modern systems of *tāla* have evolved. The following may be said about the *deśī tāla*s: that they came from many different geographical regions of the subcontinent, that they were more closely associated with song and poetic traditions than with the theater, that many were popular in origin, that in many cases they demonstrate a splintering of the rhythmic flow into an array of short and irregular patterns, that they were allied with the developing practice of improvisation, and that no overarching theoretical framework existed for their classification. Many later authors claim that the *deśī tāla*s were derived as the result of various unspecified partitionings of the *mārga tāla*s, but the profusion of patterns makes it difficult to validate this claim. While all of the conceptual apparatus of the *mārga* system was available for their classification, most of the deeper structural levels were irrelevant, and the new *tāla*s were defined simply in terms of a short, repeatable sequence of durations. Unlike the *mārga tāla*s, the gesture language was left unspecified. The trend was toward a range of much shorter durations: *laghu* replaced *guru* as the durational standard, and we see the introduction of three new units shorter than the "short" (*laghu*), in a process not unlike the splintering of rhythmic values and the demand for new notational symbols in the European Ars Nova.[54] The treatises prior to the *Saṅgītaratnākara* refer to them as *khaṇḍa* (split) *tāla*s, and it is Śārṅgadeva who was apparently the first to label them as *deśī.*[55]

Thirty such *tāla*s are mentioned in the *Mānasollāsa* of King Someśvara. By the time of the *Saṅgītaratnākara* their number had increased to 120, and it continued to swell (to more than 200) in later treatises. From all the evidence, the system seems to have remained in a state of perpetual flux, with some popular *tāla*s remaining relatively constant while others drop in or out of the system or reappear under new names or structures. Although the enormous array of patterns resisted all attempts to organize and classify them, the intent seems to have been to authorize all possible permutations of the given possibilities—a leitmotif in Indian musical thought. Nowhere, however, do we find any indication of the selection principles or arguments in favor of some patterns over others. Selection was left for *prayoga* (practice), which in the several stages and branches of India's musical tradition has tended to settle on a fairly limited selection from among the enormous number of choices offered by the theoretical system.[56]

In their search to find authority for the *deśī tāla*s in the early literature, later authors have cited a cryptic and much-disputed passage in Bharata's *Nāṭyaśāstra* (31.23–24) which refers to *miśra* (mixed) and *saṅkīrṇa* (blended) *tāla*s and mentions units of five, seven, nine, ten, and eleven *kalā*s—all the numbers, in fact, that were excluded from the rhythmic ratios of the *mārga* system.[57] The commentator Abhinavagupta attempted to identify units of these irregular lengths in the ritual forms of the ancient musical theater, but the later Indian tradition has reinterpreted this series of "mixed" numbers in the context of repeatable *tāla* patterns, not large-scale musical structure. The results are displayed in (22):

22. The five rhythmic genera (*jāti*s)

| | | |
|---|---|---|
| 3 | *tryaśra* | triangular |
| 4 | *caturaśra* | quadrangular |
| 5 | *khaṇḍa* | split |
| 7 | *miśra* | mixed |
| 9 | *saṅkīrṇa* | blended |

In this line of thinking, the terms *khaṇḍa, miśra,* and *saṅkīrṇa* have become conventional tags for the numbers five, seven, and nine. In the modern system of Karnatic music, the names listed in (22) are those of the five *jāti*s—expanded versions of the basic *tāla* structures in which a particular *aṅga* (limb) of the pattern is singled out for inflation, with its divisions marked visibly by three, four, five, seven, or nine finger counts.[58] In this manner a simple pattern may be transformed into a much more complex structure. All of this evidence suggests a long-range trend in the direction of increasing asymmetry and rhythmic irregularity, in both the individual pattern and the system as a whole. The relevant point to be extracted is that both the system of *deśī tāla*s and the *tāla*s of modern South Indian music are, to use Curt Sachs's useful terms, overwhelmingly additive rather than divisive—both in concept and in structure.[59] This is to say that they were, and are, constructed "from the bottom up" in irregular groupings of a lowest common denominator (hence, additive), not "from the top down" in a nested series of even divisions of a highest common multiple. Among all the large culture areas of world music, India is in this sense unique—not so much in her exploitation of additive rhythms as in the development of an appropriate theoretical framework for their codification.

It is clear that the *deśī tāla*s were more than abstract patterns of durations, although only the durations have been recorded. Certain *tāla*s are identical in structure and must have been differentiated by tempo, gesture, or some other means. Another problem arises in connection with several *tāla*s consisting of a string of equal durations: four shorts, five shorts, four longs, and the like. Since there was no pattern irregularity to bring forward the unique structure of the *tāla,* Sharma speculates that some definition was introduced in performance in the form of (1) the conventional alteration of one of the units; (2) the gesture sequence; or (3) in a development that seems to have occurred not earlier than the fourteenth century, devising a string of drum syllables to represent the distinctive substructure of each of the *tāla*s.[60] The tradition of reciting drum syllables is very old and appears in the *Nāṭyaśāstra,* but the attempt to capture the essence of a *tāla* with a unique set of syllables—which has become the standard practice in modern Hindustani music—belongs to the later history of the *deśī tāla* system.

Although the gesture language of the *deśī tāla*s has not been recorded in the shastric literature, we note a relevant trend. In the chironomy prescribed for the *mārga tāla*s, an audible gesture signaled the end of a *tāla* unit, with silent gestures prefixed as needed to represent the structural durations of the two expanded states; but in the *Saṅgītaratnākara,* Śārṅgadeva outlines an alternate set of eight gestures (23):[61]

23.

| | |
|---|---|
| *dhruvakā:* | an audible handclap |
| *sarpiṇī:* | hand moves to the left |
| *kṛṣṇā:* | hand moves to the right |
| *padminī:* | hand moves downward |
| *visarjitā:* | hand moves "outward" |
| *vikṣiptā:* | hand moves "inward" |
| *patākā:* | hand moves upward |
| *patitā:* | hand falls to the knee or ground |

The apparent purpose of these gestures was to demonstrate visibly the *mārga,* that is, whether each *kalā* consisted of one, two, four, or eight *mātrā*s.[62] *Dhruvakā* was always the initial, *patitā* was always the final, and the rest were inserted in regular sequence in the number needed. The essential feature here is that the *beginning* of the rhythmic unit is now marked by an audible gesture; the remaining seven are treated as suffixes that maintain the extended duration of the cycle with motions not unlike those of a modern conductor. With this innovation in the gesture language, we see the roots of the modern *tāla* practice of North and South India and most likely the system of chironomy by which the *deśī tāla*s were controlled.

In this and earlier references in this chapter, readers will not have failed to note the significant role assigned to the silent gestures. The tradition may be traced both backward and forward in Indian history: back to the style of Vedic recitation in which a gesture known as *śūnyahasta* (empty-handed) was used to mark certain conjunctions or pauses in the text, and forward to the *khālī* (empty) wave that plays a prominent role in today's Hindustani music.[63] In the present context it seems safe to infer that the beginning member of each *deśī tāla* cycle was marked by some audible gesture (and probably the beginning members of some of the internal divisions in the more complex *tāla*s), while some appropriate combination of silent motions helped to control and delineate the structure of the *tāla.*

It remains to examine a representative sampling of these patterns and assess them as a whole. In connection with the *mārga tāla*s I cautioned against the inference that their structural patterns could be expected to appear in diminution in the flow of surface rhythm. In the shorter patterns and range of durations of many of the *deśī tāla*s, we are clearly closer to the rhythmic surface. But once again it cannot be assumed that these patterns represent the fastest stream of performed rhythm. Nevertheless, they are a source of valuable information on some of the most vital aspects of rhythm in music: the preferred sequences of durations, the equilibrium of various patterns, pattern length, internal structure, and preferred ways of beginning and terminating patterns. The deductions which I draw in the following discussion are based on the listing of 120 *deśī tāla*s in chapter 5 of the *Saṅgītaratnākara.*[64] The symbols to be used and their equivalents are shown in (24), in which all durational values are either divisions or multiples of whatever value is assigned by convention to *laghu.*

24. Durations in the *deśī tāla* system

| Name | Symbol | Relative length | In Western notation | Duration |
|---|---|---|---|---|
| *pluta* | P | 3 | ♩. | protracted |
| *guru* | G | 2 | ♩ | long |
| *laghu* | L | 1 | ♪ | short |
| *druta* | D | $\frac{1}{2}$ | 𝅘𝅥𝅯 | shortest |
| *virāma*[65] | V | $\frac{1}{2}$ or $\frac{1}{4}$ | | a fractional extension of L or D |

The most interesting aspect of this series of durations is the concept of *virāma,* which may be compared to the familiar augmentation dot of Western staff notation. *Virāma* was evidently not regarded as an independent rhythmic unit with a value of its own, but it may at times have provided an internal caesura or a pause at the end of a pattern. Whether its role was extension, punctuation, or termination, *virāma* is often the element that turns an otherwise regular pattern into an asymmetric construction with a time span that cannot be measured in a whole number of *mātrās*.

Much can be deduced from the assortment of *tāla*s whose durations are encoded in such cryptic form in the *Saṅgītaratnākara.* Most important of all, the list does not represent a logical set of exclusive permutations, no matter what way we choose to examine the specifications for the 120 *tāla*s. There are numerous and obvious omissions, duplications, and puzzling anomalies in the list. The conclusion must be that we are presented with a large selection of raw data which has not yet been subjected to theoretical leveling and systematic organization, a process that was to take many centuries and was never completely successful.

First some statistics. With respect to the number of units, the *tāla*s range from a single member to as many as twenty-two (Miśravarṇa: D D D D V D D D D V D D D D V P G D D G L G). In terms of the total number of *mātrās* (L), they run from one-half (Ekatalī: D) to as many as thirty-two in the massive Siṁhanandana: G G L P L G D D G G L P L P G L L, concluding with four silent L durations.[66] Short patterns do not dominate the list to the extent we might expect (25):

25.

| Number of units | Number of *tāla*s |
|---|---|
| 1 | 3 |
| 2 | 7 |
| 3 | 15 |
| 4 | 26 |
| 5 | 31 |
| 6 | 15 |
| 7 | 12 |

How systematic is this array of *tāla*s? Let us examine some of the shorter patterns in an attempt to see how closely they approach a set of exclusive permutations. Four *tāla*s occupy a span of two *mātrā*s: G, DDDD, DDL, LDD; the obvious omission is LL. Five *tāla*s span three *mātrā*s: LG, DDLL, LLDD, and two of DDG; if an iamb, why not a trochee? Twelve *tāla*s occupy four *mātrā*s: two of LP, three of DDLG, and one each of LLG, LLLL, LDDG, LGDD, DDLLL, DDDDG, and LLDDDD. Even in this limited selection we can note a tendency to conclude with a longer duration, which provides a cadence of sorts. This tendency is typical of the list as a whole: twenty-six end with *pluta,* but only two begin with this duration; *guru* is more frequent at the end (thirty-seven) than at the beginning (twenty-six), but not by such a dramatic margin. On the other hand, thirty-five *tāla*s begin with *druta,* but only sixteen end with this duration.

There are clear signs of internal organization in the longer and more complex patterns, as demonstrated in the two I mentioned above. Miśravarṇa, as outlined in (26), falls readily into three statements of the same sequence plus an irregular string of durations at the cadence. Siṁhanandana can be analyzed into a fairly regular duple or quadruple meter and is given additional definition by a significant internal repetition of the Caccatpuṭaḥ pattern: G G L P.[67]

26. Two *deśī tāla*s

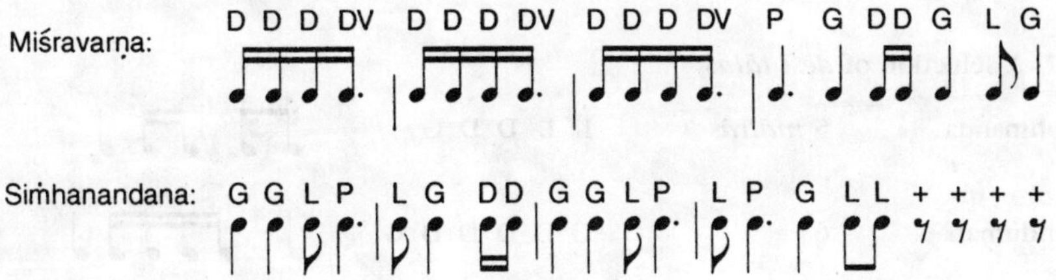


The shorter patterns, on the other hand, do not share this tendency toward internal organization: only three of the *tāla*s consist of a single repeated pattern, in effect a double foot. Eleven are palindromes, continuing the tendency we noted in the five *mārga tāla*s.[68] Many of the *deśī tāla*s are described in the cryptic language of the trisyllabic metric *gaṇa*s, a system of encoding that we shall presently explore in an attempt to discern the possible influence of poetic meters on this array of rhythmic patterns. The point I wish to make here is that the set of 120 *deśī tāla*s fails to reflect any significant influence of this code; that is, it reveals no underlying tendencies toward "threeness" or consistent sequences of any of the eight possible trisyllabic permutations of L and G.

To pursue this point, it will be useful to investigate the total pattern length in terms of *mātrā*s. Of the 120, 85 consist of a whole number of *mātrā*s, 35 of a fraction. Of the former, 35 *tāla*s occupy a total number of *mātrā*s that falls within the numerical series 1, 2, 4, 8, 16, 32; only 21 occupy a span within a ternary series of numbers, and most of these do not qualify as triple meters because of their internal structures. Fourness is more typical of this repertoire, with respect to both total length and internal division, but it is a fourness marked by considerable irregularity in contrast to the standard binary rhythms of modern Europe or the foursquare rhythmic grids of East Asia.

I conclude with a selection of typical *tāla* patterns of intermediate length, from which additional conclusions may be drawn (27). Two obstacles, among many, hinder our full understanding of how this repertoire may have been performed: we do not know the gesture sequences, and we have no evidence that indicates which *tāla*s were popular, which were not, and which may have been purely theoretical concoctions. Some inferences can be drawn on the basis of modern practice and the evidence of treatises written several centuries later, but I remain suspicious of applying the praxis of a later, settled phase of a musical tradition to the textual remains of an earlier, formative phase.

27. A selection of *deśī tālas*

| | | | |
|---|---|---|---|
| Abhinanda | 5 *mātrās* | L L D D G |  |
| Bindumati | 6 | G D D D D G |  |
| Candrakalā | 16 | G G G P P P L |  |
| Dīpaka | 7 | D D L L G G |  |
| Gauri | 5 | L L L L L |  |
| Jaya | 9 | L G L L D D P |  |
| Nissaṅka | 13 | L G G P G G L |  |
| Pratimaṇṭhaka | 8 | L L G G L L |  |
| Raṅgābharaṇa | 9 | G G L L P |  |
| Tryaśravarṇa[69] | 5 | L L D D L L |  |

## 8.9 The Influence of Metrics

In this section I focus upon an issue that cannot be avoided in any attempt to trace the early development of musical rhythm: to what extent have the rhythms of speech and poetry left their marks upon the rhythms of music? I am assuming that this is a universal process, deeply rooted in human history, and that the evolution of formal systems of musical rhythm can be interpreted as an increasingly more complex dialectic between the patterns of intoned language and the regularly pulsating rhythms of the human body. Language patterns offer a set of cultural models for the grouping of tones, models that have been authorized by long habit and a literary tradition; body rhythms provide means of entraining these groups into an organized stream of sound. The process is not fully understood, and efforts to understand it are continually frustrated because we lack most of the evidence for its formative stages.

My argument, in brief, is that while traces of ancient Indian poetic meters can be detected here and there in the structural patterns of the various *mārga* and *deśī tāla*s, their influence is most evident in the intermediate levels of musical structure, that is, in the organization of lines, phrases, and stanzas—not in the individual patterns per se nor in the longest spans of musical structure. If my contention is correct, then Indian musical rhythm managed to free itself from the surface patterns of poetry at a very early date, in striking contrast to the music of ancient and medieval Europe, which remained largely dependent upon the modal rhythms of Greek and Latin verse until the fourteenth century.[70]

For a convenient summary of the evolution of metrical principles in early Indian verse, I turn to the writings of H. D. Velankar, whose account of this process is generally respected and widely accepted.[71] In his interpretation of the evolution of Indian poetry from syllabic to quantitative and then accentual verse, Velankar has identified three distinct stages: first, a music of "voice modulation," followed by a second stage in which the music of "sound variation" was the guiding principle, and finally a music of "time-regulated accent." In (28) the main characteristics of each of the three stages are summarized; this will provide a frame of reference for the following discussion.

This summary (28) is admittedly an oversimplification of Velankar's interpretation, in that it fails to include the intermediate stages and refinements of this complex process, for which he has provided explanations and illustrations. In his view, the tonal accents and voice modulations of Vedic

28. The evolution of Indian verse according to H. D. Velankar

| Vedic and post-Vedic verse | Classical Sanskrit and the early Prakrits | Later vernaculars and popular verse |
|---|---|---|
| A music of "voice modulation" (*svara-saṅgīta*)[72] | A music of "sound variation" (*varṇa-saṅgīta*)[73] | A music of "time-regulated accent" (*tāla-saṅgīta*)[74] |
| Syllabic verse, measured in *akṣara*s and featuring tonal accents | Quantitative verse, regulated by fixed sequences of long and short syllables | Accentual verse, with regularly spaced stress accents |
| The *Sāmaveda* tradition | The classical *kāvya* tradition (lyric poetry) | Epic verse, popular song, and the accompaniment of dancing |
| Syllable quantities not fixed | Syllable quantities fixed and prescribed in terms of the trisyllabic metric *gaṇa*s[75] | Measured in "time moments" (*kāla-mātrā*s) with an invariant ratio of 1:2 between the short and long |
| Lines and stanzas of variable length, with irregular caesura (*yati*) | Stanzas of four identical lines, with regular caesura dividing the line into unequal members | Parallel couplets with regular stress after each fourth, fifth, sixth, or seventh *mātrā* |

verse eventually became the basis for the pitch structure of the various *rāgas*, just as the later *tāla* systems of Indian music evolved under the influence of the stress accents in the "time-regulated" tradition of popular-vernacular poetry. This line of argument is not without precedent and cannot be far off the mark, but his explanation offers no clues to the earlier development of rhythm in the *mārga tāla* phase. Readers may, as I do, detect a loose parallel between the *mārga* and *deśī* stages of *tāla,* on the one hand, and the *varṇa-saṅgīta* and *tāla-saṅgīta* stages of verse, on the other. But the case is difficult to build and is vulnerable to many objections, not the least of which is the problem of tracing some cause-and-effect relationship between a body of poetry and a musical repertoire that may have been influenced by it. The evidence is entirely circumstantial. The regularly recurring cycles of the *deśī tālas* would appear to be more amenable to regulation by stress accent, just as the prescribed gesture language and proportions of the *mārga tālas* may suggest a parallel to the fixed syllable sequences that are typical of classical Sanskrit verse. But I am reluctant to claim anything more than a loose historical parallel between these closely associated traditions of performed rhythm. The impact of poetic rhythm is indisputable, but it seems better to view it as a long process of gradual pressure and mutual feedback rather than as the direct influence of a particular body of metrical verse upon one specific phase in the development of musical rhythm.

Classical Sanskrit metrical theory offered a convenient system for the encoding of musical durations, a code that was adopted by Mataṅga and his successors. As usual, some of the distinctive features of a code may have found their way into the message. To represent the various sequences of short and long syllables, the metrical scholars devised the mnemonic formula *Ya mā tā rā ja bhā na sa la gaṁ,* in which each of the first eight syllables represents the first syllable of a unique trisyllabic group (each syllable is assigned a short or long duration as indicated by the presence or absence of a macron above the vowel).[76] These trisyllabic groups are the *gaṇas* or *trikas*, and they constitute the eight possible permutations of short and long durations. To accommodate metrical lines with syllable totals other than multiples of three, the final two syllables of the formula represent single *laghu* (short) and *guru* (long) durations. Thus, a line of iambic tetrameter (4 × ⏑–) would be expressed as *ja rā la gaṁ* (LGL + GLG + L + G).[77] The durations of the formula and the eight *gaṇas* are displayed in (29), together with their Greek equivalents.

29. The Sanskrit metrical code

| | |
|---|---|
| the formula: | *ya mā tā rā ja bhā na sa la gaṁ* |
| durations: | L G G G L G L L L G |

| Name of the *gaṇa* | Formulaic name | Pattern | Greek equivalent |
|---|---|---|---|
| *candra* (moon) | *bhā-gaṇa* | GLL = –∪∪ | dactyl |
| *svar* (heaven) | *na-gaṇa* | LLL = ∪∪∪ | tribrach |
| *anala* (fire) | *rā-gaṇa* | GLG = –∪– | cretic |
| *vāyu (wind)* | *sa-gaṇa* | LLG = ∪∪– | anapest |
| *ambara* (sky) | *tā-gaṇa* | GGL = ––∪ | antibacchius |
| *mārtaṇḍa* (sun) | *ja-gaṇa* | LGL = ∪–∪ | amphibrach |
| *bhūmi* (earth) | *mā-gaṇa* | GGG = ––– | molossus |
| *jala* (water) | *ya-gaṇa* | LGG = ∪–– | bacchius |

L = *laghu* (short); G = *guru* (long)

Two obvious questions arise: Why groups of three syllables, not two or four? And what have been the implications, if any, of all this "threeness" for poetry and music? There are occasional references in the music literature to *gaṇa*s of two and four units that provided a basis for permutations of di- and quadrisyllabic groupings, but they never mounted a serious challenge to the overwhelming preference for threeness in encoding syllabic durations.[78] Velankar's explanation is grounded in cultural ideology:

> In ancient India, number 3 was generally admitted as the smallest among the large and largest among the small numbers. It was adopted as the smallest unit for developing multiplicity. Thus, the smallest unit for the evolution of the manifold world in the theory of the Sāṅkhyas was the triple Pradhāna consisting of 3 guṇas, while it was the Tryaṇuka made up of 3 Aṇus or Dvyaṇukas, in the theory of the Vaiśeṣikas. The three states of life, Utpatti, Sthiti and Laya were considered as the basis of the diverse conditions of life by the Vedāntin. The three times, past, present and future, are the foundation of a convenient distribution of the ever-changing phenomenon of time. The three basic accents, high, low and middle, are sufficient to describe the many different modulations of voice[79] and the same is true of the three worlds, the upper, the lower and the middle. . . . So, both as a matter of principle and for the sake of convenience, a new unit of three letters called Trika, having 8 different forms of music or rhythm, was adopted for metrical scanning and also as a basis for defining the many different varieties of sound-variation pro-

> duced by the alternation of short and long letters in different ways that constituted shorter or longer metrical lines in classical Sanskrit metres.[80]

It cannot be disputed that this habit of thinking in threes is not only deeply rooted in Indian culture but is also ideally suited to a mnemonic code. It may also be among the reasons why Sanskrit verse, unlike Greek or Latin poetry, does not depend upon such binary principles as responsion or the opposition of arsis and thesis.[81] In the classical Sanskrit *kāvya* tradition the longer lines, which are closer to the lyric than to the stichic meters of ancient Greece, seldom fall neatly into a regular series of identical metric feet, and indeed there was no conceptual basis for identifying such a foot.[82] The trisyllabic *gaṇa*s are little more than a convenience of notation, caesura often occurs in the middle of a *gaṇa,* and no organizing principles were devised for the grouping or opposition of *gaṇa*s within a poetic line. Sometimes the *gaṇa* notation actually serves to conceal what to the Western ear would appear to be a simpler pattern: an iambic line of any length would be expressed in pairs of *ja rā gaṇa*s, that is:

LGL + GLG + LGL + GLG = ⏑–⏑–⏑–⏑–⏑–⏑–.
*ja* *rā* *ja* *rā*

This meter is among the fifty-five meters with twelve-syllable lines cited by the classical metricians, and it appears to have been fairly popular.[83] But which of its organizing rhythms would have come forward in composition and in recitation is an open question. The sequence of *gaṇa*s would surely have crossed the poet's mind, and the regular alternation of short and long syllables would just as surely not have escaped his notice. In all probability the verse he fashioned would have pulled against both of these underlying rhythms in a rich counterpoint. The longer the line, the more likely that caesura would be prescribed; but this meter has none. Of the twelve-syllable lines with obligatory caesura, we find occasional divisions into 6 + 6, but more often 7 + 5 and 8 + 4, with no obvious preference for placing the longer member at the beginning or end of the line. In their sequence of durations, many if not most of the popular poetic meters are fully as asymmetric and additive in construction as the *deśī tāla*s. It seems inescapable that the superimposition of these two rhythmic layers—the metrical patterns of verse and the rhythmic patterns of the substratum of *tāla*—would have encouraged an active rhythmic counterpoint.

Poetic lines of eight, eleven, and twelve syllables dominate the verse of the Vedic period, but later classical poets favored even longer lines. The metrical treatises mention nineteen different possibilities for lines of seventeen syllables. Of these perhaps the most famous is Mandākrāntā (literally, the "slowly advancing"), the meter in which Kālidāsa cast his masterpiece *The Cloud Messenger* (*Meghadūta*):[84]

– – – –, ⏑ ⏑ ⏑ ⏑ ⏑ –, – ⏑ – – ⏑ – ⏓

G G G G L L L L L G G L G G L G G

*mā* *bhā* *na* *tā* *tā* *ga ga*

After performing such a line with the obligatory caesuras, it is difficult to detect any traces of the underlying metric *gaṇa*s, especially when the same *gaṇa* (*tā*) is repeated in such a radically different rhythmic context. The organization of the line is clearly by members, and it is articulated by the caesuras; each of the three members displays a unique sequence of syllable quantities and thereby presents a distinct challenge to the poet's craft. The pattern contains no discernible traces of either threeness or fourness, or indeed of any overall organizing rhythm. Perhaps the best way to make sense of the profusion and persistence of asymmetric sequences is to regard them, in Velankar's words, as "fossils":

> It is interesting to note how the introduction of a Yati [a caesura] in the metrical lines helped the formation and fossilization of many different metricomusical units of varied length. . . . These fossils cannot be easily recognized by merely looking at the definition of a metre, which is couched in the terms of the Trikas; but they can be easily felt and identified when the line is actually recited or heard. Sometimes, it is found that the whole line of a metre is made up of 2 or 3 of these fossils pieced up together.[85]

It seems inescapable that a similar process of fossilization was responsible for the preservation of many of the wildly irregular rhythmic patterns in the domain of *tāla.*

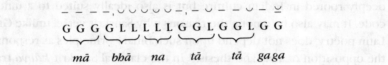

If the lines of classical Sanskrit verse surpass the lines of the Greek lyric both in length and irregularity, the Sanskrit stanza is a model of regularity and simplicity. With certain significant exceptions, the stanza with four identical lines dominates the *kāvya* repertoire. It is this sense of regularity at a deeper level of poetic structure that we find paralleled in the larger formal structures of *tāla,* especially in the typical division of a formal unit into four *pādabhāga*s.[86] It is clear that the rhythm of strophic division was a powerful influence in shaping the internal divisions of musical forms. But, lest we make too much of this, it could scarcely have been otherwise within a culture that placed such high value on vocal music and the delivery of a poetic text.

The status of *pluta,* the "protracted" or "floating" duration (three times the length of a short syllable), is markedly different in music and verse. In classical metric theory, *pluta* did not exist as an independent duration, although much the same effect may have been produced when caesura followed a long syllable. As I mentioned earlier, *pluta* occurs but three times in the entire *Ṛgveda* and fifteen times in the *Atharvaveda.*[87] It is always located at the end of a word, phrase, or line, and its evident purpose was to emphasize that final unit. *Pluta* is used, according to Whitney, at the end of a question, when calling to a distance, or to signify urgency, and it usually carries the acute tone.[88] Here is one important instance in which stress, tonal, and agogic accents coincide, revealing the same tendency toward end accent that will become even more apparent in the formal structures of *tāla.* In the *mārga tāla*s, *pluta* occurs with much greater frequency than in verse and is deployed both at the beginning and the end of patterns, with a definite preference for the latter. But this duration proved difficult to accommodate within the 1 : 2 : 4 ratio by which the manifold states of the *tāla* system were generated, so its primary role was as a structure marker in the syllabic states. With the rise of the *deśī tāla*s, however, the role of *pluta* became greatly expanded, and its divisions became the basis for a series of new fractional note values: that is, halving and quartering the duration of *pluta* produced new units of three-halves and three-fourths the value assigned to *laghu.* With its influence thus spread throughout the rhythmic system, *pluta* appears to have discarded most of its former tonal, accentual, and cadential implications and remains as just another number.

I have tried to trace the presence and influence of "deep numbers" in early Indian verse and music, with only limited success. But the issue is an important one and goes far beyond detecting traces of threeness and fourness. The principle of deep numbers—and with this expression I am attempting to suggest an analogy to the deep structures of linguistics—must be recognized as one of the basic means of building and recognizing large-scale musical forms, and I will argue the point in chapter 9. While the deep numbers embedded in Sanskrit verse are generally either a notational convenience or a conventional pulse that can be easily overridden in performance, in the ancient system of *tāla* they become a prime means of manifesting formal patterns and proportions at various hierarchical levels of musical structure.

## 8.10 The Rhythms of Indian Music

The essence of Indian musical rhythm is the interaction of independent rhythmic strata, controlled by gesture and manifesting a dense counterpoint of patterns and implications. At least four such strata can be identified in the simplest composition or performance: the metrical sequence of text syllables, the structural gesture patterns of the *mārga* or *deśī tāla*s, the melodic rhythm (vocal or instrumental) with its profusion of ornaments, and the accompanying patterns of the drummer. With a rhythmic texture of such potential complexity, problems of coordination and synchronization—such as *pāṇi* and *yati*—would inevitably have become preoccupations of the musical thinkers and would eventually have found their way into the conceptual apparatus of the musical system. But the primary means of coordinating and integrating all musical activity was the gesture language of *tāla*.

We have little evidence for the way in which text, melody, and rhythm were combined. In the ritual structures of *gāndharva,* the text was subservient to both the pitch and rhythmic dimensions, and therefore its own metric structure was easily overridden by the patterns of the *mārga tāla*s.[89] But in the freer plot songs of the early theater and the later tradition of independent song (the *prabandha*s), the metrical structure of verse became an independent stream of rhythmic activity—to which the shorter, repetitive patterns of the *deśī tāla*s were added as a continuous undercurrent. Precisely how this was accomplished must remain a matter for speculation, although as always, certain inferences may be drawn from modern performance practice.

We do not know, for example, whether the *tāla* cycle and the metrical line occupied exactly the same period, coincided at the beginning or the end of the line, or were entrained in some other way. Nor do we know just how the poetic caesuras would have been performed nor what their exact value would have been. Common sense suggests that the *tāla* cycle was performed as a continuous rhythmic background, filling in the pauses for caesura and the various cadences at the ends of lines and stanzas, over which the vocal line would become entrained—often, perhaps, beginning at a later point in the rhythmic cycle. If these assumptions are correct, the two rhythmic strata interpenetrate in a rich tangle of implications and patterns that compete for our attention, and the frequent points of confluence are experienced both as stability and as accent. Against these two streams of structural rhythms, the faster and sometimes irrational melodic rhythm and the drum rhythms will be perceived as variations superimposed upon a rhythmic ground—at times closely coordinated, and at other times developing independent patterns that cut across the established structural patterns and cycles.

My discussion has focused on the role of *tāla,* and readers should be reminded that an equally important and characteristic form of temporality in Indian music is the free genre of unmeasured rhythm that was known as *ālāpana,* the most significant beginning gambit in the music of the subcontinent.[90] Free from the constraints of *tāla,* lacking the rhythmic layer provided by the drummer(s), and in many cases lacking even the metrical structure of a text, the primary models for the time of *ālāpana* were the inner rhythms of the human body—in particular, the rhythm of the breath.

I have attempted to organize the complex evolution of rhythmic thought and practice in terms that are admittedly more simplistic than what actually happened. Within the time constraints of this study, I have pointed out a historical development in two grand stages: from *mārga* to *deśī,* theatrico-religious ritual to entertainment, strict to (relatively) free, Sanskrit to vernacular, central to regional, composed to improvised, modular to cyclical rhythm. History is never this simple, but the picture is not distorted. The constant factors in this development have been the controlling system of hand gestures and the loose collection of principles by which the system was regulated—many of which were reinterpreted to suit later practice. In the process, forms became less complex, patterns became shorter, rhythms became more repetitive, the range of activity within any single rhythmic layer became more complex, the interactions between the several rhythmic strata became somewhat simpler, and standards of measure which were once variable became fixed. None of this should be in any way surprising; we could apply much the same interpretation to the early development of rhythm in medieval Europe.

New musical needs arose, and the conceptual structure of music was revised in response to the developing practice of improvisation. The most obvious result was the institution of the rhythmic cycle as the single most important principle of musical structure. I view this development as the consequence of a long-standing cultural preference for circularity, a preference that was already so clearly expressed in the *Atharvaveda* hymn to time. The wheel of the sun chariot has become not only the Buddhist wheel of law but also the turning wheel of musical rhythm. It is no accident that the word for cycle (*āvarta*) and for a poetic meter (*vṛtta*) both mean "a turning."[91] This is how any process operates in the traditional Indian worldview—not by linear progression, but by turning and returning. With the rise of cyclical rhythm, many of the higher levels of musical structure (which we are about to examine) became irrelevant, and the overall form of Indian music became less hierarchical and was guided more by certain deep-seated formal archetypes. Music, we may say, became more a process than an object. The results have had implications that go far beyond the purely musical or the conceptual; they have profoundly affected the role of the individual musician within the fabric of Indian society.

In this as in previous chapters, I have pointed out ways in which musical organization has reflected the constant pressures of cultural ideology—in this case, how the system of *tāla* and the evolving concept of musical rhythm appear to manifest cultural intuitions of time. Among the more obvious are the ritualistic gesture language for the control of time, the plurality and mutability of temporal forms, the special value assigned to the negative aspects of rhythm (that is, to silence, inaudible gestures, and the intervals between rhythmic events), the essential relativity of the cluster of concepts that mutually define all musical timing, the organization of rhythm into repetitive cycles, and the precarious equilibrium which the Indian musician strives to maintain in the midst of a world of shifting forms and multiple perspectives.

N I N E

# FORM

As the wind, which is one, on entering creation, conforms its own form to the form of each being, so also the One, the *ātman* within all beings, assumes all forms, yet exists outside.

*Kaṭha Upaniṣad* 5.10[1]

Form is not what one should desire to understand; one should know the knower of form.

*Kauṣītaki Upaniṣad* 3.8[2]

## 9.1 Introduction

Nowhere in Indian culture is there to be found any clearer demonstration of the influence of traditional ideology upon artistic practice than in the realm of form. The Indian line of thinking on the nature of form and its relationship to substance is of great antiquity and has developed into a distinctive way of seeing and hearing the world. This chapter is an investigation of both form in music and the characteristic forms of music, internal organization and external design, building upon the concepts analyzed in chapter 8 and proceeding to an examination of the longer spans and deeper structural levels of the musical hierarchy.

Form in Indian music belongs to the domain of *tāla,* and indeed it can have no other proper home. In the musical tradition of Europe, the organization of pitch—in response to the inherent tensions and implications of the principle of harmonic tonality—has become the most powerful agent of musical form, with the significant exception of strophic and variation forms. But the structure of Indian music, from early times, has arisen from and depended upon the rhythmic impulses, energies, and implications manifested in the gesture language of *tāla.* Form in Indian music is often articulated and clarified by means of pitch, but it does not depend on it.

The thinkers of early India drew a sharp distinction between the *dṛṣṭa* and the *adṛṣṭa:* by *dṛṣṭa* (the seen) they meant the external world of phenomena and the illusions of *māyā;* they regarded the *adṛṣṭa* (the unseen) as the pathway to essential reality, via the internal world of concepts. The aim of perception is to see and hear *through* phenomena, to regard visible and audible forms as transparent symbols, not opaque objects. We shall see some of the means by which musical structures display this quality of transparency.

The two most common Sanskrit words for form are *rūpa* and *mūrti;* a brief exploration of their meanings will provide useful evidence for the traditional Indian concepts of form.[3] The primary meaning of *rūpa* is outward appearance, phenomenon, or color; its many secondary meanings include shape, figure, a beautiful form, and a likeness or image. *Rūpa* can also signify a symptom (of a disease), character, nature, mark, or sign—that is, the distinctive feature by which something or someone can be known. *Rūpa* is the lens through which perception is focused on its object, but it should not be confused with the object itself.

The compound *nāma-rūpa* is an important technical term in Indian philosophy, representing the dichotomy between "the internal world of concepts" (*nāma,* name) and external appearance (*rūpa*).[4] To know the name of someone or something, to utter that name, or to bestow a name—all of these are means of obtaining power over one's object, an insight that is reflected, perhaps, in the common avoidance of male given names in India and in many other societies. To be sure, the names we assign still represent a stage of mediation between observer and the observed, but they bring us closer to reality than the recognition of forms. The goal of all perception, ultimate reality, lies beyond the reach of *nāmarūpa.*

Our second term, *mūrti,* is a familiar element in compound surnames such as Krishnamurti or, as it is often spelled, Krishnamoorthy (having the form, or being the embodiment, of Kṛṣna). The noun *mūrti* is a derivative of the verbal root *mūrch*—to thicken, congeal, solidify, assume definite shape.[5] The semantic range of *mūrti* begins with "solid body" and "material form" and proceeds to such secondary meanings as a manifestation, embodiment, or incarnation (of someone or something), and anything with definite shape and limits. The verbal message implanted in *rūpa* and *mūrti* is not difficult to interpret: Form is a manifestation to the senses, a concrete presentation of something abstract, and an appearance of something that cannot be perceived directly but can only be inferred. Form is a sign and a way to knowledge, but in the end it can only represent reality. In this line of thinking, form is never an essential property of things—it is a single aspect among many (as in the parable of the six blind men and the elephant) and a temporary condition.

The Sanskrit lexicon of terms for form is meager when compared to the profusion of Attic Greek terms and their extremely specialized meanings: *taxis,* order; *schema,* external form or shape; *morphe,* form in general or form as opposed to content; *eidos,* essential or conceptual form (an idea which Indian thinkers would surely have found attractive); and *rhythmos,* form in motion.[6] There is impeccable logic behind India's uncharacteristic economy of terms: if form is by nature so manifold, so mutable, and so far removed from what it represents, of what value is a precise lexicon?

The epigraphs at the beginning of this chapter are testimony to a grand cultural vision—a vision of a pervasive, indivisible, and imperceptible unity (identified variously as the wind, fire, space, or the world soul) which is capable of manifestation in many different forms in the phenomenal world. They also draw the clear moral that one's attachment should be to what the form signifies, not to the form itself—an idea to which Plato would surely have subscribed. Chapter 11 of the *Bhagavadgītā* contains one of the most compelling discourses on form in all the literature of India: Arjuna, having listened to the instructions of Kṛṣṇa, his charioteer, begs the god to appear in his original form (as Viṣṇu), and Kṛṣṇa grants his wish.

The Blessed One said:
Behold My forms, son of Pṛthā,
By hundreds and by thousands,
Of various sorts, marvelous,
Of various colors and shapes. . . .

Of many mouths and eyes,
Of many wondrous aspects,
Of many marvelous ornaments,
Of marvelous and many uplifted weapons;

Wearing marvelous garlands and garments,
With marvelous perfumes and ointments,
Made up of all wonders, the god,
Infinite, with faces in all directions.

And even this glimpse of Viṣṇu's multiple forms is permitted only by the god's special grace:

This form that is right hard to see,
Which thou hast seen of Mine,
Of this form even the gods
Constantly long for the sight.

Not by the Vedas nor by austerity,
Nor by gifts or acts of worship,

Can I be seen in such a guise,
As thou hast seen Me.[7]

The *Gītā* is not often cited in discussions of aesthetics, perhaps because its uncompromising message of salvation through renunciation, self-discipline, and disinterested action appears to deny the sensory pleasures that abound in the arts of India. But it must be taken as an attempt to set our values straight. We should know appearances for what they are—only appearances. One representation does not differ in essence from another, and we should value them accordingly. And above all, we should not be so besotted with desire for the fruit of any specific action that we overlook the true goal—right action for its own sake. If the means are right, the end will take care of itself.

There is a complex message embedded in the traditional line of thinking about form: Form is not a static but a dynamic concept; form is phenomenal, a representation or manifestation of something that cannot be known through direct perception. Any individual form is only one among many possible manifestations and cannot claim to be more truthful than the others; the perspective from which we view an object can reveal only one of the many different aspects of that object. Form is the outcome of a dynamic process of playful transformations and can be revealed only in successive stages, like frames in a motion picture. (Is this among the reasons for the popularity of the film industry in modern India?) Form is many-faceted and is meant to be apprehended by means of a scanning process in which the viewer or hearer makes a mental survey of the art work from multiple aspects and perspectives.

In the case of music, the required mode of perception might be described as *circumaudition:* just as we come to know a temple by circumambulating it, in the same way we come to know a musical event by a process of gradual discovery. Form in the arts of India invites an intensely active mode of perception in which each new detail is savored by the senses, while at the same time it is held in proper perspective as one of a series of successive frames. In what Betty Heimann has described as a world of "simultaneous possibilities," no single way of seeing or hearing can exhaust a work's potential.[8] This is one of the reasons why serial forms dominate the music of India; each successive cycle reveals an additional perspective on the possibilities inherent in the *rāga* and the larger musical universe that informs each decision of the performer.

As usual, it has taken some time to get to music. But given the ideological background, it seems inescapable that form in Indian music is not medium specific, and that the subject can best be approached and discussed in connection with the other arts. Indeed, while the lexicon of terms for formal components is extensive, few of the terms are specific to music: words such as *tāla* (span), *aṅga* (limb, that is, "component"), *jāti* (genus, class), *vastu* (object, substance), and *prakaraṇa* (production) occur repeatedly in technical expositions of architecture, sculpture, painting, music, and dance. I shall argue that Horace's dictum "Ut pictura poesis" is a good piece of advice in the case of Indian music, because of its suggestion that we study musical form in the context of the other arts, as well as the implication that certain traditional cultural preferences have been causal for the entire range of Indian artistic experience.[9]

It is hard to say just how such preferences develop, but they have deep roots and seem to be the result of a process of natural selection when the preferences of one local or regional subculture come into conflict with those of another.[10] Their evolution is recorded in surviving cultural artifacts, just as the history of a canyon is recorded in the rock strata and fossil layers. But in the case of music, the earliest such artifacts are verbal descriptions. For this reason it is helpful to formulate a list of the preferences that are clearly evident in the visual arts and then see to what extent the same preferences have helped to shape the course of early Indian music.

It must be emphasized that this is not a vague notion or intuition. Art historians have long noted how certain preferences for spatial design and formal configuration differ among ancient cultures. Just as the sculptors of ancient Greece displayed an obvious relish for frontality, stasis, an erect pose, and rectilinear mass, so did their counterparts on the Indian subcontinent demonstrate their preference for an undulating, flexed pose, ovoid form, and a surface that is alive with activity.[11] I shall attempt a short list of Indian cultural preferences (some of which have been noted in earlier chapters) which may serve as a checklist for the remainder of this chapter.

1. Circular and spiral designs
2. Abundant ornamentation
3. A surface in continuous flux, modulated by superimposed patterns
4. An intensely saturated field
5. Organic development
6. Reticulated lines and patterns
7. Indefinite beginnings and predictable endings
8. Ambiguity of function and reference
9. The confluence of different streams of activity

10. Art perceived by constructing a composite mental perspective from a scanning of the object's many aspects

11. Cluster configurations preferred over linear organization[12]

The test must come with perception. My argument is that this list describes a typical performance of Indian music today just as surely as it describes the sculptures surrounding the great stupa at Sanchi or the Sun Temple at Konarak, if we make due allowance for translation from the visible to the realm of the audible. A thornier question is how far into the past these preferences can be traced on the basis of the written records. I argued in chapter 8 that the evolution of cyclical rhythm in the *deśī tāla*s—which is surely an unmistakable manifestation of circular or spiral form in music—took place late in the first millennium A.D. in response to a new set of musical requirements.[13] Nevertheless, we can detect signs of a latent preference for circularity in the prescribed repetitions (*parivarta*) of the older ritual forms and in some of the sketchy descriptions of the theatrical plot songs (the *dhruvā*s). And similarly, a preference for indefinite beginnings is already evident in the popular opening gambit known as *upohana*, which subsequently emerged as the standard Indian beginning tactic under the name of *ālāpana*.[14] Several of the remaining preferences can be deduced from the doctrines of the earliest treatises,[15] but their previous history remains obscure. The task of this chapter and chapter 10 will be to demonstrate the extent to which these and other preferences were implemented in specific musical structures and tactics, particularly the structures and tactics of the repertoire of *gāndharva* and the evolving tradition of courtly song.

## 9.2 Formal Archetypes

The approach to the rhythms of *tāla* in chapter 8 was by way of the smallest units, patterns, and spans of the musical surface. But in considering the subject of form, it seems more convenient to begin at the other extreme of the musical hierarchy, the level of whole compositions, before proceeding to the intermediate level of formal components and tactics. To see form in operation at the deepest level in music, it is useful to identify a number of archetypal designs which have been causal for the subsequent development of Indian musical structures.

What are formal archetypes? I like to think of them as powerful narrative patterns which have been developed and then maintained over the course of many centuries and which carry the implicit endorsement of the parent culture as authorized ways of making music[16]—both as models for compositional structure and as designs for shaping individual performances. Like other preferences in the domain of form, they have evolved as the result of some competitive selection process. Archetypes are slow to develop but virtually irresistible once established. Some may indeed be universals—and here I am thinking of strophic forms set to a text and the theme with variations—but others appear to be indigenous to a limited culture area. Above all, formal archetypes provide dynamic plans for shaping music over time, by drawing upon deep-seated cultural impulses—even, one might say, by resorting to local habits of story telling. Just as many of the popular musical forms of the Western European tradition have been modeled upon archetypal designs such as the so-called narrative curve[17] and the tripartite dramatic formula of exposition-conflict-denouement,[18] so do the preferred structures of Indian music reveal a number of distinctive narrative strategies. Some of these, as we would expect, are linked with typical cultural attitudes toward such things as life, creation, and process. I shall venture to point out four of these strategies and attempt to indicate what they mean as narration within the world of Indian culture.

As the name implies, an archetype has been there "from the beginning" (Greek: *archē,* "beginning," and *archētypon*), and one of its most useful characteristics is a certain flexibility and lack of definition that permits the generation of many variant structures. An archetype is by nature more like a plan or a model than a finished blueprint or a script. It is relatively unspecified with regard to overall length or the proportions of its component parts. What is fixed is the order and function of the parts and the general progression of the whole.

If, as I am arguing, Indian musical structures may be heard as versions of a relatively small number of archetypal models, it is imperative that we identify the invariant features of these models. To begin with, it can be assumed that certain popular literary forms—in particular, the Vedic stanza and the epic couplet—must have been among the likely candidates. But these poetic forms are laid out on too small a scale to be useful for generating large-scale musical forms, and we look in vain for the influence of larger models of poetic structure. One possible conclusion, to which I shall return, is that the influence of text forms is manifest at intermediate levels of musical structure but not at the level of whole compositions. If this contention is correct, we must look elsewhere for the archetypal forms that have shaped the course of Indian music from early times. As an initial proposal, I am suggesting that these include, inter alia, the structure of the human body, the principle of organic growth, the interactive patterns of sacred ritual, and the process of world creation.

Three preliminary points need to be made. First, the features of some of these archetypes are not mutually exclusive, and the similarities have often been described with identical terms, which in turn has encouraged an overly enthusiastic correlation of the separate patterns and suggested a tidier world of forms than seems to exist. The preferred formal descriptors are as usual highly metaphoric, and the range of metaphor provides valuable insights into the nature and function of the various musical parts; several of the archetypes have been deployed along the familiar metaphoric pathways outlined in chapter 2.[19] One initial conclusion must be that musical structure in this ancient tradition is more a matter of process than of object, a music more of becoming than of being, and that the dynamics and functional relationships of the successive stages in the formal pathway are ultimately more significant than the static landmarks along the way.

### 9.2.1 The Human Body

Anthropomorphic imagery has been a staple of Indian culture since antiquity. Kapila Vatsyayan, in her recent book *The Square and the Circle of the Indian Arts,* argues eloquently the role of what she has termed the "Man-Body" symbolism:

> There are two simultaneous and distinct processes, one in which the "Man-Body" is used as a metaphor and the other where the total organism of the physical Man is explored to discover its endless psychic potential. A few broad deductions emerge from these two processes, on the level of thought and consciousness and on the level of form or what scholars have termed as paradigmatic models.
>
> Briefly, these add up to conceiving the human body as a living vital symbol of the macrocosm with many inbuilt systems of organic relationships of the parts to the whole and to each other. The unity of life, the interdependence and interconnectedness of all manifestations is at the core of this vision. . . . The imagery of the Man-Body with its implicit understanding of physical anatomy and the systems, especially the nervous and the circulatory, logically give rise to a visual image of a Man-Body placed in a circle with the verticality of man representing the *stambha,* the earth-sky relationship; the extended upper limbs represent the directions . . . and the *guṇa*s [the "strands"] and *bhūta*s [the elements] are located in different parts of this Cosmic-Man image.[20] The centre of this circle is the restful stillness, and this point represents the unmanifest, corresponding to the navel of the human body. In terms of abstract design it becomes the "nave" or the

> "hub" of the wheel, the *cakra* [circle] of which both the Vedas and the Upaniṣads speak. . . . This Man-Body is placed in an eternal cosmic rhythm (*Ṛta*) of the universe.[21]

Vatsyayan proceeds to describe how this model has been implemented in the sacrificial rituals, the preparation of altars and other forms of consecrated space, the construction of a theater and the design of its dedicatory ceremonies, temple architecture, and the spatial conventions of painting. Much of the imagery is by now familiar to the reader: the stillness of the inner center, the circle of the turning wheel, the concept of a line woven from intertwined strands, the dramatic vision of *anthropos* projected against the background of a circular cosmos and oriented to the directions, the pulsating rhythms and systems of life, and a world in eternal harmony. Interestingly, the paradigm includes not only the way the human body looks but also, perhaps *especially,* the way it works. In a sense all these images are one, just as all forms and all pathways are one, but they provide the basis for a distinctive set of structural functions for the arts.

Again and again in the lexicons of the various arts, the same array of anatomical and physiological terms appears: *mukha* (mouth), for a beginning of any kind; *garbha* (womb), any section containing a seed for future development, or the seed itself; *nābhi* (navel), a point of central stasis; *śarīra* (body), for the main section of anything; *aṅga* (limb), for any articulated component; and *prāṇa* (breath), for any kind of vital current.[22] *Mukha,* for example, can signify the mouth or face of a statue, the entrance to a temple, an introductory verse of a literary work, the opening section of a musical composition, the entrance of a dancer, or the initial act of a ritual. The human body is thus a virtual ground metaphor for the representation of any structure or process, as well as a tangible symbol of the forces and rhythms of world process.

### 9.2.2 Organic Growth

The anthropomorphic model, if we properly understand its symbolism within the world of Indian culture, must be regarded as a subset of the larger model of organicism. With respect to music, however, although the archetypal form of the human body has proved most useful as a symbol of finite, closed form and has served mainly as a lexicon of formal terms applying to complex, integrated structures following the paradigm described by Vatsyayan, the archetype of organic growth is a symbol of open-ended form, manifesting what Heinrich Zimmer has termed the "phenomenon of expanding form."[23] It has become the primary model for shaping an individual performance. Here once again the emphasis is clearly upon process: not merely the physical process by which the human body functions and is maintained but that undifferentiated process by which all things work.

Critics of Indian art seldom fail to point out the animating undercurrents and relationships that are characteristic of the organic model. Basham, for example, in his general remarks on the religious art of ancient India, notes "a sensual vitality, and a feeling of growth and movement as regular and organic as the growth of living things upon earth."[24] And Heinrich Zimmer, in his *Art of Indian Asia,* is even more explicit: "A [Hindu] temple is to be fashioned as a richly decorated living form. Pure stereometry, therefore, receives no emphasis; in fact, it is regarded as of little worth, since sheer material, unsublimated matter, is, to the Indian, hardly conceivable. The world is a structure pulsing with inner life, an organism swelling with productive juices. It is a welling mass of self-transforming substance, not a concatenation of rigid masses in empty space."[25] These examples could easily be multiplied many times over. And no matter how uncomfortably some critics may react to the occasional flights of extravagant language that seem to be so easily stimulated by the sensuous forms and surfaces of the Indian arts, the idea of the organic relatedness of all creatures and things is a standard topic in Indian thought and literature—reaching back to the cosmogonic hymns of the *Ṛgveda* and especially to hymn 10.121 (addressed to Prajāpati), in which the supreme god of creation is said to have been born from a golden embryo or egg (*hiranyagarbha*).[26]

The scope of the adjective *organic* in the traditional Indian worldview transcends any of the limitations imposed in Western thought: as a concept it embraces both the physical and metaphysical realms; it is not limited to plant and animal life-forms or, in a larger, chemical sense, to compounds of carbon. It means the life principle in all its forms and kingdoms—elemental, mineral, vegetable, animal, human, demonic, and divine. Iconographically, it is not unusual to find organic imagery modulating through the various domains, as in one temple carving from Bhārhut in which the earth mother Lakṣmī, the goddess of fertility, is shown mounted on a lotus arising from a jar of water and flanked by elephants spraying water from their uplifted trunks.[27]

As a semantic field, the idea of organicism is rich with possibilities and invites application to all forms of artistic process. Among its many components are the concepts of essential unity and continuity, the seed or germ (*bīja*), incubation and swelling, fertility and abstract potentiality, energy (physical and spiritual, scarcely differentiated from each other), intensification, decorative growth, passage through successive stages and transformations, flowering out in spiral designs (such as the Tree of Life),[28] and inexhaustible abundance. It is not difficult to imagine how the many organic continuities of everyday life in early India and their visual representations would eventually encourage the development of analogies in sound.

The technical terminology of the classical theater reveals the strong influence of the organic metaphor, and given the important role of music in the theater, it must have helped to make the application to musical structure more explicit. A few examples should suffice. In the standard list of the five components (*artha-prakṛti*s) of a typical plot, *bīja* (seed) is prescribed as the "germ" whence the dramatic action arises, and *bindu* (drop) describes the action beginning to unfold like a drop of oil spreading out on a surface—when, as a Western critic might say, the plot "begins to thicken." And in the list of five dramatic moments or junctures (*sandhi*s), one of the most important was called *garbha* (womb), a section during which the plot develops as the result of some type of incubation—often the separation of the lovers.[29] Organicism has become a general model for narrative structure.

As far back as we can trace it, the organic unity of the music of India has been assured by several of its inherent properties: by the stability, continuity, and generative potential of the idea of *rāga,* which must also include those melody types from which *rāga* arose; by the rhythmic unity and many of the distinctive formal tactics in the domain of *tāla,* which we shall soon discuss; by the relationship of ornamental variations to a prior model; and above all by the general orientation toward process which we have noted in both the anthropomorphic and organic paradigms. In the closed, modular forms of the ritual theater music, both of these archetypal designs coexist in a state of equilibrium; but with the decline of the theater tradition and the rise of the tradition of solo song, the influence of the organic model begins to dominate. The general notion of musical style was gradually changing during the period of this study: away from the concept of finite, mosaic forms; toward a concept of open-ended, chainlike musical structure. In the course of this development, the processive features of music must have been singled out for special emphasis—repetitions, cycles, permutations, compressions, and other teleological features.[30] As a result they were accorded higher status in the prevailing system of musical values. The balance between composition and performance had begun to shift in favor of performance, and the concept of music as action (*karman*), much of it spontaneous, began to replace, at least in part, the older concept of a fixed musical work. The Western tradition still thinks of music mostly as a noun—an opus, or as the fifteenth-century author Johannes Tinctoris put it, *res facta*[31]—but in India it has become primarily a verb.

### 9.2.3 Ritual

One of the most durable of all Indian formal schemata may be recognized in the ceremonial discourse and liturgical structure of Vedic chant. In particular, the solo and ensemble roles of the three chanters recall the ceremonies of the Roman Catholic mass as performed by the celebrant, deacon, and subdeacon. It is not at all unusual to find similar liturgical patterns in the performing arts, which often reveal vestigial traces of their alleged origin in ancient ritual. One after another the components of solemn ceremony follow in a pleasantly rhythmic sequence, organized and articulated by a genial colloquy among the participants: convocation, response, proclamation, affirmation, reflection, transition, exposition, invocation, termination, and the like—the stuff of which human ceremonies have been crafted throughout history and adapted to local tradition and preferences. But as is often the case with long-lasting archetypal forms, later versions may have little or nothing to do with their prior context or milieu: the design has broken free of its original environment and taken on a life of its own. Such is the case with the musical forms of India.

The prototype of this design was outlined in chapter 4 with a brief explanation.[32] In the sequence of five *bhakti*s prescribed for chanting the hymns of the *Sāmagāna* we noted the following pattern: invocation, main section, response, [optional] interlude, and conclusion. Many versions of this model have appeared in the later history of Indian musical form; only two will be set forth below. The model is relatively neutral with respect to metaphor, and its components are usually identified with simple technical descriptors. As I remarked earlier, it should come as no surprise to encounter beginnings, middles, and endings: it is the in-between sections which provide much of the special interest. I shall have more to say about them. As we shall see, each component in this five-part sequence has been endowed with its own distinguishing marks, marks that often reveal distinctive cultural strategies for the delineation of form, as well as cultural attitudes toward beginnings, connections, and endings.[33]

The key features of the archetype can be summarized: there is usually a single main or "fixed" section of variable location, appropriate for the delivery of a passage of meaningful text and often preceded or followed by sections featuring the phonetic play of nonsense syllables. There may be a number of prefix, infix, or suffix sections, some of which may be optional. The fixed section can occur anywhere except at the end. The characteristic interludes vary in their function: they may be reflections on the previous section, previews of the subsequent section, or merely dividers with no integral relationship to what precedes or follows.

In the Ṛk, Gāthā, and Sāma forms mentioned by Bharata and described in greater detail by such authors as Abhinavagupta and Śārṅgadeva, the pattern is as follows:[34]

| Component | Function |
|---|---|
| *udgrāha* (grasped)[35] | an introduction |
| *anudgrāha* (not grasped) | a suffix to the introduction |
| *sambodha* (understanding) | an interlude |
| *dhruvaka* (fixed) | the principal section |
| *ābhoga* (completion)[36] | a conclusion |

And in the prescribed sequence of *dhātu*s (components) for the *prabandha*s, the eulogistic court songs of medieval India, a similar pattern may be identified:[37]

| Component | Function |
|---|---|
| *udgrāha* | an introduction |
| *melāpaka* (conjoining) | an interlude |
| *dhruvaka* | the principal section |
| *antara* (intermediate) | an optional interlude or, interestingly, a prefinal |
| *ābhoga* | a conclusion |

Still other variants of the model can be recognized in certain of the ritual forms of the ancient musical theater.[38]

### 9.2.4 Creation

Put simply, the archetypal design of creation—unquestionably the most pervasive formal design in all the later music of India—consists of a sequence of two components: a slow, exploratory section with a loose temporal organization, followed by a faster and more strictly organized section. This discussion will focus on the special rôle of the initial component which anyone who has ever heard a concert of Indian music will recognize immediately as the opening improvisation in which the performer establishes the structural outlines and characteristic features of the chosen *rāga*. There is less to say about the second component, which can assume many forms—from a long chain of variations to a complex multipart composition. Here the performance comes under the control of two interacting streams of rhythm—the *tāla* cycle and the counterpointing drum patterns.

I have discussed this archetype elsewhere, referring to it as the "free/strict archetype."[39] The same design is heard in the West in such diverse genres as the operatic recitative and aria, the baroque keyboard prelude (or toccata) and fugue, the slow introduction and sonata-allegro of the typical concert overture around 1800, and—to mention but one version from non-Western music—the first two components of the *jo-ha-kyū* sequence in many of the older musical genres of Japan.[40] Such a wide historical, geographical, and stylistic distribution indicates that this archetype is a pattern of some universal appeal, but it has been exploited to a still greater degree in India, owing in part to the heavy load of cultural symbolism that it carries. It will be useful to begin with a brief table of contrasts to introduce the cluster of meanings and associations:

| First component | Second component |
| --- | --- |
| Free | Strict |
| Slow | Faster |
| Becoming | Being |
| Vocables | Meaningful text |
| Emanation of sound | Externalization of sound |
| Improvised exposition of a *rāga* | Formal composition and/or exploration of the *rāga* |
| Brahmā as patron | Viṣṇu as patron |
| The creation of forms from primal matter | The structured universe in operation |

or to use imagery that Voltaire would have found appealing, with reference to his conception of a clockwork universe:

| | |
| --- | --- |
| The making and winding of the clock | The clock in operation |

One of the most basic distinctions drawn in Indian musical thinking is the distinction between *nibaddha* (bound, regulated) and *anibaddha* (unbound, unregulated) species of music. As the prime textual authority for this important dichotomy, most later authors cite the *Nāṭyaśāstra* (32.29–36), in which the *anibaddha* category refers specifically to the incidental music for instruments; but there is every reason to suppose that this division is of still greater antiquity. "Unbound" in the present context means a number of things: nonmetrical, with no fixed number of syllables and no prescribed caesura; unregulated by the repetitive patterns and gestures of *tāla;* and lacking the sense of regular pulsation that would be associated with one of the conventional tempos—in a word, irrational. 'Bound" varieties of music, on the other hand, unfold within the dual constraints of poetic meter and musical rhythm. The author of the *Nāṭyaśāstra* mentions another distinctive feature of the *anibaddha* genus, namely, that it is "devoid of meaning" (*arthaśūnya*) and is therefore restricted to the nonverbal sounds of instruments or to meaningless phonetic syllables.

The distinction between regulated and unregulated musical genres would appear to be a fairly uncomplicated one, but things are seldom that easy in Indian musical discourse. The terms *nibaddha* and *anibaddha* have been applied in a relative, as well as an absolute, way: a musical component may therefore be "regulated" in a general way (as opposed to a more freely conceived form), or it may be regulated with respect to some or all of the technical aspects mentioned above—poetic meter, *tāla,* or meaning. The two musical genres of the classical theater were constructed along parallel sides of this dichotomy: the ritual music was obviously stricter in organization than the incidental music, yet each of the two genres provided for a relatively free beginning gambit before proceeding with a more strictly regulated piece. *Upohana* is the term for this characteristic incipit in the ritual forms, and I shall reserve discussion until later in this chapter.[41] For now the discussion will focus upon the free style of music that has become associated with the exposition of a *rāga* and which is known variously as *rāga ālāpa, rāga ālapti, ālāpana,* or modern derivatives such as the Hindi *ālāp.*

Each of these words, with the obvious exception of the familiar *rāga,* derives from the combination of the prefix *ā* (toward, to) and the verbal root *lap* (to prate, chatter, talk, wail, and also, in the case of birds, to chirp or twitter); each of these phonetic elements provides a valuable semantic clue. *Ālāpana* is the most general of the terms: it has often been translated as "conversation," especially in the sense of a casual conversation, but as a musical term it does not suggest any kind of dialogue or interaction.[42] I take *ālāpana* in the sense of "address," with two distinct but reinforcing meanings: addressing the composition or performance and also perhaps addressing the audience. In either case, the meaning is that *ālāpana* is the approved way to initiate musical discourse and communication, thus bringing out the strong implication of "motion toward" in the prefix. The second element, *lap,* suggests communication in sounds other than meaningful words: nonsensical sounds, repetitive sounds, playful expression, rhythmic phrases and intonations that may carry a nonverbal message, and sounds that reveal the presence of human emotion. The message here is that formal musical discourse begins with sound in its elemental forms, with relatively undifferentiated musical substance, free rhythmic motion, a process of playful exploration, and clear projection of the underlying emotion.

This distinctive style of beginning must be linked with two important developments in the early medieval period: the establishment and initial expansion of the *rāga* system and the concomitant rise of the practice of improvisation. Relatively free beginning tactics, a system of mode classes, and spontaneous composition are all deeply rooted in the Indian musical tradition in one form or another, but late in the first millennium—perhaps around the time of Mataṅga's *Bṛhaddeśī*—they must all have come together. Texts from this period begin to give instruction in how to introduce, explore, and develop a *rāga;* they present short sample melodies in a rudimentary syllabic notation, and they begin to divide the opening section into a set of distinct stages.

Subtle distinctions were drawn between different procedures: *rāga ālāpa* is the term for a concise presentation of the characteristic marks, the *lakṣaṇa*s, of a *rāga; rāga ālapti* is a more elaborate plan for delineating the typical melodic outlines of the *rāga.* The distinction here is between the *rāga*'s modal features (*ālāpa*) and its tuneful features (*ālapti*). The authors also dwell on the decorative features that should be displayed prominently in a passage of *ālāpana*—the *varṇa*s (melodic contours), *alaṅkāra*s (melodic ornaments), and *gamaka*s (vocal ornaments and transitions).[43] The purpose here is to implant the *rāga*'s distinguishing marks and shapes in the creative subconscious of the performer and the aesthetic consciousness of the listeners, as a background frame of reference and a base for further development and exploration.

These definitions and distinctions seem to have become firmly established by the thirteenth century, in formulations such as the following from the authoritative *Saṅgītaratnākara.* I first present the definitions of *rāga ālāpa* and *rāga ālapti:*

> *Rāga ālāpa* is that [section] in which there is a manifestation
> Of the initial, low, [and] high notes, likewise of the final and
> confinal,
> And also of the scarceness and profusion [of certain notes] and
> of the hexatonic and pentatonic [versions of the *rāga*].
> (*SS* 2:23cd–24)[44]

> *Ālapti* is described by the experts as richly endowed with
> melodic contours and ornaments,
> Colored with vocal ornaments and shadings, and full of
> charming curves.
> (*SS* 3:202)[45]

The following passage outlines the method by which the tonal structure of a *rāga* should be established:

> Experts in song know that it [*rāga ālapti*] unfolds in four
> stages.

The *svara* with which the *rāga* begins is called the fundamental tone;[46]

The fourth step higher will be the halfway [point in the octave];
Arrival at the *svara* just below the latter is called *mukhacāla*,[47] and thus is the first register [established].

The second register [is reached] after one has moved to the halfway [step].

The eighth step above the fundamental tone is known as its double.

The *svaras* situated between the halfway and the double are the intermediate notes;
The third stage concludes after having moved into this range:
After one has proceeded to the double [and then] terminating on the fundamental tone, the fourth stage [is accomplished].
According to the wise, *rāga ālapti* [is produced] by means of these four stages.

Subsequently, the *rāga* is gradually set forth by the use of clear melodic phrases with many curves,
But chiefly by emphasizing the fundamental tone.

(*SS* 3:191–96)[48]

These informative instructions are still largely valid today, although the range covered is generally wider, perhaps up to two full octaves or more, and the fifth *svara* (*pañcama*) has assumed the role formerly assigned to the fourth step (*madhyama*). The shift in tonal equilibrium produced by dividing the octave at *pa,* instead of *ma,* means that the modal basis for the system as a whole has shifted from plagal to authentic.[49] But in other respects the process is much the same: a typical opening improvisation begins by establishing the fundamental tone (*sa*) in relation to its immediate neighbors and subsequently moves into higher registers in systematic increments—with each new stage marked by decisive arrival at one of the stable *svaras* that serve as boundaries for a particular stretch of tonal territory—before finally subsiding to the ground tone. Time seems not to be a crucial factor: *ālāpana* can run its course in a minute or two, or it may be elaborated at great length, and there are stories of legendary musicians who are reported to have sung a single *rāga* for a week or more.[50] We have no supporting evidence on this point from early sources, but it seems reasonable to conclude that the opening component was as free with respect to duration as it was with respect to rhythm, meter, and meaning. The point that needs to be emphasized is that *ālāpana* was never conceived as a free flight of fancy. On the contrary, there was a specific procedure to follow, a procedure which left considerable leeway for spontaneous performance decisions and which could be easily adapted to the musical properties of any individual *rāga,* but which demanded a disciplined and informed exposition on the part of the performer.

Much of the evidence linking the practice of *ālāpana* with the process of creation has been presented in the opening chapters: in chapter 2 we noted the significance attached to the metaphoric pathway emanating from the center of the human body and radiating outward to the external world, and in chapter 3 we followed the symbolic meanings associated with the production of sound and embodied in the theory of *nāda.* In chapter 4, we explored the important role of vocables in Indian music and the rise of one of the main streams of musical thought in the technical literature of articulatory phonetics. It is time to assemble these meanings into a coherent semantic field and provide a final interpretation.

Just as all forms are ultimately one, so do all processes manifest one process—the world process of continuous creation and dissolution, as proclaimed in the Hindu scriptures. Undifferentiated primal matter, under the creative patronage of Brahmā, is stimulated by energy, and a world of forms springs up. When the process of differentiation is complete, the newly created universe is left to run its orderly course under the watchful eye of Viṣṇu, until the time arrives for all substance to dissolve once again into its original state—under the trampling feet of Śiva as he dances his violent dance amid a circle of flames. In like manner the elemental components of music—syllables, *svara*s, durations, ornaments, and the various colors of sound—issue forth from the stream of undifferentiated sound situated at the center of the human body (an integral part of the continuum of unmanifest, universal sound). At first disjunct and free from rhythmic, metric, and semantic constraints, the *rāga* takes on substance and shape as we listen. Once its features and contours have become actualized to the performer's satisfaction, the second stage of the archetype begins, as pulsating drumbeats and the controlling rhythms of the *tāla* signal the onset of regulated musical process. There are traces of "becoming" and "being" in most creation narratives, but the Indian tradition has set a higher premium on the inchoate phase of becoming, and perhaps as a result of that decision, it has developed such a powerful musical analogy.

Creation is not a "then," as in the Genesis account; it is a continuous "now." Not every performance begins in this manner, but when performers elect to introduce a composition with a passage of *ālāpana,* they draw upon this well of primordial associations. According to the testimony of many performers, the connection I have been describing lies close to the surface of their consciousness; with others it is buried deeper, and their performance is guided more by habit, instinct, and their cultural conditioning. But conscious or unconscious, the association between the genre of *ālāpana* and the traditional view of creation has informed generations of musicians who may never have studied philosophy or cosmology.

## 9.3 Formal Components

Having examined the archetypal ideas and schemata from which the many individual forms of early Indian music arose, I turn now to the building blocks with which the ritual forms were assembled. A few preliminary observations will help to put the following discussion into perspective.

I must first emphasize the antiquity of the ritual tradition of theater music, the detail in which its structures have been described, their relative independence from the shaping principles of prosody, and the overall conception of form that these structures manifest. It is no exaggeration to say that more is known about the formal organization of this body of music than of any other body of music in the ancient world. We know many details of the ancient Greek systems of pitch and rhythm, but we know next to nothing about how the musical materials were crafted into larger structures—apart from the meager evidence of the few fragments surviving in notated form and the general conclusion that the vocal music appears to have been organized on all hierarchical levels by the structure (that is, the metric and strophic design) of the text.[51] Nothing further is known about any other categories of musical form.

In the ceremonial and incidental music for the early Indian theater, we see a tradition that was already highly developed as early as the first century A.D. Not until more than a thousand years later did the musical scholars of Europe and west Asia begin to describe the forms of music with anything approaching this level of specificity.[52] On the grounds of age alone, if for no other reason, this body of musical thought compels respect and merits detailed study, not only for what it can tell us about musical form on the Indian subcontinent but also for what it can tell us about musical form in general.

This is also an appropriate time to return to the earlier contention that the major formal structures of the early theater were essentially independent of the patterns and structures of verse, except, of course, for sections that featured the declamation of a poetic text.[53] Only at intermediate levels of structure is it possible to make a case for the possible influence of metrics and the principles of versification. While there may be a loose parallel between (1) the poetic line organized into *gaṇa*s and divided by caesuras into members and (2) the musical *mātrā* divided into a number of similar or identical *pādabhāgas*,[54] the organization of neither the rhythmic surface nor the large formal gestalts depends in any obvious way upon either the syllable sequences or the typical verse structures of Sanskrit poetry.

The reason for this must be that an independent system of musical rhythm was already at hand in the patterns and gestural language of *tāla,* and it is by means of the structural rhythms of *tāla* that the theatrical forms have been described. This is both a strength and a weakness of the early musicological literature: a strength in that the ritual forms—which are after all the musical genres that theorists and analysts take seriously, in the West and in Asia—are specified down to the individual *tāla* units in terms of durations, gestures, and their functional role; but a weakness in that virtually nothing has been set down that would permit reconstruction of the melodic and rhythmic flesh that covered the bare structural bones. The structural rhythms have survived, but not the tunes. There is little to be gained by lamenting that so little is known, but there is much to be gained by extracting the maximum information from what is known. And the continuity of the oral tradition on the Indian subcontinent permits the inference that modern practice can at least suggest how these bare bones may have been clothed in musical flesh.

With regard to the overall conception of form, the musical designs of ancient India can be described as modular and paratactic—as opposed to the integrated, cross-referenced, syntactical structures that have dominated much of the recent history of Western music; the fugue and the sonata-allegro are typical examples. Only in the theme with variations has the West approached the Indian concept of musical structure. The paratactic design is very much in harmony with the archetypal structures of ritual and the theatrical plot: sequences of episodes clearly divided from one another and embedded in a general progression of organic development. Serial forms, then, are the preferred forms of early Indian music, with few if any cross-references between nonadjacent sections and little interest in such reiterative devices as the refrain or reprise.

I shall distinguish between three levels of formal components in this discussion, referring to them as sections, lines, and affixes—or to take a grammatical parallel, paragraphs, sentences, and phrases. Indian formal terminology abounds at these levels, and the significance of many of the names is obscure. To spare the reader some of this ordeal, I shall translate only those terms which tell us something about the nature or function of the component they represent.

Entire compositions were generally divided into sections known as *an-*

*gas* (limbs) or *vastus*.[55] Forms constructed of *vastus* appear to be strophic, with few if any other types of components, so I take the *vastu* as analogous to the poetic stanza. They are generally longer and more regular than the *aṅgas*, so it is not unlikely that *vastus* may have served as appropriate vehicles for rendering a poetic text. *Aṅgas*, on the other hand, appear in a bewildering variety of shapes and sizes, and the forms assembled from *aṅgas* are much more diverse and feature more short sections and more frequent changes of pace than the stately *vastu* forms. Even without knowing anything about the texts or tunes, it is reasonable to infer that the sharp discontinuities of the *aṅga* forms reflected in some way the function they were intended to perform, perhaps as accompaniments for dancing or expressive mime.[56]

*Aṅga* in the above context is a *tālāṅga,* that is, a structural member of anything measured in terms of *tāla*. *Aṅga,* however, is also used in the sense of *varṇāṅga* (from *varṇa*), that is, a unit identified on the basis of melodic properties such as contour, cadence, prominent scale degree, and resemblance or contrast to other *aṅgas*. The information on melodic *aṅgas* is extremely sketchy in the older treatises, so most of the available material comes from the commentarial tradition. All we know about melodic style (as opposed to melodic scale) in the ritual forms must be deduced from the few cryptic references to melodic *aṅgas* in the *Nāṭyaśāstra* and the *Dattilam,* and that is precious little.[57] The relevant point here is that certain formal components were distinguished from one another by prescribed melodic features, as well as by the underlying *tāla* patterns. The knowledge that the domain of melody was conceptually and perceptibly organized in terms of melodic *aṅgas*, *varṇas*, and the ornamental *alaṅkāras*—even though these were accorded a lower priority in determining musical structure than were the *tāla* patterns—will give a more accurate picture of this musical repertoire. While a ritual composition was first and foremost a prescribed sequence of gestures, it was much more than that: the foursquare rhythmic grids and lines were overlaid with sensuous melodic arabesques, graceful ornaments, and subtle vocal transitions, and were communicated in a style drenched with emotion. Any understanding of the ritual forms as reconstructed on the basis of the textual evidence must be tempered with an awareness of what was left for the oral tradition to supply.

*Vastus* and the longer of the *aṅgas* were divided into *mātrās*, a term used here in the sense of a poetic line or a prose sentence and signifying nothing more than a unit by which the larger sections could be divided into a series of regular members.[58] A typical *vastu* comprises from three to six *mātrās*, and the *mātrā* itself was further divided into four *pādabhāgas* ("paw divisions," in analogy to the four paws of a quadruped and also to the standard four *pāda*s of a metrical couplet).[59] The process of division continues with each *pādabhāga* consisting of either two or four *tāla* gestures: that is, two in the twofold state and four in the fourfold state; the division into "paws" was discarded in the syllabic state, perhaps because it added no new information to the meaning conveyed by the individual gesture.[60] The equation (4 *tāla* units × 4 *pādabhāga*s = 1 *mātrā*) was unquestionably the most regular feature of this repertoire, and the regularity was reinforced by the repetitive background patterns of *tāla* outlined in chapter 8: *ni pra* for the twofold state and *ā ni vi pra* for the fourfold state.[61] As we shall soon see, however, the regularity is largely an illusion. What is vital to realize is that other gestures intruded into this regular sequence, gestures whose constituent patterns were to be recognized as superimpositions upon the regular metrical substratum and which were no doubt accompanied by still other melodic and rhythmic overlays.

We must recognize two additional formal elements on this same intermediate level of musical structure: *parivarta,* a prescribed repetition of a line or phrase, and *vidārī,* a caesura or the formal unit that concludes with such a caesura. Not much is known about the application of these concepts in the ritual music, and they are little used. *Parivarta* is perhaps the more informative of the two concepts, in that it testifies to the vital structural role of repetition in these forms and may also be seen as an ancestor of the rhythmic cycles by which later Indian music has been organized. It is in fact one of the few indications of anything remotely approaching cyclical practice in the ritual forms; the incidental music and songs, on the other hand, may easily have been the breeding ground for the evolution of the cyclical concept.

Affixes are a distinctive feature of this repertoire—both prefixes and suffixes, with a clear preference for the latter. The most frequent of these is known as Śīrṣaka (head), a short suffix of six units in the syllabic version of the popular Ṣaṭpitāputrakaḥ *tāla* and a palindrome.[62] Śīrṣaka is a signal of closure, both in the form of a decisive response to a longer internal component and often as the final member of a complete composition.[63] Its finality is emphasized in two important ways: by deflation to the syllabic state and by the terminal gesture of summation, *sannipāta.* It is not entirely clear to what extent the various affixes were related to the preceding or following melodic material, but the evidence of *upavartana* (to be examined in §9.4) suggests that one major role of the suffixes was to repeat the preceding segment of text and melody at twice the speed. This is another piece of evidence connecting the ancient theater tradition with South Indian music as practiced today.[64]

Each of the components just described will be illustrated, and their role should thus become clearer. But before I examine their functions as members of complete compositions, it is necessary to set forth some of the characteristic tactics by which the various formal meanings could be audibly—and visibly—conveyed.

## 9.4 Formal Tactics

The search for musical facts must always begin with quantities, but the measurable properties of music are rarely of any great intrinsic interest. If we seek out what is the most distinctive, the most flavorful, in a music, it is more likely to be found in the qualitative, functional, and processive tendencies implanted in the formal units. In these qualities, tendencies, impulses—whatever slippery words one chooses to represent these elusive properties—we see the influence of cultural ideology just as clearly as we have seen it in the archetypal schemata by which musical organization has been guided into large narrative structures with symbolic associations. In this section I shall present a number of characteristic tactics by which parts were assembled into wholes in the formal structures of the early theater music. Although the discussion will once again focus upon the ritual forms, because they are our best evidence, it will reveal formal strategies that have outlasted their original repertoire and left a permanent impression on later Indian music.

This discussion and the subsequent reconstructions of the major ritual forms build upon a number of concepts presented in chapter 8, including the list of the topics of *tāla,* the three basic time durations, the *tāla* gestures and their special roles, the five authorized *mārga tāla* patterns, the distinction between *yugma* (even, quadrangular) and *ayugma* (odd, triangular) organization, the preference for palindromes, the equations that specify the mutual timing of the variable components of *tāla* (which will present no problems in examples 30–36, because these choices will already have been made), and especially the concept of the three states—syllabic, twofold, and fourfold—which is essential to any understanding of this repertoire. The best way to make these patterns come alive is to practice the various sequences of gestures, for it is chiefly by means of the gestures that formal meaning was conveyed.

What is meant by the expression "formal meaning"? The Indian answer would include, among other things: the sense of a beginning, how one component connects with another, the feeling of motion toward a predictable goal, the feeling of expansion in the inflated states (in which the defining events lie farther apart) and the compression of events in progressing to a deflated state (as from the twofold to the syllabic),[65] the recognition of pattern beginnings and endings, the feeling of accent when superimposed patterns coincide at some structural point(s), the sense of pleasant ambiguity when one recognizes a double meaning in the counterpoint of gestures and their implications, the rhythm and rhyme of parallel lines, the syncopation that results when a triangular pattern is superimposed on a quadrangular background, sudden accelerations and decelerations of the density of gestures, the relish of following the development of a pattern through a series of systematic permutations, and the recognition of the previewing and reviewing functions of the different types of affix.

Early Indian authors would have subscribed readily to Aristotle's dictum that "wholeness means to have a beginning, a middle, and an end."[66] In fact their large formal gestalts were designed to permit and encourage multiple tactics for communicating feelings of initiation, continuity, and closure. Theirs was a multidimensional, multileveled concept of musical structure, which in its richness helps to explain why the possibility of an additional harmonic dimension has never arisen in the music of India. We shall focus first upon three structural functions that reveal distinctive cultural strategies for beginning, connecting, and terminating: *upohana, upavartana,* and *prastāra.*

### 9.4.1 *Upohana*

*Upohana* in the ritual forms is the equivalent of *ālāpana*—the (relatively) free opening component in a free-strict sequence—and is prescribed in five of the seven *gītaka* forms.[67] The name signifies "to impel toward" or "to cause to appear"—excellent clues to its musical role. *Upohana* differs from the later *ālāpana* in two important respects: its rhythm was measured (by a series of regular durations), and it was regarded as the opening segment and an integral part of a formal component, not as a detached prelude. *Upohana* was distinguished from the following musical material in two ways: the regular *tāla* gestures were replaced by a series of undifferentiated finger snaps (the *dhruva*s),[68] and nonsense syllables took the place of meaningful words. Accordingly, the opening passage of *upohana* was devoid of both metric and verbal meaning. Shorter passages of *upohana,* called *pratyupohana,* were often used to introduce subsequent sections, thus communicating a useful distinction between primary and secondary beginnings.[69]

Beginning tactics often arise for practical reasons. We hear an analogous practice in the cantorial incipits of the Roman Catholic rite, as when the celebrant of the mass intones "Credo in unum Deum" and the choir and worshipers continue with "Patrem omnipotentem" and the remainder of the Creed. I suspect that many of the musical numbers of the theatrical rituals began under the leadership of a soloist or a small group, with the full ensemble joining at a later point in the line; to be explicit, I mean the point when the regular *tāla* gestures and meaningful text begin. One of the stated purposes of *tāla*—in addition to its liturgical role in insuring "unseen benefit" (*adrṣṭa phala*)—was to maintain audible and visible communication among the members of the theater ensemble; and nowhere was this more essential than at the beginning. The syllables prescribed for *upohana* appear to be phonetic imitations of vina strokes, as in the following example provided by Abhinavagupta:[70]

One consequence of this distinctive beginning gambit is the tendency for many later Indian compositions to begin at a relatively late point in the rhythmic cycle (which we might call acephalous or afterbeat beginnings), but too early to be experienced as an upbeat or anacrusis. This characteristic mode of beginning often confuses Western listeners, who are accustomed to the strong thetic beginnings and relatively short anacruses of the European tradition.[71] In the theory of early Indian music, special concepts were devised to control the manner in which the various performers became entrained at the proper beginning point in a line or cycle: *pāṇi* (hand) signifies the process of synchronization in the *mārga tāla* system, and *graha* (grasping) represents the point of beginning in the cycles of later Indian music.[72]

The ancient ritual forms display only one other beginning tactic of any significance, that is, beginning with what we may regard as an *epigram*—a single line, a metrical couplet, or a pair of short units in parallel construction.[73] It is not as popular as *upohana,* but it is extremely unlikely that a single beginning tactic would have controlled an entire repertoire. I am assuming that this style of epigrammatic beginning was prescribed for compositions in which it was necessary to highlight the meaning of a short passage of meaningful text: either as an invocation or perhaps as a clear statement of the literary theme to be developed. Dedicatory verses are a staple of Indian literature, and it seems entirely plausible that when set to music, they would provide a convincing mode of beginning that would not suggest a need for an introductory passage of *upohana.* As a result, we see that two distinct beginning rhythms were cultivated in the ritual tradition:

| | | |
|---|---|---|
| *upohana* | | epigram |
| arsis | as opposed to | thesis |
| upbeat | | downbeat |
| indefinite | | definite |

### 9.4.2 *Upavartana*

*Upavartana* (to bring near, by means of "turning") is the most characteristic tactic of connection. It is accomplished by repetition and compression: the final segment of a component (complete with text, melody, and accompanying gestures) is repeated immediately at twice the speed, a sensation readers can easily experience for themselves by applying this technique to the last line of their national anthem or any other familiar song. This review procedure appears in suffixes and, more interestingly, as a connecting link between the end of one section and the start of another.[74] In the ritual forms *upavartana* appears almost without exception as a compression of a final segment of twelve units into the popular six-beat *tāla* called Ṣaṭpitāputrakaḥ, as illustrated below (33) in the Ovenaka form.[75] Strict temporal doubling survives today in the rhythmic practice of South India, whereas in the northern tradition tempo is altered in a series of gradual changes, perhaps as an inheritance from the waves of Persian influence.

There is quite a bit to say about this procedure. It means, among other things, a compression (of the prior musical events), a deflation (with respect to state), a repetition (of material), an intensification, a connection (of one component and another), a reflection (upon the previous material), and even a counterpoint, as often occurs when the repetition is underscored by a new sequence of gestures or by a palindrome of the gestures that accompanied the original material.[76] This is a heavy cargo of meanings for such a simple device to carry, but it illustrates the highly referential nature of Indian musical structure: the sense of form is communicated by a sonorous network of multiple allusions, implications, ambiguous meanings, and pattern transformations that compete for the listener's attention.

*Upavartana* also produces an abrupt and structurally significant change in the ratios between different rhythmic levels, ratios that I defined in chapter 8 under the term *tempo.*[77] Let us consider these ratios for a moment: In the ritual music of early India the overall pace, by any standard of measure, was extremely slow and was set by convention, but the several rhythmic levels (text, melody, gestures, durations) offer many opportunities for the simultaneous presentation of different ratios. In the special case of *upavartana,* not only do the words of the text and the melodic durations double in speed, but also the gestures—though continuing at the same rate—*imply* a doubled tempo in that a sequence of twelve beats in the twofold state has been compressed into a sequence of six syllabic beats; this is done by simply omitting all the intervening silent gestures.[78]

I draw the moral that tempo from an Indian perspective is more a matter of temporal density than of a simple temporal rate. Igor Stravinsky once remarked cryptically with reference to his *Orchestra Variations* (1964), "In my Variations, tempo is a variable and pulsation a constant."[79] We may apply the same statement to the ancient Indian conception of musical structure, in which regular pulsation is always present, but more often than not as a ground upon which more meaningful rhythmic figures are superimposed. In the technique of *upavartana* we see a typical illustration of this counterpoint between the rate of pulsation and the density of musical events.

### 9.4.3 *Prastāra*

*Prastāra* (strewing, spreading out),[80] a popular tactic of closure, is the third structural function to be examined here. Closure in this case is accomplished by constructing and then exhausting a permutation matrix, as illustrated in (33) in the section known as Anta ("the end"), the final component of three of the seven *gītaka* forms.[81] In this component a sequence of three contrasting *aṅga*s is performed first in quadruple, then in triple, and finally in "mixed" patterns: $3 \times 3 = 9$. Exploring musical possibilities through sets of systematic permutations has since become one of the basic developmental techniques of later Indian music, and *prastāra* is now recognized as one of the "ten vital breaths" of the South Indian *tāla* system.[82] Permuting tactics are by no means unknown in Western music, but nowhere has the device been as enthusiastically exploited as in India.

Once again we can draw an important formal conclusion from the popularity of *prastāra:* endings are to be signaled well in advance by the onset of some systematic musical process, a process of playful exploitation that can be followed along a course of progressively narrowed and focused expectations and that leads inexorably to a predictable conclusion. At least two traces of this technique are heard in Indian music today: the sequence of three circular melodic flourishes (*tihai* or *mora*) that often brings a performance to a close, and the practice of repeating a concluding phrase while progressively trimming off its beginning members until nothing remains but a predictable final stroke, in effect an audible colophon. But *prastāra* has symbolic overtones that transcend its local role as a simple tactic of closure: the device mimics the series of transformations through which all substance must eventually pass. And the process, like all other processes, is open-ended: any closure achieved is only temporary, and the series of available forms can never be exhausted.

Conventions of musical beginnings and endings arise from cultural attitudes—the attitudes of a culture toward beginnings and endings in general. Endings in Western music over the last several centuries have been as teleological as endings in Indian music, but in different ways. The sense of impending closure in eighteenth- and nineteenth-century musical works is often very strong, as a result of a large number of long-range strategies and short-range tactics (among them, harmonic movement, tonal implications, the liquidation of thematic material, cadential signals and clichés), but not in the sense that we can predict precisely when the final goal will be reached. And further, tonal stability and formal closure are often achieved well before the end, allowing the listener to savor the final ceremonies and reinforcing the feeling of having arrived with a period of prolonged stasis. But I know of no precise analogue to the Indian practice that permits one to predict the exact point of conclusion so far in advance. If the historical view of the Judeo-Christian tradition ends with the achievement of some final state, a final state of musical stasis will be heard as a convincing means of obtaining closure; but if one's worldview assumes a process of infinite continuity, the beginning point of any cycle—if prepared properly—is a sufficient musical goal.

So endings in the ancient music of India are more a matter of how they are approached than where they are located. We have seen that permutation, repetition, compression, deflation, and summation are the principal means by which closure was effected. The tendency toward end accent, manifest in the *tāla* patterns outlined in chapter 8, is mirrored in the design of the large formal gestalts—in the technique of suffixing and in the predictable patterning of all final components.

## 9.5 Ritual Forms

Reconstructed versions of two of the major forms of the ritual theater music will serve to summarize the preceding discussions.[83] A few introductory comments may be useful. The forms are presented in their structural outlines, with each component identified by name and diagrammed with numbered gesture units (that is, beats) and the prescribed gestures. The salient features of each form will be pointed out in the accompanying commentary. As in chapter 8, the neutral silent beats have been set in italic type, while the sounding beats—whose role is to define the musical structure—appear in roman type. Each of the reconstructions represents a choice from among authorized versions, and I have made no attempt to indicate the many performance options. The spacing within each line represents the division into *pādabhāga*s, the four "paws" of a line.[84] There are no prescribed caesuras either within or between components, but all this indicates is a continuous *structural* rhythm; the vocal and instrumental layers will obviously pause for such things as breath, melodic cadences, metric caesuras, phrase articulations, and rests between strings of nonsense syllables or drum strokes. Above all, the reader is urged to let imagination supply what the textual evidence fails to provide: the ornately curving melodic lines, the ornamental arabesques of the flute and vina, and the pulsating drum counterpoint.

As a background for the two reconstructions, I present first a conspectus of the seven major *gītaka* forms, described in terms of their Western formal equivalents, their total number of gesture units, and their estimated maximum performance times. Because the exact sense of certain of the names is obscure, several of the translations must be regarded as conjectural.

Aparāntaka (the "Western" song): two large parallel sections, each containing from five to seven short stanzas of 24 beats, separated by a short interlude and concluding with an optional short coda; 252 beat units, ca. 6:20.

Madraka (the "Northwestern" song): three or four stanzas of three lines each, concluding with a coda; 216 beat units, ca. 5:24.

Oveṇaka (?): the most complex and varied of the seven—a repeated stanza of one and one-half lines, followed by several contrasting short phrases (some with *upavartana* repetitions), then another (and different) repeated stanza, concluding with a short prefinal interlude and a permutating finale; 222 beat units, ca. 5:30.

Prakarī (the "abundant" song?): the longest of the seven—three and one-half or four stanzas of six lines each, concluding with a short coda; 384 beat units, ca. 9:36.

Rovindaka (the "bellowing" song?): a repeated stanza of six long lines, followed by a coda that is repeated several times with various types of nonsense syllables; 216 beat units, ca. 5:24.

Ullopyaka (the "eulogizing" song?): a repeated stanza of two lines (one in quadruple, the other in triple meter), followed by a short prefinal interlude and a permuting finale; 124 beat units, ca. 3:06.

Uttara (the "Northern" song, or perhaps the "last" or "best" song): an opening epigram followed by a pair of short stanzas, each with a refrain, and concluding with an ad libitum permuting finale; 94 beat units, ca. 2:20.

The Madraka and the Oveṇaka will illustrate most of the characteristic features of this repertoire: the former consists of a regular sequence of *vastus*, each beginning with a brief passage of *upohana,* and it is admirably suited to underscore a poetic text; the latter is a loose collection of contrasting *aṅgas*, bound together by frequent *upavartana* repetitions and concluding with a typical permuting final component—best suited, perhaps, to accompany a dance number or a passage of dramatic miming.

The Madraka, like several of the other ritual forms, could be performed in all three states—at least in theory.[85] I shall outline all three versions, to give a clearer demonstration of the process of structural inflation by which the manifold states were generated. The simplest and most concise version of the Madraka was a sequence of sixteen units—eight longs followed by eight shorts—of which the first three were rendered as *upohana:*

30. The syllabic Madraka

| 8 *guru* (long) durations | | | | | | | | 8 *laghu* (short) durations | | | | | | | |
|---|---|---|---|---|---|---|---|---|---|---|---|---|---|---|---|
| 1 | 2 | 3 | 4 | 5 | 6 | 7 | 8 | 9 | 10 | 11 | 12 | 13 | 14 | 15 | 16 |
| | | | śa | śa | tā | tā | śa | śa | tā | tā | śa | tā | śa | tā | S |
| *upohana* | | | | | | | | | | | | | | | |

Note especially the sequence of gestures, all audible, for they will reappear to mark the structure of the two inflated versions outlined below. As usual in this repertoire, the opening beats of *upohana* would be marked with finger snaps and nonsense syllables; meaningful text and the structural gestures begin with beat 4. Even in this briefest of forms we can observe the typical progression of gestures that marks the passage of time within a single formal component: claps of alternate hands, first in pairs and then singly until the final gesture of summation.

When this pattern is inflated to the twofold state (31), several new elements appear. First, the sequence of gestures has been expanded to cover twenty-four syllabic units, all longs; the state is therefore twofold in that the original duration has been doubled (8 longs + 8 shorts = 12 longs × 2 = 24 longs), not the number of units. This expanded version of the original sequence forms the structure of the *vastu,* which is now divided into three regular lines or *mātrās*. The composition as a whole will consist of three or four identical *vastus*,[86] ending with Śirṣaka—a short coda in the syllabic Ṣaṭpitāputrakaḥ *tāla.*[87]

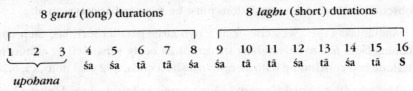

Each of the *mātrās* is further divided into four "paws" of two beats each, each paw signaled by the sequence *ni pra* (characteristic for the twofold state)—except where it is replaced by the audible series of structural gestures. This series of gestures, now in inflated form, demonstrates clearly the general principle of increasing density of events that is among the distinctive features of the entire repertoire of ritual music. At first the sounding gestures are far apart, then every second beat, and finally every beat: I like to think of this as a process of structural compression. But the progression of controlling gestures is even more precisely calibrated: each audible gesture in this twofold version marks the *end* of a duration that is twice the length of the corresponding duration in the syllabic Madraka. That is, beats 7 and 8 correspond to the former beat 4; 9 and 10 to the former beat 5; and so forth—each pair of longs replacing one long in the syllabic state, and each long replacing what was previously a short.

31. The twofold Madraka

*upohana* (beats 1–3)

| | | | | | | | | | |
|---|---|---|---|---|---|---|---|---|---|
| | 1 | 2 | 3 | 4 | 5 | 6 | 7 | 8 | (first *mātrā*) |
| | | | | *pra* | *ni* | *pra* | *ni* | śa | |
| First | 9 | 10 | 11 | 12 | 13 | 14 | 15 | 16 | (second *mātrā*) |
| *vastu* | *ni* | śa | *ni* | tā | *ni* | tā | *ni* | śa | |
| | 17 | 18 | 19 | 20 | 21 | 22 | 23 | 24 | (third *mātrā*) |
| | śa | tā | tā | śa | tā | śa | tā | S | |

followed by the remaining *vastus* and concluding with Śīrṣaka:

| | | | | | |
|---|---|---|---|---|---|
| 1 | 2 | 3 | 4 | 5 | 6 |
| S | tā | śa | tā | śa | tā |

3 : 1 : 2 : 2 : 1 : 3

A fully expanded version of the Madraka is displayed in (32), and readers who have grasped the principle of formal inflation will have no difficulty in locating the proportional sequence of structural gestures, in this case beginning four beats apart before the process of compression sets in. A complete set of *vastus* is included in (32) so that certain additional features may be illustrated. The opening is marked by eight beats of *upohana,* with meaningful text and *tāla* gestures beginning with beat 9; shorter episodes of *pratyupohana* initiate each subsequent *vastu.*[88] A curious interruption in the compression of audible gestures occurs near the end of each *vastu:* tā, which would fall predictably on beat 46, has been moved up to 45, apparently to provide a moment of recovery and collection of energies before the final beat of summation. Because this version is in the fourfold state, the background pattern of silent gestures within each *pādabhāga* is as follows: *ā ni vi pra.* Once again the structurally defining audible beats intrude upon this pattern in regular sequence.

32. The fourfold Madraka

| | | | | | | | | | | | | | | | | |
|---|---|---|---|---|---|---|---|---|---|---|---|---|---|---|---|---|
| | *upohana* | | | | | | | | | | | | | | | |
| | 1 | 2 | 3 | 4 | 5 | 6 | 7 | 8 | 9 | 10 | 11 | 12 | 13 | 14 | 15 | 16 |
| | | | | | | | | | *ā* | *ni* | *vi* | *pra* | *ā* | *ni* | *vi* | śa |
| First *vastu* | 17 | 18 | 19 | 20 | 21 | 22 | 23 | 24 | 25 | 26 | 27 | 28 | 29 | 30 | 31 | 32 |
| | *ā* | *ni* | *vi* | śa | *ā* | *ni* | *vi* | tā | *ā* | *ni* | *vi* | tā | *ā* | *ni* | *vi* | śa |
| | 33 | 34 | 35 | 36 | 37 | 38 | 39 | 40 | 41 | 42 | 43 | 44 | 45 | 46 | 47 | 48 |
| | *ā* | śa | *vi* | tā | *ā* | tā | *vi* | śa | *ā* | tā | *vi* | śa | tā | *ni* | *vi* | S |
| | *pratyupohana* | | | | | | | | | | | | | | | |
| | 1 | 2 | 3 | 4 | 5 | 6 | 7 | 8 | 9 | 10 | 11 | 12 | 13 | 14 | 15 | 16 |
| | | | *vi* | *pra* | *ā* | *ni* | *vi* | *pra* | *ā* | *ni* | *vi* | *pra* | *ā* | *ni* | *vi* | śa |
| Second *vastu* | 17 | 18 | 19 | 20 | 21 | 22 | 23 | 24 | 25 | 26 | 27 | 28 | 29 | 30 | 31 | 32 |
| | *ā* | *ni* | *vi* | śa | *ā* | *ni* | *vi* | tā | *ā* | *ni* | *vi* | tā | *ā* | *ni* | *vi* | śa |
| | 33 | 34 | 35 | 36 | 37 | 38 | 39 | 40 | 41 | 42 | 43 | 44 | 45 | 46 | 47 | 48 |
| | *ā* | śa | *vi* | tā | *ā* | tā | *vi* | śa | *ā* | tā | *vi* | śa | tā | *ni* | *vi* | S |

| | *pratyupohana* | | | | | | | | | | | | | | | |
|---|---|---|---|---|---|---|---|---|---|---|---|---|---|---|---|---|
| | 1 | 2 | 3 | 4 | 5 | 6 | 7 | 8 | 9 | 10 | 11 | 12 | 13 | 14 | 15 | 16 |
| | | | | | *ā* | *ni* | *vi* | *pra* | *ā* | *ni* | *vi* | *pra* | *ā* | *ni* | *vi* | śa |
| Third *vastu* | 17 | 18 | 19 | 20 | 21 | 22 | 23 | 24 | 25 | 26 | 27 | 28 | 29 | 30 | 31 | 32 |
| | *ā* | *ni* | *vi* | śa | *ā* | *ni* | *vi* | tā | *ā* | *ni* | *vi* | tā | *ā* | *ni* | *vi* | śa |
| | 33 | 34 | 35 | 36 | 37 | 38 | 39 | 40 | 41 | 42 | 43 | 44 | 45 | 46 | 47 | 48 |
| | *ā* | śa | *vi* | tā | *ā* | tā | *vi* | śa | *ā* | tā | *vi* | śa | tā | *ni* | *vi* | S |
| | *A | | | | | | | A | A | | | | | | | A |

*dvaigeyaka* (33–40)   *parivarta* (41–48)

| Śīrṣaka | 1 | 2 | 3 | 4 | 5 | 6 | 7 | 8 | 9 | 10 | 11 | 12 | 13 | 14 | 15 | 16 | 17 | 18 | 19 | 20 | 21 | 22 | 23 | 24 |
|---|---|---|---|---|---|---|---|---|---|---|---|---|---|---|---|---|---|---|---|---|---|---|---|---|
| | *ā* | *ni* | *vi* | *pra* | *ā* | tā | *vi* | śa | *ā* | *ni* | *vi* | tā | *ā* | *ni* | *vi* | śa | *ā* | tā | *vi* | *pra* | *ā* | *ni* | *vi* | S |

3 : 1 : 2 : 2 : 1 : 3

* The *aṁśa* must occur in the melody at the points marked A.

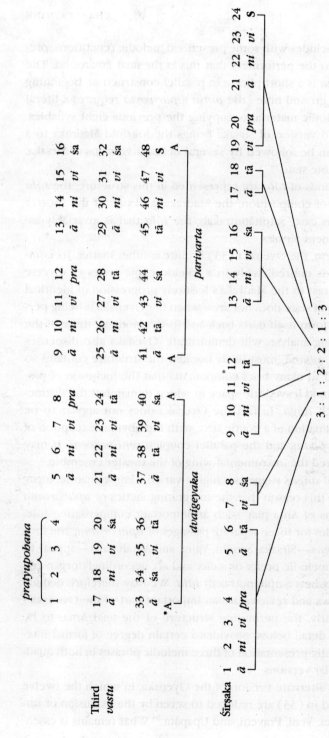

The final *vastu* concludes with some prescribed melodic repetitions, presumably as a signal to the performers that this is the final go-around. The *varṇāṅga dvaigeyaka* is a short phrase in parallel construction, beginning and ending with the ground note (the *aṁśa*); *parivarta* requires a literal repetition of the melodic material occupying the previous eight syllables. And finally an inflated version of Śīrṣaka brings the fourfold Madraka to a close. If desired it can be followed by several deflated versions of Śīrṣaka, ending with the syllabic state.[89]

In summary, two kinds of *tāla* are represented in this structure: the *tāla* of one specific type of composition, the Madraka, and one of the shorter *mārga tāla*s—in this case, Ṣaṭpitāputrakaḥ, the *tāla* that is invariably assigned to the component Śīrṣaka.

With respect to form, the Oveṇaka (33) is quite another matter. Its complex structure unfolds unpredictably in a kaleidoscopic series of diverse *aṅga*s, in sharp contrast to the Madraka's leisurely progression of identical *vastu*s. The question of state does not arise when the Oveṇaka is being performed, because the form itself darts back and forth among all three of the states, as the following analysis will demonstrate. Oveṇaka also dispenses with the gambit of *upohana,* most likely because the structure contains so many beginnings and so many brief components that the inclusion of passages of *upohana* would leave little space in which to manifest the distinctive structure of each *aṅga.* In fact the Oveṇaka does not appear to be suitable for the declamation of a poetic text, with the obvious exception of the opening pair of *pāda*s and the parallel couplet *veṇī/praveṇī.* It may therefore have featured the instrumental wing of the theater ensemble.

All this diversity of *aṅga*s suggests a highly varied, almost chaotic, form, and it is perhaps for this reason that the integrating tactics of *upavartana* and the permutations of Anta play such an important compensating role. The structure provides for three separate passages of *upavartana,* and four of the remaining *aṅga*s—Śīrṣaka, Sandhi, Vajra, and Antāharaṇa—appear to function as either a melodic prefix or suffix and are accordingly organized by the ubiquitous six-beat Ṣaṭpitāputrakaḥ *tāla.* We may therefore deduce that melodic previews and reviews are an important part of the Oveṇaka's business. And similarly, the permuting structure of the final Anta, to be discussed in greater detail below, provides a certain degree of formal integration in its systematic presentation of three melodic phrases in both quadrangular and triangular versions.

There is only one alternate version of the Oveṇaka, in which the twelve components outlined in (33) are reduced to seven by the exclusion of *upavartana,* Sampiṣṭaka, Veṇī, Praveṇī, and Upapāta.[90] What remains is essentially a ternary form: (1) the opening epigrammatic couplet and its suffix, Śīrṣaka; (2) the contrasting sequence of short *aṅga*s; and (3) the permuting finale and its prefix Antāharaṇa.

The complex structure of the Oveṇaka presents too great a wealth of detail to discuss exhaustively here, so my analysis will concentrate on four topics: (1) the various *tāla* patterns and the state of inflation they imply, (2) some details of the component Anta, (3) some interesting melodic details provided by certain authors, and (4) the occurrence of one particular deep structure (2 + 1) embedded on several hierarchical levels in the ancient ritual music.

The first thing to note about the underlying *tāla* patterns is the pervasive occurrence of single versions of Ṣaṭpitāputrakaḥ: **S** tā śa tā śa tā, or the reverse, so as to end with **S**, the gesture of summation. I count ten such occurrences plus four derivatives which I shall soon explain. As I indicated earlier, this pattern is standard for prefixes (Antāharaṇa), suffixes (Śīrṣaka), and the compressed repetitions of *upavartana* (of which there are three, emboxed in [33]). All of these are syllabic in state, which means that the proportional structure of 3 : 1 : 2 : 2 : 1 : 3 appears in the sequence of unequal durations: P, L, G, G, L, P.[91] Five remain, of which Sandhi (link), Vajra (zigzag), and the triangular (*ayugma*) version of Pravṛtta are likewise syllabic in state. (Readers will recall that this *tāla* was classified as triangular.) The list of ten is completed by the two twofold versions heard in the couplet Veṇī/Praveṇī; here all the durations are longs, and the proportional structure of the *tāla* appears in the grouping of the beats, as a reference to (19) will clarify. The other clue to the twofold state of this pair of *aṅga*s is the gesture sequence *ni pra* for each of the six *pādabhāga*s, upon which the audible beats intrude according to the pattern.

It is not as easy to account for the four derivatives—the opening pair of Pādas, Māṣaghāta ("ground beans"?), and Upapāta. Each, for different reasons, manifests a variant of the gesture pattern (that is, śa tā tā śa tā **S**, a simple exchange of the first two gestures), while seeming to discard the proportionate structure of the *tāla*. Bharata, Dattila, and Śārṅgadeva, among other early authors, have noted the close resemblance to Ṣaṭpitāputrakaḥ, so my analysis is based on more than speculation.[92] I shall argue that the pattern is indeed a genuine derivative and that the proportional structure is retained, at least in one case, and given an interesting twist.

There are two things to be explained: the change in proportions and the exchange of the first two gestures. I can suggest a tentative answer to the first problem. At first glance the opening pair of Pādas appears only to manifest the general progression of compression of the audible gestures noted

33. The Oveṇaka

| | | | | | | | | | | | | | | | | | | | | | | |
|---|---|---|---|---|---|---|---|---|---|---|---|---|---|---|---|---|---|---|---|---|---|---|
| Pāda 1: | 1 | 2 | 3 | 4 | 5 | 6 | 7 | 8 | 9 | 10 | 11 | 12 | 13 | 14 | 15 | 16 | | | | | | |
| | *ā* | *ni* | *vi* | *pra* | *ā* | *ni* | *vi* | *pra* | *ā* | *ni* | *vi* | śa | *ā* | *ni* | *vi* | tā | | | | | | |
| | 17 | 18 | 19 | 20 | 21 | 22 | 23 | 24 | | | | | | | | | | | | | | |
| | *ā* | tā | *vi* | śa | tā | *ni* | *vi* | **S** | | | | | | | | | | | | | | |
| Pāda 2: | 1 | 2 | 3 | 4 | 5 | 6 | 7 | 8 | 9 | 10 | 11 | 12 | 13 | 14 | 15 | 16 | | | | | | |
| | *ā* | *ni* | *vi* | *pra* | *ā* | *ni* | *vi* | *pra* | *ā* | *ni* | *vi* | śa | *ā* | *ni* | *vi* | tā | | | | | | |
| | 17 | 18 | 19 | 20 | 21 | 22 | 23 | 24 | | | | | | | | | | | | | | |
| | *ā* | tā | *vi* | śa | tā | *ni* | *vi* | **S** | | | | | | | | | | | | | | |
| Sīrṣaka: | 1 | 2 | 3 | 4 | 5 | 6 | | | | | | | | | | | | | | | | |
| | **S** | tā | śa | tā | śa | tā | | | | | | | | | | | | | | | | |
| Māṣaghāta and *upavartana*: | 1 | 2 | 3 | 4 | 5 | 6 | 7 | 8 | 9 | 10 | 11 | 12 | | | | | 1 | 2 | 3 | 4 | 5 | 6 |
| | *ni* | śa | *ni* | tā | *ni* | tā | *ni* | śa | tā | *pra* | *ni* | **S** | | | | | **S** | tā | śa | tā | śa | tā |
| Sandhi: | 1 | 2 | 3 | 4 | 5 | 6 | | | | | | | | | | | | | | | | |
| | **S** | tā | śa | tā | śa | tā | | | | | | | | | | | | | | | | |
| Caturaśraka: | 1 | 2 | 3 | 4 | 5 | 6 | 7 | 8 | | | | | | | | | | | | | | |
| | *ni* | śa | śa | tā | śa | tā | śa | **S** | | | | | | | | | | | | | | |
| Vajra: | 1 | 2 | 3 | 4 | 5 | 6 | | | | | | | | | | | | | | | | |
| | **S** | tā | śa | tā | śa | tā | | | | | | | | | | | | | | | | |
| Sampiṣṭaka and *upavartana*: | 1 | 2 | 3 | 4 | 5 | 6 | 7 | 8 | 9 | 10 | 11 | 12 | | | | | 1 | 2 | 3 | 4 | 5 | 6 |
| | *ni* | śa | śa | śa | tā | tā | tā | śa | tā | śa | tā | **S** | | | | | **S** | tā | śa | tā | śa | tā |

| | | | | | | | | | | | | |
|---|---|---|---|---|---|---|---|---|---|---|---|---|
| Veṇī: | 1 | 2 | 3 | 4 | 5 | 6 | 7 | 8 | 9 | 10 | 11 | 12 |
| | *ni* | *pra* | tā | śa | *ni* | tā | *ni* | śa | tā | *pra* | *ni* | **S** |
| Praveṇī and *upavartana*: | 1 | 2 | 3 | 4 | 5 | 6 | 7 | 8 | 9 | 10 | 11 | 12 |
| | *ni* | *pra* | tā | śa | *ni* | tā | *ni* | śa | tā | *pra* | *ni* | **S** |
| Upapāta: | 1 | 2 | 3 | 4 | 5 | 6 | 7 | 8 | 9 | 10 | 11 | 12 |
| | *ā* | *ni* | *vi* | tā | *ā* | tā | *vi* | śa | tā | *ni* | *vi* | **S** |
| Antāharaṇa: | 1 | 2 | 3 | 4 | 5 | 6 | | | | | | |
| | **S** | tā | śa | tā | śa | tā | | | | | | |
| Anta | | | | | | | | | | | | |
| yugma Sthita: | 1 | 2 | 3 | 4 | 5 | 6 | 7 | 8 | | | | |
| | *ni* | śa | *ni* | tā | *ni* | *pra* | *ni* | **S** | | | | |
| yugma Pravṛtta: | 1 | 2 | 3 | 4 | 5 | 6 | 7 | 8 | | | | |
| | *ni* | śa | śa | tā | śa | tā | śa | **S** | | | | |
| yugma Mahājanika: | 1 | 2 | 3 | 4 | 5 | 6 | 7 | 8 | | | | |
| | *ni* | śa | *ni* | tā | *ni* | *pra* | *ni* | **S** | | | | |
| ayugma Sthita: | 1 | 2 | 3 | 4 | 5 | 6 | | | | | | |
| | *ni* | śa | tā | *pra* | *ni* | **S** | | | | | | |
| ayugma Pravṛtta: | 1 | 2 | 3 | 4 | 5 | 6 | | | | | | |
| | **S** | tā | śa | tā | śa | tā | | | | | | |
| ayugma Mahājanika: | 1 | 2 | 3 | 4 | 5 | 6 | | | | | | |
| | *ni* | śa | tā | *pra* | *ni* | **S** | | | | | | |
| yugma Sthita: | 1 | 2 | 3 | 4 | 5 | 6 | 7 | 8 | | | | |
| | *ni* | śa | *ni* | tā | *ni* | *pra* | *ni* | **S** | | | | |
| yugma Pravṛtta: | 1 | 2 | 3 | 4 | 5 | 6 | 7 | 8 | | | | |
| | *ni* | śa | śa | tā | śa | tā | śa | **S** | | | | |
| ayugma Mahājanika: | 1 | 2 | 3 | 4 | 5 | 6 | | | | | | |
| | *ni* | śa | tā | *pra* | *ni* | **S** | | | | | | |

| | | | | | |
|---|---|---|---|---|---|
| 1 | 2 | 3 | 4 | 5 | 6 |
| **S** | tā | śa | tā | śa | tā |

elsewhere in the repertoire—first by fours, then by twos, and ultimately (after the "moment of recovery")[93] to the single final beat. Consider, however, the dual hypothesis (1) that each Pāda is conceived in the fourfold state, as signaled by the sequence *ā ni vi pra* in each of its six paws, and (2) that the spacing of the audible gestures implies successive deflations beginning at beats 13 (to the fourfold state) and 17 (to the twofold state). Viewed in this light, something remarkably similar to the original proportional structure of Ṣaṭpitāputrakaḥ emerges (34):[94]

34.

| eightfold | | fourfold | | twofold | | | | | | |
|---|---|---|---|---|---|---|---|---|---|---|
| 1 2 3 4 5 6 7 8 9 10 11 12 | ‖ | 13 14 15 16 | ‖ | 17 18 | | 19 20 | | 21 | | 22 23 24 |
| 3 | : | 1 | : | 2 | : | 2 | : | 1 | : | 3 |

The brief Māṣaghāta is clearly a twofold version of the same sequence of audible gestures, of which beats 5–12 are identical to the standard twofold Ṣaṭpitāputrakaḥ. Upapāta, which consists of three fourfold *pādabhāgas*,[95] uses only the last five gestures, probably because of its brevity. What all three of these components reveal is a familiar tendency in world poetry, a tendency toward predictable patterning in approaching a cadence, with greater freedom at the beginning of a line or other member.

As for the second problem, the initial exchange of gestures, I suspect the answer is quite simple. Because of the difficulties involved in encoding formal specifications in verbal form, it was convenient for authors to describe a pattern as a variant of another established pattern, and the variant may also have proved useful in distinguishing the function of one type of component (in this case, expository) from that of another (a preview or review).[96] Māṣaghāta was prescribed by early authors as the indispensable component in this structure, a specification that has puzzled modern interpreters. Perhaps Māṣaghāta was the essential "theme" of the Oveṇaka, a concise distillation of the melodic, textual, and rhythmic material presented at greater length in the opening pair of Pādas; in this event the similarity of the gesture pattern would have been highly appropriate. And similarly, the rapid alternation between the standard and "deviant" versions of a familiar pattern would seem to have suited admirably the playfully varied structure of the Oveṇaka.

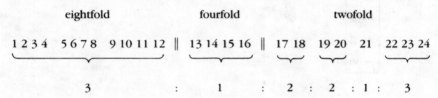

Two other patterns are worth noting before we proceed to the permutations of Anta. Both the *aṅga* Caturasraka (four-cornered) and the two occurrences of the quadrangular version of Pravṛtta (onward-moving) display a popular compound of two syllabic *tāla*s, as analyzed in (35).[97]

35.

| 1 | 2 | 3 | 4 | 5 | 6 | 7 | 8 |
|---|---|---|---|---|---|---|---|
| *ni* | śa | śa | tā | śa | tā | śa | S |
| Udghaṭṭaḥ | | | Caccatpuṭaḥ | | | | "extra" |

The *aṅga* identified as Sampiṣṭaka (crushed, ground together) is an anomalous line of twelve syllables and therefore, with no evidence to the contrary, is to be regarded as triangular. This perhaps explains the Udghaṭṭaḥ beginning (*ni* śa śa) and the grouping of śa and tā by threes, before it is compressed into what looks like yet another syllabic version of Ṣaṭpitāputrakaḥ (beats 7–12). This is the only appearance of this pattern in the major *gītaka* forms,[98] but it appears to be an obvious compound and also perhaps a triangular relative of the structural pattern of the Madraka.[99]

The second item on our analytic agenda is to show how the permutations of Anta may have been performed. We know little about the sequence of three *aṅga*s (Sthita, Pravṛtta, and Mahājanika: "steady, moving forward, and noble") except for the obvious similarity between the first and the third and the contrasting nature of Pravṛtta; but each of these must have been distinguished in performance on the basis of their text, melodic contour, or some other characteristic property. Indeed, they can be recognized only by means of some dimension other than *tāla,* because the patterns for, say, the *yugma* and *ayugma* versions of Pravṛtta are unrelated and manifest only their triangular or quadrangular nature. But whatever their melodic and textual features are, it is clear that the three contrasting *aṅga*s are first arrayed in *yugma* (even) versions, then in *ayugma* (odd) versions, and then they are performed in some combination of even and odd patterns. The formal diagram in (33) illustrates only one of the many possibilities.[100]

I have already accounted for the *tāla* structure of both forms of Pravṛtta. All occurrences of Sthita and Mahājanika are framed in the twofold state, consisting of either three or four *pādabhāga*s of two units each, with the standard *ni pra* as the background pattern of gesture. They also share the same progression of three audible gestures (śa tā **S**), a sequence which is characteristic of the system as a whole—that is, alternation of hands and ending with S—but which manifests none of the five *mārga tāla* patterns. The sense of impending closure must grow progressively stronger throughout the permutations of Anta, both in the multiple endings signaled by the gesture *sannipāta* and the growing recognition that its possibilities are about to become exhausted.

The sketchy and contradictory accounts of the early treatises do not permit any sweeping conclusions regarding the melodic materials (the *varṇāṅgas*) specified for the Oveṇaka, but I shall attempt to draw the few deductions that are possible. Four types of melodic *aṅgas* were apparently available as additional formal features of the *gītaka* forms: one ascending in contour, with up to six pauses (*vidārīs*); one descending in contour, of the same length; a pair of phrases (similar or differing in certain respects) separated by a cadence; and a single phrase.[101] Obviously the first two were appropriate for longer formal components, and the latter two were virtually the only possibilities for the shorter *tālāṅgas* in the twofold and syllabic states. In the case of the Oveṇaka form, only the initial Pādas and the Veṇī/Praveṇī couplet afforded sufficient scope for the longer melodic *aṅgas*. The two Pādas were evidently organized in parallel melodic construction, but we have no information on the specific choice of *aṅga*(s); the sequence Veṇī/Praveṇī, on the other hand, featured a combination of either (1) the ascending followed by the descending contour, or (2) the reverse. The former sounds like a more natural choice, but because the major authors differ on this crucial point, no solution is in sight. The remaining components were performed either with pairs of phrases or single phrases, depending upon their length. Applying this principle to the Oveṇaka, it seems likely that all twelve-beat components (other than those mentioned) would require a pair of melodic *aṅgas*, with all the shorter lines set to single phrases. From the standpoint of modality, the various melodic *aṅgas* were further distinguished by obligatory cadences upon the sonant note, final, or confinal, but none of the early treatises provides enough detail on this point to justify any further conclusions. What is clear is that the melodic phrasing was closely linked with the underlying *tāla* structure, and from this we can infer that the melodic dimension of the Oveṇaka featured as much variety as does the rhythmic dimension and was similarly articulated by the many abrupt changes of pace.

Finally I should like to point out two separate occurrences of one particular deep structure that may hold some archetypal significance for this body of ritual music: a parallel construction followed by a single shorter unit (2 + 1), as in the initial pair of Pādas with their Śīrṣaka suffix, and also in the Veṇī/Praveṇī sequence plus the required *upavartana.* Couplet-plus-refrain is exceedingly common in world poetry, but usually as one element in a long series, not as a single unit. Parallel couplets are indeed among the standard forms of epic Sanskrit verse, but not with single lines following. I have identified this 2 + 1 structure on several levels of the musical hierarchy: in groupings of lines (as in the present case), in groupings of larger formal components, and even in the design of entire compositions.[102] A parallel that comes to mind is the two *Stollen* plus *Abgesang* of the medieval German minnesingers. I suggest that the 2 + 1 structure arises from a typical and deep-seated formal impulse, a desire to affirm and place the final stamp of approval upon the previous textual-melodic unit by means of the usual tactics of closure in this tradition: repetition, compression, deflation, and summation—once again a musical colophon.[103]

## 9.6 Minor Forms

The repertoire of music for the theatrical rituals was augmented by a number of other forms, generally considered to be of lesser importance than the seven major *gītaka*s. Most authorities agree on seven: Chandaka (metrical), Āsārita (flowing toward), Vardhamāna (expanding), Pāṇikā ("hand," probably in the sense of measured by the hand), Ṛk (verse), Gāthā (a metrical song or verse of some non-Vedic chant), and Sāma (hymn); Kapāla (skull, a probable reference to Śiva), and Brahmagīta (the song of Brahmā) are sometimes included.[104] It is usually conceded, on the basis of their names and what little is known about them, that these compositions are considerably older and starker in design than the seven *gītaka*s.

Several of the names suggest genres of Vedic chant, and the surviving descriptions of the Ṛk, Gāthā, and Sāma confirm that they were metrical recitatives in a syllabic style appropriate for the declamation of text. They also featured interpolated vocables, that is, *stobhākṣara*s such as *au, ho, vā,* and the sacred syllables *hum* and *om.*[105] I pointed out earlier how the five *aṅga*s of these forms parallel the liturgical organization of Sāmavedic chant.[106] There is also the contradictory suggestion that these forms were somewhat lighter in character than the *gītaka*s and therefore appropriate for the delicate feminine style sometimes specified for the dedicatory ceremonies.[107] This can hardly be true for the three forms I have just mentioned, but it appears to be true in the case of Pāṇikā.[108] Its structure is: an opening epigram in parallel construction (16 + 16 syllables) in the fourfold state, followed by a main section (*śarīra,* body) of twenty-four syllabic units accompanied by four cycles of the syllabic version of Ṣaṭpitāputrakaḥ *tāla,* and concluding with a coda (Śīrṣaka) of twelve syllables set to the gesture pattern of Sampiṣṭaka as heard in the Oveṇaka.[109] This structure does not appear among the major *gītaka*s, but it is consistent with their principles.

The Āsārita and Vardhamāna are quite another matter and cannot be dismissed as easily; it is difficult to understand why early authors classified them with the lesser forms. The "expanding" Vardhamāna dance is prescribed as the first musical number after the curtain in front of the theater ensemble has been drawn: it is a dance sequence in which one female dancer after another enters, performs a passage of *abhinaya* (mime) illustrating various attributes of the patron deity of the play, and then joins with the other dancers in a group dance.[110] The expanding character of the form refers not only to the increasing number of dancers on stage and the concomitant expansion of the sung text but also to the structure of the composition. Here the principle of structural inflation finds its most typical expression. The Vardhamāna is a composite of the four possible versions of the Āsārita, arranged in order of inflation from shortest to longest—two different syllabic versions and two inflated versions—to a grand total of 132 gesture units (17 + 17 + 33 + 65, with some deletions in the inflated versions).[111] Each of the four Āsārita patterns is introduced with a passage of *upohana,* also increasing from five to eight beats to match the increasing length of each new component.

The basic *tāla* pattern of the seventeen-beat Āsarita is another compound of two of the *mārga tāla*s, as analyzed in (36):

36. The syllabic Āsārita

| the *tāla* analyzed: | Caccatpuṭaḥ | | | | Ṣaṭpitāputrakaḥ | | | | | | Ṣaṭpitāputrakaḥ | | | | | | "extra' |
|---|---|---|---|---|---|---|---|---|---|---|---|---|---|---|---|---|---|
| *tāla* gestures: | śa | tā | śa | tā | S | tā | śa | tā | śa | tā | S | tā | śa | tā | śa | tā | S |
| durations: | 2 | 2 | 1 | 3 | 3 | 1 | 2 | 2 | 1 | 3 | 3 | 1 | 2 | 2 | 1 | 3 | 3 |
| units: | 1 | 2 | 3 | 4 | 5 | 6 | 7 | 8 | 9 | 10 | 11 | 12 | 13 | 14 | 15 | 16 | 17 |

Each of the three component *tāla*s is expanded into a *vastu* in the inflated versions which follow, and here each *vastu* is constructed entirely of long syllables and organized by the appropriate inflated state of the ubiquitous Ṣaṭpitāputrakaḥ, once again demonstrating how the irregular durations of the syllabic state become translated into proportional groupings in the manifold states.

It is difficult to assess the status of these minor forms. Perhaps, as Mukund Lath has conjectured, these forms "did really have a closer affinity with the Vedic sāma music, but they were at the same time (perhaps as a corollary to their being old) comparatively simpler structures and, consequently, when the more sophisticated and intricate saptarūpa [the seven major *gītaka* forms] evolved, these older forms were relegated to a lesser position of honour."[112]

The ritual forms have provided ample evidence that most of India's artistic preferences were solidly in place during the flowering of the Gupta theatrical tradition and the production of its companion treatises. And if the preceding exposition has done its job, readers will have been reminded on numerous occasions of the pervading influence of archetypal schemata upon the nature and disposition of the many individual components, tactics, and complete forms—in the frequent metaphorical references to the parts of the human body and the process of organic growth, as well as traces of the liturgical and cosmological archetypes.

But this has inevitably presented a one-sided and overly formalistic picture of early Indian music. The sense of form in a living musical performance must arise from the interaction and combination of all the dimensions—text, melodic contour, melodic rhythm, drum counterpoint, and the controlling patterns of *tāla,* upon which this discussion has been focused. Many of the most cherished properties of the performing arts of India cannot be manifested in terms of hand gestures, accents, durations and their groupings, formal components, and their large gestalts—all of which set forth the quantitative, formalistic, and hierarchical aspects of this special body of ancient music. In particular, the spatial preferences for such things as circles, spirals, arabesques, and ornaments of all types must be fulfilled in the domain of melody, and in this respect the practice of contemporary Indian music is more informative than the early musical texts. I have emphasized that one of the main messages of the Indian conception of form is that vital continuity unites all apparently separate events—that the processes of creation, life, and growth organize a series of discrete units and stages into a regular progression of intensification and narrowed focus upon an anticipated goal. It is the business of form to quantify, arrange, and relate the separate stages, but we must not lose sight of what Indian culture has taught but which form alone cannot provide: the thread of essential unity that runs continuously throughout all process.

The nature and function of this repertoire, as accompaniment to solemn ritual and as an ensemble music, sets it apart from most subsequent Indian musical traditions and genres. Since it was a ritual music, all had to be composed in advance and rendered precisely in performance; all possible deviations had to be specified, and nothing could be left to the spur of the moment. Since it was an ensemble music, control and synchronization were essential. Because of these conditions, it was considered vital that as many of the details as possible be set down in as precise a format as language could provide, and the various formal sequences of actions, durations, patterns, and *aṅga*s were relatively easy to prescribe in words. But the same conditions no longer prevailed in later centuries. The intricate, modular structures of the theatrical prelude remained as elaborate fossils from the golden age of the early musical theater, but lighter and more popular song styles had arisen as the practice of improvisation began to flourish and music became more a matter of a duo for a soloist and a drummer. The rigorous melodic development and embellishment of a *rāga* replaced the structural rigors of the ancient *tāla* system, and with the advent of the repeating cycles of the *deśī tāla*s, both melody and the performers were freed from many of the former constraints.

Language was changing at the same time. Later developments in *tāla* and form remind us of the development from Latin to Italian, or for that matter, from classical Sanskrit to the various Prakrits. What was lost in rhetorical emphasis, grammatical subtlety, and precision of reference was replaced by gains in melodic lilt, ease of communication, spontaneity, and the swing of regular rhythmic gait. Epic Sanskrit had become a highly cultivated, ornate, even stilted tongue set on a pedestal, and literary production in the vernaculars was increasing at a rapid rate. With reference to Velankar's analysis of the changing phases of poetic meter, the "music of sound-variation" proved ultimately to be less popular than the "music of time-regulated accent."[113] Musical structure, as we might expect, took a parallel course. To follow these developments in the later Indian Middle Ages, we leave the ossified structures of *mārga tāla* and turn to the domain of solo song.

# TEN

# SONG

A pleasing arrangement of *svaras* is known as *gīta* (song).

Śārṅgadeva, *Saṅgītaratnākara* 4.1ab[1]

That *prabandha* which is sung with *rāga* at its beginning, along with ornaments, and [is] next accompanied by *tāla,* well-rendered with sol-fa and recited drum syllables, and also containing passages of meaningful text in various regional languages—this one has been declared to be Śukacañcu (parrot-beak), a favorite of people everywhere.

Mataṅga, *Bṛhaddeśī* 402–3ab[2]

## 10.1 Introduction

Song is one of the basic continuities in the history of music, with regard to both singing as a human activity and songs as products of culture. Throughout the parade of changing fashions in scales, rhythms, meters, forms, and styles, we can identify certain abiding features of song that transcend historical and geographical boundaries and have served to limit the possibilities for variation: a relative simplicity of melody, constraints of vocal range and tessitura, phrases corresponding to the length of the breath, textures and accompaniments (if any) that give maximum exposure to the vocal line, emotional expressiveness, and a common repertoire of themes—love, death, victory, praise, lamentation, dance, celebration of the seasons, and often pure nonsense.

It is easy to overlook these common properties when focusing upon those features which differ from culture to culture, or from one era to another—the text rhythms and metric patterns of the parent language, the amount and types of embellishment, the degree of rhythmic freedom permitted, the vocal quality (e.g., whether nasal, raspy, constricted), typical melodic intonations and idioms, the forms of song, and other distinctive features of a local or regional tradition. Before we examine the song descriptions found in early treatises, it will be useful to mention some of the special continuities of Indian song and to identify certain features held in common with India's neighbor regions.

My analysis proceeds from several assumptions: that song as it is heard today, although not an exact replica of them, can at least give us some idea of the song styles of one thousand to fifteen hundred years ago; that Indian song at any stage is a mixture of local, regional, national, and universal features; that the various song repertoires and regional styles heard today may be regarded as fossil records of the evolution of song on the Indian subcontinent; that they are also products of a continuous ferment between art and folk traditions; and that singing lies at the heart of the Indian concept of music and music making.

*Gīta* is the most general word for song. Śārṅgadeva's definition of *gīta* in the epigraph emphasizes the formal aspect of song as an organized disposition of tones (the *svara*s) rather than its metaphysical aspect as sound emanating from the human body. He has also emphasized its emotive aspect: the adjective *rañjaka* (translated here as "pleasing") derives from the same root as the word *rāga* and evokes the same range of meanings—to be colored (especially red), impassioned, illuminated, excited, charmed, or delighted. So to paraphrase Śārṅgadeva and amplify his laconic statement, we may define *gīta* as a disposition of the elements of melody, with the aim of conveying the underlying accents of passion and bringing delight by means of the diverse colors of human sound.

Mataṅga's description of Śukacañcu, with its somewhat forced pun on the opening exposition of *rāga* and the brightly colored beak of a parrot, sounds like the archetypal Indian song: an ornate exploration of the chosen *rāga* in the typical *ālāpana* style,[3] followed by a section of measured rhythm under the control of *tāla,* and then a highly varied mix of passages of meaningful text and meaningless vocables. The selection of forty-eight *prabandha*s set forth in the final canto of his *Bṛhaddeśī* constitutes the oldest surviving account of the Indian art song as it flourished amid the milieu of ornate court poetry near the end of the first millennium.[4] I shall present other songs from Mataṅga's selection later in this chapter.

In this chapter we will focus upon art songs, among which we must include both composed or partly composed songs and improvisations within the tradition of highly cultivated music. This is not to set a higher premium on art music but is simply a recognition of the risks involved in speculation about earlier stages of folk traditions. We know no more about village and tribal song from ancient times than we know about similar traditions in the ancient West. Ethnomusicologists have only begun to explore India's wealth of tribal musics, but the initial results are encouraging. In the case of India, the distinction between village and tribal musics is important and may not be familiar to readers. The 1961 census listed more than 314 Scheduled Tribes with a total population of more than thirty million, inhabiting pockets of aboriginal culture scattered throughout the various Indian states and union territories, but particularly in hill and forest regions.[5] Their musics are to be distinguished from the "folk" music of the surrounding population of the various regions, a music which shares the same heritage as the central tradition of art music and may be regarded simply as a less-cultivated species thereof. Ethnomusicologists have speculated that certain tribal musics may at one time have contributed to the main classical tradition, but this can no longer be the case.

I referred earlier to the idea of a creative ferment between art and folk music. The argument may be summarized along these lines: the communal music of a folk tradition—in which everyone, and therefore no one, is the composer—serves as an abiding source of fresh material and renewal, providing distinctive intonations and rhythms, energy, local color, uninhibited passion and spontaneity. With the advent of art music come such things as literacy, urban culture, increasing emphasis on the formal elements of music, theoretical concepts and systems, notations, treatises, more technologically advanced instruments, increasing specialization, professional composers and performers, an overt sense of history, a tendency toward a continuous refinement of the musical materials and their modes of organization, classification of music into precise genres, types, and individual compositions, and a gradual process of selection and transformation that emphasizes certain common features of the musical language and suppresses anomalous ingredients.

I shall not attempt a history of the long interaction of art and folk traditions of song on the Indian subcontinent. The goal is simply to suggest that the verbal descriptions of "then" may be reliably amplified with the living evidence of the "now." I begin with an instructive passage from Alan Lomax's *Folk Song Style and Culture,* the study in which the author documents his controversial cantometrics project. Here is a description of the typical song style heard today (that is, in the 1940s and 1950s) in the world area labeled "Old High Culture."

> The cantometric profile for Old High Culture shows a widely shared and a highly distinctive pattern. Probably the most important theme is "exclusive and elaborated dominance" where a solo performer . . . sings a precisely enunciated, long, and complex text. The length, wordiness, and precision of the text is combined with a complex, multiphrased melodic structure, extreme ornamentation, frequent use of rubato, and a constricted vocal style, all of which effectively prevent participation by others. Such, apparently, has been the style long employed by

> plowmen in harvest songs, and by priests and bards for the praise of gods, great beauties, and princes. Within this stylistic framework, great virtuosos and aestheticians developed scales and musical systems, poetic forms, and refinements of instrumental structure and technique. . . . The songs of Old High Culture are frequently grave and serious in tone, an effect produced by the combined use of intervals of a second or less, slow tempo, and embellishments, melismas, glissandos, and glottal tremolo.[6]

Anyone with the slightest acquaintance with Indian music will recognize this model, labeled elsewhere by Lomax as "Model A2" and characterized by elaborate solo singing, textual complexity, precise enunciation, metrical complexity, ornate embellishments, narrow pitch intervals, and a vocal quality that is "usually noisy."[7] The geographical distribution of this song style sweeps from both sides of the Mediterranean in a wide band curving across west and south Asia to the Southeast Asian archipelago. It is of further interest to note the degree of correlation among the song features exhibited in the various regions of this vast area. Lomax's technique of "homogeneity mapping" yields the following percentages of correlating features (37):[8]

37.

| Percentage | Area |
|---|---|
| 100 | Himalayas, East Asia, Mideast, Mediterranean Europe (which lies outside the area of Old High Culture) |
| 91 | Urban Southeast Asia, Tribal Southeast Asia |
| 83 | Malay, Near East |
| 74 | North Africa |
| 66 | Urban Indonesia, Australia |
| 58 | Central Asia |
| 0 | Tribal India |

There is a story buried in these correlations. Lomax's findings have been criticized on valid grounds and must be taken with more than a grain of salt, but in this case they are sufficiently strong to warrant some broad conclusions. The many disparities in style between the songs of village and tribal India are striking enough, despite the small samples of tribal music available to Lomax's analysts, to reinforce the picture of isolated pockets of tribal music embedded here and there in an otherwise homogenous region with many common musical features. And further, the 91 percent correlation between Village India (the base for the correlations of [37]) and Tribal Southeast Asia is an intriguing piece of evidence that may tell us something about the eastward migrations of Indic culture in earlier centuries.

Most of Lomax's material was recorded after 1940, when field recordings from around the world began to become available in sufficient quality and quantity to permit this type of comparative analysis. One cannot assume that the patterns he detected have remained constant throughout human history. On the contrary, time is an obvious factor in the diffusion of culture. But when contemporary analyses of folk songs reveal a high degree of correlation with the descriptions of art songs in treatises from one to two thousand years ago, it is hard to avoid the conclusion that many if not most of the distinctive properties of Indian song were well established by the beginning of the Christian era and were cultural givens by the end of the first millennium.

I have also been struck by one of the laws of musical geography proposed by Bence Szabolcsi in one of the valuable appendixes to his *History of Melody.*[9] Not all of his provocative arguments are germane to the evolution of music and musical style in India, but one particular axiom stands out in his account of the mutual interplay between art-music and folk-music cultures, which coexist, in Szabolcsi's words, "in a state of equilibrium." He continues, "In this state of equilibrium, the material collected in the peripheral areas is shaped into integrated musical language by the (art-music) centre."[10] This is an accurate account of what was accomplished during the age of *deśī* (ca. A.D. 500–1000), the movement responsible for the collecting and leveling of the many regional song styles.[11] In the texts that record these achievements, we find the earliest surviving descriptions of independent art songs.

An analogy from chemistry may help to explain how the leveling process may have operated. When musical material "is shaped into integrated musical language," I think of some kind of distillation process in which the essential ingredients of various compounds, when purified and concentrated, are discovered to have more in common with one another than is apparent from the raw state of the compounds with which one had begun. Once again, this is not to set a higher value upon art song, but merely to point out that the process of selecting, cultivating, and refocusing material found in a diverse repertoire of song tends to identify and amplify some of the most characteristic features of a tradition.

In chapter 5 I described the plot songs of the early musical theater (the *dhruvā*s).[12] These too may be regarded as art songs, some fully composed and others permitting some degree of spontaneity in performance. We know the most about their texts, when they were sung during a play, their typical emotional content, their metric structure, the appropriate metaphors and other figures of speech to be used, and a small handful of other details. It must be assumed that the *dhruvā*s shared the same musical language with the ritual forms (with respect to scales, *tāla,* and formal structure) but in a less coercive manner. *Dhruvā*s were more soloistic and less constrained in matters of rhythm, meter, and tempo; and a greater range of performance options was prescribed to accommodate the needs of the stage. This is as far back in Indian history as we can trace the roots of secular song, and it is generally assumed that later Indian art song evolved from these roots, with the aid of grafts from the many regional musics during the period of *deśī.* With the valuable *prabandha* canto of Mataṅga's *Bṛhaddeśī,* the outlines of the early art song begin to become much clearer.

## 10.2 The *Prabandhas*

*Prabandha* (bonded, well-knit) is the generic term for the independent art songs of medieval India.[13] Prior to its adoption as a musical term, the word appears in a variety of contexts in the literature of *alaṅkāraśāstra* (poetic theory), and in descriptions of the musical *prabandha*s, matters of literary style and metrical structure have often been emphasized at the expense of the purely musical features. There are two continuous ideological strands connecting the various musical and literary compositions designated by the term *prabandha,* one explicit and the other implicit: the explicit meaning is that these are strict, formal, regulated compositions, as opposed to free, unregulated improvisations; recall the important distinction drawn in chapter 9 between *nibaddha* (regulated) and *anibaddha* (unregulated) forms.[14] The implicit meaning can be deduced from their texts: most of the *prabandha*s are panegyrics, songs of praise offered to a deity or to a royal patron, and conclude with a characteristic signature mentioning the name of the patron and often the name of the singer-composer.

The meaning of *prabandha* may be further amplified through the connotations of two popular synonyms: *rūpaka* (having [good] form, figurative, and hence metaphoric) and *vastu* (essential substance, subject matter). In the later literature the three terms have acquired specialized meanings to represent various aspects of this genre of song. *Prabandha* is the most general term, *rūpaka* signifies its elevated and metaphoric poetic content, and *vastu* calls attention to the underlying formal structure.[15]

As a musical term *prabandha* enjoyed a useful life of more than a thousand years, with A.D. 1700 as an approximate terminus ad quem. The early years are obscure, and the term was taken over into music only when a need arose to designate a special genre of song in opposition to the rapidly developing practice of improvisation in the closing years of the first millennium A.D. Our first glimpse of the musical *prabandha* repertoire comes in the final canto of Mataṅga's *Bṛhaddeśī;* by the time of the *Saṅgītaratnākara,* Mataṅga's forty-eight have become several thousand. Even Mataṅga warns, in his opening remarks, that the *prabandha*s are infinite in number and that their formal complexities render them unknowable by those with "weak minds."[16] They raise the intriguing question of what constitutes a genre in ancient and medieval Indian music: it is not clear in the literature whether the *prabandha*s represent the entire repertoire of formalized art songs from all of India's regions, a specific genre of song types with common features, or a set of individual compositions—with somewhat elastic requirements—maintained by the oral tradition. And because the distinctions between the categories are blurred and have been rendered even more obscure by the garbled condition of many of the texts, we shall have to depend more upon common sense and broad deductions than upon detailed analysis of the many sticky questions that have still not been resolved.[17]

I shall devote some attention to the process by which the *prabandha*s were brought into conformity as a genre and were subdivided systematically into a large number of subgenres and structural types, because the process is interesting in itself and tells us a great deal about the intellectual pressures that influenced the analysis and description of musical works in medieval India. In particular I shall examine two important types of *prabandha*s—Jhombaḍa and the complex Elā subgenre—as examples of the twin processes of categorical expansion and cultural mapping that are prominent in the later musical texts.

The name *prabandha* became obsolete after the seventeenth century, when the term signified the final component of a four-part suite of pieces (for vina) known as Caturdaṇḍī: *rāga, ṭhāya, gīta,* and *prabandha*.[18] In recent times the *prabandha*s have disappeared as a genre and survive only in the form of a handful of individual song types. But while many of the earlier names have been discarded, their characteristic musical features remain clearly discernible.[19] So it is in this sense that we may regard the medieval *prabandha*s as the collective ancestors of the entire tradition of art song in later India. And although *prabandha* was never more than a convenient catchword for regulated, composed songs, it must be remembered that the distinction between strict and free forms of musical expression persists as one of the basic continuities of Indian musical thinking.

We can deduce three main characteristics of the *prabandha*s from the textual evidence: they were highly ornate, varied, and sectional compositions. They were ornate, both in their reliance upon elaborate poetic diction and in the abundance of vocal ornaments prescribed. They were varied, in that many of the songs featured a mixture of different languages, *rāgas*, *tālas*, and frequent alternation between meaningful text and meaningless syllables. And they were sectional, in that the *prabandhas* were divided into distinct formal components with many changes of pace. The element of pure phonetic play is also prominent in the repertoire, in the form of several categories of vocables, alliteration, puns, elaborate rhyme schemes, and special types of double entendre between the musical and text syllables.[20] And, among the chief characteristics, the typical signatures allow us to locate the *prabandhas* in the milieu of elaborate poetry and song that flourished in the courts and palaces of pleasure-loving princes.

To summarize this discussion and introduce the formal features of the *prabandhas*, I present a portion of Śārṅgadeva's exposition from the fourth canto of the *Saṅgītaratnākara*. The terms we have not previously encountered will be explained in § 10.3.

> The sages have declared *gāna* to be twofold, namely *nibaddha* (composed) and *anibaddha* (improvised). That which is composed of *dhātus* (sections) and *aṅgas* (limbs) is called *nibaddha*. *Ālapti*, which is free from such structural limitations, is known as *anibaddha*, and that has already been dealt with by us.[21] *Nibaddha* is now being expounded. *Nibaddha* has three names, viz., *prabandha, vastu,* and *rūpaka*. *Dhātu* is the structural element of *prabandha* and is shown to be fourfold: the first is *udgrāha*, then *melāpaka, dhruva,* and *ābhoga*.[22] . . . *Prabandhas* also consist of six *aṅgas*: *svara, biruda, pada, tena, pāṭa,* and *tāla;* like the limbs of the body, these are the integral parts of the configuration of a *prabandha*.[23]

## 10.3 Song Forms

In this section I will focus upon the nature and disposition of the *dhātus* and *aṅgas*, the formal components of the *prabandhas*. In chapter 9 I outlined the archetypal structure of five *dhātus*—an introduction, interlude, main section, prefinal interlude, and conclusion; the second, fourth, and fifth components were optional.[24] The fourth of these, *antara* (intermediate), seems never to have been much more than an occasional option, and later treatises generally agree on a set of four. Someśvara's testimony in the *Mānasollāsa* provides further details:

> *Udgrāha* should be the first division, then *melāpaka*,
> And next *dhruvaka* should occur, and then *ābhoga* is desired.

The song is [first] grasped (*udgrāhyate*), hence the name *udgrāha.*
*Melāpaka* (uniting) is a link binding together *udgrāha* and *dhruvaka.*
*Dhruvaka* is so-called because it is rendered again and again, and because it is obligatory (*dhruvatvāt*).
*Ābhoga* receives its name because it completes (*ābhoga*) the *dhruvaka.*

The following is considered to be a general rule pertaining to all the songs,
Namely, that *melāpaka* and *ābhoga* may or may not be included.

*Udgrāha* is said to consist of a pair of rhymed lines, followed by an ornamental passage,[25]
And then a passage of text describing the subject of the song.[26]
Thus there should be a pair of lines in *udgrāha,* and also in the third section.
Then *melāpaka* should be rendered, adorned with ornaments.
And next *dhruvaka* is to be performed, free from the regulation of metric *gaṇas*,[27]
And finally *ābhoga* is sung, incorporating the name of the singer.
Once *ābhoga* has been sung, the *dhruvaka* should be repeated by the performers.
Thus the *dhātus* have been declared to be the body of all the components of *tāla.*[28]

Some of the details in this passage are less than crystal clear, especially the division of text lines among the four sections, but the general scheme and the functions of the sections are clearly prescribed. Among the characteristic features, note in particular (1) the opening parallel couplet followed by a passage of playful elaboration (once again, the 2 + 1 structure we have identified elsewhere),[29] and (2) the requirement that the names of the patron and the singer-composer be worked into the song in the appropriate sections.

But is it true? Did this tidy four-part structure provide an organizing framework for all the early *prabandhas*? Probably not. I disagree with many of today's scholars in my contention that the sequence of *dhātus* must have been superimposed on the *prabandha* repertoire at a later stage in its development, perhaps around A.D. 1000, and I shall argue the case below.[30] In the earlier *Bṛhaddeśī* the formal structure of the various *prabandhas* is described only in terms of the six *aṅgas*, with their order left unspecified. The *aṅgas* are as follows:

> *pada* (word), a passage of meaningful text (a word, phrase, line, or stanza)
> *svara,* a passage of sol-fa syllables [31]
> *biruda* (or as it is often written, *viruda*), a passage of text extolling the subject of the song and including the singer's signature
> *tena,* a vocalise on the word *tena* with many repetitions
> *pāṭa,* a passage of recited syllables onomatopoeic of drum strokes
> *tāla,* a section regulated by one of the cyclical *deśī tālas* [32]

This is an interesting mixture of ingredients. Three of the six *aṅgas* (*svara, tena,* and *pāṭa*) are explorations in the domain of phonetics, a preference we have noted in other musical genres. *Svara* and *pāṭa* are still practiced in much the same form today, but *tena* requires a few words of explanation. *Tena* or *tenaka* (as it is sometimes written) is an offering of praise to Brahman as the supreme being and source of divine creation. The word *tena* is in the instrumental case of the masculine and neuter singular form of the demonstrative pronoun *tad* (this), and the literal meaning is something like "by means of This One." "This" refers to Brahmā, as in the so-called Great Sayings (Mahāvākyas): "Om tat sat" and "Tat tvam asi." [33] *Tena* is thus regarded as an auspicious utterance and a testimony to the divine source of musical sound.

The *aṅga* named *tāla* is unspecified as to text, but I am assuming that this type of rhythmic section would have been as appropriate for brilliant passages of recited syllables as for lines of metrical text. Its value as information lies mainly in the implication that some of the remaining *aṅgas* may not always have been measured in terms of one of the repetitive *deśī tālas*: either *svara* or *tena* may have been performed in a free rhythmic style, and a passage of *pada* may have been declaimed in a style of recitative that was controlled by the poetic meter. The precise length of the sections of meaningful text (*pada*) is not specified, and the ease with which this word can be confused with *pāda* ("paw," one of the four quarters of a couplet or other unit of verse) [34] renders it certain that the two words have been frequently mistaken for one another in the scribal tradition.

When one or more of these *aṅgas* is specified in a description of a song, it means only that they are present in the song; there is no implication that they appear in the order in which they are mentioned, nor are they necessarily equated with the formal divisions of a song; and an *aṅga* may appear in different locations over the course of the song. In this sense, then, the enumeration of the *aṅga*s of a particular *prabandha* is an entirely different kind of formal description from what we see in the sequence of *dhātu*s. It is more like a shopping list than a recipe, and it is easy to see how later authors and commentators may have become hopelessly entangled in their efforts to reconcile the none-too-clear descriptions found in early texts and to draw convincing correlations between the succession of *dhātu*s and the particular selection of *aṅga*s. I shall return to some of the problems involved in reconstructing this song tradition in my concluding remarks.

It is possible, though, to draw certain reasonable inferences about the role and order of *aṅga*s in the *prabandha* repertoire. The two syllabic components *svara* and *pāṭa* may appear anywhere in a song and may have served as introductions (especially *svara*), refrains, interludes, or developments of melodic material; when articulated rapidly in a fast tempo, accompanied by *tāla* and brilliant drumming, they may have provided a virtuoso conclusion to a *prabandha. Tena* appears to have been an interlude. *Tāla* is generally not the first component but may appear at any later stage in the progress of a song. *Pada* is a typical beginning gambit, in the form of an opening epigram or *śloka,* but it is also appropriate in later sections. *Biruda,* on the other hand, the section containing the dedicatory encomium and the composer's signature, seems appropriate at or near the end.

To reconstruct the form of a hypothetical *prabandha,* I shall attempt one possible correlation of the various elements. The opening *udgrāha* will begin with a metrical couplet (representing *pada*) setting out the main theme of the song and continuing with an elaboration of the melodic material in the form of *svara* syllables. For the interlude, *melāpaka,* I shall prescribe a brief passage of *tena.* The principal section, *dhruvaka,* returns to meaningful text but now under the rhythmic control of an appropriate *tāla* cycle; and because the rhythmic activity of the song is becoming more intense, it seems fruitful to follow this section with an *antara* (a prefinal) interlude with rapidly recited *pāṭa* syllables. For the conclusion, *ābhoga,* the *aṅga biruda* is clearly required if the song is to accomplish its goal as a panegyric, and I shall therefore take pains to insert the phrase "Rao made this *prabandha* to celebrate the Great King Devadatta's glorious deeds!" Because the *dhruvaka* section describes the ruler's heroic deeds and noble qualities, and also to follow Someśvara's instructions, a reprise of this section completes the performance—perhaps with more brilliant drumming than before. The song will thus have used all six *aṅga*s, which was not always necessary. I have described only one of a large number of formal possibilities, but two things can be said: this version would most certainly be an authorized version, in that it does not contradict in any way the evidence of the primary texts, and it would in my judgment be a typical example of the genre.

## 10.4 A Garland of Songs

Let us see some of the other possibilities. To give some further idea of the variety within the *prabandha* repertoire, I present a selection of five typical songs as described in the *Bṛhaddeśī,* with brief comments following the set of descriptions:

> That *prabandha* which contains two *tāla*s and also both meaningful text and recited drum syllables, in the form of a question and answer, is said to be Śukasārika (parrot and mynah bird); if its text is in the Karṇāṭa language or a mixture of languages, with words in the form of a conversation, this one should be known as Śukasārika.[35]
>
> Where a *prabandha* consisting of a garland of victory words such as "*vijaya*" and "*jaya*" is sung with victory as its purpose, let this one be known as Jayavardhana (victory-increasing).[36]
>
> Mātṛkā (measure) has been ordained as that *prabandha* which is sung by taking the *mātṛkā* syllables one by one, conjoined with whatever meaning is desired.[37]
>
> Among the *prabandha*s, Svarārtha (syllable-meaning) is properly sung with sol-fa syllables (*svara*s) that convey the desired meaning.[38]
>
> Varṇasvara (syllabic) is that *prabandha* which is composed of hand-stroke drum syllables, followed by *tenaka,* and which also includes sol-fa syllables, meaningful text, recited drum syllables, and *tenaka,* and is sung in conjunction with *tāla.*[39]

The dialogue format of Śukasārika is evident both from the description and the playful implications of the title—a conversation between two talking birds, apparently speaking different languages, underscored by different rhythmic patterns; and perhaps each is attempting to top the other with cheeky passages of nonsense syllables. It is also a reminder that teaching parrots and other birds to speak was among the sixty-four "arts" listed by Vātsyāyana in his *Kāmasūtra.*[40] The reference to the Karṇāṭa language of the Bangalore and Mysore districts is one of many geographical references to the south of India, and for this and other reasons I have postulated a southern origin for the *prabandha* tradition.

Jayavardhana is specified only in its subject matter, and the four repetitions of the keyword *jaya* in the space of a single metrical couplet lend a characteristic jingle to the verse and emphasize the fact that the description of a musical work was in itself an artistic accomplishment.

Mātṛkā and Svarārtha are closely related and are still practiced today in South India; each is based on the technique of verbal-musical punning. The sixteen *mātṛkā* syllables are the fourteen vowels, *visarga* (final aspiration), and *anusvāra* (nasal closure). The singer of Mātṛkā is instructed to work his way through this list, beginning each successive phrase with a new syllable and incorporating it skillfully into the meaning of the song. The medieval hymn "Ut queant laxis" and Oscar Hammerstein's "Do, a Deer, a Female Deer" are both examples of Svarārtha, in that each new line of text begins with one of the sol-fa syllables representing the successive steps of the musical scale.[41] But unlike the specifications for Mātṛkā, the syllables of Svarārtha may be taken in any desired sequence. It should be emphasized that these *prabandhas* are built on triple puns, in that the song requires one to (1) sing the syllable representing the name of a scale degree, (2) on that particular pitch, and (3) to join it with a verbal meaning.

The final *prabandha* of our short selection, Varṇasvara, prescribes all of the available *aṅgas* except *biruda* and includes an additional category of *hastapāṭa* (hand-stroke) drum syllables. In this case the two separate instances of *tenaka* suggest that this may be one of the rare occasions where the precise sequence of *aṅgas* has been specified by the author.

## 10.5 Expansion of the Genre

In a previous chapter we noted how a book, over the course of many centuries, was often expanded to the point where it could be more accurately described as a "library."[42] Musical genres underwent a similar process of expansion during the period covered by this study, a process that was almost inevitable given the inquiring habits and taxonomic proclivities of the medieval Indian mind. In this section I shall show how one particular species of *prabandha,* Jhombaḍa, was expanded during the period of three or four hundred years separating the *Bṛhaddeśī* and the *Saṅgītaratnākara.*

As a name, Jhombaḍa is meaningless, and most of the very few Sanskrit words that begin with the consonant *jh* are onomatopoeic—of the sound of drums, cymbals, whistling, the chirping of crickets, the buzzing of bees, and the splashing of water. This is our first clue. The passage of text describing Jhombaḍa in the *Bṛhaddeśī* is corrupt and garbled, but some sense may be garnered from this reconstruction:

> After having sung half a line twice, followed by the second half of the line [sung once], each with alliterations, and in the same

> manner the second, third, and fourth lines are sung, with rhyme at the end of each line, this *prabandha* is declared by the experts to be Jhombaḍa. The *tāla* named Kaṅkāla may not be employed in Jhombaḍa, but any of the other *deśī tāla*s may be used. Jhombaḍa is known for its variety of ornaments in the high register.[43]

The features to be noted here are the 2 + 1 structure of each text line or section, the jingling nature of the text, the specification of a forbidden *tāla,* its ornamental quality, and the reference to a high vocal register. This description may at one time have been an accurate description of a specific type of song, but in the later literature Jhombaḍa has apparently become an entire genre, with numerous compositional and performance variables. Śārṅgadeva's description is an attempt to interpret Jhombaḍa in terms of the four *dhatu*s:

> Wherein the first half of *udgrāha* is sung twice, then the second half once, optionally followed by *melāpaka* with a profusion of ornaments, and then singing *dhruva* twice and *ābhoga* once before concluding with another rendition of *dhruva,* the song is Jhombaḍa. These are the ten *tāla*s prescribed for Jhombaḍa [he continues to list the ten]. . . . Some also include Maṇṭha tāla, but it is not observed in actual practice.[44]

This description has been neatly reconciled with the quadripartite *dhātu* structure, and the 2 + 1 pattern has been incorporated twice: in the phrase structure of the introduction and once again in the two iterations of the main section followed by the conclusion. It is all very convincing and typical of the *prabandha* repertoire, and yet the suspicion arises that this later author has interpreted a specific song type in terms of a general framework that could accommodate a wide variety of songs. Much of the earlier individuality has been lost, although the specification of abundant ornamentation (which tells us little) and the prohibition of one particular *tāla* (a different one) still remain. After this general description Śārṅgadeva embarks on a lengthy *prastāra,* explaining how a grand total of 3,510 possible versions of Jhombaḍa result from a series of choices from among six variables. As a consequence of this scheme, Jhombaḍa is mapped across an entire registral, formal, metrical, and emotional universe.[45]

It works like this: Jhombaḍa is first divided into two types, one exploiting the high range, and the other the low range. The logic for this specification rests apparently upon the reference to a high register in Mataṅga's earlier description; if there is a version featuring the high range, then surely one featuring the low range is also appropriate. These two types then become nine: the high range may be manifested in each of the four *dhātus* of a four-*dhātu prabandha* and in each of the *dhātus* of a three-*dhātu prabandha;* and similarly, the low range may be manifested once in the former and once in the latter (4 + 3 + 1 + 1 = 9). The nine next become eighteen: nine with many ornaments and nine with few ornaments. The eighteen are then translated into ninety on the basis of the length of their text lines, that is, with four, five, six, seven, or eight trisyllabic *gaṇas* (twelve, fifteen, eighteen, twenty-one, or twenty-four syllables, respectively).[46] Each of the ninety may then be rendered in thirteen ways, depending upon the emotional content of the song (in terms of the nine *rasas* and combinations thereof),[47] to a total of 1,170 possibilities. The final option is added when each of the 1,170 may be composed either in prose, in verse, or a combination of both. To summarize the various options:

> 2 options of range × ? options with respect to formal structure = 9 × 2 options of ornamentation = 18 × 5 options of line length = 90 × 13 options of emotional content = 1,170 × 3 options of prosody = an aggregate of 3,510.

What are we to make of this staggering assortment of possibilities? We could, to be sure, prescribe a similar range of possibilities for a sonata-allegro: 2 basic varieties (1 in major, 1 in minor) × 12 possible keys = 24 × 2 (1 with and 1 without an introduction) = 48 × 2 (with coda, without coda) = 96, and so forth. But the fact that we do *not* think about musical forms in this way reveals something of the difference in habits of thought between India and the West. And such a process must be possible only in the case of a genre, not a distinct individual type. I suspect that Jhombaḍa was at one time so well-known in the oral tradition that it could be easily recognized by the ubiquitous "experts in song." But within a few hundred years one of two things had happened: either the type had become subject to so many variations that it had become a set of skeletal specifications for an entire genre, or (and this is the possibility that I favor) the song was no longer preserved in the oral tradition, and the later authors did what they could with the textual evidence available to them; in the process they made a creative reinterpretation of their material in terms of the field of song as they knew it. Whichever was the case (and each tells us something important about the tradition of Indian musical thought as it relates to practice) we confront the paradoxical situation that more variety exists within this single type of song than between one type and another. If there really *is* something that sets Jhombaḍa apart from all other *prabandhas*, the authors have withheld the information from their readers. And that is yet another lesson to be learned from this body of literature.

## 10.6 Cultural Mapping

The important subgenre of song known as Elā ("cardamom") provides another opportunity to see the process of categorical expansion at work; it is also instructive in the efforts of authors and compilers to "map" this species of song across the entire universe of Indian culture and civilization.[48] Mataṅga's account of the Elās occupies almost 45 percent of the *Bṛhaddeśī*'s *prabandha* canto, and it is clear from his descriptions that the Elā has already traveled a considerable distance on its journey of systematic expansion. Twenty-eight separate versions of the Elā are grouped into four primary categories, following a brief description of their general characteristics.[49] The flavor of Mataṅga's discussion and the many geographical references suggest that the Elās may have developed in the southern regions of the subcontinent, but that is nearly all that can be said about their origin. This passage may well be a later interpolation in the *Bṛhaddeśī,* not only because of the detailed treatment accorded this single subgenre, but also because of the internal evidence.[50] However, it unquestionably presents the Elās in an earlier phase of their evolution than we see in any of the other extant treatises. By the time of the *Saṅgītaratnākara* the Elās have grown to 356, with an "infinite" number of mixed varieties. This is surely a much more modest expansion than in the case of Jhombaḍa, perhaps because later authors hesitated to propose and populate additional categories beyond those laid down in the authoritative *Bṛhaddeśī.*

It is obvious from Śārṅgadeva's description that the Elā was regarded as auspicious and as one of the most important of the *prabandha*s. Its name is explained in a typical passage of *nirukta* analysis in which each of the phonetic elements signifies a member of an illustrious family group: analyzing the initial *e* as a diphthong (*ai*), *a* represents Viṣṇu, *i* his "flower-armed" son Kāmadeva, the god of love, and *la* his wife Lakṣmī. Elā is the first category of *prabandha* described in the *Saṅgītaratnākara,* and along with Jhombaḍa, it is one of the eight varieties of the important group of *sūḍa prabandha*s, to which the author devotes more than 40 percent of his *prabandha* canto.[51]

We begin with Mataṅga's account. Although most of his descriptions of the individual Elās are crystal clear and the condition of their text unimpeachable, the text in which he sets forth their general specifications is broken and difficult to decipher. This much can be said: the Elās were organized in five *pāda*s and concluded with a signature incorporating the names of the patron and the singer; they were metrical songs that featured alliteration and other forms of ornate poetic diction, with much melodic embellishment and an elevated emotional tone. Once again we find an ornamental repetition of the opening text phrase, along with a prescription of four particular *tāla*s—Maṇṭha, Dvitīya, Kaṅkāla, and Pratitāla.[52] The emphasis on poetic sound effects and the interaction of the several rhythmic layers (poetic meter, *tāla,* drumming, and the melodic rhythm) suggest a pleasingly active and complex rhythmic dimension. Before we examine Mataṅga's cultural map of the Elās, it will be useful to compare these specifications with those of two later authors.

The following description appears in the *Saṅgītasamayasāra* by the Jain author Pārśvadeva:

> In *udgrāha* there are two sections (*aṅghri*), with six metric *gaṇa*s in each line and [copious] alliteration. There should be *prayoga* (elaboration) at the end of the [first] line, followed by the phrase known as *pallava.* In the *pallava* there are no regulations pertaining to metric *gaṇa*s nor to syllables. Having then sung the second section in a contrasting manner, the third section follows—this would be the *melāpaka.* And thus one *gīta* is ordained, in three parts (*pāda*s). Next the *dhruva* is to be sung, with alliteration and containing the name of the patron, and then the *ābhoga,* with the signature of the singer. Having sung the *dhruva* yet another time, one concludes. Thus it is ordained in all the *Elās.*[53]

Pārśvadeva's description clarifies the picture to a degree, but possibly with the aid of some creative retouching. The five *pāda*s of the earlier description have now been reinterpreted in terms of the *dhātu*s: two in the introduction, one in the interlude, one in the main section, and one in the conclusion (not counting the final reprise of the main section). The length of the poetic line has now been fixed at eighteen syllables (six trisyllabic *gaṇa*s), while the alliteration and the signature remain. *Prayoga* (application) and *pallava* (sprouting, spreading out) are the new elements; they appear to be succes :ive elaborations of the preceding line of text, a general tendency of many of the *prabandha*s. Some metrical restrictions were retained in the *prayoga* but apparently discarded entirely in the *pallava.*

The cryptic phrase "one *gīta* . . . in three parts" lacks a clear referent. Does it refer to the combination of *udgrāha* and *melāpaka,* as I suspect was the author's intent, or to the song as a whole? The problem is exacerbated by the abundance of words for section, stanza, and line and by the authors' failure to use them in a consistent manner. Mataṅga's *pāda*s have become

Pārśvadeva's *aṅghri,* casting doubt upon the latter's use of *pāda.* And hence Śārṅgadeva, who was evidently familiar with either Pārśvadeva's treatise or an earlier common source, proceeds on the assumption that the three *pāda*s refer to the three internal divisions of the introductory *udgrāha.*[54] Textually the Elā is now divided into sixteen *pada*s (phrases or single lines of text, surely not single words):[55] twelve in the *udgrāha,* of which the twelfth serves optionally as *melāpaka,* three in the *dhruva,* and one in the concluding *ābhoga*—a division which swells the role of the introduction beyond any reasonable proportion to the rest of the song. These *pada*s are further divided among the three divisions of the *udgrāha* in an irregular way: five in the first, five in the second, and two in the third. By now the matter has become hopelessly confused, and Śārṅgadeva's two principal commentators come up with different solutions for the unresolved questions. While the ornamental, prosodic, emotional, and panegyric features of the Elā remain, its original formal specifications have become irretrievably lost, replaced by a newer formal scheme, and the technical terms are mired in a welter of confusion. Parallel sections of poetic text and ornamental elaborations continue to be regarded as distinctive features of the Elās, but there is no consensus on how they were rendered or at what length.

I have dwelt upon these matters as an example of the disintegration of a tradition at the hands of well-meaning compilers doing their best to resurrect an ancient song form by attempting to reconcile the cryptic remains of prior texts with the living musical practice of their own time. So long as a reliable *sampradāya* (a body of established doctrine transmitted orally from one teacher to another) survives, we can construe the texts with some confidence; but when the tradition has become broken or corrupt, the strengths of the shastric literature become its weaknesses. This phenomenon is not unique to India: in the West it led to unexpected results in the efforts of later scholars to resurrect the musical practice of ancient Greece, most notably in the rise of the Florentine opera around 1600.

The picture brightens when we come to the individual Elās. Although their general features have become muddled, their separate descriptions are a treasury of extremely detailed information, set forth with complete clarity in the final canto of the *Bṛhaddeśī,* to which we return. Here the problem is not how to interpret the information, but how far it can be trusted.

The author of the *Bṛhaddeśī,* perhaps with the help of later authors, editors, and compilers, visualized the Elā genre as a microcosm of the world of Indian song and devised an intricate scheme for their classification. The twenty-eight types are arrayed as follows: five *gaṇa* Elās, organized into strict eighteen-syllable lines constructed of specified metric *gaṇa*s;[56] four *mātrā* Elās, each with three stanzas of freely permuting groups of syllables; fourteen *varṇa* Elās, cataloged only by line length, tempo, and style of ornamentation; and finally, five *deśī* Elās, the freest category of all and featuring the distinctive sound preferences of five geographical regions: Gujarat, Karnataka, Bengal, Andhra Pradesh, and the Dravidian areas of Tamil Nadu and Kerala—all lying south of a line drawn between Ahmedabad and Calcutta. Metrics and poetic diction provide the main basis for these distinctions, but matters become much more specific within the first group—the *gaṇa* Elās.

There are actually four primary *gaṇa* Elās (for reasons that will soon become apparent), with provision for a fifth, "mixed" variety—a standard tactic in Indian musical classification. Mataṅga's descriptions of the four are so clear and so comprehensive that, by a happy accident of the textual tradition, the subsequent authors have been in virtually complete accord on their various features and cultural associations. Table 9 is a conspectus of the four main *gaṇa* Elās.[57]

Constructing sets of cultural correlations is a standard tactic of Indian musical explanation, but Mataṅga's detailed specifications for the four primary *gaṇa* Elās reveal the most systematic and far-reaching attempt at cultural mapping I have encountered in any early music treatise. The four song types are situated along a grid of exclusive possibilities, in at least ten separate aspects: a set of four complementary *tāla*s,[58] a spectrum of four culturally significant colors,[59] four goddesses with attitudes ranging from benevolence to malevolence,[60] the four major *rasa*s,[61] the four classes of society, four distinct literary styles borrowed from poetic theory, four modes of poetic diction representing regional stereotypes from the cardinal points of the compass, the four Vedas, and a complete set of permutations of the eight trisyllabic metric *gaṇa*s[62] after which the songs were named.

I have supplied adjective clusters to amplify the stylistic domains of *vṛtti* (style) and *rīti* (diction), and also an analysis of the metric structure, in which the eight *gaṇa*s have been traditionally associated with eight "elements": the moon, heaven, fire, wind, sky, sun, earth, and water.[63] I am unable to suggest any reason for the grouping of metric *gaṇa*s in lines of 5 + 1: although the classical metric treatises recognize thirty-seven different meters with lines of eighteen syllables, only two of the thirty-seven follow this pattern of 5 + 1 *gaṇa*s, and neither of them matches the pattern of any of the four *gaṇa* Elās.[64] So the conclusion seems inescapable that these songs have been assigned for obscure reasons to an entirely artificial category of meter, one that was neither practiced by the major Sanskrit poets nor recognized by the experts in poetic theory.

Certain additional observations suggest further ways in which the four

Table 9 The *Gaṇa* Elās as a Cultural Map of Medieval Indian Song

| | Nādāvatī | Haṁsāvatī | Nandāvatī | Bhadrāvatī |
|---|---|---|---|---|
| *Rāga* | Ṭakka | Hindola | Mālavakaiśika | Kakubha |
| *Tāla* | Manṭha: 10 possibilities | Dvitīya: DDL | Pratitāla: LLDD or LDD | Kaṅkāla: LLLLDD |
| Color | White | Red | Yellow | Black |
| Goddess | Sarasvatī | Durgā | Indrāṇī | Vārāhī |
| *Rasa* | Śṛṅgāra: the erotic | Raudra: the angry | Vīra: the heroic | Bībhatsa: the disgusting |
| Class | *Brāhmaṇa:* the priestly class | *Kṣatriya:* the warrior class | *Vaiśya:* the merchant class | *Śūdra:* the menial class |
| Style (*vṛtti*) | Kaiśikī: feminine, graceful, soft, delicate, sweet | Ārabhaṭī: masculine, fiery, warlike, powerful, proud | Sāttvatī: a weak form of Ārabhaṭī, brave, generous | Bhāratī: soft, tender, pleading |
| Diction (*rīti*) | Pāñcālī (north): moderate, leaning toward Vaidarbhī | Lāṭī (west): also moderate, leaning toward Gauḍī | Gauḍī (east): bold, ornate, vigorous | Vaidarbhī (south): simple, sweet, graceful |
| Region | Western Ganges basin | Gujarat | Bengal and Orissa | Deccan plateau |
| Veda | *Ṛg* | *Yajur* | *Sāma* | *Atharva* |
| Meter[a] (*gaṇas*) | 5 *candra* (*bhā*) + 1 *svar* (*na*) | 5 *anala* (*rā*) + 1 *vāyu* (*sa*) | 5 *ambara* (*tā*) + 1 *mārtaṇḍa* (*ja*) | 5 *bhūmi* (*mā*) + 1 *jala* (*ya*) |
| = | 5 × GLL plus 1 × LLL } 18 | 5 × GLG plus 1 × LLG } 18 | 5 × GGL plus 1 × LGL } 18 | 5 × GGG plus 1 × LGG } 18 |
| Other properties | Elaborate ornamentation, *nāda* in each stanza | An even gait, uses both *nāda* and meaningful text | Light ornaments, similar in many respects to Nādāvatī | Each stanza uses *mūrcchanā* and *dhvani* |

[a]See (29) and the accompanying explanation of the metric *gaṇas*; D = *druta* (shortest), L = *laghu* (short), G = *guru* (long).

song types were differentiated, particularly with respect to ornamentation (always an important matter) and *nāda,* which I take here to refer to the *ālāpana* style of beginning. In the present context I interpret the paired terms *mūrcchanā* and *dhvani* to mean little more than a variety of ornaments and "sounds." The four *rāga*s appear to have been chosen because of their popularity, and their specifications do not reveal any systematic scheme of organization—which would admittedly be extremely difficult to suggest in the realm of musical pitch.[65] The four *tāla*s, on the other hand, may in their earlier form have provided as complete a set of permutations as we see in the metric structure.[66]

Traces of two other organizing patterns are superimposed upon the geographical and cultural map: (1) a left-to-right progression from greater to lesser and from pure to impure, as in the sequence of colors, *rasa*s, and social classes; and (2) an important opposition between the "strong-masculine" mean pairing of Haṁsāvatī-Nandāvatī and the "weak-feminine" extreme pairing of Nādāvatī-Bhadrāvatī.[67] This opposition is conveyed not only in such obvious aspects as style, diction, and *rasa* but also by the cultural connotations of the colors and the attitudes of the four goddesses. All of this is a valuable guide to many of the questions of style to be explored in chapter 11, although some of the evidence is contradictory: the observation that Nandāvatī "is similar in many respects to *Nādāvatī*" is ludicrous in view of the sharp contrasts in virtually every domain and can be based on nothing more than the similarity of their names; and the correlation of the beloved Vaidarbhī style with the sentiment of disgust and the menial class is scarcely credible.

But putting these contradictions aside, how believable is the system as a whole? Not very. It is all too good to be true, and indeed it contradicts the very idea of genre to outline a single subgenre of song with such mutually exclusive properties and cultural connotations. As I wrote in an earlier article, "it must be regarded as an ingenious exercise in classification, not an impartial account of contemporary practice."[68] The authors and compilers of the *Bṛhaddeśī* must have seen their roles as something more than faithful recorders of tradition. They had already begun the process of grouping and classifying the songs, of identifying common properties and forms, of thinking of the Elās as both a genre and a repertoire of distinct types, and of affirming this repertoire as a representative selection of all the characteristics that were typical of India's various regions.

The result was a stylistic map of India in idealized form—from the ancient Gauḍī people of Bengal, down to the Draviḍas of the southern tip of the subcontinent, and as far west as the Lāṭas of Gujarat along the Arabian Sea.

The map is full of regional stereotypes, rhyming preferences, and the sound properties of the various provincial languages; but the map as a whole is probably about as accurate as the assumption that all New Yorkers are rude, all Texans larger than life, and all southern Californians out of touch with reality.[69] After several hundred years Śārṅgadeva found no reason to dispute the details of the scheme, so it has come down as a powerful stylistic legacy from the past, fortified and made more authoritative by the endorsements of later authors. The Elās, and especially the four upon which I have focused, provided a platform from which one could survey the entire world of Indian music and its cultural coordinates; although this survey yields unreliable information about the specific details of the songs sung in a bygone era, it nevertheless provides a treasury of valuable information about the cultural milieu within which the *prabandha*s flourished.

## 10.7 The Theory and Practice of Song

What has been learned from this survey of medieval Indian song forms and their components? A great deal about the many choices, the compositional options and performance variables, but relatively little about what differentiates one particular song or type from another. It would appear that the theorists of Indian music were relatively uninterested in defining their objects by means of differences, or by necessary and sufficient conditions. Why is this so?

The issue, I think, hinges on cultural attitudes toward freedom and constraints. What, for example, was gained by ruling out one particular *tāla* in the case of Jhombaḍa? The prohibition of one *tāla* may seem like a trivial and unnecessary constraint, but from an Indian point of view, it actually liberates by permitting all others. It has never been suggested that all the available options will be equally pleasing—that choice has been left for practice to decide. A moral that seems to arise from this body of literature is that more is to be lost by contradiction of the shastric precepts than is to be gained by observing them, an attitude that may strike many Western readers as consistent with what I referred to earlier as a "passive-negative" attitude.[70]

But the strategy of noncontradiction is not to be viewed simply as playing it safe, as treading a middle path and avoiding error. It is, I believe, typical of Indian musical thinking that their formalized songs were defined more in terms of allowable variables than of obligatory requirements, and therefore many songs were described in such similar terms that it is hard to identify their unique features. Perhaps this is an inescapable consequence of the habit of defining by characteristic features (*lakṣaṇa*s), in which any object to be defined will display a large number of appropriate features, many of which are shared with other similar objects. Against this background it is easier to recognize contradictions than to assemble the precise tally of appropriate features.

But there is more to the matter than this. In the world of medieval Indian song, it is simply not important to label a song or a type of song as something deeply individual: it is the options that provide the individuality, whether planned or spontaneous—the choice of *rāga, tāla,* tempo, ornaments, and the like—and the theorists saw little need to carve out sharply etched profiles for the songs, preferring instead to depict them in broad strokes. Indeed, all their abundance of categories and subcategories—the pure, deviant, and mixed species of song—seem more like an attempt to construct a columbarium, an elaborate edifice of individual niches within which any culturally authorized version will find its proper place. This is not done because practice has demonstrated each of the categories and now requires the theoretical seal of approval; it is done in order to permit practice to develop along valid lines. Clearly it is also a statement that right composition and right performance can occur only within guidelines already set forth in the *śāstra*s. It seems inevitable that later shastric authorities would make every attempt to determine the full intent of the guidelines when they survived in cryptic or incomplete form, and also to demonstrate to the fullest how great a range of valid options was available. This, it seems to me, is what the process of categorical expansion was intended to secure.

The evolution of Indian music has been guided not only by the shastric literature but also by *sampradāya,* defined by the commentator Kallinātha as "instruction through the tradition of teacher and taught which, even though not explicitly propounded in *śāstra* with regard to a particular subject-matter, is yet endorsed by it (in principle) and is not against it."[71] This body of oral doctrine, as I have pointed out, is one of the reasons for the laconic style of the *śāstra*s, as well as a valuable supplement to their teachings; within such a *sampradāya* there may have been no need to record the individual details of one song or another, so long as the range of variables remained within authorized guidelines. And later amplifications of earlier *śāstra*s may be implicit recognitions of many equally valid *sampradāya*s.

The response of *śāstra* to these conditions has been to resort to its traditional tools, and particularly to the practice of reflexive explanation—clarifying and amplifying the precepts of earlier texts by means of the more elaborate accounts found in later *śāstra*s. The argument goes something like this: the earlier authority found it unnecessary to mention many of the details, even the most important ones, because the musical tradition he was describing was well-known in practice; but by the time of the later author, the tradition was in danger of becoming lost, so it became necessary to set down the full details for readers who might not have the opportunity to experience it in living practice. There is something to this line of argument, but there is danger in pursuing it too enthusiastically—in assuming that all later *śāstra*s are in harmony with earlier ones—even, in Kallinātha's words, with respect to matters not explicitly propounded, such as the *dhātu*s of the *prabandha*s.

The sticky question is whether new material can be said to exist "in principle" in an earlier text: sometimes it does, and sometimes it doesn't. The formal scheme represented by the *dhātu*s existed in the musical tradition long before the *prabandha*s were described as a genre, but locating a proper precedent for them in *śāstra* is another matter. The ideal authority would be Mataṅga, but I can find no way that the present text of the *Bṛhaddeśī* authorizes this structure. But so long as the two formal traditions can be reconciled without contradiction, as Śārṅgadeva has done, that is all that matters. And it may not be possible to make sense of early Indian music without the aid of this powerful tool.

In descriptions of the *prabandha*s the boundaries between the idea of music as a whole, a genre, a repertoire, a type, a model, and an individual song have been deliberately left indistinct. This says much about the ontology of music within Indian culture. The concept of a "musical work" has not been developed as precisely as it has in the West, perhaps because of the Indian orientation toward process and the traditional hesitancy to reify that process in any one specific form. The most powerful ontological tool available to the early musical scholars was the concept of features, and to a certain extent they were indifferent about whether the features described were those of an individual work, the model on which it was built, a characteristic type, an entire genre, or *gīta* itself. We will probably never know the individual features of the many *prabandha*s enumerated in the classical treatises, but most likely these have altered over the years, as has been the case with the specifications of many of the *rāga*s mentioned in the shastric literature. It is more realistic to think of the *prabandha*s as flexible frameworks, within which a selection from among the valid options would insure right performance—so long as it was consistent with contemporary developments in musical practice.

When we attempt to reconstruct the milieu of medieval Indian song, three additional questions come to mind: What, if any, was the role of the accompaniment? Why has there been no mention of the drone? And were all of the *prabandhas* solo songs? I shall attempt to answer each of these in turn.

An accompaniment of some sort must be assumed, but the various *prabandha* cantos are silent on this important question. It is clear from many discussions of musical instruments that theirs was primarily an accompanying role, but the focus is upon hand technique, instrument construction, and the details of the musical system, not upon the specific way in which the instruments relate to a soloist in performance. Most of the useful evidence comes from discussions of drumming, but it is not very precise.[72] At the more affluent princely courts, it seems likely that the *prabandhas* would often have been performed with instrumental accompaniment, with both flute and vina available as melodic partners. Surely this would have involved imitations of the preceding phrase, occasional octave doublings, simultaneous variations (heterophony), interludes, transitions between phrases, and continuations of the vocal line during pauses for breath, memory lapses, and the like. With all the emphasis on *tāla,* we may also postulate the use of the *tāla* cymbals and an active drum counterpoint, sometimes supporting and sometimes opposing the controlling rhythms of the *tāla.* A large assortment of other percussion instruments must also have been available.

It is quite certain that the continuous drone had not yet become a standard feature of Indian music, and it would not become one until as late as the fifteenth or sixteenth century.[73] It stretches belief that such an important practice, with so many symbolic connotations and so many practical consequences for musical style, would have been ignored by all the principal authors. It is also clear that the modal system prevailing as late as the thirteenth century had not yet settled upon *sa* as a universal fundamental tone, and hence the choice of a particular ground tone for a drone would not have the same musical meaning it now holds.

Medieval accounts of musical ensembles mention the theater ensemble, which may have been featured in court performances of *prabandhas* and which usually included several singers. With this in mind, I suggest that the practice of singing in precise unison, along with occasional choral refrains, may well have been an important part of the song tradition. We cannot assume a repertoire confined to solo songs. What can be said is that none of the major treatises provides definite information on this point.

After these arguments on theoretical issues of authority, transmission, genre, and ontology, it is appropriate to conclude with a brief recapitulation of the characteristic features of Indian song, then and now: the focus on text content, precise enunciation, poetic sound effects, metrical complexity, multiple rhythmic layers, modular formal structure (in formal compositions), the phonetic play of vocables, the typical dedicatory signature, the mixture of free and strict elements, a heavy emphasis on introductory procedures, great variety, the specification of *rāga* (as melodic model) and *tāla* for any individual rendering, and above all, a florid melody with many different levels of ornamentation.[4]

# ELEVEN
# STYLE

> The ten meritorious qualities (*guṇas*) of singing are these: color, abundance, ornament, clarity, distinctness, loudness, smoothness, evenness, great delicacy, and sweetness. . . . These are the faults (*doṣas*) of singing: lack of confidence, timidity, excitement, lack of clarity, nasality, a shrill tone, a tone produced too high in the head or in the wrong register, a discordant sound, tastelessness, interruptions, rough enunciation, confusion, inability to keep time.
>
> *Nāradīyaśikṣā* 1.3.1, 11–12[1]

> Those who are possessed of [good] character, high birth, quiet behaviour and learning, are desirous of fame and virtue, impartial, advanced in age, proficient in all the six limbs of drama,[2] alert, honest, unaffected by passion, expert in playing the four kinds of musical instruments,[3] acquainted with costuming and make-up, the rules of dialect, the four kinds of histrionic representation,[4] grammar, prosody, and the various [other] *śāstras*, are very virtuous, expert in different arts and crafts, and have fine discrimination of the sentiments (*rasas*) and the [emotional] states—the foregoing are ideal spectators of the drama.
>
> Bharata, *Nāṭyaśāstra* 27:49–52[5]

## 11.1 Introduction

Style is an elusive concept. Some preliminary observations will help to indicate in what sense this useful and common term may be profitably applied to the music and musical teachings of early India.

I shall be emphasizing the composite and correlative aspects of style. Any prescription or description of style will involve clusters of individual features, but it is the package that we recognize and identify as *a* style. As Leonard Meyer has pointed out, style is essentially a matter of choices made within a set of constraints.[6] In the case of India, both the constraints and the guidelines for making correct choices have been explicitly stated and maintained with exceptional rigor in the oral tradition and the shastric literature.

There is no precise Sanskrit equivalent to the English word *style,* but there are three major contenders: *vṛtti* (mode of dramatic presentation, style of recitation, affective content), *rīti* (literary manner, poetic diction), and *gīti* (text setting, style in the sense of a specific correlation of the musical elements). All three mean about the same thing—a characteristic manner of turning (*vṛtti*), going (*rīti*), or singing (*gīti*)—and they exemplify the type of bland words so common and so useful in musical discourse, as in the Latin *modus* and *tropus,* the Greek *agoge,* and the Sanskrit *gati* (gait).[7] I introduced the concepts of *vṛtti* and *rīti* in chapter 10, and more systematic analysis will follow below. These two terms have had a long history in Indian poetic theory, and it will become evident that musical style and literary style have developed along parallel tracks with respect to both affective content and technical vocabulary.

This final chapter has been reserved for all those things that give Indian music its distinctive flavor and personality, its qualitative and affective properties, and the system of values on which Indian musical practice still depends. If this were one of the early musical *śāstra*s, the title of this chapter would be *prakīrṇa* (miscellany).[8] And I shall indeed present a collection of miscellaneous topics: (1) what the proper musical roles of men and women are, or ought to be; (2) what it takes to become an expert singer, drummer, teacher, or spectator (see the epigraph from *BN*); (3) the desirable and undesirable qualities in various fields of musical accomplishment; (4) what makes a sound beautiful or ugly, especially vocal sound (see the epigraph from *NS*); (5) the proper relationship between music and text, and the stylistic preferences of ancient India's diverse geographical regions; (6) an analysis of the ornamental and microtonal domains for a glimpse of the subtle transitions and shadings that provide much of the flavor of a music; (7) the cultural repertoire of moods and emotions and the clues by which they are communicated in composition and performance; and (8) a final assembly of the abiding values of Indian music. If these eight topics do not occupy quite the same territory as Western notions of style—the baroque concerto style, Beethoven's style, Heifetz's style—it means that these familiar concepts may need to be adjusted if they are to tell us what we want and need to know about style in the Indian musical tradition.

No one will question the musical importance of these matters, but some may argue that it is inappropriate to consider them in examining an objective tradition of music and musical thought—perhaps because they are too intangible, because the ground is too slippery, or because the qualitative and affective dimensions of music are too personal and subjective to permit valid generalization or verification. Perhaps, the argument continues, such things ought to be reserved for "tradition" to teach, a practice that seems to work well enough in the West. But does it? Analysts of nineteenth-century music can happily apply the same method to a Verdi aria and a song by Hugo Wolf, not seeing on the printed page the characteristic portamenti between certain notes that are a hallmark of the tradition of Italian opera, or the more forceful enunciation of the German consonants.

These are samples of what a tradition teaches, often well below the surface of consciousness. But in India the oral tradition has not had to carry the burden of instruction alone. The musicological literature is value laden, and values have been prescribed forcefully, not presented in an objective and impartial way. Not that terminology elsewhere is value free: on the contrary, we make implicit statements of value whenever we refer to the "dominant" note of the scale, or (in French) to the seventh degree of the scale as the *notte sensible.*[9] It is simply that the values of Indian music are more overt than those of the West, and perhaps for this reason they have remained more stable.

The evidence I will present will show the Indian system of musical values to be virtually complete by the time of the earliest musical treatises, and will show that these cultural ideals have exerted continuous pressures over the last two thousand years in prescribing right behavior and appropriate response and in shaping musical expectations. If this sounds like an Orwellian form of mind control, remember that this is precisely what any traditional society does in creating and maintaining the unwritten script by which its members live. The difference lies in the antiquity and literacy of Indian civilization; the legacy of musical and other artistic values has become progressively refined and reinforced as a result of a continuous tradition of scholarly examination and philosophical analysis. Within a musical society that looks first to the past for guidance, making valid music is an affirmation of one's cultural identity. This does not rule out change, but it sets limits to the pace and amount of change.

One implication of the English word *style* is utterly foreign to the Indian view: the distinction between style (as the form of expression) and the content that is being expressed—manner as opposed to matter. Although it is legitimate to discuss a poem, play, or song from either of these viewpoints, as in the common pairing of *vṛtti* and *rīti* in literary criticism, the Indian position accepts no possibility for opposition or disharmony between the content of the artistic message and the means for delivering that message. Style as *what* and style as *how* are one and the same, and the twin conventions of *what* and *how* have become so deeply and inseparably embedded in Indian experience that music—in all its complexity and with its entire content—occupies a familiar field in a known aesthetic universe, in which feeling, thought, and reaction have become as much a part of a person's inheritance as the color of his eyes and the other details of his genetic and cultural programming.

In the search for those clusters of particular qualities that jointly define the conventional repertoire of styles, it is appropriate to begin with the most profound and inescapable of all cultural divisions—the distinction between woman and man.

## 11.2 Gender

> *Śrutir mātā, layaḥ pitā.*
>
> Melody is the mother [of music], rhythm the father.
>
> Traditional saying[10]

> Some of the ancients called rhythm masculine and melos feminine, for melos is without actuality and formless, . . . while rhythm molds and regularly moves melos, presenting an expression of active making on the basis of the thing made.
>
> Aristides Quintilianus, *De musica* 1.19[11]

It is scarcely a new insight to point out that gender stereotypes are all around us. Yet somehow those we encounter in other cultures or in bodies of foreign literature strike us with greater impact than those we meet every day. Anyone who works with non-Western musical cultures must admit the prevalence and persistence of such attitudes and must come to terms with them if any accurate assessment of a culture is to be made. But it comes as an even greater shock when we come upon equally explicit statements about male and female roles in ancient Western literature, our own literature. The above statements speak for themselves, one an ancient Sanskrit proverb that is often quoted today, and the other from an important music treatise by the fourth-century Hellenistic author Aristides Quintilianus. There is no need to explain the similarities on the basis of cultural diffusion—they could arise, and have arisen, anywhere in the world.

It is necessary to dwell upon these matters if we are to establish a proper basis for their influence on musical thought and the delineation of artistic style. The female-male dichotomy in early Indian literature is no trivial list of duties and behavioral characteristics; on the contrary, it reaches down into the deepest strata of human experience and consciousness. The female element in the quotations was conceived as the passive source of inchoate matter and pure potentiality, the male as the active form maker and disciplining agent. Both ancient Indian and Greek cultures, by means of these and similar statements, testify to a primal concept of the origin of music: as the irrational, unstructured expression of human passion, the type of lamentation or keening that is regarded as women's music in many parts of the world, before it is brought under rational control and given form by the disciplining power of rhythm. The sophisticated language masks a primitive creation narrative.

It is also useful to point out that many world cultures have refined the concept of gender to a point far beyond any cultural instruction in duties and behavior as reckoned on the basis of natural gender. Especially, but not only, in Asian cultures, the conventional qualities of femininity and masculinity have been treated as abstractions and as natures intermingled in various combinations in different persons and types of persons. The early Greeks recognized what they termed a "medial" nature between the extremes of masculinity and femininity, but the Asian approach is even subtler. Once a tradition had managed to codify a distinctive repertoire of expressive qualities separating into well-defined feminine and masculine styles, the resulting styles became material for exploitation by performers of either sex and eventually led to such practices as the crossover roles of the Noh and Kabuki theaters of Japan.[12] Indian authors were clearly aware of tendencies toward the opposite sex, and there is early evidence that both men and women played roles of the opposite gender; but this never developed into an important practice in the classical theater. One minor but interesting exception is the long tradition of hermaphrodite mummery in the popular Indian theater, encouraged perhaps by the example of Śiva's androgynous nature and the influence of the concept of mutable form. I shall suggest that the conventional qualities of masculine and feminine expression found their way into the many lists of *guṇa*s and *doṣa*s and eventually became commonplaces in the Indian artistic universe. In this line of thinking, which is evident as early as the *Nāṭyaśāstra,* the ability to represent the qualities of the opposite sex in a convincing manner was regarded as an *alaṅkāra* (ornament), as opposed to the representation of the qualities appropriate to one's own nature.

To bring out the two stereotypes as fully as possible, I present a pair of lists assembled from the early musical *śāstra*s and the literature of dramatic criticism. Masculinity, as embodied in the Ārabhaṭī (bold) style and the archetypal masculine quality of *ojas* (fiery vital energy), was associated with an elevated style of declamation, vehemence, haughty pride, bodily strength, vigor, brightness, passion, and the sentiments of heroism, anger, and disgust. Femininity, as captured in the typical Kaiśikī (delicate) style, was associated with song, sweetness, youth, beauty, grace, charm, gentle movements, and amorous expression. The major *rasa* labeled Śṛṅgāra (the erotic sentiment) sums up these quintessential feminine qualities and will be discussed in some detail in a later section.[13]

The masculine and feminine natures outlined elsewhere in Aristides' treatise are predictably similar to the above clusters of expressive qualities.[14] Masculinity is active, representing the dry and fiery elements of nature, the thymic (intense) part of the irrational soul, harshness, somberness, strength, ruggedness, anger, and courage, and is associated with Mercury, the Sun, Mars, and Saturn. In contrast, femininity is passive, representing the earth and wetness, the epithymetic (the indulgent and pleasure loving) part of the irrational soul, gentleness, adornment, weakness, weeping, pain, and pleasure, and is associated with the Moon, Venus, and Jupiter. But not all of these cosmic coordinates work out smoothly in the course of Aristides' complex argument, and he too is forced to resort to mixed and medial natures to reconcile his contradictions.

All of this is to provide a frame of reference for the many qualitative aspects of musical style I shall explore, and I shall return to the Ārabhaṭī and Kaiśikī styles for additional analysis and examples of their correlations with other categories of style. In the list of typical masculine and feminine qualities, the opposition of the declamatory male and the songlike female style merits some comment. It has something to do with the priestly role of men in Vedic culture and men's custodianship of the tradition of sacred chant; from this it is not difficult to understand why the characteristic style of the male theater singer is described as *pāṭhya* (recitation) and that of the female singer as *gāna* (song). The basic principle was that the various utterances of the play were to be differentiated as sharply as possible on the basis of status, gender, language, and style: the deities and noble male characters recited in Sanskrit, while women and inferior characters spoke in Prakrit. From this it follows that the main function of the male singer (apart, of course, from his participation in any ensemble music) was to declaim the Sanskrit verses that are sprinkled throughout the formal text of the play, while the female singer was responsible for the many Prakrit plot songs, the *dhruvās*.

One patronizing *śloka* from the *Nāṭyaśāstra* suggests that female and male performers were measured against a different standard:

> There may be allowed a loss of proper note in women's songs and the playing of musical instruments, but this will not be sweet to the ear in the case of men. (Bharata, *Nāṭyaśāstra* 32:511)[15]

And in another verse that has often been cited, we find a general statement on preferences and taste:

> *Ācārya*s (master teachers) desire evenness [above all], while learned pandits prefer the [distinct] separation of words; women desire sweetness in music, whereas others (that is, men) prefer loudness. (Nārada, *Nāradīyaśikṣā* 1.3.14)[16]

## 11.3 Qualifications

One of the main topics of the shastric literature is the list of qualifications, the *lakṣaṇa*s, or distinguishing marks, of a proper singer, instrumentalist, teacher, student, or indeed of any profession or station in the social hierarchy—from king and priest to courtesan and burglar.[17] These job descriptions were often expounded at several levels of accomplishment, typically the ideal, the average, and the unworthy. Much can be learned from these lists with respect to style, although the qualifications often seem more like a mark to aim at than a measure of actual achievement. Bharata's prescription for the ideal spectator of a play, quoted at the beginning of this chapter, appears to be quite out of reach for most of us, but the author adds a brief postscript that not only tempers the seemingly unreasonable expectations but also tells us something about the rigidity of the prevailing system of social classes:

> All these various qualities are not known to exist in one single spectator. And because objects of knowledge are so numerous and the span of life is so brief, the inferior ones in an assembly which consists of the superior, the middling, and the inferior members cannot be expected to appreciate the performance of the superior ones. (Bharata, *Nāṭyaśāstra* 27:55–56)[18]

These comments help to explain some of the apparent contradictions in the statements of qualifications and the clusters of values we shall encounter. The prescriptions are presented as cultural shopping lists with which one is to identify as far as possible, not as specifications to be met in every detail. The traditional Indian value clusters were intended to serve as descriptions of an entire cultural universe of feeling, thought, and action, and within this universe each individual expression (superior or inferior, competent or incompetent) finds its proper place. And it is this understanding that requires Indian aesthetic theory to provide for qualities that other cultural traditions prefer to ignore.

Against this background, it will be useful to examine some sample sets of qualifications. Śārṅgadeva's job description for the master composer runs as follows:

> The best *vāggeyakāra* (one who composes both music and text) is [possessed] of these excellences: a thorough knowledge of grammar, proficiency in lexicography, knowledge of prosody, proficiency in the use of figures of speech, comprehension of aesthetic delight (*rasa*) as related to emotive states of being (*bhāva*), intelligent familiarity with local custom, knowledge of many languages, proficiency in the scientific theories of fine arts, expert knowledge of the three musical arts,[19] a lovely tone quality, good knowledge of tempo, *tāla,* and *kalā,*[20] discrimination of different intonations, a versatile genius, a beautiful musical rendering, acquaintance with regional (*deśi*) *rāga*s, cleverness in conversation for victory in debates, freedom from like and dislike, aesthetic sensitivity, a sense of propriety in expression and new melodic forms, knowledge of another's mind, maturity in the understanding of different [varieties of] *prabandha*s, the ability to compose songs at short notice, the expert knowledge of composing different verbal structures for particular melodic forms, maturity in producing *gamaka*s pervading the three registers, proficiency in [the presentation of] different [forms of] *ālāpa,* and attention (*avadhāna*). (Śārṅgadeva, *Saṅgītaratnākara* 3.3–9)[21]

Among the many requirements—which make it clear that the composer was also expected to be a competent performer—we might expect the earnest demands for expertise in so many fields of learning and also perhaps the practical admonition to know his audience, their expectations, and how their minds work. What is quintessentially Indian in this long list of qualifications is the demand that the composer be quick-witted—disputatious in argument and proficient in improvising both music and text—and also the requirement that he be free from both "like and dislike." In the latter requirement we see the influence of the *Bhagavadgītā*'s doctrine of nonattachment: the job of the composer is not to produce what brings particular delight to him; it is to produce what brings general delight to everyone. If he is able to surmount his personal desires and dislikes, the whole universe of art is open to him.

Continuing with Śārṅgadeva's exposition, we learn that a composer can earn no more than an average rating if his poetic skill fails to measure up to his musical ability, or if he fails to master the technical complexities of the *prabandha* genre. But the composer whose gift for verse surpasses his musical skill receives an even lower grade. And with respect to the balance between poetic substance and structure, he who excels in communicating the poetic content ranks higher than the poet with a knack for constructing elegant forms. At the bottom of the heap, a special place of dishonor is set aside for the composer who fits his own texts to another's music: he is dismissed contemptuously as a *kuṭṭikāra*—a "grinder," or as we might say, a hack.[22]

The qualifications for an ideal singer are no less demanding. I shall reserve full discussion of vocal quality for a later section, but the following passage will serve as a general introduction to the special qualifications expected of a master vocalist:

> The vocal experts declare him to be the best among the singers who has an attractive voice of good tone quality, who is an adept in initiating and finishing [a *rāga*]; who is well versed in [singing] the *rāgas*, . . . an expert in singing *prabandhas* and [who] knows the essentials of the different forms of *ālapti*;[23] who commands a natural access to the *gamakas* arising from all the [three] registers, and a self-controlled voice; who is aware of musical time, and is attentive and indefatigable, who knows the pure and deviant versions of compositions, who is an expert in all the specific intonations (*kāku*), who commands the movement of different shadings (*sthāyas*); who is free of all blemishes, given to regular exercise, mindful of tempo, versatile and retentive; who has the capacity to hold his breath while singing with great passion and to arrest the attention of the audience, and who excels in the exposition of *rāga* and belongs to a good tradition. (Śārṅgadeva, *Saṅgītaratnākara* 3.13c–18b)[24]

Once again the description demands both knowledge and practical skill in a large number of typical vocal accomplishments: a wide range, good vocal quality (we shall soon see what this entails), a well-disciplined technique, agility in ornament, with good breath control, personality projection, an ample memory, and sense enough to keep one's body in good physical condition. Naturally the singer must be equally adept in formal compositions and in developing a *rāga*. The list of qualifications extends into the musical microstructure with the topics *kāku* and *sthāya,* two categories that include subtle ways of shading and coloring the vocal inflections.[25] Two other qualities stand out in the list: here, as in the list of a composer's qualifications, the author has prescribed "attention" (*avadhāna*). There is a substantial body of literature on the concept of *avadhāna* as an aesthetic issue, and the presence of this word on the list is something more than a trivial reminder to maintain one's concentration. And finally, the reference to "a good tradition" invokes the important concept of *sampradāya* and reminds us that the full power of an oral tradition was expected to amplify the precepts of the *śāstra*s, informing each specific performance decision of the singer.

From the continuation of this passage we learn of a division of singers into five types: one skilled in teaching others, one who has no style of his own but imitates another's, one who becomes caught up in the underlying emotion, one who is a born entertainer and crowd pleaser, and one who has the special ability to arouse emotion in his listeners. Typically, female singers are treated separately, and in this case, in addition to the qualities required of a male singer, a few additional requirements are laid down: sweetness of manner, cleverness, and once again, youth and beauty.[26]

At some point in the vast shastric literature we can find a set of requirements for any profession and any station in the social fabric of ancient Indian culture. These descriptions proliferate in the theater treatises, but chiefly because the mission of the drama was to represent an entire universe in all its diversity. For this purpose the playwright and producer had to draw upon the full spectrum of the classified hierarchy of Indian society. The essential point here is that this proclivity for taxonomic classification was not a special property of the ancient Indian system of musical values; it had become an intellectual habit and an instinctive way of viewing the world. It reflects also a strong pedagogical impulse to improve human society, to reaffirm its development along traditional lines, and to set forth ideal models for the young to imitate. The result was a vivid picture of the world as they knew it, with some creative retouching to nudge human behavior in the direction of a more ideal society. Many of these creative touches no doubt became self-fulfilling prophecies. The pressures created by this way of thinking are largely responsible for the persistence of Indian attitudes toward human nature, human abilities, and human society over more than two thousand years.

## 11.4 *Guṇas* and *Doṣas*

The many lists of *guṇa*s and *doṣa*s (merits and demerits) in Sanskrit treatises provide more explicit evidence for the system of musical values. I have given a preliminary account of their relationship to the concepts of *lakṣaṇa*s (distinguishing marks) and *alaṅkāra*s (ornaments) in chapter 6.[27] Now it is time to examine these lists in greater detail. One typical set of *guṇa*s and *doṣa*s, from Nārada's phonetic manual, appears at the beginning of this chapter, and others will follow.

A *doṣa* is a defect, a sin of either omission or commission. *Doṣa*s can arise from the absence of some required quality, an excess or deficiency in the amount of a certain quality, or the presence of something inappropriate to the artist's purpose, or they may simply be errors. A *guṇa* is a quality, in the sense of a *good* quality—an attribute that brings merit in any evaluation. The literal meaning of *guṇa* as a "strand" (of a rope) invokes automatic associations with the influential Sāṅkhya doctrine of the three intertwined strands of reality: illumination (*sattva*), passion (*rajas*), and darkness (*tamas*).[28] This is a useful reminder, because although *guṇa*s and *doṣa*s of a composition or performance sometimes arise from a single blemish or (more rarely) some particularly impressive moment, it is more often the case that they represent pervading qualities noted in an artistic evaluation. The first step in any artistic endeavor is to avoid *doṣa*s at all costs; this is necessary if one is to escape censure and demonstrate competency, but it is not enough—to merit praise, one must also demonstrate the appropriate *guṇa*s.

The twin concepts of *guṇa*s and *doṣa*s are not indigenous to music. They appear in logical and rhetorical treatises from the early Christian era as well as in other literary genres whose aim was to insure the preservation and correct interpretation of the sacred texts; they were subsequently brought to a high state of development in the literature of poetic theory (*alaṅkāra-śāstra*) between the seventh and eleventh centuries.[29] The value system of music, with respect to both composition and performance, is thus based upon the value system of poetry, which is itself dependent on an earlier set of values pertaining to verbal communication in general and the correct recitation of the Vedic texts. As a result, each statement of musical value is located within a wide semantic field of verbal associations.

There is a lot of room for argument in such matters, and the various literary critics found much on which they could disagree. We find attempts to suggest that the *guṇa*s and *doṣa*s were linked as opposing qualities, but none of the authors managed to make the scheme work out to his satisfaction. Similarly, there was no agreement on whether a good quality is the presence of something positive or the absence of a bad quality. On the other hand, it was generally agreed that these qualities were not absolutes, and that a *doṣa* in one particular context might be a *guṇa* in another. There were *doṣa*s of sound (*śabdadoṣa*s), of meaning (*arthadoṣa*s), and of emotional tone (*rasadoṣa*s), and a *doṣa* might be partial, total, or "mixed." The broadest definition of a *doṣa* is anything that stands in the way of achieving one's purpose: a grammatical error, a metrical flaw, an inappropriate word, incorrect word order (which was seen as a particularly serious defect), a clumsy figure of speech, failure to convey one's meaning clearly, vulgarity, redundancy, a logical flaw, a word or phrase with inappropriate connotations, or the inclusion of qualities suggesting a style other than the one the poet has selected. Many of these transfer readily to musical contexts, and it is often not clear whether the author has in mind a poetic text, a recitation of such a text, a musical setting of that text, or a musical rendition. In the end it makes little difference: each of the *guṇa*s and *doṣa*s is represented by a keyword, an index term for a cluster of values and poetic associations; and these keywords combine to define the features of the various styles with clarity and precision.

To show how parallel the lists of *guṇa*s and *dosa*s tend to become in the later musicological literature, I present two passages from the *Saṅgītaratnākara:* the first is the list of ten *padaprāṇa*s, the ten "vital breaths" of poetry; the second is the list of the ten *guṇa*s of song (*gīta*).[30]

> Evenness, sweetness, intensity, beauty, brightness, orderly composition, refinement, great delicacy, clarity, [and] vigor.
>
> Clarity, abundance, distinctness, great delicacy, ornament, evenness, passion, smoothness, good articulation, and sweetness.

In the original Sanskrit several of these terms are identical, while others are common synonyms. *Guṇa*s and *doṣa*s tend to come in sets of ten, partly because ten is a significant number in Indian culture, and also because this is about the number of bi- and trisyllabic words that can be squeezed into a couplet of sixteen-syllable lines. *Mādhurya* (sweetness) and *sukumāra* (great delicacy), the typical feminine qualities, are seldom absent from the lists and are usually balanced by typical masculine qualities such as *ojas* (vigor) and *dīpta* (brilliance). A somewhat different set of qualities reflects the concerns voiced by the authors of the phonetic treatises with reference to Vedic recitation: evenness (*sama* or *samāna*), clarity (*prasanna, prasāda,* or *vyakta*), and good articulation (*vikṛṣṭa*). The attempt here is to reconcile the conflicting tendencies toward distinct articulation and musical continuity in enunciating a text. Recall the verse quoted in §11.2 and its reference to the conflicting preferences of *ācārya*s and pandits. The problem of precise articulation was particularly acute because of the highly inflected nature of the Sanskrit language and the practice of running words together (sandhi); in a social milieu in which incorrect articulation could result in cosmic disorder and divine retribution, there is every reason to lay stress upon precise enunciation.[31] And at the same time, it is easy to go too far in this zeal for separating the syllables of the text without some reminder of the need for continuity and the music of the poetic line.

Other terms reveal important Indian preferences: *ślakṣṇa* (smooth, polished, slippery), *sāndra* (oily, dense), and *snigdha* (creamy, unctuous, smooth) all suggest the ideal of fluid continuity that has been so prized in Indian aesthetics, often explained by the familiar analogy of the different grades of continuity provided by drops of water, oil, honey, and clarified butter. Still other terms apply both to composition and to performance: *samāhita* (orderly composition), *alaṅkṛta* (adorned), and *agrāmya* (refined).

Translating these terms with single keywords is always a risky exercise, because each covers a wide semantic range; and it is certain that sometimes their meanings became attenuated to bland terms such as *gentle, smooth,* or especially, *beautiful.* But the root meanings can yield valuable clues. The sweetness of *mādhurya,* for example, is the cloying sweetness of honey (*madhu*), and the delicacy of *sukumāra* is the delicacy of youth (*kumāra*) in its vulnerability to disease.[32] And the brilliance of *dīpta* is the blazing of fire. We can readily see why it is often used in tandem with, or as a substitute for, the quality of *ojas* (vigor), which Monier-Williams defines as "the principle of vital warmth and action throughout the body."[33] And we can also see why it is associated with the fiery *guṇa* of *rajas*—the chief characteristic of a *rājā,*—and the sharp-pointed flame of *tejas* (glory, splendor). Thus, in a subconscious way, the delicate sweetness of a vulnerable young girl and the fiery passion and vigorous intensity of a man have become embedded in the system of poetic and musical values.

Another popular set of terms plays on the concept of color: *rakta* (reddened, impassioned), *surakta* (well reddened, deeply colored), and *vicitra* (variegated, multicolored) all suggest poetic enhancement through the use of color. This is easy enough to understand in a land with a limited and subdued color spectrum in the natural surroundings, a concept of decoration as an essential component of beauty, a sophisticated tradition of spices in cuisine, and well-established cultural preferences for bright, vivid colors. We find references to color (*citra*) and multicolor (*vicitra*) that mean little more than "variety," but this too appears to be an attenuation of their original meaning.

Still other terms refer to qualities or levels of style: *agrāmya,* for example, means "not as in a village" (*grāma*), and hence "refined". There are also references to the type of noble, elevated, or exalted style described by Longinus—the *audārya* (lofty, noble, generous) and *udātta* (elevated) styles, usually mentioned in connection with the masculine qualities.[34]

We can sometimes learn more from the lists of *doṣa*s, which are often described with biting humor and vivid analogies. This chapter began with a passage that concludes with Nārada's fourteen *doṣa*s of song, all of them faults of performance, not composition. Some are faults of character, others are deficiencies of musical talent, and still others are defects of vocal production or enunciation. Śārṅgadeva's list is shorter: "Deviation from standard practice, deviation from the *śāstra*s, poor intonation, inability to keep time, redundancy, deviation from art, errors in order or meaning, vulgarity, uncertainty—these are the ten errors of song."[35] This is only one of many passages in the *Saṅgītaratnākara* with a set of *doṣa*s pertaining to singing; it appears in the *prabandha* canto and is a mixture of defects in performance, composition, and style. In another passage from the *prakīrṇa* canto we read of twenty-five different types of singers who deserve censure, including singers whose limbs shake, whose facial veins stand out, who close their eyes in ecstasy, who are insensitive to the emotional content of a song, or whose voice is extremely limited in range.[36] I am reserving discussion of vocal quality for §11.5.

*Guṇa*s and *doṣa*s are not always the fault of the poet, composer, or performer. In chapter 27 of the *Nāṭyaśāstra,* Bharata enumerates a number of blemishes in performance that arise from the gods or the actions of an enemy.[37] Obviously a fire in the theater, a stroke of lightning, or a stampede of elephants must be attributed to an act of god, whereas jealous or bribed spectators who talk loudly, applaud in the wrong places, or throw chips of cow dung at the performers belong in a different category. Earthquakes and meteors, on the other hand, are regarded as portents, not signs of divine displeasure. The author continues to enumerate a large number of self-made errors to be charged against the actors, musicians, or the producer, of which I shall mention only one: an actor who goes so far as to recite the benedictory verse to the wrong god is deserving of particular censure. In general, we may say that the *doṣa*s arise from a loss of control (fear, trembling, excitement), ignorance (of tradition, of the *śāstra*s, of the musical system), a lack of talent, or specific defects in sound production, the subject to which we now turn.

## 11.5 The Qualities of Musical Sound

What are the special properties of musical sound that cause us to describe it as beautiful? Anyone who has heard a sampling of folk songs and folk singers from around the world will realize that there can be no universal answer. The quality of sound must be among the most distinctive features of any musical tradition, and at the same time one of the most resistant to verbal description. Musical speculation in the West has generally avoided this issue, preferring instead to focus upon the formal and quantitative aspects of music, which can be described with greater precision. One of the most characteristic features of early Indian musical thought is the great attention devoted to the correct production of musical sound—especially vocal sound. I know of no other tradition of world music in which vocal quality has been prescribed in as consistent and systematic a manner over such a long period of time. This gives us some confidence that the sounds we hear today cannot be too different from those heard two thousand years ago. My discussion will build upon some of the gender stereotypes, the qualifications, and the *guṇa*s and *doṣa*s set forth in the previous pages.

In earlier chapters I cited various passages containing prescriptions for good vocal quality and style in Vedic recitation and chanting,[38] but our concern now is to identify the values of song. One of the oldest and most authoritative of these lists of the properties of good and bad vocal sound appears in chapter 32 of the *Nāṭyaśāstra,* where Bharata specifies six *guṇa*s and five *doṣas.*[39] We find the same qualities in many subsequent lists of *guṇa*s and *doṣa*s, and there is no evidence to suggest that this set of preferences has altered in any substantial way since Bharata's day.

The six meritorious qualities are as follows: a good voice should be, first of all, loud (*śrāvaka*)—which may mean little more than "audible"; it should also be compact (*ghana,* dense), oily (*snigdha*), sweet (*madhura*), attentive (*avadhānavān,* careful), and "splendid in the three registers" (*tristhānaśobhī*). The five flaws in a voice include gurgling with phlegm and being unsteady, bitten off with the teeth, harsh like the cawing of a crow, or nasal.

We have encountered many of these terms before, and both *snigdha* and *madhura* could refer to either style or the sound itself. The combination of *ghana, snigdha,* and *madhura* makes it clear that ideal vocal sound should be full and concentrated, oily smooth, and honey sweet. This is a vivid description of the kind of opulent vocal sound that would not be inappropriate in the bel canto style of nineteenth-century Italian opera, were it not for the implication that good vocal quality should be *senza vibrato.* It is important to point out that vibrato and tremolo are never included in the lists of vocal *guṇa*s: tonal undulations of this sort, when recognized, are considered as ornaments and are clearly defined under the general heading of *kampita* (shaking).[40] What actually happens, of course, is a much more complex matter. Of the two final *guṇa*s, the admonition to be attentive seems merely to be a reminder to the singer not to become careless in his sound production; and the reference to a voice that should display excellence in "the three registers" is an indication that it is important to have a wide range with a well-produced tone throughout. The so-called three registers do not necessarily refer to complete octaves, but it seems evident that a singer with a range smaller than two full octaves would have been considered handicapped.

The five flaws do not require as much comment. But note once again the influence of the *doṣa*s mentioned again and again in the phonetic manuals, especially in the warnings against "bitten" and nasal sounds. The early phoneticians seem to have recognized that to be aware of a particular articulatory process or source of resonance is often to emphasize it, and correct recitation of the sounds of Sanskrit demanded that the speaker or chanter distinguish clearly between dental consonants and those pronounced elsewhere in the mouth. He was also required to distinguish unequivocally between the five different nasal consonants, which, as Allen remarks, must have produced some regressive effect upon the quality of the preceding vowels.[41] Many observers hear a great deal of nasality in Indian singing today (as I do), so we can understand why the early phonetic authorities advised against overdoing it. Likewise the requirement for the precise enunciation of consonants may have invited a biting kind of articulation, and most of the *śikṣā*s quote approvingly the simile of a tigress who carries her cubs delicately by the scruff of their neck, being careful neither to bite them nor to hold them so loosely between her teeth that they might fall.[42]

The Āyurvedic tradition attributes vocal quality to the predominance of one of the three bodily humors (known also as *doṣa*s, in the sense of an imbalance): wind (*vāta*), bile (*pitta*), and phlegm (*kapha*). We return to a passage from Mataṅga's *Bṛhaddeśī* in which the sage cites the testimony of Tumburu:

> Other authorities contend that sound is fourfold, divided into the following varieties: excess of air, excess of bile, excess of phlegm, and balance of the humours. And thus Tumburu said: "Dry, higher sound is acknowledged to be *vātaja* (born of air) by the experts. Sound that is deep, solid, and continuous is to be known as *pittaja* (born of bile), while sound that is unctuous, delicate, and sweet should be known as *kaphaja* (born of phlegm). The sound resulting from a harmonious balance of these three qualities is declared to be *sannipātaja* (born of conjunction).[43]

In his account of the four types of vocal production Tumburu has resorted to several of the traditional *guṇa*s: the sound characterized by a predominance of phlegm, for example, is described by the three familiar keywords *snigdha, sukumāra,* and *madhura.* It is clear that none of the four types is to be regarded as defective.

But it remained for Śārṅgadeva to compile the most penetrating analysis of vocal sound found in any of the early musical *śāstra*s, and we shall continue with some material from his *prakīrna* canto.[44] In beginning his discussion of the ideal vocal sound, the scholarly Āyurvedic physician endorsed the concept of the three humors, enumerating thirty different mixtures of the various qualities. His basic types tally fairly well with those of Tumburu except for the voice resulting from a predominance of wind, which Śārṅgadeva describes as hollow, harsh, high, and coarse (*sthūla*)—scarcely a favorable description. The voice arising from a predominance of bile is described with Tumburu's three keywords, but with the further specification that the voice must be clear in all the three registers, perhaps as a reminder that a singer with a naturally deep voice cannot expect to rumble around in the low register and avoid exploring the upper regions. In theory, the best voice is one that combines the best properties of all three humors—on the assumption that the more the *guṇa*s, the better the voice.

All of this provides the theoretical basis for a list of *śabdaguṇa*s (*guṇa*s of sound), including four of those mentioned by Bharata and now elaborated to a set of fifteen. The ideal voice should be pure, sweet, high, shining in the three registers, soothing, rich, tender, strong, loud, inspiring pathos, compact, creamy, oily, colored, and lustrous. The eight blemishes are a voice that is dry, cracking, hollow, hoarse like the cawing of a crow, colorless, strained in the high and low registers, fragile, and broken like the braying of a donkey or the grunting of a camel.

We seem to have gotten away from the concerns voiced by the authors of the phonetic manuals; few of the later lists of the *guṇa*s and *doṣa*s of singing focus upon the character traits of the performer or his style of enunciation. And while I have emphasized the properties of vocal tone, it is clear that it is good sound in general that is being described. Vocal sound and vocal style have provided the model for instrumental sound and style since early times, and the *guṇa*s of instrumental playing draw upon the same vocabulary and set of values as do the *guṇa*s of singing. The *guṇa*s of flute playing, for example, are as follows: good flute tone should be creamy, compact, pleasing, clear, abundant, graceful, soft, resonant, spanning the three registers, loud, sweet, and "attentive."[45]

What can be deduced from these lists? The obvious contradictions provide evidence that a performer was not expected to demonstrate the entire list of *guṇa*s, any more than a single performer would display all the *doṣa*s. The faults perhaps stand out more clearly than some of the meritorious qualities: a sound that is dry, harsh, faint, thin, strained, hollow, or pallid would win no praise. The property of sweetness, which is considered so basic to good tone by all the authorities, is perhaps the hardest to define, but it is certain that the oral tradition would have left no doubt in anyone's mind as to the ideal of *mādhurya.* The image of a lustrous, well-focused, full, and rich sound with smooth liquid continuity comes through clearly in the ancient descriptions, with a supple, even, and brilliant command of a very wide range. When we add to this the traditional preferences for distinct articulation of the text and agility in ornament, the result is an accurate portrait of Indian singing as it is heard and admired today, and as it must have been heard and admired in Bharata's day. As in many other aspects of Indian life, the idea of musical sound was a cultural achievement—rooted in the phonetic observations of early language scholars, drawing upon familiar stereotypes and expressive preferences, and molded over centuries into a distinctive concept of vocal tone whose properties were then extended to encompass all the sounds of music.

## 11.6 Style as a Composite

I turn now to more complex issues, in an attempt to pin down the elusive idea of style.[46] I shall suggest in this section that Indian styles have been defined by clusters of expressive qualities, and that the value system of music came under the influence of the value system of poetic and dramatic theory at an early date, developing thereafter along a parallel course. One obvious advantage of this association was the availability of a ready-made lexicon of descriptors with precise cultural meanings. It was argued that all modalities of artistic communication—the visible and the audible, the determinate and the indeterminate—drew upon a common stock of emotions, responses, and preferences. On the strength of this argument, it was understood that a musician's job was to compose and perform music in a manner appropriate to each expressive nuance of the poetic text and its histrionic representation.

This brings up a difficult question, which I shall pose here and then defer for further consideration in a later section: Is music in the Indian tradition an independent, autonomous art, or is it a dependent art—dependent in the sense that it must rely on context and associations with the other arts to produce an emotional response and to determine the conditions on which that response will be based?[47] The question is reminiscent of the arguments for and against absolute music that preoccupied European critics for most of the nineteenth century. Indian authors have from time to time become caught up in similar arguments, but never with the same intensity and single-mindedness. The evidence to follow will suggest that style in any of the arts of India is defined by a field of cultural associations—a field involving coordinates of gender, geography, social class, emotional expression, and many other qualities—and that these associations, which arise so naturally in traditional societies, communicate on both conscious and subconscious levels of awareness. The result is a sure sense of expressive manner and of what that manner means within the parent culture.

Authors of the first millennium A.D. and their immediate successors devised a successful strategy for delineating musical style. Their solution was to classify and project the various expressive qualities across what I have referred to as a cultural map. As a basis for further analysis, I reproduce relevant portions of Mataṅga's map of the four *gaṇa* Elās (table 10).[48]

The advantages and disadvantages of such a scheme are obvious: it provides a colorful assortment of emotional, social, regional, and gender stereotypes for the poet to frame in appropriate language and the composer to match with suitable musical expression. On the other hand, it is next to impossible to combine all these cultural tags into one comprehensive arrangement without some logical contradictions.[49] If there are any natural pairings in poetic theory, they are the associations between (1) the delicate Kaiśikī *vṛtti* and the simple Vaidarbhī *rīti,* and (2) the vehement Ārabhatī *vṛtti* and the bold Gauḍī *rīti;* but Mataṅga has worked out a more complicated solution in his grid of styles. In his scheme we find a pair of "strong" styles (the mean pair) and a pair of "weak" styles (the extreme pair), enhanced by popular cultural generalizations such as the blunt, plain speech of westerners, the extravagant eloquence of the Bengalis, and the mood of wistful yearning for the sweetness and simplicity of a bygone golden age in the ancient kingdom of Vidarbha. Or taking examples from Shakespeare and reading from left to right, the nobility and submissiveness of Hermione, the fiery bravado of Hotspur, the crackjaw ranting of Petruchio, and the simple humility of Cordelia.

Some further background on the evolution of the concepts of *vṛtti* and *rīti* may help us to appreciate this arrangement and understand its musical consequences.[50] In the controversial chapter 22 of the *Nāṭyaśāstra,* Bharata outlined four modes of dramatic expression—the four *vṛtti*s—in an enigmatic passage that has become the subject of intense interpretation. His chapter was not fully understood by later authors, and while they generally retained his terms, they gradually evolved a somewhat different version of the original scheme. Bharata's four *vṛtti*s are: the graceful style (Kaiśikī), the forceful style (Ārabhaṭī), the verbal style (Bhāratī), and a fourth style (Sāttvatī) whose meaning is not entirely clear; Keith identifies it as the "grand style" and Raghavan labels it the "style of action."[51] What Bharata seems to have had in mind is feminine expression, masculine expression,

Table 10 Coordinates of Style from Mataṅga's *Bṛhaddeśī*

| | | | | |
|---|---|---|---|---|
| *Rasa* | Śṛṅgāra: the erotic | Raudra: the angry | Vīra: the heroic | Bībhatsa: the disgusting |
| Class | *Brāhmaṇa:* the priestly class | *Kṣatriya:* the warrior class | *Vaiśya:* the merchant class | *Śūdra:* the menial class |
| Style (*vṛtti*) | Kaiśikī: feminine, graceful, soft, delicate, sweet | Ārabhaṭī: masculine, fiery, warlike, powerful, proud | Sāttvatī: a weak form of Ārabhaṭī, brave, generous | Bhāratī: soft, tender, pleading |
| Diction (*rīti*) | Pāñcālī (north): moderate, leaning toward Vaidarbhī | Lāṭī (west): also moderate, leaning toward Gauḍī | Gauḍī (east): bold, ornate, vigorous | Vaidarbhī (south): simple, sweet, graceful |
| Region | Western Ganges basin | Gujarat | Bengal and Orissa | Deccan plateau |

verbal expression, and—on a somewhat different plane—an elevated style of dramatic expression that drew upon elaborate poetic diction and other "strong" qualities. It is tempting to sum up this arrangement in a neat formula (woman + man + text + action), but this would be too superficial.

Elsewhere in the literature we find references to the four *vṛtti*s as "atmospheres" or dramatic "tendencies." But whatever they are, it is apparent that Bharata has constructed a scheme with more than one dimension and has posed major problems for his interpreters. The clearest element is the familiar opposition of female and male stereotypes—Kaiśikī and Ārabhaṭī—with reference to the idea content of the drama, the emotional mood and tone, the physical actions, and the poetic language. On another level, Bhāratī pertains specifically to the composition and recitation of the text, and especially to the text of the preliminary ceremonies. What little can be deduced from Bharata's description of the Sāttvatī style—without relying entirely on his interpreters—is that it featured elevated poetic diction, focused on the elements of conflict and action in the thematic content of the play, and was associated with the *rasa*s of heroism, anger, and wonder. Because of its strong qualities, it seems inevitable that Sāttvatī would become associated with the masculine expression of Ārabhaṭī, leaving Bhāratī to gravitate in the direction of Kaiśikī, the Indian version of the "eternal feminine" style. Bharata's concept of the four dramatic *vṛtti*s may be further amplified by the correlations he drew between them and the four Vedas: the verbal Bhāratī with the *Ṛgveda,* Sāttvatī with the *Yajurveda* (with reference to the physical actions performed during a sacrifice), Kaiśikī with the *Sāmaveda* (a more graceful and musical style of recitation), and Ārabhaṭī with the magical spells and incantations of the *Atharvaveda.*[52]

By the time of the *Bṛhaddeśī,* somewhere around the ninth or tenth century, the traditional four *vṛtti*s had become detached from their earlier meanings in the theory of drama and taken up into poetic theory. The names remain the same, but Bhāratī and Sāttvatī have been converted into intermediate stages between the extremes of Kaiśikī on the one hand and Ārabhaṭī on the other. The adjective clusters I supply in table 10 will serve to summarize the expressive qualities attributed to each of the four *vṛtti*s in this phase of their evolution. In another important development, they have now become associated with the standard set of four *rīti*s—four conventional styles of poetic diction that were based on the regional stereotypes mentioned above. In his valuable account of the convoluted history of this idea, V. Raghavan states:

> The history of the concept of Rīti has three stages: first, when it was a living geographical mode of literary criticism; second,

> when it lost the geographical association and came to be stereotyped and standardized with reference to subject; and third, its re-interpretation by Kuntaka, the only Sanskrit Ālaṃkārika, who with his fine literary instinct and originality as evidenced on many other lines also, related the Rīti to the character of the poet and displaced the old Rīti-s by new ones.[53]

My discussion will not follow the concept of *rīti* beyond the second of these stages, and the stereotypical forms we encounter in discussions of medieval Indian song will reinforce Raghavan's conclusions. In the evolution of the concept, the number of *rīti*s increased from the original two (Vaidarbhī and Gauḍī) to as many as six; the two intermediate styles of Pāñcālī and Lāṭī fill out the standard set of four. If certain of the correlations in table 10 seem less than inevitable, it should be remembered that Sanskrit literary critics proposed several other schemes for linking the *vṛtti*s and *rīti*s, but without arriving at a consensus.[54]

It should be clear that "style"—qua poetic diction—is the joint product of matters of both sound and sense: in addition to their expressive qualities, the *rīti*s were distinguished from one another by such things as *prāsa* (alliteration, assonance, and other sound effects), *śleṣa* (double meanings), *samāsa* (compounding, one of the distinctive features of Sanskrit), and the numerous figures of thought and speech. Vaidarbhī and Gauḍī, the two extreme styles, differ in virtually every aspect: the former was characterized by simplicity of manner, sweetness, restraint in sound effects, direct discourse, few if any compounds, no more than light ornaments, and an avoidance of the more elaborate figures of speech; in contrast, the latter featured an elevated tone, a bold style, jingling alliterations and other similar sound effects, circumlocutions, long compounds strung together, extravagant ornamentation, hyperbolic language, and an assortment of elaborate metaphors and similes. Inevitably the tags "good" and "bad" were hung upon the two styles by generations of critics who idealized the Vaidarbhī style for its romantic associations and rejected the Gauḍī for its excesses. But this had little impact upon poetic and musical practice, where the two styles seemed to represent equally attractive poles of artistic expression. Because the remaining *rīti*s tend to gravitate toward one or another of these two poles, I am inclined to endorse Raghavan's conclusion that there are but two basic styles—one simple and one elevated.[55]

But the matter is not quite that simple. I have pointed out that the principal literary critics were not always in total agreement, and the several expressive styles may not have been as mutually exclusive as my discussion suggests. The seventh-century author Dandin's list of the ten *guṇas* of the beloved Vaidarbhī style will allow us to explore some of the contradictions:[56]

| | |
|---|---|
| *ojas:* vigor | *mādhurya:* sweetness |
| *udāratva:* elevation | *samādhi:* metaphorical expression |
| *prasāda:* clarity | *samatā:* homogeneity of sounds |
| *arthavyakti:* explicit content | *saukumārya:* great delicacy |
| *kānti:* beauty | *śleṣa:* the correlation of sound and sense |

This list corresponds in every particular to Bharata's list of the ten *guṇas* of poetry (in chapter 17 of the *Nāṭyaśāstra*), and because Bharata's aim was not to describe any one style but to identify the finest characteristics of verse in general, his *guṇas* include both simple and elevated qualities.[57] So for Daṇḍin to suggest, as he did, that the Gauḍī style was devoid of these qualities, or featured the opposite qualities, makes little sense. What this means is that the evolving field of literary criticism was in the process of sorting out the characteristic features of good poetry, so they could then be distributed in some sensible arrangement among the set of conventional styles, which they intended to be expandable. But as time went by and the number of styles grew, it required virtuoso efforts to reconcile the contradictions that arose and to maintain the integrity of the scheme the authors were attempting to construct. The critics had inherited a rich lexicon of expressive terms—in particular the array of typically feminine and masculine qualities and their poetic correlates. Their aim was to delineate a set of distinct semantic fields, each defined with precision by its *guṇas, alaṅkāras*, expressive manner, emotive content, and special use of language. It is interesting to note that a popular synonym for *rīti* was *mārga* (path), a term we have examined in connection with the temporal structure of music.[58] Here, as elsewhere in early Indian culture, we find lexical bonds between one field and another. Under the influence of a borrowed set of descriptors, and also because of the traditional associations between musical style and poetic text, the aesthetic domain of music gradually came to reflect the value systems of drama and poetry.

To explore some related developments, I return to Bharata and Dattila for their solutions to the problem of defining musical style. The term *vṛtti* is used in the same sense in both treatises, with special reference to the balance between the vocal and instrumental parts. As we shall see, however, their distinctions were elaborated by later authors into something approaching a general theory of musical style.

Dattila defines the three *vṛttis* with his usual brevity, adding that he would refrain from further detail lest his work become too lengthy: "The [three] vṛttis are: dakṣiṇā, vṛtti and citrā. In them the method is [as follows]:

in the first, song (gīta) dominates, in the second both [song and] instrumental playing (vādyaṃ) are balanced equally, and in the third, instrumental playing dominates."[59]

This passage illustrates one of the typical and confusing tactics of Indian musical discourse—using the same word for both a general category and a subcategory. As for the other terms, *dakṣiṇā* is a word loaded with "good" connotations—the right side (the side of respect), the south (in the sense of the "good old days"), capable, straightforward—so it is almost inescapable that the *dakṣiṇā vṛtti* would become linked with the simple Vaidarbhī manner, the delicate Kaiśikī literary style, and the erotic Śṛṅgāra *rasa.*[60] *Citrā* (colored) suggests the exuberant Gauḍī manner, the vehement Ārabhaṭī style, and their cognate *rasa*s. But the strategy for delineating style in music was evidently hard to reconcile with the various stylistic grids devised by the literary critics. The goal here was apparently to identify two contrasting extreme styles and then to add a third, "moderate" style midway between the two extremes. We shall soon see how this plan was implemented with the help of correlations from several musical dimensions.

I have outlined one of Bharata's contributions to the theory of musical style in chapter 5, again with reference to the relationship between vocal and instrumental performance: *tattva* (duplication), *anugata* (similarity), and *ogha* (independence).[61] The other stylistic concept in this earliest generation of musical texts involves text setting (*gīti*), this time (perhaps because of the literary associations) divided into a set of four and distinguished from one another by the syllabic content of the text and the amount of word repetition permitted in the musical setting, as shown at the bottom of table 11.[62] The stylistic correlations of the earliest layer of musical texts were gradually elaborated by later authors until a comprehensive set of three distinct musical styles emerged. Table 11 displays one such synthesis of the various stylistic coordinates, compiled on the basis of Śārṅgadeva's text in the sixth canto of the *Saṅgītaratnākara.*[63]

In addition to the predictable moderate style (in which the attempt to split the distance between the two extremes is generally successful, with the obvious exception of the category of *yati*), the table reveals clear equivalents to the two extreme styles of the literary tradition: (1) *dakṣiṇā,* an expressive vocal style, closely replicated by a discreet accompaniment, appropriate perhaps for the opening section of a *dhrupad* composition, with an extremely slow pulse, drawn-out syllables of text, extended phrases, widely spaced *tāla* gestures, and expressive deviations from the beat; and (2) *citrā,* an exciting virtuoso style based upon instrumental technique and freely accompanied, with a persistent fast tempo, many word rep-

Table 11 Coordinates of Musical Style in the *Saṅgītaratnākara*

| | | | |
|---|---|---|---|
| *Vṛtti:* style | *Citrā:* instrumental dominates | *Vṛtti:* equal blend | *Dakṣiṇā:* song dominates |
| *Gata:* "gait" | *Ogha:* independent | *Anugata:* similar | *Tattva:* duplicating |
| *Laya:* tempo | *Druta:* fast | *Madhya:* moderate | *Vilambita:* slow |
| *Yati:* progression of tempo | *Samā:* even | *Srotogatā:* accelerating | *Gopucchā:* decelerating |
| *Pāṇi:* phasing | *Avapāṇi:* accenting after the beat | *Samapāṇi:* metrical accents | *Uparipāṇi:* anticipating the beat |
| State of *tāla* | Syllabic | Twofold | Fourfold |
| *Mārga:* density of events | *Citra* (*kalā*s of 2 *mātrā*s) | *Vārttika* (*kalā*s of 4 *mātrā*s) | *Dakṣiṇa* (*kalā*s of 8 *mātrā*s) |
| *Gīti:* text setting | *Māgadhī* and *ardhamāgadhī:* many word repetitions | *Sambhāvitā:* words with many short syllables | *Pṛthulā:* rich in long syllables |

etitions, short phrases, frequent syncopations, irregular accents, and a general mood of athleticism.

But like the earlier sets of stylistic coordinates, all this is much too good to be true. The full stylistic range of Indian music can no more be defined by tables of coordinates than the full range of Sanskrit poetry can be defined by the stylistic qualities I have presented. It is perhaps better to think of these as tendencies, atmospheres, and expressive fields that fall naturally into certain broad configurations. I have also identified a number of strategies for the delineation of style: gender stereotypes, *guṇa*s and *doṣa*s, cultural mapping, lexical borrowings and the associative use of terms, grouping by culturally significant numbers, and arraying a mean between two extremes. Style does not happen—it is *made;* and the evolution of a style or set of styles must be among the most creative accomplishments of a musical culture. The process will become clearer after a survey of the decorative and emotional domains of early Indian musical thought.

## 11.7 Levels of Ornamentation

> In song, the formation of a tonal shade (*chāyā*) that emerges from a *svara*'s own *śruti* and proceeds to another *śruti* is known as a *gamaka.*
>
> Pārśvadeva, *Saṅgītasamayasāra* 1.47[64]

In this section we continue the exploration of the ornamental aspects of music, with particular emphasis on the microstructure of melody and the conceptual means that were devised to describe its intricate contours. I shall focus here on several categories of musical decoration that are finer than the relatively gross notions of *varṇa* (the melodic shape of a word or other phonetic unit) and *alaṅkāra* (ornament in the most general sense, but chiefly [1] an ornament in the abstract, or [2] a composed ornament—as opposed to one arising in performance).[65] This is slippery territory for musical documentation, and we would expect the oral tradition to have been more successful in demonstrating the various types and levels of ornament—as of course it must have been.

Ornamentation has seldom been a major issue in Western musical speculation, except in certain periods—as, for example, the seventeenth and early eighteenth centuries in Europe—when the confluence of a highly ornamental tradition, an emphasis on improvisation and virtuoso performance, and the cultivation of variation technique as one of the primary modes of musical organization stimulated a large number of treatises designed to help the composer notate his ideas properly and to teach the performer how to interpret the notation and its special signs. The same three conditions have prevailed throughout the history of Indian music, and Indian authors have responded in much the same way in their efforts to clarify the various decorative concepts and describe them verbally. The difference lies in their preference for oral notations.

Attempting to describe the melodic microstructure with words is like trying to swat a mosquito with a machine gun. The briefest glimpse of a three-dimensional melogram or any other equally sophisticated visual display of a musical segment reveals a microuniverse that is all but inaccessible to conscious intention, physical control, or aural perception—a universe of minute contours, peaks, and periodicities so complex that their correlation with the gross musical events (the individual notes) is in no way obvious.[66] It must be recorded among the major achievements of early musicians that so much progress was made in observing these subtleties of performance and capturing so many levels and dimensions of the ornamental substructure.

I shall distinguish between four specific levels of decoration: *gamaka,* which I have described as a melodic transition (although various contours were later classified under this heading); *kampita,* a shake or quiver; *kāku,* inflection in the special sense of "tone of voice," a concept borrowed from the theory of dramatic recitation; and *sthāya,* a complex and multidimensional concept that encompassed both qualitative and quantitative "shadings" of the melodic line. Although each of these terms appears here and there in the early musicological literature, it remained for later authors to sort out the concepts. Not until the *Saṅgītaratnākara* do we find the ornamental structure of music organized into a single comprehensive intellectual scheme: before this time, the twin concepts of *varṇa* and *alaṅkāra* were deemed sufficient to fix the decorative structure of the *gāndharva* repertoire, and little was said about the more flexible domain of song.

In Dattila's list of thirteen *alaṅkāra*s, we see at least three distinct types: (1) small melodic shapes that would remain within the domain of *alaṅkāra,* (2) transitive contours that would later be conceived as *gamaka*s, and (3) three types of "quiver."[67] The idea of *gamaka* (literally, "a going") as a category separate from the *alaṅkāra*s is foreign to the theater tradition of Bharata and was first mentioned by Mataṅga in connection with the *prabandha* genre, where the term clearly refers to a performed vocal ornament.[68] The words *kampa* and *kampita* appear frequently throughout the phonetic manuals and the other Vedāṅgas, both in the sense of a *doṣa* (if the shaking is excessive) and as a technical term in Vedic recitation; but the concept of tremor is not set apart as a specific category of musical ornament.[69] *Kāku* was a contribution of the theater tradition, and virtually all subsequent references to vocal inflection in dramatic recitation have been based on Bharata's exposition in chapter 19 of the *Nāṭyaśāstra*—which although it obviously involves both the pitch and timing of recitation, is not specifically concerned with singing.[70] *Sthāya* (or *ṭhāya*), as far as I am aware, was first expounded systematically by Śārṅgadeva.[71]

This is an interesting combination of the insights of several different streams of musical thought: some obvious categories of musical shape that were considered to be common property, vocal ornaments as performed in various styles of regional song, chant ornaments, and conventions of dramatic declamation. Recall my earlier suggestion that pitch consciousness developed gradually, with spoken and sung sounds not completely differentiated from one another, and that asserting even this limited degree of control over the microstructure of melody required the joint observations of several professions concerned with prescribing how the spoken, chanted, and sung sounds were to be properly rendered. It was, in effect, a committee project, and the members of that committee included priests, scientists of language, theater directors, singers, and musicologists—not to mention the royal patrons who financed their efforts.

Pārśvadeva's definition of *gamaka* is a good place to begin. It provides at least three useful insights: (1) that the entire concept of ornamentation, at any level, remains syllabic, in that it depends upon the concept of *svara;* (2) it recognizes the transitive and microtonal nature of the *gamaka*s in their traversing of the *śruti*s lying between the *svara*s; and (3) it emphasizes the essentially irrational and qualitative nature of the *gamaka*s through the connotations of the word *chāyā:* shadow, reflected image, shading or blending of colors, and in attenuated form, simply light, color, grace, and beauty.[72] The first point is perhaps not obvious: once the tonal territories of the individual *svara*s (the scale degrees) have become actualized in a specific *rāga,* any number of different transitions to other intonational steps, intrusions into the range of other *svara*s, or swings between different *śruti*s become available—impossible to catalog within any rational pitch scheme known to musicians at the time, but responding to a few simple principles (slide, tremor, oscillation, and the like).

The early history of the concept of *gamaka* demonstrates that these principles proved elusive and resistant to easy classification. In general it can be said that the ornamental types have remained much the same, while the names applied to them and their classifications have varied from author to author in the search for a successful organizing framework. In the *Bṛhaddeśī,* it is not clear which types of ornaments fall under the heading of *gamaka,* but two are mentioned frequently (without precise definitions): *bindu,* a quick touching of a single ornamental note; and *mūrcchanā,* which I take in this context as a reference to some type of ornamental cluster—the one and the many.[73] But apart from these references, the *gamaka*s are treated in a very general way in Mataṅga's text without any attempt to describe the individual varieties.

With the thirteenth-century author Pārśvadeva's lucid definitions of the seven *gamaka*s, we reach solid ground. The following passage is generally regarded as the first systematic attempt to organize the *gamaka*s into a single, comprehensive scheme:

> *Sphurita* (bursting forth), *kampita* (quivering), *līna*
> (merging), *tiripu* (meandering), *āhata* (impacted),
> *āndolita* (oscillating), and *tribhinna* (threefold) are
> proclaimed to be the seven *gamaka*s.
>
> When the *śruti*s follow rapidly one after another in ascending
> order,
> wise men know this one to be *sphurita.*
>
> When a *svara* is shaken rapidly at double speed, for this
> [reason]
> the *gamaka* is recognized by learned people as *kampita.*[74]
>
> When a *svara* melts quickly and smoothly into an adjacent
> *svara,*

it should be known as *līna.*

When the *śrutis* revolve rapidly hither and thither, the experts in song
know this one to be the *gamaka* named *tiripu.*

When a *svara* proceeds so as to impact upon the next higher *svara,*
it is declared to be *āhata.*

When there occurs a delicate oscillation of the *svaras*, the experts in song proclaim this *gamaka* to be the so-called *āndolita.*

When a *gamaka* touches without interruption [all] three [vocal] registers and [thereby] is endowed with the qualities of this and that register,
it should be known as *tribhinna.*[75]

The same seven *gamakas* appear in Śārṅgadeva's list of fifteen, some of them with different descriptions.[76] But Śārṅgadeva's *gamakas* are lumped together under the general heading of *kampita* (quivering): six are classified according to the temporal duration of the shake, five according to contour (ascending or descending, curving, returning, "crooked"), two according to the quality of sound produced (both nasal closures), and a mixed variety which is subsequently expanded into a number of subdivisions in the author's description of the ninety-six *sthāyas*.[77] It is apparent that the "experts in song" saw the unstable nature of the *gamakas* as their most distinctive feature, but their expositions are unsatisfactory in two respects. They did not manage to distinguish clearly between the *gamakas* and the *alaṅkāras*; and they failed to identify with precision the boundary conditions that would permit us to distinguish between one ornament and another—depending, for example, on whether the tremor was of definite or indefinite pitch, whether it was imposed upon a stable or an unstable *svara,* whether the ornament demonstrated a returning or continuing contour, and the like. Śārṅgadeva's approach was simply to describe as many as possible. We shall examine his classification of the *sthāyas*, which has fallen into disuse.[78]

Most of the early *gamakas* seem to have originated in a vocal tradition, but later systems (from the sixteenth and seventeenth centuries) have been based more upon instrumental practice, especially upon vina technique. For the last two hundred years Karnatic musicians have based their ornamental practice upon a system of ten *gamakas* (the *daśavidha gamakas*, or "ten graces"), which is essentially a simplification and reorganization of Śārṅgadeva's system, again with reference to vina technique.[79] As in other respects, North and South Indian traditions today differ significantly in the amount and type of *gamakas* preferred: the slowly undulating shakes and deliberate slides of modern Hindustani music contrast vividly with the rapid quivers and intricate ornamental clusters of the South.

Śārṅgadeva's classification and description of the ninety-six *sthāyas* is a bold attempt to isolate as many as possible of the microstructural details he observed in the music of his day. They are organized into four classes: ten "well-known and distinctly defined" *sthāyas*, thirty-three that are "well-known and indistinctly defined," twenty that are "obscure and distinctly defined," and another thirty-three that are "obscure and indistinctly defined."[80] Many of these open out into further subdivisions. *Vahanī,* to take but one, must have been among the most important of the "well-known and distinctly defined" *sthāyas*: it is described as a shake with a continuous tremor, either ascending, descending, or with a back-and-forth (*sañcārī*) motion. *Vahanī* is first divided into composed and improvised varieties, each of these dividing further into stable and accelerating rates of tremor, and each of these dividing once again according to the vocal register from which they arose (that is, the heart, the throat, or the head), with a few additional subcategories to keep the picture from becoming too symmetrical.[81] Nowhere do we find any indication of the duration of the *sthāyas*, so how *vahanī* would have been distinguished from the fifteen varieties of *kampita* remains obscure. Common sense suggests that the concept of *sthāya* operated at a deeper architectonic level than the *gamakas*—closer perhaps to the domain of the *alaṅkāras*—except that the category includes several of the "mixed" varieties of *gamaka.* I shall try to resolve this contradiction in a moment.

Space will not permit a detailed analysis of Śārṅgadeva's complex scheme, but the following list of the first ten *sthāyas*—those that were apparently in common practice and clearly defined—will give some idea of the scope of his classification.[82]

1. *śabda:* an ornament that begins with the final tone of a previous phrase
2. *dhāla:* a rolling motion "like a pearl"
3. *lavanī:* an extremely soft descending movement of the tones
4. *vahanī:* a continuous shake
5. *vādyaśabda:* the use of vocables representing instrumental sounds

6. *yantra:* apparently another category of ornament imitating instrumental sounds

7. *chāyā:* tonal inflections suggesting a different *rāga*, a different register, instrumental technique, or some other foreign quality[83]

8. *svaralaṅghita:* large melodic intervals produced by omitting the intervening *svaras*

9. *prerita:* the upward, downward, or oblique (?) movements of *svaras*[84]

10. *tīkṣṇa:* a "sharp" sound in the high register

Even this short list is a mixture of several different types of ornamental gestures: some defined by their motion, others by their tonal quality, and still others by their imitative properties. The picture becomes even more complicated with the remaining eighty-six, most of which—as one might by now expect—are defined in still more ambiguous language. But taken as a whole, the *sthāyas* yield a great deal of information about musical style and the extramusical models on which the performer's ornamental technique was based. We read of *sthāyas* that suggest the gait of an intoxicated elephant, *sthāyas* that exemplify tender radiance or bright delight, *sthāyas* characterized by a fullness of voice, *sthāyas* that incorporate important functional degrees of a derived *rāga* within the main *rāga* being performed, *sthāyas* that are to be performed "with great mental concentration," *sthāyas* that suggest a certain mood (pity or playfulness), *sthāyas* that are simply "appropriate" to the given situation,[85] *sthāyas* rolling like the waves of the Ganges or swirling like the water in a half-filled jar, *sthāyas* that imitate the tossing and catching of a ball, *sthāyas* that require intense effort in performance, *sthāyas* in which a single note in the upper or lower octave is quickly touched, *sthāyas* in which the volume of tone swells and is then reduced, *sthāyas* that sound like Vedic chant, *sthāyas* that are motionless,[86] and many mixed types.

This is a valiant attempt to describe an entire repertoire of expressive musical "gestures," whose principles remained obscure, but whose properties could be demonstrated clearly enough and taught to one's students. If all of these were conceived as ornaments, it is evident that the ornaments were drawn from a number of different levels and dimensions of musical experience—internal-external, quantitative-qualitative, vocal-instrumental, steady-shaking, abstract-metaphoric. We may also conclude that decoration played a far more prominent role in this repertoire than in almost any other, and Śārṅgadeva's exposition reminds us of the growing role of improvisation and the consequent demand for spontaneous ornamentation. Many of the *sthāya*s are reminiscent of the repertoire of "licks" that a jazz musician has at his command, which rise to the surface in appropriate contexts. If the *sthāya*s do not fall readily into a clearly delineated set of exclusive musical devices, it may be because our expectations are based on a foreign way of thinking about music—a pyramidal notion of music in which each of the musical dimensions (melody, rhythm, timbre) is systematically carved up into its own exclusive set of concepts and constructs. In Śārṅgadeva's presentation of the *sthāya*s, on the other hand, we see a one-dimensional concept of melody, a "unified-field" approach in which quantities and qualities are freely intermingled, and in which certain popular cultural metaphors (swings, pots, water, balls, and the like) function as accurate index terms for musical phenomena that are so well-known in practice that it needs but a word to call them forth.

Śārṅgadeva's list of the ten distinct and well-known *sthāya*s includes *chāyā,* which he defined as an inflection or intonation (*kāku*): a "shadow" or "reflection" of some extramusical quality, emotion, or specific musical property. The basic meaning of *kāku* is a tone of voice that indicates an underlying thought or emotion, so the best musical application of the term would be in the sense of an implication produced by means of some characteristic intonation. I have referred to Bharata's treatment of *kāku* as an important topic of dramatic recitation, and the wealth of musical concepts mentioned in this passage insured that later authors would have to make a place for it in their systems.[87] The opening verse is as follows: "I shall now describe the qualities of recitation. In it there are seven notes (*svara*s), three vocal registers, four contours (*varṇa*s), two modes of intonation (*kāku*), six ornaments (*alaṅkāra*s), and six limbs (*aṅga*s)."[88]

It is of course entirely reasonable to suggest that recitation can be described in terms of specific pitches, registers, contours, accents, and ornaments. Of the two types of *kāku* mentioned here, one entails expectation and one does not—with respect to both the meaning of the text and the rising or falling tone of voice. The two modes are further amplified by the six *alaṅkāra*s, which turn out to be quite different from the *alaṅkāra*s of melody. According to this concept, a specific intonation—entailing or not entailing expectation—may be high (*ucca*), excited (*dīpta*), grave (*mandra*), low (*nīca*), fast (*druta*), or slow (*vilambita*), singly or in combination with others. Certain of these intonations are appropriate to specified dramatic situations or emotional content. In combination with the other features mentioned in the above passage, Bharata's brief exposition of *kāku* contains most of the ingredients of a comprehensive theory of declamation, which, despite the large number of musical terms, does not necessarily imply any specifically musical application. Nevertheless, in Śārṅgadeva's presentation of the six types of *chāyā* or *kāku,* the idea of intonation has become translated into a musical concept of some potential value. These are the six types:

1. *svarakāku:* the shading of a particular note so as to imply another
2. *rāgakāku:* the distinctive intonations and shadings that give a particular *rāga* its individual character
3. *anyarāgakāku:* incorporating in some manner the characteristic intonations of another *rāga*
4. *deśakāku:* a distinctive shading that reflects a particular regional style or preference
5. *kṣetrakāku:* a tonal inflection produced in imitation of the distinctive quality of an individual voice or vocal register
6. *yantrakāku:* an intonation implying instrumental timbre or techniques of sound production on the flute or vina[89]

This classification may have been wholly theoretical, but it reveals a serious and provocative attempt to address some of music's most elusive properties. Among the most admirable qualities of the early musical authors was their refusal to be daunted by the inherent obstacles in their material.

## 11.8 Rasa

> When we go to the theater we do not have any inclination to think "Today I will have to accomplish something real." Rather we feel "I will listen to and see something beyond my everyday experience, something worthy [of my attention], whose essence is pure joy [from beginning] to end. I will share this experience with the whole audience." One's heart becomes like a spotless mirror, for all of one's normal preoccupations have been completely forgotten, and one is lost in aesthetic rapture, listening to the fine singing and music.
>
> Abhinavagupta, *Abhinavabhāratī*[90]

The theory of *rasa* (flavor, in this context *emotional* flavor ) is India's major contribution to the philosophy of art. The eloquent passage from Abhinavagupta's commentary on the *Nāṭyaśāstra* is an appropriate introduction to this very large subject. The idea of *rasa* arose in connection with the early theater and seems to have been solidly established by the time Bharata's treatise was assembled—perhaps as early as the first century A.D. But it received its classical formulation and definitive analysis at the hands of Abhinavagupta, the eleventh-century Kashmiri Shaivite philosopher. From dramatic criticism, the *rasa* theory was taken up into poetics and subsequently broadened into a general theory of the arts.

The critical literature on the subject of *rasa* is vast, and my brief explanation of this important concept here can give no more than a tantalizing indication of its scope, as we focus upon its role in the musical experience.[91] I once again raise the question I posed and then evaded earlier in this chapter: to what extent is the value system of early Indian music independent of, or dependent upon, the broader spectrum of cultural values demonstrated in the other arts? Some further background is necessary before I attempt an answer.

The literal meaning of *rasa* is "sap, juice, or essence," and the word invokes another of the popular metaphors of liquid continuity that we have encountered in other contexts. In the case of art, the essence is emotion. A more literary definition would go something like this: By *rasa* we mean a transcendent mode of emotional awareness by which all aspects of a performance are integrated, an awareness that rises above the circumstances which awakened it (the poetic content, the stage spectacle, and the musical clues) and generalizes the individual emotional states of the spectators into a single emotional "field." The idea has often been compared to Aristotle's concept of catharsis, as set forth in the *Poetics,* but the differences are more important.[92]

Aristotle defined catharsis as a purging of emotion, a purging that leads to a general feeling of peace and well-being; but the *rasa* theory recognizes a cultural repertoire of eight (or later nine) distinct emotional states. While catharsis occurs in the form of a discharge of the tensions built up during the play, the *rasa* is preexistent and arises gradually in the audience's experience as the various clues accumulate; it is savored, not dispersed, as one leaves the theater. And while Aristotle believed that human nature renders us automatically susceptible to the process of emotional arousal and discharge, Abhinavagupta maintained that the spectator must bring empathy (*sahṛdayatva,* "to be at heart with") to the theater, a special empathy born of cultural instruction in feeling and behavior. The *rasa* theory also requires aesthetic "distance": the spectator must remain aware that the *rasa* he hopes and expects to experience is something more than the emotion displayed by the actors and dancers, his own emotional response, or anything explicit in the emotional content of the play—it is the pure essence of emotion, distilled, clarified, organized, and flooding an entire community until they become one at heart. To return to Abhinavagupta's beautiful simile, the inner being of the instructed, sensitive, and receptive spectator becomes like a "spotless mirror"—able to reflect accurately a universe of feeling.

The standard eight *rasa*s are linked in an obvious manner with the eight permanent emotions, the *sthāyibhāvas*:[93]

| The *rasa*s | The *sthāyibhāva*s |
|---|---|
| Śṛṅgāra: the erotic | *rati:* love |
| Hāsya: the comic | *hāsa:* laughter |
| Karuṇa: the compassionate | *śoka:* sorrow |
| Raudra: the furious | *krodha:* anger |
| Vīra: the heroic | *utsāha:* energy |
| Bhayānaka: the terrible | *bhaya:* fear |
| Bībhatsa: the odious | *jugupsā:* disgust |
| Adbhuta: the wondrous | *vismaya:* wonder |

But this brief catalog of emotional states is only a general index to the Indian emotional world, a list of the main genera to which the various subspecies of feeling inevitably lead. Thirty-three transitory emotional states accompany the primary emotions: world-weariness, physical weakness, anxiety, envy, intoxication, fatigue, laziness, depression, worry, confusion, remembrance, peace of mind, shame, rashness, joy, panic, lifelessness, pride, dejection, longing, sleeping, apoplexy, dreaming, awakening, resentment, dissimulation, violence, attentiveness, sickness, insanity, death, fright, and perplexity. The array of emotional clues extends further to eight "involuntary" states, the actual stimuli (audible and visible) presented in the performance, and the mimetic changes that occur in the spectators.[94]

So the essence of style in the arts is emotional content—a remarkably explicit answer to the question, What constitutes *meaning* in music, or the arts in general? As Edwin Gerow writes,

> The *rasa* is a form of knowledge—experience abstracted from a determinate content. As Aristotle observes, learning is an activity most suited to the soul, and is pleasurable even when it is about painful things. Thus, in the context of the play, despair is experienced apart from any specific, personal despair, and this in itself is probably delightful, for the knowledge itself frees us from its consequences.
>
> It is given to the play—to art, then—to demonstrate something about ourselves that is otherwise unknown: our capacity to feel. Art that has this form, that aims this high, has no other, no extrinsic, purpose.[95]

The end of *rasa* is delight, the "aesthetic rapture" of which Abhinavagupta wrote. But it is a delight that is specifically located within a conventional universe of expressive meaning, a universe whose coordinates are clearly known and deeply felt. At the same time the awareness of *rasa* is an awareness detached not only from our personal emotions but also from all those conditions that stimulated that awareness, a form of pure idealism that is surely in harmony with the traditional doctrines of Indian philosophy. These doctrines have taught us to value the unseen above what is seen and to appreciate the emotions shared within a culture above those feelings that are attached to specific objects, persons, and concepts. In this latter sense, the experience of art is a liberation from constraints, *mokṣa.*[96]

How does the process work in the case of music, and what can be learned from the repertoire of prescribed emotional states? In Indian culture it is axiomatic that music works its effects by means of *rasa,* a belief that accords well with Gerow's definition of *rasa* as "a nondenotational state of emotional awareness."[97] It was unquestionably the important role of music in the early theater that made this linkage possible, and it is difficult to argue that music is able to evoke *rasa* without the aid of visible and verbal clues and the rich background of cultural associations. But music in the Indian tradition seldom if ever lacks the support of these clues—the content of a text, facial expressions and physical gestures, the times and seasons, and the meanings ascribed to a given *rāga* (which may include a main mood and a variety of subshadings, colors, literary motifs, iconographic symbolism, and specific types of ornament).[98]

So in the end it is pointless to consider music in the abstract, as so-called absolute music, because Indian music is never absolute—just as nothing phenomenal can ever be absolute. Formalist theories of musical aesthetics have no meaning in this context, because all forms are subordinate to their ideational and emotional content. We may legitimately contend that music is not expected to cover as wide an emotional universe as the theater, apart from the theater: despite the specification of the *rasa*s Bībhatsa or Hāsya for certain *rāga*s, which rests more on tradition than on any specific connection between the dominant emotion and the musical features of the *rāga,* I have never heard a performance where a sense of disgust or farce arose purposely. But it cannot be questioned that music evokes its own expressive universe as fully and as deeply as any of the other performing arts.

Our concern here is not for the fully developed semantic fields that inform Indian music today, but for what we can deduce about how the *rasa* theory came to be applied to musical structures between Bharata and

Śārṅgadeva. From these beginnings we can follow the development of musical and emotional associations through the later musicological literature. Virtually all of the subsequent attempts to link musical structure and emotional content rest on the authority of the opening passage in chapter 29 of the *Nāṭyaśāstra,* in which Bharata proclaimed the following connections between (1) the eight *rasa*s and (2) the note singled out for special emphasis in any scale, the sonant note or *aṁśa:*[99]

| *rasa* | *aṁśa* |
|---|---|
| the erotic | *ma* or *pa,* degrees 4 or 5 |
| the comic | *ma* or *pa* |
| the compassionate | *ga* or *ni,* degrees 3 or 7 |
| the furious | *sa* or *ri,* degrees 1 or 2 |
| the heroic | *sa* or *ri* |
| the terrible | *dha,* degree 6 |
| the odious | *dha* |
| the wondrous | *sa* or *ri* |

The table obviously does not tell the whole story: there is no one-to-one relationship between any of the *rasa*s and a particular note of tonal emphasis; and it would be trivial to conclude that the dominant emotion could be triggered in a mechanical way by the profusion of an individual scale degree around which the melodic structure gravitates. The author clearly had something much more interesting in mind. When Bharata remarked, in chapter 28, that it was the *aṁśa* on which the charm (N.B.: *rāga*) of the song depends,[100] what he meant was that the choice of *aṁśa* was the vital decision by which musical meaning—in terms of melodic function—was assigned to each of the degrees of the scale. For the choice of *aṁśa,* as we saw in §7.5, determined the essential pitch affinities (the functional relationships of consonance, dissonance, and neutrality) within the scale; it also determined which notes could be dropped and which were to be rendered as unstable tones, and it determined both the lowest and highest notes permitted.[101] The combinations shown in the table are those that were possible within the ancient modal system—the *jāti*s—as expounded in the *Nāṭyaśāstra* and the *Dattilam.*[102]

In the *jāti*s, most of which permitted a choice from among several possible *aṁśa*s, it seems quite likely that the specification of *aṁśa* may have been made in order to accommodate the desired *rasa.* I see no possible way of reconstructing the ancient scales in a manner that would demonstrate the networks of tonal relationships that would align automatically with the table of *rasa*s, but the matter cannot have been that simple: the possibilities for functional affinities and subtle shades of tuning are so numerous that it would rule out any set of one-to-one correspondences between mood and tune. I suspect the association was more a matter of belief and convention than the result of verifiable musical connections.

The situation I have just outlined does suggest at least a reasonable case for some association between the eight *rasa*s and the tonal gravitation of the individual *jāti*s. But when the same set of associations was later transferred to the *grāmarāga*s, each of which permitted only one possible *aṁśa* (and of the original set of seven, five require *sa* as the *aṁśa*), the scheme must have broken down completely.[103] There was clearly no way to reconcile the system of eight *rasa*s with a set of scales in which only three notes could function as the *aṁśa*. And if the dominant emotion was triggered by the specific gravitation of the scale degrees around their *aṁśa*, what would be the emotional range of a system of seven diatonic scales of which five would be limited to the same *rasa*s?

The way out of this dilemma seems to have been the development of still other *rāga*s with distinct musico-emotional personalities; in this way the necessary variety could be achieved. But at the same time, the idea of *rasa* as related to the *aṁśa* must have degenerated into little more than a set of conventional labels. Bharata's correlations remained unchallenged as late as the middle of the thirteenth century, and the *rasa*s were distributed among the thirty original *grāmarāga*s solely on the basis of their prescribed *aṁśa*s. The final blow must have come in later medieval times with the shift to *sa* as the common tonic note for the entire system of *rāga*s. While the *rasa*s are often mentioned in connection with modern *rāga*s, they depend not upon one particular set of pitch associations but upon an entire semantic field that has grown up around each individual *rāga*—some, to be sure, more colorful than others.

Let us take a closer look at one of these fields. A brief examination of the important Śṛṅgāra *rasa*, the erotic sentiment, will reveal the extraordinary range of meanings on which any musical application is able to draw. Śṛṅgāra has been described as *rasarājā* (the "king of *rasa*s") because of its popularity and depth of emotional content; many authors have regarded it as the supreme form of artistic expression, containing all of the other *rasa*s within its many shadings and subtleties.[104] Here is a summary of Śṛṅgāra's many cultural and theatrical associations, culled from various chapters of the *Nāṭyaśāstra*.

The aesthetic flavor of Śṛṅgāra arises from a delicate, graceful, and sweetly amorous style of expression, reminiscent of the sentimental femininity of the Victorian era: hearts, flowers, tears, vapors, and submission. Its two quintessential themes are lovers united and lovers parted, especially the familiar topic of lovers separated during the rainy season and their melancholy yearning for one another, pleasantly tinged with anticipation of their reunion. Kālidāsa's poetic masterpiece *Meghadūta* (*The Cloud Messenger*) explores the full gamut of Śṛṅgāra in its 110 ornate stanzas, of which the following is representative:

> Thou shalt know her, my second life, by the scantness of her speech,
> Like a lonely chakravaki-bird, while I, her mate, am afar;
> As these days pass heavy with intense longing, I imagine the hapless girl
> Changed in form, as a lotus blighted by the cold season.[105]

The word *śṛṅgāra* (sexual passion, yearning, enjoyment) derives from *śṛṅga:* an animal's horn or anything shaped like a horn, an elephant's tusk, a woman's breast, a mountain peak, and a symbol of anything brought to perfection. Viṣṇu is the presiding deity, an appropriate protector of conjugal love and the established world order. Its color is "dark," with a spectrum running from black to blue and green. Socially Śṛṅgāra is reserved for the young, wealthy, and highborn, with elegant, bright costumes among its distinguishing marks. Its poetic topics include enjoying the seasons, adorning oneself and the beloved with garlands, jewelry, and fragrances, listening to music, wandering through splendid palaces and elaborate gardens, enjoying water sports, pleasant conversations, and amorous dalliance. In separation, however, the emphasis turns from pleasant activities to inner states of melancholy: indifference, depression, fear, jealousy, anxiety, fatigue, sleeping, dreaming, illness, swooning, insanity, epilepsy, torpor, wasting away, and death.

Bharata proposed a large number of physical determinants to represent the many substates of Śṛṅgāra: subtle movements of the eyes and eyebrows, delicate gestures and poses, facial expressions, and gentle tones of speech. The typical mode of expression is the delicate Kaiśikī style. The appropriate type of hero is the thoughtful, restrained, noble, sensitive king—not the haughty, blustering warrior. Śṛṅgāra's proper time of day is the evening. With respect to diction, a moderate tempo (of speech and also of music) and a restrained mode of enunciation are prescribed. The poetic text should be rich in metaphoric language.

In the evolution of the expressive domain of Indian music, it seems inevitable that the early stages of the *rāga* system would have been accompanied by attempts to align the various *rasa*s with the melodic formations in some comprehensive manner. Bharata's correlations offered a simple solution which at one time may have provided a workable set of connections between emotional expression, poetic content, and melodic structure. But the authority of his text made it virtually impossible for his followers to take a fresh approach or to apply his principles in a more flexible way to the rapidly proliferating system of *rāga*s. What survived in the end was the simple conviction that each unique melodic structure was associated with, and thus possessed the power to invoke, a characteristic emotional field.

## 11.9 The Values of Indian Music

I shall attempt a summary of the value system that has emerged piecemeal from what has preceded, a value system that was substantially in place before the beginning of the shastric era and that has steadfastly resisted significant change ever since—despite the later invasions bringing Islamic ideals that differed considerably from those of Hinduism. I have argued that the system of musical values developed in close association with the values of poetry and drama and has remained in harmony with them, apart from issues that are indigenous to music. It is important to point out that in no way has the evolving scheme of musical values contradicted or undermined the larger aesthetic field within which it arose and was nourished. The most explicit link between musical aesthetics and the general philosophy of art was forged by critics of the early theater.

In comparing this value system to the values of the West, we need to make two points. First, the consensus on values has never been seriously challenged and has at no time been subject to the waves of successive revisions that we have seen in modern European aesthetics and artistic styles. And second, Indian authors from a very early time have focused on the nature of the aesthetic experience and have shown relatively little concern for the ontological status of musical objects.

The distinctive presuppositions of Indian thought have caused certain issues either to be overlooked or to be treated in a more one-sided manner than in the West. Among these nonissues and nondebates are the purpose of art (it is assumed that the main purpose of art is to bring delight, and as a more distant goal, liberation), the nature of artistic communication (it is a basic cultural assumption that essential substance can be transmitted in immaterial form from person to person), creativity in the arts (creation ex nihilo is unthinkable, so transformation of existing material is assumed), the content of art (emotional content and the suggestion of denotative meaning have been successfully explained by Indian authors), the beautiful as opposed to the sublime (a distinction that has never seemed important to Indian thinkers), art as imitation (because it is assumed that art is mimetic—of emotion, human character, and a wide range of other cultural meanings), formalism in the arts (because of the secondary role of form in the Indian worldview), and the concept of organicism in the arts (which is again assumed).

If Indian thinkers, unlike their counterparts in the West, have not been caught up in these issues, it must be because they believed themselves to be on firm ground in following the aesthetic teachings of the early *śāstras*. And with respect to the values embodied in the traditional music of India, this ground is easy to survey. Music, whether we have in mind a composition or, more often, an individual performance should be

1. flawless
2. adorned rather than plain
3. refined, a category that includes both precision and delicacy, with negative value attached to the vulgar, harsh, rough, or careless
4. continuous, in the form of a smooth, even, compact, connected, viscous stream of sound, with serene equilibrium as a goal and the process of creation as a model
5. appropriate (*aucitya*, an important category in Indian poetics)[106] with reference to the relationship between sense, sight, and sound, or any of the cultural correlations we have explored
6. intense, a category of value that includes the colorful, vivid, bright, radiant, illuminated, and impassioned, with negative value assigned to anything that is thin, bland, pallid, or dull
7. plastic, in the sense that it reveals the vital force that animates all life, as demonstrated in graceful, linear configurations, with negative value attached to the static, lifeless, and awkward
8. evocative, in that it suggests more than the explicit content, flooding the senses with meaning
9. abundant and richly fertile, with negative value assigned to what is dry, parsimonious, fragile, strained, or limited
10. clear in projection of the text, with crisply enunciated syllables
11. integrated and organically unified in an orderly manner, not disordered, broken, disjointed, or chaotic
12. comprehensive, in that the artistic contents are processed in a complete and systematic manner

It would be an interesting exercise to apply the same standards to musical works of the West, particularly those of nineteenth-century romanticism; the nineteenth century was a time when European musical values most closely resembled those of India. Frederic Chopin and Vincenzo Bellini come to mind as the composers whose music most nearly exemplifies the total set of Indian values, although few Western critics today would place them at the summit of artistic achievement. In contrast, Mozart, Beethoven, and Stravinsky would not win high ratings on the Indian criteria.

Three of the categories combine to suggest that art is valued for the manner in which it represents nature—not the appearance of nature, but the way in which nature works, pure natural *process:* the demands for continuity (the way of creation), plasticity (the way of life), and abundance (the way of all nature, at least under ideal circumstances).

I have avoided the important word *beauty,* seemingly the most crucial of all aesthetic categories. In India, as in the West, the idea of beauty is a composite of many subqualities, cannot be easily rendered by any single word, and often appears as the attenuated form of a more precise concept such as sweetness, radiance, adorned, apt, having good form, or that which brings pleasure.[107] It is clear that many of the traditional *guṇa*s—of singing, poetry, or any aspect of music—were often intended to mean little more than "beautiful" in this very general sense.

*Kānti* is perhaps the most popular word for beauty, with the following semantic range: beauty in general, especially female beauty; desire; decoration; loveliness; splendor; light; and bright color. It derives from the second verbal root *kam* (to love, have sexual intercourse with, desire, long for), and thence from the adjective *kānta* (that which is desired, pleasing, lovely). This familiar cluster of meanings reminds us of the Scholastic definition of the beautiful: "That which calms the desire, by being seen or known."[108] It is also evident that this concept of beauty is deeply rooted in typical feminine qualities, a notion unpopular in many circles today, but to gloss over it is to miss something basic in the Indian system of artistic values.

Also contributing to the general notion of beauty are a large number of other Sanskrit verbal roots that express a few fundamental ideas: to shine, be pleased, resound, appear, and enjoy. Taken together they suggest an idea that Plato would have endorsed—that beauty is an *epiphany,* a manifestation of the light of creation to the senses, bringing the taste of delight and a glimpse of the ultimate in sensible, graspable form.

As much as we must admire the systematic manner in which early musicians gradually developed their idea of music and crafted musical structures in harmony with the ideals of Indian culture, what strikes me as the single most remarkable feature of their thought is the attention they lavished on the aesthetic and qualitative properties of their music. In the light of their philosophic orientation and the nature and intensity of their cultural presuppositions, they could scarcely have done otherwise.

T W E L V E

# AFTERTHOUGHTS

It is time to step back for additional perspective. The ethnomusicologist Steven Feld, in his recent study of the music and musical life of the Kaluli people of Papua New Guinea, describes his approach as an attempt "to show how an analysis of the modes and codes of sound communication leads to an understanding of the ethos and quality of life in Kaluli society. . . . [As a result] Kaluli sound expressions are revealed as embodiments of deeply felt sentiments."[1] This struck me as an accurate description of the aims of this study, once the necessary changes have been made. After providing the appropriate historical background and cultural contexts, I too have proceeded from an initial preoccupation with the "modes and codes of sound communication" to matters that involve values and "deeply felt sentiments." But in addition to the obvious cultural differences between a small and homogeneous clan of today's New Guinea highlanders and the vast number of diverse ethnic groups of ancient and medieval India, the differences in method and orientation between our two studies will at first appear to outweigh the similarities, especially to ethnomusicologists.

My purpose in these brief final reflections is to suggest links between the findings of this study and the concerns of ethnomusicologists—especially those who are similarly committed to the study of historical ethnomusicology. The intent is not to argue on behalf of the traditional Indological model of historical investigation, but to demonstrate that some popular perceptions of the field of ethnomusicology are unnecessarily restrictive. It is true that the word *ethnomusicology* appears infrequently in this book, but this is what we have come to expect in studies of the music of India, by both foreign and domestic authors. Most students of Indian music—which is generally taken to mean India's *art* music—have addressed themselves to either the available music of the present (by learning how to perform it) or the unavailable music of the past (by investigating its theoretical systems and historical development, with the help of the methods described in chapter 6). This book is an obvious example of the latter.

Readers who have followed me this far will have rightly concluded that I am a Western musicologist with an orientation toward the theoretical and conceptual domains of music, an interest in the history of ideas, an appreciation for the methods of classical Indology, and a special concern for what documents can teach us about the early history of old high musical cultures. It seems irrelevant whether or not this cluster of interests and approaches is characteristic of ethnomusicology—we need not argue the proper sphere of ethnomusicology in order to defend the importance of studying the ancient foundations of India's musical culture.

Of the three aspects of ethnomusicology outlined by the late Alan Merriam in his celebrated model of the field (that is, concept, behavior, and sound), this study has focused primarily on concepts, with secondary attention to behavior, but with the constant assumption that the concepts framed in India's remote and more recent past are manifest in the behaviors and sounds of the present.[2] I have sought both *etic* and *emic* information:[3] *etic* (as in the word *phonetic*), "objective" knowledge obtained from analysis that does not rely on traditional cultural categories and the privileged interpretations of an insider—with reference to tunings, scales, durations, gestures, patterns, forms, and the like; and *emic* (as in *phonemic*), knowledge that arises from the subjective viewpoint and experience of a cultural insider—with reference to the mental images and constructs devised to capture and preserve these musical intuitions. In the case of etic information, India presents no unusual problems; but if emic insights are desired, India is, and always has been, a special case. It will be evident that studying music from an intramural perspective is of particular importance in assessing a culture that has for so long a time relied on the authority of the spoken and written word, a comprehensive and explicit theory of music, and a massive body of documentary evidence. It also requires, if not a complete suspension of the critical stance that ought to characterize responsible scholarship, at least a willingness to survey and evaluate our material in terms of its intramural assumptions, categories, and ways of thinking.

*Comparison, change,* and *conquest* are the keywords for the following discussion; all three are staple topics in the literature of historical ethnomusicology. Bruno Nettl's essay "Apples and Oranges" provides a useful overview of the problems of ethnomusicological comparison, and I will use it as a frame of reference for some comments.[4] In this study I have taken what might be described as a "particularist" view, resorting to occasional comparisons to clarify difficult Indian concepts or to point out some of the interesting similarities to other musics. In this respect comparisons with ancient and medieval Western music have often seemed more revealing than the quite different types of comparisons drawn between Indian music today and other world musics. Readers will understand that to make such a comparison is not to suggest that *all* things are the same—merely that here is a resemblance worth noting. I have suggested these Western analogies, not to put Indian music into a special category as the easternmost outpost of the ancient Indo-European world (a popular concept in historical linguistics because of the familial relationship between Sanskrit and its fellow Indo-European languages), but because I believe—along with the late John Blacking and many of today's ethnomusicologists—that Western music is ethnic music and deserves to be studied with modern ethnomusicological methods, as well as with the methods more often applied.[5] And indeed some of the comparisons I have made shed as much light on music in the West as they do upon Indian practice. But in general my approach has not been intended to classify the concepts, behaviors, and sounds of Indian music for filing among the musical artifacts of the world (like a collection of exotic specimens), or to dwell upon similarities or universals, but rather to increase our understanding of the distinctive features of the Indian musical tradition—to learn (as much as a foreign inquirer can hope to learn) how Indian music is and has been heard, thought, and felt. As a result we bring new light to bear on how we have become accustomed to hear, think, and feel music.

"Continuity and change" is another popular theme in ethnomusicological discourse, so much so that it has become a virtual cliché.[6] But like many other clichés, it has provided a valuable framework for the study of history and ethnography, and I offer no apology for adopting it here. As Nettl points out, "the historical aspects of ethnomusicology can be grouped into two principal classes—origin and change."[7] I have never been particularly interested in the question of origins, not for lack of curiosity but because the study of ancient music in both the East and the West has left me convinced that the quest for origins, while it may offer attractive matter for speculation, is essentially a fruitless exercise. When the earliest retrievable documents already reveal such a high level of musical and intellectual sophistication and have evidently traveled such a great distance from music's presumed "origins," it seems to me that attempts to uncover still more ancient foundations (unsupported by any pieces of solid evidence) are pointless. Those who are curious about origins will find grounds for speculation here and there in this study, especially in chapter 4, but my major concern has been for the status of Indian musical concepts in their earliest known forms and for their subsequent development. This line of thought brings us, appropriately, to the subject of change.

Let us continue with Nettl's exposition of the concerns of historical ethnomusicologists. He writes that "we are interested in the reasons for change (or for lack of change), and in its nature, degree, and rate."[8] I share these interests, and we are now in a position to draw some broad conclusions about the music and musical thinking of early India. Continuity has been present to an extraordinary degree; ideas have proved more resistant to change than the specific musical formations generated by the ideas; the degree of change has been subtle; and the rate of change can only be described as glacial. One especially interesting trend, which I documented in chapter 10, is seen in the apparent urge to construct elaborate taxonomies that can accommodate all future possibilities—to which practice has reacted by selecting preferred variations which are then subjected to still further theoretical justification. This continuing dialectic between the abundance and inventiveness of theory, restrained by the selective and often irrational habits of practice, is one of the keys to the historical development of music on the Indian subcontinent.

But what, then, are the reasons for change—such as it is—in the music and musical thinking of early India? Are they based on intrinsically musical-aesthetic criteria or upon cultural or racial criteria?[9] While it is possible to identify certain inherent properties of the musical system that tend eventually to promote instability and invite change (I am thinking here of the latent preference for circularity that seems to have encouraged the rise of the *deśī tāla*s) and also to identify certain intellectual habits that lead to similar consequences (and here I am reminded of the tendency to fill out sets of musical possibilities until some natural boundary has been reached, and to add to such sets a final, "mixed" category), it seems to me that nonmusical criteria have played a larger role in motivating musical change. I shall outline some of these.

I have avoided an evolutionary model of Indian music history in favor of what I regard as a more accurate model—a state of prolonged stasis, underscored by persistent tensions and interrupted only infrequently by major stylistic upheavals. The metaphor of a Brownian motion has been applied to music before, but in quite a different context.[10] This image of a pulsating mass (as in a gas or a fluid), within which the position of the individual particles is unpredictable while the shape and volume of the whole remain virtually unchanged, strikes me as an appropriate metaphor for the state of music in ancient and medieval India. Of course this "state" is an illusion. What we interpret from a distance as musical and intellectual stasis is revealed on closer inspection to be a tangled web of contradictory impulses and opposing tensions: the opposing demands of theory and practice, the traditional respect for authority and the human urge to deviate, the sensuousness of the musical materials and the formalism of the theoretical frameworks and systems, the rational and the irrational, the regional and the central, the world as it appears and the world as it really is.

The history of music on the subcontinent, viewed from a still larger perspective, has been marked by five periods of dramatic, sweeping change—of which only the first two fall within the time limitations of this study. (Readers will have to keep my antiquarian perspective in mind in evaluating what I have to say concerning "modern" India.) Each of the five has been in a certain sense a conquest. The initial encounter between the invading Indo-Aryans and the local Dravidian population provided the friction out of which the synthesis that we know as Indian culture arose. We can do little more than speculate about what the individual contributions to this synthesis may have been with respect to music and musical doctrines. I have detailed in various chapters the musical consequences of the second conquest (the *deśī* movement ca. A.D. 500–1000), which I interpret as a conquest of the center by the peripheries, of the one by the many. The third such conquest was the Muslim conquest of later medieval times, by which a set of foreign artistic impulses and preferences was imported, and which led eventually to a permanent schism between the musical languages of North and South India. In this connection it seems inescapable that older layers of music and musical thinking have become fossilized in the South, especially in the theory and practice of *tāla* and in the popular theater traditions of Kerala on the Malabar coast. The process by which the ancient Tamil musical system was virtually driven underground by the spread of the great "central" tradition has yet to be fully studied, but it deserves to be included in the picture I am attempting to sketch.

In each of these conquests we note a common occurrence—that foreign or peripheral influences have become assimilated into an existing tradition because of the tradition's deep roots, strength, and vitality. This is of course a commonplace of historical explanation. The result has been a fresh infusion of energy and variety into a stable tradition, not a period of dynamic change or the replacement of one music by another. We may identify the period of the British raj as a fourth conquest, one that brought foreign influences from halfway around the world but which seems to have had relatively little impact on India's deepest musical impulses and preferences. As one intriguing consequence, it is interesting to recall that both the nineteenth-century composers Tyāgarāja and Muṭṭuswami Dīkṣitar occasionally incorporated British band marches and airs into their devotional songs. This practice was described by William Jackson as knowing "winks of recognition" of a foreign culture that functioned "more like innoculations than grafts."[11]

The fifth conquest is today's electronic conquest, in which the main weapons are audio- and videocassettes. It is too soon to say what the consequences of this conquest may be. I have focused too much on the past to risk predictions of the future. India may eventually prove more resistant than some other world areas to the threat of "cultural grey-out" that some ethnomusicologists have seen in our future.[12]

If this is true, and I hope it is, there is a moral here: that a cultural area with natural geographic limitations will tend to preserve and refine its musical language and style, and will respond to external influences by accepting them as grafts onto a healthy stock. This brings a certain degree of immunity to the successive waves of new styles and culture clashes found in many other regions of the world. In this sense the example of India appears to validate one of Bence Szabolcsi's "laws" of music and cultural geography: "Regions which are enclosed from the point of view of cultural geography favour the preservation of musical styles in isolation, while the open regions encourage a more rapid circulation, a more conscious centralisation and transformation of musical styles."[13]

I have written little about music as a cultural object or social process apart from what we can deduce from its role in sacred ritual and the theater.[14] Nor have I focused on the physical evidence of early musical instruments, on the assumption (which readers may feel free to question) that the essence of Indian music is to be found more in the abstract realm of concepts than in the concrete realm of artifacts. The enduring component in the history of Indian music is the *idea,* the source from which an infinite series of fresh variations can be generated without violating established guidelines and the authority of the *śāstra*s.

But unsettling questions remain. Has this study documented the evolution of an elite music whose course has been constrained by the teachings of a ruling class of literati? Unquestionably it has. And have the authors of the *śāstra*s added some creative touches to the actual course of events in order to promote their own views? Certainly they have. What I have labeled "Indian culture," or "the Indian tradition," has never been as unified or as homogeneous as its proponents would have us believe. The unity of Indian culture is rather an ideal that has long been cultivated—an ideal that both shields and seeks to anneal the stresses and continuous ferment among the diverse groups of the subcontinent. Nevertheless, what that ideal has produced is India's heritage today.

No serious scholar will dispute the need to document such a long tradition of literate musical accomplishment, but ethnomusicologists can rightly remind us of the limits of such a study. To see the whole of Indian music in proper perspective (perhaps another unattainable ideal) we need the joint efforts of the traditional shastric scholarship and the field studies of ethnomusicologists. Each must recognize the limitations that come with a particular point of view. The bookish pursuits of Indian musicologists and classical Indologists will be enlivened by the careful study of contemporary practice. And similarly, the comparative studies of ethnomusicologists will be sharpened to the degree that they are informed by the ideologies and conceptual systems that have generated Indian music for millennia.

# NOTES

## Chapter One

1. See nn. 29 and 30.

2. Prem Lata Sharma, unpublished paper, "Contemporary *Tāla* Practice vis-à-vis *Śastraic* Tradition," n. 12, presented during a workshop, "*Śāstra* and *Prayoga* in the Performing Arts," Seventh World Sanskrit Conference (August 1987), Leiden, Netherlands.

3. For another early *nirukta* analysis of the word *bharata* in a musical context, see *MB* 277 (see n. 29); see also §3.5.

4. From the common root *bhr* (to bear, carry, maintain).

5. According to V. Raghavan's analysis in his article, "Sanskrit Drama in Performance," in *Sanskrit Drama in Performance,* ed. Rachel Van M. Baumer and James R. Brandon (Honolulu: University Press of Hawaii, 1981), 19.

6. For the early history of *gāndharva* see Lath, *Dattilam* (see n. 25), 61–79. Some scholars remain suspicious of tracing the distinction between *gāndharva* and *gāna* farther back than Abhinavagupta's analysis in *AB* (see n. 30).

7. The word *gandharva* is a cognate of the Greek *kentauros* (centaur); for further background see Lath, *Dattilam,* 62–64.

8. See §7.8.

9. I refer especially to the *Cilappatikaaram* (see below and n. 26).

10. As defined by Śārṅgadeva in *SS* 1.1.21cd (see below and n. 33).

11. As in the writings of Aristoxenus of Tarentum (4th century B.C.) and his followers; for an outline of the entire field of music see the later treatise *On Music* by Aristides Quintilianus (ca. A.D. 300), trans. and ed. Thomas J. Mathiesen (New Haven: Yale University Press, 1983), 17–18, 76–77.

12. For further analysis of this important term, see §§3.4, 4.5, 7.1–3.

13. Erich M. von Hornbostel and Curt Sachs, "Systematik der Instrumentenkunde," *Zeitschrift für Ethnologie* 46 (1914): 553–90; see also Curt Sachs, *The History of Musical Instruments* (New York: W. W. Norton, 1940), 454–67.

14. Chaps. 29, 30, 31, and 33 of the Ghosh translation of *BN* (see below and n. 24).

15. See Joseph Needham (with Kenneth Robinson), *Science and Civilisation in China,* vol. 4, pt. 1, sec. 26 (physics) (Cambridge: Cambridge University Press, 1962), 142–56.

16. For further details, see Kapila Vatsyayan, *Classical Indian Dance in Literature and the Arts* (New Delhi: Sangeet Natak Akademi, 1968), 23–141; idem, "Dance or Movement Techniques of Sanskrit Theater," in Baumer and Brandon, *Sanskrit Drama in Performance,* 45–66.

17. A. L. Basham, *The Wonder That Was India* (New York: Macmillan, 1954), 232.

18. For the background of this popular line of imagery, see Kapila Vatsyayan, *The Square and the Circle of the Indian Arts* (New Delhi: Roli Books International, 1983), 9–10; and R. F. Gombrich, "Ancient Indian Cosmology," in *Ancient Cos-*

*mologies,* ed. Carmen Blacker and Michael Loewe (London: George Allen and Unwin, 1975), 110–42.

19. *Taittirīya Upaniṣad* 1.7, Robert Ernest Hume, trans., *The Thirteen Principal Upanishads,* 2d ed. (Oxford: Oxford University Press, 1931), 279.

20. *Chāndogya Upaniṣad* 3.14.2–4, Hume, *Thirteen Principal Upanishads,* 209–10.

21. For further information, see Basham, *Wonder,* 10–43; and Debiprasad Chattopadhyaya, *History of Science and Technology in Ancient India: The Beginnings* (Calcutta: Firma KLM Pvt. Ltd., 1986).

22. Reproduced in Basham, *Wonder,* plate viii.

23. The purpose of the following series of citations (nn. 24–34) is to lead readers directly to the most accessible sources, not to provide exhaustive bibliographic details of the various editions and the secondary literature. Preference has therefore been given to English translations, even though in some cases they leave much to be desired, and to the best and most recent of the critical studies. Additional editions and sources appear in the general bibliography. For a general introduction to the early musical treatises see Emmie Te Nijenhuis, *Musicological Literature,* vol. 6, fasc. 1, of *A History of Indian Literature,* ed. Jan Gonda (Wiesbaden: Otto Harrassowitz, 1977); and two articles by V. Raghavan: "Some Names in Early *Saṅgīta* Literature," *Journal of the Music Academy, Madras* 3, nos. 1–2 (1932): 11–32; and "Some More Names in Early *Saṅgīta* Literature," *Journal of the Music Academy, Madras* 3, nos. 3–4 (1932): 94–102. For Indian history in general, readers are referred to two standard works: Basham, *Wonder;* and *Ancient India,* ed. E. J. Rapson, vol. 1 of *The Cambridge History of India* (New York: Macmillan, 1922).

24. The literature on *BN* is enormous, and numerous specific references will follow (especially in chap. 5, which includes a summary of the treatise with particular attention to the chapters on music). I will confine myself here to general references. For a complete English translation, see *The Nāṭyaśāstra,* trans. Manomohan Ghosh, 2 vols. (Calcutta: Asiatic Society, 1951–1961); all subsequent citations, unless otherwise identified, will be from this edition. Ghosh's translation is based on his own earlier edition of the Sanskrit text, which differs considerably from the text as presented in the important Baroda edition: *Nāṭyaśāstra of Bharatamuni, with the Commentary Abhinavabhāratī by Abhinavaguptācārya* (see n. 30), ed. M. Ramakrishna Kavi and J. S. Pade, 4 vols., Gaekwad's Oriental Series nos. 36, 68, 124, and 145 (Baroda: Oriental Institute, 1926–64). Several other English translations have been announced but not completed at the time of writing. I have found the following study extremely helpful: P. S. R. Appa Rao, *A Monograph on Bharata's naaTya Saastra: Indian Dramatology* (originally in Telugu), trans. P. S. R. Appa Rao and P. Sri Rama Sastry (Hyderabad: naaTya maalaa Publishers, 1967). For a valuable and accessible general introduction to *BN,* see Raghavan, "Sanskrit Drama in Performance," 18–44. See also Edwin Gerow, "Sanskrit Dramatic Theory and Kālidāsa's Plays," in *Theater of Memory: The Plays of Kālidāsa,* ed. Barbara Stoler Miller (New York: Columbia University Press, 1984), 42–62.

25. The *Dattilam* is currently available in two editions, each with an English translation and extensive commentary: Mukund Lath, *A Study of Dattilam: A Treatise on the Sacred Music of Ancient India* (New Delhi: Impex India, 1978); and E. Wiersma-te Nijenhuis, *Dattilam: A Compendium of Ancient Indian Music* (Leiden: E. J. Brill, 1970). A revised edition of Lath's study, which I consider one of the best examples of modern Indian musicological scholarship, has just been published in the Indira Gandhi National Centre for the Arts's *Kalāmūlaśāstra* Series, but was not received in time to be cited in this book; therefore all subsequent references to *D* will cite verse numbers and/or page numbers from Lath's 1978 edition.

26. See S. Ramanathan, *Music in Cilappatikaaram* (Madurai: Madurai Kamaraj University, 1979), which includes a detailed study of the musical sections of the text and English translations of 153 passages from *IC* and its commentaries.

27. At least two English translations are available: Sures Chandra Banerji, *Nāradīya-Śikṣā* (Calcutta: Rabindra Bharati University, 1983); and Usha R. Bhise, *Nāradīyā Śikṣā, with the Commentary of Bhaṭṭa Śobhākara* (Poona: Bhandarkar Oriental Research Institute, 1986). See also Lewis Rowell, "A *Śikṣā* for the Twiceborn," *Asian Music* 9, no. 1 (1977): 72–94.

28. See D. R. Widdess, "The Kuḍumiyāmalai Inscription: A Source of Early Indian Music in Notation," *Musica Asiatica* 2 (1980): 115–50; and R. Sathyanarayana, *The Kuḍimiyāmalai Inscription on Music* (Mysore: Sri Varalakshmi Academy, 1957).

29. No English translations are available apart from my translation and study of the final canto in "The Songs of Medieval India: The *Prabandhas* as Described in Mataṅga's *Bṛhaddeśī*," *Music Theory Spectrum* 9 (1987): 136—72. For the Sanskrit text see *The Bṛhaddeśī of Mataṅgamuni,* ed. K. Sāmbaśiva Śāstrī (Trivandrum: Sanskrit Series, 1928); for a reedited text, Hindi translation, and critical study, see Anil Bihari Beohar, "Mataṅgakṛta Bṛhaddeśī kā Adhyāyana" (Ph.D. diss., Banaras Hindu University, 1986). Prem Lata Sharma is currently preparing a complete English translation and critical study for publication in IGNCA's *Kalāmūlaśāstra* series. All subsequent references will cite the text of the Trivandrum edition.

30. For the best available edition of *AB,* see n. 24. Judging from the announcements I have seen, several editions and English translations have either been begun or are in the planning stages, but nothing is yet available. The best account of the condition of Abhinavagupta's text was given by the editor of the initial volume of the Baroda edition, M. Ramakrishna Kavi, when he wrote: "the originals [MSS] are so incorrect that a scholar friend of mine is probably justified in saying that even if Abhinavagupta descended from the Heaven and seen the Mss. he would not easily restore his original reading. It is in fact an impenetrable jungle through which a rough path now has been traced." For general background on A. and his thought, see Kanti Chandra Pandey, *Abhinavagupta: An Historical and Philosophical Study,* 2d ed. (Varanasi: Chowkhamba Sanskrit Series, 1963). An international seminar, "The Contribution of Abhinavagupta to Indian Culture," was held at Banaras Hindu University, Varanasi, in October 1981 and April 1982, and a selection of papers from that seminar is expected to be published soon.

31. The complete text of *NB* has yet to be published, although chaps. 1–5 were published in an edition by C. P. Desai (Khairagarh, 1961). See also R. Kavi, "King Nānyadeva on Music," *Quarterly Journal of Andhra Historical Research Society* (October 1926); and D. R. Widdess, "Tāla and Melody in Early Indian Music: A Study of Nānyadeva's Pāṇikā Songs with Musical Notation," *Bulletin of the School of Oriental and African Studies, University of London* 44, pt. 3 (1981): 481–508.

32. To the best of my knowledge, no part of *SM* has ever been translated into English. For the original text, see *The Mānasollāsa of King Someśvara,* ed. G. K. Srigondekar, 3 vols., Gaekwad's Oriental Series nos. 28, 84, and 138 (Baroda: Oriental Institute, 1925–61). The editor's introduction to vol. 2, 6–48, (in English) is particularly interesting in its vivid description of the royal enjoyments (*upabhogas*) and sports (*vinodas*) and evokes the pleasure-loving princely courts of the Middle Ages. The sections on music, dance, story telling, and drama appear in vol. 3, 1–171.

33. Thanks to the determined efforts of several of India's most distinguished musical scholars, this extremely important text will soon be available in its entirety in English translation. The standard edition of the original Sanskrit text is *Saṅgītaratnākara of Śārṅgadeva, with Kalānidhi of Kallinātha and Sudhākara of Siṁhabhūpāla,* ed. S. Subrahmaṇya Śāstrī, 4 vols. (Madras: Adyar Library, 1943–53). In

1945, C. Kunhan Raja published his English translation of vol. 1 (*svara*), and in 1976, vol. 4 (the chapter on dance) appeared in an English translation by K. Kunjunni Raja and Radha Burnier; both were published by the Adyar Library, Madras. The first volume in the Banaras Hindu University translation, produced under the supervision of Prem Lata Sharma, appeared in 1978: *Saṅgīta-Ratnākara of Śārṅgadeva,* vol. 1 (treatment of *svara*), trans. R. K. Shringy (Varanasi: Motilal Banarsidass). Shringy's second volume (chaps. 2–4) has just been released (New Delhi: Munshiram Manoharlal, 1989). The translation of chaps. 5 and 6 was completed just before Shringy's untimely death and is currently in press (also Munshiram Manoharlal). Accordingly, the B. H. U. translation (which also includes the original text, copious annotations, and summaries of what both commentators had to say) concludes with the chapter on instrumental music. Despite all its errors, irrelevant flights of fancy, and utter incomprehensibility to anyone not familiar with Indian musical terms, I cannot resist mentioning R. Rangaramanuja Ayyangar's affectionate study *"Sangeeta Ratnakaram" of "Nissanka" Sarngadeva* (Bombay: Wilco Publishing House, 1978), from which there is much to be learned.

34. A translation of *PS* is long overdue, so I was pleased to hear shortly before going to press that R. Satyanarayana is currently preparing one for IGNCA. For the standard edition of the original Sanskrit text, see *The Saṅgītasamayasāra of Saṅgītākara Śrī Pārśvadeva,* ed. T. Gaṇapati Śāstrī (Trivandrum: Sanskrit Series, 1925). A more recent but less reliable edition was published by Bṛhaspati in 1977 (Delhi: Srī Kundakundabhāratī). All subsequent references will be to the Trivandrum edition.

35. In *The Literatures of India: An Introduction,* ed. Edward C. Dimock, Jr., Edwin Gerow, C. M. Naim, A. K. Ramanujan, Gordon Roadarmel, and J. A. B. van Buitenen (Chicago: University of Chicago Press, 1974), 35.

## Chapter Two

1. Hume, *Thirteen Principal Upanishads,* 351.

2. From the root *śru* (to hear); for further analysis of *śruti* as a musical term see §§3.5, 4.5, 7.1–3. *Śruti* is also a collective term for the Vedas.

3. Richard Lannoy, *The Speaking Tree: A Study of Indian Culture and Society* (London: Oxford University Press, 1971), 272.

4. Satischandra Chatterjee and Dhirendramohan Datta, *An Introduction to Indian Philosophy* (Calcutta: University of Calcutta, 1968), 8.

5. See Walter H. Maurer's translation of *RV* 10.125 in his *Pinnacles of India's Past: Selections from the Ṛgveda* (Philadelphia: John Benjamins, 1986), 280–82.

6. Betty Heimann, *Facets of Indian Thought* (London: George Allen and Unwin, 1964), 19–23.

7. Lannoy, *Speaking Tree,* 272.

8. As in Viṣṇu's ten incarnations: as a fish (*matsya*), tortoise (*kūrma*), boar (*varāha*), man-lion (*narasiṁha*), dwarf (*vāmana*), Paraśurāma ("Rāma with the Ax"), Rāma (the hero of the *Rāmāyaṇa*), Kṛṣṇa, Buddha, and Kalkin (the incarnation yet to come).

9. For introductory surveys of Indian philosophy, see Chatterjee and Datta, *Introduction* (see n. 4); and M. Hiriyanna, *Outlines of Indian Philosophy* (London: George Allen and Unwin, 1932); for a valuable collection of more detailed essays, see *The Cultural Heritage of India,* vol. 3 (*The Philosophies*), ed. Haridas Bhattacharyya, 2d ed. (Calcutta: The Ramakrishna Mission, 1953).

10. For a concise presentation of the major doctrines of the six systems, see Basham, *Wonder,* 323–28.

11. Translated by Franklin Edgerton, in his *Bhagavad Gītā* (Cambridge: Harvard

University Press, 1972), 67–72, vv. 5, 9, and 16; see also Edgerton's essay, "Soul and Body," 139–45. For a quite different translation, see J. A. B. van Buitenen, *The Bhagavadgītā in the Mahābhārata: Text and Translation* (Chicago: University of Chicago Press, 1981), 127–29.

12. §§11.2, 11.4, and 11.6.

13. In his *Muziek, Ratio en Affect* (Antwerp: Metropolis, 1981). In December 1983, Broeckx's theses were the subject of an international symposium organized by the Communication and Cognition work group at the University of Ghent; the papers from that symposium were published in *Reason, Emotion and Music: Towards a Common Structure for Arts, Sciences and Philosophies, based on a Conceptual Framework for the Description of Music,* ed. L. Apostel, H. Sabbe, and F. Vandamme (Ghent: *Communication & Cognition,* 1986).

14. See Philip Rawson, *The Art of Tantra* (London: Thames and Hudson, 1973), 165–80, and *SS* 1.2.121–22b.

15. See §1.3.

16. See Heinrich Zimmer, *Philosophies of India,* ed. Joseph Campbell (Princeton: Princeton University Press, 1951), 414–29; and Eliot Deutsch, *Advaita Vedānta: A Philosophical Reconstruction* (Honolulu: University Press of Hawaii, 1969), 55–65.

17. *AA* 3.2.5.; see S. S. Janaki, "The Role of Sanskrit in the Development of Indian Music," *Journal of the Music Academy, Madras* 56 (1985): 68–70. Also see §5.5.

18. Described in *SS* 1.2.145c–148 as a slender flame of fire, four fingers in elevation and situated at a distance of nine fingers from the "center" of the body; see also §3.5.

## Chapter Three

1. In Raimundo Panikkar, trans., *The Vedic Experience: An Anthology of the Vedas for Modern Man and Contemporary Celebration* (Reprint, Pondicherry: All India Books, 1983), 103.

2. Hume, *Thirteen Principal Upanishads,* 327.

3. *VP* 1.1, in K. Raghavan Pillai, trans., *The Vākyapadīya: Critical Text of Cantos I and II* (Delhi: Motilal Banarsidass, 1971), 1.

4. See §3.5.

5. For an English translation, see Hume, *Thirteen Principal Upanishads,* 391–93; see also Heinrich Zimmer's translation and detailed analysis in *Philosophies of India,* 372–78; for additional background see Paul Deussen, *The Philosophy of the Upanishads* (1906; reprint, New York: Dover Publications, 1966).

6. The actual derivation may not be quite as colorful: the meaning of the noun *akṣa* is a die (as in gambling), cube, or seed, and hence the derivative *akṣi* (eye); the sense of *akṣara,* then, may be simply "unit."

7. Zimmer, *Philosophies of India,* 376–77.

8. *MU* 6.5, Hume, *Thirteen Principal Upanishads,* 426.

9. See Gombrich, "Ancient Indian Cosmology," 112–18.

10. *Chāndogya Upaniṣad* 2.23.2–3, Hume, *Thirteen Principal Upanishads,* 201.

11. *MU* 6.22.

12. See §2.4.

13. Indian mathematicians are reported to have been the first to "discover" the concept of zero; see also Ananda K. Coomaraswamy, "The Vedic Doctrine of Silence," *Indian Culture* 3 (1936–37): 559–69; and Heimann, *Facets,* 95–104.

14. *CU* 3.13.8.

15. The reference here is to the celebrated hymn to the frogs (*RV* 7.103), in which, according to Maurer, "the frogs are presented as the counterpart of the

Brahman priests in the world of nature. By their annual croaking at the culmination of the heat of spring, they are thought to bring on the monsoon rains. Their croaking is equivalent to the chanting of the Brahmans at the sacrifice, and so it has the same power to achieve its particular end." For further details and an English translation of the hymn, see Maurer, *Pinnacles,* 208–11.

16. *MU* 6.22.
17. *MU* 6.24.
18. Translation mine.
19. In Rolfe Humphries, trans., ***Lucretius, The Way Things Are: The De Rerum Natura of Titus Lucretius Carus*** (Bloomington: Indiana University Press, 1968), 133–34.
20. In this section I draw, with permission, on a number of insights and references in an unpublished paper, "Sonus: Boethian Debits and Credits," by Robert O. Gjerdingen.
21. Translated by Benjamin Jowett.
22. For an excellent survey article, see Umesha Mishra, "Physical Theory of Sound and its Origin in Indian Thought," *Allahabad University Studies* 2 (1926): 239–90; see also Brajendranath Seal, *The Positive Sciences of the Ancient Hindus* (reprint, Delhi: Motilal Banarsidass, 1985), 153–68.
23. See §3.6.
24. For the background and development of the theory of *dhvani,* see Anand Amaladass, S. J., *Philosophical Implications of Dhvani* (Vienna: Institute for Indology, University of Vienna, 1984); V. Raghavan, *Bhoja's Śṛṅgāra Prakāśa,* 3d ed. (Madras: Vasanta Press, 1978), 136–80; and K. Kunjunni Raja, *Indian Theories of Meaning,* 2d ed. (Madras: Adyar Library and Research Centre, 1969), 275–315.
25. *MB* 1.1–13; see also R. Sathyanarayana, "Śruti, Dhvani and Sphoṭa," *The Indian Theosophist* 82, nos. 10–11 (1985): 30–47; and Rowell, "Songs of Medieval India," 140–41.
26. See Maurer's translation of *RV* 10.125 in *Pinnacles,* 280–82; and Panikkar, *Vedic Experience,* 96–97.
27. See §4.5 and table 7.
28. For a thorough discussion of this controversial etymology, see R. K. Shringy's essay, "The Concept of *Śruti* as Related to *Svara,*" in *Saṅgīta-Ratnākara of Śārṅgadeva,* vol. 1 (Varanasi: Motilal Banarsidass, 1978), 398–417.
29. See chap. 2, n. 2.
30. See §7.2.
31. *NS* 1.6.16.
32. *MB* 1.17–23.
33. Literally the "knot of Brahmā," situated at the "root" of the navel and described in *SS* 1.2.145–48 as the life source of the human body; see also chap. 2, n. 18.
34. Sanskrit verbs are traditionally identified by their root (*nad*) and third person singular, present active indicative (*nadati*) forms, just as Latin nouns are cited in their nominative and genitive singular forms, e.g., *frater, fratris.*
35. See §1.2.
36. See Shringy, *Saṅgīta-Ratnākara,* 113.
37. See Rowell, "Songs of Medieval India," 146–47.
38. *Guhā,* the "secret place," sometimes used in a figurative sense for the heart but here referring to another cavity in the region of the navel.
39. As in *SS* 1.3.5; see Shringy, *Saṅgīta-Ratnākara,* 112.
40. *RV* 1.164.45 (see §§3.1–2).
41. For further details, see K. A. Subramania Iyer, *Bhartṛhari: A Study of the*

*Vākyapadīya in the Light of the Ancient Commentaries* (Poona: Deccan College, 1969), 144–46; and Pandey, *Abhinavagupta,* 497–508.

42. Pandey, *Abhinavagupta,* 498–500, 624–30.

43. Ibid., 496–502; see also Navjivan Rastogi, *The Krama Tantricism of Kashmir: Historical and General Sources,* vol. 1 (Delhi: Motilal Banarsidass, 1979), esp. 78–81.

44. Pandey, *Abhinavagupta,* 496–97.

45. In the present context *bindu* and *nāda* are used in a different sense and also a different order than in Mataṅga's explanation of *nāda-brahman.*

46. See W. Sidney Allen, *Phonetics in Ancient India* (London: Oxford University Press, 1953), 20–57; and William Dwight Whitney, *Sanskrit Grammar,* 2d ed. (Cambridge: Harvard University Press, 1889), 13–26.

47. *TU* 2.1, Hume, *Thirteen Principal Upanishads,* 283.

48. *BU* 3.8.3–11, Hume, *Thirteen Principal Upanishads,* 118–19.

49. See G. S. Kirk and J. E. Raven, *The Presocratic Philosophers: A Critical History with a Selection of Texts* (Cambridge: Cambridge University Press, 1957), 199–202.

50. For a brief survey of the history of the concept of ether, see Mary Hesse, "Ether," in *The Encyclopedia of Philosophy,* ed. Paul Edwards (New York: Macmillan, 1967), vol. 3, 66–69.

51. Used here in the most general sense of "musical sound."

52. *MB* 1.24; my translation.

53. An analogy drawn also by early Western authors, e.g., Boethius, *De institutione musica* 1.14.

54. Of the early Western authors, Vitruvius (*De architectura* 5.3.6–7) seems to have been among the first to recognize the spherical nature of sound waves, although not of course limited to the traditional ten directions of ancient Indian space; for the Mishra and Seal citations see n. 22.

55. The following section is a digest of the fuller arguments presented in several recent studies, particularly Lewis Rowell, "The Idea of Music in India and the Ancient West," in *Essays on the Philosophy of Music,* ed. Veikko Rantala, Lewis Rowell, and Eero Tarasti, *Acta Philosophica Fennica* 43 (1988): 323–42.

56. As B. C. Deva claims in his article, "The Emergence of the Drone in Indian Music," *Journal of the Music Academy, Madras* 23; the article is reprinted in B.C. Deva, *Psychoacoustics of Music and Speech* (Madras: Music Academy, 1967), 58–86.

57. I have argued this important aspect of Greek rhythmic theory in two studies: "Time in the Musical Consciousness of Old High Civilizations—East and West," in *The Study of Time 3,* ed. J. T. Fraser, N. Lawrence, and D. Park (New York: Springer-Verlag, 1978), 593–98; and "Aristoxenus on Rhythm," *Journal of Music Theory* 23, no. 1 (1979), 77–78 n. 26.

58. Fragment 115, trans. Philip Wheelwright, in his *The Presocratics* (New York: Odyssey Press, 1966), 78.

59. Ibid., fragments 116 and 117; see also Edward A. Lippman's brilliant analysis in his *Musical Thought in Ancient Greece* (New York: Columbia University Press, 1964), 10–12.

60. According to the testimony of Theon of Smyrna, *Mathematica* (trans. E. Hiller) 1.

61. Generally low-order integral ratios of the equal (e.g., 1:1), multiple (e.g., 2:1), and superparticular (e.g., 3:2) classes; for the Aristoxenian doctrine of rhythmic substance (*rhythmizomenon*), see Rowell, "Aristoxenus on Rhythm," 67–68, 71.

62. As in Boethius, *De institutione musica* 1.2; for an English translation, see *Fundamentals of Music [of] Anicius Manlius Severinus Boethius,* trans. Calvin M. Bower (New Haven: Yale University Press, 1989), 9–10.

63. Needham, *Science and Civilisation,* vol. 4, pt. 1, sec. 26, 131.

64. Ibid., 205.

65. For additional background of the important yin-yang theory, attributed to the philosopher Tsou Yen (340–260 B.C.?), see William Theodore de Bary, Wing-tsit Chan, and Burton Watson, comps., *Sources of Chinese Tradition* (New York: Columbia University Press, 1960), 96–97, 200–226.

66. Needham's conclusion in *Science and Civilisation,* 135.

67. For further details see Kenneth J. DeWoskin, *A Song for One or Two: Music and the Concept of Art in Early China* (Ann Arbor: Center for Chinese Studies, The University of Michigan, 1982), 37–39 and numerous indexed passages; Needham, *Science and Civilisation,* 133–41, 205–9; and David Pollard, "*Ch'i* in Chinese Literary Theory," in *Chinese Approaches to Literature from Confucius to Liang Ch'i-ch'ao* (Princeton: Princeton University Press, 1978), 43–66.

68. For an excellent discussion of the theory and a table of correspondences for the Five Agents system, see de Bary et al., *Sources of Chinese Tradition,* 214–26.

69. Needham, *Science and Civilisation,* vol. 4, pt. 1, 134–41, 178–84, and 186–92.

## CHAPTER FOUR

1. Hume, *Thirteen Principal Upanishads,* 275.

2. All translations from the *NS* (chap. 1, n. 27), which will be featured in this chapter, are mine.

3. For an introduction to the early phonetic literature see Allen, *Phonetics in Ancient India,* 1–7; and Vidhata Mishra, *A Critical Study of Sanskrit Phonetics* (Varanasi: Chowkhamba Sanskrit Series, 1972), 1–60; Rowell, "*Śikṣā* for the Twice-born" (chap. 1, n. 27) is a study of the *NS* with translations of many verses.

4. Used here in the sense of "evenness," which was the ideal in recitation; the word is unrelated to the *sāma* (from *sāman,* hymn) in *Sāmaveda.*

5. As in *NS* 1.1.5.

6. *Indraśatruḥ* means "Indra-enemy." Vṛtra intended to say "May the enemy of Indra prevail!" but his misaccentuation resulted in the meaning: "May Indra, the enemy, prevail!" For the grammatical details, see Bhise, *Nāradīyā Śikṣā,* 76.

7. The word *ṛc* (verse of praise) appears also as *ṛk* and *ṛg* (as in *Ṛgveda*), depending on the place of articulation of the following consonant.

8. *RV* 10.71.11, Panikkar, *Vedic Experience,* 95.

9. For a valuable introduction to the *Ṛgveda,* see Maurer, *Pinnacles,* 5–9.

10. Panikkar, *Vedic Experience,* 94.

11. Wayne Howard, *Sāmavedic Chant* (New Haven: Yale University Press, 1977), 2.

12. See §4.6 and the references mentioned in nn. 98–106.

13. See §4.5.

14. See §4.5.

15. For a valuable introduction, see Howard, *Sāmavedic Chant,* 1–25.

16. See Willi Apel, *Gregorian Chant* (Bloomington: Indiana University Press, 1958), 139 and 246 n. 1.

17. The variations among the Kauthuma, Rāṇāyanīya, and Jaiminīya schools are spelled out in Howard, *Sāmavedic Chant,* with many transcriptions and analyses; see also Wayne Howard, *The Decipherment of the Sāmavedic Notation of the Jai-*

*minīyas* (Helsinki: Finnish Oriental Society, 1988); and J. F. Staal, *Nambudiri Veda Recitation* (The Hague: Mouton, 1961), esp. 64–86.

18. See chap. 9 and an earlier study: Lewis Rowell, "Form in the Ritual Theatre Music of Ancient India," *Musica Asiatica* 5 (1988): 140–90.

19. I am indebted to Wayne Howard for this suggestion.

20. See Howard, *Sāmavedic Chant,* 8–9 and 14–25.

21. The three versions of this verse (*SV* 1.1.2.5) are taken from Alain Danielou's commentary, "Vedic Recitation and Chant" (The Music of India 1, no. 6, in the UNESCO series of phonodiscs entitled *A Musical Anthology of the Orient*), Bärenreiter-Musicaphon BM 30 L 2006.

22. See Howard, *Sāmavedic Chant,* 29–75.

23. For a brief introduction to the Vedic meters, see Basham, *Wonder,* 508–12; see also the standard work on Vedic meters: E. V. Arnold, *Vedic Metre in its Historical Development* (Cambridge: Cambridge University Press, 1905).

24. As in *RV* 1.1; for metrical analysis and discussion, see A. A. Macdonell, *A Vedic Reader* (London: Oxford University Press, 1917), 3–10.

25. *RV* 3.62.10, Panikkar, *Vedic Experience,* 38, with extensive commentary; see also Basham, *Wonder,* 162.

26. See especially the *Bṛhadāraṇyaka Upaniṣad* 5.14, in Hume, *Thirteen Principal Upanishads,* 155–57.

27. See §8.9.

28. For details, see Howard, *Sāmavedic Chant,* 16–25.

29. For *upohana,* see §9.4.1; for *ālāpana,* see §9.2.4.

30. See §9.2.3.

31. See §10.3.

32. *CU* 2.12.1, Hume, *Thirteen Principal Upanishads,* 195–96.

33. See Navjyoti Singh's appendix 7 ("Illustration of Various Kinds of Recitations of Ṛgveda Which Were Devised to Preserve Long Compositions Orally") in Debiprasad Chattopadhyaya, *History of Science and Technology in Ancient India: The Beginnings* (Calcutta: Firma KLM Pvt. Ltd., 1986), 506–13.

34. For illustrations, see Howard, *Sāmavedic Chant,* 78–91, 106–8, and 220–48.

35. See §4.6; and *NS* 1.6.1.–14, 1.7.1–5.

36. For the auspicious role of the right hand in Vedic ceremonies, see J. Gonda, *Vedic Ritual* (Leiden: E. J. Brill, 1980), 57–62. A more mundane reason for the priority of the right hand in daily life lies in the standard use of the left hand to wipe after a bowel movement.

37. A particularly rich selection of hand diagrams appears in Joseph Smits van Waesberghe, *Musikerziehung: Lehre und Theorie der Musik im Mittelalter* (Leipzig: VEB Deutscher Verlag für Musik, 1969), 120–43.

38. See §8.5.

39. That is, to emphasize the rising tone at the end of a question or when calling to a distance (Allen, *Phonetics in Ancient India,* 84).

40. *PS* 49, Allen, *Phonetics in Ancient India,* 84.

41. *NS* 1.6.21; also *Ṛk-Prātiśākhya* 13.46.49.

42. *ML* 11; see Wayne Howard, trans. and ed., *Mātrālakṣaṇam* (New Delhi: Indira Gandhi National Centre for the Arts, 1988), 14–15.

43. *ML* 11–12.

44. See §8.6.

45. *TP* 23.4–10, William Dwight Whitney, *Journal of the American Oriental Society* 9 (1871).

46. *CU* 2.22.1, Hume, *Thirteen Principal Upanishads,* 199–200.

47. Hume, *Thirteen Principal Upanishads,* 458.

48. See §2.2.

49. Mishra, *Sanskrit Phonetics,* 18–21.

50. Yugalakiśora Vyāsa, ed., *Śikṣā-Saṃgraha: A Collection of Śikṣās by Yājñavalkya and Others* (Varanasi: Benares Sanskrit Series, 1893).

51. As in the *Sarvasaṃmataśikṣā,* ed. and trans. A. O. Franke (Göttingen, 1886), 49.

52. Siddheshwar Varma, *Critical Studies in the Phonetic Observations of Indian Grammarians* (London: Royal Asiatic Society, 1929), introduction.

53. Allen, *Phonetics in Ancient India,* 6.

54. Arthur A. Macdonell, *A Sanskrit Grammar for Students,* 3d ed. (London: Oxford University Press, 1927), 10.

55. For the *gamakas*, see §11.7.

56. See table 6; see also Allen, *Phonetics in Ancient India,* 33–39.

57. For samples of the drum syllables, see Harold S. Powers's subsection, "Theory and Practice of Classical Music," in the entry on "India," sec. 2, no. 5, in *The New Grove Dictionary of Music and Musicians,* ed. Stanley Sadie, vol. 9, 118–25.

58. As cited in Plutarch, *De Plac. Phil.* iv.21.903C.

59. See Allen, *Phonetics in Ancient India,* 40–46.

60. As in *NS* 1.3.12; see §11.4.

61. *ṅ, ñ, ṇ, n,* and *m* (see table 6).

62. The model for this table appears in M. B. Emeneau and B. A. van Nooten, *Sanskrit Sandhi and Exercises,* 2d rev. ed. (Berkeley and Los Angeles: University of California Press, 1968), 1. Similar charts, with slightly different vocabulary and layout, appear in Allen, *Phonetics in Ancient India,* 20, and Whitney, *Sanskrit Grammar,* 73.

63. Such as nasality, aspiration, voicing, closure, constriction, and the like.

64. *PS* 9–10, trans. W. S. Allen.

65. For *svara,* see §§4.5 and 7.1–3; for *kāla,* see §§8.3 and 8.7; for *sthāna,* see §4.5.

66. See §3.5.

67. See J. A. B. van Buitenen, "Notes on *Akṣara,*" *Bulletin of the Deccan College Research Institute* 17, no. 2 (1955): 204–15.

68. See §11.7.

69. The other two are the *Lomasīśikṣā* and the *Gautamīśikṣā,* both considerably shorter than the *NS;* for their contents see Mishra, *Sanskrit Phonetics,* 15.

70. Especially 1.3, which is nonmetrical.

71. The first-century-A.D. Greek author Cleonides used the word *tone* (*tónos*) in four distinct senses: as a note, as an interval (equivalent to the modern whole step or whole tone), as "region of voice" (by which he meant one of the thirteen keys), and as pitch (high or low). See Oliver Strunk, comp. and ed., *Source Readings in Music History* (New York: W. W. Norton, 1959), 44.

72. The author is drawing an analogy between the three vocal registers and the three *savanas* (the pressings of the soma juice at sunrise, noon, and sunset).

73. *NS* 1.1.7–8.

74. See §§7.4–5.

75. See §3.4.

76. *NS* 1.2.4.

77. See §3.4.

78. 1.5.7–9.

79. For additional background, see Gustave Reese, *Music in the Middle Ages*

(New York: W. W. Norton, 1940), 149–51; the passage from Guido's *Epistola de ignoto cantu,* in which he explains and illustrates his system, is translated in Strunk, *Source Readings,* 121–25.

80. The basic meaning of *grāma* is "village," an assembly. Many scholars of Indian music have objected to the standard translation as "scale," preferring instead "collection" (of pitches)—which admittedly retains the force of the word *grāma.* I have never understood the basis for their objections: although the term "scale" implies a consecutive ordering of the notes (as in the Italian *scala,* ladder), this arrangement is no more than an abstraction drawn from the musical materials, and in no way does it imply that these notes must appear in consecutive order in performance or composition. Also, the term "scale" is appropriate in another sense—as the proportionate division of the pitch spectrum. So I shall insist on retaining the traditional translation.

81. 1.2.7; for the eccentric structure of this celestial scale, see chap. 7, n. 3.

82. For details, see §§7.2–6.

83. I will mention briefly a problem in interpreting this passage: all versions of the text that I have seen equate *mandra* with *dha* and *atisvāra* with *ni,* and hence the correlations in table 8. Because there is no evidence whatsoever that the seven *svara*s of the secular scale have ever been listed in a different order, many scholars have inferred that the Sāmavedic scale had a crooked (*vakra*) gamut. I find this utterly unconvincing and am more inclined to suspect an error in Nārada's text as it has come down to us. I have seen no indications that the question can be resolved by the study of modern Sāmavedic practice, so I stand by my interpretation in (3). It is clear that the conceptual basis of the *svara*s was different in the two systems; in this connection see Howard, *Samavedic Chant,* 38.

84. See §7.2.

85. For many of the reasons suggested by Robert Gauldin in his provocative article "The Cycle-7 Complex: Relations of Diatonic Set Theory to the Evolution of Ancient Tonal Systems," *Music Theory Spectrum* 5 (1983): 39–55.

86. See Table 8; the ranking of the four social classes is as follows: *brāhmaṇa* (the priestly class), *kṣatriya* (the warrior class), *vaiśya* (the merchant class), and *śūdra* (the menial class); for additional background, see Basham, *Wonder,* 137–51.

87. Curt Sachs, *The Rise of Music in the Ancient World—East and West* (New York: W. W. Norton, 1943), 64.

88. As demonstrated in the studies cited in nn. 17 and 102.

89. The word derives from the verbal root *rañj,* "to be colored (especially red), to feel affect," and consequently evokes subconscious associations with color, passion, desire, and beauty; for further analysis see §7.8.

90. *NS* 1.4.7–8.

91. The compound *grāma-rāga* can be analyzed in several ways, but its meaning is probably little more than "scalar mode."

92. See §7.8.

93. An attractive coinage in Harold S. Powers's article, "Mode," *The New Grove,* vol. 12, 377; see also Powers's valuable discussion of the concept of *rāga* in the same volume (428–36) and his article "India" (vol. 9) in which *rāga* is defined as "a continuum with scale and tune as its extremes" (98).

94. For an explanation of the Greek octave species, see Isobel Henderson, "Ancient Greek Music," in *Ancient and Oriental Music,* ed. Egon Wellesz, vol. 1 of *The New Oxford History of Music* (London: Oxford University Press, 1957), 352–58.

95. See §7.2.

96. N. Ramanathan, "The Concept of *Śruti-Jāti*-s," *Journal of the Music Academy, Madras* 51 (1980): 99–112.

97. *NS* 1.7.18.
98. See table 7 and (3).
99. *Aṣṭādhyāyī* 1.2.29–32.
100. 3.1.
101. Staal, *Nambudiri Veda Recitation,* 23.
102. J. E. B. Gray, "An Analysis of Nambudiri Ṛgvedic Recitation and the Nature of the Vedic Accent," *Bulletin of the School of Oriental and African Studies* 22, pt. 3 (1959): 519–20.
103. The following chapters pertain specifically to the *RV:* 1.8 and 2.1–7.
104. 1.8.8.
105. See above.
106. J. E. B. Gray, "Analysis of Ṛgvedic Recitation," *Bulletin of the School of Oriental and African Studies* 22, pt. 1 (1959): 87.
107. *RV* 8.48.3 and 13, Maurer, *Pinnacles,* 76–79.
108. See Maurer, *Pinnacles,* 75–88; and Basham, *Wonder,* 235–36.
109. Maurer, *Pinnacles,* 85–88; for an eloquent account of the symbolism associated with the *stambha* (or *skambha*), see Kapila Vatsyayan, *The Square and the Circle of the Indian Arts* (New Delhi: Roli Books International, 1983), 10–20 and passim.
110. R. Gordon Wasson has proposed the mushroom *Amanita muscaria* (the fly agaric) as the original soma plant; see Wasson, *Soma, Divine Mushroom of Immortality* (reprint, New York: Harcourt Brace Jovanovitch, 1971), and *Soma and the Fly-Agaric: Wasson's Rejoinder to Professor Brough* (Cambridge: Botanical Museum of Harvard University, 1972).
111. 2.8.passim.
112. 2.8.29.
113. 2.8.10 and 19.
114. 2.7.10.
115. 2.8.27.
116. 2.8.21.
117. See §3.2.
118. See §4.2.
119. *NS* 1.6.2–5.
120. *NS* 1.7.1–2.
121. See §11.4; the references in this paragraph are taken from *NS* 1.6.11–19 and 2.8.17 and 30.
122. For an index of this material and analysis, see Rowell, "Paradigms for a Comparative Mythology of Music," *Journal of the Indian Musicological Society* 18, no. 2 (1987): 14–29.
123. *NS* 1.5.3–4.
124. See (3).
125. For color symbolism in ancient India, see Gonda, *Vedic Ritual,* 44–47; I have not managed to locate a convincing explanation for the particular selection of colors in the *NS* 1.4.1–2.

## Chapter Five

1. Translated by Edwin Gerow, in *Theater of Memory: The Plays of Kālidāsa,* ed. Barbara Stoler Miller (New York: Columbia University Press, 1984), 257.
2. Umā is one of the many names for Pārvatī, Śiva's consort, and represents the feminine aspect of his dual nature; Śiva himself is often referred to as *ardhanārīśvara,* the "god who is half female." For the role of gender stereotypes in classifications of musical style, see § 11.2.

3. See §2.3.
4. See §11.8.
5. See the frontispiece and the accompanying commentary.
6. That is, the five elements, the sun and moon, and the priest who performs a sacrifice; see also §8.3.
7. As it still does today, especially in the many regional dance and dramatic genres of Kerala, e.g., Kathākalī and Kūṭiyāṭṭam; see also Raghavan, "Sanskrit Drama in Performance," 19.
8. For translations of Kālidāsa's three extant plays see Miller, *Theater of Memory;* translated plays by other major authors appear in Rachel Van M. Baumer and James R. Brandon, eds., *Sanskrit Drama in Performance* (Honolulu: University Press of Hawaii, 1981); and J. A. B. van Buitenen, trans., *Two Plays of Ancient India* (New York: Columbia University Press, 1968). For two standard introductions to the classical Indian theater, see A. Berriedale Keith, *The Sanskrit Drama in its Origin, Development, Theory and Practice* (London: Oxford University Press, 1924); and Henry W. Wells, *The Classical Drama of India* (London: Asia Publishing House, 1963).
9. The common epithet for an empathetic spectator is *sahṛdaya,* one who is "of similar heart," as defined by Abhinavagupta in his *Locana:* "Those people who are capable of identifying with the subject matter, as the mirror of their hearts has been polished through constant repetition and study of poetry, and who sympathetically respond in their own hearts." Translated by J. L. Masson and M. V. Patwardhan, in their *Śāntarasa and Abhinavagupta's Philosophy of Aesthetics* (Poona: Bhandarkar Oriental Research Institute, 1969), 78. See also §11.8.
10. Dimock et al., *Literatures of India,* 93–95.
11. See n. 9 and §11.8.
12. Keith, *Sanskrit Drama,* 12–68.
13. See in particular K. Kunjunni Raja, *Kutiyattam: An Introduction* (New Delhi: Sangeet Natak Akademi, 1964).
14. Baumer and Brandon, *Sanskrit Drama in Performance,* xiv–xv.
15. See §9.2.1–4.
16. See §§11.2 and 11.6.
17. *BN* 1.106–9, trans. Ghosh.
18. See §1.2.
19. *BN* 36.80–82, translation mine.
20. Chaps. 7 and 8, respectively.
21. V. Raghavan, "Sanskrit Drama in Performance," in Baumer and Brandon (see n.8), 18–19.
22. *BN* 1.13–14.
23. *BN* 1.17–18; for additional background and analysis, see Vatsyayan, *Square and the Circle,* 48–51; and idem, "Dance or Movement Techniques of Sanskrit Theater," in Baumer and Brandon, *Sanskrit Drama in Performance,* 48–50.
24. V. Raghavan, "Sanskrit Drama in Performance," 19.
25. Vatsyayan, "Dance or Movement Techniques of Sanskrit Theater," 51.
26. For a translation and study of Bharata's exposition of *rasa* and Abhinavagupta's comments, see J. L. Masson and M. V. Patwardhan, *Aesthetic Rapture: The Rasādhyāya of the Nāṭyaśāstra,* 2 vols. (Poona: Deccan College, 1970).
27. In 27.21–22, Bharata points out how a jealous, hostile, or bribed audience can ruin a performance by "screaming, buzzing, noisy clapping, throwing of cow-dung, clods of earth, grass and stones."
28. Ghosh translation, vol. 2, 1–28.
29. Ghosh translation, vol. 2, 29–49.

30. Ghosh translation, vol. 2, 53–105; the *tāla* system will be analyzed in chap. 8 and the ritual forms will be outlined in chap. 9.

31. Ghosh translation, vol. 2, 106–60.

32. In the Baroda edition these twenty-three verses are treated as a separate chapter (vol. 4, 393–402).

33. This point will be amplified in §6.2.

34. See chap. 1, nn. 25 and 30.

35. For an elaborate exposition and analysis of Abhinavagupta's explanation, see Lath, *Dattilam,* 61–90.

36. See §1.2.

37. See §5.4.

38. J. A. B. van Buitenen, *Two Plays of Ancient India,* 51.

39. See Lath, *Dattilam,* 82–86.

40. *BN* 5.8–21; see also Keith, *Sanskrit Drama,* 339.

41. Including the director, his assistant, the leading man and lady, the jester (*vidūṣaka*), courtesan, "parasite," fop, and servant—roles that are as precisely delineated as those of the members of a modern Gilbert and Sullivan troupe. See *BN* 35.66–90.

42. For a selection, see §9.5.

43. For further analysis, see Vatsyayan, *Square and the Circle,* 60–64; it is probable that the ancestral rites of the later *pūrvaraṅga* may have included human sacrifice.

44. For a brief explanation and references, see Margaret Stutley and James Stutley, *A Dictionary of Hinduism* (London: Routledge and Kegan Paul, 1977), 297–98.

45. See n. 9 and §11.8.

46. Ghosh translation, vol. 2, 156.

47. Chap. 33 in the Ghosh edition, vol. 2, 161–200; see §5.5 for a summary of this chapter.

48. Translation by Gerow, in Miller, *Theater of Memory,* 278.

49. *BN* 32.228–29, trans. Ghosh, vol. 2, 128.

50. *BN* 32.232–33, trans. Ghosh, vol. 2, 128.

51. For the special significance of even and odd numbers in ancient metric theory and practice, see §8.9.

52. *BN* 32.360–64.

53. *BN* 32.364–70.

54. *BN* 32.392.

55. *BN* 32.384–91.

56. *BN* 32.399.

57. *BN* 32.4–6. The eighteen are: Mukha, Pratimukha, Vaihāyasika, Sthita, Pravṛtta, Vajra, Sandhi, Saṁharaṇa, Prastāra, Upavarta, Māṣaghāta, Caturásra, Upapāta, Praveṇī, Śirṣaka, Saṁpiṣṭaka, Antāharaṇa, and Mahājanika. Most of these are illustrated and analyzed in chap. 9, and a particularly rich selection is included in the Oveṇaka *gītaka* (33), analyzed in §9.5.

58. *BN* 32.382.

59. *BN* 32.369–70, trans. Ghosh, vol. 2, 144.

60. See Paul Cravath's translation in Baumer and Brandon, *Sanskrit Drama in Performance,* 195–97.

61. *BN* 33.129–69.

62. See §9.2.2 and chap. 9, n. 29.

63. V. Raghavan, "Sanskrit Drama in Performance," 38–39.

64. For the topic of "qualifications," see §11.3.

65. See below for a chapter summary and further discussion of this point.
66. *Adhyāya* 5.
67. The conclusion reached by B. C. Deva in his article, "The Emergence of the Drone in Indian Music," reprinted in B. Chaitanya Deva, *Psychoacoustics of Music and Speech* (Madras: Music Academy, 1967), 58–86.
68. See §7.8.
69. For further discussion, see S. S. Janaki, "The Role of Sanskrit in the Development of Indian Music," *Journal of the Music Academy, Madras* 56 (1985): 68–70.
70. See §11.2.
71. *BN* 33.37–40; several of these topics (*laya, mārga, pāṇi,* and *yati*) are also among the topics of *tāla* (see §8.3).
72. Which include fasting, a haircut, white clothes, the choice of an auspicious day, mental preparation, the making of *maṇḍalas* (circular diagrams) with cowdung that is "free from bad smell," and offerings of honey, garlands, and perfumes (*BN* 33.259–71).
73. *BN* 33.250–51, trans. Ghosh, vol. 2, 195.
74. Curt Sachs, *Rhythm and Tempo* (New York: W. W. Norton, 1953), 105.
75. For comparative analyses of early rhythmic systems, see Rowell, "Time in the Musical Consciousness of Old High Civilizations—East and West," in *The Study of Time 3,* ed. J. T. Fraser, N. Lawrence, and D. Park (New York: Springer-Verlag, 1978), 578–611; and idem, "The Subconscious Language of Musical Time," *Music Theory Spectrum* 1 (1979): 96–106.
76. See Henry W. Wells's analysis in his *Classical Drama of India,* 6–19.

### Chapter Six

1. Translated by Sheldon Pollock, in his "Theory of Practice and the Practice of Theory in Indian Intellectual History," *Journal of the American Oriental Society* 105, no. 3 (1985): 508. This chapter draws upon many of the insights in this and two other articles by the same author: "The Idea of Śāstra in Traditional India," and "Playing by the Rules: Śāstra and Sanskrit Literature," in *Shastraic Traditions in Indian Arts,* ed. Anna Libera Dallapiccola, 2 vols. (Stuttgart: Steiner Verlag Wiesbaden GMBH, 1989), vol. 1, 17–26 and 301–12, respectively. I am indebted to Professor Pollock for sharing copies of the latter two papers with me in advance of publication.
2. Translation adapted from J. A. B. van Buitenen, *The Bhagavadgītā in the Mahābhārata: Text and Translation* (Chicago: University of Chicago Press, 1981), 135; cf. Franklin Edgerton's verse translation in his *Bhagavad Gītā* (Cambridge: Harvard University Press, 1972), 78.
3. Cited (in slightly different form) by Pollock in "Idea of Śāstra," 17.
4. *De institutione musica* 1.33, trans. Oliver Strunk in his *Source Readings,* 85.
5. See §6.3.
6. van Buitenen, *Bhagavadgītā in the Mahābhārata,* introduction, 14.
7. Ibid., 133–35.
8. For a general survey of the scientific literature, see M. Winternitz, *A History of Indian Literature,* vol. 3, pt. 2, trans. Subhadra Jhā (Delhi: Motilal Banarsidass, 1967); see also Sures Chandra Banerji, *Aspects of Ancient Indian Life—From Sanskrit Sources* (Calcutta: Punthi Pustak, 1972); see also a recent collection of valuable essays: Anna Libera Dallapiccola, ed., *Shastraic Traditions in Indian Arts,* 2 vols. (Stuttgart: Steiner Verlag Wiesbaden GMBH, 1989).
9. For additional background and English translations of representative passages, see William Theodore de Bary, Stephen N. Hay, Royal Weiler, and Andrew Yarrow, comps. and eds., *Sources of Indian Tradition* (New York: Columbia University Press, 1958), 205–15.

10. Readers who remain unconvinced are referred to Lee Siegel, *Laughing Matters: Comic Tradition in India* (Chicago: University of Chicago Press, 1987).

11. van Buitenen, *Two Plays of Ancient India,* 85–89.

12. A. B. Keith, *A History of Sanskrit Literature* (London: Oxford University Press, 1920), 410–11.

13. *Ars Poetica,* 361–65; for additional background on the history of this concept, see John Graham's survey article, "Ut pictura poesis," in *Dictionary of the History of Ideas,* ed. Philip P. Wiener (New York: Scribner's, 1973), vol. 4, 465–76.

14. See §3.2.

15. See §4.2.1 and the references cited in chap. 4, n. 33.

16. For the characters of the Devanagari script, see William Dwight Whitney, *Sanskrit Grammar,* 2d ed. (Cambridge: Harvard University Press, 1889), 2–3.

17. Dimock et al., *Literatures of India,* 35.

18. See §1.4 and chap. 1, n. 29.

19. See Lath, *Dattilam,* 1.

20. See §6.4.

21. Winternitz, *History of Indian Literature,* vol. 3, pt. 2, 419 and 428.

22. See §4.6 and *NS* 2.8.19.

23. See §10.7.

24. Translation adapted from R. K. Shringy's version in *SS,* vol. 2 (see chap. 1, n. 33); for an analysis of this passage and its context, see §§10.2–3.

25. *D* 55–62; see §7.8; see also Lath, *Dattilam,* 268–78; and Rowell, "Early Indian Musical Speculation and the Theory of Melody," *Journal of Music Theory* 25, no. 2 (1981): 230–41.

26. As in Cleonides *Intro.* 5 and Aristides Quintilianus *De musica* 1.7.

27. Translated by K. Kunjunni Raja and Radha Burnier, in their *The Saṃgītaratnākara of Śārṅgadeva,* vol. 4, chapter on dancing (Madras: Adyar Library and Research Centre, 1976), 1.

28. See frontispiece and accompanying commentary; also see §8.3.

29. See Raghavan, "Sanskrit Drama in Performance," 22–36.

30. For bibliographical details, see chap. 1, n. 33.

31. *MB* 6.

32. As in the verse analyzed above.

33. See §§8.6, 8.9, and 9.4.3.

34. For *guṇa*s and *doṣa*s in the musicological literature, see §11.4.

35. According to Bharata in *BN* 29.75.

36. *BN* 6.31–37.

37. For the metrical structure see Basham, *Wonder,* 511–12.

38. *SS* 3.202.

39. Both *ir* and *ā* are feminine singular endings in the nominative case.

40. "*Ālapti* has been proclaimed [to be]" = – – – ∪ ∪ – ∪ –.

41. See §8.9.

42. *NS* 1.6.17 and 2.8.27; see also §4.6.

43. For the pitch notations, see Isobel Henderson, "Ancient Greek Music," in *Ancient and Oriental Music,* ed. Egon Wellesz, vol. 1 of *The New Oxford History of Music* (London: Oxford University Press, 1957), 358–76; for the rhythmic notation, see Thomas J. Mathiesen, "Rhythm and Meter in Ancient Greek Music," *Music Theory Spectrum* 7 (1985): 169–80.

44. See D. R. Widdess, "Tāla and Melody in Early Indian Music: A Study of Nānyadeva's Pāṇikā Songs with Musical Notation," *Bulletin of the School of Oriental and African Studies, University of London* 44, pt. 3 (1981): 481–508; see also Wid-

dess's forthcoming study, *The Rāgas of Early Indian Music: Modes, Melodies and Musical Notations c. 600–1250* (Oxford: Oxford University Press).

45. See Robert O. Gjerdingen's provocative exploration of this problem, with particular reference to Indian singing, in his article, "Shape and Motion in the Microstructure of Song," *Music Perception* 6, no. 1 (Fall 1988): 35–64.

46. For a brief account, see Richard H. Hoppin, *Medieval Music* (New York: W. W. Norton, 1978), 57–62.

47. See Howard, *Sāmavedic Chant,* 29–75.

48. See §§3.4 and 4.5.

49. See §4.4; for some survivals of this practice in modern Hindustani drumming, see Harold S. Powers, "India," sec. 2, 5, in *The New Grove,* vol. 9, 122–25.

50. In a draft version of his forthcoming study, *The Rāgas of Early Indian Music* (see n. 44), which Dr. Widdess was kind enough to share with me.

51. See §§8.4 and 9.5.

52. See chap. 1, n. 28.

53. For the microlevels of ornamentation, see §11.7.

## Chapter Seven

1. Translation by Shringy, in his *Saṅgīta-Ratnākara,* vol. 1, 134–35.

2. See §§3.4 and 4.5.

3. This would appear to be no more than a slight discrepancy between two otherwise identical scales, but its consequences are multiplied throughout the system (in that each derivative scale must be traced back to one of the two parent scales to establish its proper tuning). This in turn must have stimulated efforts to put the system of tuning on a more scientific footing and prove that the *śruti*s actually existed and could be demonstrated in practice. For additional background and an account of Bharata's celebrated demonstration with two identically tuned vinas (*BN* 28.24–28, Ghosh translation, vol. 2, 7–9), see Lath, *Dattilam,* 212–17. Because the *ma-grāma* was conceived as running from lower *ma* to upper *ma,* readers may encounter it in other sources with the following sequence of *śruti*s: 3, 4, 2, 4, 3, 2, 4 (the equivalent of the Western Mixolydian mode, running from *g* to *g'*). It is important to point out, however, that the *svara* names remained the same: *do,* in the ancient Indian system, was fixed, not movable. And it should also be remembered that the two *grāma*s were nothing more than neutral background collections of pitches with no built-in tendencies for tonal gravitation—until actualized in a particular *jāti* or *grāmarāga* with a particular *svara* designated as the focal tone or *aṁśa* (§7.5). This being the case, it is a moot point whether a scale was conceived as "running" from *sa* or *ma.* To complete the picture, the sequence of *śruti*s in the *ga-grāma* (see §4.5 and chap. 4, n. 81) as reported by Śārṅgadeva in *SS* 1.4.3c–5 is as follows: 4, 3, 3, 3, 4, 3, 2. I have not dealt with this scale, not only because there is little support for it in the *śāstra*s but because I fail to find it credible. Note that there is only one semitone. It remains a historical curiosity, and it is probable that only someone with the expertise of the celestial musicians would be able to make anything out of it. It is clearly lacking in the properties that ancient musicians found valuable in the *sa-* and *ma-grāma*s.

4. For a brief introduction to the scales of ancient Greece and the medieval church modes, see Donald J. Grout and Claude V. Palisca, *A History of Western Music,* 4th ed. (New York: W. W. Norton, 1988), 9–23, 74–82.

5. For details, see J. Murray Barbour, *Tuning and Temperament: A Historical Survey,* 2d ed. (East Lansing: Michigan State University Press, 1953); J. Murray Bar-

bour and Fritz A. Kuttner, *The Theory and Practice of Just Intonation* (New York: Musurgia Records, 1958); and Easley Blackwood, *The Structure of Recognizable Diatonic Tunings* (Princeton: Princeton University Press, 1985).

6. See, in particular, articles by Antsher Lobo, R. Sathyanarayana, and K. K. Verma in "Music and Science," pt. 2, *Sangeet Natak* 17 (1970): 5–74; see also N. A. Jairazbhoy, "An Interpretation of the 22 Śrutis," *Asian Music* 6, nos. 1–2 (1975): 38–59.

7. For details and calculations, see Ellis's English translation of Hermann L. F. Helmholtz, *On the Sensations of Tone* (reprint, New York: Dover, 1954), appendix xx, 431, 446–57. In the following text the centitone equivalents for the various intervals mentioned have been rounded to the nearest whole number.

8. The four are the diatonic semitones (e.g., C/D flat): 16:15 = 111.7, 27:25 = 133.2; the chromatic semitones (e.g., C/C sharp): 25:24 = 70.7, 135:128 = 92.2.

9. And also, by the same procedure, the difference between the Pythagorean major third (81:64 = 407.8) and the just major third (5:4 = 386.3), since the former is the result of 2 × 9:8 and the latter, of 9:8 + 10:9. For details on the special role of the syntonic comma, see Blackwood, *Diatonic Tunings,* 46–48.

10. See §6.3.

11. *MB* 1.27–42.

12. Not vice versa. For an analysis of this passage and its subtle arguments, see R. K. Shringy's appendix 3, "The Concept of *Śruti* as Related to *Svara,*" in his *Saṅgīta-Ratnākara,* vol. 1, 398–417.

13. *MB* 1.43.

14. See R. Sathyanarayana, "*Śruti:* The Scalic Foundation," *Sangeet Natak* 17 (1970): 58–74.

15. The atomistic nature of much of ancient Greek musical thought is reflected in the frequent use of the word *semeion* (a point, as in geometry) for the basic units of pitch and especially of time, as well as for the signs by which these units were notated.

16. Sathyanarayana, "*Śruti,*" 64–65.

17. *MB* 1.44–47; see also Lath, *Dattilam,* 221–25.

18. The *schemata* (see Cleonides *Intro.* 9 and chap. 4, n. 94).

19. I am indebted to Prem Lata Sharma for calling my attention to some relevant passages.

20. It must be of some significance that these *svaras* were situated within the only two four-*śruti* intervals unaffected by the choice of *grāma* (*ga/ma,* degrees 3 and 4; and *ni/sa,* degrees 7 and 8); and the variable status of *pa* in the two basic scales may help to explain the greater stability of *ma* (the fourth degree) in the ancient system as a whole. It is not clear whether the two altered scale degrees were substitutes for *ga* and *ni* or whether they could appear as partners within the same scale formation; and the documentary evidence is confusing. N. A. Jairazbhoy clears up some of the confusion in his article, "Bharata's Concept of *Sādhāraṇa,*" *Bulletin of the School of Oriental and African Studies, University of London* 21 (1958): 54–60, but some troubling questions remain. Bharata apparently drew a distinction between deploying these notes as permanent members of a scale and as what we in the West call "accidentals." As permanent members (*svara-viśeṣa*), *antara-ga* was restricted to the *ma-grāma, kākalī-ni* to the *sa-grāma;* when this was the case, the regular forms of *ga* and *ni* did not appear. As accidentals (*antara-svaras*), their role was more limited and they could appear together and in combination with their unaltered forms. However, many of the specifications for the early *grāmarāgas* and *rāgas* contradict Bharata's teachings in that the two altered *svaras* are prescribed

together; his doctrines apply more fully to the system of *jātis* (§7.8). Jairazbhoy concludes that "the implications of the system of *grāmas*, the *sādhāranas*, and the *jātis*, had already been forgotten by Śārṅgadeva's time (thirteenth century)."

21. *BN* 28.34; Lath, *Dattilam,* 262; see also Jairazbhoy, "Bharata's Concept of *Sādhāraṇa,*" 54.

22. As in the *jātis* (see §7.8).

23. The special role of *ma* will be argued below, and readers are urged to keep in mind that *sa* (the first scale degree) had not yet become the common tonic for the entire modal system; if anything, *ma* was at this time the pivotal tone for the system.

24. The category of those with *ma* is by far the larger category, as we might surmise. In the system of seventy-two *melakarta rāgas* (see §7.8 and n. 74), *melas* 1–36 specify *śuddha* or natural *ma,* whereas *melas* 37–72 contain *prati* or raised *ma.* One of the few generalizations that we can make is that the latter are usually assigned to the evening. Harold S. Powers, in his dissertation, "The Background of the South Indian Rāga-System" (Princeton University, 1958), estimates that (1) there are only about seven or eight *rāgas* in common use that use the raised fourth degree, and (2) that "a good eighty percent of the music heard in concert" is in *rāgas* using the natural fourth degree (vol. 1, 24–25).

25. See Sachs, *Rise of Music,* 64–65.

26. Bence Szabolcsi, *A History of Melody,* trans. Cynthia Jolly and Sara Karig (London: Barrie and Rockliff, 1965), 37–39.

27. Jean-Philippe Rameau, *Treatise on Harmony,* trans. Philip Gossett (New York: Dover Publications, 1971), esp. 65 and 237.

28. *SS* 1.3.50b–51, trans. Shringy, in his *Saṅgīta-Ratnākara,* vol. 1, 149.

29. Translation adapted from N. Ramanathan, "*Vādī, Samvādī, Vivādī,* and *Anuvādī Svara*-s," *Journal of the Music Academy, Madras* 54 (1983): 62.

30. For the concept of interval class, see Allen Forte, *The Structure of Atonal Music* (New Haven: Yale University Press, 1973), 13–15.

31. Deva, "The Emergence of the Drone" (see chap. 3, n. 56).

32. I can report some progress. I have long suspected that set theory could provide some explanations for the early formation and development of musical scales—not, perhaps, for the mental processes by which ancient musicians formalized their musical preferences, but for the underlying musical instincts and impulses. After hearing John Clough and Jack Douthett's paper, "Maximally Even Sets" (read at the joint meeting of the American Musicological Society and the Society for Music Theory, October 1989, Austin, Texas), I sent relevant portions of this chapter to the authors and asked whether their theory might shed some light on the present problem. Their response far exceeded my expectations. It turns out that the concept of maximal evenness (which involves restrictions on the specific sizes of diatonic intervals—seconds, thirds, etc.) does indeed help to explain both (1) the derivation of the seven-note diatonic set from the chromatic universe of twenty-two *śrutis* and (2) the derivation of the several pentatonic versions from their heptatonic source scales. More work needs to be done, and our conclusions are still too tentative to present in any detail; I will simply make a few pertinent comments.

The theory of maximally even (ME) sets has so far failed to provide a comprehensive explanation for the derivation of the hexatonic collections, though it is consistent with my conclusions regarding these collections in what follows. The theory does, however, suggest that the pathway from the twenty-two *śrutis* to the seven *svaras* is a lawful one and that the resulting heptatonic scales can be derived either (1) as "second-order ME sets" (postulating an intermediate twelve-note scale); or

(2) on the basis of a requirement for sonant relationships, as defined above, coupled with a requirement that step sizes, measured in *śrutis*, comprise three consecutive integers.

And further, my comment below that the pentatonic versions are obtained "by insuring that the scale contains two nonconsecutive gaps of minimal size, instead of two consecutive gaps or a single larger interval" is—as Clough points out in a personal communication (29 June 1990)—"logically equivalent to the formal definition of a ME pentatonic set drawn from a heptatonic set." As he concludes, with respect to the entire pathway from 22 (through 12), to 7, and 5, "There is a fine orderliness, a lovely (if incomplete) design in the *ways* evenness and sonance present themselves in the Indian scheme."

All of this lends support to my instinctive conclusion that many of the apparent anomalies in ancient scale systems are the result, not of caprice or idiosyncracy or ingenious attempts to reconcile the conflicting preferences of various ethnic traditions, but rather of our failure to understand fully the impulses that motivated early musicians to select satisfying and flexible pitch collections from a larger universe of possibilities. Clough, Douthett, N. Ramanathan, and I are preparing a further study of the ancient Indian system of scales, a study that so far appears to offer interesting extensions of the findings in their Austin paper (to be published in the spring 1991 issue of the *Journal of Music Theory*). For additional background, see John Clough and Gerald Myerson, "Variety and Multiplicity in Diatonic Systems," *Journal of Music Theory* 29 (1985): 249–70; a different version of this paper appeared in *American Mathematical Monthly* 93, no. 9 (1986): 695–701.

33. That is, the pentatonic scale without semitones (as in the pattern of black keys on the piano); see Szabolcsi, *History of Melody,* 11–35, and his essay on "Pentatonicism and Cultural History," 216–43. Each of these sets would have been available in a complete set of rotations and with different sonant relationships: in other words, they are not yet *rāgas*.

34. Translation adapted from Ghosh, vol. 2, p. 39.

35. For the microlevels of ornamentation, see §11.7.

36. Cleonides *Intro.* 14.

37. According to Lath, *Dattilam,* 300–303.

38. *BN* 29.17–76.

39. *SS* 1.6.1–65b, Shringy, *Saṅgīta-Ratnākara,* vol. 1, 234–65.

40. *D* 99B–108, Lath, *Dattilam,* 304–10.

41. *SS* 1.6.64c–65b, trans. Shringy.

42. For the *gamakas* and a translation of Pārśvadeva's exposition, see §11.7; for the later history of the idea of *gamaka,* see Powers, "India," *New Grove,* vol. 9, 105–7.

43. Translation by D. R. Widdess, from an unpublished talk, "Aspects of the Aesthetics of Indian Music: *Rāga,*" used by permission.

44. *NS* 2.7.12.

45. For the full range of meanings, see M. Monier-Williams, *A Sanskrit–English Dictionary,* new edition (Oxford: Clarendon Press, 1899), 861B.

46. *BN* 28.76–78; for the concept of sonance see §7.5; see also Lath, *Dattilam,* 269–70.

47. Powers, "India," *New Grove,* vol. 9, 98; see §4.5.

48. *D* 48–97A and *BN* 28.38–151; for analysis and historical background see Lath, *Dattilam,* 265–99.

49. Allen, *Phonetics in Ancient India,* 90; the reference here is to Kallinātha's commentary on *SS* 1.3.7.

50. Also known as Niṣādavatī.

51. See §7.2.
52. Ṣāḍjī was apparently unavailable in pentatonic form.
53. For the concept of *lakṣaṇa,* see §6.3.
54. This limitation would apply to *jātis* with *aṁśas* higher than *ga;* for additional background, see Lath, *Dattilam,* 271–73.
55. Interestingly, the one such exception mentioned by Bharata (when *ga* is the final, one is permitted to move down as far as *ri*) produces a semitone below the final, in contrast to the convention of Western chant that prohibits the *subsemitonium modi,* as in mode 5 (Lydian). I rely here on Lath's reading in *Dattilam,* 273.
56. Apparently in consonant relationship, following the requirement noted in §7.6 in the case of the pentatonic *tānas*, which reinforces the suspicion that a consistent, although unstated, algorithm dictates the process by which heptatonic collections were converted into hexatonic and pentatonic versions. In this connection see n. 32.
57. Reckoned on the basis of the twenty-five possible *aṁśas* in the system of seven pure *jātis.*
58. One from the Andhra region on the Bay of Bengal and "Northern" versions of Ṣāḍjī, Gāndhārī, and Madhyamā; this type of classification is reminiscent of the *deśī* movement (see §§1.2 and 8.8).
59. I have analyzed this *jāti* in greater detail in "Early Indian Musical Speculation and the Theory of Melody," *Journal of Music Theory* 25, no. 2 (1981): 238–39.
60. See (12).
61. *NS* and *K* (chap. 1, nn. 27 and 28).
62. And subdivided into five categories: the pure (*śuddha*), deviant (*bhinna*), extravagant (*gauḍa*), passionate (*vesara*), and mixed (*sādhāraṇī*) species.
63. Widdess, *Rāgas of Early Indian Music* (see chap. 6, n. 44).
64. R. F. Wolpert, "Lute Music and Tablatures of the Tang Period" (Ph.D. diss., University of Cambridge, 1975), 106–11.
65. Cf. §7.2.
66. For similar displays and additional background, see Harold Powers, "An Historical and Comparative Approach to the Classification of *Rāgas* (with an Appendix on Ancient Indian Tunings)," *Selected Reports,* vol. 1, no. 3, Institute of Ethnomusicology, UCLA (1970), 4–6, 59–63.
67. In Western terms, two "Dorians," two "Mixolydians," and three "Ionians" (one of the last a deficient version).
68. See §7.4 and n. 20; because the literature records no lasting consensus on the role of the two altered *svaras* in the early *rāga* system, it is useful to bear in mind that their function could at various times be described as (1) a permanent member of the scale, (2) a note that alternated with the regular form of *ga* or *ni,* or (3) a temporary auxiliary.
69. Gauldin, "Cycle-7 Complex," 53.
70. As in the tension between the thetic and dynamic *mesai* of ancient Greek music and the functional roles of the final and dominant in medieval Western chant.
71. Of the several diatonic tunings cited by Greek authors such as Archytas, Aristoxenus, and Ptolemy, only one—the Ditonic Diatonic—featured whole steps of identical size. The model for my hypothesis is the standard tetrachord of just intonation:

| T | T | S | = | perfect fourth |
|---|---|---|---|---|
| 9:8 | 10:9 | 16:15 | = | 4:3 |
| 204 | 182 | 112 | = | 498 cents |

72. Powers, "Classification of *Rāgas,*" 62.

73. See Basham, *Wonder,* 302.

74. S. Subrahmanya Śāstri, ed., *The Caturdaṇḍī Prakāśika of Śrī Venkaṭamakhin of Tanjore* (Madras: Music Academy, 1934). For a lucid introduction to the system of seventy-two *melakarta rāgas*, see S. Sambamoorthy, *South Indian Music,* vol. 3, 6th ed. (Madras: Indian Music Publishing House, 1964), 30–77. For a useful chart, see A. Krishnaswamy, *Melakarta and Janya Rāga Chart* (Madras: Sakthi Priya Publications, n.d.).

75. In V. N. Bhātkhaṇḍe, *Kramik Pustak Mālikā* (Hathras: Saṅgīt Kāryālay, 1954–59); for an explanation of the system, see N. A. Jairazbhoy, *The Rāgs of North Indian Music: Their Structure and Evolution* (London: Faber and Faber, 1971), 46–64.

CHAPTER EIGHT

1. Translated by Raimundo Panikkar, in his "Time and History in the Tradition of India: *Kāla* and Karma," in *Cultures and Time* (Paris: UNESCO Press, 1976), 63; for a different translation and Helārāja's commentary, see Peri Sarveswara Sharma, *The Kālasamuddeśa of Bhartṛhari's Vākyapadīya* (Delhi: Motilal Banarsidass, 1972), 87–89.

2. Hume, *Thirteen Principal Upanishads,* 434.

3. See §§8.2 and 9.2.

4. But without any of their special connotations in Heinrich Schenker's theory of musical structure.

5. Translation mine, with reference to Maurice Bloomfield, *Hymns of the Atharva-Veda* (Oxford: Clarendon Press, 1897), 224–25, 681–88; Panikkar, "Time and History," 65–66; and William Dwight Whitney, *Atharva-Veda-Saṃhitā,* rev. and ed. C. R. Lanman (Cambridge: Harvard University Press, 1905), 987–91.

6. See Gombrich, "Ancient Indian Cosmology," 110–42; and Heinrich Zimmer, *Myths and Symbols in Indian Art and Civilization,* ed. Joseph Campbell (reprint, New York: Harper and Row, 1962), 11–19.

7. For the significance of naming and the philosophical doctrine of *nāmarūpa,* see §9.1.

8. *Maitri Upaniṣad* 6.15.

9. *RV* 10.90, Maurer, *Pinnacles,* 271–76.

10. Panikkar, "Time and History," 63–71.

11. *AB* 31.42.

12. For additional background, see Heimann, *Facets,* 95–104.

13. *Vākyapadīya* 3.9.4 and 15; see Sharma, *Kālasamuddeśa,* 45–51.

14. See Kanti Chandra Pandey, *Comparative Aesthetics,* vol. 1 (Indian Aesthetics), 2d ed. (Varanasi: Chowkhamba Sanskrit Series, 1959), 122–24.

15. *BN* 31, translation mine; for an English translation of the verse that stimulated Abhinavagupta's poetic imagination, see *The Nāṭyaśāstra,* trans. Ghosh, vol. 2, 53.

16. *D* 110A; see Lath, *Dattilam,* 101–6, 313.

17. See below for further discussion of these terms.

18. For background see C. Sivaramamurti, *Naṭarāja in Art, Thought, and Literature* (New Delhi: National Museum, 1974), 31–33; and Zimmer, *Myths and Symbols,* 151–75; for a poetic interpretation of this epithet in the benedictory verse from Kālidāsa's *Śākuntala,* see the frontispiece and accompanying commentary.

19. For the symbolism of Śiva's trident (the *triśūla*) and literary references, see Stutley and Stutley, *Dictionary of Hinduism,* 305.

20. For the full semantic range of these words, see Monier-Williams, *Sanskrit-English Dictionary,* 440B and C, 444C–445A.

21. For additional background, see Rowell, "Tālā," in *Kalātattvakośa: A Lexicon of Fundamental Concepts of the Indian Arts,* vol. 2, ed. Bettina Bäumer (New Delhi: Indira Gandhi National Centre for the Arts, 1990).

22. See Hoppin, *Medieval Music,* 362–67.

23. See (16).

24. For a comparison of the *tāla* topics in *BN* and *D,* see Lath, *Dattilam,* 22–29.

25. That is, *samā* (even), *srotogatā* (gaining speed like a river), and *gopucchā* (tapering like a cow's tail); see Lath, *Dattilam,* 365–67.

26. *Prakaraṇa* means "production" or "accomplishment"; for descriptions and reconstructions of representative forms, see §9.5.

27. For *parivarta,* see §§8.10 and 9.3; for *upavartana* (a related device), see §9.4.2.

28. See Sambamoorthy, *South Indian Music,* vol. 3, 107–11, and vol. 4, 169–84.

29. For the complete list, see Sambamoorthy, *South Indian Music,* vol. 4, 169–70.

30. See §8.8.

31. The sources do not indicate how the *dhruva* snaps were spaced between the other gestures.

32. This symbol (a boldface capital **S**) will appear frequently in the various diagrams and reconstructions below and in chap. 9; readers who are familiar with the traditional Indian system of rhythmic notation shown in parentheses in (18) and explained in the accompanying text are warned not to confuse this symbol with the similar symbol representing the long (*guru*) duration.

33. For which the normative pattern of accent is **1 2 3 4**.

34. Especially in passages of *upohana* (§9.4.1).

35. See §8.6.

36. Note here that inflating a pattern from twice to four times its original length also requires the prefixing of additional silent gestures, that is,

*ni* *pra*

becomes

*ā* *ni* *vi* *pra*

37. See (18).

38. See §8.9.

39. *D* 122B–130A, *BN* 31.7–23. Only the first three *tāla*s in (18) are expounded in *D;* see Lath, *Dattilam,* 320–35.

40. With a clear preference for reversing this pattern in the manifold states, so as to end with the gesture *sannipāta,* which I describe below as a gesture of summation.

41. In an essay on Claude Debussy's *Prélude à "L'Après-midi d'un faune."*

42. This *tāla* has three names: Uttara (the "last" or "northern" *tāla*), Pañcapāṇi ("five-handed," probably a reference to the fingers), and the nonsensical Ṣaṭpitāputrakaḥ ("son of six fathers," a mnemonic formula for the sequence of six durations as shown in long and short syllables at the bottom of [18]).

43. For additional background, see N. Ramanathan, "*Kalā, Mātrā, Laya,* and *Mārga,*" *Journal of the Indian Musicological Society* 11, nos. 3–4 (1980): 14–27.

44. For analysis and additional references, see Rowell, "Paradigms for a Comparative Mythology of Music," *Journal of the Indian Musicological Society* 18, no. 2 (1987): 16–17.

45. M. M. (= Maelzel metronome) ♩ = 60 indicates a rate of sixty quarter notes per minute.

46. Wallace Berry, *Structural Functions in Music* (Englewood Cliffs, N.J.: Prentice-Hall, 1976), 305.

47. Varma, *Critical Studies,* 170–78; see also §4.2.3.
48. Chattopadhyaya, *Science and Technology,* 223–37.
49. Sharma, "*Śāstra* and *Prayoga*" (chap. 1, n. 2), 1.
50. See (16).
51. Cf. (19) and (20).
52. In this section I draw on many of the valuable insights in Sharma, "*Śāstra* and *Prayoga,*" 10–14.
53. These verses have been collected in Anil Bihari Beohar, "Mataṅgakṛta Bṛhaddeśī kā Adhyāyana" (Ph.D. diss., Banaras Hindu University, 1986), appendix 2, vol. 1, 347–48.
54. See Hoppin, *Medieval Music,* 353–57.
55. Sharma, "*Śāstra* and *Prayoga,*" n. 4.
56. A point emphasized in many of the papers presented in the workshop, "*Śāstra* and *Prayoga* in the Performing Arts," during the Seventh World Sanskrit Conference (August 1987), Leiden, Netherlands.
57. Sharma, "*Śāstra* and *Prayoga,*" n. 3.
58. See Powers, "India," sec. 2, 5, in *New Grove,* vol. 9, 118–22.
59. Sachs, *Rhythm and Tempo,* 21–32.
60. Sharma, "*Śāstra* and *Prayoga,*" n. 9.
61. Ibid., 9–10.
62. See (20) and (21).
63. Sharma, "*Śāstra* and *Prayoga,*" nn. 7 and 16; see also Joan L. Erdman, "The Empty Beat: *Khālī* as a Sign of Time," *American Journal of Semiotics* 1, no. 4 (1982): 21–45.
64. I am indebted to N. Ramanathan for assistance in deciphering Śārṅgadeva's metrical code.
65. *Virāma* signifies a pause, stop (as at the end of a sentence), or metrical caesura; also the oblique substroke placed under a final consonant to indicate that no vowel follows.
66. See (26).
67. See (18).
68. See §8.5 and (18).
69. A name that emphasizes the conceptual "triangularity" of this *tāla* and suggests that the structural numbers were manifested more by the number and grouping of the units than by the total time span they occupy (as measured in *mātrās*).
70. I argue this point in "Form in the Ritual Theatre Music of Ancient India," *Musica Asiatica* 5 (1988): 185–86; for the tradition of modal rhythm in the European Middle Ages, see Hoppin, *Medieval Music,* 221–31.
71. Especially in H. D. Velankar, *Jayadāman: A Collection of Ancient Texts on Sanskrit Prosody and a Classified List of Sanskrit Metres . . .* (Bombay: Haritosha Samiti, 1949); idem, "Sanskrit Metres: Their Evolution and Principles of Division," in *The Cultural Heritage of India,* vol. 5, ed. Suniti Kumar Chatterji, 2d ed. (Calcutta: The Ramakrishna Mission Institute of Culture, 1978), 303–11.
72. *Svara,* that is, in the sense of the three Vedic accents (see §4.5); *saṅgīta,* with reference to the "music" of the verse.
73. *Varṇa,* in the sense of the letters representing individual syllables and hence a type of verse whose music resides in the durations of the syllables, not their pitch.
74. *Tāla,* in the sense of the stress accent produced by "beating time" (in this case, with the voice) at more or less regular intervals.
75. See below and (29).

76. See (29); for additional background on Sanskrit metrics, see Keith, *Sanskrit Literature,* 415–421.
77. Velankar, *Jayadāman,* 121; see below for a similar, longer line.
78. For some exceptions, see Rowell, "The Songs of Medieval India," *Music Theory Spectrum* 9 (1987): 148–50.
79. In recitation, that is, not in music proper.
80. Velankar, *Jayadāman,* 17–18.
81. For the concept of responsion, see Paul Maas, *Greek Metre,* trans. Hugh Lloyd-Jones (Oxford: Clarendon Press, 1962), 23–51.
82. For the lyric and stichic meters, see D. S. Raven, *Greek Metre* (London: Faber and Faber, 1962), 17–20.
83. Velankar, *Jayadāman,* 128.
84. For the Sanskrit text, an excellent English translation, and a discussion of the meter (introduction, 4–5), see Kālidāsa, *The Cloud Messenger,* trans. Franklin Edgerton and Eleanor Edgerton (Ann Arbor: University of Michigan Press, 1964).
85. Velankar, *Jayadāman,* 19–20.
86. See §§9.3 and 9.5.
87. Whitney, *Sanskrit Grammar,* 27.
88. Ibid.
89. According to Lath, *Dattilam,* 112–16.
90. See §9.2.4.
91. From the common verbal root *vṛt* (to turn); see also the derivatives *parivarta* (§§8.3 and 9.3), *upavartana* (§9.4.2), and *vṛtti* (§§11.1 and 11.6).

Chapter Nine

1. Panikkar, *Vedic Experience,* 666.
2. Hume, *Thirteen Principal Upanishads,* 327.
3. Monier-Williams, *Sanskrit-English Dictionary,* 824, 885–86.
4. Zimmer, *Philosophies of India,* 23–27.
5. For the full range of meanings, see Monier-Williams, *Sanskrit-English Dictionary,* 823.
6. For ancient Greek concepts of form, see Rowell, "Aristoxenus on Rhythm," *Journal of Music Theory* 23 (1979): 68–70.
7. Edgerton, in *Bhagavad Gītā,* 55–61 (vv. 5, 10–11, 52–53).
8. Heimann, *Facets,* 31–36.
9. See chap. 6, n. 13.
10. As in the *deśī* movement: see §§1.2, 8.8, 10.1, and 10.6.
11. For a comparative study, see Robert L. Scranton, *Aesthetic Aspects of Ancient Art* (Chicago: University of Chicago Press, 1964).
12. For a comparative study of Indian and Japanese musical preferences, see Rowell, *Thinking about Music* (Amherst: University of Massachusetts Press, 1983), 194–98.
13. See §8.10.
14. See §§9.2.4 and 9.4.1.
15. Rowell, "Early Indian Musical Speculation," 218–28.
16. For further arguments and illustrations from Western music, see Rowell, *Thinking about Music,* 170, 173–75, 197–98.
17. See Barney Childs, "Time and Music: A Composer's View," *Perspectives of New Music* 15 (1977): 195–96.
18. As in the standard three sections of the eighteenth-century sonata-allegro: exposition, development, and recapitulation.

19. See §2.4.

20. This imagery is strikingly reminiscent of the medieval European concept of macrocosm and microcosm; for the background of this idea and a rich selection of illustrations, see S. K. Heninger, Jr., *The Cosmographical Glass: Renaissance Diagrams of the Universe* (San Marino, Calif.: Huntington Library, 1977), esp. 144–58.

21. Vatsyayan, *Square and the Circle,* 18–19.

22. For survey articles on two of these terms, *śarīra* (Prem Lata Sharma) and *prāṇa* (H. N. Chakravarty), see *Kalātattvakośa: A Lexicon of Fundamental Concepts of the Indian Arts,* vol. 1, ed. Bettina Bäumer (New Delhi: Indira Gandhi National Centre for the Arts, 1988), 71–96, 97–115.

23. Zimmer, *Myths and Symbols,* 130–36.

24. Basham, *Wonder,* 347.

25. Heinrich Zimmer, *The Art of Indian Asia: Its Mythology and Transformations,* comp. and ed. Joseph Campbell (Princeton: Princeton University Press, 1955), vol. 1, 269–70.

26. For an annotated translation, see Maurer, *Pinnacles,* 268–70; see also F. D. K. Bosch, *The Golden Germ: An Introduction to Indian Symbolism* (The Hague: Mouton, 1960).

27. Zimmer, *Myths and Symbols,* 90–102.

28. For tree symbolism in Indian culture see Lannoy, *Speaking Tree,* xxv–xxvi; and Zimmer, *Myths and Symbols,* 66–68.

29. The following table is a conspectus of the elements that contribute to the structure of a typical dramatic plot (*itivṛtta,* a "thus turning"), especially the plot structure of the heroic romance or *nāṭaka* as described in *BN* 21. For detailed analysis and references, see M. Christopher Byrski, *Concept of Ancient Indian Theatre* (New Delhi: Munshiram Manoharlal, 1974), 101–43; idem, "Sanskrit Drama as an Aggregate of Model Situations," in *Sanskrit Drama in Performance,* ed. Rachel Van M. Baumer and James R. Brandon (Honolulu: University Press of Hawaii, 1981), 141–66; and Edwin Gerow, "Sanskrit Dramatic Theory and Kālidāsa's Plays," in *Theater of Memory,* ed. Barbara Stoler Miller (New York: Columbia University Press, 1984), 42–62. For an English translation of Bharata's text, see Ghosh, *The Nāṭyaśāstra,* vol. 1, 380–400.

| The 5 stages of a plot (*avasthās*) | The 5 dramatic junctures (*sandhis*) | The 5 plot components (*arthaprakṛtis*) |
|---|---|---|
| *ārambha:* motivation | *mukha* (face): a beginning | *bīja* (seed): the germ whence the action arises |
| *prayatna:* effort to achieve the object | *pratimukha* (reflection of the face): a progression | *bindu* (drop): action beginning to unfold like a drop of oil spreading out on the water |
| *prāptyāśā:* vision of the possibility of success | *garbha* (womb): a development, often by incubation or separation | *patākā:* an episode or a secondary plot |
| *niyatāpti:* frustration by an obstacle | *vimarśa:* a moment of reflection, a crisis | *prakarī:* an interlude |
| *phalāgama:* attainment of success | *nirvahaṇa:* a conclusion | *kārya:* denouement |

30. See §§9.3 and 9.4–9.4.3.

31. Or *cantus compositus,* as opposed to improvised music (*super librum cantare*); see Johannes Tinctoris, *The Art of Counterpoint,* trans. Albert Seay (Rome: American Institute of Musicology, 1961), 5–6, 102–10.

32. See §4.2.

33. See §9.3–9.4.3.

34. For analysis and textual references, see Lath, *Dattilam,* 135–44; and N. Ramanathan, "A Critical Study of the Treatment of *Gīta* in *Saṅgīta-Ratnākara* of Śārṅgadeva" (Ph.D. diss., Banaras Hindu University, 1979), 504–12.

35. A common metaphor for the act of beginning in many world languages; see Carl Darling Buck, *A Dictionary of Selected Synonyms in the Principal Indo-European Languages* (Chicago: University of Chicago Press, 1949), 976–78.

36. *Ābhoga* has an interesting and attractive etymology: from the prefix *ā* (to, toward) plus either the first verbal root *bhuj* (to bend, curve) or the third root *bhuj* (to enjoy); the word thus implies closure by a conflation of the two root meanings, i.e., to come full circle and to achieve completion by becoming satisfied. See Monier-Williams, *Sanskrit-English Dictionary,* 145–46.

37. See §10.3.

38. See §9.6 for the structure of the Pāṇikā, which omits the second and fourth components but may still be a distant relative.

39. Rowell, "The Creation of Audible Time," in *The Study of Time 4,* ed. J. T. Fraser, N. Lawrence, and D. Park (New York: Springer-Verlag, 1981), 204–8.

40. For the concept of *jo* (introduction)-*ha* ("breaking apart" or exposition)-*kyū* ("rushing to conclusion" or denouement), see William P. Malm, *Japanese Music and Musical Instruments* (Rutland, Vt.: Charles E. Tuttle, 1959), 102–4, 110–12, and 209.

41. See §9.4.1.

42. Modern renditions of *ālāpana* often feature the violin or another instrument as an answering voice, but there are no indications that this is what was meant when the term was first coined.

43. See §§7.7 and 11.7.

44. Translation mine.

45. For a slightly different translation of this verse and analysis of the literary style, see §6.4.

46. *Sthāyi* (the steady or abiding note), identified by the commentator Kallinātha as the *aṁśa* or sonant note; the final line of this excerpt includes another synonym—*jīvasvara,* the vital or living tone.

47. "That which moves the mouth," according to R. K. Shringy's comments, taking *mukhacāla* as the general term for the first phase of the exposition; see n. 48.

48. Translation mine, with reference to R. K. Shringy, *Saṅgīta-Ratnākara of Śārṅgadeva,* vol. 2 (New Delhi: Munshiram Manoharlal, 1990), 199–201.

49. "Plagal" describes a modal octave divided 1-4-8, "authentic," an octave divided 1-5-8, both in general terms and with specific reference to the church modes of the European Middle Ages. See Sachs, *Rise of Music,* 64–70. I agree with Sachs's contention that plagal organization is much older than authentic in the early history of world scale systems.

50. See Sambamoorthy, *South Indian Music,* vol. 3, 346. Stories such as this are common in the didactic literature and are not intended to be taken literally. Rather, they should be recognized as attempts to encourage right habits by drawing upon the mythical background. In this connection, see §4.6.

51. For a general discussion of the problem, transcriptions, and analyses of four

of the fragments, see Thomas J. Mathiesen, "Rhythm and Meter in Ancient Greek Music," *Music Theory Spectrum* 7 (1985): 159–80.

52. The treatise *De Musica* by Johannes de Grocheo (ca. 1300) is one of the first Western works to provide descriptions of a wide range of musical forms, although they are sketchy; see Johannes de Grocheo, *Concerning Music,* trans. Albert Seay (Colorado Springs: Colorado College Music Press, 1967).

53. See §8.9.

54. See below and the reconstructions in (31–33).

55. *Vastu,* from the fifth root *vas* (to dwell or abide), is also an important philosophical term for any object or substance that *really* exists or persists.

56. As I argue below (§9.5) in connection with the function of the Oveṇaka.

57. See Lath, *Dattilam,* 352–60.

58. For the other meaning of *mātrā* (as a measure for the durations of verse), see §8.7.

59. See §6.4; for an illustration see (31).

60. And also perhaps because the paws would no longer be of equal length.

61. See (17).

62. See (18) and (19).

63. The former is demonstrated in the Oveṇaka (33), the latter in the Madraka (31) and (32).

64. In the music of South India, tempo changes are abrupt and are accomplished by doubling or halving the previous pulse, whereas in North Indian music the tempo changes occur in gradual increments; for *upavartana,* see §9.4.2.

65. As in *upavartana* (see §9.4.2).

66. *Metaphysics* delta.26.

67. The Aparāntaka, Madraka, Prakarī, Rovindaka, and Uttara (see §9.5).

68. See §8.4 and (16).

69. As in the fourfold Madraka (32).

70. Syllables supposedly uttered by Brahmā (*AB* 31.104).

71. There are, to be sure, many exceptions to the latter, and the typical slow introduction to the eighteenth-century symphony may be regarded as a huge upbeat to the subsequent fast movement.

72. For the three species of *pāṇi,* see Lath, *Dattilam,* 362–64; for the modern concept of *graha,* see Sambamoorthy, *South Indian Music,* vol. 3, 108–10.

73. As in the Oveṇaka (33).

74. As in the final *vastu* of the Aparāntaka; see Rowell, "Ritual Theatre Music," 155, 168–69.

75. See (33).

76. As in the *upavartana* that follows the component Praveṇī (33).

77. See §8.7.

78. Again, as in the *upavartana* that follows Praveṇī (33).

79. Record liner notes for Col. MS 7386, subsequently reprinted (with minor changes) in Igor Stravinsky, *Themes and Conclusions* (Berkeley and Los Angeles: University of California Press, 1982), 63.

80. As in strewing straw for a bed or the spreading out of vegetation.

81. The Oveṇaka, Ullopyaka, and Uttara; for the finale of the Oveṇaka, see (33) and the accompanying discussion.

82. See §8.3.

83. For reconstructions and analyses of the seven *gītaka*s, see Rowell, "Ritual Theatre Music."

84. See §9.3.

85. I strongly suspect that the syllabic version is merely a theoretical distillation of the manifold versions; see Rowell, "Ritual Theatre Music," 159–63.

86. According to Dattila, but three appears to be the standard version.

87. See (18).

88. The passages of *pratyupohana* were of variable length (*D* 167A)—at least two but not more than four units; see Lath, *Dattilam,* 375–76.

89. See (19).

90. All occurrences of *upavartana.*

91. See (18).

92. For these references, see Lath, *Dattilam,* 400–401.

93. See above.

94. Cf. (19).

95. Triangular *tāla*s normally divide into three "paws," stretching the metaphor to the breaking point.

96. That is, exposition as in the Pāda and Māṣaghāta, preview as in the Antāharaṇa, and review as in the Śīrṣaka and all occurrences of *upavartana.*

97. See (18).

98. The same pattern occurs in the final component of the minor Pāṇikā form; see §9.6; and Widdess, "*Tāla* and Melody," 505.

99. Cf. (30).

100. For the options, see Rowell, "Ritual Theatre Music," 176.

101. Lath, *Dattilam,* 348–60.

102. Rowell, "Ritual Theatre Music," 158–59.

103. See §§6.3 and 9.4.3.

104. For details see Lath, *Dattilam,* 135–44; and Ramanathan, "Treatment of *Gīta,*" 504–12.

105. See §§3.2 and 4.2.

106. See §§4.2 and 9.2.3.

107. See §5.3.

108. According to Abhinavagupta, as cited in Lath, *Dattilam,* 142.

109. For notated examples and analysis, see Widdess, "*Tāla* and Melody."

110. See §5.3.

111. By trimming off the appropriate number of beginning units, so that the pattern could be recognized from its typical sequence of terminal gestures; for details see Lath, *Dattilam,* 416–22.

112. Ibid, 144.

113. See §8.9, esp. (28).

## Chapter Ten

1. Translation mine; for background, see Shringy, *Saṅgīta-Ratnākara,* vol. 2, 209–11; see also Ramanathan, "Treatment of *Gīta.*"

2. For analysis and a slightly different translation, see Rowell, "The Songs of Medieval India: The *Prabandhas* as Described in Mataṅga's *Bṛhaddeśī,*" *Music Theory Spectrum* 9 (1987): 136–72.

3. For *ālāpana* see §9.2.4.

4. For a detailed study and complete English translation, see Rowell, "Songs of Medieval India."

5. Sudhibhusan Bhattacharya, *Ethnomusicology and India* (Calcutta: Indian Publications, 1968), 22–23.

6. Alan Lomax, *Folk Song Style and Culture* (Washington: American Association for the Advancement of Science, 1968), 97–99.

7. Ibid., 18.
8. Ibid., 96.
9. An essay entitled "Music and Geography," in Szabolcsi, *History of Melody,* 267–87.
10. Ibid., 284.
11. See §1.2.
12. See §5.4.
13. For additional background on the *prabandhas*, see Rowell, "Songs of Medieval India," 141–42.
14. See §9.2.4.
15. See Shringy, *Saṅgīta-Ratnākara,* vol. 2, 212–13.
16. *MB* 376.
17. See §10.7.
18. S. Seetha, *Tanjore as a Seat of Music* (Madras: University of Madras, 1981), 42–43.
19. For some examples, see Prem Lata Sharma, *Saṅgītarāja by Mahārāṇā Kumbhā* (Varanasi: Banaras Hindu University, 1963), 149–50.
20. See Rowell, "Songs of Medieval India," 144–45.
21. For *ālapti,* see §9.2.4.
22. See §9.2.3.
23. Translation adapted from Shringy, *Saṅgīta-Ratnākara,* vol. 2, 212––16.
24. See §9.2.3.
25. In my interpretation, this "ornamental passage" refers to the *melāpaka* interlude.
26. That is, the main section (*dhruvaka*).
27. See §8.9.
28. *SM* 4.16.440–47 (vol. 3); see chap. 1, n. 32.
29. See §§9.4.1 and 9.5.
30. See §§10.5–7.
31. See §4.5.
32 See §8.8.
33. Two of the twelve sacred utterances of the Upanishads: "Om! This One exists!" and "This Thou art!"; for background, see Deussen, *Philosophy of the Upanishads,* 126–79.
34. See §6.4.
35. *MB* 410–11.
36. *MB* 420cd–21ab.
37. *MB* 503cd–4ab.
38. *MB* 504cd–5ab.
39. *MB* 506cd–7.
40. *The Kama Sutra of Vatsyayana,* trans. Sir Richard Burton and F. F. Arbuthnot (Frogmore, St Albans, Herts: Panther Books, 1963), 18–24.
41. See §4.5.
42. See §6.2.
43. *MB* 496–500ab.
44. *SS* 4.155–58; translation adapted from Shringy, *Saṅgīta-Ratnākara,* vol. 2, 259.
45. Ibid., 260–61.
46. For the *gaṇas*, see §8.9 and (29).
47. For the *rasas*, see §11.8.
48. For fuller analysis of many of the issues in the following section, see Rowell, "Songs of Medieval India," 148–60.

49. *MB* 431cd–95.
50. I am indebted to Harold S. Powers for this suggestion.
51. Shringy, *Saṅgīta-Ratnākara,* vol. 2, 223–65 (*SS* 4.33cd–181ab).
52. See table 9.
53. *PS* 4.130–34 (see §1.4 and chap. 1, n. 34).
54. *SS* 4.33cd–41 (Shringy, *Saṅgīta-Ratnākara,* vol. 2, 223–27).
55. Despite R. Rangaramanuja Ayyangar's claim in *"Sangeeta Ratnakaram,"* 163 (chap. 1, n. 33).
56. See (29) and table 9.
57. For additional analysis, see Rowell, "Songs of Medieval India," 150–57.
58. This is not evident from the table, but see the arguments in Rowell, "Songs of Medieval India," 153–54.
59. For color symbolism in ancient India, see Gonda, *Vedic Ritual,* 44–48.
60. From left to right: (1) the gentle river goddess of fertility, speech, eloquence, and learning; (2) Pārvatī, Śiva's consort, in her wrathful aspect; (3) the wife of Indra (the thunder god and chief deity in Vedic mythology); and (4) the sow goddess, representing the female "energy" (*śakti*) of Viṣṇu in his incarnation as a boar.
61. See §11.8.
62. Cf. (29).
63. See (29).
64. Velankar, *Jayadāman,* 139–40.
65. The four *rāga*s are transcribed and analyzed in Rowell, "Songs of Medieval India," 157.
66. Ibid., 154.
67. See §§11.2 and 11.6.
68. Rowell, "Songs of Medieval India," 150.
69. For the cultural geography of the *prabandha* tradition, see Rowell, "Songs of Medieval India," 149 (for the *deśī* Elās) and 159.
70. See §§8.2 and 8.7.
71. As cited by Shringy in *Saṅgīta-Ratnākara,* vol. 2, 153.
72. See §5.4.
73. Deva, "Emergence of the Drone."
74. See §§7.7 and 11.7.

CHAPTER ELEVEN

1. Translation mine; for the context of this passage, see Rowell, "*Śikṣā* for the Twiceborn," 85–91.

2. This is a puzzling reference. I know of no canonical list of the six "limbs" (*aṅga*s, in the sense of "components") of *nāṭya,* and nowhere else in *BN* is there any such enumeration. If there is an authoritative list of the components of drama, it must be the set of eleven topics set forth in *BN* 6.10–the *saṅgraha* (digest) or table of contents for the rest of the treatise: *rasa* (§11.8), *bhāva* (emotion), *abhinaya* ("representation," see below, n. 4), *dharmī* (acting), *vṛtti* (style, see §§10.6 and 11.6), *pravṛtti* (regional characteristics), *siddhi* ("success," the objectives of drama), *svara* (music in the abstract), *ātodya* (instrumental music), *gāna* (singing), and *raṅga* (stagecraft). Abhinavagupta apparently did not know what the original author had in mind, for he merely remarked that the drama is a source of satisfaction for people because it has six *aṅga*s—a typical commentarial evasion.

I am indebted to Edwin Gerow for another suggestion: because the opening chapters of *BN* refer to *Nāṭyaśāstra* as a fifth Veda, created by Brahmā himself at the request of Indra and the other gods, the implication here may be that the "Veda of Drama" has its own six Vedāṅgas ("limbs of the Vedas") modeled upon the set of six ancillary disciplines (i.e., phonetics, ritual, grammar, etymology, metrics, and astronomy) that contribute to the correct understanding and performance of the Vedas and their accompanying rituals. Professor Gerow was also kind enough to refer my question to a friend, with the following interesting results.

In a paper entitled "*Ṣaḍaṅga-Nāṭya*" (The six limbs of drama) and presented at the Thirty-Third International Congress of Asian and North African Studies (August 1990, Toronto, Canada), Ashok Aklujkar investigates this problem along two lines: (1) by comparing the present translation (see n. 5) with other published interpretations of this passage, and (2) by looking beyond the immediate context in Abhinavagupta's commentary to see if there are any other sets of "six *aṅgas*" that might possibly qualify as an explanation for Bharata's expression. Aklujkar concludes that Abhinavagupta took the six *aṅgas* to mean the four types of *abhinaya* (see below, n. 4) plus vocal and instrumental music. A second set of six *aṅgas* appears in *BN* 19.51–52, with reference to the purposes served by the dramatic junctures (the *sandhis*; see chap. 9, n. 29): "The purpose of the *aṅgas* as seen in the Śāstras is six-fold: constructive arrangement of the desired matter; non-loss or non-dwindling [i.e., presence and continuity] of the (essential) happenings in the plot; securing attraction or pleasure for the dramatic performance; concealment of things which deserve to be concealed; narrative representation of things full of surprise and wonder; open presentation of things that deserve to be disclosed" (translated by G. K. Bhatt, in his *Bharata's Nāṭya-Mañjarī* [Poona: Bhandarkar Oriental Research Institute, 1975], 177). I am not convinced that either of these explanations offers the key to what Bharata had in mind. For other subdivisions of the subject of drama, see §1.2; see also Rao, *Monograph on Bharata's naaTya Saastra,* 5–7, and Vatsyayan, *Square and the Circle,* 47–51.

3. That is, stringed, hollow, solid, and covered (see §1.2 and [1], and also §5.5).

4. That is, the four types of *abhinaya:* representation by means of voice and speech (*vācika*), by movement (*āṅgika*), by costume and makeup (*āhārya*), and by emotion (*sāttvika*). See also §6.3.

5. Translation adapted from Ghosh, vol. 1, 519.

6. Leonard B. Meyer, "Toward a Theory of Style," in *The Concept of Style,* ed. Berel Lang, rev. ed. (Ithaca: Cornell University Press, 1987), 21–71.

7. For *vṛtti* and *rīti,* see §11.6.

8. As in the third canto of *SS* (see Shringy, *Saṅgīta-Ratnākara,* vol. 2, 145–208).

9. As pointed out in §7.5.

10. For analysis, see Rowell, "Paradigms," 16–17.

11. Translated by Thomas J. Mathiesen, in Aristides Quintilianus, *On Music in Three Books* (New Haven: Yale University Press, 1983), 102–3.

12. A phenomenon not unknown in Western opera, particularly in the trouser roles for women (e.g., Cherubino, Octavian, Siebel).

13. See §11.8.

14. Arist. Quint., *On Music* 2.8 (129–31), 2.12–14 (140–46), and 3.21 (190–92).

15. Ghosh translation, vol. 2, 159.

16. Translation mine.

17. See §6.1.

18. Translation adapted from Ghosh, vol. 1, 520.

19. That is, song, instrumental music, and dance.

20. For *kalā,* see §8.7.

21. Shringy, *Saṅgīta-Ratnākara,* vol. 2, 147–48.

22. *SS* 3.10–12b (ibid., 148–49).

23. For *ālapti,* see §9.2.4.
24. Shringy, *Saṅgīta-Ratnākara,* vol. 2, 151–53.
25. See §11.7.
26. *SS* 3.19c–24 (Shringy, *Saṅgīta-Ratnākara,* vol. 2, 153–55).
27. See §6.3.
28. See §2.3.
29. For a comprehensive history of the two concepts, see V. Raghavan, *Bhoja's Śṛṅgāra Prakāśa,* 3d ed. (Madras: Vasanta Press, 1978), 203–43 (the *doṣas*) and 244–343 (the *guṇas*).
30. *SS* 4.47–48, 374–78.
31. See §4.1.
32. Monier-Williams, *Sanskrit-English Dictionary* (292A), explains the etymology of the word *kumāra* as "easily dying." Viewers of the recent British television series "The Jewel in the Crown" will agree that Hari Kumar, the victim of the story, was aptly named.
33. Monier-Williams, *Sanskrit-English Dictionary,* 235.
34. Longinus, *On the Sublime,* trans. W. Hamilton Fyfe, Loeb Classical Library (Cambridge: Harvard University Press, 1927).
35. *SS* 4.379–80; translation mine.
36. *SS* 3.25–38 (Shringy, *Saṅgīta-Ratnākara,* vol. 2, 156–58).
37. Ghosh translation, vol. 1, 513–18.
38. See §4.6.
39. Vv. 514–24 (Ghosh translation, vol. 2, 159–60).
40. See §11.7.
41. Allen, *Phonetics in Ancient India,* 40–41.
42. As in *NS* 2.8.30.
43. *MB* 1.24.
44. *SS* 3.39–86 (Shringy, *Saṅgīta-Ratnākara,* vol. 2, 158–71).
45. *SS* 6.654–55.
46. For a variety of perspectives on the idea of style, see Lang, *Concept of Style;* see also Leonard B. Meyer, *Style and Music: Theory, History, and Ideology* (Philadelphia: University of Pennsylvania Press, 1989).
47. See §11.8.
48. See §10.6 and table 9.
49. For some examples, see §10.6.
50. For the development of the concepts of *vṛtti* and *rīti* in poetic theory, see V. Raghavan, *Studies on Some Concepts of the Alaṃkāra Śāstra,* rev. ed. (Madras: Adyar Library and Research Centre, 1973), 147–213; see also Keith, *Sanskrit Literature,* 372–86.
51. Keith, *Sanskrit Drama,* 326–38; Raghavan, *Alaṃkāra Śāstra,* 201.
52. *BN* 22.24 (Ghosh translation, vol. 1, 403); for analysis see Vatsyayan, *Square and the Circle,* 48–51.
53. Raghavan, *Alaṃkāra Śāstra,* 147.
54. Ibid., 162–72.
55. Ibid., 178–82.
56. Raghavan, *Bhoja's Śṛṅgāra Prakāśa,* 268–75.
57. That is, *ojas, udāratva, samādhi,* and *śleṣa* belong clearly to the elevated style.
58. See §8.7.
59. *D* 43–44, Lath, *Dattilam,* 257.
60. See §11.8.
61. §5.4.

62. See Lath, *Dattilam,* 425–26.
63. *SS* 6.165–70.
64. Translation mine.
65. See §7.7.
66. For a graphic demonstration, see Gjerdingen, "Shape and Motion," 39–62.
67. See §7.7 and Lath, *Dattilam,* 304–10.
68. *MB* 416.
69. See Howard, *Sāmavedic Chant,* 104, 518.
70. Ghosh translation, vol. 1, 335–54.
71. *SS* 3.97c–189b.
72. See Monier-Williams, *Sanskrit-English Dictionary,* 406.
73. As in *MB* 456d; the same terms are paired in *SS* 6, with reference to single and multiple vina strokes.
74. The reference to "double speed" (*drutadviguṇavegataḥ*) is probably not to be taken literally.
75. *PS* 1.47–55; translation mine.
76. *SS* 3.87–97b (Shringy, *Saṅgīta-Ratnākara,* vol. 2, 171–74).
77. See below.
78. For the history of the *sthāyas*, see Prem Lata Sharma, "The Concept of *Sthāya* in Indian *Saṅgītaśāstra,*" *Indian Music Journal* 3–5 (1965).
79. See Sambamoorthy, *South Indian Music,* vol. 4, 3d ed., 138–40.
80. Shringy, *Saṅgīta-Ratnākara,* vol. 2, 174–98.
81. *SS* 3.114c–119b (ibid., 178).
82. Ibid., 176–80.
83. See below.
84. In this context "oblique" probably means *vakra* (crooked), as opposed to ascending or descending motion.
85. The *sthāya* known as *ucita* (*SS* 3.149b), related by its name to *aucitya,* one of the most important aesthetic categories in Indian poetics.
86. *Baddha* (*SS* 3.169a), apparently a prolonged single tone, suggesting that the absence of motion or melodic activity was itself regarded as an ornament (as in Western violin playing when *senza vibrato* is indicated).
87. *BN* 19 (Ghosh translation, vol. 1, 335–54).
88. *BN* 19.37–38 (Ghosh translation, vol. 1, 346).
89. *SS* 3.120c–125b (Shringy, *Saṅgīta-Ratnākara,* vol. 2, 179–80).
90. J. L. Masson and M. V. Patwardhan, *Aesthetic Rapture: The Rasādhyāya of the Nāṭyaśāstra* (Poona: Deccan College, 1970), vol. 1, 33.
91. Bharata's exposition of the theory of *rasa* is found in chaps. 6 and 7 of *BN* (Ghosh translation, vol. 1, 100–147). For a better translation of chap. 6, with copious annotations and translations of selected passages from Abhinavagupta's commentary (*AB*), see Masson and Patwardhan, *Aesthetic Rapture.* For additional background and perspectives on the subject of *rasa,* see Eliot Deutsch, "Reflections on Some Aspects of the Theory of *Rasa,*" in Baumer and Brandon, *Sanskrit Drama in Performance,* 214–25; Edwin Gerow, "*Rasa* as a Category of Literary Criticism," ibid., 226–57; idem, "The *Rasa* Theory of Abhinavagupta and its Application," in Dimock et al., *Literatures of India,* 216–27; Raniero Gnoli, *The Aesthetic Experience According to Abhinavagupta,* 2d ed. (Varanasi: Chowkhamba Sanskrit Series Office, 1968); K. C. Pandey, *Comparative Aesthetics,* vol. 1, *Indian Aesthetics,* 2d ed. (Varanasi: Chowkhamba Sanskrit Series Office, 1959), 20–71, 188–256; and V. Raghavan, *The Number of Rasa-s,* 3d ed. (Madras: Adyar Library and Research Centre, 1975).

92. Aristotle, *The Poetics*, trans. W. Hamilton Fyfe, Loeb Classical Library (Cambridge: Harvard University Press, 1927), 22–23.

93. *BN* 6.17 (Ghosh translation, vol. 1, 102).

94. *BN* 6.18–22 (Ghosh translation, vol. 1, 102–3).

95. Gerow, "*Rasa* as a Category," 238–39.

96. See §6.1.

97. Gerow, "*Rasa* as a Category," 234.

98. For the iconography of *rāga* in North Indian miniature painting, see Klaus Ebeling, *Ragamala Painting* (New Delhi: Ravi Kumar, 1973).

99. *BN* 29.1–16 (Ghosh translation, vol. 2, 29–31). I should add here that I am aware of Lath's contention (*Dattilam*, 124–25) that the intent of this passage was to relate these correlations of *rasa*s and *svara*s not to the *jāti*s but to derivative *rāgas*. Because his interpretation is based entirely on the later commentarial tradition, I remain unconvinced.

100. *BN* 28.76 (Ghosh translation, vol. 2, 19).

101. See §7.5.

102. For the *jāti*s, see §7.8; and Lath, *Dattilam*, 265–99.

103. For the *grāmarāga*s, see §7.8.

104. Sambamoorthy, *South Indian Music*, vol. 5, 2d ed., 160–68.

105. Verse 79, Edgerton and Edgerton, *Cloud Messenger*, 61.

106. For a history of the concept of *aucitya* in poetic theory, see Raghavan, *Alaṃkāra Śāstra*, 214–81.

107. For the evolution of the idea of beauty in Western thought, see Herbert Dieckmann, "Theories of Beauty to the Mid-Nineteenth Century," in *Dictionary of the History of Ideas: Studies of Selected Pivotal Ideas*, ed. Philip P. Wiener (New York: Scribner's, 1968), vol. 1, 195–206; Władysław Tatarkiewicz, *A History of Six Ideas* (The Hague: Martinus Nijhoff, 1980), 121–219.

108. Saint Thomas Aquinas, *Summa theologia* (trans. Dominican Fathers) 1. Q. 27. art. 1.

## Chapter Twelve

1. Steven Feld, *Sound and Sentiment: Birds, Weeping, Poetics, and Song in Kaluli Expression* (Philadelphia: University of Pennsylvania Press, 1982), 3.

2. Alan Merriam, *The Anthropology of Music* (Evanston: Northwestern University Press, 1964), 32.

3. For the emic-etic dichotomy, see Bruno Nettl, *The Study of Ethnomusicology: Twenty-nine Issues and Concepts* (Urbana: University of Illinois Press, 1983), 140–41.

4. Ibid., 52–64.

5. John Blacking, *How Musical Is Man?* (Seattle: University of Washington Press, 1973), 30–31.

6. See Nettl's discussion of this theme in his *Study of Ethnomusicology*, 172–86.

7. Bruno Nettl, *Theory and Method in Ethnomusicology* (New York: Free Press, 1964), 226.

8. Ibid., 227.

9. Ibid., 230–38.

10. Pierre Boulez, *Boulez on Music Today*, trans. Susan Bradshaw and Richard Rodney Bennett (Cambridge: Harvard University Press, 1971), 67.

11. William J. Jackson, "Domesticating Others' Tunes: The Assimilation of Western Elements in the Works of Tyāgarāja and Dīkṣitar," paper delivered at the Thirty-

Third International Congress of Asian and North African Studies, 20 August 1990, Toronto.

12. Nettl, *Study of Ethnomusicology,* 345–54.
13. Szabolcsi, *History of Melody,* 284.
14. See §§1.3, 4.2, 4.6, 5.1, 5.3–6, and 11.3.

# GLOSSARY

This word list focuses on technical terms and words that appear frequently throughout the text. It excludes proper nouns and words that occur only once or twice or are defined immediately. In most cases, only musical meanings are given.

***abhinaya*** dramatic representation, pantomime (in acting or dancing)
***ābhoga*** a concluding section in chant or in a *prabandha*
***ākāśa*** atmosphere, ether
***akṣara*** syllable
***alaṅkāra*** ornament
***ālāpana*** a nonmetrical exposition of a *rāga* at the beginning of a composition or performance
***ālapti*** a version of *ālāpana* that emphasizes the typical melodic contours of the chosen *rāga*
***aṁśa*** the tonic or sonant note (the most prominent note in a *jāti* or *grāmarāga*)
***aṅga*** "limb," a part of anything, often in the sense of a formal component
***anibaddha*** unregulated
***Anta*** the final component of a *gītaka*
***Antara*** an interlude
***anudātta*** a grave accent in Vedic recitation
***anuvādi*** a neutral or subordinate note
***ātman*** soul, self, the world soul
***avanaddha*** "covered" instruments, i.e., drums
***āvāpa*** one of the four silent *tāla* gestures (right palm up with fingers folded)
***āvarta*** a rhythmic cycle, as in the later *tāla* systems
***ayugma*** "odd," with reference to triple patterns and meters
***bhāva*** emotion
***bindu*** "drop," in the sense of (1) a single ornamental tone, or (2) a metaphorical reference to the spreading properties of a drop of liquid
***biruda*** a panegyric, often the final component of a *prabandha*
***Cācapuṭaḥ*** one of the five *mārga tāla* patterns, with a proportional structure of 2:1:1:2

***Caccatpuṭaḥ*** one of the five *mārga tāla* patterns, with a proportional structure of 2 : 2 : 1 : 3

***caturaśra*** "quadrangular," with reference to quadruple patterns and meters

***deśī*** regional, provincial; the assimilation of regional musical traditions ca. A.D. 500–1000

***dha, dhaivata*** the sixth scale degree

***dhātu*** "element," in the sense of (1) a formal component of a *prabandha;* (2) an instrumental finger stroke

***dhruva*** a finger snap used to mark time

***dhruvā*** a song sung during the performance of a play

***dhruvaka*** the main section of a *prabandha*

***dhvani*** (1) sound in general; (2) the implications of a sound

***doṣa*** a defect or blemish

***ga, gāndhāra*** the third scale degree

***gamaka*** a melodic transition or vocal ornament

***gaṇa*** a metrical foot, usually of three syllables

***gāna*** the genre of incidental music for the ancient theater

***gandharva*** a celestial musician

***gāndharva*** the genre of ritual music performed during the prelude to a play

***ghana*** the "solid" category of instruments, i.e., idiophones

***gīta*** song

***gītaka*** one of the compositions performed during the ritual prelude to a play

***gīti*** (1) mode of text setting; (2) style in general

***graha*** a beginning, mode of beginning

***grāma*** scale

***grāmarāga*** a scalar mode

***guṇa*** "quality," in the sense of (1) a meritorious quality; or (2) the three interwoven strands of existence (goodness, passion, and darkness) as expounded in the Sāṅkhya philosophy

***guru*** (1) a teacher; (2) a long duration in music and poetry

***jāti*** genus, species, especially in the sense of (1) one of the ancient mode classes; or (2) the rhythmic genera

***kāku*** intonation in dramatic recitation, vocal inflection

***kalā*** (1) a conceptual unit of time; (2) a silent gesture initiating such a unit

***kāla*** time in general

***kampita*** a melodic quiver or oscillation

***karman*** action, the consequences of one's actions

***kriyā*** an action, especially (in music) a *tāla* gesture

***laghu*** a short duration in music and poetry

***lakṣaṇa*** a distinguishing mark or feature

***laya*** the timing of musical events in terms of the interval that separates them, i.e., tempo
***ma, madhyama*** the fourth scale degree
***mandra*** low, the lowest note permitted
***mantra*** a recited formula
***mārga*** "path"; (1) the ancient musical system; (2) a measure of the density of musical events
***mātrā*** (1) a time unit in verse or music; (2) a phrase or line within a larger formal component
***melāpaka*** the second component of a *prabandha,* usually an ornamental interlude
***mudrā*** a hand gesture (in Vedic recitation, chant, dance, or pantomime)
***mukha*** "face," an opening section
***mūrcchanā*** "expanding, spreading," as in (1) the rotations of the basic scales; and also (2) with reference to ornamental melodic clusters or multiple instrumental finger strokes
***nāda*** "causal sound," the metaphysical theory of sound
***nāṭya*** drama
***ni, niṣāda*** the seventh scale degree
***nibaddha*** regulated
***nirukta*** etymological analysis
***niṣkrāma*** one of the four silent *tāla* gestures (right palm down with fingers extended)
***nṛtta*** nonrepresentational dance
***nṛtya*** representational dance, mime
***nyāsa*** the final note
***pa, pañcama*** the fifth scale degree
***pada*** "word," in the sense of (1) text in general; or (2) a passage of music set to a meaningful text (as opposed to nonsense syllables)
***pāda*** "paw," a formal division of a larger unit, usually a quarter part
***pādabhāga*** one segment of a line divided into four parts
***pāṇi*** a measure of the synchronization of melody and accompaniment
***parivarta*** a repetition
***pāta*** an audible *tāla* gesture
***pāṭa*** a passage of recited drum syllables (one of the *aṅgas* of a *prabandha*)
***pāṭhya*** (1) recitation; (2) the male singer in the theater ensemble
***pluta*** a protracted duration in music or poetry
***prabandha*** an art song
***prakaraṇa*** "production," a collective term for the *gītakas*
***prakīrṇa*** miscellany (as a musical topic)
***prakṛti*** elemental substance
***pramāṇa*** a criterion or standard of measure
***prāṇa*** (1) breath; (2) a metaphorical term for any kind of vital current

***prastāra*** permutations
***praveśa*** one of the four silent *tāla* gestures (right palm down with fingers closed)
***prāyoga*** "application," practice (as opposed to theory)
***pūrvaraṅga*** the ritual prelude to a play
***rāga*** a melodic framework, mode
***rajas*** passion, the principle of stimulation
***rasa*** a pervading emotional flavor
***ri, ṛṣabha*** the second scale degree
***rīti*** style of poetic diction
***rūpa*** form
***rūpaka*** a synonym for *prabandha* (with reference to its poetic content)
***sa, ṣaḍja*** the first scale degree
***śabda*** sound
***sādhāraṇa*** an altered note in a scale or *rāga*
***sāman*** a Sāmavedic chant or hymn
***Sampakveṣṭākaḥ*** one of the five *mārga tāla* patterns, with a proportional structure of 3:2:2:2:3
***sampradāya*** an oral tradition
***saṁvādi*** a consonant note
***śamyā*** one of the four audible *tāla* gestures (right hand slaps down)
***sandhi*** (1) a phonetic alteration when words are run together; (2) a dramatic juncture or situation
***saṅgīta*** music
***sannipāta*** one of the four audible *tāla* gestures (hands clap together)
***saptaka*** "the set of seven," i.e., the degrees of the heptatonic scale
***sargam*** the seven sol-fa syllables as an oral or written notation
***śāstra*** (1) a treatise; (2) a field of study, "ology"
***Ṣaṭpitāputrakaḥ*** the most popular of the five *mārga tāla* patterns, with a proportional structure of 3:1:2:2:1:3
***sattva*** goodness, the principle of illumination
***śikṣā*** (1) articulatory phonetics; (2) a phonetic manual
***Śīrṣaka*** a short internal or final coda of six units
***śloka*** a metrical couplet
***smṛti*** "tradition," as distinguished from *śruti,* q.v.
***śruti*** (1) intonation in general; (2) the twenty-two divisions of the octave; (3) revealed knowledge, i.e., the Vedas, as distinguished from *smṛti,* q.v.
***sthāna*** register, i.e., high, medium, low
***sthāya*** an ornamental phrase
***stobha*** an interpolated nonsense syllable in Sāmavedic chant
***śuddha*** pure
***suṣira*** the "hollow" category of instruments, i.e., the flute

***sūtra*** an aphorism
***sūtradhāra*** the "string holder," i.e., the director-producer in the ancient theater
***svara*** (1) pitch in general; (2) one of the seven scale degrees; (3) a Vedic accent
***svarita*** a circumflex accent in Vedic recitation
***tāla*** (1) the rhythmic/metric system; (2) one of the four audible *tāla* gestures (left hand slaps down)
***tamas*** darkness, the principle of inertia and obscuration
***tāna*** a pentatonic or hexatonic variant of one of the basic scales
***tāra*** high, the highest note permitted
***tata*** stringed instruments
***tattva*** a topic (in philosophy)
***tena, tenaka*** a vocalise on the auspicious word *tena,* one of the six *aṅga*s available for use in a *prabandha*
***trika*** a trisyllabic metric foot
***tryaśra*** "triangular," with reference to triple patterns and meters
***udātta*** an acute accent in Vedic recitation
***uddeśa*** a list of the topics to be expounded in a treatise or section of a treatise
***Udghaṭṭaḥ*** one of the five *mārga tāla* patterns, with a proportional structure of 2:2:2
***udgrāha*** the opening component of a *prabandha,* often an epigram or metrical couplet
***upavartana*** a connecting tactic in the *gītaka*s, in which a final unit of text and melody is repeated at double speed
***upohana*** a melodic incipit sung to meaningless syllables
***vāc*** (1) speech; (2) the goddess of speech or divine speech principle
***vādi*** the sonant note in a scale, equivalent to the *aṁśa*
***vādya*** (1) instrumental music; (2) in a more restricted sense, drumming
***vakra*** "crooked," with reference to a scale or *rāga* that does not follow a straight path in ascent or descent
***varṇa*** (1) a phonetic unit of any kind; (2) the letter representing such a unit; (3) a melodic contour (e.g., ascending or descending); (4) color; (5) one of the four main social classes
***vastu*** (1) a large formal section in a *gītaka;* (2) a synonym for *prabandha* (with reference to its formal structure)
***vidārī*** (1) a pause or melodic cadence; (2) a unit ending with a prescribed pause or cadence
***vikṛta*** distorted, impure, derivative
***vikṣepa*** one of the four silent *tāla* gestures (right hand cast to the right)
***vīṇā*** a stringed instrument
***vivādi*** a dissonant note

***vṛtta*** a poetic meter

***vṛtti*** (1) the four modes of dramatic expression in *BN*; (2) poetic and/or musical style; (3) the tempo of recitation

***yati*** (1) in metrics, a caesura; (2) in music, the progression of tempo, i.e., even, accelerating, decelerating

***yugma*** "even," with reference to quadruple patterns and meters

# BIBLIOGRAPHY


Allen, W. Sidney. *Phonetics in Ancient India.* School of Oriental and African Studies, University of London, London Oriental Series, vol. 1. London: Oxford University Press, 1953.

Amaladass, Anand, S.J. *Philosophical Implications of Dhvani: Experience of Symbol Language in Indian Aesthetics.* Vienna: Institute for Indology, University of Vienna, 1984.

Annapurni, K. "Poetic Metres and Their Influence on the Growth of the Tāla System." M. Litt. thesis, University of Madras, 1955.

Arnold, E. V. *Vedic Metre in Its Historical Development.* Cambridge: Cambridge University Press, 1905.

Ayyangar, R. Rangaramanuja. *History of South Indian (Carnatic) Music: From Vedic Times to the Present.* Madras: [the author], 1972.

Bake, A. A. "The Aesthetics of Indian Music." *British Journal of Aesthetics* 4 (1964): 47–57.

———. "The Music of India." In *Ancient and Oriental Music,* edited by Egon Wellesz, The New Oxford History of Music, vol. 1, 195–227. London: Oxford University Press, 1957.

Balslev, Anindita Niyogi. *A Study of Time in Indian Philosophy.* Wiesbaden: Otto Harrassowitz, 1983.

Banerji, Sures Chandra. *Aspects of Ancient Indian Life—From Sanskrit Sources.* Calcutta: Punthi Pustak, 1972.

Basham, A. L. *The Wonder That Was India.* New York: Macmillan, 1954.

Basham, A. L., ed. *A Cultural History of India.* Oxford: Oxford University Press, 1975.

Bäumer, Bettina, ed. *Kalātattvakośa: A Lexicon of Fundamental Concepts of the Indian Arts.* Vol. 1. New Delhi: Indira Gandhi National Centre for the Arts, 1988.

Baumer, Rachel Van M., and James R. Brandon, eds. *Sanskrit Drama in Performance.* Honolulu: University Press of Hawaii, 1981.

Beohar, Anil Bihari. "Mataṅgakṛta Bṛhaddeśī kā Adhyāyana." Ph.D. diss., Banaras Hindu University, 1986.

[Bharata?] *Le Gītālaṃkāra.* Translated and edited by Alain Daniélou and N. R. Bhatt. Pondicherry: Institut Français D'Indologie, 1987.

Bharata. *Nāṭyaśāstra of Bharatamuni, with the Commentary Abhinavabhāratī by Abhinavaguptācārya.* Edited by M. Ramakrishna Kavi and J. S. Pade. 4 vols. Gaekwad's Oriental Series nos. 36, 68, 124, and 145. Baroda: Oriental Institute, 1926–1964.

———. *The Nāṭyaśāstra.* Translated by Manomohan Ghosh. 2 vols. Calcutta: Asiatic Society, 1951–1961.

Bhattacharya, Arun. *A Treatise on Ancient Hindu Music.* Calcutta: K. P. Bagchi, 1978.

Bhattacharya, Sudhibhusan. *Ethnomusicology and India.* Calcutta: Indian Publications, 1968.

Bhattacharyya, Haridas, ed. *The Cultural Heritage of India.* Vol. 3, *The Philosophies.* 2d reprint ed. Calcutta: Ramakrishna Mission Institute of Culture, 1983.

Bhise, Usha R. "Development of the Indian Musical Scale." *Journal of the Oriental Institute, Baroda* 25 (1975–76): 181–84.

Blacker, Carmen, and Michael Loewe, eds. *Ancient Cosmologies.* London: George Allen and Unwin, 1975.

Blacking, John. *How Musical Is Man?* Seattle: University of Washington Press, 1973.

Bosch, F. D. K. *The Golden Germ: An Introduction to Indian Symbolism.* The Hague: Mouton, 1960.

Brough, John. "Some Indian Theories of Meaning." *Transactions of the Philological Society* (1953): 161–76.

———. "Theories of General Linguistics in the Sanskrit Grammarians." *Transactions of the Philological Society* (1951): 27–46.

Buitenen, J. A. B. van. "Notes on Akṣara." *Bulletin of the Deccan College Research Institute* 17, no. 2 (1955): 204–15.

Buitenen, J. A. B. van, trans. *Two Plays of Ancient India.* New York: Columbia University Press, 1968.

Byrski, M. Christopher. *Concept of Ancient Indian Theatre.* New Delhi: Munshiram Manoharlal, 1974.

Chatterjee, Satischandra, and Dhirendramohan Datta. *An Introduction to Indian Philosophy.* 7th ed. Calcutta: University of Calcutta Press, 1968.

Chattopadhyaya, Debiprasad. *History of Science and Technology in Ancient India: The Beginnings.* Calcutta: Firma KLM, 1986.

Coomaraswamy, A. K. "The Vedic Doctrine of Silence." *Indian Culture* 3 (1936–37): 559–69.

Dallapiccola, Anna Libera, ed. *Shastric Traditions in Indian Arts.* Beiträge zur Südasienforschung, South Asia Institute, University of Heidelberg, Band 125. 2 vols. Stuttgart: Franz Steiner Verlag, 1989.

Dandekar, R. N. "Man in Hindu Thought." *Annals of the Bhandarkar Oriental Research Institute* 43 (1962): 1–57.

Davies, C. Collin. *An Historical Atlas of the Indian Peninsula.* Reprint. London: Oxford University Press, 1954.

de Bary, William Theodore, Stephen N. Hay, Royal Weiler, and Andrew Yarrow, comps. and eds. *Sources of Indian Tradition.* Columbia University, Records of Civilization, Sources and Studies, no. 56. New York: Columbia University Press, 1958.

Deussen, Paul. *The Philosophy of the Upanishads.* Translated by A. S. Geden. Reprint. New York: Dover Publications, 1966.

Deutsch, Eliot. *Advaita Vedānta: A Philosophical Reconstruction.* Honolulu: University Press of Hawaii, 1969.

Deva, B. Chaitanya. *Psychoacoustics of Music and Speech.* Madras: Music Academy, 1967.

Dimock, Edward C., Jr., Edwin Gerow, C. M. Naim, A. K. Ramanujan, Gordon Roadarmel, and J. A. B. van Buitenen. *The Literatures of India: An Introduction.* Chicago: University of Chicago Press, 1974.

Durga, S. A. K. "A Comparative Study of the Methodologies of Ethno Musicologists and Indian Musicologists." *Vivekananda Kendra Patrika* (Music India) 13, no. 2 (August 1984): 305–8.

Erdman, Joan L. "The Empty Beat: *Khālī* as a Sign of Time." *American Journal of Semiotics* 1, no. 4 (1982): 21–45.

———. "Play with *Laya:* Tempo, Pace, and Cadence in Indian Music and Culture." In

*Poetics East and West,* edited by Milena Doleželová-Velingerová, 111–34. Toronto: Toronto Semiotic Circle Monograph Series 4, 1989.

Fiske, A. M. "Notes on *Rasa* in Vedic and Buddhist Texts." *Mahfil* 8 (1971): 215–28.

Gauldin, Robert. "The Cycle-7 Complex: Relations of Diatonic Set Theory to the Evolution of Ancient Tonal Systems." *Music Theory Spectrum* 5 (1983): 39–55.

Gnoli, R. *The Aesthetic Experience According to Abhinavagupta.* Reprint. Varanasi: Chowkhamba Sanskrit Series, 1968.

Gombrich, R. F. "Ancient Indian Cosmology." In *Ancient Cosmologies,* edited by Carmen Blacker and Michael Loewe, 110–42. London: George Allen and Unwin, 1975.

Gonda, Jan. *Vedic Ritual: The Non-Solemn Rites.* Leiden: E. J. Brill, 1980.

Heimann, Betty. *Facets of Indian Thought.* London: George Allen and Unwin, 1964.

———. *Indian and Western Philosophy: A Study in Contrasts.* London: George Allen and Unwin, 1937.

Hillebrandt, Alfred. *Vedic Mythology.* Translated by Sreeramula Rajeswara Sarma. Delhi: Motilal Banarsidass, 1980.

Hiriyanna, M. *Outlines of Indian Philosophy.* Bombay: George Allen and Unwin (India), 1973.

Hopkins, E. Washburn. *Epic Mythology.* Varanasi: Indological Book House, 1968.

Hoppin, Richard H. *Medieval Music.* New York: W. W. Norton, 1978.

Howard, Wayne. *The Decipherment of the Sāmavedic Notation of the Jaiminīyas.* Studia Orientalia 63. Helsinki: Finnish Oriental Society, 1988.

———. *Sāmavedic Chant.* New Haven: Yale University Press, 1977.

Howard, Wayne, trans. and ed. *Mātrālakṣaṇam.* New Delhi: Indira Gandhi National Centre for the Arts, 1988.

Hume, Robert Ernest, trans. *The Thirteen Principal Upanishads.* 2d rev. ed. London: Oxford University Press, 1931.

Iyer, K. A. Subramania. *Bhartṛhari: A Study of the Vākyapadīya in the Light of the Ancient Commentaries.* Poona: Deccan College, 1969.

Jairazbhoy, N. A. "An Interpretation of the 22 *Śrutis.*" *Asian Music* 6 (1975): 38–59.

———. "Bharata's Concept of *Sādhārana.*" *Bulletin of the School of Oriental and African Studies, University of London* 21 (1958): 54–60.

Janaki, S. S. "The Role of Sanskrit in the Development of Indian Music." *Journal of the Music Academy, Madras* 56 (1985): 66–98.

Kale, Pramod. *The Theatric Universe (A Study of the Nāṭyaśāstra).* Bombay: Popular Prakashan, 1974.

Kanta, Surya, ed. *Ṛktantram: A Prātiśākhya of the Sāmaveda.* Delhi: Meharchand Lachhmandas, 1970.

Katz, Jonathan. "Indian Musicological Literature and its Context." *Puruṣārtha* 7 (1983): 57–75.

Kaufmann, Walter. *Musical Notations of the Orient: Notational Systems of Continental East, South, and Central Asia.* Bloomington: Indiana University Press, 1967.

Kay, G. R. *Hindu Astronomy: Ancient Science of the Hindus.* New Delhi: Cosmo Publications, 1924.

Keith, A. Berriedale. *A History of Sanskrit Literature.* London: Oxford University Press, 1920.

———. *The Sanskrit Drama in its Origin, Development, Theory and Practice.* London: Oxford University Press, 1924.

Kerman, Joseph. *Contemplating Music: Challenges to Musicology.* Cambridge: Harvard University Press, 1985.

Kosambi, Damodar Dharmanand. *An Introduction to the Study of Indian History.* Bombay: Popular Book Depot, 1956.

Kramrisch, Stella. *Exploring India's Sacred Art: Selected Writings of Stella Kramrisch.* Edited by Barbara Stoler Miller. Philadelphia: University of Pennsylvania Press, 1983.

Lannoy, Richard. *The Speaking Tree: A Study of Indian Culture and Society.* London: Oxford University Press, 1971.

Lath, Mukund. *A Study of Dattilam: A Treatise on the Sacred Music of Ancient India.* New Delhi: Impex India, 1978.

Law, Bimala Churn. *Historical Geography of Ancient India.* Paris: Asiatic Society of Paris, 1954.

Lomax, Alan. *Folk Song Style and Culture.* Washington: American Association for the Advancement of Science, 1968.

McAllester, David P. *Readings in Ethnomusicology.* Reprint. New York: Johnson Reprint Corp., 1971.

Macdonell, Arthur A. *A History of Sanskrit Literature.* New York: D. Appleton, 1900.

Mahar, J. Michael. *India: A Critical Bibliography.* Tucson: University of Arizona Press, 1964.

Mandal, Kumar Kishore. *A Comparative Study of the Concepts of Space and Time in Indian Thought.* Varanasi: Chowkhamba Sanskrit Series, 1968.

Masson, J. L., and M. V. Patwardhan. *Aesthetic Rapture: The Rasādhyāya of the Nāṭyaśāstra.* 2 vols. Poona: Deccan College, 1970.

———. *Śāntarasa and Abhinavagupta's Philosophy of Aesthetics.* Poona: Bhandarkar Oriental Research Institute, 1969.

Mataṅga. *The Bṛhaddeśī of Mataṅgamuni.* Edited by K. Sāmbaśiva Śāstrī. Trivandrum: Sanskrit Series, 1928.

Maurer, Walter H., trans. *Pinnacles of India's Past: Selections from the Ṛgveda.* Philadelphia: John Benjamins, 1986.

Merriam, Alan P. *The Anthropology of Music.* Evanston: Northwestern University Press, 1964.

Meyer, Leonard B. *Style and Music: Theory, History, and Ideology.* Philadelphia: University of Pennsylvania Press, 1989.

Miller, Barbara Stoler, ed. *Theater of Memory: The Plays of Kālidāsa.* New York: Columbia University Press, 1984.

Mishra, Umesha. "Physical Theory of Sound and its Origin in Indian Thought." *Allahabad University Studies* 2 (1926): 239–90.

Mishra, Vidhata. *A Critical Study of Sanskrit Phonetics.* Varanasi: Chowkhamba Sanskrit Series, 1972.

Moore, Charles A., ed. *The Indian Mind: Essentials of Indian Philosophy and Culture.* Honolulu: East-West Center Press, 1967.

———. *Philosophy and Culture—East and West: East-West Philosophy in Practical Perspective.* Honolulu: University of Hawaii Press, 1968.

Nakamura, Hajime. *A Comparative History of Ideas.* Rev. ed. London: KPI, 1986.

Nārada. *Nāradīya-Śikṣā.* Translated and edited by Sures Chandra Banerji. Calcutta: Rabindra Bharati University, 1983.

———. *Nāradīyā Śikṣā, with the Commentary of Bhaṭṭa Śobhākara.* Translated and edited by Usha R. Bhise. Poona: Bhandarkar Oriental Research Institute, 1986.

Nettl, Bruno. "Historical Aspects of Ethnomusicology." In *Readings in Ethnomusicology,* edited by David P. McAllester, 150–63. Reprint. New York: Johnson Reprint Corp., 1971.

———. *The Study of Ethnomusicology: Twenty-Nine Issues and Concepts.* Urbana: University of Illinois Press, 1983.

———. *Theory and Method in Ethnomusicology.* New York: Free Press, 1964.

Neuman, Daniel. *The Life of Music in North India.* Reprint. Chicago: University of Chicago Press, 1990.

Noblitt, Thomas, ed. *Music East and West.* Essays in Honor of Walter Kaufmann. New York: Pendragon Press, 1981.

Pandey, Kanti Chandra. *Abhinavagupta: An Historical and Philosophical Study.* 2d rev. ed. Varanasi: Chowkhamba Sanskrit Series, 1963.

———. *Comparative Aesthetics.* Vol. 1, *Indian Aesthetics.* 2d ed. Varanasi: Chowkhamba Sanskrit Series Office, 1959.

Panikkar, Raimundo. "Time and History in the Tradition of India: *Kāla* and Karma," with an appendix on the "Empirical Apperception of Time" by Bettina Bäumer. In *Cultures and Time: At the Crossroads of Culture,* 63–88. Paris: UNESCO Press, 1976.

———. *The Vedic Experience (Mantramañjarī): An Anthology of the Vedas for Modern Man and Contemporary Celebration.* Reprint. Pondicherry: All India Books, 1983.

Pārśvadeva. *The Saṅgītasamayasāra of Saṅgītākara Śrī Pārśvadeva.* Edited by T. Gaṇapati Śāstrī. Trivandrum: Sanskrit Series, 1925.

Patterson, Maureen L. P. *South Asian Civilizations: A Bibliographic Synthesis.* Chicago: University of Chicago Press, 1981.

Pollock, Sheldon Ivan. *Aspects of Versification in Sanskrit Lyric Poetry.* New Haven: American Oriental Society, 1977.

———. "The Theory of Practice and the Practice of Theory in Indian Intellectual History." *Journal of the American Oriental Society* 105, no. 3 (1985): 499–519.

Potter, Karl H. *Presuppositions of India's Philosophies.* Englewood Cliffs, N.J.: Prentice-Hall, 1963.

Potter, Karl H., comp. and ed. *Encyclopedia of Indian Philosophies.* Vol. 1, *Bibliography.* 2d rev. ed. Delhi: Motilal Banarsidass, 1983.

Powers, Harold S. "An Historical and Comparative Approach to the Classification of *Rāgas* (with an Appendix on Ancient Indian Tunings)." *Selected Reports* 1, no. 3, Institute of Ethnomusicology, UCLA (1970): 1–78.

———. "India." (Sections 1 and 2.) In *The New Grove Dictionary of Music and Musicians,* edited by Stanley Sadie, vol. 9, 69–141. London: Macmillan, 1980.

———. "Indian Music and the English Language: A Review Essay." *Ethnomusicology* 9 (1965): 1–12.

———. "Mode." In *The New Grove Dictionary of Music and Musicians,* edited by Stanley Sadie, vol. 12, 376–450. London: Macmillan, 1980.

———. "The Structure of Musical Meaning: A View from Banaras." *Perspectives of New Music* 14, no. 2/15, no. 1 (1976): 308–34.

Prajñānānanda, Swāmī. *Historical Development of Indian Music: A Critical Study.* 2d ed. Calcutta: Firma K. L. Mukhopadhyay, 1973.

———. *A History of Indian Music.* Vol. 1, *Ancient Period.* Calcutta: Ramakrishna Vedanta Math, 1963.

Radhakrishnan, Sarvepalli, and Charles A. Moore, eds. *A Source Book in Indian Philosophy.* Princeton: Princeton University Press, 1957.

Raghavan, V. *Abhinavagupta and His Works.* Varanasi: Chaukhamba Orientalia, 1980.

———. *Bhoja's Śṛṅgāra Prakāśa.* 3d ed. Madras: Vasanta Press, 1978.

———. "Later *Saṅgīta* Literature." *Bulletin of the Sangeet Natak Akademi* 17 (1960): 1–24, and 18 (1961): 1–18.

———. "Music in Ancient Indian Drama." *Journal of the Music Academy, Madras* 25 (1954): 79–92.

———. *The Number of Rasa-s.* 3d rev. ed. Madras: Adyar Library, 1975.

———. "Sanskrit Drama in Performance." In *Sanskrit Drama in Performance,* edited by Rachel Van M. Baumer and James R. Brandon, 9–44. Honolulu: University Press of Hawaii, 1981.

———. "Some More Names in Early *Saṅgīta* Literature." *Journal of the Music Academy, Madras* 3, nos. 3–4 (1932): 94–102.

———. "Some Names in Early *Saṅgīta* Literature." *Journal of the Music Academy, Madras* 3, nos. 1–2 (1932): 11–32.

———. *Studies on Some Concepts of the Alaṃkāra Śāstra.* Rev. ed. Madras: Adyar Library, 1973.

Raghavan, V., comp. and ed. *The Indian Heritage.* Bangalore: Indian Institute of Culture, 1956.

Raja, K. Kunjunni. *Indian Theories of Meaning.* Reprint. Madras: Adyar Library, 1977.

Ramanathan, N. "A Critical Study of the Treatment of *Gīta* in *Saṅgītaratnākara* of Śārṅgadeva." Ph.D. diss., Banaras Hindu University, 1979.

———. "*Kalā, Mātrā, Laya,* and *Mārga.*" *Journal of the Indian Musicological Society* 11, nos. 3–4 (1980): 14–27.

———. "*Śruti-s* According to Ancient Texts." *Journal of the Indian Musicological Society* 12, nos. 3–4 (1981): 31–37.

———. "*Vādī, Saṃvādī, Vivādī,* and *Anuvādī Svaras.*" *Journal of the Music Academy, Madras* 54 (1983): 60–82.

Ramanathan, S. *Music in Cilappatikaaram.* Madurai: Madurai Kamaraj University, 1979.

Rao, P. S. R. Appa. *A Monograph on Bharata's naaTya Saastra.* Translated by P. S. R. Appa Rao and P. Sri Rama Sastry. Hyderabad: naaTya maalaa Publishers, 1967.

Rapson, E. J., ed. *The Cambridge History of India.* Vol. 1, *Ancient India.* New York: Macmillan, 1922.

Rastogi, Navjivan. *The Krama Tantricism of Kashmir: Historical and General Sources.* Vol. 1. Delhi: Motilal Banarsidass, 1979.

Ray, Niharranjan. *An Approach to Indian Art.* Chandigarh: Punjab University, 1974.

Reyna, Ruth. "Metaphysics of Time in Indian Philosophy and Its Relevance to Particle Science." In *Time in Science and Philosophy: An International Study of some Current Problems,* edited by Jiří Zeman, 227–39. Amsterdam: Elsevier, 1971.

Rowell, Lewis. "Abhinavagupta, Augustine, Time, and Music." *Journal of the Indian Musicological Society* 13, no. 2 (December 1982): 18–36.

———. "The Ancient *Tāla* System: A Comparative Approach." *Journal of the Music Academy, Madras* 57 (1986): 83–99.

———. "Early Indian Musical Speculation and the Theory of Melody." *Journal of Music Theory* 25, no. 2 (1981): 217–44.

———. "Form in the Ritual Theatre Music of Ancient India." *Musica Asiatica* 5 (1988): 140–90.

———. "The Idea of Music in India and the Ancient West." In *Essays on the Philosophy of Music,* edited by Veikko Rantala, Lewis Rowell, and Eero Tarasti, 323–42. *Acta Philosophica Fennica* 43. Helsinki: Philosophical Society of Finland, 1988.

———. "Paradigms for a Comparative Mythology of Music." *Journal of the Indian Musicological Society* 18, no. 2 (December 1987): 14–29.

———. "A *Śikṣā* for the Twiceborn." *Asian Music* 9, no. 1 (1977): 72–94.

———. "The Songs of Medieval India: The *Prabandhas* as Described in Mataṅga's *Bṛhaddeśī*." *Music Theory Spectrum* 9 (1987): 136–72.

———. "The Subconscious Language of Musical Time." *Music Theory Spectrum* 1 (1979): 96–106.

———. *Thinking about Music: An Introduction to the Philosophy of Music.* Amherst: University of Massachusetts Press, 1983.

———. "Thinking Time and Thinking *about* Time in Indian Music." *Communication & Cognition* 19, no. 2 (1986): 229–40.

———. "Time in the Musical Consciousness of Old High Civilizations—East and West." In *The Study of Time* 3, edited by J. T. Fraser, N. Lawrence, and D. Park, 578–611. New York: Springer-Verlag, 1978.

Royce, Anya Peterson. *The Anthropology of Dance.* Bloomington: Indiana University Press, 1977.

Sachs, Curt. *Rhythm and Tempo.* New York: W. W. Norton, 1953.

———. *The Rise of Music in the Ancient World—East and West.* New York: W. W. Norton, 1943.

———. *The Wellsprings of Music.* Edited by Jaap Kunst. New York: McGraw-Hill, 1965.

Sambamoorthy, P. *South Indian Music.* 6 vols. Madras: Indian Music Publishing House, 1960–69.

Sanyal, Ritwik. *Philosophy of Music.* Bombay: Somaiya Publications, 1987.

Śārṅgadeva. *The Saṃgītaratnākara of Śārṅgadeva.* Vol. 4, Chapter on Dancing. Translated by K. Kunjunni Raja and Radha Burnier. Madras: Adyar Library, 1976.

———. *Saṅgītaratnākara of Śārṅgadeva.* Vol. 1, chap. 1. Translated by C. Kunhan Raja. Madras: Adyar Library, 1945.

———. *Saṅgīta-Ratnākara of Śārṅgadeva.* Vol. 1, Treatment of *Svara.* Translated by R. K. Shringy, under the supervision of Prem Lata Sharma. Varanasi: Motilal Banarsidass, 1978.

———. *Saṅgītaratnākara of Śārṅgadeva, with* [the commentaries] *Kalānidhi of Kallinātha and Sudhākara of Siṁhabhūpāla.* Edited by S. Subrahmaṇya Śāstrī. 4 vols. Madras: Adyar Library, 1943–53.

Sathyanarayana, R. "Śruti, Dhvani, and Sphoṭa." *The Indian Theosophist* 82, nos. 10–11 (1985): 30–47.

———. "Śruti: The Scalic Foundation." *Sangeet Natak* 17 (1970): 58–74.

Schayer, Stanisław. *Contributions to the Problem of Time in Indian Philosophy.* Kraków: Polska Akademia Umiejetności, 1938.

Scranton, Robert L. *Aesthetic Aspects of Ancient Art.* Chicago: University of Chicago Press, 1964.

Seal, Brajendranath. *The Positive Sciences of the Ancient Hindus.* Reprint. Delhi: Motilal Banarsidass, 1985.

Sharma, Peri Sarveswara. *The Kālasamuddeśa of Bhartṛhari's Vākyapadīya.* Delhi: Motilal Banarsidass, 1972.

Sharma, Prem Lata. "The Concept of *Sthāya* in Indian *Saṅgītaśāstra.*" *Indian Music Journal* 3–5 (1965).

———. "Rasa Theory and Indian Music." *Sangeet Natak* 16 (1970): 57–64.

———. *Saṅgītarāja by Mahārāṇā Kumbhā.* Vol. 1. Varanasi: Banaras Hindu University Press, 1963.

Siegel, Lee. *Laughing Matters: Comic Tradition in India.* Chicago: University of Chicago Press, 1987.

Simonsson, Nils. "Some Philological Problems in Indian Musicological Literature." *Acta Orientalia* 37 (1976): 127–63.

Sinha, Jadunath. *Indian Psychology.* 3 vols. Reprint. Delhi: Motilal Banarsidass, 1986.

Sivaramamurti, C. *Naṭarāja in Art, Thought, and Literature.* New Delhi: National Museum, 1974.

Someśvara. *The Mānasollāsa of King Someśvara.* Edited by G. K. Srigondekar. 3 vols. Gaekwad's Oriental Series nos. 28, 84, and 138. Baroda: Oriental Institute, 1925–61.

Staal, J. F. *Nambudiri Veda Recitation.* Disputationes Rheno-Trajectinae 5, edited by J. Gonda. The Hague: Mouton, 1961.

Strangways, A. H. Fox. *The Music of Hindostan.* Oxford: Clarendon Press, 1914.

Stutley, Margaret, and James Stutley. *A Dictionary of Hinduism: Its Mythology, Folklore and Development 1500 B.C.–A.D. 1500.* London: Routledge and Kegan Paul, 1977.

Szabolcsi, Bence. *A History of Melody.* Translated by Cynthia Jolly and Sara Karig. London: Barrie and Rockliff, 1965.

Te Nijenhuis, Emmie. *Indian Music: History and Structure.* Leiden: E. J. Brill, 1974.

———. *Musicological Literature: A History of Indian Literature,* edited by Jan Gonda, vol. 6, fasc. 1. Wiesbaden: Otto Harrassowitz, 1977.

Varma, K. M. *Nāṭya, Nṛtta, and Nṛtya: Their Meaning and Relation.* Calcutta: Orient Longmans, 1957.

Varma, Siddheshwar. *Critical Studies in the Phonetic Observations of Indian Grammarians.* London: Royal Asiatic Society, 1929.

Vatsyayan, Kapila. *Classical Indian Dance in Literature and the Arts.* New Delhi: Sangeet Natak Akademi, 1968.

———. *The Square and the Circle of the Indian Arts.* New Delhi: Roli Books International, 1983.

Velankar, H. D. "Sanskrit Metres: Their Evolution and Principles of Division." In *The Cultural Heritage of India,* vol. 5, edited by Suniti Kumar Chatterji, 2d ed., 303–11. Calcutta: Ramakrishna Mission Institute of Culture, 1978.

Velankar, H. D., comp. and ed. *Jayadāman: A Collection of Ancient Texts on Sanskrit Prosody and a Classified List of Sanskrit Metres.* Bombay: Haritosha Samiti, 1949.

Vyāsa, Yugalakiśora, ed. *Śikṣā-Saṃgraha: A Collection of Śikṣās by Yājñavalkya and Others.* Varanasi: Benares Sanskrit Series, 1893.

Walimbe, Y. S. *Abhinavagupta on Indian Aesthetics.* Delhi: Ajanta Publications, 1980.

Wayman, Alex. "The Significance of Mantra-s, from the Veda down to Buddhist Tantric Practice." *Adyar Library Bulletin* 39 (1975): 65–89.

Wellesz, Egon, ed. *Ancient and Oriental Music.* The New Oxford History of Music, vol. 1. London: Oxford University Press, 1957.

Wells, Henry W. *The Classical Drama of India: Studies in Its Values for the Literature and Theatre of the World.* London: Asia Publishing House, 1963.

Whitney, William Dwight. *Sanskrit Grammar.* 2d ed. Cambridge: Harvard University Press, 1889.

Widdess, D. R. "The Kuḍumiyāmalai Inscription: A Source of Early Indian Music in Notation." *Musica Asiatica* 2 (1980): 115–50.

———. *The Rāgas of Early Indian Music: Modes, Melodies and Musical Notations c 600–1250.* Forthcoming.

———. "Sugar, Treacle and Candy: History and the Concept of *Rāga* in Indian Music." In *Ethnomusicology and the Historical Dimension,* ed. Margot Lieth Philipp, 71–81. Papers presented at the European Seminar in Ethnomusicology, School of Oriental and African Studies, University of London, May 1986. Ludwigsburg: Philipp Verlag, 1989.

———. "Tāla and Melody in Early Indian Music: A Study of Nānyadeva's Pāṇikā Songs with Musical Notation." *Bulletin of the School of Oriental and African Studies, University of London* 44, part 3 (1981): 481–508.

Winternitz, Maurice. *A History of Indian Literature.* Vols. 1 and 2. Translated by S. Ketkar and H. Kohn. 2d ed. New Delhi: Oriental Books Reprint Corp., 1977. Vol. 3, fasc. 1. Translated by H. Kohn. Calcutta: University of Calcutta Press, 1959. Vol. 3, part 2. Translated by Subhadra Jhā. Delhi: Motilal Banarsidass, 1967.

Zimmer, Heinrich. *The Art of Indian Asia: Its Mythology and Transformations.* Completed and edited by Joseph Campbell. Bollingen Series no. 39. Princeton: Princeton University Press, 1955.

———. *Myths and Symbols in Indian Art and Civilization.* Edited by Joseph Campbell. Bollingen Series no. 6. Reprint. New York: Harper and Row, 1962.

———. *Philosophies of India.* Edited by Joseph Campbell. Bollingen Series no. 26. Princeton: Princeton University Press, 1951.

# INDEX

Unless otherwise identified, entries pertain specifically to India (e.g., geography, cultural). Because the line dividing "music" from the rest of the world of early India is often fuzzy, information on musical and nonmusical concepts has often been indexed under the same entry (e.g., form). For the purposes of a common index, Sanskrit words have been alphabetized in Latin alphabetical order, letter-by-letter, and disregarding diacritics, except in those cases where otherwise identical words are distinguished only by diacritics (in these cases, letters unaffected by diacritics appear first, e.g., *kalā, kāla*). Sanskrit words are treated as they appear in the text, i.e., generic terms in italics and lowercased, proper nouns in roman and capitalized.


*Abhinavabhāratī* of Abhinavagupta, 20, 101, 186, 249, 347n.30; on *rasa,* 327–30; on time, 188–90

Abhinavagupta (author), 7, 93, 102–3, 108, 249. See also *Abhinavabhāratī* of Abhinavagupta; Kashmir Shaivism

*abhinaya* (mime), 10, 15, 266; four components of, 132, 295, 376n.4

*ābhoga* (a concluding section), 237, 276–77, 279–80, 282, 285

accent(s): agogic, 199; evolution of, in Sanskrit verse, 215–17, 268; in *tāla,* determined by context, 194, 196; tendency toward end—, 133, 200, 221, 251–52, 262, 373n.111; three Vedic, 58–59, 83–85

accompaniment: drum, 116; of songs, 111, 292–93; three styles of, 112, 318–19

acoustics: Chinese, Greek, Indian compared, 51–55; a philosophy of mind, 50. *See also* sound

action, 120–21, 235. *See also* karma

aesthetics, 312–13, 330, 334–37; *rasa* theory, 327–34. *See also* beauty; preferences, artistic; values

affixes, formal: in ritual forms, 244, 246; in Sāmaveda tradition, 64. *See also* Ṣaṭpitāputrakaḥ; Śīrṣaka; *upavartana*

Agni (god), 11, 45

*Aitareya Āraṇyaka,* 33, 115

*ākāśa* (atmosphere), 2–4; contrasted to ether, 49; the medium of sound, 40–41, 47–50; in the Sāṅkhya system, 29–30, 40; in the Vaiśeṣika system, 29

*akṣara* (syllable), 48, 202–7; etymology of, 36, 75, 349n.6. See also *Om; stobha;* syllable(s); vocables

*alaṅkāra* (ornament): in dramatic representation, 299; of *kāku,* 326; musical ornaments, 162–66, 320–21; a topic of criticism, 134. *See also* ornament(s)

*alaṅkāraśāstra* (literary theory), 305

*ālāpana* (exposition of a *rāga*), 63, 223, 230, 239–43, 289

*ālapti* (a subspecies of *ālāpana*), 137–38, 239–41

Allen, W. Sidney, 67, 70, 168, 310

altered note(s). See *sādhāraṇa*

ambiguity, 194–96, 229

*aṁśa* (the predominant note), 155, 158–60, 167–73, 331–32

Ānandavardhana (author), 42

*aṅga* (component), 233; formal components, 244–47; melodic, 245, 258, 264; in Oveṇaka, 258–59, 262–64; six—of drama, 295, 375n.2; six—of *prabandha,*

*aṅga* (component) (*continued*)
276–80; a topic of *tāla,* 191–92. *See also* form
*anibaddha* (unregulated), 130, 238–39, 274, 276
Anta (a permuting final component), 251–52, 261, 263–64
*antara* (an interlude), 237, 276–77, 279–80
*anuvādi* (a neutral or subordinate note), 158–60
Aparāntaka (a type of composition), 253
Ārabhaṭī (masculine style), 288, 299–300, 313–15, 318. *See also* style
archetypes, formal, 230–43
Archytas of Tarentum, 39
Aristides Quintilianus, 298, 300, 345n.11
Aristotle, 39, 49, 54, 121, 248, 328, 329
art music, 270–71, 338
Āsārita (a type of composition), 266
Aśvaghoṣa (author), 92
*Atharvaveda,* 10, 15, 57–58; hymn to time, 182–84. *See also* Vedas
*ātman* (self; soul), 3, 16, 29, 39, 48; analyzed in *Kaṭha Upaniṣad,* 23; forms of, 36–38; as sound principle, 51–55
Augustine, Saint, 186
authority, 6; in *śāstra,* 119–24, 289–92; of testimony, 25, 125
authorship, of Sanskrit treatises, 6–7, 21–22, 24–25, 129–30
*avadhāna* (attention), 302–3
*āvarta* (cycle), 192, 223. *See also* cycle, rhythmic
Āyurvedic doctrines, 44, 310–11

Basham, A. L., 15, 234
beauty, 307, 336. See also *guṇas*; preferences, artistic; values
beginnings, musical: epigram, 249–50; free/strict archetype, 237–43; indefinite preferred, 230; *rāga,* 269–70; tactics, 63–64, 248–49; *udgrāha,* 276–79; *upohana,* 248–50. See also *ālāpana*
Berry, Wallace, 203
*Bhagavadgītā,* 27, 31, 119, 121, 227–28, 302
Bharata (author): etymology, 10–11, 97. See also *Nāṭyaśāstra* of Bharata
*Bharatabhāṣya* of Nānyadeva, 20–21, 166, 347n.31
Bhāratī (a style), 288, 313–15. *See also* style
Bhāsa (author): *The Vision of Vāsavadattā,* 92, 111
Bhātkhaṇḍe, V. N., 179
*bindu* (drop), 44–45, 47, 235, 322, 370n.29
*biruda* (a panegyric), 278–79. See also *prabandha*
Blacking, John, 340
body, human: as center of universe, 16–18, 232–33; five sheaths, 33; significance of, 232–33; source of formal terms, 233
Boethius, 120
book making, 125–26
Brahmā (god), 25, 106; knot of, 34, 43–44, 350n.33
Brandon, James R., 94
breath, 17; aspiration in Sanskrit, 71–72; as sacrifice, 185–86; significance of, in music, 186; in sound production, 33–34, 39–40, 44–45; and spirit, 51–55; three forms of vital—, 36–37. See also *prāṇa*
*Bṛhad-Āraṇyaka Upaniṣad,* 48
*Bṛhaddeśī* of Mataṅga, 7, 20, 42, 142, 321–22, 347n.29; cultural mapping, 287–90, 313–14; display of *sa-grāma,* 152; Elā, 284–90; explanation of sonance, 158; exposition of *nāda,* 43–47; five *prabandhas,* 280–81; Jhombaḍa, 281–82; lost *tāla* canto, 207–8; manuscript sources, 127; philosophical arguments on *śruti* and *svara,* 149–52; *prabandhas,* 275, 292; Śukacañcu, 269–70; on vocal sound, 50, 310
Broeckx, Jan L., 32
Buddhism, 19, 27; views on sound, 41; views on time, 187

Cācapuṭaḥ (a *tāla*), 197
Caccatpuṭaḥ (a *tāla*), 197, 263, 266
caesura, 219–20
catharsis, 328
center: of the body, symbolism of, 232–33; the source of sound, 16–18, 29. *See also* body, human; cosmology
centonization, 59
*Chāndogya Upaniṣad,* 16–17, 38, 68
chant, 56–90. *See also* recitation; *Ṛgveda; Sāmaveda; śikṣā*
*chāyā* (shading), 319, 322, 325, 326–27

*chhi*, 51–55
China, ancient: classification of instruments, 14; concept of sound, 51–55; rhythm and drumming, 117
chironomy, 13; of *deśī tāla*s, 210–11; notations for, 142; in *Sāmaveda* recitation, 65–66, 87; of *tāla* system, 193–96. *See also* gesture(s); mnemonics
*Cilappatikaaram* of ILankoo, 20, 347n.26
Cleonides, 163, 354n.71
Clough, John, 363n.32
colophons, in Sanskrit texts, 132–33
color, symbolism of, 67, 88–89, 287–88, 307, 356n.125
commentarial tradition, 6–7; method, 24, 126; style, 128–30
composers, 302–3
consonance. *See* sonance
cosmology, 16–18, 47–49, 182–86. *See also* creation; process
creation, 2–3, 6; as formal archetype, 237–43; in Hindu worldview, 25, 242; sound as agent of, 35–36; three phases, 188–90
cycle, rhythmic, 180, 184–86, 190, 192–93, 222–24, 230. *See also* rhythm; *tāla*

dance, 10; categories of, 15
Daṇḍin (author), 316–17
dating of Indian literature, 21–22, 27, 69–70
Dattila (author). See *Dattilam* of Dattila
*Dattilam* of Dattila, 20, 100–101, 346n.25; five *mārga tāla*s, 196–99; *lakṣaṇa*s of *jāti*, 131; thirteen *alaṅkāra*s, 164, 321; three musical styles, 317–18
Decsey, Ernest, 200
Descartes, René, 49
*deśī* (provincial), 7, 178, 273, 342; as opposed to *mārga*, 10, 12–13, 192–93; *tāla*s, 198–99, 203, 207–14
*dhātu*s (elements; components): natural elements, 2–4, 16, 29–30, 217–18, 287–88; components of *prabandha*s, 130, 236–37, 276–80, 282, 285–86, 292
*dhruva, dhruvaka* (the main section of a song), 237, 276–77, 279–80, 282, 285
*dhruvā* (a theater song), 100, 108–12, 273–74
*dhvani* (sound), 42, 288–89, 350n.24. *See also* sound
diatonicism, 80, 146, 176–77, 363n.32. See also *grāma; mūrcchanā; svara*
Dīkṣitar, Muttuswami (composer), 342
dissonance. *See* sonance
*doṣa*s: blemishes, 72, 133–34, 295, 304–8, 309–12; humors, 310
Douthett, Jack, 363n.32
drama, Sanskrit: early history of, 92–96; plot structure, 235, 370n.29; ritual origins, 97–98; six limbs of, 375n.2; sources for, 357n.8. *See also* theater
drone, 114–15, 159, 178, 292–93
drumming, 14, 100; *BN*, chap. 33 summarized, 116–17; counter-dimension to pitch, 116; notations, 141–42, 354n.57; percussion vs. timekeeping, 116; in *prabandha*s, 292–93; three accompaniment styles, 112, 318–19
durations, rhythmic: in *deśī tāla*s, 211–12; in *mārga tāla*s, 196–97, 204–5; in recitation, 67–68; in verse, 221. *See also* state(s) of *tāla; tāla;* timing
dynamics, 68

Einstein, Albert, 49
Elā (song genre), 284–90
elements, the five, 2–4, 16; in the Sāṅkhya system, 29–30; symbolism of, in metrics, 217–18, 287–88; in the Vaiśeṣika system, 29
Ellis, A. J., 147
emic-etic dichotomy, 339
emotion, 10, 15, 90, 97, 118, 166–67, 179. See also *rasa*
endings, musical: Anta, 251, 263–64; permutations, 251–52; tactics of closure, 252, 265. *See also* accent, tendency toward end —
equal temperament, 147–49, 176–77. *See also* tuning
ether in Western thought, 48–49, 351n.50
ethics, Indian and Western compared, 120–21
ethnomusicology, 270–71, 338–44

Feld, Steven, 338
flute, 14, 99, 115–16, 311
folk music vs. art music, 271–73
form, 225–68; affixes, 64, 246; an-

form (*continued*)
thropomorphic, 232–33; archetypes, formal, 230–43; components, 243–47; in Indian thought, 225–30, 267; later history of musical, 235, 268; meaning of, 247–48, 267; mutable, 3–4, 26–27, 228; organic, 233–35; preferences for, 59, 228–30, 244; in ritual theater music, 252–68; in *Sāmaveda* tradition, 61–64; song forms, 276–80; structural inflation, 195, 199–201; tactics of, 247–52, 265; 2 + 1 grouping, 264–65, 277; in Vedic liturgy, 61–64, 236–37
free/strict archetype, 237–43
function, tonal. *See* sonance

*gamaka* (transition; ornament), 71, 163–66, 319–24, 364n.42; seven, in *PS*, 164–65, 319, 322–23
gamut, musical: circular display of, in *MB*, 152; evolution of, 77–85; and its tuning, 145–49; and its variables, 152–57. See also under *mūrcchanā; sthāna; svara*
*gaṇas* (metrical feet), 196, 213, 217–20; in Elā, 286–89. *See also* meter, poetic
*gāna* (song genre), 10–12, 300; according to Abhinavagupta, 101; analysis of, in *SS*, 130, 276; as opposed to *gāndharva*, 11–12
*gandharvas* (celestial musicians), 11, 345n.7
*gāndharva* (ritual music), 10–12, 222, 345n.6; according to Abhinavagupta, 101–3; as opposed to *gāna*, 11–12
Ganeṣa (god), 3
Gāthā (a type of composition), 265
Gauḍī (a mode of poetic diction), 288–89, 313–14, 316–18. *See also* style
Gauldin, Robert, 176
Gāyatrī (a poetic meter), 62–63, 87
gender stereotypes, 91, 298–301, 306, 313–15
genre(s): expansion of, 281–84, 284–90, 291; constitution of, 275
geography, cultural, 343; in *gaṇa* Elās, 286–90, 313–14; of song styles, 271–73
Gerow, Edwin, 329–30
gesture(s), 15; for *deśī tālas*, 210–11; meaning of, 194–96; in *Sāmaveda* recitation, 65–66, 87; sequences, 197–99; significance of, in music, 186; silent, 210–11. *See also* chironomy; *tāla*
*gīta* (song), 5–6, 269–70; a component of *saṅgīta*, 9–10, 13. *See also* song(s)
*gītakas* (ritual compositions), 191–92, 253–68. *See also* form
*gīti* (style, text setting), 191–92, 296, 318–19. *See also* style
Gjerdingen, Robert O., 350n.20
*graha* (a musical beginning), 170, 192, 249
*grāma* (scale), 78–79, 82, 153, 355n.80; with altered degrees, 154–56; circular projection, in *MB*, 152; evolution of Vedic scale, 80; *ga-grāma*, 361n.3; omission of notes, 160–62; *sa-* and *ma-grāmas* compared, 146, 361n.3. See also *svara*
*grāmarāgas* (ancestors of *rāgas*), 173–79, 332, 355n.91; in *K*, 142; in *NS*, 81
Gray, J. E. B., 84
Great sayings, 278, 374n.33
Great utterances [*Vyāhṛtis*], 37–38, 87
Greece, ancient: concept of music, 5; diatonic scale, 146; emphasis on pitch intervals, 148–49; formal preferences, 229; gender, music and, 298–300; musical definitions, 131; musical system, 95; musical thought, atomistic, 362n.15; notations, musical, 140–41, 360n.43; rhythm modeled on principles of verse, 117; typical text format, 131; views on musical sound, 51–55, 150; views on sound in general, 38–39; words for form, 226–27
Guido of Arezzo: hand, 66; sol-fa syllables, 42, 79
*guṇas* (qualities): and *doṣas*, 133–34, 295, 304–8, 309–12; in the Sāṅkhya philosophy, 31–32, 91, 190, 305; of Vaidarbhī *rīti*, 317

harmony, Western concept of, 51–55, 116
Heimann, Betty, 26, 228
Heraclitus, 25, 49, 53
hierarchy, temporal, 181, 191–92. *See also* form; *tāla*
history, Indian, 341–44; chronology, 19–21; problems of, 7–8
Horace, 124, 229
Hornbostel, E. M. von, 14

Howard, Wayne, 58
humors, 32; and vocal sound, 49–50, 310–11

ILankoo (author). See *Cilappatikaaram* of ILankoo
improvisation, 11–12, 81–82, 110, 268
India: cultural geography of, 271–73, 286–90, 313–14, 343; history of, 7–8, 19–21, 341–44
individual, in Indian thought, 16–18, 232–33; five sheaths, 33. *See also* body, human; cosmology
Indo-Aryan conquest, 18–19, 23, 342
Indus Valley civilizations, 18, 204
instruments, 112–17; categories of, 10, 13–14, 99, 112–17, 295; four strands of ideas about, 113–14; limited role in Indian thought, 14, 40; role in accompaniment, 292–93; theater ensemble, 103, 293; three musical styles, 112. *See also* drumming; flute; *tāla,* cymbals; vina
intervals, musical: consonant and dissonant, 158–60; Greek and Indian views compared, 152–53; role of octave, 78, 152–53, 168; tuning of, 146–49. *See also* sonance

Jackson, William, 342–43
*jātis*: *lakṣaṇas* of, in *D,* 131, 170–71; mode classes, 166–67, 168–73, 175–79, 331–32; rhythmic genera, 209; in *tāla,* 192. See also *svara*
Jayavardhana (a type of song), 280–81
Jhombaḍa (song genre), 281–84, 290
just intonation, 147–48. *See also* tuning

*Kaiśikī* (feminine style), 288, 299–300, 313–15, 318, 333. *See also* style
*kāku* (vocal inflection), 303, 320–21, 326–27
*kalā:* conceptual unit of rhythm, 202–7; four silent gestures, 194–96; as a topic of *tāla,* 188–93. *See also* rhythm; *tāla*
*kāla* (time), 74, 180, 188–89, 192, 205. *See also* time
Kālidāsa (author): *Mālavikā and Agnimitra,* 91, 109; *Meghadūta,* 220, 333; *Śākuntala,* 2–4, 92
Kallinātha (commentator), 21, 291–92
*Kāmasūtra* of Vātsyāyana, 122, 280
*kampita* (tremor; ornament), 309, 320–24. *See also* ornament(s)
karma, doctrine of, 26, 29, 50, 119–21
Kashmir Shaivism, 7; role of time, 188; topics of, 30–31; views on sound, 46–47. *See also* Abhinavagupta
*Kaṭha Upaniṣad,* 23, 225
*Kauṣītaki Upaniṣad,* 35, 225
Keith, A. B., 93, 122–23, 313
knowledge: acquired from multiple perspectives, 3; analyzed in *Kaṭha Upaniṣad,* 23; distrust written, 86, 125, 129; six obstacles to, 86. *See also* teaching and learning
*kriyā* (an action), 192
Kuḍumiyāmalai rock inscription, 20, 142, 347n.28
*kuṇḍalinī yoga,* 33

*lakṣaṇa* (distinguishing mark; feature): definition by features, 131, 134; of *jāti,* 170–71; as opposed to *lakṣya,* 120; qualifications, 301–4; of songs, 290–91. *See also* scholarship, Indian musical; shastric tradition
Lannoy, Richard, 25, 26
Lāsya (feminine style of theater prelude), 107
Lāṭī (a mode of poetic diction), 288–89, 314, 316. *See also* style
*laya* (tempo), 188–89, 191–92, 202–7, 298, 319. See also *tāla*
life, four ends of, 121–22. See also *mokṣa*
literature, musicological, 19–22, 119–43, 346n.23. *See also* Sanskrit; scholarship, Indian musical; texts, Sanskrit
Lomax, Alan, 271–73
Lucretius, *De rerum natura,* 38–39, 41

Macdonell, A. A., 70
macrocosm and microcosm, 16–18, 232–33. *See also* cosmology
Madraka (a type of composition), 253–58
*Maitri Upaniṣad,* 36–38, 68, 180–81, 185
*Mānasollāsa* of Someśvara, 21, 208, 347n.32; structure of *prabandha,* 276–77
*Māṇḍūkya Upaniṣad,* 36
*maṅgalācaraṇa* (a dedicatory verse), 131–32, 188–90
mantra, 17, 50, 57

mapping, cultural, 284–90, 313–17. *See also* style
*mārga*: density of time, 191–92, 202–7, 210, 319; as opposed to *deśī*, 10, 12–13, 192–93, 217; *tāla*s, five, 196–99, 203
Mataṅga (author). See *Bṛhaddeśī* of Mataṅga
*mātrā* (unit of measure): in metrics, 193, 204; in *Sāmaveda* recitation, 67–68; in *tāla* system, 191–93, 202–7, 245–46; as a topic of phonetic theory, 56–57
*Mātrālakṣaṇam*, 67
Mātṛkā (a type of song), 280–81
Maurer, Walter H., 185
maya, 25, 29, 30, 225
meaning, musical, 179, 329–30. *See also* aesthetics; values
mediation, 25
*melāpaka* (an interlude), 237, 276–77, 279–80, 282, 285
melody, Indian: contour, 163–66; decorative aspects, 162–63; demonstrates spatial preferences, 267; develops by permutations, 154; displays feminine qualities, 298–300; evolution of, 60; Indian and Western concepts contrasted, 66; influence of sandhi, 71; microstructure of, 164–65, 320–27. *See also* preferences, Indian artistic; values
Merriam, Alan, 339
metaphor(s): animal, 32–33, 86–90, 134, 310; anthropomorphic, 33, 232–33; Brownian motion, 341; fluid continuity, 306–7; in Indian explanation, 32–34; outward spiral, 33–34, 38, 151; for sound, 51–55
meter, musical. See *tāla*
meter, poetic: Anuṣṭubh, 61; codes, 140, 217–20; evolution of, in Indian verse, 215–17; fossils, 220; *gaṇa*s, 217–21; *gaṇa* Elās, 286–90; influence upon musical rhythm, 215, 243–44; *śloka*, 128, 135–40; Vedic, 353n.23
Meyer, Leonard B., 295
microtones. See *śruti*
Mīmāṁsā, philosophical system of, 28, 40–41. *See also* philosophy, Indian
Mishra, Umesha, 50–51
Mishra, Vidhata, 69
mnemonics, 125, 193, 353n.33; names of *tāla*s, 197; in Vedic recitation, 64–65
mode. See *grāmarāga*s; *jāti*s; *rāga*
*mokṣa* (liberation), 3, 18, 29, 121–22, 330
*mudrā* (gesture), 65–66, 87–88. *See also* chironomy; gesture(s)
*mukha* (face), 233
*mūrcchanā*: octave species, rotating, 78–79, 82, 153–54; ornament, 288–89, 322
*mūrti* (form), 226. *See also* form
music, 5–6, 124, 150–51; in ancient Greece, 5, 150; the being of, 51–55, 292; the divisions of, 9–16; and ritual, 185

*nāda* (causal sound): five grades of, 44–47; four meanings of, 45; in *gaṇa* Elās, 288–89. See also under *Bṛhaddeśī* of Mataṅga
*nādabrahman* (sound as agent of creation), 36, 43–47
*nāmarūpa* (philosophical term), 226
Nānyadeva (author). See *Bharatabhāṣya* of Nānyadeva
Nārada (author). See *Nāradīyaśikṣā* of Nārada
*Nāradīyaśikṣā* of Nārada, 20, 56–57, 67, 129, 140, 347n.27; contents, 75–85; dating of, 70; equation of Vedic and secular scales, 80, 355n.83; exposition of pitch, 75–85; *guṇa*s and *doṣa*s of singing, 295, 304, 307–8; instructions for recitation, 86–88; milieu of Sāmavedin, 85–90; mythology in, 88–90; preferences for recitation, 301. *See also* phonetics; *śikṣā*
*nāṭya* (acting, drama), 10, 15. *See also* drama; theater
*Nāṭyaśāstra* of Bharata, 11, 14, 19, 96, 163, 299, 346n.24; on *alaṅkāra*, 162; chaps. on music summarized, 99–101; contents, 96–101; date, 93; demonstration of *śruti*s, 147–48; *doṣa*s of performance, 308; on drumming, 116–17; five *mārga tāla*s, 196–99; four modes of dramatic expression, 313–15; *guṇa*s and *doṣa*s of singing, 309–10; *guṇa*s of poetry, 317; incidental theater music, 108–12; on instruments, 112–17; irregular *tāla*s, 209; on *kāku*, 326–27; *nibaddha/anibaddha* distinction, 238–39; production of *rasa*, 331–32; *pūrvaraṅga*, 101–8; on *rasa*, 327–34; on *sādhāraṇa*, 155; sexist performance

standards, 300; spectator, qualifications of ideal, 295, 301; Śṛṅgāra *rasa,* 332–34; on *tāla,* 188–90; textual problems, 100–101; theater songs, 109–11, 273–74; three styles of accompaniment, 112, 318–19
Nettl, Bruno, 339–41
*nibaddha* (regulated), 130, 238–39, 274, 276
*nirukta* (etymology), 9–11, 44–45, 284
nirvana, 29
noncontradiction, strategy of, 290–91
notations, musical, 7, 140–43; characteristics, 140; drum, 141–42; for durations, 197; in *K,* 142; limitations of, 141, 143; numerals, 141; preference for oral, 320; *sargam,* 141, 143; syllabic, 140–41; for *tāla,* 142, 193–94. *See also under* syllable(s)
*nṛtta* (abstract dance), 9–10, 15
*nṛtya* (representational dance), 15. See also *abhinaya*
numbers, musical significance of: in *Sāmaveda* recitation, 61–64; threeness, 77–78, 218–19; triangular/quadrangular *tāla*s, 198, 213–14
*nyāsa* (final), 171–75
Nyāya, philosophical system of, 28, 40–41. *See also* philosophy, Indian

octave, 78, 152, 168
*ojas* (vital energy), 299, 307
Old High Culture, 271–72
*Om* (a sacred syllable): analysis of, 36; recitation of, 17; in *Sāmaveda* recitation, 63, 73, 87; symbolic associations of, 36–38. See also *akṣara;* syllable(s)
oral tradition, 7, 22, 123, 286, 291, 296–97, 304; aims of, 128, 135; notations, 140–41; as testimony, 125
organicism, 233–35
ornament(s): *alaṅkāra*s, 134, 162–66, 320–21; classification of, 309; *gamaka*s, 163–66, 319–24, 364n.42; in *gaṇa* Elās, 288–89; in Indian aesthetics, 165–66; *kāku,* 303, 320–21, 326–37; levels of, 319–27; *sthāya*s, 320–21, 324–27; *varṇa*s, 163–64, 320, 326

*pada* (word; unit of text): a component of *saṅgīta,* 13; a component of *prabandha,* 276–80
*pāda* ("paw"; a quarter part of anything), 135–39, 246, 254, 278, 284–86
*pādabhāga* (division into fours), 191, 220, 245–46, 253
palindrome, 199, 213
Pāñcālī (a mode of poetic diction), 288–89, 314, 316. See also *rīti;* style
*pāṇi* (phasing), 191–93, 249, 318–19
Pāṇikā (a type of song), 265
Panikkar, Raimundo, 58, 185–86
Pāṇini (author), 57, 83–84
*Pāṇinīyaśikṣā,* 67, 69–70, 74
*parivarta* (repetition), 191–92, 246, 258
Pārśvadeva (author). See *Saṅgītasamayasāra* of Pārśvadeva
*pāta* (beat): four audible gestures, 194–96; as a topic of *tāla,* 191–93. See also *tāla*
*pāṭa* (recited drum syllables), 278–79. *See also* drumming; syllable(s)
*pāṭhya* (reciter; recitation), 10, 111, 300
permutation(s), 154, 183, 192, 196; of metrical feet, 217–18; as tactic of closure, 251–52, 263–64
*phalasūtra,* 134
philosophy, Indian: common doctrines, 28–29; four main phases, 27; epistemology and ontology contrasted, 30–31; heterodox schools, 27; informal, 32–34; introduction to, 23–24, 348nn. 9, 10; six orthodox systems, 26, 27–32; views on sound, 40–41; views on time, 186–88
phonetics: alterations in *Sāmaveda* recitation, 59–61; distinctive features of Sanskrit, 70–75; oppositions, as basis for musical notations, 72, 141–42; six topics of, 56–57; Sanskrit consonants, 46–47, 310; treatises, genres of, 68–70; Vedic accents, 83–85. *See also* Sanskrit; syllable(s); vocables
pitch: early Indian system of, 79; evolution of—concepts, 76–85, 321; organization of, 176–77. See also *śruti; svara*
Plato, 227; *Timaeus,* 39
*pluta* (a protracted duration), 67, 196–97, 204–5, 211, 221
Powers, Harold S., 167, 168, 177
*prabandha* (art song): characteristic features, 275–76; cultural mapping of Elā, 284–90; defined, 274; expansion of Jhombaḍa, 281–84; formal components,

*prabandha* (art song) (*continued*) 276–80; as a genre, 292; history of, 274–76; performance practice, 292–93. *See also* song(s)
Prajāpati (god), 37, 182, 234
Prakarī (a type of composition), 253
*prakīrṇa* (miscellany), 132, 296
*prakṛti* (elemental substance), 29–32, 155, 165
*pramāṇa* (criterion), 25; measure of rhythm, 206–7; *pramāṇa-śruti,* 147–48
*prāṇa* (breath), 16–17; forms of, 36–37; and sound production, 44–45; vital substance, 115. *See also* breath
*prastāra* (permutations), 183, 192, 196, 251–52. *See also* Anta; permutation(s)
*prātiśākhya* (a phonetic treatise), 69–70. *See also* phonetics; *śikṣā*
*prayoga* (practice), 120, 124. *See also* theory
preferences, Indian artistic, 26, 180, 334–37; for decoration, 165–66; for fluid continuity, 306–7; musical, 334–37; for musical form, 59, 228–30, 244; in recitation, 301; for singing, 312; for spatial organization, 267. *See also* aesthetics; beauty; style; values
priestly life, 16–18; described in *NS,* 85–90. See also *Sāmaveda*
process: Hindu worldview, 25–26, 189, 242; in Indian philosophy, 30; natural, 336; organic, 233–35. *See also* cosmology; creation
*puruṣa* (philosophical term), 29
*Puruṣa-Sūkta,* 185
*pūrvaraṅga* (ritual prelude to a play), 101–8
Pythagoreans, 53–54
Pythagorean tuning, 147

qualifications: of composers, 302–3; of singers, 303–4; of spectators, 295, 301
quotation(s) in Sanskrit treatises, 7–8, 21–22, 24, 125; convention of *iti,* 133. *See also* scholarship, Indian musical; texts, Sanskrit

*rāga* (melodic framework, mode): affective properties, 330; ancestors of, 166–77; beginning tactics, in *prabandha,* 269–70; concept of, 166–68; defined, 10, 81–82; early notations of, 142–43; etymology, 166–67; expansion of the system, 12–13; exposition of, 45, 239–42; later history of, 177–79; and musical meaning, 179
*rāga ālāpa* (a modal exposition), 239–40. See also *ālāpana*
*rāga ālapti* (a melodic exposition), 137–38, 239–41. See also *ālāpana*
Raghavan, V., 96–97, 112, 313, 315–16
Rājaśekhara (author), 119
Ramanathan, N., 83
Rameau, Jean-Philippe, 157
*rasa* (emotional flavor), 10, 15, 17, 91, 110–11, 327–34, 378n.91; in *gaṇa* Elās, 287–89, 314
recitation, Vedic: preferences for, 301, 306; procedure, 87–88; significance of, 17; three speeds, 67–68, 204. *See also* chant; *Ṛgveda; Sāmaveda*
*Ṛgveda,* 10, 15, 19, 35, 57–58, 234; on *soma,* 85–86; style of recitation, 58–59; three accents, 83–85. *See also* Vedas
rhythm: additive/divisive, 209; in ancient China, Greece, India, 117; assigned masculine gender, 298–300; cyclical, 180, 184–86, 190, 192–93, 222–24, 230; durations, 67–68, 196–97, 204–5, 211–12, 221; evolution of, 223–24; fossils, 220; patterns, 196–99; and percussion, 116; ratios, 202–7, 246; in Sāmavedic chant, 61–64; significance of *BN* chap. 31, 99; strata, 222–23; tempo and, 67–68, 202–7; triangular/quadrangular, 198, 218–21, 263. See also *tāla*
*rīti* (poetic diction): distinctive features, 316; four modes, in *gaṇa* Elās, 287–90; history of, 315–17; and style, 295–97
ritual: formal archetype of, 61–64, 236–37; in the Gupta theater, 97–98, 101–8; and time, 184–86. *See also* chant; chironomy; gesture(s); *Sāmaveda*
Ṛk (a type of composition), 265
*Ṛk-Prātiśākhya,* 83–84
Rovindaka (a type of composition), 253
*ṛta* (cosmic order), 17, 62, 86, 233. *See also* cosmology
*rūpa* (form), 226. *See also* form

*śabda* (sound), 41–42. *See also* sound
*śabdabrahman* (sound as agent of creation), 35–36
Sachs, Curt, 14, 80–81, 117, 209
sacrifice, in Indian tradition, 2–4, 17, 184–86, 189; drama as sacrifice, 91, 97–98, 107–8
*sādhārana* (altered notes), 154–57, 362n.20
Sāma (a type of composition), 265
*Sāmaveda,* 10, 15, 57–68; durations and tempo, 67–68; dynamics, 68; gestures, 65–66; liturgy, 62–64; melodic composition in, 59; mnemonics, 64–65; musical form, 61–64; musical scale, 80–81; notations, 352n.17; performance practices, 59–68, 87–88; phonetic alterations, 59–61; style of recitation, 58–59; text, 59; tonal inflections, 82–83. *See also* chant; Vedas
Sampakveṣṭākaḥ (a *tāla*), 197
*sampradāya* (an oral tradition), 286, 291, 303–4
*saṁskāra* (philosophical term), 151
*saṁvādi* (a consonant note), 158–60
sandhi (junction): five, in a dramatic plot, 112, 235, 370n.29; in Sanskrit texts, 65, 70–71, 306
*saṅgīta* (music), 5; divisions of, 9–15; three performing components of, 13. *See also* music
*Saṅgītaratnākara* of Śārṅgadeva, 5, 21, 347n.33; analogy for sonance, 158, 160; analysis of *gāna,* 130; benedictory verse in dance canto, 132–33; canto topics, 132; coordinates of musical style, 318–19; *deśī tāla*s, 208, 210–14; *doṣa*s of singing, 308; Elā, 284, 286, 290; *gamaka*s, 323–24; *gīta* defined, 269–70; *guṇa*s of poetry and song, 306; Jhombaḍa, 282–84; *kāku,* 326–27; *prabandha*s, 276, 292; purpose of *alaṅkāra*s, 164; qualifications of composers, 302–3; qualifications of singers, 303–4; *rāga ālāpa,* 240–41; *rāga ālapti,* 137–39, 240–41; sound, 38–40; *sthāya*s, 324–27; *svara* defined, 144; vocal quality, 311–12
*Saṅgītasamayasāra* of Pārśvadeva, 21, 27–28, 348n.34; Elā, 285–86; seven *gamaka*s, 164–65, 319, 321–23
*saṅgītaśāstra* (musicology), 119. See also *śāstra;* scholarship, Indian musical; texts, Sanskrit
Sāṅkhya, philosophical system of, 28–32, 40–41, 90, 190, 218. *See also* philosophy, Indian
Sanskrit: aspiration in, 71–72; classification of sounds, 46–47, 73–74; code expressions, 139–40; distinctive features of, 70–75; identification of verbs, 350n.34; nasality in, 72–73, 310; and Prakrits, 268, 300; pronunciation, xv–xvi; prosody, 215–21; role of syllable, 74–75; sandhi, 70–71; scripts for, 126, 141; stanza, as formal model, 220–21; verse from *SS* analyzed, 137–39; words for form, 226–27; words for theory and practice, 120
*saptaka* (heptatonic collection), 152–53, 168. See also *svara*
*saptarūpa*s (the seven *gītaka* forms), 191–92. *See also* form
Sarasvatī (goddess), 42, 287–88
*sargam* notation, 42, 78–79, 141, 143
Śārṅgadeva (author). See *Saṅgītaratnākara* of Śārṅgadeva
*śāstra* (treatise; "ology"), 119–43; etymology, 121; and *prayoga,* 120, 124, 341. *See also* scholarship, Indian musical; texts, Sanskrit
Sathyanarayana, R., 151
Ṣaṭpitāputrakaḥ (a *tāla*), 197, 207; in Āsārita, 266; in Madraka, 254–58; in Oveṇaka, 258–62; in Pāṇikā, 265; in Śīrṣaka, 246; in the three states, 200–201; in *upavartana,* 250
Sāttvatī (a style), 288, 313–15. *See also* style
scales, heptatonic. See *grāma; grāmarāga*s; *jāti*s; *svara*
scales, hexatonic and pentatonic. See *tāna*s
scholarship, Indian musical: assumptions of, 124–25; commentaries, 123, 128–30; definitions, 131; distinctive features, 7–9, 21–22; emphasis upon values, 133–34; organization of pitch, 145, 176; reflects shastric tradition, 123–24; the scribal tradition, 125–26; strategies of explanation, 130–34; trends in, 341–42; verse forms and techniques, 134–40. See also *śāstra;* texts, Sanskrit

Seal, Brajendranath, 50–51
self in Indian thought, 29–31, 124; according to *Katha Upaniṣad,* 23. See also *ātman;* body, human; individual in Indian thought
Sharma, Prem Lata, 8, 204, 210
shastric tradition: categorical nature, 122–23; characteristic features, 6–9; classifications of society, 304; early history, 121–23, 359n.8; parody of, 122; reflexive explanation, 291–92; valid options, 291–92. See also *śāstra;* scholarship, Indian musical
*śikṣā* (phonetics): phonetic treatises, 68–70; six topics of, 56–57. See also *Nāradīyaśikṣā* of Nārada; phonetics
*Śikṣāsaṁgraha,* 69
silence, 36–38, 187, 224
Simhabhūpāla (commentator), 21
singers, types of, 303–4. *See also* singing; song(s)
singing: merits and demerits of, 295, 304–8; standards for, 300–301, 303–4; style, 269–73, 312; tone quality, 271–72, 308–11. *See also* singers; song(s)
Śīrṣaka (a short coda), 246, 254–61, 265
Śiva (god), 2–4, 26; androgynous nature, 91, 299, 356n.2; five activities, 3; four attributes, 132; as Lord of the Dance, 3–4, 132, 189; octoform, 2–4, 91, 188–90; patron of the theater, 102, 107; three eyes, 190
*śloka* (metrical couplet), 24; analyzed, 137–39; meter, 128, 135–40
*smṛti* (tradition), 24, 69
social class, 89, 355n.86; correlations in *gaṇa* Elās, 287–89; correlations in *NS,* 88–90; as depicted in drama, 17–18
*soma* (a ritual drink), 85–86, 356n.110
Somānanda (author), 46
Someśvara (author). See *Mānasollāsa* of Someśvara
sonance, 148, 157–60
song(s), 269–94; accompaniment of, 111–12, 292–93, 318–19; art and folk, 270–74; continuities of, 269; cultural correlations, 286–90; forms, 276–80; influenced by literary style, 287–90; *prabandhas,* 274–76; solo/group performance, 293; style, Indian, 271–74, 293–94, 312; theater, 100, 108–12, 273–74; theory and practice of, 290–94
sound, 2–4, 35–55; articulation of, 68, 74; as emanation of vital substance, 33–34, 43–47, 52–53; four divisions of, 35–38; good and bad qualities of, 308–12; in Indian philosophies, 40–41; measurement of, 76–77; medium of, 47–50; multidimensional concept of musical, 59; multiple stages of, 46–47; musical modeled upon vocal sound, 6, 36–37, 40, 311; power of, the, 15–17, 25, 40, 50, 63–64; propagation of, 50–51, 51–55; Sanskrit words for, 41–43; theories of, 38–40; three ancient conceptions of musical, 51–55. *See also* breath
space, 40–41, 48. See also *ākāśa*
*sphoṭa* (sound), 42, 151
Śṛṅgāra (a major *rasa*), 300, 314, 318, 332–34. See also *rasa*
*śruti:* microtones, 43, 145–49, 152–56, 157–60, 160–62, 174, 361n.3; philosophical arguments on — and *svara,* 149–52; qualities of sound, 50; revealed truth, 24, 69; tonal inflections, in *NS,* 82–83; tuning of, 145–49
Staal, J. F., 84
*stambha* (pillar of the universe), 86, 232, 356n.109
state(s) of *tāla,* 195, 319; Madraka diagrammed, in three, 254–58; in Ovenaka, 258–63; three, 199–201
*sthāna* (register), 74, 77–78, 153, 309–10
*sthāyas* (ornamental phrases), 303, 320–21, 324–27. *See also* ornament(s)
*stobha* (an interpolated syllable), 60–61, 71, 265. *See also* syllable(s)
Stoics, 49
Stravinsky, Igor, 251
style, 295–337; as a composite, 312–19; correlations of *vṛtti* and *rīti,* 287–90, 313–17; four modes of dramatic expression, in *BN,* 313–15; gender stereotypes, 298–301; *guṇas* and *doṣas,* 304–8; in Indian music and musical thought, 295–98; levels of ornamentation, 319–27; lists of qualifications, 301–4; qualities of musical sound, 308–12; *rasa,* 327–34; strategies for delineating, 296, 319; three styles of accompani-

ment, 112, 318–19; three musical styles, 317–19. *See also* values
substance, 3, 26–27, 30–32; musical, 51–55; in Vaiśeṣika system, 29; vital, 17, 39–40. See also *ākāśa;* breath
Śūdraka (author): *Little Clay Cart,* 92, 102, 122
Śukacañcu (a type of song), 269–70
Śukasārika (a type of song), 280
sutra, 24, 27, 127
*sūtradhāra* (theater producer/director), 16–18, 102–6; as a metaphor for time, 187–88
*svara* (pitch; scale degree), 144–79; altered scale degrees, 154–55; a band of sound, 151; the basis for ornaments, 319, 321–22; a component of *prabandha,* 278–79; defined, 13, 42–43, 144; as expounded in *NS,* 78–79; marked by gesture, 65–66, 87; mythological correspondences, in *NS,* 89; ranking of, 80–81, 156–57; as scale degree, 42–43; seven scale degrees, 78–79; significance of *ma,* 156–57; sonant relationships, 157–60; and *śruti,* philosophical arguments on, 149–52; three aspects of, 59; three Vedic accents, 58, 83–85; as a topic in phonetics, 56–57; topics of, 145; tuning of, and *śrutis*, 145–49; Vedic and secular scales compared, 80
*svaramaṇḍala* (circle of *svaras*): definition of, in *NS,* 78; diagram of, in *MB,* 152; marked on the hand, 87. See also *svara*
Svarārtha (a type of song), 280–81
syllable(s): drum, 72, 354n.57; meaningless, role of, 106; in musical notations, 140–43; role in Indian music, 74–75, 205; the sacred — *Om,* 36–38; Sāmavedic infixes, 59–61; sol-fa, 42, 78–79, 141; syllabic components of *prabandha,* 278–81; in *tāla* practice, 205, 210. See also *akṣara;* vocables
Szabolcsi, Bence, 157, 273, 343

*Taittirīya Prātiśākhya,* 68
*Taittirīya Upaniṣad,* 3, 16, 48, 56
*tāla:* a component of *prabandha,* 278–79; compounds, 262–63, 266; cymbals, 14, 194, 293; defined, 10, 13; *deśī tālas*, 207–14; etymology, 190; five *mārga tālas*, 196–99; in *gaṇa* Elās, 286–90, 290; gesture notations, 142; gestures, 193–96; and musical form, 225; patterns, 196–99; and percussion contrasted, 116; performance of, 222–23; as ritual action, 186; three states of, 195, 199–201; timing, 193, 202–7; topics of, 191–93. *See also* chironomy; form; rhythm
Tamil civilization, music in ancient, 13, 342
*tānas* (hexatonic and pentatonic collections), 78–79, 153–54, 160–62
Tantra (mystical cult), 7, 33, 40, 44–45
*tattvas* (topics): of Kashmir Shaivism, 30–31; of the Sāṅkhya system, 29–30; of the Vaiśeṣika system, 29. *See also* philosophy, Indian
teaching and learning, 7, 86, 124–25
tempo, 67–68, 202–7, 250–51. See also *laya*
*tena* (a vocalise), 278–79
texts, Sanskrit: chronology of, 19–21; codes, 133; colophons, 132–33; format, 131–34; physical materials, 125; problems in reconstructing, 7–8, 21–22, 125–30; punctuation, 136; treatment of quotations, 133; verse preferred, 134–35. *See also* scholarship, Indian musical; *śāstra;* Sanskrit
theater, classical Sanskrit, 11–12, 91–118; early history, 92–96; incidental music, 11–12, 108–12; influence upon musical thought and practice, 95–96; instrumental music, 111–12, 112–17; milieu, 16–18; plot structure, 235, 370n.29; ritual music, 11–12, 101–8; ritual origins, 97–98; role of the producer/director, 16–18; six limbs of drama, 375n.2; songs, 100, 108–11, 273–74; spectators, 295, 301
theory: disinterest in intervals, 152–53; incompatible objectives, 175–76; of music, evolution of, 144–45; and practice, 120, 154, 176, 208, 290–92, 341, 359n.1; preference for bland words, 296. *See also* scholarship, Indian musical
thought, Indian: categorical nature of, 6, 123–24; continuities of, 23–27; distinctive patterns, 6–9; dynamic, 25–26; habits, 46; hylozoistic, 26; orthodox

thought, Indian (*continued*)
systems of, 27–32; presuppositions, aesthetic, 334–35; taxonomic, 24–25; typical analogies, 32–34; views on form, 225–30. *See also* metaphor(s); philosophy, Indian
time, 180–224: cyclical, 182–86; in Hindu worldview, 26; idea of, in ancient India, 182–88; in Indian philosophy, 29–30, 186–88; musical hierarchy, 181; organization of, in Indian music, 180–81; as represented by *om,* 36–37; and ritual, 184–86; and sacrifice, 185–86; *tāla,* 188–93; two streams of, 181, 186. *See also* rhythm; *tāla*
timelessness, 180–82. *See also* time
timing, 193, 202–7. See also under *tāla*
Tinctoris, Johannes, 235
tonality, 156–57, 157–60, 176–77, 178
treatise. See *śāstra;* scholarship, Indian musical
tribal music, 270–73
Tumburu (author), 50, 166, 310
tuning: of intervals and scales, 145–49, 156, 177, 361n.3; Western tuning systems, 361n.5
Tyāgarāja (composer), 342

*uddeśa* (table of contents), 9, 78, 132
Udghaṭṭaḥ (a *tāla*), 197, 263
*udgrāha* (an opening section), 237, 276–77, 279–80, 282, 285
Ullopyaka (a type of composition), 253
*upavartana* (a compressed repetition), 246, 250–51, 254, 258–59, 264
*upohana* (a melodic incipit), 63, 230, 248–50, 254–57, 258
Uttara (a type of composition), 253

Vāc (goddess), 25, 42, 44, 46, 52, 57–58
*vādi* (the sonant note), 158–60
*vādya* (instrumental music), 9–10, 103, 111–12, 112–17; classification of instruments, 10, 13–14. *See also* instruments
Vaidarbhī (a mode of poetic diction), 288–89, 313–14, 316–18; *gunas* of, 317. See also *rīti;* style
Vaiśeṣika, philosophical system of, 28–29, 40, 218. *See also* philosophy, Indian
*Vākyapadīya* of Bhartṛhari, 35–36, 46, 180, 187–88, 202
values: decoration, 165–66; formal, 228–30; of Indian music, 297, 334–37; influenced by cultural ideology, 52–53, 224; inward/outward pathways, 33–34; musical, based on poetic, 305; in musicological literature, 297. *See also* aesthetics; preferences, Indian artistic
van Buitenen, J. A. B., 22, 92–93, 120, 126
Vardhamāna (a type of composition), 265–66
Varma, Siddheshwar, 69
*varṇa:* melodic contour, 163–64, 320–21, 326; mythology, in *NS,* 88–90; a topic in phonetic theory, 56–57
Varṇasvara (a type of song), 280–81
*vastu* (formal component), 191–92, 245–47, 372n.55; in Madraka, 254–58; a synonym for *prabandha,* 274
Vatsyayan, Kapila, 97–98, 232–33
Vātsyāyana (author). See *Kāmasūtra* of Vātsyāyana
Vedāṅgas (Limbs of the Vedas), 69
Vedānta, philosophical system of, 28, 33, 40–41, 218. *See also* philosophy, Indian
Vedas: contribution to Sanskrit theater, 10, 15, 97, 315; four — compared, 57–58; and *gaṇa* Elās, 287–89; represented by divisions of *om,* 37; testimony on time and sacrifice, 185. See also *Atharvaveda; Ṛgveda; Sāmaveda; Yajurveda*
Velankar, H. D., 215–19, 220, 268
Veṅkaṭamakhī (author), 179
vidārī (cadence), 191–92, 246
vina, 14; in *BN* chap. 29, 99; *gātravīṇā,* 87; symbolism of, 33, 115–16
*virāma* (fractional extension of a duration), 211–12
Viṣṇu (god), 26, 178, 227–28, 348n.8
*vivādi* (a dissonant note), 158–60
vocables, 74–75, 205, 238, 265; in *Sāmaveda* recitation, 60–61, 63; in the theater, 106. *See also* syllable(s)
Voltaire, 238
*vṛtti:* four modes of dramatic expression, 313–15; four literary styles, in *gaṇa* Elās, 287–90; four styles in poetic theory, 314–15; general word for style, 295–97; three musical styles, 317–19; three speeds of recitation, 67–68, 204; three styles of accompaniment, 112, 318–19. *See also* style

Whitney, William Dwight, 221
Widdess, D. R., 142, 173
Winternitz, Maurice, 128

*Yajurveda,* 10, 15, 57–58. *See also* Vedas
yang, yin, 52–55, 352n.65
Yāska (author), 9–10. See also *nirukta*
*yati:* caesura, 220; progression of tempo, 191–93, 318–19
Yoga, philosophical system of, 28, 33–34, 37, 45, 187, 190. *See also* philosophy, Indian

Zeno, 25, 72
Zimmer, Heinrich, 233–34